D0348864

Croatia

Zagorje
p71

Zagreb
p40

Slavonia
p84

Istria
p97

Kvarner
p134

Northern
Dalmatia
p160

Split &
Central Dalmatia
p197

Dubrovnik &
Southern Dalmatia
p250

THIS EDITION WRITTEN AND RESEARCHED BY

Anja Mutić

Peter Dragicevich

PLAN YOUR TRIP

Welcome to Croatia 4

Croatia Map 6

Croatia's Top 17 8

Need to Know 16

What's New 18

If You Like 19

Month by Month 22

Itineraries 26

Travel with Children 34

Regions at a Glance 36

ON THE ROAD

ZAGREB 40

Lonjsko Polje Nature Park . . 68

Medvednica Nature Park . . 70

ZAGORJE 71

Varaždin 74

Varaždinske Toplice 78

Trakošćan Castle 79

Krapina 81

Veliki Tabor Castle 82

Kumrovec 83

Klanjec 83

Marija Bistrica 83

SLAVONIA 84

Osijek 85

Baranja 91

Vukovar 94

Ilok 96

ISTRIA 97

The Istrian Coast 99

Pula 99

Brijuni Islands 107

Rovinj 108

Poreč 115

The Istrian Interior . . . 120

Labin 121

Vodnjan 123

Svetvinčenat 124

Pazin 124

Gračišće 126

Buzet 126

Motovun 129

Istarske Toplice 131

Grožnjan 132

Momjan 133

KVARNER 134

Rijeka 136

Opatija 142

Cres &
Lošinj Islands 146

Beli 147

Cres Town 148

Valun 150

Lubenice 151

Osor 151

Mali Lošinj 152

Veli Lošinj 156

Krk Island 157

Malinska 158

Krk Town 159

Punat 161

Vrbnik 161

Baška 162

Rab Island 163

Rab Town 164

Lopar 168

NORTHERN
DALMATIA 169

Lika 171

Plitvice Lakes
& Around 171

Around Gospić 173

Paklenica
National Park 174

Pag Island 176

Pag Town 176

Central Pag 177

Novalja & Around 178

Zadar 179

Dugi Otok 186

Sali 187

Božava 188

Veli Rat 188

Šibenik-Knin
County 188

Kornati Islands 188

Tisno & Murter Island . . . 189

Šibenik 190

DUBROVNIK P251

SUSAK P155

GARY JOHN NORMAN /GETTY IMAGES ©

VUK8691 /GETTY IMAGES ©

Contents

SPLIT P200

Krka National Park......194
Knin 198

SPLIT & CENTRAL DALMATIA........197
Split 200
Šolta 217
Solin (Salona)..........217
Trogir & Around 218
Makarska Riviera 223
Makarska..............223
Brela.................226

Brač Island 226
Supetar 227
Bol....................233
Hvar Island 235
Hvar Town 236
Stari Grad 242
Jelsa.................243
Vis Island............244
Vis Town..............245
Komiža................248
Biševo................249

DUBROVNIK & SOUTHERN DALMATIA........250
Dubrovnik 251
Cavtat................270
Lokrum Island.........271
Trsteno Arboretum......271
Elafiti Islands 272
Mljet Island 273
Pelješac Peninsula 274
Ston & Mali Ston 274
Central Pelješac 275
Orebić................276
Korčula Island.......277
Korčula Town..........279
Lumbarda 283
Vela Luka.............284

UNDERSTAND

Croatia Today 286
History 288
The Croatian Mindset 303
The Cuisine 308
Architecture in Croatia 314
The Natural Environment 316
The Arts.............319

SURVIVAL GUIDE

Directory A–Z 324
Transport 332
Language............337
Index................345
Map Legend..........351

SPECIAL FEATURES
Itineraries 26
Croatia's Coast......228
Dubrovnik Old Town 264
Cuisine............308

Welcome to Croatia

If your Mediterranean fantasies feature balmy days by sapphire waters in the shade of ancient walled towns, Croatia is the place to turn them into reality.

Coastal Croatia

Croatia's extraordinary island-speckled coastline is indisputably its main attraction. Part of the appeal lies in its diversity. You'll find glitz and glamour in places like Hvar, where fancy yachts and fancier threads are *de rigueur*. In other locales Croatian families get busy with buckets and spades, Aussie backpackers slop about in flip-flops and German naturists free themselves from the tyranny of apparel altogether. For those wanting peace and quiet, there are plenty of secluded coves and Robinson Crusoe–style islets to discover.

The Edge of Empires

Precariously poised between the Balkans and Central Europe, this land has been passed between competing kingdoms, empires and republics for millennia. If there's an upside to this continual dislocation, it's in the rich cultural legacy that each has left behind. Venetian palazzos snuggle up to Napoleonic forts, Roman columns protrude from early Slavic churches, and Viennese mansions face off with Socialist Realist sculpture. Excellent museums showcase treasures from most key stages of Europe's history, telling a story that is in equal parts fascinating and horrifying.

Beauty on the Inside

Shift your gaze for just a moment from the glittering waters and chances are an almighty mountain will loom into view. The Dinaric Alps, which stretch all the way from Italy to Albania, hug much of the coast. The limestone karst has bequeathed a wonderland of craggy peaks, underground caverns, river canyons, dramatic waterfalls and ridiculously picturesque lakes. Head further inland and things flatten out again into rolling farmland. Active types will find plenty of chances to get amongst it on the numerous hiking and biking trails.

Cultural Feast

If you're lucky enough to cross the tourist/guest barrier and be invited into a local's home, you'll soon become acquainted with the refrain '*Jedi! Jedi! Jedi!*' (Eat! Eat! Eat!). It's little wonder that sharing food and drink plays such a big part in the culture here, when the country is blessed with such top-notch ingredients from the land and sea. Simple home-style cooking is a feature of family-run taverns, but increasingly a new breed of chefs are bringing a more adventurous approach to the table. Meanwhile Croatian wines and olive oils are making their mark on the world stage, garnering top awards.

Why I Love Croatia

By Peter Dragicevich, Author

I'll admit, I'm more than a little biased, but Croatia is quite simply my favourite country to visit. For me, it offers a unique combination of all the things I love: breathtaking natural beauty, great swimming, summertime sun, oodles of history, interesting architecture, incredible wine, delicious seafood... I could go on. True, Croats don't always present the sunniest face to complete strangers, but break through that initial reserve and you'll discover the friendliest, most hospitable people you could hope to meet. I'm sure that even if my grandparents didn't hail from here, I'd still adore the place.

For more about our authors, see page 352

Above: Dubrovnik (p251)

Croatia

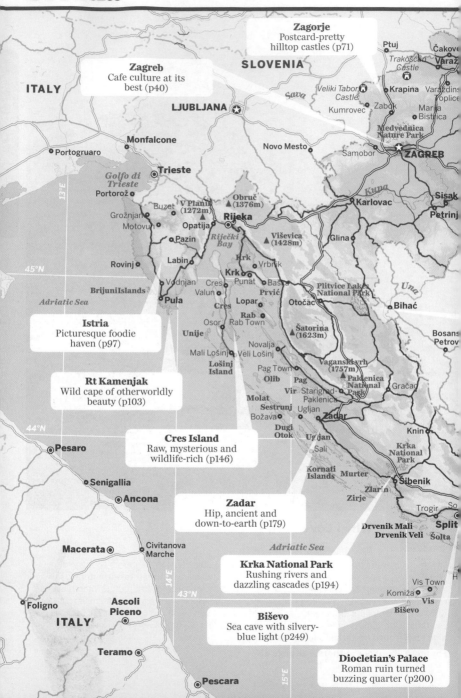

Zagorje
Postcard-pretty
hilltop castles (p71)

Zagreb
Cafe culture at its
best (p40)

Istria
Picturesque foodie
haven (p97)

Rt Kamenjak
Wild cape of otherworldly
beauty (p103)

Cres Island
Raw, mysterious and
wildlife-rich (p146)

Zadar
Hip, ancient and
down-to-earth (p179)

Krka National Park
Rushing rivers and
dazzling cascades (p194)

Biševo
Sea cave with silvery-
blue light (p249)

Diocletian's Palace
Roman ruin turned
buzzing quarter (p200)

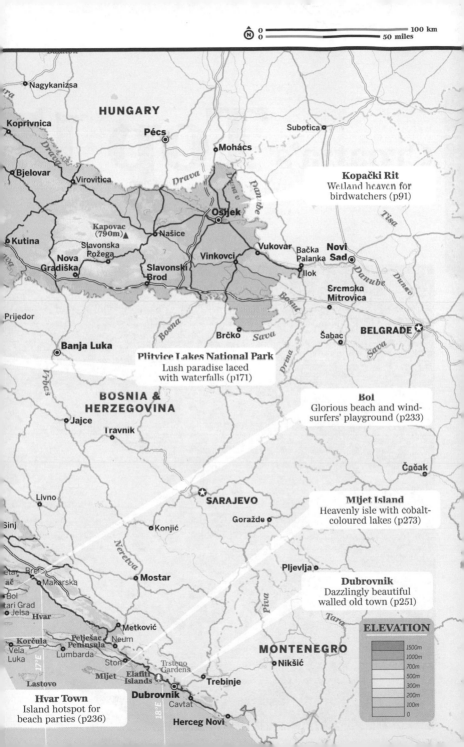

N | 0 ⟶ 100 km
0 ⟶ 50 miles

HUNGARY

Nagykanizsa

Koprivnica

Pécs

Mohács

Subotica

Kopački Rit
Wetland heaven for
birdwatchers (p91)

Bjelovar

Virovitica

Drava

Osijek

Tisa

Kapovac
(790m)▲

Našice

Kutina

Slavonska
Požega

Vukovar

Bačka
Palanka

**Novi
Sad**

Nova
Gradiška

Vinkovci

Ilok

Danube

Dunav

Slavonski
Brod

Sremska
Mitrovica

Prijedor

Bosna

Brčko

Sava

Šabac

BELGRADE

Banja Luka

Plitvice Lakes National Park
Lush paradise laced
with waterfalls (p171)

Drina

Sava

**BOSNIA &
HERZEGOVINA**

Bol
Glorious beach and wind-
surfers' playground (p233)

Jajce

Travnik

Vrbas

Livno

Čačak

SARAJEVO

Goražde

Mljet Island
Heavenly isle with cobalt-
coloured lakes (p273)

Sinj

Neretva

Pljevlja

Brel

Makarska

Mostar

Dubrovnik
Dazzlingly beautiful
walled old town (p251)

Bol

tari Grad

Jelsa

Hvar

Piva

Tara

Metković

Korčula

Vela
Luka

Pelješac
Peninsula

Neum

Lumbarda

Ston

MONTENEGRO

Nikšić

ELEVATION

Lastovo

Mljet

Elafiti
Islands

Trsteno
Gardens

Trebinje

1500m
1000m
700m
500m
300m
200m
100m
0

Hvar Town
Island hotspot for
beach parties (p236)

Dubrovnik
Cavtat

Herceg Novi

Croatia's Top 17

Plitvice Paradise

1 A turquoise ribbon of crystal water and gushing waterfalls in the forested heart of continental Croatia, Plitvice Lakes National Park (p171) is an awesome sight. There are dozens of lakes – from 4km-long Kozjak to reed-fringed ponds – all in an incredible hue that's a product of the karst terrain. Travertine expanses covered with mossy plants divide the lakes, while boardwalks allow you to step right over this exquisite water world. Follow hiking trails through beech, spruce, fir and pine trees to escape the crowds on the lakeshore.

All That is Dubrovnik

2 Croatia's most popular attraction, Dubrovnik (p251) is a Unesco World Heritage Site for good reason. This historic walled city was relentlessly shelled during Croatia's 1990s 'Homeland War'. Now, its mighty walls, monasteries, medieval churches, graceful squares and fascinating residential quarters all look magnificent again. For an unrivalled perspective of this Adriatic pearl, first take the cable car up to Mt Srd, then get up close to the city by walking Dubrovnik's walls, as history unfolds from the battlements.

ANDREW BURKE / GETTY IMAGES ©

Party-Happy Hvar

3 Come high summer, there's no better place to get your groove on than Hvar Town (p236). Gorgeous tanned people descend from their yachts in droves for round-the-clock fun on this glam isle. With après-beach parties as the sun drops below the horizon far out in the Adriatic, designer cocktails sipped seaside to fresh house tunes spun by DJs, and full-moon beach parties, Hvar caters to a well-dressed, party-happy crowd. Plus there's Hvar beyond the party scene, with its gorgeous interior largely uncharted by tourist crowds.

Marvel at Mljet

4 Cloaked in dense pine forests, marvellous Mljet (p273) is an island paradise. Legend has it that Odysseus was marooned here for seven years, and it's easy to appreciate why he'd take his time leaving. The entire western section is a national park, where you'll find two sublime, cobalt-coloured lakes, an island monastery and the sleepy little port of Pomena, which is as pretty as a picture. Don't neglect eastern Mljet, home to some tranquil little beaches and the excellent Stermasi restaurant.

Coffee Fix in Zagreb

5 Elevated to the status of ritual, having coffee in one of Zagreb's outdoor cafes (p63) is a must, involving hours of people-watching, gossiping and soul-searching, unhurried by waiters. To experience the truly European and vibrant cafe culture, grab a table along the pedestrian cobbled Tkalčićeva, with its endless streetside cafes, or one of the pavement tables on Trg Petra Preradovića or Bogovićeva. Don't miss the Saturday morning *špica*, the coffee-drinking and people-watching ritual in the city centre that forms the peak of Zagreb's weekly social calendar.

Wine & Dine in Istria

6 *La dolce vita* reigns supreme in Istria (p97), Croatia's top foodie destination. The seafood, truffles, wild asparagus and a rare breed of Istrian beef called *boškarin* all stand out, as do myriad regional specialities and award-winning olive oils and wines by small local producers. Slow food is a hit here: you can sample the ritual in upmarket restaurants in seafront towns, in traditional family-run taverns in medieval hilltop villages, and in converted olive mills high up in the hills of the peninsula's verdant interior.

Hit the Waves in Bol

7 Bol (p233), on the southern coast of Brač Island, is home to the illustrious Zlatni Rat beach, with its tongue-like shape and golden pebbles. The town is a favourite among windsurfers: the channel between the islands of Brač and Hvar provides ideal wind conditions, thanks to the westerly *maestral* that typically blows between May and late September. The wind picks up slowly in the morning, an excellent time for beginners to hit the waves. By afternoon, the winds are very strong, perfect for those looking to get an adrenalin kick. Zlatni Rat (p233)

6

7

MEREDITH ANDREWS / LONELY PLANET ©

Pastries & Ice Cream

8 Croatia is a superior spot to indulge your sweet tooth. You absolutely must not miss the *slastičarnas* (pastry shops) found in towns and villages across the country. Indulge in the Austrian-style creamy cakes, homemade strudels, and the very local *kremšnite* (custard pies) of Samobor (p69). In the summertime, head straight for the ice-cream counters, which typically showcase 10 to 20 flavours of fresh ice cream made on the premises. Croatian *sladoled* (ice cream) gives Italian gelato a run for its money.

Blue Magic on Biševo

9 Of the numerous caves around the remote limestone island of Biševo (p249), the Blue Grotto (Modra Špilja) is the most spectacular. The light show produced by this rare natural phenomenon will amaze you. On a clear morning, the sun's rays penetrate through an underwater hole in this coastal cave, bathing the interior in a mesmerising silvery-blue light. Beneath the turquoise water, rocks glimmer silver and pink, creating an unearthly effect. Swimming inside is a surreal must-have experience, worth a trip to this far-out island.

Ferry Fun in the Adriatic

10 From short jaunts between nearby islands to overnight rides along the length of the Croatian coast, sea travel (p334) is a great and inexpensive way to see the Croatian side of the Adriatic. Take in the stunning coastline as you whiz past some of the country's 1244 islands, including the popular Hvar (p235) and Brač (p226) and more offbeat options such as Vis (p244). If you have cash to splash, see the islands in style by chartering a sailboat, propelled by winds and sea currents.

Cracking Krka

11 There are Roman ruins, historic watermills and two fascinating monasteries (one on an island and one built over ancient catacombs), but the star of this highly scenic national park (p194) is the Krka River itself, rushing through canyons, broadening into lakes and splashing over numerous falls and cascades. You can stroll along boardwalks and marvel at the multitude of fish darting through the emerald waters, and then cap off your visit with a dip in a lake at the foot of a mighty waterfall.

Go Wild in Rt Kamenjak

12 It's the wild rugged beauty and end-of-the-world vibe of this small peninsula just south of Pula that have earned it cult status among Croatian beach-goers. An undeveloped protected nature reserve, Rt Kamenjak (p103) showcases a carpet of heath plants, shrubs and wildflowers, criss-crossed by a maze of dirt tracks. It's fringed by a string of pebble bays and secluded rocky beaches, surrounded by blue-green sea. It gets busy in summer but there's always an empty beach to escape to, plus a fun beach bar for socialising.

The Soul of Split

13 Experience life as it's been lived for thousands of years in Diocletian's Palace (p200), one of the world's most imposing Roman ruins. The mazelike streets of this buzzing quarter, the heart and soul of Split, are full of bars, shops and restaurants. Getting lost in the labyrinth of narrow streets, passageways and courtyards is one of Croatia's most enchanting experiences – and it's small enough that you'll always find your way out easily. Escape the palace walls for a drink on the palm-fringed Riva along the water's edge. Diocletian's Palace

Storybook Castles of Zagorje

14 Don't miss the postcard-perfect medieval castles of Zagorje. Although it dates to 1334, Trakošćan Castle (p79) was restored in neo-Gothic style, a style still in evidence today. Learn about Croatian aristocracy in its well-presented museum and wander the 215-acre castle grounds landscaped into a English-style park with exotic trees and an artificial lake. The hilltop castle of Veliki Tabor (p82) is worth a visit for its interiors that now house a museum, the pentagonal exterior of its towers, and the bucolic landscapes that surround it. Veliki Tabor

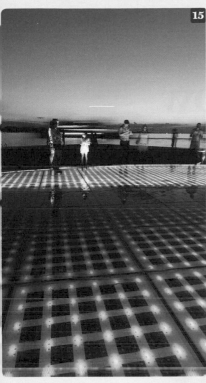

INE ALEN GURUVIC / ALAMY ©

ALAN COPSON / GETTY IMAGES ©

Discover Zadar

15 Set on a peninsula shaped like a hitchhiker's thumb, Zadar (p179) is well worth stopping for. The old town has history and culture in spades: Roman ruins protrude from the city streets, while museums and churches lurk around every other corner. Artsy types, students and style-mavens rub shoulders in bars ranging from utterly classy to deliciously divey, while food-lovers frequent the many excellent eateries. Backpackers are well served by some brilliant hostels, while families gravitate to the surrounding beach resorts, and boutique hotels reel in the romantics. Sun Salutation (p182), architect Nikola Basic

Kopački Rit – a Wetland Wonder

16 A flood plain of the Danube and Drava Rivers, Kopački Rit Nature Park (p91) – part of a Unesco biosphere reserve – offers breathtaking scenery and some of Europe's best birdwatching. Join a boat trip and keep your eyes peeled for white-tailed and imperial eagles, black storks, purple herons and woodpeckers – just some of the nearly 300 species recorded here. Mammals such as red deer and wild boar are common, too. Explore a flooded forest by canoe, hike the nature trails or saddle up and ride a horse.

De-Stress in Cres

17 Leafy, sparsely populated and never overwhelmed by tourists, the island of Cres (p146) is unique amongst Croatia's Adriatic isles. Strolling through the Tramuntana region in the north you might even begin to believe the old people's stories about elves lurking in the ancient forests. At the other end of the island, tiny Osor (p151) is as sleepy a walled town as you'll find on the entire coast. Scattered in between are gorgeous beaches, lost-in-time hilltop villages and the pretty pastel-hued harbour of Cres Town. Cres Town (p148)

Need to Know

For more information, see Survival Guide (p324)

Currency
Kuna (KN)

Language
Croatian

Visas
Generally not required for stays of up to 90 days. Some nationalities, such as South Africans, do need them.

Money
ATMs widely available. Credit cards accepted in most hotels and restaurants. Smaller restaurants, shops and private accommodation owners only take cash.

Mobile Phones
Users with unlocked phones can buy a local SIM card, which are easy to find. Otherwise, you'll be roaming.

Time
Central European Time (GMT/UTC plus one hour)

When to Go

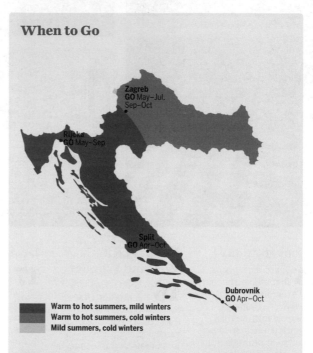

Zagreb
GO May–Jul,
Sep–Oct

Rijeka
GO May–Sep

Split
GO Apr–Oct

Dubrovnik
GO Apr–Oct

Warm to hot summers, mild winters
Warm to hot summers, cold winters
Mild summers, cold winters

High Season
(Jul & Aug)

➡ Peak season brings the best weather. Hvar Island gets the most sun, followed by Split, Korčula Island and Dubrovnik.

➡ Prices are at their highest and coastal destinations at their busiest.

Shoulder
(May–Jun & Sep)

➡ The coast is gorgeous, the Adriatic is warm enough for swimming, the crowds are sparse and prices are lower.

➡ In spring and early summer, the steady *maestral* wind makes sailing great.

Low Season
(Oct–Apr)

➡ Winters in continental Croatia are cold and prices are low.

➡ Holiday season brings buzz to the streets, even with the snow, plus there's skiing too.

Useful Websites

Adriatica.net (www.adriatica.net) Books hotels, apartments and lighthouses all along the coast.

Croatian National Tourist Board (www.croatia.hr) The best starting point to plan your holiday.

Like Croatia (www.likecroatia. hr) An information-packed online guide to Croatia.

Lonely Planet.com (www.lonely planet.com/croatia) Destination information, hotel bookings, traveller forum and more.

Taste of Croatia (www. tasteofcroatia.org) Excellent informative website.

Important Numbers

To call from outside Croatia, dial your international access code, then the Croatian country code, the area code (without the initial 0) and the local number.

Country code	🕿 385
International access code	🕿 00
International directory assistance	🕿 11802
Local directory assistance	🕿 11888
Roadside assistance	🕿 1987

Exchange Rates

Australia	A$1	5.32KN
Canada	CA$1	5.30KN
Europe	€1	7.63KN
Japan	100Y	5.48KN
New Zealand	NZ$1	4.79KN
UK	UK£	9.57KN
US	US$1	5.88KN

For current exchange rates, see www.xe.com.

Daily Costs

**Budget:
Less than 450KN**

➡ Dorm bed: 150KN

➡ Campsite: 40KN

➡ Meal in a local tavern: 60KN

➡ Bus, tram or train ticket: 10–150KN

Midrange:
450–1000KN

➡ Double room in a hotel: 650KN

➡ Meal in a decent restaurant: 120KN

➡ A city tour by bike: 175KN

➡ Short taxi trip: 30KN

**Top End:
More than 1000KN**

➡ Double room in a four-star hotel: 850KN

➡ Meal in a top-tier restaurant: 300KN

➡ Private sailing trip: 1000KN

➡ Car rental per day: 250KN

Opening Hours

Opening hours vary throughout the year. We've provided high-season opening hours; hours will generally decrease in the shoulder and low seasons.

Banks 8am or 9am–8pm weekdays, 7am–1pm or 8am–2pm Saturday

Cafes and Bars 8am–midnight

Restaurants noon–11pm or midnight

Shops 8am–8pm weekdays, till 2pm or 3pm Saturday

Arriving in Croatia

Zagreb Airport (p67) Croatia Airlines bus (30KN) leaves from the airport every half-hour or hour from about 4.30am to 8pm. Taxis to the centre cost between 110KN and 200KN (20 minutes).

Split Airport (p215) Catch local bus 37 to Domovinskog Rata stop in the city centre (21KN, 50 minutes). Buses by Pleso Prijevoz depart Split airport (30KN) to Obala Lazareta several times daily. Taxis cost between 200KN and 250KN (30 minutes).

Dubrovnik Airport (p269) Atlas runs the airport bus service (35KN, 30 minutes), timed around flights. Buses to Dubrovnik stop at the Pile Gate and the bus station. A taxi to the old town costs about 250KN.

Getting Around

Transport in Croatia is reasonably priced, quick and generally efficient.

Car Useful for travelling at your own pace, or for visiting regions with minimal public transport. Cars can be hired in every city or larger town. Drive on the right.

Bus Reasonably priced, with extensive coverage of the country and frequent departures.

Boat Extensive network of car ferries and catamarans all along the coast and the islands.

Train Less frequent and much slower than buses, with limited network.

For much more on **getting around**, see p334

PLAN YOUR TRIP NEED TO KNOW

What's New

Mundoaka Street Food, Zagreb

Funky new eatery that's ever buzzing, right off the main square, where the menu showcases American classics and globally inspired dishes, plus delicious cakes and muffins. (p59)

Mali Plac na Tavanu, Zagreb

This Saturday food market is a gathering of small producers who hawk their edible wares in the funky attic of food blogger and stylist Jelena Nikolić, or in one of the offbeat locations around town. (p65)

Lighting Giants, Pula

Pula's latest attraction is a spectacular lighting display at Uljanik shipyard, where iconic cranes come alive four times every evening, lit up in 16,000 different colour schemes. (p101)

Coastal Hostels

A flurry of independent hostel openings has greatly improved the quality of budget accommodation on the coast, with excellent options springing up in Rijeka, Novalja, Zadar, Šibenik and Dubrovnik.

Sea Turtle Rescue Centre, Mali Lošinj

It might be tiny but this centre plays an important role in nursing injured sea turtles back to health and returning them to the wild. (p153)

Zrće Beach Festivals, Pag

Every year the calendar of electronic dance music festivals at Zrće Beach on Pag Island gets more scorching. Hot tickets include Hideout, Sonus and hip-hop-flavoured Fresh Island. (p178)

Aquarium Split

Croatia's biggest aquarium has 130 Adriatic species swimming in tanks among original amphorae and antique marine memorabilia, on the ground floor of an old villa on the Vranjic peninsula 8km from Split. (p202)

Paradigma, Split

On the culinary cutting edge of Dalmatia, this new restaurant has a rooftop terrace featuring Riva views, a superb wine list and Mediterranean-inspired dishes. (p211)

Peninsula, Pelješac

Some of Croatia's best wine is grown and made on the Pelješac Peninsula and neighbouring Korčula. This newbie wine bar offers you the chance to sample 60 different drops under one roof. (p276)

D'vino, Dubrovnik

Let the well-informed staff guide you through themed tasting flights of Croatia's best wine at this cute little bar set on one of Dubrovnik's cobbled lanes. (p268)

Croatian Design Superstore

Launched in summer 2014, this hybrid of design exhibition and pop-up shop showcases the best of contemporary Croatian design in offbeat locations around the country (www.croatiandesignsuperstore. com).

For more recommendations and reviews, see lonelyplanet. com/croatia

If You Like

Islands

Croatia's coast is speckled with a multitude of magnificent islands that range from tiny, verdant and unpopulated to massive, arid and buzzing.

Hvar People come to party on Croatia's sunniest isle, thanks to its glam hub Hvar Town. (p236)

Vis Remote, mysterious and off-limits to foreigners for decades, it has top beaches, seaside towns and food. (p244)

Mljet Long, slender and beguiling, with a lagoonlike sea lake, an island monastery and superb scenery. (p273)

Cres Among Croatia's least touristy islands, with awe-inspiring landscapes, medieval villages and a pretty port capital. (p146)

Brač Sports Croatia's most famous beach, the alluring Zlatni Rat in the pretty town of Bol. (p226)

Rab Kvarner isle with the most diverse landscapes, plus sandy beaches and the enchantingly ancient Rab Town. (p163)

Pag Sun-scorched scenery akin to the moon, foods featuring the famously pungent cheese and hard-core beach parties. (p176)

Korčula Rich in vineyards, olive groves and scenic hamlets, and featuring the marvellous medieval Korčula Town. (p277)

Kornati Comprised of 147 mostly uninhabited islands, islets and reefs, it's the Adriatic's largest archipelago. (p188)

Lošinj Beautiful bays, lush vegetation featuring 1100 plant species, plus a pair of pretty port towns. (p146)

Outdoor Activities

There's plenty for active and outdoorsy types to do in Croatia. Start with swimming in the Adriatic and progress to mountain biking, windsurfing, kayaking, climbing, river rafting and more.

Sailing Glide between beautiful Croatian islands, docking at popular destinations like Hvar Town and exploring remote islands. (p218)

Hiking The numerous national parks – including Plitvice (p171), Paklenica (p174) and Krka (p194) – are fantastic for hikers.

Diving Plunge in and discover marine beauties off the islands of Hvar (p237), Brač (p226), Krk (p157) and Kornati (p188).

Cycling Ride through the flat countryside of Baranja (p91), along Istria's Parenzana route, or on the islands. (p122)

Naturism Croatia has been a prime spot for going starkers since the 1930s, and still is. (p104)

Rafting Hit the rapids of the Cetina, the longest river in central Dalmatia, best accessed from Makarska. (p223)

Windsurfing Ride the waves of *maestral*, a strong westerly best experienced in Bol. (p233)

Rock-climbing Paklenica has rock-climbing routes ranging from beginner's level to borderline suicidal. (p174)

Horseback riding Explore the wilds of the Velebit mountains on horseback from Linden Tree Retreat & Ranch. (p174)

Nightlife

Croatia has become a hot ticket on Europe's nightlife circuit, pulsating with a variety of options – from beach parties to megaclubs.

Hvar Get your groove on at Hvar Town, with its après-beach and full-moon parties. (p236)

Pag Croatia's answer to Ibiza, the clubbing mecca of Zrće on Pag Island provides round-the-clock fun. (p176)

Poreč Istria's party capital has nightlife hawks hitting its late-night clubs. (p115)

Tisno This cute little coastal town hosts a series of high-profile music festivals. (p189)

Split Tops for nightlife, its palace walls throb with music and action, especially in summer. (p212)

Zagreb Croatia's capital offers a modest but ever-developing art and music scene. (p60)

Architecture

Croatia has it all – from Roman, baroque, Renaissance and Romanesque to Venetian, Gothic and contemporary architecture.

Dubrovnik One of Europe's most visually arresting cities, ringed by monumental walls. (p251)

Trogir Pocket-sized seaside town full of well-preserved Romanesque and Renaissance buildings, and a lovely cathedral. (p218)

Zadar Showcasing an array of architectural styles, from Roman ruins through to the contemporary 'Sea Organ'. (p179)

Roman Amphitheatre Pula's most imposing sight is this 1st-century amphitheatre overlooking the harbour, built entirely from local limestone. (p101)

Diocletian's Palace One of the world's most impressive Roman ruins still functions as the city's living heart. (p200)

Varaždin A showcase of scrupulously restored baroque architecture, Croatia's former capital has an extraordinarily refined old town. (p74)

Euphrasian Basilica This 6th-century World Heritage Site in Poreč is one of Europe's finest examples of Byzantine art. (p116)

St James' Cathedral The crowning architectural glory of the Dalmatian coast, this Šibenik cathedral features Gothic-Renaissance style. (p191)

Top: Preparing a fish dish with Croatian olive oil (p310)
Bottom: Lubenice (p151)

Zagreb The Museum of Contemporary Art in a stunning city icon designed by local star architect Igor Franić. (p50)

Hotel Lone Rovinj's showpiece hotel is a stunner revamp by Croatia's leading architecture studio 3LHD. (p112)

Beaches

Get your kit off or don the latest designer swimsuit on one of the many gorgeous beaches that dot Croatia's coastline and islands.

Pakleni Islands Pine-shaded beaches for naturists and swimsuit wearers alike. (p240)

Bačvice Fun and bursting at the seams with local life. (p202)

Zrće Croatia's summer clubbing capital. (p179)

Lubenice Small, secluded, sensational and difficult to reach. (p151)

Zlatni Rat A tongue-shaped stretch of golden pebbles packed with beach bodies and activities galore. (p233)

Lokrum A rocky beach with clear waters, it is heaven for nudies, and always peaceful. (p271)

Paradise Beach A sandy stunner with shallow waters and the shade of pine trees. (p168)

Stiniva A spectacular and secluded cove of pebble stones flanked by high rocks. (p246)

Brela A string of beautiful palm-fringed coves with soft pebbles. (p226)

Rt Kamenjak Thirty unspoilt kilometres of inlets, coves, pebbles and rocks. (p103)

National Parks

Croatia's appeal is grounded in nature – its waterfalls, forests, mountains and the dazzling Adriatic coast. Luckily, much of it is protected – Croatia has eight national parks covering 961 sq km.

Plitvice Lakes This startling natural phenomenon contains sublime waterfalls, turquoise pools and forests. (p171)

Krka Explore stupendous waterfalls and visit a remote monastery. (p194)

Paklenica Experience nature on a big scale, with canyons and great hiking and climbing. (p174)

Risnjak Shady trails through dense forests and meadows rich in wildflowers. (p140)

Kornati Islands The isles' stark beauty is the ultimate resort free Adriatic escape. (p188)

Mljet Find Mediterranean paradise on this serene, peaceful and unspoilt island. (p273)

Brijuni This archipelago off the coast of Istria is the most cultivated of Croatia's national parks. (p107)

Food & Drink

Gastronomic culture is on the rise in Croatia. You'll find top-quality homegrown ingredients such as olive oil, truffles, seafood and smoked ham – plus a burgeoning wine scene.

Slow food Check out this movement promoting local, fresh and seasonal ingredients, and enjoying the ritual of eating. (p308)

Olive oil Follow the marked olive-oil routes of Istria to visit local producers and taste their oils. (p310)

Wine From Istria's white *malvazija* to *dingač* of Pelješac Peninsula and Slavonia's *graševina*, wines abound. (p311)

Truffles The prized fungus grows in the forests of Istria, where you can go truffle-hunting during autumn. (p127)

Markets Don't miss the food markets, including Zagreb's offbeat Mali Plac na Tavanu. (p65)

Rakija Sample Croatia's famous *rakija* (grappa), with flavours ranging from plum and grape to mistletoe. (p311)

Coffee The social ritual of sipping coffee is a must-do when in Croatia. (p311)

Low-Key Hideaways

The good thing about Croatia – even in peak season in the most touristy of spots, there's always some place to escape the hubbub.

Stari Grad On Hvar Island's north coast, a more quiet and offbeat affair than its stylish sister. (p242)

Cavtat Pretty coastal town that's a lot more 'local' than its neighbour Dubrovnik just to the north. (p270)

Lumbarda A laid-back beach town that's a much quieter retreat from the busy Korčula Town. (p284)

Beli Skip Cres Town for this ancient village that clings to a hill above a pebbly beach. (p147)

Bale Make a beeline from Rovinj for medieval Bale, an offbeat town and among Istria's best-kept secrets. (p115)

Samobor Escape Croatia's capital for the small-town vibe and delicious cakes of nearby Samobor. (p69)

Month by Month

TOP EVENTS

Rijeka Carnival, February

Cest is D'Best, June

Motovun Film Festival, July

Ultra Europe, July

Unknown Festival, September

January

As the country goes back to work after the holidays, snow makes roads difficult to tackle on the continent while strong winds on the coast and islands limit the ferry schedule.

🏃 Skiing on Sljeme

Hit the downhill slopes right outside Zagreb at Sljeme, the main peak of Mt Medvednica, complete with ski runs, lifts and even a triple chairlift. Skiing is a popular pastime for sporty Croats. (p53)

⊙ Beat the Crowds on the Coast

If you want to explore Croatia's coastal cities, this is the prime time to save some cash. Many hotels offer discounts of up to 50% at this time.

February

Enjoy scenic snowy hikes on the continent but still be mindful on the roads. Bura winds blow along the Adriatic, ferries run infrequently and many hotels in coastal towns shut down.

✨ Carnival

For colourful costumes, plenty of dancing and the nonstop revelry of this pre-Lent celebration, head to Rijeka, where Carnival is the pinnacle of the year's calendar. Zadar and Samobor host colourful Carnival celebrations, too. (p139)

✨ Feast of St Blaise, Dubrovnik

On 3 February each year, the streets of Dubrovnik perk up with folk dancing, concerts, food, processions and lots of street action, all happening in honour of the city's patron saint, St Blaise. (p259)

March

Days start to get longer and temperatures begin to rise, especially on the seaside. As winter ice melts, it's a great time to catch the waterfalls in Plitvice and Krka. Most action is still indoors.

☆ Zagrebdox

Catch documentary films from around the globe during this annual festival in Zagreb, the international Zagrebdox. Starting in late February and continuing into March, it draws a small crowd of avid doco lovers. (p54)

April

Soak up some sunshine and enjoy the solitude on southern islands and the coastline. Continental Croatia is still chilly but trees start to blossom and, as rivers swell with water, rafting and kayaking are tops.

☆ Music Biennale Zagreb

Held in the capital city each April during odd-numbered years since the 1960s, this is Croatia's most high-profile contemporary music event. By 'contemporary', do not read 'pop' – this prestigious fest celebrates modern-day classical music. (p53)

✖ Wild Asparagus Harvest, Istria

During early spring, the fields and meadows of in-land Istria become dotted with wild asparagus. Do like the locals do and head out to pick some, and then cook up a mean asparagus *fritaja* (omelette).

◉ Holy Week, Korčula

Holy Week celebrations are particularly elaborate in Korčula. The week before Easter is devoted to ceremonies and processions organised by the local religious brotherhoods dressed in traditional costumes (p282).

May

It's sunny and warm on the coast, and you can take a dip in the sea. Hotels are cheaper, too, and crowds have yet to come. Cafe life in Zagreb and Split kicks into full gear.

✦ Subversive Festival, Zagreb

Mingle with Europe's activists and revolutionaries who storm Zagreb for this two-week festival each May. The first week hosts a series of film screenings, while the second week's program includes lectures and panels by left-leaning movers and shakers. (p54)

☆ Ljeto na Strossu, Zagreb

Kicking off in late May is this ultra-fun summer-long event that features free outdoor film screenings, concerts by local bands, artsy workshops, best-in-show mongrel dog competitions

and other quirky happenings, all along the leafy Strossmayer Promenade. (p54)

▢ Open Wine Cellar Day, Istria

On the last Sunday in May each year, renowned wine makers and winegrowers of Istria open the doors to their wine cellars for free tastings and wine fuelled merrymaking.

June

Swim in the Adriatic, take in great festivals across the country and enjoy outdoor activities galore. Ferries start their summer schedule, high-season prices haven't kicked in and hotels are still not packed.

☆ INmusic Festival, Zagreb

Get your groove on during this three-day music extravaganza, which takes over leafy Jarun Lake with multiple stages and spots for camping. This is Zagreb's highest-profile music festival; The Black Keys and Pixies fronted a recent year's line-up. (p54)

✦ Cest is D'Best, Zagreb

For several days in early June, Zagreb's streets come alive with music, dance, theatre, art, sports and other fun events. This street festival is a much-loved affair, with several stages around the city centre and around 200 international performers. (p54)

☆ For Festival, Hvar

Kicking off the summer season for four days in June, this intimate music event puts a boutique spin on Croatia's busy festival scene – only 2500 tickets go on sale. It showcases live performances in a converted monastery and at Carpe Diem Beach.

July

Tourist season is in full swing: hotels along the coast get booked and beaches are full. Ferries run on their maximum schedule and there are festivals aplenty. A good time to explore Croatia's crowd-free continent.

☆ Hideout, Zrće

The festival that put Zrće on the electronic-dance-music map takes over the beach bars and clubs in late June/early July. Expect big-name DJs and multiple nights of mayhem. (p178)

☆ Dubrovnik Summer Festival

Kicking off in the middle of July and lasting into late August, this festival has been taking place in Dubrovnik since the 1950s. It features classical music, theatre and dance at different venues around town, including the Lovrjenac Fort. (p259)

☆ Dance & Nonverbal Theatre Festival, Svetvinčenat

The otherwise sleepy Istrian town of Svetvinčenat comes alive during this mid-July fest, which showcases contemporary dance pieces, street theatre, circus and mime acts, and other nonverbal forms of expression. (p124)

☆ Motovun Film Festival, Istria

This film festival, Croatia's most fun and glamorous, presents a roster of independent and avant-garde films in late July each year. Nonstop outdoor and indoor screenings, concerts and parties take over the medieval streets of this hilltop town. (p129)

☆ Soundwave, Tisno

Kicking off for five nights in the middle of July, this dance-music extravaganza features live acts from the alternative, dub and world-music end of the dance-music spectrum. (p190)

☆ Ultra Europe, Split

One of the world's largest electronic-music festivals takes over Split's Poljud stadium for three days in July, and wraps it up on the fourth day with a beach party outside the city. (p205)

August

Tourist season peaks in the Adriatic, with the hottest days and sea temperatures, swarming beaches and highest prices. Zagreb is hot but empty, as people escape to the coast.

★ Full Moon Festival, Zadar

During this festival held on the night of the full moon, Zadar's quays are lit with

Top: Croatian National Theatre (p64), a major venue for the World Theatre Festival, Zagreb

Bottom: Hideout festival (p178), Zrće

torches and candles, stalls sell local delicacies and boats lining the quays become floating fish markets. (p183)

☆ Sonus, Zrće

Five days and nights of electronic music in mid-August take over Pag Island's iconic Zrće beach. In previous years the festival has featured the likes of John Digweed and Laurent Garnier. (p178)

☆ Špancirfest, Varaždin

In late August this eclectic festival enlivens the parks and squares of Varaždin with a rich repertoire of events that range from world music (Afro-Cuban, gypsy, tango and more) to acrobats, theatre, traditional crafts and illusionists. (p76)

☆ Vukovar Film Festival, Slavonia

The annual Vukovar Film Festival in late August shows features, documentaries and shorts, mainly from Danubian countries. Visiting is a great way to support this city, as it is still recovering from the war. (p95)

September

The summer rush is over, but sunshine is still plentiful, the sea is warm and the crowds have largely gone – it's a great time to visit Croatia. Zagreb becomes alive again, after the summer exodus to the coast.

☆ World Theatre Festival, Zagreb

High-quality contemporary theatre comes to Zagreb for a couple of weeks each year, often extending into early October and delighting the country's die-hard theatre buffs. (p55)

☆ Varaždin Baroque Evenings

Baroque music takes over the baroque city of Varaždin for two to three weeks each September. Local and international orchestras play in the cathedral, churches and theatres around town. (p76)

☆ Unknown Festival, Rovinj

Artsy live-music fest in a forest just outside Rovinj wraps up the summer season in September with five days of concerts, boat and island parties and offbeat art installations.

October

Children are back in school, parents are at work and the country sways to its regular rhythms. Ferries change to their winter schedule but the weather is still pretty mild.

☆ Zagreb Film Festival

Don't miss this major cultural event that takes place in mid-October each year, with film screenings, accompanying parties and international film directors competing for the coveted Golden Pram award. (p55)

⚔ Truffle Hunting, Istria

Go hunting for the prized white and black truffles that grow in the forests around Motovun and Buzet in Istria's interior. Then cook up the smelly fungus and eat it in risotto, pasta and omelettes. (p127)

November

The continent chills but the seaside can still be sunny, albeit not warm. A number of the hotels along the coast shut their doors for the season, as do many restaurants.

⚑ Feast of St Martin

Martinje (St Martin's Day) is celebrated in all the wine-producing regions across Croatia on 11 November. There are wine celebrations and lots of feasting and sampling of new wines.

Plan Your Trip
Itineraries

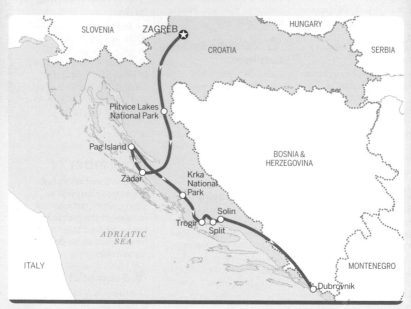

Essential Croatia

2 WEEKS

Take in the heavyweights of Croatia in this two-week journey from the continent to the coast, including the capital city, a national park and the gems of the Dalmatian coast.

Start in the capital, **Zagreb**, and set aside a long weekend to delve into its booming cafe culture, cutting-edge art scene, simmering nightlife and choice museums such as the quirky Museum of Broken Relationships. En route south, spend the day at the World Heritage–listed **Plitvice Lakes National Park** exploring its verdant maze of turquoise lakes and cascading waterfalls by foot or on one of the park's boats and buses for a whirlwind tour.

Next, head down to **Zadar**, one of Croatia's most underrated cities. It's a real find: historic, modern, active and packed with attractions, such as the unique sound-and-light spectacle of the Sea Organ and Sun Salutation, so stick around for two days. From here take an overnight trip to **Pag Island** to try some of that famously pungent and dangerously delicious cheese and indulge in its hopping beach party scene, if it's the height of summer. En route further

Zadar (p179)

south, swim under the stupendous falls at **Krka National Park** and do the hour-long loop along boardwalks connecting little islands in the emerald green river; end the outing at Skradinski Buk, the park's largest waterfall.

Take an afternoon stroll through the pretty streets of the postcard-perfect town of **Trogir,** the World Heritage star of Central Dalmatia. Next up, prepare yourself for one of the region's best sights: Diocletian's Palace in **Split** is a living part of this exuberant seafront city, a throbbing ancient quarter that's home to 220 historic buildings within its boundaries and about 3000

people. Base yourself here for three days of sightseeing, beach fun and nightlife action. Don't miss a jaunt to the nearby town of **Solin** for an afternoon, to meander around its impressive Roman ruins.

Next, take it easy down the winding coastal road to **Dubrovnik**, a magnificent walled city whose beauty is bound to blow you away. Spend the next two days taking in the jaw-dropping sights of its old town, ringed by mighty defensive walls and sparkling blue Adriatic.

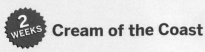

Cream of the Coast

2 WEEKS

Discover the stunners of Croatia's coast in two weeks – from Istria's favourite getaways to the jewels of Kvarner bay and all the way south to Dalmatia's greatest hits, both on the mainland and the islands.

Start your journey in Istria's coastal resort town of **Poreč** for an afternoon, admiring its showpiece, the World Heritage–listed Euphrasian Basilica that stands as one of Europe's finest intact examples of Byzantine art with magnificent 6th-century frescos. Then head south for the Venetian-inspired architecture and enchanting cobblestone streets of **Rovinj** for a two-day sojourn. Take in this star attraction of coastal Istria with its fishing-port vibe, the hilltop Church of St Euphemia, steep streets and piazzas and a lovely little art scene. Then it's on to **Pula** to tour its evocative Roman ruins and the 1st-century amphitheatre that overlooks the harbour. Spend a day exploring the historic highlights of Istria's capital before moving down the coast.

Make a pit stop in the old Habsburg resort of **Opatija** for a stroll along the elegant seaside promenade and killer views of the Kvarner coast. From nearby **Rijeka**, Croatia's third largest city and a lively port with a notable cafe scene, you can take a catamaran to pretty **Rab Town** on Rab Island. Spend a day exploring the ancient stone alleys of its old quarter and the four elegant bell towers that rise above it.

Next, devote another day to historic **Zadar** for its wealth of museums, churches, cafes and bars. Then travel south to the buzzing Dalmatian city of **Split** for a two-day fling focused on Diocletian's Palace.

Hop over to chic **Hvar Island** for a taste of its happening nightlife and for some clothing-optional sunbathing on its offshore **Pakleni Islands**. Alternatively, opt for a couple of days of real rest, rustic food and top diving on the more remote and uncrowded **Vis Island**. From Split, drive down to **Dubrovnik** to spend the next two days exploring its old town's gleaming marble streets, vibrant street life and fine architecture. Don't miss a hop to the gorgeous island of **Mljet** with its national park, where the verdancy, salt lakes and tranquillity heal the soul.

Top: Hvar Town (p236)
Bottom: Rab Town (p164)

Highlights of Istria

PLAN YOUR TRIP ITINERARIES

Explore the Istrian peninsula for its coastal resorts, pretty beaches, hilltop medieval towns, top-rated food, award-winning wines and lovely rural hotels.

Start your trip in **Pula**, the peninsula's coastal capital, home to the remarkably well-preserved Roman amphitheatre that overlooks the city's harbour. Arena, as it's known locally, once hosted gladiatorial contests, seating up to 20,000 spectators; today you can tour its remains and take in the small museum in the chambers downstairs. Base yourself in Pula for two days to see the smattering of other Roman ruins and take at least an afternoon to explore nearby **Rt Kamenjak** cape by bike or on foot. This entirely uninhabited cape, Istria's southernmost point, features rolling hills, wildflowers (including 30 species of orchid), medicinal herbs and around 30km of virgin beaches and coves.

Next drive up to **Rovinj** and set aside at least two days for the coast's showpiece resort town. Discover its steep cobbled streets and piazzas leading up to the Church of St Euphemia with its 60m-high tower that punctuates the peninsula, plus take in its verdant beaches and some of the 14 green islands that make up the Rovinj archipelago just offshore. Take a side trip to the captivating town of **Bale**, an offbeat place and one of Istria's best-kept secrets. Then zip up the coast to **Poreč** to gape at its World Heritage–listed Euphrasian Basilica; you'll be blown away by its medieval frescoes.

Don't miss exploring the peninsula's wooded interior, so end your trip with two nights in the hilltop town of **Buzet**, known as Istria's truffle epicentre. From here, make side trips to see the highlights of the interior. Istria carries the foodie crown of Croatia for its delicate truffles, air-dried ham, yummy olives and excellent wines; stop at the scenic village of **Zrenj**, home to a pair of top eating choices for simple but utterly delicious Istrian farm food (reserve ahead). Wander around the world's smallest town, the adorable **Hum**. Drive on to the artsy hilltop settlements of **Motovun**, known for its summer film festival, and the music-filled **Grožnjan**. Head south towards **Pazin** to walk through its famous chasm, which once inspired Jules Verne, then stroll through scenic **Svetvinčenat**, with its Renaissance-era square featuring a castle.

Top: Rovinj (p108)
Bottom: Roman Amphitheatre (p101), Pula

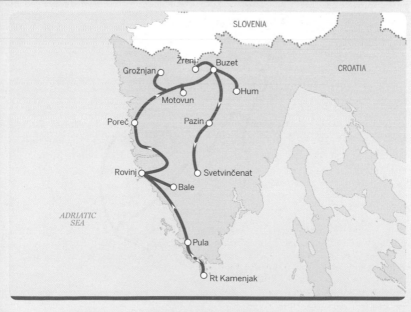

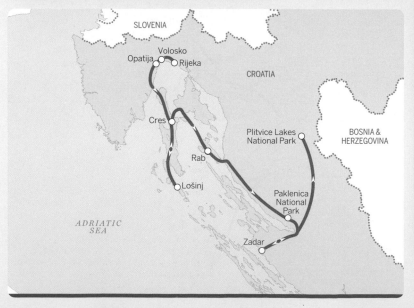

10 DAYS Kvarner & Northern Dalmatia

Take in the delights of Croatia's northern coastal stretches and their wild hinterland, starting with the Kvarner Gulf and moving south to northern Dalmatia with its wide spectrum of appealing sights.

Start in the capital of Kvarner, **Rijeka**, Croatia's third largest city and a thriving port with a laid-back vibe and a lively cafe scene. Take a day to explore this under-visited city and another to take in the elegant seaside resort town of **Opatija** and its leafy Riviera, just 13km west of Rijeka. Take in the beautiful belle époque villas and ample gardens of this town that once was the stomping ground of Viennese elite during the days of the Austro-Hungarian Empire. While you're at it, be sure to stroll Lungomare, a picturesque path that winds along the coast through exotic bushes and thickets of bamboo to **Volosko**, a pretty fishing village that's become one of Croatia's gastro meccas; make sure you have lunch or dinner in one of its acclaimed restaurants.

Next hop over to one of the Kvarner islands for two days – the interconnected **Cres** and **Lošinj** are the most offbeat. Wilder, greener Cres has remote camping grounds, pristine beaches, a handful of medieval villages and an off-the-radar feel, while more populated and touristy Lošinj sports a pair of pretty port towns, a string of beautiful bays and lush and varied vegetation throughout, with 1100 plant species and 230 medicinal herbs, many brought from faraway lands by sea captains. Spend another two days chilling on **Rab**, lounging on the sandy beaches of Lopar peninsula and exploring the postcard-pretty Rab Town with its ancient stone alleys and four bell towers that rise from them.

Back on the mainland, if you're feeling adventurous, don't miss a hike through the alpine trails and stunning canyons of **Paklenica National Park**. Next head down to **Zadar** for an amble through this vibrant coastal city with its medley of Roman ruins, Habsburg architecture and a lovely seafront; stick around for two days to take it all in. En route back inland, spend the day exploring the dazzling nature wonderland of **Plitvice Lakes National Park** with its gorgeous turquoise lakes linked by a series of waterfalls and cascades.

Top: Plitvice Lakes National Park (p171)
Bottom: Church of St Nicholas (p314), Nin, Zadar (p179)

Plan Your Trip
Travel with Children

With safe beaches, hiking and biking tracks to suit all abilities, a clutch of interactive museums, and lots of ancient towns and fortresses for would-be knights and princesses to explore, Croatia offers entertainment aplenty for those with children in tow.

Best Regions for Kids

Dubrovnik & Southern Dalmatia
Offers lots of beach action and unique experiences; let the littl'uns off the leash in Dubrovnik's car-free old town.

Split & Central Dalmatia
Wander the maze that is Diocletian's Palace and then head to the beaches of the Makarska Riviera.

Northern Dalmatia
Kids are fascinated by Zadar's nature-powered Sun Salutation and Sea Organ. Šibenik hosts an excellent children's festival.

Istria
Poreč and Rovinj are great bases for exploring nearby caves, dinosaur parks and beaches.

Zagreb
Ride the funicular, check out the many museums, get active at Jarun and Bundek, and hike up to the mountain peak of Sljeme.

Zagorje
Savour a slice of Croatian country life at Vuglec Breg and Grešna Gorica, tour the interactive museum in Krapina and visit medieval castles.

Croatia for Kids

Croatia has a lot of open spaces, playgrounds aplenty and pedestrian zones where there's no danger of traffic. Most seaside towns have a *riva* (seafront promenade) away from the water's edge that's perfect for strolling and letting the toddlers run around.

There are beaches galore, although some of what are referred to as 'beaches' are rocky indentations with steep drop-offs. Many of the sandy beaches are extremely shallow; perfect for toddlers but not so great for the teens. The numerous pebble beaches tend to offer better swimming.

Keep in mind that some of Croatia's smaller seaside towns can be too quiet for fun-seeking teenagers. They (and you in turn) will be a lot happier in the more happening coastal destinations where there are buzzy cafes and seasonal funfair rides.

Children's discounts are widely available for everything from museum admissions to hotel accommodation. The cut-off age is often nine, when student discounts kick in. Many attractions offer free entry for the little ones.

Eating with Kids

The generally relaxed dining scene means that you can take the children almost anywhere. Even the more upmarket restaurants will have a kid-friendly pasta, pizza or rice dish on the menu. Children's portions are easily arranged. However, you won't often find high chairs for the tinier tots and dining establishments are rarely equipped with nappy-changing facilities.

Locals are quite happy to take their children out for dinner to restaurants, and you'll often see kids running around on the local square while the adults are eating, drinking and chatting. Children eat mostly the same food as the adults, and everyone tucks into an ice cream at the end of the meal.

Babies

Breastfeeding in public is uncommon, but is generally accepted if done discreetly. Specific baby-friendly facilities are still thin on the ground, although that is slowly changing.

Baby food, disposable nappies and powdered baby formulas are easily found at supermarkets and pharmacies.

Hazards

Those spending a lot of time in forests during spring, summer or early autumn should make sure that they check the kids for ticks. There has been a rise in tick-borne diseases in recent years, so if you do find one, go to the doctor immediately. Be mindful of the numerous sea urchins in the shallows, particularly on rocky beaches; invest in some plastic water shoes for safer playing.

Children's Highlights

Beaches

Baška, Krk Island A 2km-long crescent of beach with a little waterpark at one end. (p162)

Cres & Lošinj Islands Lots of family-friendly campsites set right by the beach. (p146)

Crveni Otok, Rovinj Two connected islets awash with pebble beaches. (p114)

Lopar, Rab Island Shallow, sandy beaches which are perfect for toddlers. (p168)

Mljet Island The small saltwater lake is warm and perfect for babies. (p273)

Museums & Sights

➡ **Technical Museum, Zagreb** A quirky museum with a planetarium and a replica mine. (p59)

➡ **Museum of the Krapina Neanderthal, Krapina** Get up close and personal with our ancestors. (p81)

➡ **Batana House, Rovinj** Multimedia interactive displays illustrate Rovinj's fishing history. (p110)

➡ **Staro Selo Museum, Kumrovec** An entertaining slice of traditional village life. (p83)

➡ **Sun Salutation, Zadar** Come sunset, tots have a ball racing around this marvellous light display. (p182)

➡ **Istralandia, Istria** (www.istralandia.hr) Shoot down the slides and ride the waves in this big new water park.

Planning

Consider renting a private apartment – they're usually cheaper than a hotel room and give you more flexibility. Make sure you ask for specifics about the facilities – whether there's air-conditioning, a full kitchen, laundry facilities and how far the beach is, for example.

Hotels may have cots, but numbers are usually limited and sometimes there's a surcharge. Kids under three often stay for free, while those under nine get a considerable discount. Most properties in Croatia are family friendly but few are family specialists. Of those, the best are Club Funimation Borik (p183) near Zadar and Hotel Vespera (p154) in Mali Lošinj.

Children under five years old are required to travel in a suitable child seat. Make sure you're very clear with your hire-car company about your needs before you turn up.

No vaccinations are required for Croatia.

When to Go

The coastal city of Šibenik hosts a renowned International Children's Festival in late June/early July, with craft workshops, music, dance, children's film and theatre, puppets and parades. July and August coincide with the European school holidays, so they tend to have the most laid on for kids. If you'd prefer fewer people and lower prices, June and September are the best times, as the sea is warm enough for swimming and the days are sunny.

Regions at a Glance

Zagreb

Cafe Culture
Museums & Galleries
Food

Saturday Ritual of Špica

Zagreb is a bastion of Europe's famed cafe culture. The prime time to experience the peak of its social calendar is during the coffee-sipping and people-watching ritual known as *špica,* which happens on warm-weather Saturday mornings, when everyone and their mother comes out to show off their latest outfits.

Broken Hearts & Contempo Art

Zagreb's cultural flagship, the Museum of Contemporary Art brought an artistic flavour to the city's streetscapes, while the quirky Museum of Broken Relationships quickly became a favourite since opening a couple of years ago.

Croatia's Culinary Scene

On the food front, there is plenty to explore in Croatia's capital, where the culinary scene has diversified in recent years. A handful of destination restaurants showcase Croatia's own style of cooking, prepared with high-quality ingredients from around the country.

p40

Zagorje

Medieval Castles
Architecture
Countryside

Storybook Sights

Postcard-perfect fairytale castles dot the wooded hills of this bucolic region. The neo-Gothic Trakošćan offers an intimate insight into the life of former Croatian nobility, while the formidable Veliki Tabor, complete with towers, turrets and other castle trimmings, looks down from a verdant hilltop.

Baroque Delights

Soak up the baroque architecture of Varaždin. Its 18th-century buildings shine bright in their fully restored glory, with facades freshly painted in the original pastels: ochres, pinks, pale blues and creams.

Farm Life

The pretty pastoral panoramas of Zagorje's vineyard-covered hills, cornfields, dense forests and gingerbread cottages are the stuff of storybooks. Savour traditional Croatian farm life as it unfolds away from the tourist hullabaloo down south.

p71

Slavonia

Nature
Culture
History

Birdwatching

One of Europe's most important wetlands, Kopački Rit Nature Park occupies the floodplain where the Danube meets the Drava. Internationally famed for its diverse birdlife, the park is best visited during the spring or autumn migrations.

An Undiscovered Capital

Slavonia's capital, Osijek, is one of the greenest cities in Croatia, with a picturesque riverside promenade. It's also one of the most culturally rich areas, with a fascinating Habsburg quarter bursting with authentic restaurants ideal for trying the local paprika-rich food, including *fiš paprikaš*.

War Memorials

Eastern Slavonia suffered terribly during Croatia's Homeland War, when the region was pummelled by heavy artillery. In Vukovar you can visit stirring reminders of the war, including the exhibit about the siege in the newly reopened Castle Eltz Museum.

p84

Istria

Food
Architecture
Beaches

Truffles & Wines

Indulge in *la dolce vita* Istrian-style, feasting on superfine meals prepared in creative ways. From white truffles and wild asparagus to award-winning olive oils and wines, dining and wining is a highlight of any stay in Istria, Croatia's most foodie-friendly place.

Amphitheatres & Medieval Hilltowns

Istria's hotchpotch of architecture includes Roman-era amphitheatres, Byzantine basilicas, Venetian-style townhouses and medieval hilltop towns, all packed tightly and prettily into one small peninsula.

A Beach for Everyone

From pine-fringed, activity-packed pebble beaches a hop and a skip from Pula, Rovinj and Poreč, to the wild landscapes of Rt Kamenjak and its string of secluded coves, Istria has a beach for every taste (except for die-hard fans of sand).

p97

Kvarner

Food
Wildlife
Architecture

Gourmet Villages

The tiny cove of Volosko outside Rijeka is a gastronomic hotbed of authentic Croatian cooking, with a clutch of high-quality, atmospheric *konobas* (taverns) and restaurants.

Dolphins & Sea Turtles

The connected islands of Lošinj and Cres each boast excellent wildlife projects: in tiny Veli Lošinj you'll find a fascinating Adriatic dolphin research centre, while up in Mali Lošinj there's a new centre devoted to rescuing sea turtles.

Medieval Island Towns

Krk Town has a beautifully preserved medieval core, while the small but perfectly formed Rab Town features a string of historic churches and belltowers. The townhouses in Cres Town, Veli Lošinj and Mali Lošinj all show strong Venetian influences.

p134

Northern Dalmatia

Nature
Cities
Sailing

Inland Hikes & Swims

Most visitors come here for the coast, but this region has inland appeal in abundance. Krka and Plitvice showcase lovely lakes and exquisite waterfalls. Head to Paklenica for soaring mountains and great hiking.

Ancient Quarters

Northern Dalmatia's two cities both offer culture and history while being far from touristy. Šibenik arguably has Croatia's most elegant cathedral and a remarkable old quarter, while Zadar offers up intriguing sights, hip bars and restaurants.

Sails in the Sun

See the Mediterranean as it looked to the ancients, sailing between the isles of Kornati National Park, the largest and densest archipelago in the Adriatic, with 147 mostly uninhabited islands.

p169

Split & Central Dalmatia

Beaches
Architecture
Activities

Sand & Pebbles

From fun-filled Bačvice, Split's adored city beach, to the round pebbles of pine-fringed Brela and the tongue-shaped Zlatni Rat on Brač Island, Central Dalmatia has some of Croatia's best beaches – both popular and off the well-worn trail.

Medieval Quarters

Two Unesco World Heritage Sites sit a quick drive from one another in Central Dalmatia: the buzzing Roman-era quarter that is Diocletian's Palace in Split, and the architectural medley of Trogir's compact old town.

Outdoor Delights

Be it sailing, mountain biking, sea kayaking, diving, hiking, river rafting or windsurfing, active travellers will find it all in Central Dalmatia's varied landscapes.

p197

Dubrovnik & Southern Dalmatia

History
Nature
Wine

Walled Towns

One of the world's most evocatively situated and historic cities, Dubrovnik is a dream to look at, a delight to explore and a wrench to leave. The much smaller but gorgeous Korčula Town offers a similar experience.

Islands in the Sun

The thinly populated, pine-forested islands of Mljet and Korčula are rightfully acclaimed for their natural beauty and cove beaches. But don't neglect little Lokrum and the lovely Elafitis.

Dalmatian Grapes

The unspoilt Pelješac Peninsula is one of Croatia's emerging wine districts. Try rich, vibrant local reds like *postup* and *dingač* on a tour of its vineyards. Neighbouring Korčula is renowned for its white wines from the *pošip* and *grk* grapes.

p250

On the Road

Zagorje p71

Zagreb p40

Slavonia p84

Kvarner p134

Istria p97

Northern Dalmatia p169

Split & Central Dalmatia p197

Dubrovnik & Southern Dalmatia p250

Zagreb

01 / POP 792,875

Includes ➡

Around Zagreb 68

Lonjsko Polje
Nature Park 68

Medvednica
Nature Park 70

Best Places to Eat

➡ Vinodol (p59)

➡ Mundoaka Street Food (p59)

➡ Lari & Penati (p60)

➡ Karijola (p60)

Best Places to Stay

➡ Studio Kairos (p57)

➡ Esplanade Zagreb Hotel (p57)

➡ Hobo Bear Hostel (p55)

➡ Hotel Dubrovnik (p57)

Why Go?

Zagreb has culture, arts, music, architecture, gastronomy and all the other things that make a quality capital city – it's no surprise that the number of visitors has risen sharply in the last couple of years. Croatia's coastal attractions aside, Zagreb has finally been discovered as a popular city-break destination in its own right.

Visually, Zagreb is a mixture of straight-laced Austro-Hungarian architecture and rough-around-the-edges socialist structures, its character a sometimes uneasy combination of the two elements. This small metropolis is made for strolling the streets, drinking coffee in the permanently full cafes, popping into museums and galleries, and enjoying the theatres, concerts and cinema. It's a year-round outdoor city: in spring and summer everyone scurries to Jarun Lake in the southwest to swim or sail, or dance the night away at lakeside discos, while in autumn and winter Zagrebians go skiing at Mt Medvednica (only a tram ride away) or hiking in nearby Samobor.

When to Go
Zagreb

Apr & May The city takes off its winter coat and pavement cafes become a beehive of activity.

Jun Some of Zagreb's best festivals liven up its streetscapes and provide plenty of cultural fodder.

Sep & Oct People return from holidays and the city buzzes with summer energy.

History

Zagreb's known history begins in medieval times with two hills: Kaptol, now the site of Zagreb's cathedral, and Gradec. When the two settlements merged in 1850, Zagreb was officially born.

The space now known as Trg Bana Jelačića became the site of Zagreb's lucrative trade fairs, spurring construction around its edges. In the 19th century the economy expanded with the development of a prosperous clothing trade and a rail link connecting Zagreb with Vienna and Budapest. The city's cultural life blossomed, too.

Zagreb also became the centre for the Illyrian movement. Count Janko Drašković, lord of Trakošćan Castle, published a manifesto in Illyrian in 1832 and his call for a national revival resounded throughout Croatia. Drašković's dream came to fruition when Croatia and its capital joined the Kingdom of Serbs, Croats and Slovenes after WWI.

Between the two world wars, working-class neighbourhoods emerged in Zagreb between the railway and the Sava River, and new residential quarters were built on the southern slopes of Mt Medvednica. In April 1941 the Germans invaded Yugoslavia and entered Zagreb without resistance. Ante Pavelić and the Ustaše Croatian Liberation Movementmoved quickly to proclaim the establishment of the Independent State of Croatia (NDH; Nezavisna Država Hrvatska), with Zagreb as its capital. Although Pavelić ran his fascist state from Zagreb until 1944, he never enjoyed a great deal of support within the capital, which maintained support for Tito's Partisans.

In postwar Yugoslavia, Zagreb (to its chagrin) took second place to Belgrade but continued to expand. Zagreb was made the capital of Croatia in 1991, the same year that the country became independent.

◉ Sights

As the oldest part of Zagreb, the Upper Town (Gornji Grad), which includes the neighbourhoods of Gradec and Kaptol, has landmark buildings and churches from the earlier centuries of Zagreb's history. The Lower Town (Donji Grad), which runs between the Upper Town and the train station, has the city's most interesting art museums and fine examples of 19th- and 20th-century architecture.

◉ Upper Town

Museum of Broken Relationships　MUSEUM
(www.brokenships.com; Ćirilometodska 2; adult/concession 25/20KN; ⊙9am-10.30pm) Explore mementos that remain after a relationship ends at Zagreb's quirkiest museum. The innovative exhibit toured the world until it settled here in its permanent home. On display are donations from around the globe, in a string of all-white rooms with vaulted ceilings and epoxy-resin floors.

Exhibits hit on a range of emotions, from a vinyl record that was played during a teenage breakup forty years ago to a stun gun that never got to be used. Check out the lovely adjacent store – the 'bad memories eraser' is a bestseller – and the cozy cafe with sidewalk tables. There are jazz nights on Thursdays during summer and fall.

Dolac Market　MARKET
(⊙6.30am-3pm Mon-Fri, to 2pm Sat, to 1pm Sun) Zagreb's colourful fruit and vegetable market is just north of Trg Bana Jelačića. Traders from all over Croatia come to sell their products at this buzzing centre of activity. Dolac has been heaving since the 1930s, when the city authorities set up a market space on the 'border' between the Upper and Lower Towns.

The main part is on an elevated square; the street level has indoor stalls selling meat and dairy products and (a little further towards the square) flowers. The stalls at the northern end of the market are packed with locally produced honey, handmade ornaments and cheap food.

**Cathedral of the Assumption
of the Blessed Virgin Mary**　CATHEDRAL
(Katedrala Marijina Uznešenja; Kaptol 31; ⊙10am-5pm Mon-Sat, 1-5pm Sun) Kaptol Square is dominated by this cathedral, formerly known as St Stephen's. Its twin spires – seemingly permanently under repair – soar over the city. Although the cathedral's original Gothic structure has been transformed many times over, the sacristy still contains a cycle of frescoes dating from the 13th century. An earthquake in 1880 badly damaged the cathedral; reconstruction in a neo-Gothic style began around the turn of the 20th century.

Inside, don't miss the baroque marble altars, statues and pulpit, or the tomb of Cardinal Alojzije Stepinac by Ivan Meštrović.

Zagreb Highlights

1 Sipping coffee and cocktails alfresco along **Tkalčićeva** (p60).

2 Gaping at the remains of failed romances at the **Museum of Broken Relationships** (p41).

3 Strolling along the winding streets of the ancient **Upper Town** (p41).

4 Tapping into Croatia's current art beat in Zagreb's **Museum of Contemporary Art** (p50).

5 Picnicking and strolling in rambling **Maksimir Park** (p50).

6 Contemplating mortality amid the trees and tombs in **Mirogoj** (p50).

7 After a day hike, gorging on delicious *kremšnite* (custard pies) in **Samobor** (p69).

8 Trekking the trails of **Medvednica Nature Park** (p70), visiting mountain huts en route.

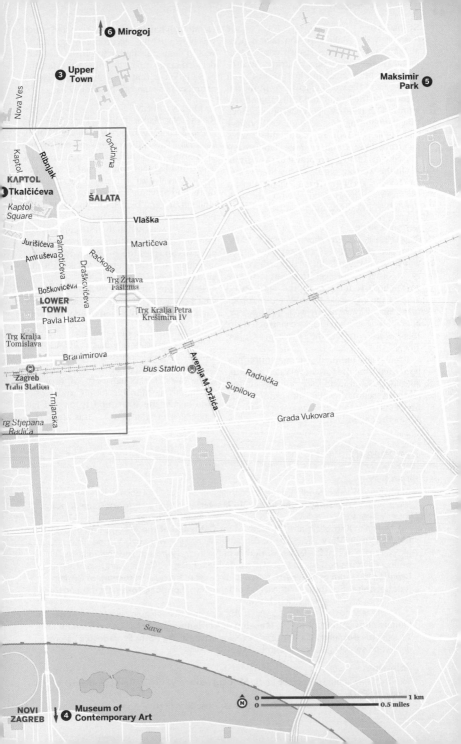

Stone Gate
GATE

(Kamenita Vrata) Make sure you take a peek at the Stone Gate, the eastern gate to medieval Gradec Town, now a shrine. According to legend, a great fire in 1731 destroyed every part of the wooden gate except for the painting of the Virgin and Child (by an unknown 17th-century artist). People believe that the painting possesses magical powers and come regularly to pray, light candles and leave flowers. Square stone slabs are engraved with thanks and praise to the Virgin.

On the western facade of the Stone Gate you'll see a statue of Dora, the hero of an 18th-century historical novel, who lived with her father next to the Stone Gate.

Lotrščak Tower
HISTORIC BUILDING

(Kula Lotrščak; Strossmayerovo Šetalište 9; adult/concession 20/10KN; ⊙9am-9pm) The tower was built in the middle of the 13th century in order to protect the southern city gate. Climb it for a sweeping 360-degree view of the city. Near the tower is a **funicular railway** (www.zet.hr/english/funicular.aspx; ticket 4KN; ⊙6.30am-10pm), constructed in 1888, which connects the Lower and Upper Towns.

For the last hundred years a cannon has been fired from the tower every day at noon, allegedly to commemorate one day in the mid-15th century, when the cannon was fired at noon at the Turks, who were camped across the Sava River. On its way down, the cannonball happened to hit a rooster, which was blown to bits – according to legend, this was so demoralising for the Turks that they decided not to attack the city. (A less fanciful explanation is that the cannon shot allows churches to synchronise their clocks.)

St Mark's Church
CHURCH

(Crkva Svetog Marka; Trg Svetog Marka 5; ⊙Mass 7.30am & 6pm Mon-Fri, 7.30am Sat, 10am, 11am & 6pm Sun) This 13th-century church is one of Zagreb's most emblematic buildings. Its colourful tiled roof, constructed in 1880, has the medieval coat of arms of Croatia, Dalmatia and Slavonia on the left side, and the emblem of Zagreb on the right. The Gothic portal, composed of 15 figures in shallow niches, was sculpted in the 14th century. The interior contains sculptures by Ivan Meštrović. You can enter the anteroom only during opening hours; the church itself is open only at Mass times.

From late April to October there's a guard-changing ceremony outside the church every Saturday and Sunday at noon.

Croatian Museum of Naïve Art
MUSEUM

(Hrvatski Muzej Naivne Umjetnosti; ☎01-48 51 911; www.hmnu.org; Ćirilometodska 3; adult/concession 20/10KN; ⊙10am-6pm Tue-Fri, to 1pm Sat & Sun) If you like Croatia's naive art – a form that was highly fashionable locally and worldwide during the 1960s and 1970s and has declined somewhat since – this small mu-

---

ZAGREB IN...

Two Days

Start your day with a stroll through Strossmayerov trg, Zagreb's oasis of greenery. Take a look at the **Strossmayer Gallery of Old Masters** and then walk to **Trg Bana Jelačića**, the city's centre.

Head up to **Kaptol Square** for a look at the **Cathedral of the Assumption of the Blessed Virgin Mary**, the centre of Zagreb's religious life. While in the Upper Town, pick up some fruit at the **Dolac Market** or have lunch at **Amfora**. Then get to know the work of Croatia's best sculptor at **Meštrović Atelier** and see its naive art legacy at the **Croatian Museum of Naïve Art**, followed by a visit to the quirky **Museum of Broken Relationships**. See the lay of the land from the top of **Lotrščak Tower**, then spend the evening bar-crawling along **Tkalčićeva**.

On the second day, tour the Lower Town museums, reserving an hour for the **Museum Mimara** and another one for the **Museum of Contemporary Art**. Lunch at **Vinodol** and digest in the **Botanical Garden**. Early evening is best at **Trg Petra Preradovića** before dining and sampling some of Zagreb's nightlife.

Four Days

Your third day should take in the lovely **Mirogoj** cemetery, with a stop at **Medvedgrad** or **Maksimir Park**.

On day four, take a trip out to **Samobor** for a big dose of small-town charm.

seum will be a feast. It houses around 1900 paintings, drawings and some sculptures by the discipline's most important artists, such as Generalić, Mraz, Rabuzin and Smajić.

Meštrović Atelier   GALLERY
(01-48 51 123; Mletačka 8; adult/concession 30/15KN; 10am-6pm Tue-Fri, to 2pm Sat & Sun) Croatia's most recognised artist is Ivan Meštrović. This 17th-century building is his former home, where he worked and lived from 1922 to 1942. The excellent collection it houses has some 100 sculptures, drawings, lithographs and pieces of furniture from the first four decades of his artistic life. Meštrović, who also worked as an architect, designed many parts of the house himself.

City Museum   MUSEUM
(Muzej Grada Zagreba; 01-48 51 926; www.mgz.hr; Opatička 20; adult/concession/family 30/20/50KN; 10am-6pm Tue-Fri, 11am-7pm Sat, 10am-2pm Sun;) Since 1907, the 17th-century Convent of St Claire has housed this historical museum, which presents the history of Zagreb through documents, artwork and crafts, as well as interactive exhibits that fascinate kids. Look for the scale model of old Gradec. Summaries of the exhibits are posted in English.

Galerija Klovićevi Dvori   GALLERY
(01-4851926; www.galerijaklovic.hr; Jezuitskitrg4; admission varies by exhibit, up to 40KN; 11am-7pm Tue-Sun) Housed in a former Jesuit monastery, this gallery is among the city's most prestigious spaces for exhibiting modern Croatian and international art. Past exhibits have included Picasso and Chagall, as well as collections of Croatia's prominent fine artists. The gallery's gift shop has arty souvenirs, and there's a nice cafe attached. The gallery closes in summer months, typically in August and part of September.

Jesuit Church of St Catherine   CHURCH
(Crkva Svete Katarine; Katarinin trg bb; Mass 6pm Mon-Fri, 11am Sun) This fine baroque church was built between 1620 and 1632. Although battered by fire and earthquake, the facade still gleams and the interior contains a fine altar dating from 1762; the interior stucco work dates from 1720. Look for the 18th-century medallions depicting the life of St Catherine on the ceiling of the nave.

Croatian Natural History Museum   MUSEUM
(Hrvatski Prirodoslovni Muzej; 01-48 51 700; www.hpm.hr; Demetrova 1; adult/concession 20/15KN; 10am-5pm Tue-Wed & Fri, to 8pm Thu, to 7pm Sat, to 1pm Sun) This museum houses a collection of prehistoric tools and bones excavated from the Krapina cave, as well as exhibits showing the evolution of animal and plant life in Croatia. Temporary exhibits often focus on specific regions.

Sabor   HISTORIC BUILDING
(Trg Svetog Marka 6) The eastern side of Markov trg is taken up by the Croatian *sabor* (parliament), built in 1910 on the site of baroque 17th- and 18th-century town houses. Its neoclassical style is quite incongruous on the square, but the historical importance of this building is undeniable – Croatia's secession from the Austro-Hungarian Empire was proclaimed from its balcony in 1918.

Lower Town

Trg Bana Jelačića   SQUARE
Zagreb's main orientation point and its geographic heart is Trg Bana Jelačića – it's where most people arrange to meet up. If you enjoy people-watching, sit in one of the cafes and watch the tramloads of people getting out, greeting each other and dispersing among the newspaper and flower sellers

The square's name comes from Ban Jelačić, the 19th-century *ban* (viceroy or governor) who led Croatian troops into an unsuccessful battle with Hungary in the hope of winning more autonomy for his people. The equestrian statue of Jelačić stood in the square from 1866 until 1947, when Tito ordered its removal because it was too closely linked with Croatian nationalism Franjo Tuđman's government dug it up out of storage in 1990 and returned it to the square.

Museum Mimara   MUSEUM
(Muzej Mimara; 01-48 28 100; www.mimara.hr; Rooseveltov trg 5; adult/concession 40/30KN; 10am-7pm Tue-Fri, to 5pm Sat, to 2pm Sun) This is the diverse private art collection – Zagreb's best – of Ante Topić Mimara, who donated over 3750 priceless objects to his native Zagreb (even though he spent much of his life in Salzburg, Austria). Housed in a neo-Renaissance former school building (1883), the collection spans a wide range of periods and regions.

Inside you'll find an archaeological section with 200 items; exhibits of ancient Far Eastern artworks; a glass, textile and furniture collection that spans centuries; and 1000 European art objects. In the painting

ZAGREB SIGHTS

Zagreb

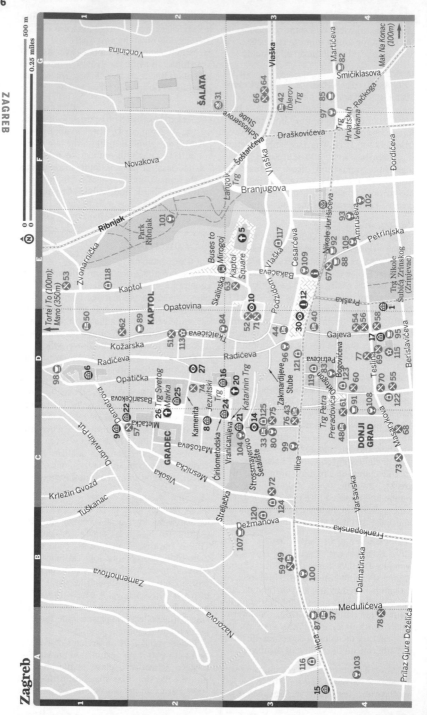

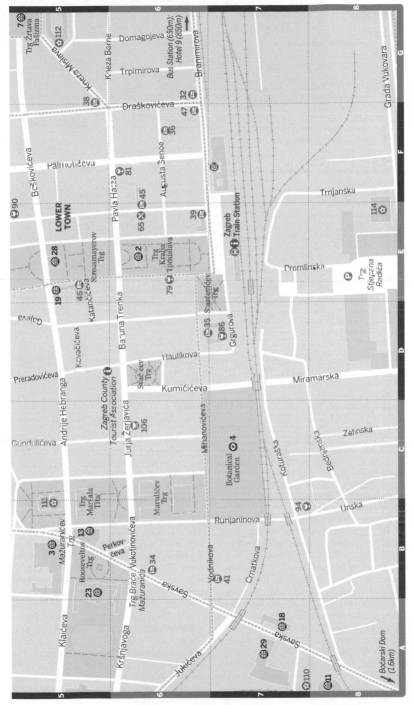

Zagreb

⊚ Sights
1 Archaeological Museum E4
2 Art Pavilion E6
3 Arts & Crafts Museum B5
4 Botanical Garden C7
5 Cathedral of the Assumption of
   the Blessed Virgin Mary E3
6 City Museum D1
7 Croatian Association of Artists G5
8 Croatian Museum of Naïve Art C2
9 Croatian Natural History
   Museum C1
10 Dolac Market E3
11 Dražen Petrović Memorial
   Museum A8
12 Equestrian Statue...................................E3
13 Ethnographic Museum.......................... B5
14 Funicular Railway................................... C3
15 Galerija Greta A4
16 Galerija Klovićevi Dvori D2
17 Galerija Nova D4
18 Galerija Studentski Centar A7
19 Gallery of Modern Art.............................E5
20 Jesuit Church of St Catherine.............. D3
21 Lotrščak Tower C3
22 Meštrović Atelier.....................................C1
23 Museum Mimara......................................B5
24 Museum of Broken
   Relationships.. C3
25 Sabor.. D2
26 St Mark's Church C2
27 Stone Gate D2
28 Strossmayer Gallery of Old
   Masters..E5
29 Technical Museum A7
30 Trg Bana Jelačića....................................D3

⊕ Activities, Courses & Tours
31 Sports & Recreational Centre
   Šalata...G2

⊜ Sleeping
32 Arcotel Allegra G6
33 Chillout Hostel Zagreb
   Downtown...C3
34 Croatian YHA B6
35 Esplanade Zagreb Hotel D6
36 Evistas...F6
37 Hobo Bear Hostel A4
38 Hostel Day and Night G5
39 Hotel Central..E6
40 Hotel Dubrovnik......................................D3
41 Hotel Garden..B7
42 Hotel Jadran...G3
43 Hotel Jägerhorn.......................................C3
44 Main Square Apartment.........................D3
45 Omladinski Hostel E6
46 Palace Hotel...E5
47 Palmers Lodge Hostel Zagreb F6
48 Shappy Hostel C4
49 Swanky Mint Hostel B3
50 Taban Hostel D1

⊗ Eating
51 Agava D2
52 Amfora D3
53 Baltazar...E1
54 Boban..D4
55 Burgeraj D4
56 Čušpajz...D4
57 Didov San C1
58 Dinara..D4
59 Dinara..B3
60 Dinara..D4

collection, check out works by Raphael, Caravaggio, Rembrandt, Bosch, Velázquez, Goya, Manet, Renoir and Degas.

**Strossmayer Gallery of
Old Masters** GALLERY
(Strossmayerova Galerija Starih Majstora; ☑01-48 95 117; http://info.hazu.hr/the_strossmayer_gallery_of_old_masters; Trg Nikole Šubića Zrinskog 11; adult/concession 30/10KN; ⊙10am-7pm Tue, to 4pm Wed-Fri, to 1pm Sat & Sun) This museum is housed in the 19th-century neo-Renaissance Croatian Academy of Arts and Sciences – this lovely building showcases the impressive fine-art collection donated to the city by Bishop Strossmayer in 1884. It includes Italian masters from the 14th to 19th centuries, such as Tintoretto, Veronese and Tiepolo; Dutch and Flemish painters such as Brueghel the Younger; and the classic Croatian artists Medulić and Benković.

The interior courtyard contains the **Baška Slab** (Bašćanska Ploča), a stone tablet from the Krk Island, which features the oldest example of Glagolitic script, dating from 1102. There is also a **statue of Bishop Strossmayer** by Ivan Meštrović.

Archaeological Museum MUSEUM
(Arheološki Muzej; ☑01-48 73 101; www.amz.hr; Trg Nikole Šubića Zrinskog 19; adult/concession/ family 20/10/30KN; ⊙10am-6pm Tue-Wed, Fri & Sat, to 8pm Thu, to 1pm Sun) The artefacts housed here stem from prehistoric times onwards. Among the most interesting are the **Vučedolska golubica** (Vučedol Dove), a 4000-year-old ceramic censer found near the town of Vukovar – the 'bird' has since become a symbol of Vukovar and peace. The courtyard, with a collection of Roman monuments dating from the 5th to 4th centuries BC, functions as an open-air cafe in summer.

61	Green Point	C4
62	Ivica i Marica	D1
63	Kaptolska Klet	E3
64	Karijola	G3
65	Lari & Penati	E6
	Le Bistro	(see 35)
66	Mali Bar	G3
67	Mundoaka Street Food	E4
68	Nishta	C4
69	Pingvin	D4
70	Ribice i Tri Točkice	D4
71	Rubelj	D3
72	Stari Fijaker 900	C3
73	Tip Top	C4
74	Trilogija	D2
75	Vallis Aurea	C3
76	Vincek	C3
77	Vinodol	D4
	Zinfandel's	(see 35)
78	Zrno	A4

Drinking & Nightlife
79	Bacchus	E6
80	Basement Wine Bar	C3
81	Beertija	F6
82	Booksa	G4
83	Bulldog	D4
84	Cica	D2
85	Divas	G4
86	Dramatic	D7
87	Eliscaffe	A3
88	Express	F4
89	Funk	D2
90	Hotpot	E5
91	Kino Europa	C4
92	Klub Kino Grič	E4
93	Kolaž	E4

94	KSET	B7
95	Lemon	D4
96	MK Krolo	D3
97	Mojo	F4
98	Palainovka	D1
99	Pepermint	C3
100	Pivnica Medvedgrad	B3
101	Rock Klub Ribnjak	E2
102	Rush Club	F4
103	Sedmica	A4
104	Stross	C3
105	Time	E4
106	U Dvorištu	C6
107	Velvet	B3
108	Vimpi	C4
109	VIP Club	E3

Entertainment
110	Cibona Tower	A7
111	Croatian National Theatre	B5
112	Koncertna Direkcija Zagreb	G5
113	Melin	D2
114	Vatroslav Lisinski Concert Hall	E8
115	Zagrebačko Kazalište Mladih	D4

Shopping
116	Antiques Market	A3
117	Aromatica	E3
118	Bornstein	E1
119	Croata	D3
120	I-GLE	B3
121	Nama	D3
122	Natura Croatica	D4
123	Profil Megastore	D4
124	Prostor	C3
125	Take Me Home	C3

Also inside are some fascinating Egyptian mummies, with ambient sounds and light designed to provoke pondering. The coin collection is one of the most important in Europe, containing some 260,000 coins, medals and medallions.

Ethnographic Museum MUSEUM
(Etnografski Muzej; ☎ 01-48 26 220; www.emz. hr; Mažuranićev trg 14; adult/concession 15/10KN; ⊙ 10am-6pm Tue-Thu, to 1pm Fri-Sun) The ethnographic heritage of Croatia is catalogued in this museum housed in a domed 1903 building. Out of 70,000 items, about 2750 are on display, such as ceramics, jewellery, musical instruments, tools, weapons and folk costumes – including gold-embroidered scarves from Slavonia and lace from the island of Pag. Thanks to donations from the Croatian explorers Mirko and Stevo Seljan, there are

also artefacts from South America, Ethiopia, China, Japan and Australia.

Arts & Crafts Museum MUSEUM
(Muzej za Umjetnost i Obrt; ☎ 01-48 82 123; www. muo.hr; Trg Maršala Tita 10; adult/concession/family 30/20/50KN; ⊙ 10am-7pm Tue-Sat, to 2pm Sun) Built between 1882 and 1892, this museum exhibits furniture, textiles, metal, ceramic and glass ranging from the Middle Ages to today. You can see Gothic and baroque sculptures from northern Croatia, as well as paintings, prints, bells, stoves, rings, clocks, bound books, toys, photos and industrial design. The museum hosts frequent temporary exhibitions.

Art Pavilion GALLERY
(Umjetnički Paviljon; ☎ 01-48 41 070; www.umjet-nicki-paviljon.hr; Trg Kralja Tomislava 22; adult/concession 30/15KN; ⊙ 11am-7pm Tue-Sat, 10am-1pm

Sun) The yellow Art Pavilion presents changing exhibitions of contemporary art. Constructed in 1897 in stunning art-nouveau style, the pavilion is the only space in Zagreb that was specifically designed to host large exhibitions. In some years, the gallery shuts its doors from mid-July through August; check the website for details.

Gallery of Modern Art GALLERY
(Moderna Galerija; 📞 01-60 41 040; www.moderna-galerija.hr; Andrije Hebranga 1; adult/concession 40/20KN; ⊘ 11am-7pm Tue-Fri, to 1pm Sat & Sun) Take in this glorious display of Croatian artists of the last 200 years, including such 19th- and 20th-century masters as Bukovac, Mihanović and Račić. It's a fine overview of the nation's vibrant arts scene.

Botanical Garden GARDENS
(Botanički Vrt; 📞 01-48 98 060; Marulićev trg 9A; ⊘ 9am-2.30pm Mon & Tue, to 7pm Wed-Sun Apr-Oct) **FREE** If you need a change from museums and galleries, take a break in this lovely, verdant retreat. Laid out in 1890, the garden has 10,000 species of plants and plenty of restful corners and paths.

◉ Novi Zagreb

Museum of Contemporary Art MUSEUM
(Muzej Suvremene Umjetnosti; 📞 01-60 52 700; www.msu.hr; Avenija Dubrovnik 17; adult/concession 30/15KN; ⊘ 11am-6pm Tue-Fri & Sun, to 8pm Sat) Housed in a stunning city icon designed by local star architect Igor Franić, this swanky museum displays both solo and thematic group shows by Croatian and international artists in its 17,000 sq metres. The permanent display, called *Collection in Motion,* showcases 620 edgy works by 240 artists, roughly half of whom are Croatian. There's a packed schedule of film, theatre, concerts and performance art year-round.

Inside, note the fun interactive *Double Slide* piece by Belgian artist Carsten Holler, and the stirring *Ženska Kuća* installation by Croatia's foremost artist, Sanja Iveković, dealing with the theme of violence against women.

Admission is free on the first Wednesday of each month.

◉ North of the Centre

Mirogoj CEMETERY
(Aleja Hermanna Bollea 27; ⊘ 6am-8pm Apr-Sep, 7am-6pm Oct-Mar) A 10-minute ride north of the city centre (or a 30-minute walk through leafy streets) takes you to one of the most beautiful cemeteries in Europe, sited at the base of Mt Medvednica. It was designed in 1876 by Austrian-born architect Herman Bollé, who created numerous buildings around Zagreb. The majestic arcade topped by a string of cupolas looks like a fortress from the outside, but feels calm and graceful on the inside.

The lush cemetery is crisscrossed by paths and dotted with sculptures and artfully designed tombs. Highlights include the grave of poet Petar Preradović and the bust of Vladimir Becić by Ivan Meštrović.

Take bus 106 from the Cathedral of the Assumption of the Blessed Virgin Mary.

Medvedgrad FORTRESS
(admission 15KN; ⊘ 11am-7pm Tue-Sun) The medieval fortress of Medvedgrad, just above the city on the southern side of Mt Medvednica, is Zagreb's most important medieval monument. Built from 1249 to 1254, it was erected to protect the city from Tartar invasions. Today you can see the rebuilt thick walls and towers, a small chapel with frescoes and the **Shrine of the Homeland**, which pays homage to those who died for a free Croatia. On a clear day, it offers beautiful views of Zagreb and surrounds.

To get there, take bus 102 from Britanski trg and get off at the church in Šestine; continue on foot following hiking trail #12 (from Lagvić to Medvedgrad).

◉ East of the Centre

Maksimir Park PARK
(📞 01-23 20 460; www.park-maksimir.hr; Maksimirski perivoj bb; ⊘ info centre 10am-3pm Mon-Fri, to 6pm Sat & Sun) The park, a peaceful wooded enclave covering 18 hectares, is easily accessible by trams 11 and 12 from Trg Bana Jelačića. Opened to the public in 1794, it was the first public promenade in southeastern Europe. It's landscaped like an English garden, with alleys, lawns and artificial lakes.

The most photographed structure in the park is the exquisite Bellevue Pavilion, constructed in 1843. There is also the Echo Pavilion, as well as a house built to resemble a rustic Swiss cottage. The **zoo** (www.zoo.hr; adult/children 30/20KN, children under 7 free; ⊘ 9am-8pm, ticket booth to 6.30pm) has a modest collection of the world's fauna and daily feeding times for seals, sea lions, otters and piranhas.

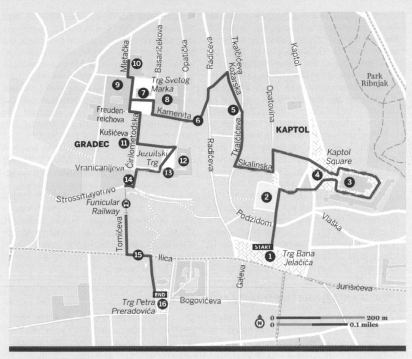

🏃 City Walk
Architecture, Art & Street Life

START TRG BANA JELAČIĆA
FINISH TRG PETRA PRERADOVIĆA
LENGTH 1KM; 1½ HOURS

You can pick up a copy of *Step by Step* free from any tourist office. It suggests two walking tours around the town centre exploring both the Upper Town and Lower Town.

The natural starting point of any walk in Zagreb is the buzzing ❶ **Trg Bana Jelačića**. Climb the steps up to ❷ **Dolac Market** and pick up some fruit or a quick snack before heading for the neo-Gothic ❸ **Cathedral of the Assumption of the Blessed Virgin Mary**. Cross ❹ **Kaptol Square**, lined with 17th-century buildings, walk down Skalinska and come out at Tkalčićeva. Wander up the street and climb the stairs next to the terraced bar ❺ **Melin**, which will take you up to ❻ **Stone Gate**, a fascinating shrine. Next, go up Kamenita and you'll come out at Trg Svetog Marka, the site of ❼ **St Mark's Church**, Zagreb's most emblematic building;

the ❽ **Sabor**, the country's parliament; and ❾ **Banski Dvori**, the presidential palace.

Wander about the winding streets of the Upper Town, and take in different aspects of Croatia's art world in ❿ **Meštrović Atelier**. Walk back across Trg Svetog Marka and down Ćirilometodska, stepping into one of the country's most singular museums, the ⓫ **Croatian Museum of Naïve Art**. Cross Jezuitski trg and enter ⓬ **Galerija Klovićevi Dvori**, where local and international contemporary art exhibitions await. When you're finished with art, gaze up at the gorgeous ⓭ **Jesuit Church of St Catherine**, before finally emerging at ⓮ **Lotrščak Tower**. Take in the cityscape and, if you fancy, go down in the funicular. Otherwise descend the verdant stairway – both will leave you on the side of ⓯ **Ilica**, Zagreb's commercial artery.

Cross Ilica and walk to ⓰ **Trg Petra Preradovića**, where you can take a break at one of the many alfresco cafes.

Croatian Association of Artists GALLERY
(Hrvatsko Društvo Likovnih Umjetnika; ☑ 01-46 11
818; www.hdlu.hr; Trg Žrtava Fašizma 16; adult/concession 20/10KN; ⊙ 11am-7pm Tue-Fri, 10am-2pm
Sat & Sun) East of the centre, this gallery is
housed in one of the few architectural works
by Ivan Meštrović and has a diverse repertoire
of art shows and various events – a must on
the art circuit of Zagreb. The building itself
has also had several fascinating incarnations,
reflecting the region's history in a nutshell.

Originally designed by Meštrović in 1938
as an exhibition pavilion, the structure honoured King Petar Karađorđević, the ruler of
the Kingdom of Serbs, Croats and Slovenes –
which grated against the sensibilities of Croatia's nationalists. With the onset of a fascist
government, the building was renamed the
Zagreb Artists' Centre in May 1941; several
months later Ante Pavelić, Croatia's fascist
leader, gave orders for the building to be
evacuated of all artwork and turned into a
mosque (claiming it was to make the local
Muslim population feel at home). There were
murmurs of disapproval from the artists, but
the building was significantly restructured
and eventually surrounded by three minarets.

With the establishment of Socialist Yugoslavia, however, the mosque was promptly
closed and the building's original purpose
restored – though it was renamed the
Museum of the People's Liberation. A permanent exhibition was set up and in 1949
the government had the minarets knocked
down. In 1951 an architect called V Richter
set about returning the building to its original state according to Meštrović's design.

The building has remained an exhibition
space ever since, with a non-profit association of Croatian artists making use of it.
Despite being renamed the Croatian Association of Artists in 1991 by the country's new
government, everyone in Zagreb still knows
it as 'the old mosque'.

ZAGREB'S CONTEMPORARY ART GALLERIES

Zagreb's palpable creative energy is driven by a host of young, ambitious artists and
curators who think outside the box. Here are some of the places where you can catch
home-grown art, much of it dealing with Croatia's society in transition. Note that most of
these shut their doors in August so check before you head there.

Lauba (☑ 01-63 02 115; www.lauba.hr; Baruna Filipovića 23a; adult/concession 25/10KN;
⊙ 2-10pm Mon-Fri, 11am-10pm Sat) This private art collection, housed in a former textile
weaving mill in an industrial area of western Zagreb, provides an insight into Croatian contemporary art from the 1950s to today. Works on display change frequently, with an exciting roster of events, and there's a cool **bistro** (⊙ 9am-11pm Mon-Fri, 11am-11pm Sat) on site.

Galerija Greta (www.greta.hr; Ilica 92; ⊙ 4-8pm Mon-Sat) **FREE** This storefront gallery in an
old textile shop hosts fun Monday night openings, showcasing different art forms: fine
arts, video, sound installations, sculptures, projections and performances.

Galerija Nova (☑ 01-48 72 582; www.whw.hr; Teslina 7; ⊙ noon-8pm Tue-Fri, 11am-2pm Sat)
FREE This independent art space is run by the WHW (Što, Kako i za Koga?) curatorial
collective, known for their probing of politically and socially sensitive topics. The small
space has a lively line-up of exhibits, performances, happenings and talks.

Galerija Studentski Centar (☑ 01-45 93 602; www.galerija.sczg.hr; Savska 25; ⊙ noon-
8pm Mon-Fri, 10am-1pm Sat) **FREE** You'll see works by some of Croatia's youngest artists at
this space, just southwest of the centre. With a focus on conceptual art, it puts on installations, site-specific works, performances and interactive projects, as well as theatre
pieces, concerts and festivals.

Galerija Galženica (☑ 01-62 21 122; www.galerijagalzenica.info; Trg Stjepana Radića 5, Velika
Gorica; ⊙ 10am-4pm Mon-Fri, to 1pm Sat & Sun) **FREE** This cutting-edge gallery in the nearby
town of Velika Gorica is worth the trek. Emphasis is placed on art that has arisen out of
the social, political and cultural changes Croatia has experienced in the past 15 years.
Check whether there's an exhibit on before you head out there.

Galerija Miroslav Kraljević (www.g-mk.hr; Šubićeva 29; ⊙ noon-7pm Tue-Fri, 11am-1pm
Sat) **FREE** Founded in 1986, this contemporary art space east of the city centre dedicates
itself to visual art. It has a dynamic repertoire of exhibitions, lectures, presentations and
residency programs.

🏃 Activities

Sports Park Mladost
SWIMMING, TENNIS

(☑ 01-36 58 553; Jarunska 5, Jarun; weekend day ticket adult/child/family 30/25/100KN, weekdays 25/20/60KN; ⊙ noon-7pm Mon-Fri, 10am-7pm Sat & Sun) Set by the Sava River, this park has outdoor and indoor Olympic-size swimming pools, as well as smaller pools for children, a gym and tennis courts. To get to Jarun, take tram 5 or 17.

Sports & Recreational Centre Šalata
SWIMMING, SKATING

(☑ 01-46 17 255; Schlosserove Stube 2; weekend day ticket adult/child/family 30/20/60KN, weekdays 20/15/40KN; ⊙ 1.30-6pm Mon-Fri, 11am-7pm Sat & Sun) This centre offers outdoor and indoor tennis courts, a gym, a winter ice-skating rink and two outdoor swimming pools (open June through September). There's also an indoor ice-skating rink that rents out skates.

Sljeme
SKIING, HIKING

(www.sljeme.hr) Although Zagreb is not normally associated with winter sports, you can ski right outside town at Sljeme, the main peak of Mt Medvednica, if the snow lasts long enough. It has four ski runs, three ski lifts and a triple chairlift; call the ski centre (☑ 01-45 53 382) or check the website for information on snow conditions.

Jarun Lake
SWIMMING, WATER SPORTS

Jarun Lake in south Zagreb is a popular getaway for residents at any time of the year, but especially in summer, when the clear waters are ideal for swimming. Although part of the lake is marked off for boating competitions, there is plenty of space to enjoy a leisurely swim.

On arrival, head left to Malo Jezero for swimming and canoe or pedal-boat rental, or right to Veliko Jezero, where there's a pebble beach and windsurfing.

Take tram 5 or 17 to Jarun and follow signs to the *jezero* (lake).

👉 Tours

There's a variety of tours to choose from in Zagreb. For more options than we've listed, browse the Zagreb City Tours section on the tourism board website (www.zagreb-touristinfo.hr).

Zagreb Bites
GUIDED TOUR

(☑ 091 52 88 723; www.zagrebites.com) For a guided tour of Zagreb's hottest restaurants and wine bars you wouldn't easily find yourself, book with this new venture, started by a pair of Croatia's renowned food bloggers. They also run excursions to the wine regions near Zagreb.

ZET
BUS TOUR

(☑ 060 100 001; www.zet.hr; adult/child 70/35KN; ⊙ May-Sep) Zagreb's public transportation network operates open-deck tour buses on a hop-on/hop-off basis in the warmer months. Buses depart from Kaptol Square and take in the old town (this route is marked red on maps) and the outlying parks and Novi Zagreb (marked green). Children under 7 years ride for free.

Funky Zagreb
TOURS

(www.funky-zagreb.com) Personalised tours that range in theme from wine tasting (340KN for 2½ to three hours) to hiking in Zagreb's surroundings (from 720KN per person for a day trip).

Blue Bike Tours
BIKE TOUR

(☑ 098 18 83 344; www.zagrebbybike.com) To experience Zagreb on a bike, book one of the tours – choose between Lower Town, Upper Town or Novi Zagreb – departing daily at 10am and 2pm from Trg Bana Jelačića 15. Tours last around two hours and cost 175KN.

Zagreb Talks
WALKING TOUR

(☑ 091 25 12 336; www.zagrebtalks.com) Tours include 'Do You Speak Croatian?', which teaches you basic language skills. By appointment only. Prices vary by number of people in the group.

Segway City Tour
GUIDED TOUR

(www.segwaycitytourzagreb.com) See Zagreb by Segway. This tour has daily departures, by prior booking, starting at 250KN for a fifty-minute ride.

✨ Festivals & Events

For a complete listing of Zagreb events, see www.zagreb-touristinfo.hr. Croatia's largest international fairs are the Zagreb spring (mid-April) and autumn (mid-September) grand trade fairs.

Music Biennale Zagreb
MUSIC

(www.mbz.hr) Croatia's most important contemporary music event is held in April during odd-numbered years.

Urban Festival
ARTS

(www.urbanfestival.blok.hr/13) A contemporary art festival centred around a yearly theme, Urban Festival places art in public spaces; typically held in spring or autumn.

LOCAL KNOWLEDGE

IVANA VUKŠIĆ: FOUNDER & DIRECTOR OF ZAGREB'S STREET ART MUSEUM

Founded in spring 2010, Zagreb's **Street Art Museum** (www.muu.com.hr) doesn't have a fixed physical home, opening hours, curators or pompous openings, or at least that's how the museum's director, Ivana Vukšić, describes the initiative, conceived as a series of projects. The first was successfully completed when over 80 artists were given 450m of the wall that separates Branimirova street from railway tracks. The latest projects beautified the otherwise drab Dugave and Siget neighbourhoods in Novi Zagreb with colourful street art.

Here Ivana lets us in on the latest happenings in the art and culture scene of Zagreb.

Top Art Galleries

The most interesting galleries for discovering new art trends in Croatia are Galerija Studentski Centar (p52), Galerija Nova (p52), Lauba (p52) and the Croatian Association of Artists (p52). The programs at these spaces always surprise with their fresh concepts and quality work presented in unpretentious environments.

Top Cultural Events

For film buffs, three must-see events are Zagreb Film Festival (p55), **Zagrebdox** (www.zagrebdox.net) and 25 FPS – International Experimental Film and Video Festival (p55).

The delightful festival of street performance Cest is D'Best (below) awakes Zagreb each summer, transforming it into a circus that doesn't stop. For site-specific and conceptual works, don't miss Urban Festival (p53).

Also be sure to check out the program of **Pogon Jedinstvo** (www.upogoni.org) for interesting events, and browse the website of **Kontejner** (www.kontejner.org), another collective worth following for their art productions.

Subversive Festival   CULTURE
(www.subversivefestival.com) Europe's activists and philosophers descend on Zagreb in droves for film screenings and lectures over two weeks in May.

Ljeto na Štrosu   CULTURE
(www.ljetonastrosu.com) From late May through late September, this quirky annual event stages free outdoor film screenings, concerts, art workshops and best-in-show mongrel dog competitions, all along the leafy Strossmayer Šetalište.

INmusic Festival   MUSIC
(www.inmusicfestival.com) A three-day extravaganza every June, this is Zagreb's highest-profile music festival. Previous years have seen Massive Attack, Iggy Pop and Morrissey take to the Jarun Lake main stage.

World Festival of Animated Film   FILM
(www.animafest.hr) Held in June, this prestigious festival has taken place in Zagreb since 1972 – odd-numbered years are devoted to feature films and even-numbered ones to short films.

Cest is D'Best   CULTURE
(www.cestisdbest.com) This street festival delights Zagreb citizens for a few days in early June each year, with five stages around the city centre, around 200 international performers, and acts that include music, dance, theatre, art and sports.

International Folklore Festival   CULTURE
(www.msf.hr) Taking place in Zagreb since 1966, this festival features folk dancers and singers from Croatia and other countries dressed in traditional costumes. There are free workshops designed to introduce you to Croatian folk culture. Held in July.

Zagreb Summer Evenings   MUSIC
This festival presents a cycle of concerts in the Upper Town each July. The atrium of Galerija Klovićevi Dvori (p45), on Jezuitski trg, and the Gradec stage are used for performances of classic music, jazz, blues and world tunes.

International Puppet Theatre Festival   PUPPETRY
(http://public.carnet.hr/pif-festival) Typically taking place during the last week of August or first week of September, this prominent

puppetry festival, around since 1968, show-cases star ensembles, workshops on puppet making and puppetry exhibits.

World Theatre Festival THEATRE
(www.zagrebtheatrefestival.hr) High-quality contemporary theatre comes to Zagreb for a couple of weeks each September, often extending into early October.

25 FPS – International Experimental Film and Video Festival FILM
(www.25fps.hr) This offbeat festival presents alternative visual expressions during one week of screenings, typically in late September.

Zagreb Film Festival FILM
(www.zagrebfilmfestival.com) If you're in Zagreb in mid-October, don't miss this major cultural event, with film screenings and accompanying parties. Directors compete for the Golden Pram award

Fuliranje CHRISTMAS MARKET
This alfresco holiday market, which uses various locations around the city centre, is held from late November though December. The focus is on street food, mulled wine and much merriment despite the below-zero temperatures. Check the Facebook page for this year's location.

🛏 Sleeping

Zagreb's accommodation scene has been undergoing a noticeable change with the arrival of some of Europe's budget airlines. The budget end of the market has picked up greatly and hostels have mushroomed in the last couple of years – as of writing, there were over thirty in Zagreb, from cheap backpacker digs to more stylish hideaways. Several of them have organised a pub crawl three nights per week, with free entrance to clubs and shots to boot (enquire at your hostel).

The city's business and high-end hotels are in full flow, thanks to Zagreb's role as an international conference hot spot.

Prices usually stay the same in all seasons, but be prepared for a 20% surcharge if you arrive during a festival or major event (in particular the autumn fair).

🛏 Upper Town

Taban Hostel HOSTEL €
(✆01-55 33 527; www.tabanzagreb.com; Tkalčićeva 82; dm 140KN, s/d/apt 220/400/600;

Ⓟ Ⓐ Ⓦ) Great location for partying, right on Tkalčićeva. Some rooms come with TVs, fridges and private bathrooms. A one-bedroom apartment is also available. There's a buzzing bar downstairs with live music events.

🛏 Lower Town

Chillout Hostel Zagreb Downtown HOSTEL €
(✆01-48 49 605; www.chillout-hostel-zagreb.com; Tomićeva 5a; dm 105-125KN, s/d 300/350KN; Ⓟ ❄ Ⓐ Ⓦ) Located in the tiny pedestrian street with the funicular, this cheerful spot has no less than 170 beds just steps away from Trg Bana Jelačića. The trimmings are plentiful, and the vibe friendly. Breakfast is available.

Hobo Bear Hostel HOSTEL €
(✆01-48 46 636; www.hobobearhostel.com; Medulićeva 4; dm from 153KN, d from 436KN; ❄ Ⓐ Ⓦ) Inside a duplex apartment, this sparkling five-dorm hostel has exposed brick walls, hardwood floors, free lockers, a kitchen with free tea and coffee, a common room and book exchange. The three doubles are across the street. Take tram 1, 6 or 11 from Trg Bana Jelačića.

Shappy Hostel HOSTEL €
(✆01 48 30 483; www.hostel-shappy.com; Varšavska 8; dm 137-190KN, d from 530KN; Ⓟ ❄ Ⓐ Ⓦ) This 14-room hostel is a peaceful oasis tucked away in a courtyard. Rooms range in size and theme – from the Romantic for Two and six bed Happy Room to a ten-person dorm; there's also a two-room apartment. On site is a bar with a terrace.

Palmers Lodge Hostel Zagreb HOSTEL €
(✆+385 1 889 28 68; www.palmerslodge.com.hr; Kneza Branimira 25; dm 120-150KN, d from 450KN; Ⓟ ❄ Ⓐ Ⓦ) Convenient for late arrivals, this hostel – part of the namesake British hostel chain – sits steps from the train station. The dorms aren't spectacular, but each comes with its own bathroom, plus there's a common space, a shared kitchen and excursions.

Omladinski Hostel HOSTEL €
(✆01-48 41 261; www.hfhs.hr; Petrinjska 77; dm 125-140KN, s/d 290/385KN; Ⓦ) Although spruced up, this socialist-era spot still maintains a bit of its old gloomy feel. The rooms are sparse and clean, and dorms have three or six beds. It's central and has many rooms, so it's a good back-up if you can't find a bed elsewhere.

Hotel Garden
HOTEL €€

(☑01-48 43 720; www.gardenhotel.hr; Vodnikova 13; s/d 471/547KN; ❄️🖥️) A newcomer on Zagreb's hotel scene, this contemporary three-star has clean-lined rooms with a full range of amenities. It's right by the Botanical Garden, hence the name. A great midrange choice, with a convenient location near the train station and close to the main square.

Swanky Mint Hostel
HOSTEL €€

(☑01-40 04 248; www.swanky-hostel.com/mint/; Ilica 50; dm 125-160KN, s/d 320/520KN, apt 620-760KN; @🖥️) Inside a restored textile-dye factory from the 19th century, this new hostel at the heart of town combines industrial chic with creature comforts in its rooms, dorms and apartments. Freebies include wi-fi, lockers, towels and a welcome shot of *rakija* (grappa). The garden bar serves breakfasts and drinks.

Hotel Jägerhorn
HOTEL €€

(☑01-48 33 877; www.hotel-jagerhorn.hr; Ilica 14; s/d/apt 835/911/1217KN; P❄️@🖥️) A charming, recently renovated little hotel that sits right underneath Lotršćak Tower (p44), the 'Hunter's Horn' has friendly service and 18 spacious, classic rooms with good views (you can gaze over leafy Gradec from the top-floor attic rooms). The downstairs terrace cafe is charming.

Hotel Jadran
HOTEL €€

(☑01-45 53 777; www.hotel-jadran.com.hr; Vlaška 50; s/d 560/650KN; P❄️@🖥️) This six-storey hotel has a superb location that is only minutes from Jelačić square. The 49 rooms are laid out in a cheery style and the service is friendly. Rates are negotiable depending on availability.

Hotel Central
HOTEL €€

(☑01-48 41 122; www.hotel-central.hr; Branimirova 3; s/d 550/660KN; ❄️@🖥️) The best midpriced place to stay if you have a train to catch, the Hotel Central is in a square concrete building with 76 comfy, if a little pokey, rooms. The larger top-floor rooms face the leafy courtyard.

A HOME OF YOUR OWN

Short-term apartment rentals in Zagreb are becoming increasingly popular, and are a good way to experience the city like a local. You can book prior to arrival through an agency or directly from the owners. The choice of apartments can be dizzying, so we've outlined the best agencies and highlighted a terrific find of a private apartment right on the main square. Plus there's a sweet cottage a short drive outside the city for those who want a taste of the Croatian countryside. Note that one-night stays sometimes have a surcharge.

ZIGZAG Integrated Hotel (☑01-88 95 433; www.zigzag.hr; Petrinjska 9; r/apt from 450/720KN; P❄️🖥️) The top agency in Zagreb, with 11 four-star apartments and five rooms around the centre of town, and great customer service.

Evistas (☑01-48 39 554; www.evistas.hr; Augusta Šenoe 28; s/d/apt from 220/290/320KN; ❄️🖥️) This agency can find you private accommodation. It's recommended by the tourist office and is the closest one to the train station.

InZagreb (☑01-65 23 201; www.inzagreb.com; apt 490-670KN; ❄️🖥️) Centrally located apartments with a minimum two-night stay. The price includes wi-fi, pick-up from the train or bus station and bike rental in most apartments.

Main Square Apartment (☑098 494 212; www.apartment-mainsquare.com; Trg Bana Jelačića 3; two people 608KN, three to four people 684KN; ❄️🖥️) This stylish apartment on the main square, steps from Dolac Market, has all the trimmings imaginable and a friendly host full of with insider tips you'll feel like a local in no time. Two more apartments in the building are joining the fray shortly.

Kućica (☑091 54 98 118; www.kuchica.com; weekdays/weekends 450/750KN; P) A great option if you have a car and crave a taste of Croatia's countryside, this Hansel-and-Gretel-style retreat in the hills (only 30 minutes from the city) is in a traditional cottage made of 120-year-old oak wood. Outside are orchards, vineyards, an organic garden and a hammock, while inside you'll find restored antique furniture, a wood oven and colourful rustic decor.

★**Esplanade Zagreb Hotel** HOTEL €€€
(☑ 01-45 66 666; www.esplanade.hr; Mihanovićeva 1;
s/d 1385/1500KN; ⓟ ✳ @ ⓢ) Drenched in
history, this six-storey hotel was built next
to the train station in 1925 to welcome the
Orient Express crowd in grand style. It has
hosted kings, artists, journalists and politi-
cians ever since. The art-deco masterpiece
is replete with walls of swirling marble, im-
mense staircases and wood-panelled lifts.

While you're there, take a peek at the
magnificent Emerald Ballroom and have a
meal at superb Zinfandel's restaurant (p60).

Palace Hotel HOTEL €€€
(☑ 01-48 99 600; www.palace.hr; Strossmayerov
trg 10; s/d from 779/890KN; ⓟ ✳ @ ⓢ) This
classy hotel, the oldest in Zagreb, oozes European charm. Its grand Secessionist mansion (built in 1891) has elegant rooms and
suites outfitted with the latest modern comforts. Try to get a front room for fantastic
views over the park. Look for the frescoes in
the back of the ground-floor cafe, which has
a unique Austro-Hungarian finesse.

Hotel Dubrovnik HOTEL €€€
(☑ 01-48 63 555; www.hotel-dubrovnik.hr; Gajeva 1;
s/d from 740/885KN; ⓟ ✳ ⓢ) Smack on the
main square, this glass New York wannabe is a city landmark, and the 245 well-
appointed units have old-school classic style.
It buzzes with business travellers who love
being at the centre of the action – try to get a
view of Trg Bana Jelačića and watch Zagreb
pass by under your window. Enquire about
packages and specials.

⌂ East of the Centre

Funk Lounge Hostel HOSTEL €
(☑ 01-55 52 707; www.funkhostel.hr; Rendićeva
28b; dm 135-180KN, s/d 450/450KN; ✳ @ ⓢ) Located steps from Maksimir Park, this outpost
of the original Funk Hostel (southwest of the
centre) has friendly staff, neat rooms and a
range of freebies, including breakfast, a shot
of *rakija,* toiletries and lockers. On site is a
restaurant and bar, and a full kitchen.

Hostel Day and Night HOSTEL €
(☑ 01-45 54 303; www.hosteldayandnight.com;
Kneza Mislava 1; dm 90-120KN, d 350KN; ✳ @ ⓢ)
Contemporary hostel a five-minute walk
from the train station and just ten minutes
from the main square, with dorms that sleep
four, six or eight; there's one double room.
Facilities are comprehensive, and it offers
tours.

Ravnice Hostel HOSTEL €
(☑ 01-23 32 325; www.ravnice-youth-hostel.hr; Prve
Ravnice 38d; dm/s/d 119/157/274KN; ⓟ @ ⓢ) A
20-minute tram ride (on lines 11 or 12) from
the centre, this pioneer of Zagreb hostels has
clean rooms, a rambling garden and freebies
such as lockers, coffee and tea and breakfast.
Musicians and performers get a free night's
stay in exchange for an hour's performance
for fellow guests.

★**Studio Kairos** B&B €€
(☑ 01-46 40 680; www.studio-kairos.com; Vlaška
92; s 340-420KN, d 520-620KN; ✳ ⓢ) This adorable B&B in a street-level apartment has four
well-appointed rooms decked out by theme –
Writers', Crafts, Music and Granny's – and
there's a cosy common space where delicious
breakfast is served. The interior design is gorgeous and the friendly owners are a fountain
of info. Bikes are also available for rent.

Arcotel Allegra HOTEL €€€
(☑ 01-46 96 000; www.arcotelhotels.com;
Branimirova 29; s/d from 730/840KN; ⓟ ✳ @ ⓢ)
Zagreb's first designer hotel has 151 airy
rooms and a marble reception area acces-
sorised with exotic fish. The bed throws are
printed with faces of Kafka, Kahlo, Freud
and other iconic personalities. The top-floor
wellness and workout area has great city
views.

Hotel 9 HOTEL €€€
(☑ 01-56 25 040; www.hotel9.hr; Avenija Marina
Držića 9; s/d 680/900KN; ✳ ⓢ) This recent hotel addition, steps from the main bus station,
is also Zagreb's most boutiquey option –
it's ideal for design hawks with its twenty
swanky rooms on three floors. Breakfast is
served on the rooftop terrace, with all the
trimmings thrown in.

✖ Eating

You'll have to love Croatian and Italian food
to enjoy Zagreb's restaurants, but new places
are branching out to include Japanese and
other world cuisines, as well as some vegetarian options (see p60). The city centre's
main streets, including Ilica, Teslina, Gajeva
and Preradovićeva, are lined with fast-food
joints, bakeries and inexpensive snack bars.

Note that many restaurants close in August for their summer holiday, which typically lasts anywhere from two weeks to a
month.

✗ Upper Town

Amfora
SEAFOOD €
(Dolac 2; mains from 40KN; ⊗6am-5pm) This locals' lunch favourite serves fresh seafood straight from the market next door, paired with off-the-stalls vegies. Just a hole in the wall, it has a few tables outside and an upstairs gallery with a nice market view.

Kaptolska Klet
TRADITIONAL CROATIAN €
(Kaptol 5; mains from 50KN; ⊗11am-midnight) This friendly restaurant has a huge outdoor terrace and a brightly lit, beer-hall-style interior. Although famous for its Zagreb specialities, such as grilled meats, lamb and veal under *peka* (a domed baking lid), and homemade sausages, it also turns out a nice vegetable loaf.

Rubelj
FAST FOOD €
(Dolac 2; mains from 25KN; ⊗9am-11pm) One of the many Rubeljs across town, this Dolac branch is a great place for a quick portion of *ćevapčići* (small spicy sausage of minced beef, lamb or pork) – they come pretty close to those in Bosnia and Hercegovina, the spiritual home of the dish.

Didov San
DALMATIAN €€
(✑01-48 51 154; www.konoba-didovsan.com; Mletačka 11; mains from 60KN; ⊗10am-midnight) This Upper Town tavern features a rustic wooden interior with ceiling beams and tables on the streetside deck. The food is based on traditional cuisine from the Neretva River delta in Dalmatia's hinterland, such as grilled frogs wrapped in proscuitto. Reserve ahead.

Trilogija
MEDITERRANEAN €€
(Kamenita 5; mains from 70KN; ⊗11am-11pm Mon-Sat) Right by the Stone Gate, in a location that has seen many a restaurant open and close – though this one seems to be here to stay. The secret lies in the quality of its fresh Croatian-Mediterranean food, friendly staff and friendly prices.

Mano
INTERNATIONAL €€
(www.mano.hr; Medvedgradska 2; mains from 100KN; ⊗noon-1am Mon-Sat) Swish steakhouse in a beautiful brick building steps from the Kaptol Centar, with an airy interior featuring exposed stone walls, steel pillars and a glass-enclosed kitchen. The lighting is moody and the mains innovative. Think wild-boar polenta with gorgonzola.

Ivica i Marica
TRADITIONAL CROATIAN €€
(www.ivicaimarica.com; Tkalčićeva 70; mains from 70KN; ⊗noon-11pm) Inspired by the Brothers Grimm story *Hansel and Gretel,* this little restaurant and cake shop is made to look like the gingerbread house from the tale, with waiters clad in traditional costumes. It has veggie and fish dishes plus meatier fare. The ice creams, cakes and *štrukli* (baked cheese dumplings) are great.

Baltazar
CROATIAN €€
(www.restoran-baltazar.hr; Nova Ves 4; mains from 90KN; ⊗noon-midnight Mon-Sat, to 5pm Sun) All kinds of meat – duck, lamb, pork, beef and turkey – are grilled and prepared the Zagorje and Slavonian way at this upmarket old-timer. There's a good choice of Mediterranean dishes and local wines. The summer terrace is a great place for dining under the stars.

Agava
INTERNATIONAL €€
(www.restaurant-agava.hr; Tkalčićeva 39; mains from 80KN; ⊗9am-11pm) The best thing about this smart spot on the main strip is its terrace. Food ranges from starters such as swordfish carpaccio to mains of steak and truffle. The wine list features plenty of Istrian and Slavonian choices.

✗ Lower Town

Tip Top
DALMATIAN €
(Gundulićeva 18; mains from 40KN; ⊗7am-11pm Mon-Sat) How we love Tip Top and its wait staff, who still sport old socialist uniforms and scowling faces that eventually turn to smiles. But we mostly love the excellent Dalmatian food. Every day has a different set menu.

Burgeraj
BURGERS €
(Preradovićeva 13; burgers from 35KN; ⊗11am-11pm Mon-Thu, to 2am Fri & Sat) American-style burger bar that whips up tasty, if slightly pricey, double and triple burgers, and serves Brooklyn Brewery beers. Chow down at the counter or grab one of few tables.

Ribice i Tri Točkice
SEAFOOD €
(Preradovićeva 7/1; mains from 50KN; ⊗9am-11pm) Funky and fun seafood spot offering simple but good Dalmatian mainstays, with daily specials announcing what's freshest. Sit inside in the colourful upstairs or at the sidewalk tables on Teslina.

Stari Fijaker 900
TRADITIONAL CROATIAN €
(Mesnička 6; mains from 50KN; ⊗11am-11pm) This restaurant and beer hall was once

ZAGREB FOR CHILDREN

Zagreb has some wonderful attractions for kids, but getting around with small children can be a challenge. Between the tram tracks, high curbs and cars, manoeuvring a stroller on the streets isn't easy. Buses and trams are usually too crowded to accommodate strollers, even though buses have a designated stroller spot. Up to the age of seven, children travel free on public transport. If you choose taxis, make sure they have working seat belts for the kids.

Kids will be fascinated by the bug collection at the Croatian Natural History Museum (p45). The **Technical Museum** (Tehnički Muzej; www.tehnicki-muzej.hr; Savska 18; general admission 15KN; ☉9am-5pm Tue-Fri, to 1pm Sat & Sun) features a planetarium and collections including steam-engine locomotives, scale models of satellites and space ships, and a replica of a mine; note that the planetarium might not appeal to very young kids. The little ones love the slide at the Museum of Contemporary Art (p50) though, and the interactive exhibits at the City Museum (p45).

For open-air activity, the best place for tots to work off some steam is **Bočarski Dom** (Prisavlje 2). The park has the best in playground equipment, playing fields and a roller-blading ramp. There's also a relaxing path along the Sava River for parents to enjoy. To get there, take tram 17 west to the Prisavlje stop.

Another good spot is **Bundek Lake** in Novi Zagreb, with water fit for swimming (in summer) and two playgrounds, one for children up to seven years and another for seven-plus. To get there, take tram 14 from Trg Bana Jelačića.

There are two playgrounds and a zoo inside Maksimir Park (p50), which are all great for little ones. Aquatically minded kids will like the pools in the Sports Park Mladost (p53) and Šalata (p53). Head to Jarun Lake (p53) for other recreational options, such as biking, rollerblading and kids' parks.

---

the height of dining out in Zagreb, and its decor of banquettes and white linen still has a staid sobriety. Tradition reigns in the kitchen, so try the homemade sausages and *štrukli*, or one of the cheaper daily dishes.

Valis Aurea   TRADITIONAL CROATIAN €
(Tomićeva 4; mains from 37KN; ☉9am-11pm Mon-Sat) This true local eatery has some of the best home cooking you'll find in town, so it's no wonder that it's chock-a-block at lunchtime for its *gableci* (traditional lunches). Located right by the lower end of the funicular.

Pingvin   SANDWICHES €
(Teslina 7; sandwiches from 15KN; ☉10am-4am Mon-Sat, 6pm-2am Sun) This quick-bite institution, around since 1987, offers tasty designer sandwiches and salads, which locals savour on a couple of bar stools.

Vincek   BAKERY €
(Ilica 18; pastries from 6KN; ☉8.30am-11pm Mon-Sat) This institution of a *slastičarna* (pastry shop) serves some of Zagreb's creamiest cakes. They have some serious competition, however, with **Torte i To** (Nova Ves 11, 2nd fl, Kaptol Centar; pastries from 3KN; ☉8am-11pm

Mon-Sat, 9am-11pm Sun) on the 2nd floor of Kaptol Centar, and the recently opened **Mak Na Konac** (Dukljaninova 1; pastries from 8KN; ☉9am-9pm Mon-Sat).

Dinara   BAKERY €
(Gajeva 8; pastries from 3.50KN; ☉5.30am-10.30pm) The best bakery in town churns out an impressive variety of baked goodies. Try the *bučnica* (filo pie with pumpkin). It also has branches at Ilica 71 and Preradovićeva 1.

★**Mundoaka Street Food**   INTERNATIONAL €€
(☑01-78 88 777; Petrinjska 2; mains from 45KN; ☉8am-midnight Mon-Thu, to 1am Fri, 9am-1am Sat) This adorable new eatery clad in light wood, with tables outside, serves up American classics – think chicken wings and pork ribs – and a global spectrum of dishes, from Spanish tortillas to *shakshuka* eggs. Great breakfasts, muffins and cakes, all prepared by one of Zagreb's best-known chefs. Reserve ahead.

★**Vinodol**   CROATIAN €€
(www.vinodol-zg.hr; Teslina 10; mains from 56KN; ☉noon-11pm) The well-prepared Central European fare here is much-loved by local and overseas patrons. On warm days, eat on the

covered patio (entered through an ivy-clad passageway off Teslina); the cold-weather alternative is the dining hall with vaulted stone ceilings. Highlights include the succulent lamb or veal and potatoes cooked under *peka*, as well as *bukovače* (local mushrooms).

Lari & Penati MODERN CROATIAN €€
(Petrinjska 42a; mains from 60KN; ☉noon-11pm Mon-Fri, to 5pm Sat) Small stylish bistro that serves up innovative lunch and dinner specials – they change daily according to what's market-fresh. The food is fab, the music cool and the few sidewalk tables lovely in warm weather. Closes for two weeks in August.

Boban ITALIAN €€
(www.boban.hr; Gajeva 9; mains from 70KN; ☉11am-11pm) Italian is the name of the game in this cellar restaurant owned by the Croatian football star Zvonimir Boban. The menu features a robust range of pasta, risotto, gnocchi and meat dishes. Its cafe next door, Čušpajz (mains from 38KN; ☉11am-6pm Mon-Sat), is a great quick-bite alternative for delicious lunchtime stews.

Zinfandel's INTERNATIONAL €€€
(☑01-45 66 644; www.esplanade.hr/cuisine/; Mihanovićeva 1; mains from 170KN; ☉6am-11pm Mon-Sat, 6.30am-11pm Sun) The tastiest, most creative dishes in town are served with flair in the dining room of the Esplanade Zagreb Hotel (p57). For a simpler but still delicious dining experience, head to French-flavoured Le Bistro (www.esplanade.hr/french-chic/; Mihanovićeva 1; mains from 95KN; ☉9am-11pm), also in the hotel – and don't miss its famous *štrukli* pastry.

East of the Centre

Karijola PIZZA €
(Vlaška 63; pizzas from 42KN; ☉11am-midnight Mon-Sat, to 11pm Sun) Locals swear by the crispy, thin-crust pizza churned out of a clay oven at this newer location of Zagreb's best pizza joint. Pizzas come with high-quality ingredients, such as smoked ham, olive oil, rich mozzarella, cherry tomatoes, rocket and shiitake mushrooms.

Mali Bar TAPAS €€
(☑01-55 31 014; Vlaška 63; dishes 35-120KN; ☉12.30-11pm Mon-Sat) This spot owned by star chef Ana Ugarković shares the terraced space with Karijola, hidden away in a *veža* (alleyway). The interior is cosy and earth-tone colourful, and the food focused on globally inspired tapas-style dishes. Book ahead.

Drinking & Nightlife

In the Upper Town, the chic Tkalčićeva is throbbing with bars and cafes. In the Lower Town, there's bar-lined Bogovićeva, just south of Trg Bana Jelačića, which turns into prime meet-and-greet territory on spring and summer days and balmy nights. Trg Petra Preradovića (known locally as Cvjetni trg) is the most popular spot in the

ZAGREB GOES VEGGIE

In the last couple of years, even a carnivore-pleasing place like Zagreb woke up to the growing needs of vegetarians and vegans. Several options now exist for those who don't eat meat.

Zrno (www.zrnobiobistro.hr; Medulićeva 20; mains from 47KN; ☉noon-9.30pm Mon-Sat; 🖉) This contemporary 'bio-bistro' (as it dubs itself) is tucked away in a courtyard a ten-minute walk from the main square and serves tasty options, from brown-rice gomoku to greenpeace pasta, a daily 'makroplata' meal, and desserts like *crostata* (baked tart) with seasonal fruit.

Nishta (www.nishtarestaurant.com; Masarykova 11/1; mains from 50KN; ☉11am-11pm Mon-Sat; 🖉) This newcomer on the scene, the offshoot of its Dubrovnik namesake, serves imaginative, globally inspired dishes in a chintzy, artsy space. The menu ranges from *ćevapovrčići* (a veggie version of the spicy sausage dish *ćevapčići*) to Mexican burritos, with many vegan and gluten-free options.

Green Point (www.green-point.hr; Varšavska 10; dishes from 20KN; ☉9am-10pm Mon-Sat; 🖉) For a quick, healthy bite on the go, grab a burger (take your pick from seitan, hemp or tofu) or one of the wok dishes or salads at this vegetarian storefront, smack in the centre of town.

Lower Town for street performers and occasional bands. With half a dozen bars and sidewalk cafes between Trg Preradovića and Bogovićeva, the scene on some summer nights resembles a vast outdoor party. Things wind down by midnight though, and get quieter from mid-July through late August, when half of Zagreb storms the coast.

In terms of nightclubs, admittedly Zagreb doesn't register high on the scale, but it does have an ever-developing art and music scene, and a growing influx of fun-seeking travellers. Nightclub entry ranges from 20KN to 100KN, depending on the evening and the event. Clubs open around 10pm but most people show up around midnight. Many clubs are open only from Thursday to Saturday.

Upper Town

★ Cica
BAR

(Tkalčićeva 18; ⊙10am-2am) This tiny storefront bar is as underground as it gets on Tkalčićeva. The funky interior has cutting-edge work by local artists and cool flea-market finds. Sample one or if you dare – all of the 25 kinds of *rakija* that the place is famous for. Herbal, nutty, fruity: if you can think it, they've got it.

Stross
BAR

(Strossmayerovo Šetalište; ⊙from 9.30pm daily Jun-Sep) A makeshift bar is set up most nights in summer at the Strossmayer promenade in the Upper Town, with cheap drinks and live music. The mixed-bag crowd, great city views and leafy ambience make it a great spot to while away your evenings.

Funk
CAFE, BAR

(Tkalčićeva 52; ⊙11am-2am) Sip coffee and watch people during the day, and at night go down the spiral staircase and you'll see why this cult spot has locals at its beck and call. In a small basement with stone vaulted ceilings, DJs spin house, jazz, funk and broken beats to a boogie-happy crowd.

Palainovka
CAFE

(Ilirski trg 1; ⊙8am-midnight Mon-Thu, to 2am Fri & Sat, 9am-11pm Sun) Claiming to be the oldest cafe in Zagreb (dating from 1846), this Viennese-style place serves delicious coffee, tea and cakes under pretty frescoed ceilings.

Lower Town

Booksa
CAFE

(www.booksa.hr; Martićeva 14d; ⊙11am-8pm Tue-Sun; 🔊) Bookworms and poets, writers and performers, oddballs and artists...basically anyone creative in Zagreb comes here to chat and drink coffee, browse the library, surf with free wi-fi and hear readings at this lovely, book-themed cafe. There are English-language readings here, too; check the website. Closes for three weeks from late July.

Basement Wine Bar
WINE BAR

(Tomićeva 5; ⊙9am-2am Mon-Sat, 4pm-midnight Sun) A city-centre hotspot for sampling Croatian wines by the glass, this basement bar (with a few sidewalk tables) sits right by the funicular. Pair the tipple with meat and cheese platters.

Bacchus
BAR

(Trg Kralja Tomislava 16; ⊙11am-midnight Mon-Fri, noon-midnight Sat) You'll be lucky if you score a table at Zagreb's funkiest courtyard garden, lush and hidden in a passageway. After 10pm the action moves inside the artsy subterranean space, which hosts poetry readings and classic-rock nights. Things get quiet in the summer.

Kino Europa
CAFE, BAR

(www.kinoeuropa.hr; Varšavska 3; ⊙8.30am-midnight Mon-Thu, to 4am Fri & Sat, 11am-11pm Sun; 🔊) Zagreb's oldest cinema, from the 1920s, now houses a splendid cafe, wine bar and *grapperia*. At this glass-enclosed space with an outdoor terrace, you can enjoy great coffee, over 30 types of grappa and free wi-fi. The cinema hosts film screenings and occasional dance parties.

Time
BAR

(Petrinjska 7; ⊙7am 2am Mon-Fri, 9am-2am Sat, 10am-10pm Sun) A newcomer on the scene, this cavernous former ironmonger's store is now a swish coffee-drinking hangout during the day and a buzzing American-style bar with DJ music come nightfall. The adjacent restaurant (⊙11am-11pm Mon-Sat) serves contemporary food.

MK Krolo
BAR

(Radićeva 7; ⊙8am-1am Mon-Thu, to 2am Fri & Sat, to 11pm Sun) This darling of Zagreb's dive bars is the gathering spot for the city's artists, bohos, media types and local drunks. Socialist chic at its best.

Pivnica Medvedgrad BREWERY
(www.pivnica-medvedgrad.hr; Ilica 49;
◷10am-midnight Mon-Sat, noon-midnight Sun)
Sip on one of five house-brewed beers at this
beer hall, which offers up reliably cheap and
tasty grub and a bustling atmosphere. It's
accessed through a shopping passageway
off Ilica, with a large, chestnut-tree-shaded
courtyard.

U Dvorištu CAFE, BAR
(Jurja Žerjavića 7/2; ◷9am-11pm Mon-Sat) A
sweet little cafe-bar tucked away inside a
courtyard, serving excellent organic and
fair-trade coffee and tea. There are occasional live-music performances and art
exhibitions.

Limb BAR
(Plitvička 16; ◷8am-2am Mon-Sat) A secret
spot only the locals know about, and probably the most understatedly hip little bar in

---

---

town, right by KSET (p63). A slightly older
boho crowd packs the two small, colourful
rooms and the glassed-in terrace with a tree
in the middle.

Klub Kino Grič CAFE, BAR
(Jurišićeva 6; ◷7am-midnight) This old-school
cinema has been revamped into a colourful,
two-floor bar and a small basement club
(weekends only). It has since become a locals' favourite, with art exhibits and film
screenings in the cosy projection room.

Beertija BAR
(Hatzova 16; ◷8am-midnight Mon-Wed, to 1am Thu,
to 4am Fri & Sat, 10am-midnight Sun) Zagreb's
popular beer hall, with a huge terrace and
the biggest selection of beers from around
the world – plus pub grub and various
events.

Sedmica BAR
(Kačićeva 7a; ◷8am-midnight Mon-Sat, 5pm-
midnight Sun) This low-key bar is hidden in an
alleyway off Kačićeva, with just a big Guinness sign marking the entrance. A gathering
point for Zagreb's boho-intellectual crowd,
it has a pokey interior with a mezzanine
and an outside patio that buzzes in warmer
months.

Velvet CAFE, BAR
(Dežmanova 9; ◷8am-10pm Mon-Fri, to 3pm
Sat, to 2pm Sun) Stylish spot for a good (but
pricey) cup of java and a quick bite amid the
minimalist-chic interior decked out by owner Saša Šekoranja, Zagreb's hippest florist.
The **Velvet Gallery** bar next door, known
as 'Black Velvet', stays open till 11pm (except
Sunday).

Lemon CAFE, BAR
(www.lemon.hr; Gajeva 10; ◷9am-midnight Mon-
Thu, to 5am Fri & Sat) A great spot for summer
cocktails on the terrace of the Archaeological Museum (p48), surrounded by ancient
slabs of stone. During autumn and winter,
boogie in the club downstairs.

Eliscaffe CAFE
(Ilica 63; ◷8am-7pm Mon-Fri, to 4pm Sat, to 2pm
Sun) The award-winning coffee from 100%
arabica beans here is tops. Try the smooth
triestino (similar to a macchiato) and pair
it with delicious *macarons* (made by Mak
Na Konac bakery, p59). Closes at 2pm daily
in summer.

Express
CAFE

(Petrinjska 4; 7am-11pm Mon-Fri, 8am-10pm Sat, 9am-2pm Sun) Tiny little cafe with tables outside, serving some of Zagreb's best coffees and teas.

Bulldog
PUB

(Bogovićeva 6; 9am-1am) The sidewalk tables here are prime for people-watching on this busy pedestrian street. At night, it's a good place to meet for drinks.

VIP Club
CLUB

(www.vip-club.hr; Trg Bana Jelačića 9; 8pm-5am Tue-Sat, closed summer) This newcomer on the nightlife scene has quickly become a local favourite. A swank basement place on the main square, it offers a varied program, from jazz to Balkan beats. It closes in summer months.

Pepermint
CLUB

(www.pepermint-zagreb.com; Ilica 24; 10pm-5am Tue-Sat, closed Aug) Small and chic city centre club clad in white wood, with two levels and a well-to-do older crowd. Programs change weekly, ranging from vintage rockabilly and swing to soul and house.

KSET
CLUB

(www.kset.org; Unska 3; 9am-4pm & 8pm-midnight Mon-Thu, 9am-4pm & 8pm-1am Fri, 10pm-3am Sat) Zagreb's top music venue, with everyone who's anyone performing here, from ethno to hip-hop acts. Saturday nights are dedicated to DJ music, when youngsters dance till late. You'll find gigs and events to suit most tastes.

Medika
CLUB

(www.pierottijeva11.org; Pierottijeva 11) This artsy venue in an old pharmaceutical factory calls itself an 'autonomous cultural centre'. It's the city's first legalised squat, with a program of concerts, art exhibits and parties fuelled by cheap beer and *rakija*.

Rock Klub Ribnjak
CLUB

(www.purgeraj.hr; Park Ribnjak 1; 10pm-5am Fri & Sat, 9pm-1am Sun-Thu) Live rock, blues and avant-garde jazz are on the music menu at this funky space. Programs feature a fusion of disco, house, breakbeat, pop and '80s music.

Sirup
CLUB

(www.sirupclub.com; Paromlin; 1am-8am Fri & Sat Oct-Jun) A serious party crowd frequents this new warehouse club in the landmark Paromlin building behind the train station.

Hotshot local and international DJs churn out techno.

North of the Centre

Jabuka
CLUB

(Jabukovac 28; Fri & Sat 10pm-3am) 'Apple' is an old-time fave, with 1980s hits played to a 30-something crowd that reminisces about the good old days when they were young and alternative. It's a taxi ride or a walk through the woods, set away in a posh area.

East of the Centre

Divas
CAFE

(Martićeva 17; 7am-11pm Mon-Fri, 8am-11pm Sat, 9am-5pm Sun) Great for daytime hanging out in the chintzy chic interior or the sidewalk tables, this boho little cafe is on the up-and-coming Martićeva street.

Mojo
BAR

(Martićeva 5; 7am-2am Mon-Fri, 8am-2am Sat, 8am-midnight Sun) Smoky basement hangout where live music and DJ-spun tunes are on every night. On warm nights, take your pick among 70 *rakijas* and liqueurs and sample them on the sidewalk tables out front.

Masters
CLUB

(Ravnice bb) Zagreb's smallest club also has the most powerful sound system, the feel of a private party and top-notch local and international DJ acts spinning deep house, tech-house, dub and reggae.

Katran
CLUB

(Radnička 27; 11pm-3am Fri & Sat) Former factory turned club, outside the centre near Zagreb's new CBD, it hosts varied weekend events, sometimes two parties on one floor, resulting in a diverse crowd and tunes. Events are posted on their Facebook page.

 South & West of the Centre

Sherry's Coffee & Wine Lab WINE BAR
(Andrije Žaje 63; ⊙7am-midnight Mon-Sat) This hot newcomer on the Zagreb wine bar scene is worth a trek out to Trešnjevka neighborhood, southwest of the city centre. You'll find more than 150 wine labels (mostly Croatian) by the glass or bottle, a friendly vibe and tasty nibbles.

Aquarius CLUB
(www.aquarius.hr; Aleja Matije Ljubeka bb, Jarun Lake) Past its heyday but still fun, this lakeside club has a series of rooms that open onto a huge terrace. House and techno are the standard fare but there are also hip hop and R&B nights. During summer, Aquarius sets up shop at Zrće on Pag (p179).

Močvara CLUB
(www.mochvara.hr; Trnjanski Nasip bb) In a former factory on the banks of the Sava River, 'Swamp' is one of Zagreb's best venues for the cream of alternative music and attractively dingy charm. Live acts range from dub and dancehall to world music and heavy metal.

☆ Entertainment

Zagreb's theatres and concert halls present a great variety of programs throughout the year. Many are listed in the monthly brochure *Zagreb Events & Performances,* available from the main tourist office. The back pages of daily newspapers *Jutarnji List* and *Večernji List* show the current offerings on the art and culture circuit.

Many open-air events in the city are free, but admission is usually charged for indoor concerts. Prices depend upon the concert, but tickets for most musical events can be purchased from **Koncertna Direkcija Zagreb** (☑01-45 01 200; www.kdz.hr; Kneza Mislava 18; ⊙9am-6pm Mon-Fri) as well as several music shops around town.

☆ Live Music

Melin JAZZ BAR
(Kožarska 19; ⊙9.30am-2am) Popular jazz hangout on Tkalčićeva, with live music most nights, a diverse crowd and a colourful outdoor terrace.

Tvornica LIVE MUSIC
(www.tvornicakulture.com; Šubićeva 2; ⊙cafe 7am-11pm, club 11pm-4am) Excellent multimedia venue showcasing a variety of live music performances, from Bosnian *sevdah* to alternative punk rock. Check out the website to see what's on.

☆ Theatre

Theatre tickets are usually available for purchase last-minute, even for the most in-demand shows.

Zagrebačko Kazalište Mladih THEATRE
(☑01-48 72 554; www.zekaem.hr; Teslina 7; ⊙box office 10am-8pm Mon-Fri, to 2pm Sat & Sun, plus 1hr before the show) Zagreb Youth Theatre, better known as ZKM, is the cradle of Croatia's contemporary theatre. It hosts several festivals and many visiting troupes from around the world.

Croatian National Theatre THEATRE
(☑01-48 88 418; www.hnk.hr; Trg Maršala Tita 15; ⊙box office 10am-7pm Mon-Fri, to 1pm Sat & 1hr before the show) This neobaroque theatre, established in 1895, stages opera and ballet performances. Check out Ivan Meštrović's sculpture *The Well of Life* (1905) standing out front.

Vatroslav Lisinski Concert Hall CONCERT HALL
(☑01-61 21 166; www.lisinski.hr; Trg Stjepana Radića 4; box office 10am-8pm Mon-Fri, 10am-2pm & 6-8pm Sat & Sun) This is the city's most prestigious venue in which to hear symphony concerts, jazz and world-music performances; it also stages theatrical productions.

☆ Sport

Jarun Lake (p53) hosts competitions in rowing, kayaking and canoeing during summer.

Cibona Tower BASKETBALL
(☑01-48 43 333; www.cibona.com; Savska 30; tickets 30-100KN) Basketball is popular in Zagreb, which is home to the Cibona basketball team. Tickets can be purchased at the door or online. Learn more about the team's most famous player at the nearby **Dražen Petrović Memorial Museum** (☑01-48 43 146; www.drazenpetrovic.net; Trg Dražena Petrovića 3; adult/child 20/10KN; ⊙10am-5pm Mon-Fri; closed mid-Jul–mid-Aug), next to the Technical Museum.

Stadion Maksimir FOOTBALL
(☎ 01-23 86 125; www.gnkdinamo.hr; Maksimirska 128; tickets 250-550KN) Dinamo is Zagreb's most popular football team; it plays matches at Stadion Maksimir, on the eastern side of Zagreb. Take trams 4, 7, 11 or 12 to Maksimirska.

 Shopping

Ilica is Zagreb's main shopping street, with fashionable international brands peeking out from the staid buildings. Most stores are closed on Sunday.

Prostor FASHION
(www.multiracionalnakompanija.com; Mesnička 5; ☺ noon-8pm Mon-Fri, 10am-3pm Sat) A fantastic little art gallery and clothing shop, that features some of the city's best independent artists and young designers. Check out the Prostor website for details of exhibition openings.

Natura Croatica FOOD
(www.naturacroatica.com; Preradovićeva 8; ☺ 9am-9pm Mon-Fri, 10am-4pm Sat) Over 300 Croatian products and souvenirs are sold at this shop, from *rakija,* wines and chocolates to jams, spices and truffle spreads. A perfect pit stop for gifts.

Take Me Home SOUVENIRS
(Tomićeva 4; ☺ 10am-8pm Mon-Fri, to 3pm Sat) Great choice of cool souvenirs, all by Croatian designers.

Profil Megastore BOOKS
(Bogovićeva 7) Inside an entryway, this most atmospheric of Zagreb bookstores has a great selection of books (including a whole section of titles in English) and a nice cafe.

Aromatica BEAUTY
(www.aromatica.hr; Vlaška 7; ☺ 8am-8pm Mon-Fri, to 3pm Sat) Flagship store of a small chain showcasing all-natural skincare products, from handcrafted soaps to fragrant oils, with a focus on local herbs. Great gift baskets, too.

Bornstein WINE
(www.bornstein.hr; Kaptol 19; ☺ 9am-8pm Mon-Fri, to 4.30pm Sat) If Croatia's wine and spirits have gone to your head, get your fix here. Stocks an astonishing collection of brandy, wine and gourmet products.

I-GLE FASHION
(www.i-gle.com; Dežmanova 4; ☺ 10am-2pm & 4pm-8pm Mon-Fri, 10am-2pm Sat) Get one of the almost sculptural yet wearable creations by Nataša Mihaljčišin and Martina Vrdoljak-Ranilović, the movers and shakers of Croatia's fashion industry since the 1990s.

MARKET DAYS

Zagreb doesn't have many markets but those it does have are stellar. The weekend **antiques market** (Britanski trg; ☺ 7am-2pm Sat, 7.30am-2.30pm Sun) on Britanski trg, for example, is one of central Zagreb's joys.

But to see a flea market that's unmatched in the whole of Croatia, you have to make it to **Hrelić** (☺ 7am-3pm Wed & Sun). It's a huge space packed with everything from car parts and antique furniture to clothes, records, kitchenware – you name it. All goods are, of course, secondhand, and bargaining is the norm. Apart from the shopping, it's a great experience in itself and is a side of Zagreb you probably won't see anywhere else – expect lots of Roma people, music, general liveliness and grilled meat smoking in the food section. If you're going in the summer months, take a hat and put on some sunscreen, as there's no shade. Take bus 295 (15KN, 20 minutes, on Sunday only) to Sajam Jakuševac from behind the railway station. By tram, take number 6 in the direction of Sopot, get off near the bridge and walk 15 minutes along the Sava to get to Hrelić; or take tram 14, get off at the last stop in Zapruđe and do the 15-minute walk from there.

If it's a Saturday and you're into food, don't miss **Mali Plac na Tavanu** (Little Market in the Attic; ☎ 095 91 52 711; www.tavan.info; Sinkovićeva 8; ☺ 11am-6pm Sat Sep–mid-Jun, 6pm-midnight Sat mid-Jun–Jul, closed Aug) , a weekly gathering of small producers who hawk their wares in the funky attic of food blogger and stylist Jelena Nikolić; you'll find anything from organic citrus fruits and sage honey to hemp oil and hummus, plus hand-crafted natural cosmetics. At time of research the market was planning to move locations, so check for the latest on the website.

ℹ️ ZAGREB CARD

If you're in Zagreb for a day or three, getting the **Zagreb Card** (www.zagreb-card.fivestars.hr) is a pretty good way to save money. You can choose either 24 or 72 hours (60KN or 90KN) and you get free travel on all public transport, a 50% discount on museum and gallery entries, and even discounts in some bars and restaurants, on car rental and so forth. A booklet lists all the places that offer discounts. The card is sold at the main tourist office and in many hostels, hotels and shops.

Croata · CLOTHING
(www.croata.hr; Oktogon Passage, Ilica 5; ⊙8am-8pm Mon-Fri, to 3pm Sat) Since the necktie originated in Croatia, nothing could make a more authentic gift – this is the place to get one. The locally made silk neckties are priced from 249KN to 2000KN.

Nama · DEPARTMENT STORE
(Ilica 4; ⊙8am-8.30pm Mon-Fri, to 3pm Sat) Zagreb's immortal, old-time department store, with a wide assortment of items at low prices.

ℹ️ Information

EMERGENCY
Police Station (📞01-45 63 311; Petrinjska 30)

INTERNET ACCESS
There are a number of smaller internet cafes along Preradovićeva.
Sublink (📞01-48 19 993; www.sublink.hr; Teslina 12; per hr 19KN; ⊙9am-11pm Mon-Wed, to 1am Thu-Sat, 3-11pm Sun) The city's first cybercafe, still going strong.

MEDICAL SERVICES
Dental Emergency (📞01-48 97 688; Runjaninova 4; ⊙10pm-6am)
KBC Rebro (📞01-23 88 888; Kišpatićeva 12; ⊙24hr) East of the city; provides emergency aid.
Pharmacy (📞01-48 16 198; Trg Bana Jelačića 3; ⊙24hr)

MONEY
There are ATMs at the bus and train stations, the airport, and at numerous locations around town. Some banks in the train and bus stations accept travellers cheques.
Exchange offices can be found in the Importanne Centar on Starčevićev trg, as well as in other locations around town.

POST
Post Office (📞01-66 26 453; Jurišićeva 13; ⊙7am-8pm Mon-Fri, to 1pm Sat) Has a telephone centre.
Main Post Office (📞01-72 30 3304; Branimirova 4; ⊙7am-midnight) Holds poste restante mail. Right by the train station.

TOURIST INFORMATION
The **Main Tourist Office** (📞information 0800 53 53, office 01-48 14 051; www.zagreb-tourist info.hr; Trg Bana Jelačića 11; ⊙8.30am-9pm Mon-Fri, 9am-6pm Sat & Sun Jun-Sep, 8.30am-8pm Mon-Fri, 9am-6pm Sat, 10am-4pm Sun Oct-May) Distributes free city maps and leaflets, and sells the Zagreb Card.
Other branches can be found at Lotrščak Tower (⊙9am-9pm Mon-Sat, 10am-9pm Sun Jun-Sep, 9am-5pm Mon-Fri, 10am-3pm Sat & Sun Oct-May), the airport (📞01-62 65 091; ⊙9am-9pm Mon-Fri, 10am-5pm Sat & Sun), the train station (⊙9am-9pm Mon-Fri, 10am-5pm Sat & Sun) and the bus station (⊙9am-9pm Mon-Fri, 10am-5pm Sat & Sun).
Zagreb County Tourist Association (📞01-48 73 665; www.tzzz.hr; Preradovićeva 42; ⊙8am-4pm Mon-Fri) has information and materials about attractions surrounding Zagreb, including wine roads and bike trails.

TRAVEL AGENCIES
Atlas Travel Agency (📞01-48 07 300; www.atlas-croatia.com; Zrinjevac 17) Tours around Croatia.
Croatia Express (📞01-49 22 224; www.croatia-express.com; Trg Kralja Tomislava 17) Train reservations, car rental, air and ferry tickets, hotels around the country and a daily trip to the beach from June to September (90KN round trip to Crikvenica).
CYHA Travel Section (📞01-48 29 294; www.hfhs.hr; Savska 5; ⊙8.30am-4.30pm Mon-Fri) The travel branch of the Croatian YHA can provide information on HI hostels throughout Croatia and make advance bookings.
Zdenac Života (📞01-48 16 200; www.zdenac-zivota.hr; 2nd fl, Vlaška 40; ⊙10am-4pm Mon-Fri) In addition to thematic sightseeing tours of Zagreb, this small agency does active day trips from the capital and multi-day adventures around Croatia.

ℹ️ Getting There & Away

AIR
Croatia Airlines (📞01-66 76 555; www.croatiaairlines.com; Zrinjevac 17) The country's national carrier operates international and domestic flights to and from Zagreb.

Zagreb Airport (☎ 01-45 62 222; www.zagreb-airport.hr) Located 17km southeast of Zagreb, this is Croatia's major airport, offering a range of international and domestic services.

BUS

Zagreb's **bus station** (☎ 060 313 333; www.akz.hr; Avenija M Držića 4) is 1km east of the train station. If you need to store bags, there's a **garderoba** (per hour 5KN; ⊘ 24hr). Trams 2 and 6 run from the bus station to the train station. Tram 6 goes to Trg Bana Jelačića.

Before buying your ticket, ask about the arrival time – some of the buses take local roads and stop in every town en route.

Note that listed schedules are somewhat reduced outside high season.

TRAIN

The **train station** (☎ 060 333 444; www.hznet.hr; Trg Kralja Tomislava 12) is in the southern part of the city centre. As you come out of it,

you'll see a series of parks and pavilions directly in front of you, which lead into the town centre.

It's advisable to book train tickets in advance because of limited seating. The station also has a **garderoba** (lockers per 24hr 15KN; ⊘ 24hr) if you need to store bags.

ⓘ Getting Around

TO/FROM THE AIRPORT
Bus

The Croatia Airlines bus to the airport (30KN) leaves from the bus station every half-hour or hour from about 4.30am to 8pm, and returns from the airport on the same schedule.

Taxi

Costs from 110KN to 200KN to the city centre.

CAR

Zagreb is a fairly easy city to navigate by car (main streets are wide, and parking in the city

BUSES FROM ZAGREB

DOMESTIC DESTINATION	COST (KN)	DURATION (HR)	DAILY SERVICES
Dubrovnik	205-250	9½-11	9-12
Korčula	264	11	1
Krk	113-219	3-4½	8-10
Makarska	175-230	6½	12-15
Mali Lošinj	287-312	5-6	3
Osijek	131-144	4	10
Plitvice	92-106	2-3	11-15
Poreč	156-232	4-4½	11
Pula	105-196	3½-5½	17-20
Rab	207-219	4-5	5
Rijeka	91-155	2½-4	20-25
Rovinj	150-195	4-6	9-11
Šibenik	151-165	4½-7	20-22
Split	115-205	5-8½	32-34
Varaždin	65-87	1-2	19-23
Zadar	105-139	3½-5	31

INTERNATIONAL DESTINATION	COST (KN)	DURATION (HR)	DAILY SERVICES
Belgrade	220	6	5
Florence	481	10½	1
Ljubljana	87-125	2½-3½	4-6
Munich	375	9½	6
Paris	798	24	1 weekly
Sarajevo	160-210	7-8	4-5
Vienna	225-247	5-6	3

ZAGREB AROUND ZAGREB

TRAINS FROM ZAGREB

DOMESTIC DESTINATION	COST (KN)	DURATION (HR)	DAILY SERVICES
Osijek	132-150	5-6	5
Rijeka	111-118	4-6	6
Šibenik	183	8	4
Split	197-208	5-7	4
Varaždin	64-71	2-3	11

INTERNATIONAL DESTINATION	COST (KN)	DURATION (HR)	DAILY SERVICES
Banja Luka	111	4½-5	1
Belgrade	188	6½	1
Budapest	224	6-7	1
Ljubljana	127	2½	4
Mostar	300	11½	1
Munich	785	7-8½	2
Sarajevo	238	8-9½	1
Vienna	520	6-7	2

centre, although scarce, costs 6KN per hour). Watch out for trams buzzing around.

A number of international car-hire companies are represented in Zagreb. Bear in mind that local companies will usually have lower rates.

H&M (☑ 01-37 04 535; www.hm-rentacar.hr; Grahorova 11) Local car-rental company; also at airport.

Hertz (☑ 01-48 46 777; www.hertz.hr; Grada Vukovara 274)

Oryx (☑ 01-62 60 800; www.oryx-rent.hr; Grada Vukovara 74) Local car-rental company; also at aiport.

Hrvatski Autoklub (HAK, Croatian Auto Club; ☑ 01-46 40 800; www.hak.hr; Avenija Dubrovnik 44) Motorists can call ☑ 1987 for help on the road.

TAXI

Radio Taxi (☑ 060 800 800, 1777) charges 10KN for a start and 5KN per kilometre; waiting time is 40KN per hour. **Ekotaxi** (☑ 060 77 77, 1414) charges similar rates.

You'll have no trouble finding idle taxis, usually at blue-marked taxi signs; note that these are Radio Taxi stands.

For short city rides, **Taxi Cammeo** (☑ 060 71 00, 1212) is typically the cheapest, as the 15KN start fare includes the first two kilometres (it's 6KN for every subsequent kilometre).

TRAM

Zagreb's public transport (www.zet.hr) is based on an efficient network of trams, although the city centre is compact enough to make them almost unnecessary. Tram maps are posted at most stations, making the system easy to navigate.

Buy tickets at newspaper kiosks or from the driver for 10KN. You can use your ticket for transfers within 90 minutes, but only in one direction. A *dnevna karta* (day ticket) is valid on all public transport until 4am the next morning; it's available for 30KN at most newspaper kiosks.

Make sure you validate your ticket when you get on the tram by pressing it on the yellow box.

AROUND ZAGREB

The area around Zagreb is rich with quick getaway options, from picturesque towns with great food to peaceful hikes and nature reserves.

Lonjsko Polje Nature Park

Lonjsko Polje (☑ 044-672 080; www.pp-lonjsko-polje.hr; Čigoć; adult/concession 40/30KN; ☺ 8am-4pm) is a fascinating mix of several diverse delights. It's packed with 19th-century wooden architecture, and birdwatchers (well, stork lovers) can have a field day here, as can those who appreciate all things equestrian. Nominated for World Heritage Site status in January 2008, Lonjsko Polje is a 506-sq-km stretch of swampland (*polje* means 'field') in the Posavina region, between the Sava River and Mt Moslavačka Gora. Seated along Lonja River, a Sava tributary that gives the park its name, this huge retention basin is famed for the diversity of its flora and fauna.

The area is divided into several villages. Čigoć is a world-famous 'stork meeting point' – the storks nest on top of Čigoć's lovely wooden houses. The birds flock here in late March and early April, hanging around and munching on the swampland insects up until late August, when they start their two-to three-month flight back towards southern Africa. If you're here during autumn and winter, you might catch sight of a few year-round storks who are content to hang out and be fed by the villagers. Čigoć is home to the park's information point and ticket office, and a small ethnographic collection owned by the Sučić family.

The heritage village of **Krapje** is known for its well-preserved traditional wooden houses and rich fishing and hunting areas. Check out the covered external staircases, porches and pillars, and various farm buildings with their barns, drying sheds, pigsties and hen houses. From April through October an information centre in one of the wooden houses is staffed with a guide who will be happy to enlighten you about the

---

WORTH A TRIP

SAMOBOR: SWEET TREATS & HIKES

Stressed-out city dwellers head to Samobor, 25km west of Zagreb, to wind down and get their fix of hearty food, creamy cakes and pretty scenery. A shallow stream curves through the town centre, which is composed of trim pastel houses and several old churches. For a great meal, stop by **Gabreku 1929** (Starogradska 46; mains from 55KN), a classic restaurant a short walk from the town centre that has been run by the same family since the 1920s; it's known for its 35 types of sweet and savoury *palačinke* (crêpes). Don't miss the town's famous *kremšnite* (custard pies), served at **U Prolazu** (Trg Kralja Tomislava 5).

Samobor is a good jumping-off point for **hiking** into the Samoborsko Gorje, a mountain system (part of the Žumberak Range) that links the high peaks of the Alps with the karstic caves and abysses of the Dinaric Range. Carpeted with meadows and forests, it's the region's most popular hiking destination, and has been the cradle of organised mountaineering activity in Croatia since 1875. Most of the hikes are easy and there are several mountain huts that make pleasant rest stops. Many are open weekends only (except in high season); more information is available through the **Croatian Mountaineering Association** (Hrvatski planinarski savez; ☑ 01-48 23 624; www.hps.hr). In 1999 the whole area, covering 333 sq km, was proclaimed a nature park because of its biodiversity, forests, karst caves, river canyons and four waterfalls.

The range is divided into three sections: the Oštrc group in the centre, the Japetić group to the west and the Plešivica group to the east. Both the Oštrc and Japetić groups are accessible from the Šoićeva Kuća mountain hut and restaurant, 10km west of Samobor, reachable by bus 144. From there it's a rather steep 30-minute climb to the medieval hill fort of Lipovac and an hour's hike to the peak of Oštrc (752m), with another mountain hut.

Another popular hike is the 1½-hour climb from Šoićeva Kuća to Japetić (879m), the highest peak of Samobor Hills and a famous **paragliding** spot (see www.parafreek. hr for information). You can also follow a path from Oštrc to Japetić (two hours). The Plešivica group has ruins of a medieval fort and a protected park forest area, and it's also a famous **rock-climbing** spot; you can access it from the village of Rude (bus 143 services Rude and Braslovje). From Rude, head east to the hunting cabin Srndać on the mountain saddle of Poljanice (12km), from where it's a rather steep 40-minute hike to the peak of Plešivica (779m).

Samobor is easy to reach by public transport. Get a Samoborček bus from the main bus station in Zagreb (28KN, 30 minutes, half-hourly). For plentiful brochures and maps of Samobor, as well as maps and hiking information for Samoborsko Gorje and Žumberačko Gorje (another nearby mountain range), pop by the **tourist office** (☑ 01-33 60 044; www.tz-samobor.hr; Trg Kralja Tomislava 5; ⊙ 8am-5pm Mon-Fri, 9am-5pm Sat, 10am-5pm Sun) in the town centre.

cultural heritage of the area. Look out for the *posavski* horse, a local breed that grazes in the oak forests of Lonjsko Polje. You can go horse riding here, too – ask at the information office in Čigoć.

Also worth a visit is the village of **Mužilovčica**, known for its swallows. Don't miss a meal at the Ravlić family farm here.

Lonjsko Polje is 50km southeast of Zagreb. The best way to visit is with your own transport or on a tour, as public transport is poor and makes moving around the park quite difficult. Private accommodation is available in various wooden houses inside the park; more information is available on the website.

Medvednica Nature Park

Medvednica Nature Park (www.pp-medvednica.hr), just to the north of Zagreb, offers excellent **hiking** opportunities. There are several popular and well-marked routes. You can take tram 14 to the last stop and then change to tram 15 and take it to its last stop. Walk straight through the tunnel, which takes you directly to Dolje park entrance; this leads to the popular and easy Lojstekova trail, which ends at Sljeme, the top of Mt Medvednica. Along the way you can stop at one of Sljeme's oldest huts, **Runolist** (www.runolist-sljeme.com; mains from 40KN), which offers beautiful views of the city and traditional food and drink.

Alternatively you can hike in the direction of the **Puntijarka** (www.puntijarka.com; mains from 50KN) and **Hunjka** mountain huts. These are very popular on weekends for their home-cooked traditional Croatian dishes served in a rustic setting. This second Bikčevićeva path starts at the Bliznec entrance to Medvednica Nature Park. Follow the tunnel path, but then cross to the left side of the road at the former funicular station. This is a shorter but also steeper and more intense path.

You can also take bus 102 from Britanski trg, west of the centre on Ilica, to the church in Šestine and take the easy hiking route from there. There are two huts along the way: **Risnjak** and **Grafičar**. For more info about these, see the park website.

Allow about three hours return for any of these hikes – and remember that this is a heavily wooded mountain with ample opportunities to get lost. Take warm clothes and water, and make sure to return before sundown. There is also a danger of disease-carrying ticks in spring, so wear trousers and long sleeves, and examine your body after the hike. For more information, contact the Zagreb tourist office (p66).

In winter there's skiing at the **Sljeme ski resort** (www.sljeme.hr), which has five slopes of varying difficulty. The website provides the up-to-date status of each slope.

Zagorje

Includes ➡
Varaždin 74
Varaždinske Toplice . . .78
Trakošćan Castle 79
Krapina. 81
Veliki Tabor Castle 82
Kumrovec 83
Klanjec 83
Marija Bistrica 83

Best Places to Eat

➡ Vuglec Breg (p80)

➡ Grešna Gorica (p82)

➡ Majsecov Mlin (p80)

➡ Mala Hiža (p79)

Best Places to Stay

➡ Vuglec Breg (p80)

➡ Villa Magdalena (p82)

➡ Spa & Sport Resort Sveti Martin (p79)

➡ Hiže na Bregu (p80)

Why Go?

Despite its proximity to Zagreb, the bucolic northern region of Zagorje receives few tourists, even at the height of summer – especially surprising given the delightful villages, medieval castles, endless vineyards and thermal springs that speckle its rolling hills. These leafy landscapes, with Austrian-influenced food and architecture (and the same prices year-round), present a nice alternative to the busy Mediterranean south and a good escape from the summer heat. You'll find it blissfully crowd-free, although slightly less so on weekends, when day-tripping families from Zagreb storm the area.

The Zagorje region begins north of Mt Medvednica (1035m), near Zagreb, and extends west to the Slovenian border, and as far north as Varaždin, a showcase of baroque architecture. Whether you want to feast on hearty cuisine at rustic restaurants, dip into the hot springs, get a taste of village life or tour ancient castles, with Zagorje you're in for an offbeat treat.

When to Go

Varaždin

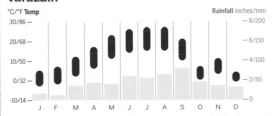

Jun Summer weather kicks in, perfect for touring the hills, castles and thermal spas.

Aug Špancirfest in Varaždin has world music, theatre and other fun performances.

Sep Enjoy folklore and traditional food at Krapina's Festival of Kajkavian Songs.

Zagorje Highlights

1 Admiring the immaculately preserved baroque architecture of **Varaždin** (p74).

2 Experiencing the life of Croatian nobility at **Trakošćan Castle** (p79).

3 Getting an insight into traditional village life at **Staro Selo Museum** (p83) in Kumrovec.

4 Sampling Croatian culinary specialties at **Vuglec Breg** (p80), near Krapinske Toplice.

5 Learning about our Neanderthal ancestors at the **Museum of the Krapina Neanderthal** (p81) in Krapina.

6 Catching **Špancirfest** (p76), an event that rocks the streets of Varaždin.

7 Touring the wine roads of the **Međimurje region** (p79), which stretches northeast of Varaždin.

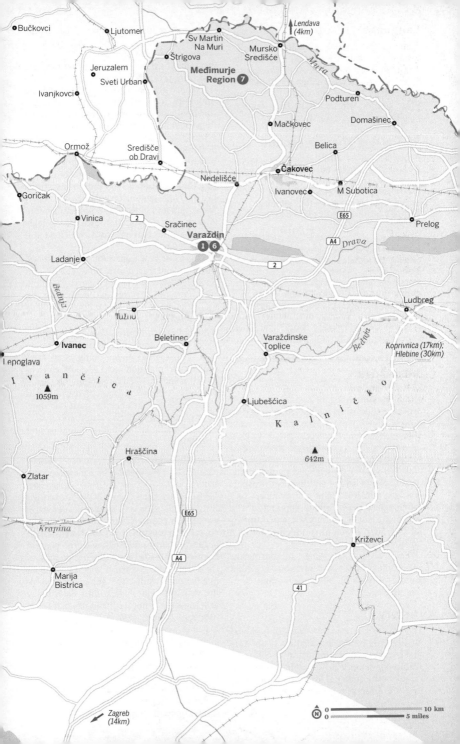

Language

Many of the region's inhabitants speak a local dialect called Kajkavski, named after *kaj*, their word for 'what'. After Croatian or Kajkavski, the second language is likely to be German. Few people speak English and those who do will mostly be from younger generations.

ⓘ Getting There & Around

Although the cities and attractions of Zagorje are linked to Zagreb by bus and train, the connections are sporadic, so it helps to have your own wheels to fully appreciate the area. Renting a car for a day or two and setting off along Zagorje's twisting country roads is the best way to take in its rustic charms.

Otherwise, you can book excursions with **Viatica Travel** (www.viatica-travel.hr), specialising in cultural, spa and adventure tourism in Zagorje; its offshoot agency, **Zagreb Tours** (www.zagreb-tours.com), arranges outings from Zagreb to Zagorje. Trips include romantic weekends as well as guided visits to castles, wineries, rural taverns and archaeological sites. Other agencies in Zagreb, such as Funky Zagreb (p53) and Zdenac Života (p66), also organise day trips.

Varaždin

🕿 042 / POP 47,055

Varaždin, 81km north of Zagreb, is a largely overlooked destination that's often used as a mere transit point on the way to or from Hungary. Yet the town is worth a visit in its own right – its centre is a showcase of scrupulously restored baroque architecture and well-tended gardens and parks. It was once Croatia's capital and its most prosperous city, which explains the extraordinary refinement of its buildings. Topping off the symphony is the gleaming-white and turreted Stari Grad (Old Town), which contains a city museum.

The pedestrian zone of attractive 18th-century buildings centres on Trg Kralja Tomislava, with old streets radiating from this square.

History

The town of Garestin (now Varaždin) played an important role in Croatia's history. It first became a local administrative centre in 1181 under King Bela III, and in 1209 it was raised to the status of a free royal borough by King Andrew II, receiving its own seal and coat of arms.

When Croatia was under siege by the Turks, Varaždin was the most powerful stronghold and the residence of choice for generals. Once the Ottoman threat receded, Varaždin prospered as the cultural, political and commercial centre of Croatia. Its proximity to northern Europe facilitated the boom of baroque architecture, which flourished in Europe during this period. Top artisans and builders flocked to Varaždin, designing mansions, churches and public buildings.

The town was made the capital of Croatia in 1767, a position it held until a disastrous fire in 1776, when the Croatian *ban* (viceroy) packed up and moved his administration to Zagreb. The still-thriving town was quickly rebuilt in the baroque style, which is still visible today.

The town is a centre for textiles, shoes, furniture and agricultural products. It's also an increasingly popular day-trip destination, with a recently spruced-up historic core.

◎ Sights

Varaždin's town centre offers a fine ensemble of baroque buildings, a number of which have been turned into museums. Many of its aristocratic mansions and elegant churches are being restored as part of the town's bid to be included in Unesco's list of World Heritage Sites. Conveniently, most buildings have plaques with architectural and historical explanations in English, German and Croatian.

Town Museum   MUSEUM
(Gradski Muzej; www.gmv.hr; Strossmayerovo Šetalište 7; adult/concession 25/15KN; ⊙9am-5pm Tue-Fri, to 1pm Sat & Sun) This whitewashed fortress, a gem of medieval defensive architecture housed inside Stari Grad, is surrounded by a manicured park. Construction began in the 14th century, with the present Gothic-Renaissance structure dating back to the 16th century, when it was the regional fortification against the Turks. The building was in private hands until 1925; today as a museum it houses furniture, paintings, watches, ceramics, decorative objects, insignia and weapons, amassed over centuries and displayed throughout 30 exhibition rooms.

Even more interesting than the historic collections is the architecture: enter via a drawbridge and wander around to view the archways, courtyards and chapels of this sprawling castle-fortress.

Varaždin

Varaždin

⊙ Sights
1 Cathedral of the Assumption B2
2 Croatian National Theatre B2
3 Franciscan Church & Monastery
   of St John the Baptist B1
4 Gallery of Old & Modern
   Masters B1
5 Patačić-Puttar Palace B2
6 Town Hall B1
7 Town Museum A1
8 Traditional Crafts Square A1
9 World of Insects B2

🛏 Sleeping
10 Garestin B3
11 Hotel Istra B1
12 Hotel Turist B3
13 Hotel Varaždin D2

14 Maltar B3
15 Studentski Centar Varaždin D1

✕ Eating
16 Angelus B2
17 Market B1
18 Palatin A2
19 Park B2
20 Verglec B1

🍷 Drinking & Nightlife
21 Lounge Bar Ritz B2
22 Mea Culpa B1
23 My Way A1
24 The Office Bar B1

ⓘ Information
   Varaždin Concert Bureau .... (see 2)

Varaždin Cemetery   CEMETERY
(Hallerova Aleja; ⊙ 7am-9pm May-Sep, to 8pm Mar
& Apr, to 5pm Jan, Feb, Nov & Dec) A 10-minute
stroll west of Stari Grad takes you to this serene horticultural masterpiece, designed in
1905 by Viennese architect Hermann Helmer. Meander amid tombstones, avenues,
promenades and over 7000 trees, including
magnolia, beech and birch.

**Gallery of Old &
Modern Masters**   ART GALLERY
(Galerija Starih i Novih Majstora; Trg Miljenka Stančića
3; adult/concession 25/15KN; ⊙ 9am-5pm Tue-Fri, to
1pm Sat & Sun) The rococo-style Sermage Palace
that houses the gallery was built in 1759. Note
the carved medallions on the facade and visit the museum, which displays portraits and
landscapes from Croatian, Italian, Dutch, German and Flemish schools.

World of Insects
MUSEUM

(Entomološka Zbirka; Franjevački trg 6; adult/concession 25/15KN; ⊙ 9am-5pm Tue-Fri, to 1pm Sat & Sun) This fascinating entomological collection, housed in the classicist Hercer Palace, comprises nearly 4500 exhibits of the bug world, including 1000 insect species. The examples of insect nests, habitats and reproductive habits are informative and well displayed, with interactive stations and free audioguides.

Franciscan Church & Monastery of St John the Baptist
CHURCH

(Crkva Svetog Ivana Krstitelja; Franjevački trg 8; ⊙ 6.30am-noon & 5.30-7.30pm) Built in 1650 in baroque style on the site of an earlier structure, this church contains the town's tallest tower (54.5m) and houses an ancient pharmacy ornamented with 18th-century ceiling frescoes. Next door is a copy of the bronze statue of Bishop Grgur Ninski that Ivan Meštrović created for Split. Touch the statue's big toe and good luck will come your way (so the story goes).

Cathedral of the Assumption
CATHEDRAL

(Katedrala Uznesenja Marijina; Pavlinska 5; ⊙ 7am-12.30pm & 3.30-7.30pm) This former Jesuit church, located southeast of Trg Kralja Tomislava, was built in 1646. The facade is distinguished by an early-baroque portal bearing the coat of arms of the noble Drašković family. Occupying the central nave is the altar, which has elaborate engravings and a gilded painting of the Assumption of the Virgin Mary. Famous for its great acoustics, the cathedral is the site of concerts during the Baroque Evenings festival.

Town Hall
HISTORIC BUILDING

(Gradska Vijećnica; Trg Kralja Tomislava 1) This striking Romanesque-Gothic structure has been the town hall since the 16th century. Notice the town's coat of arms at the foot of the tower and the carved portal dating from 1792. There's a guard-changing ceremony every Saturday at 11am from May to September.

Traditional Crafts Square
SQUARE

(Trg Tradicijskih Obrta; ⊙ 10am-6pm Mon-Sat Apr-Oct) Demonstrations of pottery, weaving, beekeeping and hat-making re-create the olden times.

Patačić-Puttar Palace
PALACE

(Palača Patačić-Puttar; Zagrebačka 2) Check out this eye-catching mixture of baroque and classical styles. The richly decorated stone portal features the coat of arms of the Patačić family.

Croatian National Theatre
HISTORIC BUILDING

(Hrvatsko Narodno Kazalište; Augusta Cesarca 1) This stunning theatre was built in 1873 in neo-Renaissance style, following the designs of Hermann Helmer.

Drava River Waterfront
WATERFRONT

A 15-minute walk northeast of the town centre takes you to this verdant, tranquil riverfront, bordered by footpaths and several outdoor cafes at which to kick back.

🎭 Festivals & Events

Špancirfest
ARTS FESTIVAL

(www.spancirfest.com) In late August, the eclectic Špancirfest enlivens the town's parks, streets and squares with world music, street performances, theatre, creative workshops, traditional crafts and contemporary arts.

Varaždin Baroque Evenings
MUSIC

(www.vbv.hr) Varaždin is famous for its baroque music festival, which takes place over two weeks each September. Local and international orchestras play in the cathedral, churches and theatres around town. Tickets range from 75KN to 250KN (depending on the event), and become available one hour before the concert at travel agencies or the **Varaždin Concert Bureau** (☎ 042-212 907; Augusta Cesarca 1, Croatian National Theatre).

Trash Film Fest
FILM FESTIVAL

(www.trash.hr) This annual extravaganza of low-budget action flicks is screened at different locations around town, over two to four days in mid-September.

🛏 Sleeping

Most hotels in Varaždin are clean, well maintained and offer decent value for money, and are generally less expensive than in Zagreb. The clientele consists mostly of visiting businessfolk from Zagreb and neighbouring countries, which means hotels are likely to be busy on weekdays and empty on weekends.

If you're looking for private accommodation, turn to the tourist office (p78), which has listings of single/double rooms from about 180KN/410KN. There is generally no supplement for a single night's stay.

Studentski Centar Varaždin
HOSTEL €

(☎ 042-332 910; www.hostel.hr; Julija Merlića bb; s/d 199/298KN; @) This student hall and hostel has recently renovated rooms, each equipped with a TV, cable internet and a fridge. There's laundry service too, and breakfast (25KN).

Garestin
PENSION €

(☑042-214 314; Zagrebačka 34; s/d 257/416KN; P❄) Locals frequent the popular restaurant of this establishment a stone's throw from the centre, while visitors kick back in 13 comfy rooms upstairs, each outfitted with a minibar.

Maltar
GUESTHOUSE €€

(☑042-311 100; www.maltar.hr; Prešernova 1; s/d 248/488KN, ste 465KN-595KN; P❄@) Good value for money can be had at this cheerful little family-run guesthouse near the centre. Rooms, with TV, are well kept. Four suites (which sleep two or three people) have kitchenettes.

Hotel Varaždin
HOTEL €€

(☑042-290 720; www.hotelvarazdin.com; Kolodvorska 19; s/d 388/576KN; P❄@🛜) Contemporary rooms at the city's nicest hotel, opposite the train station, are jam-packed with amenities such as minibars. On the premises is a restaurant with a bar and terrace.

Hotel Turist
HOTEL €€

(☑042-395 395; www.hotel-turist.hr; Kralja Zvonimira 1; s/d from 337/474KN; P❄@) The lack of character here is balanced by solid facilities and nearly four decades of service. Pricier 'business-class' rooms come with minibars and air-conditioning.

Hotel Istra
HOTEL €€€

(☑042-659 659; www.istra-hotel.hr; Ivana Kukuljevića 6; s/d from 490/780KN; P❄@🛜) The expected facilities, an unbeatable location and in-room perks are all in place at this 11-room property, Varaždin's only four-star hotel (though wowed you won't be).

🍴 Eating

While it doesn't stand out as a gourmet destination, Varaždin offers plentiful opportunities to try Croatia's continental cuisine, suitable for all budgets. There is a daily **market** (Augusta Šenoe 12), open until 1pm. Many bakeries sell *klipić*, Varaždin's savoury, finger-shaped bread.

Verglec
TRADITIONAL CROATIAN €

(☑042-211 131; Kranjčevića 12; mains from 40KN; ⊙9am-11pm Mon-Fri, to midnight Sat, 10am-11pm Sun) No-frills but great-value *gableci* (cheap filling lunches, served on weekdays) are popular with locals at this eatery in the town centre, known for its wide range of traditional dishes and family weekend lunches from 50KN.

Palatin
CROATIAN €

(☑042-398 300; Braće Radića 1; mains from 35KN; ⊙7.30am-11pm) An ambitious menu, a great wine list of over 50 wines and great lunch specials daily. Sit in the vaulted basement or on the covered terrace outside.

Angelus
ITALIAN €

(☑042-303 868; Alojzija Stepinca 3; pizzas/mains from 30/45KN; ⊙10am-11pm Mon-Sat, noon-10pm Sun) Housed in a vaulted basement, this cosy pizzeria-trattoria churns out excellent pizza, pasta (from gnocchi to tagliatelle), risottos and meat mainstays.

Park
CROATIAN €

(☑042-211 499; Jurja Habdelića 6; mains from 48KN; ⊙8am-10pm Mon-Sat, 10am-10pm Sun) The grilled meats and salad buffets are pretty standard here – what's special are the terrace with leafy views, the old-school vibe and the inexpensive lunches.

🍷 Drinking

Mea Culpa
LOUNGE

(Ivana Padovca 1; ⊙6.30am-11.30pm Mon-Thu, to 4am Fri & Sat, 7.30am-11.30pm Sun) Get your caffeine or cocktail fix at this swanky lounge bar. There are two floors inside and, on sunny days, tables extending out on Trg Miljenka Stančića.

My Way
CAFE, BAR

(Trg Miljenka Stančića 1; ⊙6.30am-11.30pm Mon-Thu, to 4am Fri & Sat, 7.30am-11.30pm Sun) This cafe-bar has tables on the square and an intimate and toned-down interior.

Lounge Bar Ritz
BAR

(Franjevački trg 1; ⊙8am-10pm Sun-Thu, 9am-midnight Fri & Sat) Great spot to unwind and refresh during your daytime wanderings, and to pop in at night for a quiet drink or one of the occasional theme parties.

The Office Bar
CAFE, BAR

(Trg Kralja Tomislava 2; ⊙7.30am-11pm Mon-Thu, to 1am Fri, 8am-1am Sat, to 11pm Sun) The town's best spot for a good cup of coffee – with a top-notch selection of beers, too. Right on the main square.

BUSES FROM VARAŽDIN

DESTINATION	COST (KN)	DURATION	SERVICES
Berlin (Germany)	851	15 hours	2 weekly
Munich (Germany)	380	8 hours	1 daily
Trakošćan Castle	36	1¾ hours	9 daily
Varaždinske Toplice	21	30 minutes	hourly
Vienna (Austria)	219	5 hours	1 daily
Zagreb	81	1¾ hours	hourly

ℹ️ Information

INTERNET ACCESS

The entire city centre has free wi-fi.

Caffe Bar Aquamarin (Gajeva 1; ☺7am-midnight Mon-Thu & Sun, to 2am Fri & Sat) Free access to the computer terminal with purchase of a drink.

TOURIST INFORMATION

Tourist office (☑042-210 987; www.tourism-varazdin.hr; Ivana Padovca 3; ☺8am-6pm Mon-Fri, 10am-5pm Sat May-Oct, 8am-4pm Mon-Fri, 10am-1pm Sat Nov-Apr) A wealth of information and plenty of colourful brochures are available here.

TRAVEL AGENCIES

Horizont Travel (☑042-395 111; www.horizont-travel.hr; Kralja Zvonimira 1) Located inside Hotel Turist, this agency offers tours around the city and Zagorje region, as well as northern Croatia.

ℹ️ Getting There & Away

The **bus station** (Zrinskih i Frankopana bb) lies just to the southwest of the town centre. The **train station** (Kolodvorska 17) is to the east, at the opposite end of town. About 1km apart, the stations are linked by a minibus (5KN to 15KN) that serves the town and nearby villages (though not on Sundays). Both offer left luggage services; at the bus station you can leave your bags at the **garderoba** (per bag 7KN; ☺4.30am-8.30pm); there's also a **garderoba** (per day 15KN; ☺5am-8.20pm) at the train station.

Bus Varaždin is a major transport hub in north Croatia, with bus and train lines running in all directions. Northbound buses originate in Zagreb and make a stop at Varaždin, but they cost the same whether you buy the ticket in Zagreb or Varaždin. Most buses to the coast go through Zagreb. Note that service to Trakošćan Castle and Varaždinske Toplice is greatly reduced on weekends.

Train There are 12 daily trains to Zagreb (65KN, 2½ hours); connect in Zagreb for trains to the coast. Two trains run daily to Budapest, Hungary (222KN, 6½ hours), with a change in Koprivnica.

Varaždinske Toplice

☑042 / POP 6973

Sulphurous thermal springs at a steaming temperature of 58°C (136°F) have been attracting weary visitors to Varaždinske Toplice since the Romans first established a health settlement here in the 1st century AD. Gentle, wooded hills surround this appealing spa town, which has an assortment of churches and historic buildings, including the baroque castle of **Stari Grad**. Behind its neo-Gothic facade hides the **tourist office** (☑042-633 133; www.toplice-vz.hr; Trg Slobode 16; ☺8am-4pm Mon-Fri), which distributes brochures and info about relaxing health therapies, and can help you find private accommodation.

Adjacent is the **city museum** (www.zmvt.com.hr; Trg Slobode 16; adult/concesssion 20/15KN; ☺9am-2.30pm Mon, Wed & Fri, to 5pm Tue & Thu, to 1pm Sat), which showcases a sculpture of Minerva from the 3rd century AD. History buffs should stroll around **Aqua Iasae**, the remains of the Roman spa built between the 1st and 4th centuries AD, located just a quick stroll up from Stari Grad.

The spa is 12km southeast of Varaždin and 69km northeast of Zagreb. There are numerous buses from Varaždin.

🛏️ Sleeping & Eating

Ozis GUESTHOUSE €

(☑042-250 130; www.ozis.hr; Zagrebačka 7; s/d 180/300KN; ⓟ@) This charming, family-run guest house at the town entrance has 10 spick-and-span rooms and three suites, plus a lovely courtyard.

Hotel Minerva HOTEL €€

(☑042-630 831; www.minerva.hr; Trg Slobode 1; s/d 400/520KN; ⓟ🏊) This hotel is built around the thermal pools, which are said to have curative powers, especially for rheumatic ailments. The unsightly concrete building features rooms with balconies, indoor and outdoor pools, an aqua park and a fitness room. Guests have free access to the pools; day visitors pay 35KN on weekdays and 40KN on weekends.

Zlatne Gorice CENTRAL EUROPEAN €
(☑042-666 054; www.zlatne-gorice.eu; Breg Banjščina 104, Gornji Kneginec; mains from 60KN; ⊙11am-10pm Mon-Sat, to 8pm Sun) If you have your own wheels, stop for lunch at this sparkling restored mansion, set 3km from Toplice along the old road to Varaždin. Surrounded by vineyards, it serves central European fare (think schnitzels, stews and veal medallions) in the four interior salons, or on a terrace with pastoral views.

There's a wine trail, a garden labyrinth and three cozy doubles (300KN) upstairs. Reserve ahead on weekends.

Trakošćan Castle

Among continental Croatia's most impressive castles, **Trakošćan Castle** (☑042-796 281; www.trakoscan.hr; adult/concession 30/15KN; ⊙9am-6pm Apr-Oct, to 4pm Nov-Mar), 80km northwest of Zagreb, is worth a visit for its well presented museum and attractive grounds. The exact origin of its construction is unknown, but the first official mention dates to 1334. Not many of the castle's original Romanesque features were retained when it was restored in neo-Gothic style in the mid-19th century; the 215-acre castle grounds were landscaped into a romantic

---

WORTH A TRIP

EN ROUTE TO HUNGARY: MEĐIMURJE

The undulating landscapes of Međimurje stretch northeast of Varaždin, towards the borders with Hungary and Slovenia. Fertile, scenic and packed with vineyards, orchards, wheat fields and gardens, this area sees few tourists. That is slowly changing, however, as its attractions, such as up-and-coming wine cellars and the spa village of Sveti Martin, become uncovered.

Foodies from Zagreb travel to **Mala Hiža** (www.mala-hiza.hr; Balogovec 1, Mačkovec; mains from 70KN; ⊙9.30am-11pm) in the village of Mačkovec (4km north of Čakovec, the region's capital), for its lauded and awarded seasonal cuisine done up with flair. Served in an old wooden Međimurje cottage, it showcases creative local mainstays and over 150 wine labels, at least 30 of which are from Međimurje. Don't miss its take on *medimurska gibanica*, the local dessert.

To sample the region's top wines in an authentic family environment, head to **Lovrec vineyard** (☑040-830 171; www.vino-lovrec.hr; Sveti Urban 133, Štrigova; tour & tasting 85KN; ⊙by appointment) in the village of Sveti Urban, 20km northwest of Čakovec. The guided tour of this country estate tells you about the boutique wine production and its fascinating history, which spans six generations of winemakers. You'll peek into the 300-year-old wine cellar (featuring ancient wine presses and barrels), rest in the shade of two towering plane trees, take in the vistas of the 6-hectare vineyards, and top it off with tasting about 10 wine varieties, from chardonnay to local *graševina*.

A few kilometres away along verdant hilly roads, the pleasant village of Sveti Martin Na Muri showcases the four-star **Spa & Sport Resort Sveti Martin** (☑040-371 111; www.spa-sport.hr; Grkaveščak bb; s/d 615/930KN; ❄). It has a series of outdoor, indoor and thermal pools, a water park, tennis courts, forest trails, shops, restaurants and a golf course. Adjacent to the resort are swanky apartment-style units, each with a living room, a kitchen and a balcony (from 420KN). For nonguests, day tickets to the pools start at 40KN (60KN on weekends); the price drops by 10KN after 1pm. Other facilities include a fitness room (40KN per day), a sauna complex (125KN for three hours) and various body therapies, including mud wraps (320KN per hour) and chocolate massages (300KN for 45 minutes).

At **Goričanec farm** (☑040-868 288; Dunajska 26), about 4km from Sveti Martin, you can try horse riding, fishing or hunting. **Potrti Kotač** (☑040-868 318; Jurovčak 79; mains from 50KN), 1km uphill from the spa, serves good local food and has an apartment for rent (250KN).

TOP RURAL RETREATS

Rural retreats that offer food and accommodation have been mushrooming around Zagorje in the last few years. Weekends at these hideaways are typically packed with Zagreb day trippers, but come on a weekday and you'll have them practically to yourself. All of the following are best reached with your own wheels.

Vuglec Breg (☑ 049-345 015; www.vuglec-breg.hr; Škarićevo 151, Škarićevo; s/d 390/550KN, mains from 75KN; P @ 🖢) This delightful rural inn has a scenic location in the village of Škarićevo, 4km from Krapinske Toplice. The four traditional cottages (with seven rooms and three suites) sit amid hills, vineyards and forests. The restaurant serves fantastic Zagorje specialties from the bread oven – such as *purica s mlincima* (slow-roasted turkey with baked noodles) and *štrukli* (baked cheese dumplings) – on a terrace with panoramic vistas.

The grounds feature tennis courts, hiking trails and a wine cellar. Mountain bikes are available for rent (70KN per day), plus there's a playground, a badminton court and pony riding to keep the little ones busy.

Bolfan Vinski Vrh (☑ 099 70 31 797; www.bolfanvinskivrh.hr; Gornjaki 56, Hraščina; mains from 75KN; ⊘ noon-8pm Wed-Sat, to 6pm Sun) For tastings of award-winning wines, head to Bolfan Vinski Vrh in the village of Hraščina, near the town of Zlatar. Inside this beautiful hilltop *klet* (typical Zagorje cottage), with vineyards sloping down and some of Zagorje's best views, is a great restaurant (open Wednesdays to Sundays) and a handful of rustic rooms (s/d 350/600KN).

If you want to try one of its specialties, like veal baked under *peka* (a domed baking lid), you must order a day ahead. Otherwise, you can always do cheeses, cold cuts and wine. Look out for its fun, musical blues evenings, advertised on the website.

Klet Kozjak (☑ 049-228 800; www.klet-kozjak.hr; Kozjak 18a, Sveti Križ Začretje; mains from 45KN; ⊘ 8am-10pm) Klet Kozjak in Sveti Križ Začretje, southeast of Krapina, is an adorable little cottage that serves traditional food from the region – such as homemade nettle pasta with cheese and vegetable sauce – and pairs it with sweeping views of the hills and valleys from the terrace.

Run by a local family that has been in the goat-breeding business for generations, it is known for its excellent goat cheese and oven-baked kid goat. If you want to stay, there are a few rooms (s/d 315/475KN).

Majsecov Mlin (☑ 049-288 092; www.majsecov-mlin.com; Obrtnička 47, Donja Stubica; mains from 65KN; ⊘ 9am-11pm) Housed in two traditional cottages near the village of Donja Stubica, Majsecov Mlin serves up local mainstays, seasonally inspired and cooked up by one of Zagorje's best chefs. Try the delicious steak with nettle chips and Zagorje-style pesto.

On site is an old mill, which to this day grinds maize for use in corn flour. In summer months, small producers sell their edible wares at the small market here. You can also spend the night in one of five rooms (s/d 200/360KN).

Hiže na Bregu (☑ 098 92 90 881; www.hizenabregu.com; Hižakovec; s/d 150/250KN) The new Hiže na Bregu, in the village of Hižakovec (near Donja Stubica), is an adorable hideaway on the northern foothills of Medvednica mountain. The traditional Zagorje cottage, clad in wood, has three sweet rooms – two doubles (one with a private bathroom) and a single – and lovely surroundings that include an orchard and garden for guest use.

English-style park with exotic trees and an artificial lake.

Occupied by the aristocratic Drašković family until 1944, the castle features three floors of exhibits that display the family's original furniture, a plethora of portraits, an armament's collection of swords, and a period kitchen in the basement. The series of rooms range in style from neo-Renaissance to Gothic and baroque.

After soaking up the history, go for a wander along the verdant paths down to the wooden jetty at the lake, where you can rent a two-person paddleboat (30KN for 30 minutes).

No buses operate between Zagreb and Trakošćan but there are weekday connections from Varaždin, making a day trip here possible.

Krapina

🗷 049 / POP 12,950

Krapina is a busy provincial town at the heart of a pretty rural region. The main reason to visit is one of Europe's largest Neanderthal excavation sites, now a high-tech museum.

In 1899 an archaeological dig on the Hušnjakovo hill unearthed findings of human and animal bones from a Neanderthal tribe that lived in a cave from 100,000 BC to 35,000 BC. Alongside stone tools and weapons from the Palaeolithic Age, the remains of 876 humans were found, including 196 single teeth belonging to several dozen individuals. Once you've connected with our long-gone ancestors and briefly meandered around town, though, Krapina offers little to keep you entertained.

The main road that runs through town is Zagrebačka ulica, which becomes Ljudevita Gaja in the centre and Magistratska at the northern end. The town centre is Trg Stjepana Radića, between Zagrebačka and Ljudevita Gaja.

⊙ Sights

Museum of the Krapina Neanderthal MUSEUM
(www.mkn.mhz.hr; Šetalište Vilibalda Sluge bb; adult/concession 50/25KN; ⊙ 9am-7pm Tue-Sun Apr-Jun & Sep, 9am-7pm Tue-Fri, to 4pm Sat & Sun Jul & Aug, 9am-6pm Tue-Sun Mar & Oct, 9am-5pm Tue-Sun Nov-Feb) This is Krapina's highlight, just west of the centre. Built into a vertical rock and fronted with a glass wall, this cavernous two-floor space has high-tech exhibits tracing the history and geology of the region, with trilingual signage.

After an introductory video in the main hall, the walk through the museum is designed to emulate a journey of discovery back to the origins of the Neanderthals, with subterranean chambers, hyper-realistic dioramas and lots of interactive games. Don't miss the entrance to the 2nd floor, set in a dark passageway with funky lights.

The outdoor part of the museum, the leafy hill where the remains were found, contains a display of sculpted life-sized models of Neanderthals engaged in everyday activities, such as wielding clubs and throwing stones.

Last admission for the day is one hour before the official closing time.

Franciscan Monastery MONASTERY
Peek into this baroque monastery just west of the centre, which once housed a philosophy and theology school. The adjoining church has evocative frescoes by the Pauline monk Ivan Ranger in the sacristy.

City Art Gallery ART GALLERY
(Magistratska 25; adult/concession 10/5KN; ⊙ 10am-1pm Mon-Fri, to 2pm Sat & Sun) Features rotating exhibits of Croatian artists.

✪ Festivals & Events

At the beginning of September, the annual **Festival of Kajkavian Songs** (Festival Kajkavske Popevke) features folkloric performances, poetry readings and traditional Zagorje food.

🛏 Sleeping

Hostel Barrock HOSTEL €
(🗷 098 18 23 863; www.hostel-barrock.com; Magistratska 36; dm adult/child 122/75KN; ❄@🛜)
A new hostel just two minutes from the main square, this sweet little spot has three dorms – two with four beds and one that sleeps seven – as well as a kitchenette and common area, a backyard with a BBQ and a cool cafe-bar on site.

Pod Starim Krovovima PENSION €
(Trg Ljudevita Gaja 15; s/d 205/326KN) This pleasant *pansion* (guest house) in the centre has eight plain but clean en suite units. On weekdays, cheap and tasty *gablec* (lunch) can be had at the downstairs restaurant for 25KN.

🍴 Eating & Drinking

Neandertal Pub BARBECUE €
(Šetalište Vilibalda Sluge bb; mains from 50KN; ⊙ 8am-10pm Tue-Sun May-Sep, to 8pm Tue-Sun Oct-Apr) This Neanderthal-themed cafe-restaurant at the entrance to the museum claims to dish out barbecue from a recipe that's 130,000 years old.

Ilir CAFE, BAR
(Trg Ljudevita Gaja 3; ⊙ 8am-11pm Mon-Thu & Sun, to midnight Fri & Sat) For a coffee break in the sun, grab an outside table at this loungey spot. Or you can soak up the old-fashioned vibe inside.

ℹ Information

Tourist office (☑ 049-371 330; www.tzg-krapina.hr; Magistratska 28; ⊙8am-3pm Mon-Fri, to noon Sat) Not particularly helpful but does offer some brochures and scant information.

ℹ Getting There & Away

One early-morning bus runs Monday to Saturday from Zagreb to Krapina (45KN, one hour), but there are none on Sunday. There are up to 11 trains on weekdays from Zagreb (40KN, 1½ hours); of those only two are direct, while the rest have to change at Zabok. Trains run less frequently on weekends.

The train station is about 300m to the south, on Frana Galovića. The bus terminal is another 600m away along the same street, at number 15.

Veliki Tabor Castle

As you approach the hilltop castle of Veliki Tabor, 57km northwest of Zagreb, what unfolds is a pleasing panorama of hills, cornfields, vineyards and forests. The rural vistas alone make a visit worthwhile, as does good traditional dining nearby.

The Croatian aristocracy began building fortified castles in the region – to stave off the Turkish threat – at the end of the 16th century. The pentagonal **Veliki Tabor Cas-**tle (www.velikitabor.com; Košnički Hum 1, Desinić; adult/concession 20/10KN; ⊙9am-5pm Tue-Fri, to 7pm Sat & Sun Apr-Sep, 9am-4pm Tue-Sun Oct-Mar), which was recently renovated and now houses a museum, was built on the grounds of an earlier medieval structure in the early 16th century, with the four semicircular towers added later. Strategically perched on top of a hill, the golden-yellow castle-fortress has everything a medieval master could want: towers, turrets and holes in the walls for pouring tar and hot oil on the enemy. It even houses the skull of Veronika Desinić, a poor village girl who, according to local lore, was punished for her romance with the castle owner's son and bricked up in the walls.

The castle hosts the **Tabor Film Festival** (www.taborfilmfestival.com) in June or July, an extravaganza of international short films with screenings in the castle (as well as at several locations in nearby Kumrovec).

To admire the castle from a distance, grab an alfresco table at **Grešna Gorica** (☑049-343 001; www.gresna-gorica.com; Taborgradska Klet 3, Desinić; mains from 40KN; ⊙9am-9pm daily), a rustic eatery often overtaken by day-tripping families from Zagreb on weekends. The place is a tad gimmicky but great for kids, with farm animals roaming around, a playground and lots of open space. Adults will appreciate the countryside views and the well-prepared

---

WORTH A TRIP

SWEET SPA SPOTS IN THE HILLS

While lots of Zagorje's spas cater to an ageing clientele with time-induced ailments, they are worth an outing if you want to spend a day steaming the travel stress away and/or you want to see these remnants of the socialist era. In most of these spa towns, the discovery of thermal waters with purportedly healing properties spurred often unseemly development. But there is a charm to these spots regardless – and if you like to soak and be pampered, they provide a welcome outing.

Krapinske Toplice (www.krapinsketoplice.com), about 17km southwest of Krapina, is a spa town set amid the rolling hills of the Zagorje countryside. The showpieces are the four thermal springs, rich in magnesium and calcium and never below 39°C. You can stay at the **Villa Magdalena** (☑049-233 333; www.villa-magdalena.net; Mirna Ulica 1; s/d 690/960KN; P ❄ @ 🛜) guest house, a pink-themed lap of luxury featuring swanky and spacious suites with Jacuzzis and balconies, an á la carte restaurant and an outdoor pool.

Tuheljske Toplice (www.tuheljsketoplice.com), a short drive from Zagreb in the pretty village of Tuhelj, en route to Kumrovec, has been a longstanding favorite for urbanites. it recently got a boost with an unveiling of the four-star **Hotel Well** (☑049-203 751; www.terme-tuhelj.hr; Ljudevita Gaja 4, Tuheljske Toplice; s/d €109/188; ❄), with a series of swimming pools, a swanky wellness centre and an adventure park.

Another worthwhile spa destination is **Hotel Terme Jezerčica** (☑049-200 600; www.terme-jezercica.hr; Toplička 80, Donja Stubica; ❄), in the village of Donja Stubica, which has a new swimming-pool complex.

Zagorje staples, such as *štrukli* (dumplings with cottage cheese) and *srneći gulaš* (venison goulash). The restaurant can be found about 2km east of Veliki Tabor; a marked trail leads from the back of the castle to the restaurant (40 minutes on foot).

There are several daily buses from Zagreb to Desinić (62KN to 70KN, 1½ to two hours) from Monday to Saturday, and four on Sunday. You will have to walk 3km northwest to Veliki Tabor.

Kumrovec

☑ 049 / POP 1854

The Zagorje region was the birthplace of several celebrated Croats, most notably Tito, who was born as Josip Broz in Kumrovec. Nestled in the Sutla River valley near the Slovenian border, this pretty village has been thoughtfully transformed into an open-air ethnographic museum. A re-creation of a 19th-century village, the **Staro Selo Museum** (http://mdc.hr/kumrovec/eng/index.html; Kumrovec bb; adult/concession 20/10KN; ⊙ 9am-7pm Apr-Sep, 9am-4pm Oct-Mar) features 40 restored houses and barns made of pressed earth and wood. These *hiže* (traditional Zagorje huts) are now filled with furniture, mannequins, toys, wine presses and baker's tools (all accompanied by English captions) in order to evoke the region's traditional arts, crafts and customs.

With a stream bubbling through the idyllic setting, the museum presents a vivid glimpse of peasant traditions and village life. Note the life-sized bronze sculpture of Marshal Tito outside his humble place of birth, with the original furniture, letters from foreign leaders and random memorabilia inside. On some weekends from April to September, the museum hosts demonstrations of blacksmithing, candlemaking, pottery making and flax weaving. For Tito's birthday, on 25 May, the village comes alive with devotees from all over former Yugoslavia.

There are two daily buses between Zagreb and Kumrovec (52KN, 1¼ hours) on weekdays, but none on weekends.

Klanjec

☑ 049 / POP 3234

Another notable Croat from Zagorje was sculptor Antun Augustinčić (1900–79), who created the *Monument to Peace* in front of the UN building in New York. Klanjec, his pleasant home town, has the **Antun Augustinčić Gallery** (http://www.mdc.hr/augustincic/eng/home.html; Trg Antuna Mihanovića 10; adult/concession 20/10KN; ⊙ 9am-5pm Apr-Sep, to 3pm Tue-Sun Oct-Mar) devoted to his opus, plus lots of headless bronze torsos and a huge replica of the *Peace* statue. There's a small sculpture garden outside and the sculptor's memorial to fallen Partisans nearby.

Once you've seen the gallery, you'll be strapped for more sightseeing, but do stroll around the charming town to see the 17th-century **baroque church** and the **Franciscan monastery** (admission 8KN) opposite the gallery, and to take in the views of surrounding hills. If you make an appointment with the **tourist office** (☑ 550 235; Trg A. Mihanovića 3; ⊙ 8am-4pm Mon-Fri, to 1pm Sat) ahead of time, you can take a look at the two recently restored sarcophagi of the noble Erdody family; these elaborate findings from the baroque era are hidden in the monastery's crypt.

The two daily buses running from Zagreb to Kumrovec stop in Klanjec (51KN, 1 to 1½ hours) on weekdays. Note that there are no buses on weekends.

Marija Bistrica

☑ 049 / POP 6612

Croatia's largest pilgrimage centre is in Zagorje at Marija Bistrica, a village 37km north of Zagreb on the slopes of Mt Medvednica. What steals the show here is the **Marija Bistrica Church** (Hodočasnička Crkva Marije Bistričke), which contains a wooden Gothic statue of the Black Madonna created in the 15th century. The statue's alleged miraculous power dates back to the 16th-century Turkish invasions, when it was saved from destruction. It was further proven when a disastrous 1880 fire destroyed everything but the statue.

Behind the church is the **Way of the Cross**, a path leading up Calvary Hill, with 14 stations marked with works by Croatian sculptors and paired with excellent vistas. To witness a display of serious religious devotion, visit on 15 August for the most popular pilgrimage of **Velika Gospa** (Assumption of the Virgin Mary).

There are up to 22 buses a day from Zagreb to Marija Bistrica (36KN to 58KN, 40 minutes to one hour) on weekdays, fewer on weekends.

Slavonia

Includes ➡

Osijek 85
Baranja 91
Vukovar 94
Ilok 96

Best Places to Eat

➡ Kod Ruže (p89)
➡ Baranjska Kuća (p93)
➡ Piroš Čizma (p94)
➡ Zelena Žaba (p92)

Best Places to Stay

➡ Maksimilian (p87)
➡ Zdjelarević (p93)
➡ Ivica i Marica (p93)
➡ Stari Podrum (p96)

Why Go?

Pancake-flat, river-rich Slavonia is all but untouched by tourism, with unique natural wonders and delicious regional cuisine. The wetlands of Kopački Rit are one of Europe's finest ornithological reserves, perfect for boat tours, biking and hiking. Osijek, Slavonia's largest town, has a lovely riverfront setting and fortress quarter, while the Baranja region is renowned for its wineries.

The impact of the war hit hardest in southeast Slavonia, where historic Vukovar is slowly regaining its role as an important regional city and Ilok, on the Serbian border, is again attracting visitors to its fine wine cellars and historic old town.

Bordered by three major rivers (Sava, Drava and Danube), this fascinating region has long held strong connections with Hungary, Serbia and Germany. Slavonia's key appeal lies in this culturally intriguing mix that makes it closer to central Europe than coastal Croatia.

When to Go
Osijek

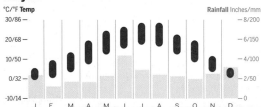

Apr–May Spring in Slavonia is a real delight, with mild temperatures and almost no mosquitoes.

Jun–Sep Catch any number of festivals, from urban music to sculpture.

Oct–Mar The short days are an ideal time to savour paprika-rich Slavonian stews and game.

History

Before the 1991 war displaced tens of thousands of inhabitants, Slavonia contained one of the most ethnically diverse populations in Europe. Settled by Slavic tribes in the 7th century, the region was conquered by the Turks in the 16th century. Catholic residents fled, and Serbian Orthodox settlers, who were better received by the Turks, arrived en masse.

In 1690 Serb supporters of Vienna, in their battles with the Turks, left Kosovo and settled in the Srijem region around Vukovar. The Turks ceded the land to Austria in 1699 and the Habsburgs turned a large part of the region into a Vojna Krajina (Military Frontier).

The Muslim population left but more Serbs arrived, joined by German merchants; Hungarian, Slovak and Ukrainian peasants; Catholic Albanians; and Jews. Much land was sold to German and Hungarian aristocrats, who built huge baroque and classical mansions around the towns of Osijek, Vukovar and Ilok.

The large Serbian community prompted Slobodan Milošević to attempt to incorporate the region into a 'Greater Serbia'. This assault began with the destruction of Vukovar and the shelling of Osijek in 1991. A ceasefire prevailed in 1992, but it wasn't until January 1998 that the region was returned to Croatia as part of the Dayton peace agreement.

The fighting may be over but the war's impact remains profound. In towns such as Vukovar, Serbs and Croats lead almost totally separate lives. Efforts are being made to bring the communities together, but with limited success so far.

🛈 Dangers & Annoyances

Osijek and its surrounds were heavily laid with landmines during the war in the 1990s. Although the city and its outskirts along the main road have been de-mined and are completely safe, it would be unwise to wander through the swampland north of the Drava River, which leads to Kopački Rit. Most mined areas are marked; be on the lookout for signs.

In summer, Kopački Rit is besieged by mosquitoes. Wear long sleeves and trousers or slather on plenty of repellent.

Osijek

🗗 031 / POP 107,784

A historic, leafy university town with a stunning waterfront promenade along the broad Drava River and an imposing 18th-century fortress, Osijek is well worth a visit.

The city suffered terribly in the 1990s from Serb shelling and pockmarks still scar some structures, but most of Osijek's grand buildings (including some fine 19th-century Secessionist mansions) have been renovated.

This elegant regional capital is steadily regaining its poise, boosted by the return of exiles, booming student numbers, new hotels and restaurants and an increasing flow of tourists. You'll find Osijek perfect as an intriguing, cosmopolitan and enjoyable base for day trips to Slavonia's countryside and the wonderful Kopački Rit Nature Park.

⊙ Sights

◎ Tvrđa

Built under Habsburg rule as a defence against Turkish attacks, the 18th-century citadel was relatively undamaged during the recent war. This baroque complex of cobblestone streets, spacious squares and stately mansions reveals a remarkable architectural unity, lending it the feel of an open-air museum.

The main square, Trg Svetog Trojstva, is marked by the elaborate **Holy Trinity Monument**, a baroque pillar erected in 1729 to commemorate the victims of the 18th-century plague that swept the city.

Gloria Maris Museum   MUSEUM
(www.gloria maris.hr; Svodovi bb; adult/concession 20/10KN; ⊙10am-4pm Tue, Wed & Fri, to 8pm Thu, to 1pm Sat & Sun) Housed inside vaults of the old citadel, this museum is dedicated to seashells and marine and freshwater life. It's the labour of love of Vladimir Filipović, who has amassed around one million shells in his 48 years of collecting, from all corners of the globe. Enter through the street to the right side of the church.

Check out the most poisonous creature in the ocean (the remains of an octopus from the Philippines), fossils from 650 million years ago, a megalodon tooth and a vast array of exotic shells.

Museum of Slavonia   MUSEUM
(Muzej Slavonije Osijek; www.mso.hr; Trg Svetog Trojstva 6; adult/concession 15/10KN; ⊙9am-7pm Tue-Fri, 10am-2pm Sat & Sun) Houses a huge collection of treasures and artefacts relating to Slavonian history, including Bronze Age implements, Roman artefacts from the colony of Mursa, beautiful textiles, weavings, jewellery and fine furniture. Exhibits rotate

Slavonia Highlights

1 Exploring **Kopački Rit Nature Park** (p91), one of Europe's largest wetlands and a birdwatchers' paradise.

2 Feasting on Slavonian specialties in Osijek's fortress quarter, **Tvrđa** (p85).

3 Visiting the haunting war memorials in **Vukovar** (p94).

4 Travelling the wine roads of **Baranja** (p91).

5 Spending a day taking in the impressive cultural sights of **Osijek** (p85).

6 Enjoying an outstanding museum then sampling local fare in pretty **Ilok** (p96).

7 Savouring rustic life in the ethno-village of **Karanac** (p93).

8 Viewing the Danube from the imposing war memorial of **Batina** (p94).

every few months. From June to September the museum is open till 10pm on Thursday nights.

A joint ticket for Museum of Slavonia, Archaeological Museum and the Gallery of Fine Arts costs 25KN.

Archaeological Museum of Osijek MUSEUM
(Arheološki Muzej Osijek; Trg Svetog Trojstva 2; adult/concession 15/5KN; ⊙9am-7pm Tue-Fri, 10am-2pm Sat & Sun) The building itself – a renovated city-guard structure – is stunning, with a lovely oak-block floor and glass dome over an arcaded patio. It showcases finds from Roman stones to Celtic helmets, with explanations also in English. Open till 10pm on Thursdays from June to September.

⊙ Upper Town

Church of St Peter & Paul CHURCH
(Pavla Pejačevića 1; ⊙noon-7pm Mon, 7am-7pm Tue-Sun) FREE Looming over Trg Ante Starčevića, this church's 90m-high tower is surpassed in height only by the cathedral in Zagreb. Built in the 1890s, this red-brick, neo-Gothic structure features an interior with 40 elaborate stained-glass windows in Viennese style and vividly coloured frescoes by Croatian painter Mirko Rački.

Gallery of Fine Arts ART GALLERY
(Galerija Likovnih Umjetnosti; www.gluo.hr; Europska Avenija 9, adult/concession 15/5KN; ⊙10am-6pm Tue, Wed & Fri, to 8pm Thu, to 1pm Sat & Sun) Housed in an elegant neoclassical mansion, the Gallery of Fine Arts contains a collection of paintings and sculptures by Slavonian artists from the 18th century onwards.

⊙ Beyond the Centre

Zoo Osijek ZOO
(www.zoo-osijek.hr; Sjevernodravska Obala 1; adult/concession 20/10KN; ⊙9am-7pm) As an escape from museums and churches, take a free ride on the emblematic *kompa* (a wooden pedestrian ferry propelled by the water current) from the shore of Gornji Grad to Zoo Osijek, on the other side of the Drava. Croatia's largest zoo spreads over 11 verdant riverside hectares, with 80 animal species and a reptile-filled aquarium.

The *kompa* operates from 9am to 7pm April to October.

★✦ Festivals & Events

Urban Fest Osijek MUSIC
(www.ufo.com.hr) June music event showcasing hip-hop, rock and electronic artists.

Pannonian Challenge SPORTS
(www.pannonian.org) Extreme sports (and music) festival in August.

🛏 Sleeping

For private rooms ask at the tourist office (p91) or OK Tours (p90).

★ Maksimilian GUESTHOUSE €
(☑031-497 567; www.maksimilian.hr; Franjevačka 12; s 230-320KN, d 330-420KN; ❋@☎) In the heart of the old town, this superb guest house is run by a hospitable, English-speaking team. All 14 rooms in the historic 1860 building come with satellite TV, high ceilings and good fittings (most have air-con). There's a kitchen, free coffee and tea, generous breakfast (included), bike rental and a downstairs terrace where they're soon to open a cafe and an info point for cyclists.

Hostel Tufna HOSTEL €
(☑031-215 020; www.tufna.com.hr; Franje Kuhača 10; dm per person 100KN; @☎) Osijek's only backpacker joint, this quirky hostel has three cramped, five-bed dorms plus one double, and a guests' lounge and kitchen with mismatched '70s decor. It's directly above a nightclub, so pack those earplugs for weekends. Ring the number at the door if nobody answers the buzzer.

Hi Smještaj Osijek PENSION €€
(☑091 30 07 070; www.smjestaj-osijek.com; Adolfa Waldingera 12; s/d 450/700KN; ❋☎) The most stylish spot in town, with only three rooms and no services (the reception is mostly unstaffed) but great interior design and all the in-room trappings. Breakfast is available on request. Make sure you ask about discounts, as these can be considerable.

Hotel Drava HOTEL €€
(☑031-250 500; www.hotel-drava.com; Ivana Gundulića 25a; s/d 413/606KN; P❋☎) Inviting hotel close to the train and bus stations that has 11 colourful, well-appointed rooms with a little kitsch thrown in. There are discounts if you pay in cash.

Waldinger HOTEL €€€
(☑031-250 450; www.waldinger.hr; Županijska 8; pension s/d 340/440KN, hotel s/d 650/950KN; P❋@☎) This is a grand little hotel of two

SLAVONIA

Osijek

Drava

Kopački Rit
Nature Park
(12km)

4 🏛

● 7

Trg Svetog
Trojstva

1 🏛 5 🏛

Trg J
Križanica

9 🔢
Franje Kuhača

16 ✕ 14 ✕ Kamila Firingera

12
🔢 17
Franjevačka
20

🏛 6 🛈 ●
18 ❶

Perivoj
Kralja
Tomislava

Europska Avenija

Park
Kralja
Držislava

Kralja Zvonimira

Park Kralja Petra
Krešimira IV

Istarska

D Cesarca

Vukovarska

Zagrebačka

Bartula Kašića

Kneza Trpimira

Trg
Baruna
Trenka

Reljkovitma

Trg A
Senoe

D Neumana

3 🏛

Trg LJ
Gaja

Stjepana Radića

Reisnerova

Osijek 🅺
Trg L Ružičke

🅺

Zimska Luka

Šamačka

🔢 11

Lučki Prilaz
Kapucinska

Adamovića

Školska

Lorenza Jägera

Sunčana

A Kačića M

Trg L
Ružičke

🅺

Kompa
(100m)

Ribarska

Trg Ante
Starčevića

Pejačevića

⊕ 2

Trg L Mirskog

✪ 19

Jägerov
prolaz

Hrvatske Republike

Ivana Gundulića

J Andrića

Zrinjevac

🔢 10

Strossmayera

🔢 8

15 🔀

🔢 13

Županijska

Ružina

Vinkovačka

N
0 —— 200 m
0 —— 0.1 miles

Osijek

◎ **Sights**
1 Archaeological Museum of
  Osijek...F1
2 Church of St Peter & Paul.....................A1
3 Gallery of Fine Arts...............................D2
4 Gloria Maris Museum............................G1
5 Holy Trinity Monument.........................F2
6 Museum of Slavonia..............................G2
7 Tvrđa G1

⊜ **Sleeping**
8 I Il Smještaj Osijek................................A1
9 Hostel Tufna...F2
10 Hotel Drava..D3
11 Hotel Osijek..C1
12 Maksimilian...G2

13 Waldinger B2

⊗ **Eating**
  Kavana Waldinger ....(see 13)
14 Kod Ruže F2
15 Rustika A1
16 Slavonska Kuća F2

◉ **Drinking & Nightlife**
17 Old Bridge Pub.....................................G2
18 St Patrick's Pub F2

✪ **Entertainment**
19 Croatian National Theatre....................B2
20 Exit...G2
  Tufna ....(see 9)

SLAVONIA OSIJEK

halves. The bedrooms in the main building offer lashings of old-school charm, with plush furnishings and thick carpets. The pension in the back is a humbler abode, with functional rooms. The hotel offers discounts for midsummer stays; rates drop by 25% on weekends.

A fine breakfast is served in the stately dining room and there's an upscale restaurant, an atmospheric cafe and a top-floor fitness area with a sauna.

Hotel Osijek   HOTEL €€€
(☏031-230 333; www.hotelosijek.hr; Šamačka 4; s/d 840/935KN; P☀@☎) Right on the river, this towering concrete landmark is the town's most luxurious hotel, drawing business travellers in droves. The 147 rooms and suites are city-slicker smart, with a nod to modernist style; most have spectacular views. The wellness centre on the 14th floor has a Turkish bath, Jacuzzi and sauna.

✕ Eating

Osijek is the place to sample hearty and spicy Slavonian cuisine. The local food is strongly influenced by neighbouring Hungary, with paprika sprinkled on almost every dish, and meat and freshwater fish featuring strongly. *Fiš paprikaš* (fish stewed in a paprika sauce, served with noodles) is the signature regional meal.

★Kod Ruže   SLAVONIAN €
(Kuhačeva 25a; mains from 50KN; ◷10am-11pm Mon-Sat, to 4pm Sun) The rustic paraphernalia is laid on pretty thick here (think taxidermy galore) but this is certainly a highly atmos-

pheric place for a Slavonian meal, especially at weekends, when a live band plays gypsy music. Try the *čobanac* meat stew or one of the substantial salads, such as the *alas salata* with river fish.

Slavonska Kuća   SLAVONIAN €
(Kamila Firingera 26; mains from 45KN; ◷10am-10pm Mon-Sat) This is a great choice for authentic Slavonian food, with lots of *pečena riba* (baked fish), including delicious catfish. Prices are moderate and portions hearty. Wash your meal down with *graševina,* a fruity white wine.

Rustika   PIZZA €
(Pejačevića 32; mains from 35KN; ◷9am-11pm) Popular spot steps from from the cathedral, where pizzas and grilled meats are the order of the day, dished out in a rustic interior with a contemporary touch, or on the terrace in the back.

Kompa   SLAVONIAN €
(Splavarska 1; mains from 35KN; ◷10am-10pm Mon-Sat) The locals' favourite joint on the riverfront, across from the zoo. This is a no-frills spot with a tiny interior and tables right on the river. Good for mainstays and low prices – although there's no menu in English, nor is English spoken here.

Galija   INTERNATIONAL €
(Gornjodravska Obala bb; mains from 40KN; ◷11am-11pm) This is the best of Osijek's boat restaurants, situated a little bit west of the hubbub that surrounds Hotel Osijek. A range of international and regional dishes is paired with river views, particularly pretty at sunset.

WORTH A TRIP

ĐAKOVO

The peaceful provincial town of Đakovo, just 35km to the south of Osijek, makes an easy day trip. There are three major reasons to visit: its impressive cathedral, the Lipizzaner horses and a wonderful folk festival every summer.

The town's pride and glory is the red-brick **cathedral** (Strossmayerov Trg 6; ⊘6.30am-noon & 3-7.30pm), which dominates the town centre with its two 84m-high belfries. Commissioned by Bishop Strossmayer in 1862, this neo-Romanesque structure features a three-nave interior colourfully painted with biblical scenes.

Đakovo is famous for its Lipizzaner horses, a noble purebred with a lineage that can be traced back to the 16th century. They are bred on a farm outside town and trained at **Ergela** (www.ergela-djakovo.hr; Augusta Šenoe 45; adult/concession 20/10KN; ⊘7am-5pm Mon-Fri, 9am-1pm Sat Mar-Jul & Sep-Oct, 7am-3pm Mon-Fri, 9am-1pm Sat Aug), a short walk from the cathedral. About 30 horses undergo daily training for their eventual work as high-class carriage and riding horses.

Đakovački Vezovi (Đakovo Embroidery) is a festival featuring a display by the Lipizzaner horses and a folklore show on the first weekend in July each year, complete with folkloric dancing and traditional songs.

Kavana Waldinger CAFE €
(Županijska 8; cakes from 12KN; ⊘7am-11pm) Dignified cafe that attracts local notables for its proper service and a range of cakes that are worth every calorie.

🍷 Drinking & Nightlife

The outdoor cafe-bars that line the riverfront around Hotel Osijek are popular when the weather permits. Otherwise your best bet for bar action is the Tvrđa area, where you'll find everything from British-style pubs to raucous turbo-folk joints.

Old Bridge Pub PUB
(www.oldbridgepub.com; Franje Kuhača 4; ⊘10am-1am Mon-Thu & Sun, to 4am Fri & Sat) A dead ringer for a London boozer, the Old Bridge has three levels and a slim outdoor terrace – the top floor is a classy space with elegant Chesterfield sofas. There's a live band on weekend nights.

St Patrick's Pub PUB
(Franje Kuhača 15; ⊘7am-midnight Mon-Wed & Sun, to 1am Thu & Fri, 8am-2am Sat) Your best bet to start the evening is this sociable, welcoming pub, with an intimate interior of dark wood and neon and a huge terrace on the main square.

Tufna CLUB
(www.tufna.com.hr; Franje Kuhača 10; ⊘10pm-5am Thu-Sat) A small club with an underground vibe. DJs play eclectic electronic sounds – anything from house anthems to drum 'n' bass.

Exit CLUB
(Franje Kuhača 5; ⊘10pm-5am Thu-Sat) Popular club on two levels, where you can boogie to house, jazz, hip hop and rock.

☆ Entertainment

Croatian National Theatre THEATRE
(Hrvatsko Narodno Kazalište; ☑031-220 700; www.hnk-osijek.hr; Županijska 9) Grand theatre that features a regular program of drama, ballet and opera performances.

ℹ Information

There's free wi-fi around both the Gornji Grad area and the Tvrđa.

Hospital (☑031-511 511; Josipa Huttlera 4)

OK Tours (☑031-212 815; www.ok-tours.hr; Trg Slobode 7) Tours, information and some private accommodation.

Panturist (☑031-638 580; www.panturist.hr; Kapucinska 19) Slavonia's largest travel agency. Runs buses to the coast as well as to international destinations.

Post office (Kardinala Alojzija Stepinca 17; ⊘7am-8pm Mon-Sat) Phone calls and cash advances on MasterCard.

Press Cafe (Lorenza Jägera 24; internet access per hour 15KN; ⊘7am-11pm) Surf the net inside a bar.

Privredna Banka (Stjepana Radića 19) Has an ATM.

Tourist Information Centre (☑031-210 120; www.tzosijek.hr; Trg Svetog Trojstva 5; ⊘10am-4pm Mon-Fri, 9am-1pm Sat) Friendly info point in the same building as Museum of Slavonia.

Tourist office (☏ 031-203 755; www.tzosijek. hr; Županijska 2; ⊙ 8am-8pm Mon-Fri, to noon Sat mid-Jun–mid-Sep, 8am-4pm Mon-Fri, to noon Sat mid-Sep–mid-Jun) A well-briefed office with plentiful brochures, booklets and maps.

Zlatna Greda (☏ 091 42 11 424; www.zlatna-greda.org) An excellent environmental agency, which organises canoe trips along the Danube and into Kopački Rit, as well as hikes, birdwatching expeditions, city tours by boat, photo safaris, horseback-riding jaunts and bike tours.

ⓘ Getting There & Away

Osijek is a major transport hub, with buses and trains arriving and departing in all directions.

AIR

Klisa Airport (☏ 060 339 339; www.osijek-air port.hr) is 20km from Osijek on the road to Vukovar. Klisa is a very minor airport with only a few Croatia Airlines flights to Dubrovnik and Zagreb.

BUS

A full list of international buses can be found at the station, located on Bartula Kašića.

TRAIN

Osijek's train station is located on Trg Lavoslava Ružičke, just south of the centre. Trains run to Rijeka (220KN, nine to 10 hours, once daily) and Zagreb (130KN, 4½ hours, five daily).

ⓘ Getting Around

A free shuttle bus for Ryan Air flights meets arrivals at the airport and heads to the city centre. It departs from the bus station on Mondays and Fridays, before their scheduled flights.

There's an excellent, very affordable taxi service in the city. **Cammeo** (☏ 1212) has modern cars with meters; most rides in town cost just 20KN.

Osijek has two tram lines. Line 2 connects the train and bus station with Trg Ante Starčevića in the centre, and line 1 goes to Tvrđa. The fare is 10KN, which you pay to the driver.

Buses connect Osijek to nearby Bilje; from the bus station take the Panturist bus heading to Beli Manastir and ask to get off in Bilje (15minutes, 16KN).

Baranja

☏ 031

A small triangle in the far northeast of Croatia at the confluence of the Drava and Danube Rivers, Baranja stretches east of Osijek towards Serbia, north towards the town of Beli Manastir and southwest towards Đakovo. The Hungarian influence is strongly felt in this largely agricultural area: all the towns have bilingual names.

In the last few years this scenic area of swamps, vineyards, orchards and wheat fields has been on the rise as eastern Croatia's most interesting tourist destination. That's thanks in part to its star attraction, the bird sanctuary of Kopački Rit, but also to a clutch of authentic farmstays, regional restaurants and splendid wineries.

Kopački Rit Nature Park

Only 12km northeast of Osijek, **Kopački Rit Nature Park** (Park Prirode Kopački Rit;

BUSES FROM OSIJEK

DOMESTIC DESTINATIONS	COST (KN)	DURATION	DAILY SERVICES
Đakovo	35	45 minutes	26
Dubrovnik	340	14 hours	1
Ilok	62	two hours	4
Rijeka	270	7 hours	1
Split	290	11 hours	1
Toplice	48	one hour	6
Vukovar	34	45 minutes	12
Zagreb	131	four hours	8

INTERNATIONAL DESTINATIONS	COST (KN)	DURATION	DAILY SERVICES
Belgrade	122	3½ hours	4
Vienna	295	9 hours	1
Zürich	882	19½ hours	1 weekly

www.kopacki-rit.com; adult 20KN, children under 2 free; ⊙ 9am-5pm mid-Mar–Oct, 8am-4pm Nov–mid-Mar) is one of the largest wetlands in Europe: 293 bird species have been recorded here. Formed by the meeting of the Drava and Danube rivers, this vast floodplain has two main lakes, Sakadaško and Kopačevo, surrounded by a remarkable variety of vegetation, from aquatic and grassland flora to willow, poplar and oak forests. Depending on the season, you can find water lilies, sedges, water ferns, duckweeds, reeds and ryegrass. The Drava and Danube rivers, together with the Mura River, were pronounced a biosphere reserve by Unesco in July 2012.

Beneath the waters lie 44 species of fish, including carp, bream, pike, catfish and perch. Above the water buzz 21 kinds of mosquito (bring a tonne of repellent!) and on land roam red deer, wild boar, beaver, pine marten and foxes. But it's really about the birds here – look for the rare black storks, white-tailed eagles, great crested grebes, purple herons, spoonbills and wild geese. The best time to come is during the spring and autumn migrations.

The park was heavily mined during the war and closed for many years as a result. Most mines have now been cleared: safe trails have been marked. The park has a **visitor centre** (☑ 031-752 320; www.kopacki-rit.com; ⊙ 8am-7pm) located at the main entrance, along the Bilje–Kopačevo road. You can walk the two educational trails nearby; there are also various **guided tours** offered. A tour of the zoological reserve by boat, taking in a castle complex and farm, costs 70KN for adults and 50KN for children and students; a wildlife tour in a small boat is 100KN per hour (maximum four people). Tours depart from an embarkation point about 1km from the visitor centre. Book in advance, especially during spring and autumn.

At the northern end of the park, 12km from the visitor centre, is an Austro-Hungarian castle complex and bio-ecological research station, **Dvorac Tikveš** (☑ 031-752 320; www.kopacki-rit.com; per person 160KN), where the seven pleasant en suite rooms have leafy views. Once used by Tito as a hunting lodge, the castle was occupied by Serbs during the 1990s and forests around the complex are still mined, so don't wander off by yourself. The best lunch to be had here is on the very edge of the park at **Kormoran** (☑ 031-753 099; Podunavlje bb, Podunavlje; mains from 50KN; ⊙ 11am-10pm), which serves the full roster of local dishes.

There's no public transport to the park, but you can take a local Osijek bus to Bilje and walk the remaining 3km. Alternatively, you can rent a bike in Osijek at **Šport za Sve** (☑ 031-208 135; Istarska bb; per day 40KN; ⊙ 9am-1pm Mon-Fri).

Zlatna Greda (☑ 091 42 11 424; www.zlatnagreda.org; tours €10-30) also runs superb tours of Kopački Rit and has its own ecocentre in a deserted village – now a protected cultural heritage sight – on the border of the park, 28km north of Osijek. Hikes, birdwatching trips, horseback riding and canoe adventures begin here. It's a work in progress, but Zlatna Greda plans to open a hostel, a restaurant and an adrenalin-inducing fun park.

Around Kopački Rit

Bilje, 5km north of Osijek, is a dormitory suburb for the city, with lots of inexpensive accommodation. It makes an alternative base for exploring Kopački Rit. **Bilje Plus** (☑ 091 55 15 711; www.biljeplus.hr; per person 155KN) is an association of three B&Bs that rents out rooms and bikes (70KN per day). Family-run **Mazur** (☑ 031-750 294; www.mazur.hr; Kneza Branimira 2, Bilje; s/d 176/312KN; P ❋ 🛜) is also a good bet, with four neat rooms with private bathrooms and filling breakfasts.

Cycling is an increasingly popular activity in the region, and a cycle path connects Bilje with Osijek. The Pannonian Peace Route is an 80km ride from Osijek to the Serbian city of Sombor, along the Danube and through Kopački Rit. For more info and a map, browse www.zeleni-osijek.hr, a local association for environmental protection. Also popular is the 138km-long Danube Route, which traces easternmost Croatia along its borders with Hungary and Serbia.

The quiet village of **Kopačevo**, on the edge of Kopački Rit, is home to an outstanding regional restaurant – **Zelena Žaba** (Green Frog; ☑ 031-752 212; Ribarska 3, Kopačevo; mains from 40KN; ⊙ 10am-10pm), named after the thousands of squatters bellowing in the backyard swamp. Don't miss the house speciality: *fiš perkelt,* a fish stew with homemade noodles, soft cheese and bacon.

WINE TASTING IN SLAVONIA

Vines have been cultivated in Slavonia for millennia – it's thought that the name Baranja is derived from the Hungarian for 'wine mother' – and after a period of stagnation the region is undergoing a serious renaissance. White wines with local grapes, including *graševina*, are justifiably renowned, and earthy reds are also produced, primarily from *frankovka* (*blaufränkisch*), merlot and cabernet sauvignon. You should call ahead at all these cellars to make sure somebody is there to show you around.

Kutjevo (☑ 0800 600 006; www.kutjevo.com; Kralja Tomislava 1, Kutjevo; guided tour 30KN; ☺ by appointment), in the town of the same name, is home to a medieval wine cellar dating from 1232, formerly of the Cistercian Abbey. You can visit on a guided tour and sample three of its wines.

Nearby are two of Slavonia's top wineries: **Krauthaker** (☑ 099 22 23 013; www.krauthaker.hr; Ivana Jambrovića 6, Kutjevo; tasting 28KN), whose *graševina* and sweet wines regularly win top awards, and **Enjingi** (☑ 034-267 200; www.enjingi.hr; Hrnjevac 87, Vetovo; tasting & tour 50KN), one of Croatia's leading ecological producers, with winemaking experience dating back to 1890 – try the award-winning Venje white blend. The winery also offers accommodation overlooking the vineyards. For a complete selection of Kutjevo's wines, visit **Kolijevka Graševine** (☑ 098 363 312; Republike Hrvatske 56, Kutjevo), a wine shop and tasting room in the town centre.

In Baranja, grape cultivation has been revived on the gentle hills around Kneževi Vinogradi. Up-and-coming winegrowers, mainly in the villages of Zmajevac and Suza, work along well-marked wine trails. Traditionalist in its approach to winemaking, **Gerštmajer** (☑ 091 35 15 586; Šandora 31, Zmajevac) offers tasting tours of its 11 hectares of vineyard and the cellar. Just down the hill is the area's biggest producer, **Josić** (☑ 098 252 657; www.josic.hr; Planina 194, Zmajevac), which also has a fine restaurant. **Kolar** (☑ 031-733 006; Maršala Tita 141, Suza; ☺ 9am-5pm) offers a restaurant, shop and wine tastings in its 100-year old cellar, located on the main road in nearby Suza.

Slavonia also boasts the ancient cellars in Ilok, as well as Croatia's first wine hotel, **Zdjelarević** (☑ 035-427 775; www.zdjelarevic.hr; Vinogradska 65, Brodski Stupnik; s/d 345/534KN), located in Brodski Stupnik (near Slavonski Brod), set among beautiful rolling hills and fish ponds. The hotel has marked bicycle and educational paths through the vineyards. There's a terrace restaurant serving haute cuisine paired with local wines and vineyard views, nicely appointed rooms and guided cellar tours. For a more downhome experience, visit **Sobe Tonkić** (☑ 035-273 408; www.sobe-tonkic.hr; Zagrebačka 348, Slavonski Brod; r 200KN), a rustic, family-run guest house and restaurant featuring home-cooked local specialities and family wines.

Karanac & Around

Located in the far north of Baranja, 8km east of Beli Manastir, the ethno-village and farming community of Karanac provides an authentic slice of Slavonian village life and is well set up to welcome visitors. Lined with cherry trees and lovingly tended gardens, it is home to three churches (Reformist, Catholic and Orthodox) and some well-preserved Pannonian architecture.

Several accommodation options are available in Karanac, including the atmospheric **Sklepić** (☑ 031-720 271; www.sklepic.hr; Kolodvorska 58, Karanac; s/d 225/370KN; P ☎) with its lovely little rustic, en suite rooms. **Ivica i Marica** (☑ 091 13 73 793; www.ivica-marica.com; Ivo Lola Ribara 8a, Karanac; s/d 350/450KN; P ☎)

is another excellent choice: an upmarket working farm on the edge of the village, run by a young couple and offering delightful pine-trimmed rooms and suites, as well as bike rental (100KN per day), good kids' facilities and fun such as horse-drawn carriage rides (350KN per hour).

You'll find several excellent restaurants and wineries in this part of Baranja. **Baranjska Kuća** (☑ 031-720 180; www.baranjska-kuca.com; Kolodvorska 99, Karanac; mains from 50KN; ☺ 10am-11pm Mon-Thu, to 1am Fri & Sat, to 5pm Sun) is one of these, with many traditional dishes, such as fish stews. There's a chestnut-tree-shaded backyard with a 'street of forgotten time' – a barn, a blacksmith's workshop and other huts with old-fashioned crafts. Another great food option on a traditional Slavonian farm (known as a *salaš*), **Tri Mudraca** (☏ 091 21 01 212; www.trimudraca. com; Ive Lole Ribara 27, Karanac; mains from 40KN; ⊘ 10am-11pm Thu-Sun) does elaborate dishes (on request), like duck glazed with honey, or pork neck in a sauce of reduced merlot and root veggies – or just show up and eat whatever the cook has whipped up (with local ingredients) that day. Sit in the back garden for a view of rolling fields and vineyards. The family who runs the place also offer adventure tours on request (starting at 100KN), including all-terrain vehicle (ATV) riding, geocaching, off-road jeep jaunts, expeditions to an abandoned basalt mine and archery.

Josić (☏ 099 73 65 945; www.josic.hr; Planina 194, Zmajevac; mains from 50KN; ⊘ 1-10pm Wed-Thu & Sun, to midnight Fri & Sat), in the nearby village of Zmajevac, is an upmarket alternative, with tables set in vaulted cellars; meat is the strong suit here. Try the duck *perkelt* stew and be sure to visit the wine cellar for tastings of local *graševina*. Reserve ahead in September and October.

Also nearby, in the small village of Suza, the Hungarian-run **Kovač Čarda** (Maršala Tita 215, Suza; mains from 40KN; ⊘ 10am-11pm) is a no-frills roadside eatery at the far end of the village, known for the best *fiš paprikaš* in Baranja (the cooks make it spicy, so ask for paprika on the side). The area's most interesting stop food-wise is **Piroš Čizma** (☏ 031-733 806; www.piroscizma.hr; Maršala Tita 101, Suza; mains fom 50KN; ⊘ noon-10pm); this excellent restaurant, headed up by an Italian chef, is on the roadside when you enter Suza. It serves up gourmet Slavonian dishes, focusing on seasonal ingredients and prepared with a twist – think marinated catfish on an endive base with lemon, honey and mustard emulsion, and beef steak in a sauce of grapes with a *frankovka* wine reduction. It doubles as a hotel, with 25 pleasant rooms (s/d 250/360KN) in two buildings, all well equipped and featuring breakfasts of local fresh cheeses, jams and cold cuts, such as *kulen*, from a local producer.

Right on the tripartite border where Croatia touches Serbia and Hungary is **Batina**, a striking memorial from the communist era that commemorates a key victory of Soviet-led forces over the Nazis in WWII. A colossal female statue sits on high ground, which offers spectacular views over the Danube.

Vukovar

☏ 032 / POP 27,683

When you visit Vukovar today, it's a challenge to visualise this town as it was before the war. A pretty place on the Danube, with roots that stretch back to the 10th century and a series of elegant baroque mansions, it once bustled with art galleries and museums. All that changed with the siege of 1991, which destroyed its economy, culture, physical infrastructure, civic harmony and soul.

Since the return of Vukovar to Croatia in 1998, there has been much progress in repairing the damage. In the centre are new buildings, but many pock-marked and blasted facades remain. The former water tower on the road to Ilok has been left as a testament to destruction.

Less progress has been made in restoring harmony. Serbs and Croats live in parallel and hostile universes, socialising in separate spheres. Children attend separate schools and their parents drink in either Serb or Croat cafes. International organisations are trying to encourage more integration, but forgiveness comes hard to those who have lost family members and livelihoods.

Inevitably, many of Vukovar's sights deal with the war. You may find visiting them an emotionally wrenching experience.

◉ Sights

Castle Eltz   MUSEUM
(Županijska 2; adult/concession 25/15KN, Wed after 2pm free; ⊘ 10am-6pm Tue-Fri, to 1pm Sat & Sun) Closed for several years following the war, the 18th-century Eltz Palace reopened its doors after renovations in 2014. It now showcases four levels of exhibits, many with interactive multimedia features and all marked in English. Don't miss the moving 3rd-floor exhibit about the siege of Vukovar.

Place of Memory:
Vukovar Hospital   MUSEUM
(☏ 091 45 21 222; Županijska 37; adult/concession 15/7KN; ⊘ 8am-3pm Mon-Fri, or by appointment) This multimedia museum recounts the tragic events that took place in the hospital during the 1991 siege. The stirring tour takes you through a series of sandbag-protected corridors, with video projections of war footage, bomb holes and the claustrophobic atomic shelter where newborn babies and the nurses' children were kept. There are small cubicles where you can listen to

THE SIEGE OF VUKOVAR

Before the war, Vukovar had a multi-ethnic population of about 44,000, of which Croats comprised 44% and Serbs 37%. As Croatia edged away from the former Yugoslavia in early 1991, tensions mounted between the two groups. In August 1991, the federal Yugoslav force launched a full-scale artillery and infantry assault in an attempt to seize the town.

By the end of August all but 15,000 of Vukovar's original inhabitants had fled. Those who remained cowered in bomb-proof cellars, living on tinned food and rationed water while bodies piled up in the streets above them. For several months of the siege, the city held out as its pitifully outnumbered defenders warded off the attacks.

After weeks of hand-to-hand fighting, Vukovar surrendered on 18 November. On 20 November Serb Yugoslav soldiers entered Vukovar's hospital and removed 400 patients, staff and their families, 194 of whom were massacred near the village of Ovčara, their bodies dumped in a mass grave nearby. In 2007 at the War Tribunal in the Hague, two Yugoslav army officers, Mile Mrkšić and Veselin Šljivančanin, were sentenced to 20 and five years in prison, respectively, for their role in this massacre. Mrkšić's sentence was upheld in a 2009 appeal, while Šljivančanin's was increased to 17 years for aiding and abetting the murders.

In all, it's estimated that 2000 people – including 1100 civilians – were killed in the defence of Vukovar. There were 4000 wounded, several thousand who disappeared (presumably into mass graves), and 22,000 who were forced into exile.

interviews and speeches by the victims and survivors.

Ovčara Memorial
MEMORIAL

(☉10am-5pm) **FREE** Around 6km out of town en route to Ilok there's a turn-off to the Ovčara Memorial, which is another 4km down the road. This is the hangar where the 194 victims from the hospital were beaten and tortured. Inside the dark room are projections of the victims' photos, with a single candle burning in the middle. The victims met their death in a cornfield another 1.5km down the road, now marked with a black marble gravestone that's covered with candles and flowers.

Ada
BEACH

Head out to this sandy island in the Danube, where on a summer weekend you'll find lots of locals swimming, lounging on the beaches and hanging out at the cafe. Boats depart from the restaurant **Vrške** (Parobrodarska 3) and charge 35KN for a seasonal ticket (unlimited rides).

✦ Festivals & Events

Vukovar Film Festival
FILM FESTIVAL

(www.vukovarfilmfestival.com) Held in late August, this annual festival shows features, documentaries and shorts, mainly from Danubian countries.

🛏 Sleeping & Eating

Vila Rosa
GUESTHOUSE €

(☎091 52 04 036; vilarosavukovar@gmail.com; Josipa Rukavine 2b; s/d 200/350KN; P❀🛜) This guest house is run by a pair of kooky but friendly owners. The five en suite rooms have hardwood floors and modern trimmings; there's a shared kitchen where breakfast is served (25KN) and you have the Danube right across the road.

Hotel Lav
HOTEL €€€

(☎032-445 100; www.hotel-lav.hr; JJ Strossmayera 18; s/d 640/1000KN; P❀🛜) A modern, well-run, four-star hotel. Rooms and suites are spacious and well equipped; many have lovely river views. There's a good bar, a coffee room, a restaurant, a small fitness room and a terrace.

Dunavska Golubica
SLAVONIAN €€

(Dunavska Šetnica 1; mains from 50KN; ☉7am-11pm daily) Pleasant restaurant by the riverside, with an excellent reputation for Slavonian specialties (it does great boneless *fiš paprikaš*) and live music on summer weekends.

ℹ Information

There are banks with ATMs at several locations along Strossmayera, the main drag.

Danubium Tours (☎032-445 455; www.danubiumtours.hr; Olajnica 6/21) Offers biking trips, kayaking on the Danube and various activities in and around Vukovar.

Tourist office (☎ 032-442 889; www.turizam-vukovar.hr; JJ Strossmayera 15; ⊘7am-3pm Mon-Fri, 8am-1pm Sat) The staff here do their best to help visitors.

❶ Getting There & Away

The town has good bus connections to Osijek (35KN, one hour, 10 daily), Ilok (35KN, one hour, 12 daily) and Zagreb (166KN, five hours, five daily). There are also regular services to Belgrade (99KN, 2½ hours, four daily) in Serbia.

Ilok

☑ 032 / POP 7000

The easternmost town in Croatia, 37km from Vukovar, Ilok sits perched on a hill overlooking the Danube and the Serbian region of Vojvodina, across the river. Surrounded by the wine-growing hills of Fruška Gora, famous for viniculture since Roman times, this well-preserved medieval town has a landmark castle that's now one of Slavonia's best museums.

Occupied by Serbia in the early 1990s, Ilok was reintegrated into Croatia in 1998. Wine production has since been revived – the area now has 17 wineries you can tour – and the fortified town centre is being renovated following recent archaeological excavations.

◉ Sights & Activities

The **medieval town** is a leafy place surrounded by the remains of huge city walls. It has two rare specimens of Ottoman heritage: a 16th-century **hammam** and a **turbe**, the grave of a Turkish nobleman.

City Museum MUSEUM
(Muzej Grada Iloka; Šetalište Oca Mladena Barbarića 5; adult/concession 20/10KN; ⊘9am-3pm Tue-Thu, to 6pm Fri, 11am-6pm Sat) Ilok's principal attraction is this excellent municipal museum located in the Odescalchi palace high above the Danube, with spectacular river views. The castle was built on the foundations of a 15th-century structure, which the Italian family Odescalchi later rebuilt in today's baroque-classicist style.

The museum's displays are very well presented, with illustrated information panels in English and Croatian. Sabres and muskets represent the town's Turkish period, there's fine

19th-century furniture and art, and a tombstone and tapestry from an ancient synagogue.

Iločki Podrumi WINE TASTING
(☎032-590 088; www.ilocki-podrumi.hr; Šetalište OM Barbarića 4; tours 30KN; ⊘7am-11pm) The old wine cellars adjacent to the castle are well worth a look. Be sure to taste the *traminac*, a dry white wine served at the coronation of Queen Elizabeth II. A 30-minute tour takes you to the atmospheric underground cellar with its oak barrels. There's also a terrific wine store. Tours in English need to be arranged in advance.

⌂ Sleeping & Eating

Old Town Hostel HOSTEL €
(☎098 92 22 512; www.cinema.com.hr; Julija Benešića 42; dm/s/d 100/250/400KN; P❋@☎) Inside a restored old cinema, this hostel just below the old town has four colourful dorms upstairs, a funky bar with vinyl-plastered walls and a disco on weekend nights.

Stari Podrum HOTEL €€
(☎032-590 088; www.ilocki-podrumi.hr; s/d 350/500KN; P❋@☎) The motel-style accommodation block in the back has 18 large, modern rooms, all with Danube views and plush decor. Located inside the castle's old wine cellars are banqueting rooms lined with wood panelling and giant oak barrels, a splendid setting for a hearty meal of Ilok pork sausages and shepherd's stew with dumplings (mains from 50KN). The wine list is, of course, superb.

Hotel Dunav HOTEL €€
(☎032-596 500; www.hoteldunavilok.com; Julija Benešića 62; s/d 300/500KN; P@☎) Right on the Danube, this fine hotel has 16 attractive rooms with verdant views, some with balconies overlooking the river, and a lovely terrace cafe on the riverfront.

❶ Information

Tourist office (☎032-590 020; www.turizam-ilok.hr; Trg Nikole Iločkog 2; ⊘9am-5pm Mon-Fri) Can recommend rural hotels and walking routes around Ilok and has a lot of local information. Call ahead, as opening hours are sporadic.

❶ Getting There & Away

The bus stops in the town centre just steps from the medieval town. Ilok is connected to Osijek by four daily buses (60KN, 1¾ hours), all passing through Vukovar.

Istria

📞 052

Includes ➡

Pula................99
Brijuni Islands.......107
Rovinj..............108
Poreč..............115
Labin..............121
Vodnjan...........123
Svetvinčenat.......124
Pazin..............124
Gračišće...........126
Buzet..............126
Motovun...........129
Istarske Toplice......131
Grožnjan...........132
Momjan..........133

Why Go?

Continental Croatia meets the Adriatic in Istria (Istra to Croats), the heart-shaped, 3600-sq-km peninsula just south of Trieste in Italy. The bucolic interior of rolling hills and fertile plains attracts artsy visitors to Istria's hilltop villages, rural hotels and farmhouse restaurants, while the verdant indented coastline is enormously popular with the sun-and-sea set. While vast hotel complexes line much of the coast and the rocky beaches are not Croatia's best, facilities are wide ranging, the sea is clean and secluded spots are still plentiful.

The coast, or 'Blue Istria', as the tourist board calls it, gets flooded with tourists in summer, but you can still feel alone and undisturbed in 'Green Istria' (the interior), even in mid-August. Add acclaimed gastronomy (starring fresh seafood, prime white truffles, wild asparagus, top-rated olive oils and award-winning wines), sprinkle it with historical charm and you have a little slice of heaven.

Best Places to Eat

➡ Konoba Batelina (p105)
➡ Monte (p113)
➡ Kantinon (p113)
➡ Marina (p122)

Best Places to Stay

➡ Villa Meneghetti (p115)
➡ Monte Mulini (p112)
➡ Hotel Kaštel (p131)
➡ Vela Vrata (p127)

When to Go

Pula

[Climate chart for Pula showing temperature (°C/°F Temp) and rainfall (Rainfall Inches/mm) by month from January to December. Temperature axis: 30/86, 20/68, 10/50, 0/32, -10/14. Rainfall axis: 8/200, 6/150, 4/100, 2/50, 0.]

Apr Celebrate spring by heading out to the fields to pick some wild asparagus.

Jul–Aug A festival roster of classical music, jazz, films and art sets Istrian towns alight.

Sep The white-truffle season kicks off with the Festival of Subotina in Buzet.

Istria Highlights

1 Admiring the mosaics at **Euphrasian Basilica** (p116) in Poreč.

2 **Truffle hunting** (p127) in the forests around Buzet.

3 Taking in Rovinj's fishing history at **Batana House** (p110).

4 Walking the trails of the legendary **Pazin Chasm** (p125).

5 Catching alfresco screenings during the summer film festival of **Motovun** (p129).

6 Soaking up the communist chic at Tito's playground of **Brijuni** (p107).

7 Exploring the wild landscapes of **Rt Kamenjak cape** (p103) near Pula.

History

Towards the end of the 2nd millennium BC, the Illyrian Histrian tribe settled the region and built fortified villages on top of the coastal and interior hills. The Romans swept into Istria in the 3rd century BC and began building roads and more hill forts as strategic strongholds.

From AD 539 to 751, Istria was under Byzantine rule, the most impressive remnant of which is the Euphrasian Basilica in Poreč. In the period that followed, power switched between Slavic tribes, the Franks and German rulers until an increasingly powerful Venice wrestled control of the Istrian coast in the early 13th century.

With the fall of Venice in 1797, Istria came under Austrian rule, followed by the French (1809–13) and then the Austrians. During the 19th and early 20th centuries, most of Istria was little more than a neglected outpost of the Austro-Hungarian Empire.

When the empire disintegrated at the end of WWI, Italy moved quickly to secure Istria. Italian troops occupied Pula in November 1918 and, in the 1922 Treaty of Rapallo, the Kingdom of Serbs, Croats and Slovenes ceded Istria along with Zadar and several islands to Italy, as a reward for joining the Allied powers in WWI.

A massive population shift followed as 30,000 to 40,000 Italians arrived from Mussolini's Italy and many Croats left, fearing fascism. Their fears were not misplaced, as Istria's Italian masters attempted to consolidate their hold by banning Slavic speech, education and cultural activities.

Italy retained the region until its defeat in WWII when Istria became part of Yugoslavia, causing another mass exodus, as Italians and many Croats fled Tito's communists. Trieste and the peninsula's northwestern tip were points of contention between Italy and Yugoslavia until 1954, when the region was finally awarded to Italy. As a result of Tito's reorganisation of Yugoslavia, the northern part of the peninsula was incorporated into Slovenia, where it remains.

THE ISTRIAN COAST

At the tip of the Istrian peninsula is Pula, the coast's largest city. The Brijuni Islands, Tito's former playground, are an easy day trip from here. The east coast of Istria centres on the modern seaside resort of Rabac, just below the ancient hilltop town of Labin. The west coast is the tourist showcase. Rovinj is the most enchanting town and Poreč the easiest – and cheaper – holiday choice, with lodging and entertainment options aplenty. Just across the water is Italy, and the pervasive Italian influence makes it seem even closer. Italian is a second language in Istria, many Istrians have Italian passports and each town name has an Italian counterpart.

Pula
POP 57,765

The wealth of Roman architecture makes otherwise workaday Pula (ancient Polensium) a standout among Croatia's larger cities. The star of the show is the remarkably well-preserved Roman amphitheatre, smack in the heart of the city, which dominates the streetscape and doubles as a venue for summer concerts and festivals.

Historical attractions aside, Pula is a busy commercial city on the sea that has managed to retain a friendly small-town appeal. Just a short bus ride away, a series of beaches awaits at the resorts that occupy the Verudela Peninsula to the south. Although marred with residential and holiday developments, the coast is dotted with fragrant pine groves, seaside cafes and a clutch of good restaurants. Further south along the indented shoreline, the Premantura Peninsula hides a spectacular nature park, the protected cape of Kamenjak.

History

In 1853, during Austro-Hungarian rule, the monarchy chose Pula as the empire's main naval centre. The construction of the port and the opening of its large shipyard in 1886 unleashed a demographic and economic expansion that transformed Pula into a military and industrial powerhouse.

The city fell into decline once again under Italian fascist rule, which lasted from 1918 to 1943, when the city was occupied by the Germans. At the end of WWII, Pula was administered by Anglo-American forces until it became part of postwar Yugoslavia in 1947. Pula's industrial base weathered the recent war relatively well and the city remains an important centre for shipbuilding, textiles, metals and glass.

Pula

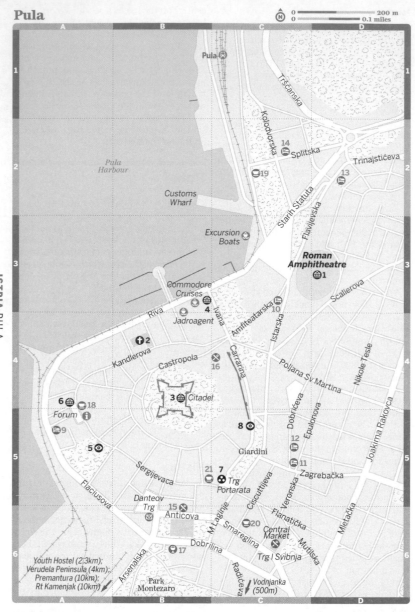

Sights

The oldest part of the city follows the ancient Roman plan of streets circling the central citadel, while the city's newer portions follow a rectangular grid pattern. Most shops, agencies and businesses are clustered in and around the old town as well as on Giardini, Carrarina, Istarska and Riva, which runs along the brand-new harbour. With the exception of a few hotels and restaurants in the old town, most others, as well as the beaches, are 4km to the south on the Ver-

Pula

◉ Top Sights
1 Roman Amphitheatre........................... D3

◉ Sights
2 Cathedral B4
3 Historical & Maritime Museum
of Istria B4
4 Museum of Contemporary Art of
Istria B3
5 Roman Floor Mosaic............................ A5
6 Temple of Augustus A4
7 Triumphal Arch of Sergius................... C5
8 Zerostrasse C5

◉ Sleeping
9 Hostel Pipištrelo.................................... A5

10 Hotel Amfiteatar C3
11 Hotel Galija C5
12 Hotel Omir C5
13 Hotel Scaletta D2
14 Riviera Guest House C2

◉ Eating
15 Fresh B6
16 Jupiter.. C4

◉ Drinking & Nightlife
17 Club Uljanik B6
18 Cvajner... A4
19 Pietas Julia C2
20 Scandal Express C6
21 Uliks... B5

udela Peninsula; these can be reached by walking south on Arsenalska, which turns into Tomasinijeva and then Veruda.

If you plan on taking in all the sights, it's worth buying the Pula Card for 120KN (70KN for children over seven), which allows you free entry to all of the sights below.

★ **Roman Amphitheatre** HISTORIC BUILDING
(Arena; Flavijevska bb; adult/concession 40/20KN; ◷ 8am-midnight Jul & Aug, to 9pm May-Jun & Sep, to 7pm Oct-Apr) Pula's most famous and imposing sight is this 1st-century amphitheatre, overlooking the harbour northeast of the old town. Built entirely from local limestone, the amphitheatre, known locally as the Arena, was designed to host gladiatorial contests, with seating for up to 20,000 spectators.

On the top of the walls is a gutter that collected rainwater. You can still see the slabs used to secure the fabric canopy, which protected spectators from the sun. In the chambers downstairs is a small museum with a display of ancient olive-oil equipment. Pula Film Festival is held here every summer, as are pop and classical concerts.

Check out the weekly Spectacvla Antiqva, an evening summer event that re-creates gladiator fights, workshops featuring ancient Roman clothing and hairstyles and tasting of Roman food and drinks. It costs 70KN for adults, 30KN for children.

Temple of Augustus HISTORIC BUILDING
(Forum; adult/concession 10/5KN; ◷ 9am-10pm Mon-Fri, to 3pm Sat & Sun) This is the only visible remnant from the Roman era on the Forum, Pula's central meeting place from antiquity through the Middle Ages. It used to contain temples and public buildings, but today this temple, erected from 2 BC to AD 14, is the showcase. When the Romans left, it became a church and then a grain warehouse. Reconstructed after a bomb hit it in 1944, it now houses a small historical museum with captions in English.

Zerostrasse HISTORIC SITE
(adult/concession 15/5KN; ◷ 10am-10pm Jun-mid-Sep) This underground system of tunnels was built before and during WWI to shelter the city's population and serve as storage for ammunition. Now you can walk through several of its sections, which all lead to the middle, where a photo exhibit shows early aviation in Pula. There are three entrances – one by the Forum (in a tiny unmarked street off Kandlerova), another by the Archaeological Museum and the third by the taxi stand on Giardini.

Lighting Giants PUBLIC ART
(Pula harbour) Don't miss Pula's latest attraction, a stunning lighting display at the city's c 1856 Uljanik shipyard, one of the world's oldest working shipyards. Renowned lighting designer Dean Skira has lit up the shipyard's iconic cranes in 16,000 different colour schemes, which come alive four times every evening on the hour, starting at 9pm for 15 minutes.

Triumphal Arch of Sergius RUIN
Along Carrarina are Roman walls, which mark the eastern boundary of old Pula. Follow these walls south and continue down Giardini to this majestic arch erected in 27 BC to commemorate three members of the Sergius family who achieved distinction in Pula.

Museum of Contemporary Art of Istria
MUSEUM

(Ivana 1; admission 10KN; ⊙11am-2pm & 5-9pm Tue-Sun) Pop in to Pula's contemporary-art museum, inside the old printing house off the harbour, for a look at Istria's art from the second half of the 20th century up until today. Rotating exhibits change frequently.

Cathedral
CATHEDRAL

(Katedrala; Trg Svetog Tome 2; ⊙10am-6pm) The main altar of Pula's 5th-century cathedral is a Roman sarcophagus holding relics of saints from the 3rd century. The floor reveals fragments of 5th- and 6th-century mosaics. Stones from the amphitheatre were used to build the bell tower in the 17th century.

Historical & Maritime Museum of Istria
MUSEUM

(Gradinski Uspon 6; adult/concession 20/10KN; ⊙8am-9pm) Housed in a 17th-century Venetian hilltop fortress in the old town's centre, the meagre exhibits here deal mostly with the maritime history of Pula, but the views from the citadel walls are worth a stop.

Roman Floor Mosaic
HISTORIC SITE

Located just off Sergijevaca, this mosaic dates from the 3rd century. In the midst of remarkably well-preserved geometric motifs is the central panel, which depicts bad girl Dirce from Greek mythology being punished for the attempted murder of her cousin.

🏃 Activities

An easy 41km cycling trail from Pula to Medulin follows the path of Roman gladiators. The tourist centre (p106) can provide information on the trail, including a map.

Istria Bike
CYCLING

(www.istria-bike.com) This website run by the tourist board outlines trails, packages and agencies that offer cycling trips.

Orca Diving Center
DIVING

(☑098 409 850; www.orcadiving.hr; Hotel Histria) At this centre on the Verudela Peninsula, you can arrange boat and wreck dives.

Windsurf Bar
WATER SPORTS, CYCLING

(☑091 5123 646; www.windsurfing.hr; windsurfing equipment/courses per hour from 70/200KN) In addition to windsurfing, this Premantura outfit offers cycling (250KN) and kayaking (300KN) excursions, and rents bikes (30KN per hour/100KN per day).

Tours

Every Monday evening during the high season, a guided walking tour (narrated in several languages) departs from the Arena at 8.30pm; it costs 76KN for adults and 54KN for children and lasts an hour and 30 minutes. On Wednesdays at the same time, you can do a guided two-hour gourmet tour that features traditional food and wine tastings; it costs 145KN for adults, 100KN for children. Admission for both of the above tours includes entrance to the Arena. Tickets can be bought on the spot or from travel agencies in town.

Most travel agencies offer trips to Brijuni, Limska Draga, Rovinj and inner Istria, but it's often cheaper to book with one of the boats at the harbour. These run regularly and offer fishing picnics (220KN), two-hour 'panorama' excursions to Brijuni (150KN) and a jaunt to Rovinj, Limska Draga and Crveni Otok (300KN).

Only two ships go to Brijuni and actually stop and tour: *Martinabela* and *Arena*.

Martinabela
BOAT

(www.martinabela.hr; tours 280KN) Runs twice daily in summer to Brijuni.

🎉 Festivals & Events

Pula Film Festival
FILM

(www.pulafilmfestival.hr; ⊙Jul) Now in its 62nd year, this July film festival is the town's most important event, with screenings of mainly Croatian and some international films in the Roman Amphitheatre and other locations around town.

Seasplash Festival
MUSIC

(www.seasplash.net; ⊙Jul) Each July, this hopping music fest, featuring wide-ranging live performances – from reggae and ska to dancehall and hip hop – alights Štinjan's Punta Christo Fort, just northwest of Pula.

Outlook Festival
MUSIC

(www.outlookfestival.com; ⊙Sep) Europe's largest bass-music and sound-system culture festival, taking place in early September in Punta Christo Fort in Štinjan, just outside Pula.

Jazzbina
MUSIC

A year-long program of jazz concerts, many featuring world-renowned musicians, on Portarata square during the summer and in theatres and clubs other times of year.

🛏 Sleeping

Pula's peak tourist season runs from the second week of July to late August. During this period it's wise to make advance reservations.

The tip of the Verudela Peninsula, 4km southwest of the city centre, has been turned into a vast tourist complex replete with hotels and apartments. It's not especially attractive, except for the shady pine forests that cover it, but there are beaches, restaurants, tennis courts and water sports. Any travel agency can give you information and book you in to one of the hotels, or you can contact Arenaturist (p106).

The travel agencies in Pula can find you private accommodation, but there is little available in the town centre. Count on paying from 250KN to 490KN for a double room and from 300KN to 535KN for a two-person apartment. You can also browse the list of private accommodation at www.pulainfo.hr.

Hostel Pipištrelo
HOSTEL €

(☎ 052-393 568; www.pipistrelo.com; Flaciusova 6; dm/r 138/367KN; ❄@⏰) With its colourful facade, this recent addition to Pula's hostel scene sits right across the harbour. Its quirky thematic rooms were done up by young Pula designers. It is cash only and closed Sundays, so call ahead. The shipyard across the way brings in some noise.

Youth Hostel
HOSTEL €

(☎ 052-391 133; www.hfhs.hr; Valsaline 4; dm 135KN, caravan 155KN, campsites per person/tent 80/15KN; ◉) Overlooks a beach in Valsaline Bay, 3km south of central Pula. There are dorms, caravans split into two tiny four bed units and campsites. To get here, take bus 2A or 3A to the 'Veruda 2' stop, walk back towards the city to the first street, then turn left and look for the hostel sign.

Camping Stoja
CAMPGROUND €

(☎ 052-387 144; www.arenacamps.com; Stoja 37; campsites per person/tent 62/39KN; ◷Apr–Oct) The closest camping ground to Pula, 3km southwest of the centre. It has lots of space

ISTRIA PULA

BEACHES

Pula is surrounded by a half-circle of rocky beaches, each one with its own fan club. Like bars or nightclubs, beaches go in and out of style. The most tourist-packed are undoubtedly those surrounding the hotel complex on the **Verudela Peninsula**, although some locals will dare to be seen at the small turquoise-coloured **Hawaii Beach** near the Hotel Park.

For seclusion, head out to the wild **Rt Kamenjak** (www.kamenjak.hr; pedestrians & cyclists free, per car/scooter 35/20KN; ◷7am–10pm) on the **Premantura Peninsula**, 10km south of Pula. Istria's southernmost point, this gorgeous, entirely uninhabited cape has lovely rolling hills, wild flowers (including 30 species of orchid), low Mediterranean shrubs, fruit trees and medicinal herbs, and around 30km of virgin beaches and coves. It's criss-crossed with a maze of gravel roads and paths, making it nice and easy to get around. The views to the island of Cres and the peaks of Velebit are extraordinary. Leave no trace – be sure to use the plastic bag and the eco-ashtray you get at the entrance for all your rubbish. Watch out for strong currents if swimming off the southern cape.

Stop by the visitor centre in the old school building in the centre of Premantura, which has an informative bilingual display about the park's ecosystems. Nearby Windsurf Bar rents out bikes and windsurfing equipment. It also offers trial windsurfing courses.

Kolombarica Beach, on the southern end of the peninsula, is popular with daring young men who dive from the high cliffs and swim through the shallow caves at the water's edge. Just above it is a delightful **beach bar**, Safari, half-hidden in the bushes near the beach, about 3.5km from the entrance to the park. A shady place with lush alcoves, lots of driftwood, found objects and a bar that serves tasty snacks, it's a great place to while away an afternoon. For the wildest and least-discovered stretch of the cape, head to **Gornji Kamenjak**, which lies between the village of Volme and Premantura.

Getting to Rt Kamenjak by car is the easiest option, but drive slowly in order not to generate too much dust, which is detrimental to the environment. A more ecofriendly option is taking city bus 28 from Pula to Premantura (20KN), then renting a bike to get inside the park. On full-moon nights in summer, an organized 10km bike ride, adapted to all ages, leaves from Premantura.

TAKING IT OFF IN ISTRIA

Naturism in Croatia enjoys a long and venerable history that began on Rab Island around the turn of the 20th century. It quickly became a fad among Austrians influenced by the growing German Freikörperkultur movement, which loosely translates as 'free body culture'. Later, Austrian Richard Ehrmann opened the first naturist camp on Paradise Beach in Lopar (on Rab), but the real founders of Adriatic naturism were Edward VIII and Wallis Simpson, who popularised it by going skinny-dipping along the Rab coast in 1936.

The coast of Istria now has many of Croatia's largest and most well-developed naturist resorts. Naturist camping grounds are marked as FKK, an abbreviation of Freikörperkultur.

Start in the north at **Camp Kanegra** (www.istracamping.com), north of Umag, a relatively small site on a long pebbly beach. Continuing south along the coast, you'll come to **Naturist Centre Ulika** (www.plavalaguna.hr) in Červar, just outside Poreč, which has 559 pitches, as well as caravans and mobile homes available for rent. For those who prefer to stay in an apartment, **Naturist Resort Solaris** (www.valamar.hr) is the ideal choice. Only 12km north of Poreč, on the wooded Lanterna Peninsula, the complex also includes a naturist campground. South of Poreč, next to the fishing village of Funtana, is the larger **Naturist Camping Istra** (www.valamar.hr), which sleeps up to 3000 people. Continue south past Vrsar and you come to the mother ship of naturist resorts, **Koversada** (www.campingrovinjvrsar.com). In 1961 Koversada islet went totally nude and the colony soon spread to the nearby coast. Now this behemoth can accommodate up to 8000 people in campsites, villas and apartments. If that seems a little overwhelming, keep going south to **Valalta Naturist Camp** (www.valalta.hr), on the other side of the Lim Channel north of Rovinj. It has a manageable number of apartments, bungalows, caravans, mobile homes and campsites. If you prefer to be within easy reach of Pula, travel down the coast to Medulin and **Camp Kažela** (www.arenacamps.com), which has mobile homes for rent, plus campsites right by the sea.

on the shady promontory, with a restaurant, dive centre and swimming off the rocks. Take bus 1 to Stoja.

Hotel Amfiteatar
HOTEL €€

(☑ 052-375 600; www.hotelamfiteatar.com; Amfiteatarska 6; s/d 529/636KN; P ❉ @ 🛜) The swankiest spot in town, right by the amphitheatre, this newish hotel has contemporary rooms with upscale trimmings such as minibars and flat-screen TVs. Rooms range in size and view. The restaurant is one of Pula's best. There's a surcharge for stays of less than two nights.

Hotel Scaletta
HOTEL €€

(☑ 052-541 025; www.hotel-scaletta.com; Flavijevska 26; s/d 505/732KN; P ❉ 🛜) There's a friendly family vibe at this cosy hotel. The rooms have tasteful decor and a bagful of trimmings (such as minibars). Plus it's just a hop and a skip from town, and a short walk from the amphitheatre and the waterfront.

Hotel Galija
HOTEL €€

(☑ 052-383 802; www.hotelgalija.hr; Epulonova 3; s/d 523/747KN; P ❉ 🛜) This two-part hotel sits a stone's throw from the central market. Standard rooms are in the building above

the restaurant, while the newer, more modern rooms (for 75KN extra) are in the building that houses the reception.

Hotel Omir
HOTEL €€

(☑ 052-213 944; www.hotel-omir.com; Dobrićeva 6; s/d 450/600KN; ❉ 🛜) The best budget option smack in the heart of town, Hotel Omir has modest but clean and quiet rooms with TVs. Rooms on the 2nd and 3rd floors are more spacious. There's no elevator.

Riviera Guest House
HOTEL €€

(☑ 052-211 166; www.arenaturist.hr; Splitska 1; s/d 450/600KN; 🛜) This once-grand property in a neobaroque 19th-century building is in dire need of a thorough overhaul. The saving grace: it's in the centre of town and the front rooms have water views.

Park Plaza Histria Pula
HOTEL €€€

(☑ 052-590 000; www.arenaturist.hr; Verudella 17; s 750-950KN, d 1200-1400KN; P ❉ @ 🛜 ≋) Extensive four-star facilities, renovated rooms with balconies and easy beach access make up for the lack of character at this concrete behemoth on the Verudela Peninsula. There are indoor and outdoor swimming pools and a spa. Reserve online for the best prices.

Eating

The centre of Pula is full of tourist traps, so for the best food and good value you'll have to head out of town. To grab a cheap quick bite, browse around the central market. For a reliably good meal, head to the alfresco restaurant of Hotel Amfiteatar.

City Centre

Vodnjanka   ISTRIAN €
(Vitezića 4; mains from 40KN; ☺noon-4pm & 7.30-10pm Mon-Sat Jun-Sep, 11am-4pm Mon-Sat Oct-May) Locals swear by the real-deal home cooking at this no-frills spot. It's cheap, casual and cash-only, and there's a small menu that concentrates on simple Istrian dishes. To get here, walk south on Radićeva to Vitezića.

Fresh   SANDWICHES €
(Anticova 5; salads & sandwiches from 12KN, cakes from 9KN; ☺6am-4.30pm) Best for a quick and wholesome bite, this sandwich-and-salad bar serves a mean ham-and-cheese toast plus tasty vegetarian/vegan dishes (think spinach and chicory quiche) and traditional Croatian savoury pies like *zlevanka*.

Jupiter   PIZZA €
(Castropola 42; pizzas 30-96KN; ☺10am-midnight) Good thin-crust pizzas and decent pasta dishes served on the upstairs terrace.

South & East of the City

Fish-Food More   SEAFOOD €
(Rizzijeva 47; mains from 50KN; ☺8am-11pm Mon-Sat Jun-Jul & Sep, also Sun in Aug) Simple seafood joint in a residential area some 15 minutes' walk from the central market (part of it uphill). It buzzes with locals at lunchtime, who come for fresh fish dishes. The marinated sardines are to die for. Walk south on Radićeva to Rizzijeva.

★Konoba Batelina   SEAFOOD €€
(☎052-573 767; Čimulje 25, Banjole; mains from 85KN; ☺5-11pm Mon-Sat) The superb food that awaits at this family-run tavern is worth a trek to Banjole village, 3km southeast of Pula. The owner, fisherman and chef, David Skoko, dishes out seafood that's some of the best, most creative and lovingly prepared you'll find in Istria. Reserve ahead.

Gina   ISTRIAN €€
(Stoja 23; mains from 60KN; ☺noon-11pm) This low-key eatery near Stoja camping ground draws in a local crowd for its well-prepared Istrian mainstays, cosy decor and lovely sea views. Try the cream fish soup with *malvazija* wine and the lavender semifreddo with a hot sauce of figs and pine nuts.

Farabuto   MEDITERRANEAN €€
(Sisplac 15; mains from 70KN; ☺11am-midnight daily Jun-Sep, closed Sun Oct-May) It's worth a trek to this nondescript residential area about 1.5km southwest of the centre for stylish decor, but more importantly, stellar Mediterranean fare with a creative touch. There are daily specials and a well curated wine list; try the house wine from Piquentum winery.

Milan   MEDITERRANEAN €€
(www.milanpula.com; Stoja 4; mains from 85KN; ☺noon-11pm) An exclusive vibe, seasonal specialties, four sommeliers and an olive-oil expert on staff all create one of the city's best dining experiences. The five-course fish menu is well worth it. There's also a 12-room upscale hotel (single/double 590/850KN) out the back.

🍷 Drinking & Nightlife

Most of the nightlife is out of the town centre, but in mild weather the cafes on the Forum and along the pedestrian streets Kandlerova, Flanatička and Sergijevaca are lively people-watching spots. To mix with Pula's young crowd, grab some beers and head to the Lungomare coastal strip, where music blasts out of parked cars.

For beach-bar action, head to Verudela or Medulin.

★Cabahia   BAR
(Širolina 4; ☺8am-midnight Mon-Sat, 10am-midnight Sun) This artsy hideaway, 2km south of the centre in Veruda, has a cosy wood-beamed interior, eclectic decor of old objects, dim lighting, South American flair and a great garden terrace out the back. It hosts concerts and gets packed on weekends. If it's too full, try the more laid-back **Bass** (Širolina 3), just across the street.

Cvajner   CAFE
(Forum 2; ☺8am-10pm) Snag a prime alfresco table at this art-filled cafe right on the buzzing Forum and check out rotating exhibits in the funky interior, which showcases works by up-and-coming local artists.

Pietas Julia   CAFE, BAR
(Riva 20; ☺8am-midnight Mon-Thu & Sun, to 4am Sat; 🛜) At this trendy bar on the harbour,

things start to get happening late on weekends, as it stays open till 4am. During the day, there are breakfasts and snacks. Great spot for a sundowner.

Scandal Express   CAFE, BAR
(Ciscuttijeva 15; ⊙ 7am-midnight Mon-Fri, 7am-2pm & 6pm-midnight Sat & Sun) Mingle with a mixed-bag crowd of locals at this popular gathering spot with a cool train-carriage vibe and lots of posters. Try *pašareta*, a local Istrian soda. Smoking is allowed.

Uliks   CAFE
(Trg Portarata 1; ⊙ 6am-2am Mon-Fri, from 7am Sat, from 9am Sun) James Joyce once taught in this apartment building, where you can now linger over a drink at the ground-floor cafe, pondering *Ulysses* or Pula's pebble beaches.

Zeppelin   BEACH BAR
(Saccorgiana Bay; ⊙ 10am-2am Mon-Thu & Sun, to 4am Fri & Sat) Après-beach fun is on the menu at this beach bar in Saccorgiana bay on Verudela, but it also does night parties ranging in theme from vodka to reggae and karaoke to martini.

Club Uljanik   CLUB
(www.clubuljanik.hr; Dobrilina 2; ⊙ 8am-5am Thu-Sat) Going strong since the 1960s, the legendary Pula club these days caters to a young party crowd who come for its range of themed weekend parties.

☆ Entertainment
You should definitely try to catch a concert in the spectacular amphitheatre – the tourist office has schedules and there are posters around Pula advertising live performances.

Rojc   CULTURAL CENTRE
(www.rojcnet.pula.org; Gajeva 3) For an arty underground experience, check the program at Rojc, a converted army barracks that now houses a multimedia art centre and studios with occasional concerts, exhibitions and other events. Head south of Park Montezaro, just below the centre of Pula, and follow Gajeva to reach Rojc.

❶ Information

INTERNET ACCESS
There's free wi-fi all around town – on the Forum, Portarata, Giardini, Flanatička street, Kaštel and Narodni trg.

MEDICAL SERVICES
Hospital (☑ 052-376 500; Zagrebačka 30)

Tourist Ambulance (☑ 052-210 085; Flanatička 27; ⊙ 8am-9.30pm Mon-Fri)

POST
Main post office (Danteov trg 4; ⊙ 7am-8pm Mon-Fri, to 2pm Sat) You can make long-distance calls here. Check out the cool staircase inside.

TOURIST INFORMATION
Tourist Information Centre (☑ 052-219 197; www.pulainfo.hr; Forum 3; ⊙ 9am-9pm) Knowledgable and friendly staff provide maps, brochures and schedules of events in Pula and around Istria. Pick up two useful booklets: *Domus Bonus*, which lists the best-quality private accommodation in Istria, and *Istra Gourmet*, with a list of all restaurants.

TRAVEL AGENCIES
Active Travel Istra (☑ 052-211 889; www.activa-istra.com; Scalierova 1) Excursions around Istria, adventure trips and concert tickets.
Arenaturist (☑ 052-529 400; www.arenaturist.hr; Riviera Guest House, Splitska 1a) Books rooms in the network of hotels it manages and offers guide services and excursions.
IstrAction (☑ 095 700 7822; www.istraction.com; Kolodvorska 5) Offers fun half-day tours to Rt Kamenjak and around Pula's fortifications, as well as medieval-themed full-day excursions around Istria.
Maremonti Travel Agency (☑ 052-384 000; www.maremonti-istra.hr; Flavijevska 8) Books accommodation and rent cars and scooters (from 150KN to 300KN per day). It also rents bikes for 75KN per day and offers a guided cycling tour around Pula for 300KN.

❶ Getting There & Away

AIR
Pula Airport (☑ 052-530 105; www.airport-pula.hr) is located 6km northeast of town. There is one daily flight to Zagreb (40 minutes). In summer, there are low-cost and charter flights from major European cities, such as with Ryanair and Germanwings. **Croatia Airlines** (☑ 062 500 505; www.croatiaairlines.hr; Valtursko polje 210) has an office at the airport.

BOAT
Pula's harbour is located just west of the amphitheatre and a handy 500m southwest of the bus station. **Jadroagent** (☑ 052-210 431; www.jadroagent.hr; Riva 14; ⊙ 7am-3pm Mon-Fri) has schedules and tickets for Jadrolinija boats connecting Istria with the islands and south of Croatia.
    Commodore Cruises (☑ 052-211 631; www.commodore-travel.hr; Riva 14) Sells tickets for the Wednesday boat service to Venice (540KN, 3½ hours) between June and September.

BUSES FROM PULA

DOMESTIC DESTINATION	COST (KN)	DURATION	DAILY SERVICES
Dubrovnik	600	15hr	1
Labin	42	45min	10
Poreč	72	1hr	7
Rijeka	97	2½hr	9
Rovinj	38	45min	17
Split	392	10hr	3
Zadar	255	7hr	3
Zagreb	190	4hr	11

INTERNATIONAL DESTINATION	COST (KN)	DURATION	DAILY SERVICES
Ljubljana	165	5hr	1 (summer only)
Milan	424	9½hr	1 weekly
Padua	235	6hr	1 (none Sun)
Trieste	107	3hr	2
Venice	171	5hr	1 (none Sun)

BUS

The Pula **bus station** (☑ 060 304 091; Šijanska 4) is 500m northeast of the town centre, and has a **garderoba** (per hour 2.50KN; ☺ 24hr) for those who need to store bags. Buses head from the bus station to Rijeka (97KN, 1½ hours) almost hourly. In summer, reserve a seat a day in advance and be sure to sit on the right-hand side of the bus for a stunning view of the Kvarner Gulf.

TRAIN

Less than 1km north of town, the train station is near the sea along Kolodvorska. There is one direct train daily to Ljubljana (180KN, 4½ hours) and three to Zagreb (160KN, nine hours), but you must board a bus for part of the trip, from Lupoglav to Rijeka.

There are three daily trains to Buzet (56KN, two hours).

ⓘ Getting Around

An airport bus (30KN) departs from the bus station several times weekly, coinciding with Ryanair flights; check at the bus station. Taxis cost about 120KN.

The city buses of use to visitors are 1, which runs to Camping Stoja, and 2A and 3A to Verudela. The frequency varies from every 15 minutes to every half-hour (from 5am to 11.30pm). Tickets are sold at *tisak* (news stands) for 6KN, or from the driver for 11KN.

Brijuni Islands

The Brijuni (Brioni in Italian) archipelago consists of two main pine-covered islands and 12 islets off the coast of Istria, just northwest of Pula across the 3km-wide Fažana Channel. Only the largest island, Veli Brijun, can be visited. Covered by meadows, parks and oak and laurel forests – and some rare plants such as wild cucumber and marine poppy – the islands were pronounced a national park in 1983.

Even though traces of habitation go back more than 2000 years, the islands owe their fame to Tito, the extravagant Yugoslav leader who turned them into his private retreat.

Each year from 1947 until just before his death in 1980, Tito spent six months in Brijuni at his hideaway. To create a lush comfort zone, he introduced subtropical plant species and created a safari park to house the exotic animals gifted to him by world leaders. The Somali sheep you'll see roaming around came from Ethiopia, while a Zambian leader gave a gift of waterbuck.

At his summer playground, Tito received 90 heads of state and a bevy of movie stars in lavish style. Bijela Vila on Veli Brijun was Tito's 'White House': the place for issuing edicts and declarations as well as entertaining. The islands are still used for official state visits, but are increasingly a favourite on the international yachting circuit, and a

ISTRIA BRIJUNI ISLANDS

holiday spot of choice for royalty from obscure kingdoms and random billionaires who love its bygone aura of glamour.

Every summer, theatre aficionados make their way across the channel to the Minor Fort on Mali Brijun for performances by **Ulysses Theatre** (www.ulysses.hr).

◉ Sights

As you arrive on Veli Brijun, after a 15-minute boat ride from Fažana, you'll dock in front of the Hotel Neptun-Istra, where Tito's illustrious guests once stayed. A guide will take you on a four-hour island tour on a miniature tourist train, beginning with a visit to the 9-hectare **safari park**. Other stops on the tour include the ruins of a **Roman country house**, dating from the 1st century BC, an **archaeological museum** inside a 16th-century citadel, and **St Germain Church**, now a gallery displaying copies of medieval frescoes in Istrian churches.

Most interesting is the **Tito on Brijuni** exhibit in a building behind Hotel Karmen. A collection of stuffed animals occupies the ground floor. Upstairs are photos of Tito with film stars such as Josephine Baker, Sophia Loren, Elizabeth Taylor and Richard Burton, and world leaders including Indira Gandhi and Fidel Castro. Outside is a 1953 Cadillac that Tito used to show the island to his eminent guests. These days, you can pay 55KN for a photo op inside or rent it for a measly 2750KN for 30 minutes. Bikes (35KN per hour or 110KN per day) and electric carts (300KN per hour) are a cheaper option, and a great way to explore the island.

⌷ Sleeping & Eating

There is no private accommodation on Veli Brijun but there are three luxurious villas (7660KN per day for the smallest one, which sleeps four) available for rent through the national park office. Boat transport to and from the mainland is included in the following hotel prices; both are on Veli Brijun. Veli Brijun's hotel restaurants are the only places to eat.

Hotel Neptun-Istra   HOTEL €€€
(☑ 052-525 807; www.brijuni.hr; s/d 840/1430KN; @ 🛜) This is the ultimate in communist chic. Even though it's spruced up and comfy, rooms retain their plain utilitarian look. Each comes with a balcony; some have forest views, too. You can just imagine Tito's famous guests lounging here.

Hotel Karmen   HOTEL €€€
(☑ 052-525 807; www.brijuni.hr; s/d 600/1000KN; @) Designers and architects from Zagreb flock to this spot on the harbour for its authentic communist design – it's trashy, real and feels as if it's still in the 1950s. Let's just hope they don't renovate.

❶ Getting There & Away

A number of excursion boats leave from the Pula waterfront for the islands. Instead of booking an excursion with one of the travel agencies in Pula, Rovinj or Poreč, you could take public bus 21 from Pula to Fažana (15KN), 8km away, then sign up for a tour at the **national park office** (☑ 052-525 888; www.brijuni.hr; tours 125-210KN), near the wharf. In July and August, tours cost 210KN per person (children 105KN). It's best to book in advance, especially in summer, and request an English-speaking tour guide.

Check along the Pula waterfront for excursion boats to Brijuni. Note that many of the two-hour 'panorama' trips from Pula to Brijuni (150KN) don't actually stop at the islands; *Martinabela* and *Arena* are the only ones that do.

Rovinj

POP 14,365

Rovinj (Rovigno in Italian) is coastal Istria's star attraction. While it can get overrun with tourists in summer, and residents have developed a sharp eye for maximising profits by upgrading hotels and restaurants to four-star status, it remains one of the last true Mediterranean fishing ports. Fishers haul their catch into the harbour in the early morning, followed by a horde of squawking gulls, and mend their nets before lunch. Prayers for a good catch are sent forth at the massive Church of St Euphemia, the 60m-high tower of which punctuates the peninsula. Wooded hills and low-rise hotels surround the old town, which is webbed with steep cobbled streets and piazzas. The 14 green islands of the Rovinj archipelago make for a pleasant afternoon away; the most popular islands are Sveta Katarina and Crveni Otok (Red Island), also known as Sveti Andrija.

The old town is contained within an egg-shaped peninsula. About 1.5km south is the Punta Corrente Forest Park and the wooded cape of Zlatni Rt (Golden Cape), with its

Rovinj

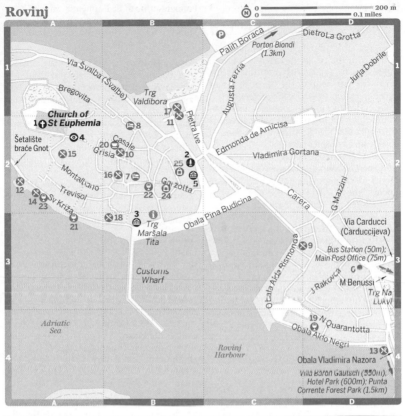

Rovinj

◎ Top Sights
1 Church of St Euphemia.........................A2

◎ Sights
2 Balbi Arch...B2
3 Batana House......................................B3
4 Grisia..A2
5 Heritage Museum...............................B2

✿ Activities, Courses & Tours
6 Adistra..D3

🛏 Sleeping
7 Casa Garzotto.....................................B2
8 Villa Valdibora.....................................B2

✕ Eating
9 Kantinon..D3
10 Da Sergio..B2

11 Grota...B2
12 Puntulina..A2
13 Maestral..D4
14 Male Madlene.....................................A2
15 Monte..A2
16 Ulika..B2
17 Vegetable Market...............................B1
18 Veli Jože...B3

☕ Drinking & Nightlife
19 Havana..D4
20 Limbo..B2
21 Monte Carlo..A3
22 Piassa Granda....................................B2
23 Valentino...A2

🛍 Shopping
24 Galerija Brek.......................................B2
25 Zdenac 13...B2

age-old oak and pine trees and several large hotels. There are two harbours: the northern open harbour and the small, protected harbour to the south.

ISTRIA ROVINJ

History

Originally an island, Rovinj was settled by Slavs in the 7th century and began to develop a strong fishing and maritime industry. In 1199 Rovinj signed an important pact with Dubrovnik to protect its maritime trade, but in the 13th century the threat of piracy forced it to turn to Venice for protection.

From the 16th to 18th centuries, its population expanded dramatically with an influx of immigrants fleeing Turkish invasions of Bosnia and continental Croatia. The town began to develop outside the walls put up by the Venetians, and in 1763 the islet was connected to the mainland and Rovinj became a peninsula.

Although the town's maritime industry thrived in the 17th century, Austria's 1719 decision to make Trieste and Rijeka free ports dealt Rovinj a blow. The decline of sailing ships further damaged its shipbuilding industry, and in the middle of the 19th century it was supplanted by the shipyard in Pula. Like the rest of Istria, Rovinj bounced from Austrian to French to Austrian to Italian rule before finally becoming part of postwar Yugoslavia. There's still a considerable Italian community here, who speak a particular dialect.

⊙ Sights

★ **Church of St Euphemia**   CHURCH
(Sveta Eufemija; Petra Stankovića; ⊙ 10am-6pm Jun-Sep, to 4pm May, to 2pm Apr) The town's showcase, this imposing church dominates the old town from its hilltop location in the middle of the peninsula. Built in 1736, it's the largest baroque building in Istria, reflecting the period during the 18th century when Rovinj was its most populous town. Inside, look for the marble **tomb of St Euphemia** behind the right-hand altar.

Rovinj's patron saint was tortured for her Christian faith by Emperor Diocletian before being thrown to the lions in AD 304. According to legend, the body disappeared one dark, stormy night only to appear off the coast of Rovinj in a spectral boat. The townspeople were unable to budge the heavy sarcophagus until a small boy appeared with two calves and moved it to the top of the hill, where it still stands in the present-day church. On the anniversary of her martyrdom (16 September), devotees congregate here.

Modelled on the belfry of St Mark's in Venice, the 60m bell tower is topped by a copper statue of St Euphemia, which shows the direction of the wind by turning on a spindle. You can climb the tower (to the left of the altar) for 15KN.

Batana House   MUSEUM
(Pina Budicina 2; adult/concession 10/5KN, with guide 15KN; ⊙ 10am-2pm & 7-11pm) On the harbour, Batana House is a museum dedicated to the *batana,* a flat-bottomed fishing boat that stands as a symbol of Rovinj's seafaring and fishing traditions. The multimedia exhibits inside the 17th-century town house have interactive displays, excellent captions and audio with *bitinada,* which are typical fishers' songs. Check out the *spacio,* the ground-floor cellar where wine was kept, tasted and sold amid much socialising (open on Tuesday and Thursday).

Grisia   STREET
Lined with galleries where local artists sell their work, this cobbled street leads uphill from behind the Balbi Arch to St Euphemia. The winding narrow backstreets that spread around Grisia are an attraction in themselves. Windows, balconies, portals and squares are a pleasant confusion of styles – Gothic, Renaissance, baroque and neoclassical. Notice the unique *fumaioli* (exterior chimneys), built during the population boom when entire families lived in a single room with a fireplace.

Punta Corrente Forest Park   PARK
Follow the waterfront on foot or by bike past Hotel Park to this verdant area, locally known as Zlatni Rt, about 1.5km south. Covered in oak and pine groves and boasting 10 species of cypress, the park was established in 1890 by Baron Hütterott, an Austrian admiral who kept a villa on Crveni Otok. You can swim off the rocks or just sit and admire the offshore islands.

Heritage Museum   MUSEUM
(www.muzej-rovinj.com; Trg Maršala Tita 11; adult/concession 15/10KN; ⊙ 10am-2pm & 6-10pm Tue-Sun Jun-Sep, closed Sun Oct-May) This museum in a baroque palace contains a collection of contemporary art and old masters from Rovinj and elsewhere in Croatia, plus archaeological finds, a maritime section and occasional special exhibits.

Balbi Arch   MONUMENT
The elaborate Balbi Arch was built in 1679 on the location of the former town gate. The top of the arch is ornamented with a Turkish

head on the outside and a Venetian head on the inside.

Activities

Most people hop aboard a boat for **swimming**, **snorkelling** and **sunbathing**; boat trips across to Crveni Otok or Sveta Katarina are easily arranged through operators along the waterfront.

Nadi Scuba Diving Centar (052-813 290; www.scuba.hr) and **Petra** (052-812 880; www.divingpetra.hr) offer daily boat dives. The main attraction is the **Baron Gautsch wreck**, an Austrian passenger steamer sunk in 1914 by a sea mine in 40m of water.

There are 80 **rock-climbing routes** in a former Venetian stone quarry at Punta Corrente Forest Park (Zlatni Rt), many suitable for beginners.

Cycling around Rovinj and the Punta Corrente Forest Park is a superb way to spend an afternoon.

Birdwatchers can bike to the **ornithological reserve** at Palud Marsh, 8km southwest of Rovinj.

Tours

Most travel agencies in Rovinj sell day trips to Venice (390KN to 520KN), Plitvice (500KN to 600KN) and Brijuni (380KN to 470KN). There are also fish picnics (250KN), panoramic cruises (100KN) and boat outings to Limska Draga Fjord (150KN). These can be slightly cheaper if booked through one of the independent operators that line the waterfront.

Delfin   TOURS
(052 848 265) A reliable independent tour operator on the waterfront.

Adistra   KAYAKING
(095 838 3797; www.adistra.hr; Carera 69) Adistra runs kayaking tours, including 9km jaunts around the Rovinj archipelago and a 14km outing to the Lim fjord; both cost 280KN and include picnic lunch and snorkelling gear. It also offers a sunset paddle (190KN) with wine, cheese and olives.

White Dust Sailing   BOAT TOUR
(www.whitedust-sailing.com) For a unique sailing experience, charter a boat through White Dust Sailing, which runs excellent daily tours as well as thematic weeklong sails (adventure, family, gastronomy) to undiscovered nautical routes and off-the-radar beaches; high-season sails start at €500.

★ Festivals & Events

The city's annual events include various regattas from late April through August.

From late June to mid-September, on Tuesdays and Thursdays, there's a **procession of batanas** with lanterns. It departs at 8.30pm and costs 60KN, or 220KN for procession and dinner at a traditional tavern. Reserve a couple of days ahead at Batana House. On Sundays and Wednesdays in summer there's a **traditional fish festival** outside the museum, with *bitinada* music and cheap seafood snacks.

Avantgarde Jazz Festival   JAZZ
(www.avantgardejazzfestival.com, May-Jul) This festival brings big-name jazz performers to the old tobacco factory on the waterfront and to the main square, from May through July.

Rovinj Summer Festival   MUSIC
(Jul & Aug) Rovinj Summer Festival is a series of classical concerts that take place in the Church of St Euphemia and the Franciscan monastery.

Grisia Art Show   CULTURE
(Aug) The second Sunday in August sees the town's most renowned event, when narrow Grisia becomes an open-air art exhibition. Anyone from children to professional painters display their work in churches, studios and on the street.

☐ Sleeping

Rovinj has become Istria's destination of choice for hordes of summertime tourists, so reserving in advance is strongly recommended. Prices have been rising steadily and probably will continue to do so.

If you want to stay in private accommodation, there is little available in the old town, where there's also no free parking and accommodation costs are higher. Double rooms start at 220KN in the high season, with a small discount for single occupancy; two-person apartments start at 330KN. Out of season, prices go down considerably.

The surcharge for a stay of less than three nights is up to 50%, and guests who stay only one night are sometimes punished with a 100% surcharge. Outside summer months, you should be able to bargain the surcharge away. You can book through one of the travel agencies.

ISTRIA ROVINJ

Except for a few private options, most hotels and campgrounds in the area are managed by **Maistra** (www.maistra.com).

Porton Biondi
CAMPGROUND €

(☏ 052-813 557; www.portonbiondi.hr; Aleja Porton Biondi 1; campsites per person/tent 53/40KN; ⊙ mid-Mar–Oct) This beachside camping ground, which sleeps 1200, is about 700m north of the old town.

Polari Camping
CAMPGROUND €

(☏ 052-801 501; www.campingrovinjvrsar.com; Polari bb; campsites per person/tent 81/92KN; ⊙ Apr-Sep; @ � ⩫) On the beach about 3km southeast of town, it features swimming pools, restaurants and playgrounds.

Villa Baron Gautsch
GUESTHOUSE €€

(☏ 052-840 538; www.baron-gautsch.com; IM Ronjgova 7; incl breakfast s/d 293/586KN; ⊛ �) This German-owned *pansion* (guesthouse), up the leafy street leading up from Hotel Park, has 17 spick-and-span rooms, some with terraces and lovely views of the sea and the old town. Breakfast is served on the small terrace out the back. It's cash (kuna) only.

Monte Mulini
HOTEL €€€

(☏ 052-636 000; www.montemulinihotel.com; A Smareglia bb; s/d 2600/3300KN; P ⊛ @ � ⩫) This swanky hotel slopes down towards the peaceful Lone bay, a 10-minute stroll from the old town along the Lungomare. Balconied rooms all have sea views and upscale trimmings. The spa is tops, as is the renowned Wine Vault restaurant. There are three outdoor pools and the overall design is bold and bright.

Hotel Lone
DESIGN HOTEL €€€

(☏ 052-632 000; www.lonehotel.com; Luje Adamovića 31; s/d 1800/2300KN; P ⊛ @ �) Croatia's first design hotel, this 248-room powerhouse of style is a creation of Croatia's starchitects 3LHD. It rises over Lone bay like a ship dropped in the forest. Light-flooded rooms come with private terraces and five-star trimmings. Facilities include a couple of restaurants, an extensive spa and a brand-new beach club.

Villa Valdibora
HOTEL €€€

(☏ 052-845 040; www.valdibora.com; Silvano Chiurco 8; s/d 1176/1568KN; ⊛ �) The 11 rooms, suites and apartments in this old-town building come with cool stone floors and upscale trimmings such as hydromassage sauna showers. There's a fitness room, massages (150KN to 450KN) and bikes for guest use.

Casa Garzotto
GUESTHOUSE €€€

(☏ 052-811 884; www.casa-garzotto.com; Via Garzotto 8; incl breakfast s/d 1000/1221KN; P ⊛ @ �) Rooms and apartments in this historic town house have original details such as fireplaces and wooden beams, an antique touch and up-to-the-minute amenities. The use of bikes is complimentary. The complex has three other buildings nearby, one with more basic rooms (830KN).

Hotel Istra
HOTEL €€€

(☏ 052-802 500; www.maistra.com; Crveni Otok; s/d 1100/1400KN; P ⊛ @ ⩫) The renowned wellness centre and spa and good facilities for children are chief assets of this four-star complex, a 10-minute boat ride away on Crveni Otok. There's a restaurant in an old castle on-site.

Hotel Park
HOTEL €€€

(☏ 052-808 000; www.maistra.com; IM Ronjgova bb; s/d 1100/1400KN; P ⊛ @ � ⩫) It's conveniently close to the ferry dock for Crveni Otok and has such crowd-pleasing amenities as two outdoor pools, a fitness room with a range of classes and a sauna. Most rooms have balconies.

✖ Eating

Picnickers can get supplies at the supermarket next to the bus station or at one of the Konzum stores around town. For a cheap bite, pick up a *burek* (heavy pastry stuffed with meat or cheese) from one of the kiosks near the **vegetable market** (⊙ 7am-6pm).

Most of the restaurants that line the harbour offer the standard fish and meat mainstays at similar prices. For a more gourmet experience, you'll need to bypass the water vistas. Note that many restaurants shut their doors between lunch and dinner.

Male Madlene
TAPAS €

(☏ 052-815 905; Svetog Križa 28; snacks from 30KN; ⊙ 11am-2pm & 7-11pm May-Sep) This is an adorable spot in the owner's tiny living room hanging over the sea, where she serves up creative finger food with market-fresh ingredients, based on old Italian recipes. Think tuna-filled zucchini, goat-cheese-stuffed peppers and bite-size savoury pies and cakes. A 12-snack plate for two is 100KN. There are also great Istrian wines by the glass. Reserve ahead, especially for evenings.

Da Sergio
PIZZA €

(Grisia 11; pizzas 28-71KN; ⏱11am-3pm & 6-11pm) It's worth waiting in line to get a table at this old-fashioned two-floor pizzeria that dishes out Rovinj's best thin-crust pizza, which locals swear by. The best is Gogo, with fresh tomato and arugula (rocket) and prosciutto.

Konoba Bruna
ISTRIAN €

(🗷098 9567 836; Monsena 7a; mains from 50KN; ⏱5-11pm May-Sep) For a different experience, head to this family-run *agroturizam* that serves seasonal dishes using its own veggies and fish and meat under *peka* (a domed baking lid, from 110KN). Sit at the tables scattered around a field of olive trees, enjoying a chilled-out vibe fuelled by shots of homemade *rakija* (grappa; try the pomegranate). Reserve ahead. It's a five-minute taxi ride out of town.

Grota
SNACKS €

(Valdibora bb; snacks from 35KN; ⏱7am-7pm) Right by the city market, this tiny barrel-lined spot serves daytime snacks like local cheese and proscuitto, paired with carefully curated wines from the region (the owner is a winemaker). It gets busy with foodies who flock here for après-beach bites.

Maestral
MEDITERRANEAN €

(Vladimira Nazora bb; mains from 45KN; ⏱11am-midnight) Grab an alfresco table at this tavern on the sea edge for great views of the old town and well-prepared simple food that's priced just right. Its *ribarska pogača* (pizza-like pie with salted fish and veggies) is delicious. It's in an old stone house away from the tourist buzz.

Veli Jože
SEAFOOD €

(Svetog Križa 3; mains from 50KN; ⏱11am-11pm) Graze on good Istrian standards, either in the eclectic interior crammed with knickknacks or at the clutch of outdoor tables with water views.

★ Kantinon
SEAFOOD €€

(Alda Rismonda bb; mains from 70KN; ⏱noon-11pm) Recently unveiled in its new incarnation, this top eating choice is headed up by a stellar team – one of Croatia's best chefs and an equally amazing sommelier. The food is 100% Croatian, with ingredients as local and fresh as they get, and lots of seafood based on old-fashioned fishers' recipes. Don't miss the sardines *na savor*.

Ulika
MEDITERRANEAN €€

(Porečka 6; mains from 100KN; ⏱12.30-3pm & 6.30-midnight) Tucked away in an alleyway, this small pretty tavern with streetside seating excludes staples of Adriatic food kitsch (pizza, calamari, *čevapčići*) and instead features well-prepared if pricey Mediterranean fare.

Monte
MEDITERRANEAN €€€

(🗷052-830 203; Montalbano 75; mains from 190KN; ⏱noon-2.30pm & 6.30-11pm) Rovinj's top restaurant, right below St Euphemia Church, is worth the hefty cost. Enjoy beautifully presented dishes on the elegant glassed-in terrace. Don't want to splurge? Have a pasta or risotto (from 124KN). Try the fennel ice cream. Reserve ahead in high season.

Puntulina
MEDITERRANEAN €€€

(🗷052-813 186; Svetog Križa 38; mains from 100KN; ⏱noon-11pm) Sample creative Med cuisine on one of the three alfresco terraces. Pasta dishes are more affordable (from 70KN). At night grab a cushion and sip a cocktail on the rocks below this converted town house. Reservations recommended.

🍷 Drinking & Nightlife

Limbo
CAFE, BAR

(Casale 22b; ⏱10am-1am) Cosy cafe-bar with small candlelit tables and cushions laid out on the stairs leading to the old town's hilltop. It serves tasty snacks and good prosecco.

Piassa Granda
WINE BAR

(Veli trg 1; ⏱10am-1am) This stylish little wine bar with red walls and wood-beamed ceilings has 150 wine labels, mainly Istrian, 20 *rakija* (Croatian grappa) varieties and delicious snacks.

Valentino
COCKTAIL BAR

(Svetog Križa 28; ⏱6pm-midnight) Premium cocktail prices at this high-end spot include fantastic sunset views from cushions scattered on the water's edge.

Havana
COCKTAIL BAR

(Aldo Negri bb; ⏱10am-1am) Tropical cocktails, Cuban cigars, straw parasols and the shade of tall pine trees make this open-air bar a popular spot.

Monte Carlo
COCKTAIL BAR

(Svetog Križa 21; ⏱10am-1am) This low-key cafe-bar has great views of the sea and Sveta Katarina across the way.

ISTRIA ROVINJ

Shopping

Rovinj is jam-packed with galleries, many touting overpriced souvenirs. A few stand out, including **Galerija Brek** (Fontica 2), which sells diverse works by local artists, and **Zdenac 13** (Zdenac 13), which sells beautiful ceramic pieces from the ground floor of a gorgeous old town house.

Information

INTERNET ACCESS
A-mar (☑ 052-841 211; Carera 26; per 10min 6KN; ⊘ 9am-10pm) Conveniently located. There's also free wi-fi in the town centre.

MEDICAL SERVICES
Medical Centre (☑ 052-813 004; Istarska bb)

MONEY
There are banks with ATMs all around town. Most travel agencies and many hotels will change money.

POST
Main post office (Matteo Benussi 4; ⊘ 8am-9pm Mon-Sat)

TOURIST INFORMATION
Tourist office (☑ 052-811 566; www.tzgrovinj.hr; ⊘ 8am-10pm Jun-Sep, to 8pm Apr-May & Oct-Nov) Has plenty of brochures and maps. Just off Trg Maršala Tita.

TRAVEL AGENCIES
Globtour (☑ 052-814 130; www.globtour-turizam.hr; Alda Rismonda 2) Excursions and private accommodation.

Kompas (☑ 052-813 211; www.kompas-travel.com; Trg Maršala Tita 5) Offers daily excursions.

Planet (☑ 052-840 494; www.planetrovinj.com; Svetog Križa 1) Good bargains are available on private accommodation. It doubles as an internet cafe (6KN per 10 minutes) and has a printer.

Getting There & Away

The bus station is just to the southeast of the old town, and offers a **garderoba** (per day 10KN; ⊘ 6.30am-8pm).

Getting Around

You can rent bicycles at many agencies around town for around 20KN per hour or 70KN per day. Scooters are also available from around 240KN per day.

Around Rovinj

Crveni Otok & Sveta Katarina

A popular day trip from Rovinj is a boat ride to lovely Crveni Otok (Red Island). Only 1.9km long, the island includes two islets, **Sveti Andrija** and **Maškin**, connected by a causeway. In the 19th century, Sveti Andrija became the property of Baron Hütterott, who transformed it into a luxuriantly wooded park. The Hotel Istra complex now dominates Sveti Andrija, where a playground and small gravel beaches make it popular with families. Maškin is quieter, more wooded and has plenty of secluded coves. Bring a mask for snorkelling around the rocks.

Right across the peninsula is Sveta Katarina, a small island forested by a Polish count in 1905 and now home to **Hotel Katarina** (☑ 052-804 100; www.maistra.com; Otok Sveta Katarina; s/d 700/1000KN; P � 🖀).

In summer, there are hourly boats from 5.30am till midnight to Sveta Katarina (return 30KN, 10 minutes) and to Crveni Otok (return 40KN, 15 minutes). They leave from just opposite Hotel Adriatic and also from the Delfin ferry dock near Hotel Park.

BUSES FROM ROVINJ

DESTINATION	COST (KN)	DURATION	DAILY SERVICES
Dubrovnik	628	15-16hr	1
Labin	80	1½-2hr	3
Poreč	35-45	35-50min	4
Pula	35-45	50min	11
Rijeka	95-127	2½-3hr	4
Split	444	11hr	1
Trieste (Italy)	100	2hr	2
Zagreb	145-180	4-6hr	6

MEDIEVAL BALE

In the southwestern section of Istria, between Rovinj and Vodnjan, the medieval town of Bale is one of Istria's best-kept secrets. Only 7km from the sea, it features a maze of narrow cobblestone streets and ancient town houses that developed around the recently restored Gothic-Renaissance castle of the Bembo family. Dominated by the 36m-high belfry of the baroque St Julian church, it also has several old churches and a town hall with a 14th-century loggia. The 9km stretch of shoreline nearby is the most pristine in Istria, with delightful beaches and shallow water.

Bale draws a spiritually minded and bohemian crowd for its apparently very powerful energy – a fact you won't find in the tourist brochures. Come here to meet kindred spirits and spend endless hours talking, drinking, dreaming and scribbling

The boutique **La Grisa Hotel** (☎052-824 501; www.la-grisa.com; La Grisa 23; s/d 520/715KN; ⓟ❋❖) has 22 tasteful rooms and suites in eight interconnected buildings on the edge of the old town, with an ambitious restaurant (try the dishes with *boškarin*, Istrian ox) and a small spa with a sauna, Jacuzzi and massages (from 150KN).

For a splurge, book one of four rooms at the exclusive **Villa Meneghetti** (www.meneghetti.info; r from 1368KN; ⓟ❋❖❖) in the secluded countryside near Bale, known for its olive oil, wines and renowned food served at the on-site restaurant.

Head to **Kamene Priče** (Stone Tales; www.kameneprice.com; Castel 57; meals from 100KN), an artsy oasis amid the ancient stone. There's no real menu as such at this restaurant-bar-performance space; the food depends on the season and the chef's mood. The whimsical decor, a plethora of bizarre objects and two terraces out the back make this the perfect place for whiling the day away.

The small but excellent **Last Minute Open Jazz Festival** takes place in early August. Other times you may find poetry readings, theatre performances, stand-up comedy – there's always something happening at Kamene Priče. Tomo, the owner, is a great source of info about 'the other side of Bale'. There are four apartments upstairs for those who want to stay (670KN per night).

Limska Draga Fjord

About 10km long, 600m wide and with steep valley walls that rise to a height of 100m, the Limska Draga Fjord (Limski Kanal) is the most dramatic sight in Istria. The inlet was formed when the Istrian coastline sank during the last Ice Age, allowing the sea to rush in and fill the Draga Valley. The deep-green bay has a hillside cave on the southern side where the 11th-century hermit priest Romualdo lived and held ceremonies. Fishing, oyster and mussel farming and excursion boating are the only activities found here.

At the fjord you'll find souvenir stands and two waterside restaurants that serve up superbly fresh shellfish, right from the source. Of the two, **Viking** (Limski Kanal 1; mains from 55KN; ⊙11am-11pm) is the better option. Enjoy oysters (11KN per piece), great scallops (22KN per piece) and mussels, or fish (priced by the kilogram) on a terrace overlooking the fjord. There's also a picnic area, a waterside cafe with wooden tables

and chairs and a swimming cove behind the other restaurant (named Fjord).

Small excursion boats will take you on a one-hour boat ride for 75KN per person (negotiable); these run frequently in July and August, and sporadically in June and September. To get to the fjord, you can take an excursion from Rovinj, Pula or Poreč, or follow the signs to Limski Kanal past the village of Sveti Lovreč.

Poreč

POP 16,700

The ancient Roman town of Poreč (Parenzo in Italian; Parentium in Roman times) and the surrounding region are entirely devoted to summer tourism. Poreč is the centrepiece of a vast system of tourist resorts that stretches north and south along the west coast of Istria. The largest is Zelena Laguna, with a full range of facilities and accommodation.

These holiday villages and tourist camps offer a rather industrialised package-type experience, with too much concrete and plastic and too many tour buses for some tastes. The hotels, restaurants, tourist offices and travel agencies, however, are almost universally staffed with multilingual people who make an effort to welcome visitors.

While this is not the place for a quiet getaway (unless you come out of season), there's a World Heritage–listed basilica, a medley of Gothic, Romanesque and baroque buildings and well-developed tourist infrastructure, and the pristine Istrian interior is within easy reach. It's also become the party hub of Istria in the last couple of years, drawing in young partygoers from all corners of Europe and beyond.

History

The coast of Poreč measures 37km, islands included, but the ancient town is confined to a peninsula 400m long and 200m wide. The Romans conquered the region in the 2nd century BC and made Poreč an important administrative centre, from which they were able to control a sweep of land from the Limska Draga Fjord to the Mirna River. Poreč's street plan was laid out by the Romans, who divided the town into rectangular parcels marked by the longitudinal Decumanus and the latitudinal Cardo.

With the collapse of the Western Roman Empire, Poreč came under Byzantine rule between the 6th and 8th centuries. It was during this time that the Euphrasian Basilica, with its magnificent frescoes, was erected. In 1267 Poreč was forced to submit to Venetian rule.

With the decline of Venice, the town oscillated between Austrian and French dominance before the Italian occupation that lasted from 1918 to 1943. Upon the capitulation of Italy, Poreč was occupied by the Germans and damaged by Allied bombing in 1944 before becoming part of postwar Yugoslavia and, more recently, Croatia.

◉ Sights

The compact old town is squeezed onto the peninsula and packed with hundreds of shops and agencies. The ancient Roman Decumanus, with its polished stones, is still the main street running through the peninsula's middle. Hotels, travel agencies and excursion boats are on the quayside Maršala Tita, which runs from the small-boat harbour to the tip of the peninsula.

★ Euphrasian Basilica   BASILICA
(Eufrazijeva bb;   adult/concession 40/20KN; ⊙9am-6pm Mon-Sat, 2-6pm Sun Apr-Sep) The main reason to visit Poreč is to see the 6th-century Euphrasian Basilica, a World Heritage Site and one of Europe's finest intact examples of Byzantine art. Built on the site of a 4th-century oratory, the sacral complex includes a church, an atrium and a baptistery. What packs in the crowds are the glittering wall **mosaics** in the apse. These 6th-century masterpieces feature biblical scenes, archangels and Istrian martyrs.

Notice the group to the left, which shows Bishop Euphrasius, who commissioned the basilica, with a model of the church in his hand. The belfry, accessed through the octagonal baptistery, affords an invigorating view of the old town. Make sure to pop into the adjacent Bishop's Palace, which contains a display of ancient stone sculptures, religious paintings and 4th-century mosaics from the original oratory.

Trg Marafor   SQUARE
The Roman Forum, where public gatherings took place, once stood on the site of the present-day Trg Marafor. The original pavement has been preserved along the northern row of houses on the square. West of this rectangular square, inside a small park, are the ruins of the 2nd-century **Temple of Neptune**, dedicated to the god of the sea.

Venetian Towers   RUIN
The town has three 15th-century towers that date from the Venetian rule and once formed the city walls: the gothic **Pentagonal Tower** at the beginning of Decumanus; the **Round Tower** on Narodni trg; and the **Northern Tower** on Peškera Bay.

Sveti Nikola   ISLAND
On this small island that lies opposite Poreč harbour, there are pebble and concrete beaches to choose from, as well as rocky breakwaters, shady pine forests and great views of the town across the way. From May to October there are **passenger boats** (adult/concession 20/10KN) travelling to Sveti Nikola. They depart every 30 minutes (from 6.45am to 1am) from the wharf on Maršala Tita.

🏃 Activities

Nearly every activity you might want to enjoy is on offer outside the town in either Plava Laguna or Zelena Laguna. Most of the

Poreč

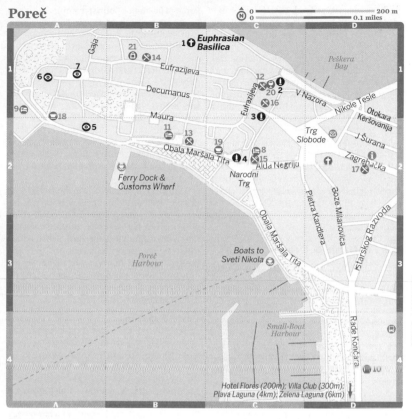

Poreč

◎ Top Sights
1 Euphrasian Basilica	B1

◎ Sights
2 Northern Tower	C1
3 Pentagonal Tower	C1
4 Round Tower	C2
5 Sveti Nikola	A2
6 Temple of Neptune	A1
7 Trg Marafor	A1

🛏 Sleeping
8 Hostel Papalinna	C2
9 Hotel Palazzo	A1
10 Hotel Poreč	D4
11 Valamar Riviera Hotel	B2

⊗ Eating
12 Buffet Horizont	C1
13 Dva Ferala	B2
14 Gourmet	B1
15 Konoba Ćakula	C2
16 Konoba Ulixes	C1
17 Nono	D2
Peterokutna Kula	(see 3)

🍷 Drinking & Nightlife
18 Epoca	A1
19 Saint & Sinner	C2
Torre Rotonda	(see 4)
20 Vinoteka Bacchus	C1

🛍 Shopping
21 Koza	B1

sports and recreational centres (there are 20) are affiliated with hotels and have tennis, basketball and volleyball courts, windsurfing, rowing, bungee jumping, paintball, golf, waterskiing, parasailing, boat rentals, go-karting and canoeing. If the weather turns bad, you can always work out in a fitness centre or get a massage at one of the spas. For details, pick up the annual *Poreč Info & Events* booklet, which lists all the recreational facilities in the area, from the tourist office.

The gentle rolling hills of the interior and the well-marked paths make **cycling** and **hiking** prime ways to explore the region. The tourist office (p120) issues a free map of roads and trails stemming from Poreč, along with suggested routes. You can rent a bike at many agencies around town.

There is good diving in and around shoals and sandbanks in the area, as well as at the nearby *Coriolanus,* a British Royal Navy warship that sank in 1945. At **Diving Centre Poreč** (☑ 052-433 606; www.divingcenter-porec. com), boat dives start at 135KN (more for caves or wrecks) or 355KN with full equipment rental.

✦✦ Festivals & Events

Poreč Annale   CULTURE
(☉ Jul & Aug) One of the oldest Croatian contemporary-art exhibitions is curated around a single theme.

Street Art Festival   PERFORMING ARTS
(☉ Aug) Held for a week in August, the Street Art Festival attracts international artists performing anything from acrobatics to theatre and music in the old town squares and streets.

Classical Music Concerts   MUSIC
(www.concertsinbazilika.com; ☉ Jul & Aug) Classical music concerts take place at the Euphrasian Basilica several times a week during summer; tickets can be purchased one hour before the concert at the venue.

Jazz Concerts   MUSIC
(www.jazzinlap.com; ☉ Jun-Aug) There are jazz concerts between late June and late August, held once a week in the courtyard of the regional museum, beside Lapidarium.

Poreč Summer   MUSIC
(☉ Jul & Aug) Free concerts take place on Trg Slobode as part of Poreč Summer.

🛏 Sleeping

Accommodation in Poreč is plentiful but gets booked ahead of time, so advance reservations are essential if you come in July or August.

The old town has a handful of hotels, though most of the camping grounds, hotels, apartment complexes and resorts spread along the coast north and south of

Poreč. The major tourist complexes are in Brulo, 2km south of town; Plava Laguna, 4km south of the old town; and Zelena Laguna, 2km further south. North of Poreč are the tourist settlements of Borik and Špadići. Some 20 hotels and a dozen apartment complexes are planted in these wooded areas. Most hotels are managed by **Valamar Hotels & Resorts** (☑ 052-465 000; www.valamar. com) or **Laguna Poreč** (☑ 052-410 101; www. lagunaporec.com). All hotels are open from April to October; several remain open all year. For stays shorter than three nights during peak season, some impose a 20% surcharge.

Many travel agencies can help you find private accommodation. Expect to pay between 200KN and 300KN for a double room with private bathroom in the high season, plus a 30% surcharge for stays shorter than three nights during peak season. There is a limited number of rooms available in the old town, which has no parking. Look for the *Domus Bonus* certificate of quality in private accommodation.

Hostel Papalinna   HOSTEL €
(☑ 052-400 900; www.hostelpapalinna.com; Vladimira Nazora 9; dm from 190KN; ✳🛜) Steps from the seaside, this new hostel in a restored 1885 building features 22 comfortable dorms (sleeping four or eight) with ensuite bathrooms and a boutique touch. You get free lockers and towels, 24-hour reception, lovely views of the old town and a bar terrace for mingling. Good choice for partygoers.

Camping Zelena Laguna   CAMPGROUND €
(☑ 052-410 147; www.lagunaporec.com; Zelena Laguna; campsites per person/tent 65/150KN; ☉ mid-Apr–Sep; ✳@🛜☀) Well equipped for sports, this camping ground 5km from the old town can house up to 2700 people. It has access to many beaches, including a naturist one.

Hotel Flores   HOTEL €€
(☑ 052-408 800; www.hostin.hr; Rade Končara 4; s/d 690/1005KN; P✳@🛜☀) This unassuming hideaway in verdant parkland just steps from the bus station has 39 well-equipped rooms, each with a balcony. An indoor swimming pool, a fitness room, a Turkish bath and a sauna are nice perks, as is the pebble beach only 70m away.

Hotel Poreč   HOTEL €€
(☑ 052-451 811; www.hotelporec.com; Rade Končara 1; s/d 496/760KN; P✳🛜) While the rooms inside this concrete box have unin-

spiring views over the bus station and the shopping centre opposite, they're acceptable, with balconies and an easy walk from the old town.

Valamar Riviera Hotel   HOTEL €€€

(☑052-465 000; www.valamar.com; Maršala Tita 15; s/d 975/1295KN; P ❄ 🛜) Rather swanky four-star incarnation right on the harbourfront. The rooms with seafront balconies are lovely but considerably more expensive. There's a private beach on Sveti Nikola that you can reach by boat (free) every 30 minutes. Down the seafront promenade is the recently renovated **Villa Parentino** (☑052-465 000; Maršala Tita 18; ste 1940KN; P ♨ 🛜), which has eight luxury suites. Look out for online specials and packages.

Hotel Palazzo   HOTEL €€€

(☑052-858 800; www.hotel-palazzo.hr; Maršala Tita 24; s/d 1120/1375KN; P ❄ @ 🛜 ☲) Housed in a 1910 building on the seafront, this recent addition to Poreč's hotel scene has 70 rooms and four suites plus a spa, restaurants and bars. The style is elegant historic, blending modern design with classical beauty. Rooms 120 to 126 have open-sea and lighthouse views – and higher prices.

🍴 Eating

★Konoba Daniela   ISTRIAN €

(☑052-460 519; Veleniki 15a; mains from 65KN; ◷noon-11.30pm) In the sweet little village of Veleniki 4.5km northeast of town, this family-run tavern in an 1880s house with rustic decor and a big terrace is known for its steak tartare and seasonal Istrian mainstays. Taxis charge 80KN to 100KN one way.

Buffet Horizont   FAST FOOD €

(Eufrazijeva 8; mains from 30KN; ◷11am-midnight) For cheap and tasty seafood snacks such as sardines, shrimp and calamari, look for this yellow house with wooden benches outside.

Nono   PIZZA €

(Zagrebačka 4; pizzas from 30KN; ◷noon-midnight) Nono serves the best pizza in town, with puffy crusts and toppings such as truffles. Other dishes are also tasty.

Dva Ferala   ISTRIAN €

(Maršala Tita 13; mains from 60KN; ◷noon-midnight) Savour well-prepared Istrian specialities, such as *istarski tris* (a copious trio of homemade pastas) for two, on the terrace of this pleasant *konoba* (tavern).

Konoba Ćakula   ISTRIAN €€

(Vladimira Nazora 7; mains from 70KN; ◷10am-11pm) This tavern with a subtly hipster vibe does interesting cold appetisers and solid mains. Great spot to come for tapas, paired with a glass of wine.

Gourmet   ITALIAN €€

(Eufrazijeva 26; mains from 70KN; ◷11am-1am) Comforting Italian concoctions come in all shapes and forms here – penne, tagliatelle, fusilli, gnocchi and so on. There are also pizzas from a wood-fired oven as well as meat and seafood dishes. Tables spill out on to the square.

Peterokutna Kula   INTERNATIONAL €€

(Decumanus 1; mains from 70KN; ◷noon-midnight) Inside the medieval Pentagonal Tower, this upmarket restaurant has two alfresco patios in a stone vault, and a roof terrace with great vistas. It serves a full spectrum of fish and meat dishes, although the service is spotty and the food can be hit-and-miss.

Konoba Ulixes   MEDITERRANEAN €€

(Decumanus 2; mains from 75KN; ◷noon 4pm & 6pm-midnight) The fish and shellfish are excellent at this tavern. Try the salt-encrusted fish baked in the oven, which first gets deboned right in front of you. There's a good selection of Istrian wines.

🍷 Drinking & Nightlife

In the last couple of years, Poreč has turned into Istria's party capital, with nightlife hawks coming from all parts of Europe to let loose in its late-night clubs.

Byblos   CLUB

(www.byblos.hr; Zelena Laguna 1; ◷11pm-6am) On weekends, celeb guest DJs such as David Morales crank out electro house tunes at this humongous open-air club, one of Croatia's hottest places to party.

Villa Club   BEACH CLUB

(www.villa-club.net; Rade Končara 4a; ◷9am-6am) Popular beach bar and club that draws in a party crowd for a boogie to DJ-spun tunes each night in summertime.

Vinoteka Bacchus   WINE BAR

(Eufrazijeva 10) Sweet little wine shop with a clutch of tables outside, where you can try local wines on tap from 9KN per glass. Try the *malvazija* and the *refošk*.

BUSES FROM POREČ

DESTINATION	COST (KN)	DURATION	DAILY SERVICES
Pula	58-63	1–1½hr	7
Rijeka	82-89	1½hr	7
Rovinj	35-43	45min	6
Zagreb	150-215	4–4½hr	5

Saint & Sinner CAFE, BAR
(Maršala Tita 12; ☺8pm-4am) A black-and-white plastic theme runs throughout this waterfront hangout, where the young ones sip chococcinos during the day and strawberry *caipiroskas* late into the night.

Epoca CAFE, BAR
(Maršala Tita 24; ☺8am-2am) Kick back by the water and watch the sun go down, grab a quick espresso or have a leisurely nightcap cocktail at this low-key cafe-bar.

Torre Rotonda CAFE, BAR
(Narodni trg 3a; ☺8am-2am) Take the steep stairs to the top of the historic Round Tower and grab a table at the open-air cafe to watch the action on the quays.

 Shopping

Koza ACCESSORIES
(Eufrazijeva 28; ☺10am-10pm) Don't miss the great leather items designed and handmade by a brother-and-sister team at this tiny storefront with cool bags, flip-flops, briefcases and wallets.

 Information

INTERNET ACCESS
The entire town centre has free wi-fii access.

MEDICAL SERVICES
Poreč Medical Centre (☑052-451 611; Maura Gioseffija 2)

MONEY
You can exchange currency at any of the many travel agencies or banks. There are ATMs all around town.

POST
Main post office (Trg Slobode 14; ☺7am-8pm Mon-Fri, to 2pm Sat) Has a telephone centre.

TOURIST INFORMATION
Tourist office (☑052-451 293; www.to-porec. com; Zagrebačka 9; ☺8am-9pm Mon & Thu-Sun, to 6pm Tue & Wed) Gives out lots of brochures and useful info.

TRAVEL AGENCIES
Fiore Tours (☑052-431 397; www.fiore.hr; Mate Vlašića 6) Handles private accommodation and adventure travel.
Sunny Way (☑052-452 021; www.sunnyway. hr; Alda Negrija 1) Specialises in boat tickets and excursions to Italy and around Croatia.

🛈 **Getting There & Away**

Venezia Lines (www.venezialines.com) operates a daily fast catamaran to Venice in high season (one way 450KN, return 900KN; two hours); **Commodore Cruises** (www.commodore-cruises.hr) has two weekly catamarans (one way 450KN, return 750KN).

The **bus station** (☑060 333 111; K Huguesa 2) is just outside the old town, behind Rade Končara. The station's **garderoba** (left luggage; per hour 10KN; ☺6am-9pm) will store your bags.

Between Poreč and Rovinj the bus runs along the Limska Draga Fjord. To see it clearly, sit on the right-hand side if you're travelling south, or on the left if you're northbound.

🛈 **Getting Around**

You can rent bikes for about 90KN per day. From April to October, a tourist train operates regularly from Šetalište Antona Štifanića, by the marina, to Brulo (10KN), Plava Laguna (20KN) and Zelena Laguna (20KN). There are passenger boats (10KN to 25KN) that make the same run from the ferry landing. The frequent buses to Vrsar stop at Plava Laguna, Zelena Laguna and the other resorts south of the city.

THE ISTRIAN INTERIOR

Head inland from the Istrian coast and you'll notice that crowds dissipate, hotel complexes disappear and what emerges is an unspoilt countryside of medieval hilltop towns, pine forests, fertile valleys and vineyard-dotted hills. The pace slows down considerably, defined less by the needs of tourists and more by the demands of harvesting grapes, hunting for truffles, picking wild asparagus and cultivating olive groves.

ISTRIA POREČ

Farmhouses are opening their doors to visitors looking for an authentic holiday experience, rustic taverns in the middle of nowhere serve up slow-food delights and Croatia's top winemakers provide tastings in their cellars. Remote hilltop villages that once seemed doomed to ruin are attracting colonies of artists and artisans as well as well-heeled foreigners. While many compare the region to Tuscany – and the Italian influence can't be denied – it's a world all of its own: unique, magnetic and wholesome.

You will need a car to explore this area, as the bus and train connections are sporadic. Good news – you're never far from the sea!

Labin

POP 11,700

Perched on a hilltop just above the coast, Labin is the undisputed highlight of eastern Istria, as well as its historical and administrative centre. The showcase here is the old town, a beguiling potpourri of steep streets, cobbled alleys and pastel houses festooned with stone ornamentation.

Surrounding it below is a grubby new town that has sprouted as a result of the coal-mining industry. Labin was the mining capital of Istria until the 1970s, its hill mined so extensively that the town began to collapse. Mining stopped in 1999, the necessary repairs were undertaken and the town surfaced with a new sense of itself as a tourist destination.

Labin has plenty to offer for a day-long visit. The labyrinth of its old town hides an unusual museum in a baroque palace, a wealth of Venetian-inspired churches and palaces, and a sprinkling of craft shops and galleries. The coastal resort of Rabac, 5km southwest of Labin, is overdeveloped with tightly packed holiday houses, hotels and apartment blocks, but its beaches are decent and it can be a nice place to spend an afternoon.

◎ Sights

Wandering the medieval streets of Labin is the highlight of any visit. Labin is divided into two parts: the hilltop old town with most of the sights and attractions; and Podlabin, a much newer section below the hill, with most of the town's shops and services.

Town Museum
MUSEUM

(Gradski Muzej; 1 Maja 6; adult/concession 15/10KN; ⊙10am-1pm & 5-10pm Mon-Sat) The ground floor of this museum, housed in the baroque 18th-century Battiala-Lazzarini Palace, is devoted to archaeological finds. Upstairs is a collection of musical instruments with some fun interactive features, and the top floor has a contemporary art gallery. The museum is over a coal pit that has been turned into a realistic re-creation of an actual coal mine.

Fortress
FORTRESS

(Forica) This fortress at the western edge of town is the highest point in Labin. To get there, walk along Ulica 1 Maja or take the long way around by following Šetalište San Marco along the town walls. What unfolds below you is a sweeping view of the coast, the Učka mountain range and Cres island.

Loggia
HISTORIC BUILDING

(Titov Trg) This 1550 loggia served as the community centre of Labin in the 16th century. News and court verdicts were announced here, fairs were held and those guilty of waywardness were punished on the pillar of shame.

☆ Festivals & Events

Labin Art Republic
ARTS

(Labin Art Republika; ⊙Jun-Sep) Labin Art Republic takes over this artsy town – there are more than 30 artists living and working here – from mid-June through early September. During the festival, the town comes alive with street theatre, concerts, plays, clown performances and open studios. Every Tuesday at 9.30pm, free guided tours (in various languages) depart from the tourist office in the old town and show you the highlights.

⊨ Sleeping

There are no hotels in Labin itself but choices abound just below in Rabac. Most of the lodging is of the large hotel-resort kind, with a few smaller properties. Valamar (www.valamar.com) manages nine properties here, including two premium four-star options (newly renovated Hotel & Casa Valamar Sanfior and Valamar Bellevue Hotel & Residence), three three-star properties (hotels and apartments), and four two-star properties that include apartments and a tourist village. Peak season (read August) prices range greatly, from 1565KN to 1945KN in a

ISTRIA LABIN

double room at a four-star hotel (half board), to 760KN at a two-star hotel. A surcharge is applied for stays under three nights.

Two independent hotels with more character are **Hotel Amfora** (☑ 052-872 202; www.hotel-amfora.com; Rabac bb; s/d 375/1100KN;

ISTRIA'S DIVERSE HIDEAWAYS

Istria has many more highlights for those willing to explore. Here's a rundown.

Novigrad is an attractive old town crammed onto a peninsula, only 20 minutes (18km) north of Poreč. It has one of Istria's best restaurants, **Damir & Ornella** (☑ 052-758 134; www.damirornella.com; Zidine 5; mains from 70KN; ☺ 12.30-3.30pm & 7.30-11.30pm), a 28-seat tavern famous for its raw-fish specialities. The Mediterranean-style sashimi is to die for; reserve ahead. On par is **Marina** (Antona 38; mains from 80KN; ☺ noon-3pm & 6-11pm), a restaurant headed up by one of Croatia's best chefs, Marina Gaši, who whips up playful versions of Croatia's mainstays in this contemporary space right by the marina. The six-course tasting menu (370KN) is worth the splurge.

The fishing village of **Savudrija** is Croatia's westernmost point and home to Istria's oldest **lighthouse** (www.lighthouses-croatia.com), built in 1818. The lighthouse is now available for weekly rental (5312KN per week for two people).

Vrsar, located roughly between Rovinj and Poreč, is a delightful fishing town rising on a hilltop in a jumble of medieval buildings. It's quieter than its neighbours and has an outdoor sculpture park featuring the work of renowned Croatian sculptor Dušan Džamonja. The story goes that Casanova frequented Vrsar back in the day, which the town today celebrates each June during **Casanovafest** (www.casanovafest.com; ☺ Jun), the Love and Erotica Festival.

Also within easy reach of Poreč is the **Baredine Cave** (www.baredine.com; adult/concession/child 6-12 60/45/35KN; ☺ 9.30am-6pm Jul & Aug, 10am-5pm May, Jun & Sep, 10am-4pm Oct & Apr), whose subterranean chambers are replete with stalagmites and stalactites; various agencies offer excursions.

In the interior, art aficionados should head to **Beram**, near Pazin, to take in the amazing 15th-century frescoes in the Church of St Mary of Škriljine; the Pazin tourist office has details. **Vela Vrata** (mains from 40KN; ☺ 1-11pm), the village konoba (tavern), serves great homemade pastas, good meat and mean crêpes with skuta (ricotta) and honey, paired with leafy views.

Near Labin is Istria's youngest town, **Raša**, a showcase of modernist functionalist architecture that sprang up under Mussolini's rule in the 1930s. Nearby, in the fishing village of Trget, wrapped around a small bay, is one of Istria's best seafood restaurants, **Martin Pescador** (Trget 11a; mains from 45KN; ☺ noon-11pm). This Istrian konoba, right on the water, with a boat-shaped bar inside and a lovely terrace right on the sea, serves a mean fish soup and excellent seafood.

On a hilltop north of Motovun is **Oprtalj**, less developed than its neighbour, with cypress trees and fantastic views of the surrounding scenery. Four kilometres to the southeast, amid scenic hills, is the gorgeous **Ipša Estate** (☑ 052-664 010; www.ipsa-maslinovaulja.hr), worth a visit for the taste of its award-winning olive oils; call ahead.

Foodies shouldn't miss the scenic village of **Zrenj** northeast of Oprtalj, which has a couple of top eating choices where Istrian farm food is concerned. For a light meal of truffle-infused antipastos served with homemade bread, like cheese drowned in olive oil, truffles and butter, Istrian prosciutto and truffle fritaja (omelette), look no further than **Agroturizam Nežić** (☑ 052-644 285; Zrenj 11; mains from 50KN; ☺ Sundays only). The farm owners Paolo and Nadia serve up these lovingly prepared snacks on Sundays in their traditional stone tavern; be sure to call ahead. For a more solid meal featuring the best lamb and potatoes under peka (a domed baking lid), head to the renowned **Agroturizam Tončić** (☑ 052-644 146; www.agroturizam-toncic.com; Čabarnica 42, Zrenj; mains from 50KN; ☺ weekends only) at the end of the village, where tasty food is dished out in the rustic interior or on the terrace with stunning views of Čićarija mountains. Try the cumin rakija (grappa) and ask to see the farm animals. Reserve ahead, as it's hugely popular and sometimes receives big groups.

P✱@⟲) in town, and the posh **Villa Annette** (☑052-884 222; www.villaannette.hr; Raška 24; s/d 1117/1397KN; P✱@☎⟲), up on a hill slope; the latter has an outdoor pool overlooking the bay.

Sidro (☑052-881 010; www.sidro-istra.hr; Aldo Negri 20) travel agency finds double rooms (225KN) and apartments (320KN) in Labin (but not the old town). Note there's a 30% surcharge at all of the above accommodations for stays of less than three nights. Gostiona Kvarner has several simple rooms to rent; 400KN for single, 535KN for double.

✖ Eating

Labin is known for its *krafi,* ravioli-like pasta which is served either sweet or savoury. Rabac has plenty of restaurants serving seafood standards, but most cater to the unfussy tourist crowds.

Gostiona Kvarner   ISTRIAN €€
(Šetalište San Marco bb; mains from 70KN; ☺10am-midnight Jun-Sep) Steps from Titov trg, this restaurant has a terrace overlooking the sea, good food and a loyal local following.

ℹ Information

Tourist office (☑052-852 399; www. rabac-labin.com; Titov trg 2/1; ☺8am-9pm Mon-Fri, 10am-2pm & 6-9pm Sat & Sun) At the entrance to the old town.

ℹ Getting There & Away

Labin is well connected by bus with Pula (47KN, one hour, eight daily). In summer, the bus to Rabac (12KN), via the old town, departs 12 times daily.

ℹ Getting Around

Buses stop at Trg 2 Marta in Podlabin, from where you can catch a local bus to the old town. This bus continues on to Rabac in the peak season.

Vodnjan

POP 3615

Connoisseurs of the macabre can't miss Vodnjan (Dignano in Italian), located 10km north of Pula. Lying inside a sober church in this sleepy town are the mummies that constitute Vodnjan's primary tourist attraction. These desiccated remains of centuries-old saints, whose bodies mysteriously failed to decompose, are considered to have magical powers.

There's not much going on in the rest of the town, which has Istria's largest Roma population. The centre is Narodni trg, composed of several neo-Gothic palaces in varying stages of decay and restoration.

◉ Sights

St Blaise's Church   CHURCH
(Crkva Svetog Blaža; Župni trg 1; Collection of Sacral Art admission incl mummies 75KN, mummies only 55KN, Collection of Sacral Art only 55KN, church only 15KN; ☺9.30am-7pm Mon-Sat, noon-5pm Sun) A few steps from Narodni trg, this handsome neobaroque church was built at the turn of the 19th century, when Venice was the style setter for the Istrian coast. With its 63m-high **bell tower** as high as St Mark's in Venice, it's the largest parish church in Istria, and worth a visit for its magnificent altars alone. The **mummies** are in a curtained-off area behind the main altar.

In the dim lighting, the complete bodies of Nikolosa Bursa, Giovanni Olini and Leon Bembo resemble wooden dolls in their glass cases. Assorted body parts of three other saints complete the display. As you examine the skin, hair and fingernails of these long-dead people, a tape in English narrates their life stories. Considered to be Europe's best-preserved mummy, the body of St Nikolosa is said to emit a 32m bioenergy circle that has caused 50 miraculous healings.

If the mummies have whetted your appetite for saintly relics, head to the **Collection of Sacral Art** (Zbirka Sakralne Umjetnosti) in the sacristy. Here there are hundreds of relics belonging to 150 different saints, including the casket with St Mary of Egypt's tongue. Make sure you cover up as the eccentric parish priest is known for turning away 'inappropriately dressed' people.

✖ Eating

Vodnjanka   ISTRIAN €
(Istarska bb; mains from 60KN; ☺5-11pm daily Jul & Aug, closed Sun Sep-Jun) This excellent regional restaurant has several rustic rooms, lots of style and personal service. Specialties include *fuži* (homemade egg pasta twisted into a unique shape) topped with truffles and various kinds of *fritaja* (omelette). The terrace has pretty views of the old-town rooftops and the church spire.

ISTRIA VODNJAN

Drinking & Nightlife

Lighthouse Music Club CLUB
(www.lighthouseclub.com; Krnjaloža 1; ⊘ midnight-6am Fri & Sat, to 2am Sun) On the road between Bale and Vodnjan, this newish club has quickly become one of Istria's best places to party, with big-name DJs and jazz concerts.

ℹ Information

Tourist office (☑ 052-511 700; www.istra.hr/vodnjan; Narodni trg 3; ⊘ 8am-3pm & 7-9pm Mon-Sat, 9am-1pm Sun) Located on the main square.

ℹ Getting There & Away

Vodnjan is well connected with Pula by bus during the week (15KN, 30 minutes, 10 daily); there are only four buses on Saturday and one on Sunday.

Svetvinčenat

POP 180

Lying halfway between Pazin and Pula in southern Istria, Svetvinčenat (also known as Savičenta) is an endearing little town. First settled by Benedictines, it centres on a Renaissance town square. With its surrounding cypress trees, harmoniously positioned buildings and laid-back ambience, it's a delightful place for a wander.

◉ Sights

Morosini-Grimani Castle CASTLE
The northern part of the main square is occupied by this beautifully preserved 13th-century palace. A Venetian makeover in the 16th century added towers that served as a residence and a prison. The site held feasts, parades, fairs and witch burnings.

The castle is home to a seasonal **medieval park** (adult/child under 15 20KN/free; ⊘ 11am-2pm & 6-9pm Mon-Fri Jul & Aug); on weekends, visitors can roam around the castle on their own.

Church of Mary's Annunciation CHURCH
This parish church on the east side of the main square has a trefoil Renaissance facade made of local cut stone, and five elaborate Venetian marble altars inside.

✱ Festivals & Events

Dance & Nonverbal Theatre Festival DANCE
(www.svetvincenatfestival.com; ⊘ Jul) The time to be in Svetvinčenat is mid-July, during this annual festival featuring contemporary dance pieces, street theatre, circus and mime acts, and various other nonverbal forms of expression. This international event hosts performers from Croatia and Europe, its acts ranging from Finnish hip hop to Brazilian capoeira.

⊨ Sleeping & Eating

Stancija 1904 RURAL INN €€€
(☑ 052-560 022; www.stancija.com; Smoljanci 2-3; d from 925KN; 🅿) In the village of Smoljanci, just 3km from Svetvinčenat on the road to Bale, this traditional stone Istrian house has been stylishly converted by a Swiss-Croatian family. Surrounded by fragrant herb gardens and shaded by tall old-growth trees, it offers elaborate breakfasts (request these when booking). There's a surcharge of 30% for one-night stays.

Kod Kaštela ISTRIAN €
(Savičenta 53; mains from 50KN; ⊘ 10am-11pm) Right at the heart of town, with great views of the castle and the square, this regional restaurant serves homemade pastas and tasty *pršut* (prosciutto).

ℹ Information

Tourist office (☑ 052-560 349; www.tz-svetvincenat.hr; Svetvinčenat 20; ⊘ 8am-7pm Mon-Fri, 11am-6pm Sat & Sun) Located opposite the main square. It has information about private accommodation in and around town (from 150KN per person), brochures and a map of a bike path that takes you on a 35km circuit from Svetvinčenat, with information boards explaining the local history, flora and fauna in English.

Pazin

POP 5000

Most famous for the gaping chasm that inspired Jules Verne, and for its medieval castle, Pazin is a workaday provincial town in central Istria. It deserves a stop mainly for the chasm and the castle, but part of the appeal is its small-town feel and the lack of fashionable foreigners stomping its streets. Most of the town centre is given over to pedestrian-only areas, while rolling Istrian countryside surrounds the slightly unsightly outskirts.

Lying at the geographic heart of Istria, Pazin is the county's administrative seat and is well connected by road and rail to virtually every other destination in the region. The hotel and restaurant pickings in town are skimpy – you're better off visiting on a day

MATHIAS SANDORF & THE PAZIN CHASM

The writer best known for going around the world in 80 days, into the centre of the earth and 20,000 leagues under the sea found inspiration in the centre of Istria. The French futurist-fantasist Jules Verne (1828–1905) set *Mathias Sandorf* (1885), one of his 27 books in the series Voyages Extraordinaires, in the castle and chasm of Pazin.

In the novel, later made into a movie, Count Mathias Sandorf and two cohorts are arrested by Austrian police for revolutionary activity and imprisoned in Pazin's castle. Sandorf escapes by climbing down a lightning rod but, struck by lightning, he tumbles down into the roaring Pazinčica River. He's carried along into the murky depths of the chasm, but our plucky hero holds on fast to a tree trunk and (phew!) six hours later the churning river deposits him at the tranquil entrance to the Limska Draga Fjord. He walks to Rovinj and is last seen jumping from a cliff into the sea amid a hail of bullets.

Verne never actually visited Pazin – he spun Sandorf's adventure from photos and travellers' accounts – but that hasn't stopped Pazin from celebrating it at every opportunity. There's a street named after Jules Verne as well as special Jules Verne days.

trip since you're within an hour of most other Istrian towns. However, the countryside around Pazin offers plentiful activities, such as hiking, free climbing, ziplining, cycling and visiting local honey makers.

◎ Sights

Pazin Chasm　　　　　　　　CAVE
(www.pazinska-jama.com; adult/concession 30/15KN; ☉10am-7pm Jun-Aug) Pazin's most renowned site is undoubtedly this deep abyss of about 100m, through which the Pazinčica River sinks into subterranean passages forming three underground lakes. Its shadowy depths inspired the imagination of Jules Verne, as well as numerous Croatian writers. Visitors can walk the 1.3km **marked path** inside the natural canyon, which takes about 45 minutes and involves a gentle winding climb.

There are two entrances, one by Hotel Lovac and one by the footbridge that spans the abyss 100m from the castle. You can enter the cave with an expert speleologist (150KN), if arranged in advance through the tourist office, and even zipline across it. If the trip into the abyss doesn't appeal, there's a viewing point just outside the castle.

Castle　　　　　　　　　　CASTLE
(Trg Istarskog Razvoda 1) Looming over the chasm, Pazin's Kaštel is the largest and best-preserved medieval structure in all of Istria. First mentioned in AD 983, it is a medley of Romanesque, Gothic and Renaissance architecture. There are two **museums** (adult/concession 25/18KN; ☉10am-6pm daily Jul & Aug, 10am-6pm Tue-Sun mid-Apr–Jun & Sep–mid-Oct, 10am-3pm Tue-Thu, 11am-4pm Fri,

10am-4pm Sat & Sun mid-Oct–mid-Apr) inside; one ticket gets you into both. The **town museum** has a collection of medieval Istrian church bells, an exhibition about slave revolts, and torture instruments in the dungeon. The **Ethnographic Museum** has about 4200 artefacts portraying traditional Istrian village life, including garments, tools and pottery.

🏃 Activities

The Pazin tourist office distributes a map of hiking trails and honey spots (you can visit beekeepers and taste their delicious acacia honey), and a brochure about wine cellars around Pazin. It can also hook you up with ziplining over the Pazin Chasm (120KN) and horseback riding near town.

🎊 Festivals & Events

The first Tuesday of the month is **Pazin Fair**, featuring products from all over Istria.

Days of Jules Verne　　　　CULTURE
(www.julesvernedays.com; ☉Jun) Held in the last week of June, this festival is Pazin's way of honouring the writer who put the town on the cultural map. There are races, re-enactments from the novel and journeys retracing the footsteps of Verne's hero Mathias Sandorf.

🛏 Sleeping

The tourist office helps to arrange private accommodation, which is generally reasonably priced. Count on spending from 100KN per person for a room.

Hotel Lovac HOTEL €€

(☑ 052-624 324; Šime Kurelića 4; s/d 268/550KN; P ❋ ☎) The late-1960s architecture of Pazin's only hotel could be a hit, if only the rooms were done up right. Request one of the spruced-up rooms with a chasm view. On the western edge of town.

❶ Orientation

The town is relatively compact, stretching little more than 1km from the train station on the eastern end to the Kaštel on the western end. The old part of town comprises the 200m leading up to the Kaštel.

❶ Information

Tourist office (☑ 052-622 460; www.central-istria.com; Franine i Jurine 14; ☉10am-7pm Mon-Fri, to 1pm Sat). The best source of information about Pazin. Also manages the entire central Istrian region.

❶ Getting There & Away

The **bus station** (☑ 060 306 040; Miroslava Bulešića 2) is 200m west of the **train station** (☑ 052-624 310; Stareh Kostanji 1). Services at both are reduced on weekends.

Gračišće

Gračišće, 7km southeast of Pazin, is a sleepy medieval town surrounded by rolling hills, and is one of Istria's well-kept secrets. Its collection of ancient buildings includes the 15th-century Venetian-Gothic **Salamon Palace**, the Romanesque **Church of St Euphemia**, and the **Church of St Mary** from 1425.

Most of these buildings are unrestored (although some work is being done). You won't need more than 30 minutes to circle the tiny town, but the ambience is truly lovely. There's an 11.5km circular **hiking trail** that leads from here, which is well marked with signs.

Istrian specialties are served at **Konoba Marino** (Gračišće 75; mains from 35KN; ☉11am-11pm Thu-Tue Jun-Sep), a cosy tavern that dishes out copious portions of *fuži* (homemade egg pasta twisted into a unique shape) with game and *ombolo* (boneless pork loin) with cabbage. The same owners run a restored town house steps away with four charming rustic rooms (150KN per person, with breakfast).

Buzet

POP 6115

It may not be Istria's most fascinating town, but sleepy Buzet, 39km northeast of Poreč over the Mirna River, offers a whiff of the timeless grace of old Istria. First settled by the Romans, Buzet achieved real prominence under the Venetians, who endowed it with walls, gates and several churches. With its grey-stone buildings in various stages of decay and restoration, and the cobblestone streets nearly deserted (most of Buzet's residents resettled at the foot of the hill in the unbecoming new part of town long ago), the old town is a quiet but charming place.

Enjoy a wander around the maze of Buzet's narrow streets and squares, its sights all well marked with English plaques. The other reason to come here is the glorious truffle. Self-dubbed the city of truffles, Buzet takes its title seriously. Lying at the epicentre of the truffle-growing region, it offers a variety of ways to celebrate the smelly fungus, from sampling it at the old town's restaurant to various truffle-related activities, including the Festival of Subotina.

◉ Sights

Most commerce is in the new Fontana section of town at the foot of the hilltop old town. If you have wheels, you must park your car by the cemetery on the hill and make the five-minute walk up to the old town.

Regional Museum MUSEUM
(Zavičajni Muzej Buzet; Ulica Rašporskih Kapetana 5; adult/concession 15/10KN; ☉9am-3pm Mon-Fri) Buzet's main sight is housed inside a 17th-century palace. The museum displays a collection of prehistoric and Roman artefacts as well as some ethnological items such as field tools and folk costumes.

Baroque Well LANDMARK
On a square a few metres north of the Regional Museum is this exquisite well, which was restored in 1789 and sports a Venetian lion relief.

⚡ Activities

Pick up a guide from the tourist office (p128) to wine, olive oil and truffle roads throughout the region, as well as various activities such as hiking (check out the seven trails in the area), cycling (there are 14 trails around town), free climbing, hot-air ballooning and paragliding.

Istriana Travel
ADVENTURE

(☑ 091 5412099; www.istrianatravel.hr; Vrh 28) offers truffle-hunting excursions, a fresco workshop, wine and olive-oil tours, bike jaunts, hiking, caving, paragliding and more.

Truffle Hunting
CULINARY

(☑ 052-667 304; www.karlictartufi.hr; Paladini 14; tour per person 260-965KN) If you want to experience truffle hunting, contact the friendly Karlić family, who live in the village of Paladini, 12km from Buzet; request a tour in English ahead of time. The tour includes cheese and truffle tasting, a story about truffles and a hunt in the forest that lasts up to two hours.

✴✶ Festivals & Events

Festival of Subotina
FOOD

(☺ Sep) Buzet's top truffle event is on the second Saturday in September, marking the start of the white-truffle season (which lasts through December). The pinnacle of it all is the preparation of a giant truffle omelette –

with over 2000 eggs and 10kg of truffles – in a 1000kg pan.

🛏 Sleeping & Eating

A number of farmhouses in the surrounding area have rooms and apartments to rent (from 100KN to 150KN per person). The tourist office has details.

Vela Vrata
BOUTIQUE HOTEL €€

(☑ 052-494 750; www.velavrata.net; Šetalište Vladimira Gortana 7; s/d 593/810KN; ✳🔊) This lovely boutique hotel on the edge of the old town, with panoramic views of the surrounding hills, has revitalized Buzet's hilltop. Twenty rooms in five interconnected buildings are tasteful and well-equipped. Room 11 has a gorgeous vista from its balcony. There's a restaurant and a cafe on-site and a small spa.

Stara Oštarija
ISTRIAN €€

(☑ 052-694 003; Petra Flega 5; mains from 75KN; ☺ noon-9pm) This is the place to try truffles in the old town. The restaurant even serves pannacotta with truffle honey. For a splurge, order a slow-food truffle menu of six courses

---

THE TRUFFLE TRADE IN ISTRIA

The truffle trade is less like a business than a highly profitable cult. It revolves around an expensive subterranean fungus allegedly endowed with semimagical powers, which is picked in dark woods and then sent across borders to be sold for a small fortune. Devotees claim that once you've tasted this small, nut-shaped delicacy, all other flavours seem insipid.

There are 70 sorts of truffle in the world, of which 34 come from Europe. The traditional truffle-producing countries are Italy, France and Spain, but Istrian forests boast three sorts of black truffles as well as the big white truffle – one of the most prized in the world, at 34,000KN per kilogram. Croatia's largest exporter of Istrian truffles is Zigante Tartufi, with its share of the overall Croatian export market being about 90%. In 1999 the company's owner, Giancarlo Zigante, along with his dog Diana, found the world's largest truffle in Istria, weighing 1.31kg and making it into *Guinness World Records*.

The Istrian truffle business is relatively young. In 1932, when Istria was occupied by Italy, an Italian soldier from the truffle capital of Alba allegedly noticed similarities in vegetation between his region and Istria. He returned after his military service with specially trained dogs, which, after enough sniffing and digging, eventually uncovered the precious commodity.

Because no sign of the truffle appears above ground, no human can spot it, so dogs (or, traditionally, pigs) are the key to a successful truffle hunt. Istrian *breks* (dogs) may be mongrels, but they are highly trained. Puppies begin their training at two months, but only about 20% of them go on to have fully fledged careers as truffle trackers.

The truffle-hunting season starts in early October and continues for three months, during which time at least 3000 people and 9000 to 12,000 dogs wander around the damp Motovun forests. The epicentre of the truffle-growing region is the town of Buzet.

Some people believe truffles are an aphrodisiac, though scientific research has failed to prove this. Conduct your own experiment!

(790KN for two) and enjoy views of the valley below. Reserve ahead.

Shopping

Zigante Tartufi   FOOD
(www.zigantetartufi.com; Trg Fontana; ⊘9am-8pm) Stock up on truffles in various shapes and forms – whole, hand-sliced, puréed, and with olives or mushrooms. Zigante stores are ubiquitous in Istria.

❶ Information

Tourist office (🖉 052 662 343; www.tz-buzet. hr; Šetalište Vladimira Gortana 9; ⊘8am-3pm Mon-Fri, 9am-2pm Sat). In a swanky new space next to Vela Vrata. Has info about accommodation and plentiful maps and brochures about regional activities.

❶ Getting There & Away

Buzet is connected by bus with Poreč (55KN, one hour, three daily), Rijeka (55KN to 70KN, one hour, five daily) and Pula (60KN, 1½ hours, one daily). The **bus station** (🖉 663 285; Riječka bb) is in the new part of town.

Around Buzet

The rolling hills, woods, pastures and vineyards around Buzet make for a memorably scenic drive. You really need your own wheels to explore this region.

Roč

Small and sleepy Roč, 8km southeast of Buzet, is snug within its 15th-century walls. A meander will reveal the Romanesque **Church of St Anthony**, a 15th-century **Renaissance house** in the square next to the church, and a **Roman lapidarium** within the town gate. The **tourist office** (⊘9am-5pm) has keys to all the town's churches, so ask here if you want to see the interiors. It also has information about the fresco workshop that's on offer in town.

Roč slumbers most of the year, roused only by the annual **Accordion Festival** on the second Sunday in May, which gathers accordion players from Croatia, Italy and Slovenia.

There are private rooms in town for about 100KN per night; the tourist office has details.

One of the town's stone buildings houses a regional restaurant, **Ročka Konoba** (mains from 30KN; ⊘noon-10pm Tue-Sun), which has

outdoor tables and a fireplace indoors. Discover Istrian specialties such as *fuži* (hand-rolled pasta), homemade sausages and *maneštra* (vegetable-and-bean soup). At the **Biskoteka** (Roč 14) shop you can try about 30 *rakija* varieties, including seven brands of *biska* (mistletoe grappa).

Hum

Outside Roč is **Glagolitic Alley**, a series of 11 outdoor sculptures placed along the road commemorating the area's importance as a centre of the Glagolitic alphabet. There's horseback riding at an equestrian club near here; the tourist office in Buzet has details.

Don't miss the abandoned ancient village of **Kotli**, just 2.5km off the main road between Roč and Hum. Set on the Mirna River, this protected rural complex has preserved courtyards, outer staircases, arched passages and picturesque chimneys.

Continuing southwest, the road ends in Hum, a beautifully preserved place that bills itself as the world's smallest town, with a permanent population of 24. Legend has it that the giants who built Istria had only a few stones left over and they used them to build Hum.

In summer, this tiny and adorable town gets a steady stream of visitors who come to meander around the narrow lanes and to visit **Aura** (⊘10am-7pm) FREE, which displays some old village tools but serves mostly as a souvenir shop.

It takes just 30 minutes to see the town on a self-guided tour, as each church and building is marked with informative multilingual plaques. Don't miss the 12th-century frescoes in the Romanesque **Chapel of St Jerome** (Crkvica Svetog Jerolima), which depict the life of Jesus in unusually vivid colours. The chapel, by the cemetery outside the town gates, is locked, but you can get the key at the town tavern.

That very tavern is reason enough to come to Hum. **Humska Konoba** (www.hum. hr; Hum 2; mains from 30KN; ⊘11am-10pm) not only serves first-rate Istrian mainstays, but also has a lovely outdoor terrace offering panoramic views. Start with a shot of sweet *biska* (white mistletoe grappa made according to an ancient Celtic recipe), then go on to *maneštra s kukuruzom* (bean and fresh maize soup), continue with truffle-topped *fuži* and end with *kroštuli* (fried crispy dough covered in sugar). If you like *biska,* stock up at the Imela shop, which is run by the restaurant owners and has olive oils, truffles, jams, wines, honey and souvenirs. It lies where the village ends.

On the last Sunday of October, about 4000 visitors pour into Hum for **Dan Rakije** (Day of Grappa). During this fun event, you get a tasting glass and sip on different-flavored grappas produced in the area, till they run out.

Sovinjsko Polje

The sleepy hamlet of Sovinjsko Polje is up in the hills off the road from Buzet to Istarske Toplice (follow the signs for about 4km along a narrow curvy road).

The reason to come to this tiny hamlet is **Toklarija** ([☑]091 9266769; Sovinjsko Polje 11; 6-course meal incl wine 400-500KN; ⊙1-10pm Wed-Mon), which offers one of Istria's finest dining experiences. At this beautifully converted 600-year-old olive mill (bought by his grandfather in the 1950s), eccentric owner Nevio Sirotić serves delectable, homemade Istrian slow food. A meal can take up to four hours in a well-timed string of delicate courses. The menu changes daily and features dried Istrian ham, porcini mushrooms, asparagus salad, truffles and juicy meats. Ninety percent of the food is local, all fruit and vegetables come from the family's gardens, and even the bread and pasta are homemade. It's all paired with local wines such as *teran* and *malvazija*. Reserve ahead.

Motovun

POP 480

Motovun is a captivating little town perched on a 277m hill in the Mirna River Valley, about 25km northeast of Poreč. It was the Venetians who decided to fortify the town in the 14th century, building two sets of thick walls.

There are a number of galleries and shops before you enter the old town and between the town gates, including a wine-tasting shop and a Zigante food store. Within the walls, an atmospheric cluster of Romanesque and Gothic buildings houses a smattering of artist studios. Newer houses have sprung up on the slopes leading to the old town, where the popular film festival takes place every summer – the very film fest that has, in recent years, made Motovun the most touristy of Istria's hilltop towns.

A Venetian lion scowls down from the outer gate, beyond which sprawls a terrace with a baroque loggia and a cafe's outside tables, perfect for watching the sun go down below the valley. A cheerier lion adorns the inner gate, which holds a long-running restaurant. Inside is a tree-shaded square with the town's hotel, an old well and the Church of St Stephen.

◉ Sights & Activities

Church of St Stephen　　　　　CHURCH
(Svetog Stjepana; Trg Andrea Antico) The town highlight is the Renaissance Church of St Stephen. Designed by Venetian artist Andrea Palladio, the interior is currently under renovation and opening hours are sporadic. Along the inner wall that encloses the old town rises a 16th-century bell tower.

Ramparts　　　　　CITY WALLS
Be sure to walk on the outer walls of the ramparts for memorable vistas over vineyards, fields and oak woods below. Take a break in the hidden cafe on the city walls, by the post office.

Paragliding　　　　　PARAGLIDING
([☑]098 922 8081; www.istraparagliding.com; per person 550KN) Jump off Motovun's hilltop for a tandem glide (with an instructor) with stunning vistas over Istria's hills. Book ahead.

Parenzana Train　　　　　TOURIST TRAIN
(www.parenzana.hr; adult/child aged 2-12 yr 130KN/65KN) The recently revived route takes visitors along the old Parenzana train line from Motovun to the scenic hill town of Vižinada above the Mirna River valley. The ride stops in the village of Ratokule, where you taste homemade Istrian treats from a local farm. There are five daily departures; the trip lasts one hour and 40 minutes; you can return for free. The trip can also be done from Vižinada to Motovun.

⚞ Festivals & Events

Motovun Film Festival　　　　　FILM
(www.motovunfilmfestival.com; ⊙Jul) The Motovun Film Festival presents a roster of independent and avant-garde films in late July. Since its inception in 1999, this small event has become pretty popular and now attracts quite a crowd, with nonstop outdoor and indoor screenings, concerts and parties.

ISTRIA MOTOVUN

🛏 Sleeping

Motovun Camping
CAMPGROUND €

(☑052-681 557; www.motovun-camping.com; 2-person sites for 1 night 180KN, subsequent nights 108KN) This small campging round is run by Hotel Kaštel and offers 12 pitches that are situated right below town. Campers get free use of the swimming pool at the hotel, and they also receive a 10% discount at the hotel's restaurant.

Villa Borgo
B&B €€

(☑052-681 708; www.villaborgo.com; Borgo 4; s/d incl breakfast from 384/480KN; ☎) Gorgeous spot at the top of the old town, with 10 rooms of different styles and configurations – some with shared bathroom, some with panoramic views (for 70KN more), others overlooking the street. The decor is clean-lined and minimalist, and there's a lovely shared terrace with sweeping valley views, a

---

ISTRIA'S TOP RURAL RETREATS

Agritourism is an increasingly popular accommodation option in Istria's interior. Some of these residences are working farms engaged in producing wine, vegetables and poultry; some are country houses with apartments to let; while others are plush modern villas with swimming pools. Whatever you choose, the highlights are hiking and cycling opportunities and, in some, wholesome food.

The Istrian tourist office has a brochure with photos and information about rural holidays throughout Istria. You'll need your own car to reach most of these lodgings, as many are located in the middle of nowhere. There's often a supplement for stays of less than three nights.

Agroturizam Ograde (☑052-693 035; www.agroturizam-ograde.hr; Katun Lindarski 60; per person incl breakfast 250KN; P☎☜☷) At leafy Agroturizam Ograde, in the village of Katun Lindarski, 10km south of Pazin, you'll hang out with horses, sheep, chickens, pigs and geese. The food, served in a dark and cool konoba (tavern), is a real-deal affair: veggies from the garden, home-cured meats and wine from the cellar. Accommodation is in two separate houses, one with a pool.

Pruga (☑091 78 17 263; www.apartments-pruga.com; Lovrinići 14; apt in Jul & Aug 750KN, in Jun & Sep 610KN) In the village of Lovrinići, 9.5km from Pazin, this is a lovely choice for a quiet getaway. Choose one of two beautifully renovated apartments in an original limestone Istrian house, each showcasing rustic chic, original details and fully equipped kitchens. Breakfast of local cheese, homemade jams and cakes is served outside among fruit trees and forests.

For meals, don't miss **Konoba Puli Pineta** (Karlov Vrt 1, Žminj; mains from 60KN; ⊘5-10pm), known around Istria for its top-notch pastas and great grilled meats. It's in the nearby town of Žminj.

Agroturizam San Mauro (☑052-779 033; www.sinkovic.hr; San Mauro 157; per person incl breakfast 176KN) Near the hilltop town of Momjan, Agroturizam San Mauro specialises in tastings of its award-winning wines (40KN), truffle dishes and homemade jams, honeys and juices that you get to sample for breakfast. Some of the apartments, each with a kitchenette, have terraces and sea vistas. There's a small surcharge for one-night stays, and payments are cash only.

La Parenzana (☑052-777 460; www.parenzana.com.hr; Volpia 3; s/d 295/590KN; P@☎) La Parenzana is a notable rural inn, situated 3km from Buje in the village of Volpia. It features 16 rooms with rustic wood-and-stone decor, and a konoba (tavern) popular for its Istrian food, such as čripnja (roast meat or fish cooked with potatoes in a cast-iron pot over an open fire). There's bike rental (75KN per day) and tours on request.

San Rocco (☑052-725 000; www.san-rocco.hr; Srednja Ulica 2, Brtonigla; s/d from 897/1380KN; P☀@☎☷) This family-run boutique inn in the village of Brtonigla, near Buje, is a rural hideaway with 14 stylish rooms – no two are alike, but all are equipped with modern conveniences and graced with original detail. There's an outdoor swimming pool, a top-rated restaurant and a small spa.

gallery shop downstairs plus a ground-floor apartment that sleeps four.

Hotel Kaštel
HOTEL €€

(☑ 052-681 607; www.hotel-kastel-motovun.hr; Trg Andrea Antico 7; s/d 460/780KN; P @ 🛜 ☒) The town's only hotel is an utterly charming little place in a restored 17th-century palazzo, with 33 simply furnished rooms. For 1170KN get one of three rooms with air-con and balconies overlooking the leafy square. There's a good restaurant offering truffles and Istrian wines, bike rental (110KN per day) and a wellness centre.

✖ Eating & Drinking

Konoba Dolina
ISTRIAN €

(Gradinje 59/1; mains from 38KN; ⊘ noon-10pm Wed-Mon) If you have wheels, this low-key locals' favourite is worth the drive for its unassuming vibe and honest simple fare featuring Istrian dishes, many with truffles. Wash it down with local Favorit beer.

From Motovun, take a right turn towards Buzet, continuing till the left turnoff for Gradinje; it's 2.5km from here. Closed for holidays for three weeks in late June each year.

Pod Napun
ISTRIAN €

(Gradizol 33; mains from 60KN; ⊘ noon-10pm) Great choice at the beginning of the old town as you walk uphill, this cozy restaurant has a terrace with sweeping valley views and whips up well-prepared traditional dishes from the area.

Pod Voltom
ISTRIAN €

(Trg Josefa Ressela 6; mains from 60KN; ⊘ noon-10pm daily) In a vaulted space within the town gates, this wood-beamed place serves simple down-home Istrian cuisine and pricier truffle dishes. From June to September, grab a seat in the loggia with great valley views.

Mondo
ISTRIAN €€

(Barbacan 1; mains from 75KN; ⊘ noon-3.30pm & 6-10pm) Just before the outer town gate, this little tavern with a small side terrace serves up well-prepared Istrian mainstays, many featuring truffles. Wash it down with wines from Tomaz winery.

Restaurant Zigante
GASTRONOMIC €€€

(☑ 052-664 302; www.zigantetartufi.com; Livade 7, Livade; mains from 185KN; ⊘ noon-11pm) Gourmets from afar come to this destination restaurant a few kilometres below Motovun in the village of Livade. Expect five-star fancy dining, with truffles as the showcase – goose liver with banana potato and black truffle, and even black-truffle ice cream.

ⓘ Information

There's an ATM just past the town entrance, on the right.

Montona Tours (☑ 052-681 970; www.montonatours.com; Kanal 10) is a great source of info; it can help with accommodation in central Istria, rural stays and private apartments and rents bikes for 105KN per day.

Tourist office (☑ 052-681 726; www.tz-motovun.hr; Trg Andrea Antico 1; ⊘ 10am-6pm) Located on the main square, right below Hotel Kaštel.

ⓘ Getting There & Away

It's not easy to visit Motovun without your own car. There are bus connections from Pazin (35KN, 40 minutes, three daily) and Poreč (35KN, 45 minutes, one daily), but on weekdays only during the school year.

ⓘ Getting Around

There are three parking areas in town. The first is at the foot of the village, from where it's a steep 2km hike up to the city gates. Another is 300m below the old town. The last one is for residents and hotel guests. Unless you're staying at the hotel, there's a 20KN charge per day from April to October at the other two parking lots.

ISTRIA ISTARSKE TOPLICE

Istarske Toplice

Dating from the Roman era, Istarske Toplice (www.istarske-toplice.hr) is one of Croatia's oldest, most scenic thermal spas. Beneath an 85m-high cliff and surrounded by greenery, the complex features a concrete-box-style hotel, a wellness centre and, like most spas in Croatia, a slightly geriatric touch. The rotten-egg smell is from the high sulphur content of the large pool, where temperatures reach 34°C.

It's not worth spending the night (unless you love spas), but come for a few hours to indulge. The treatments menu is wide and varied, and includes anything from hot stone (350KN for 1¼ hours) to signature body treatments with wine, honey and lavender (330KN each). Or simply spend time paddling around in the thermal pool (40KN for three hours) or sweating it all away in the sauna (170KN for three hours). The thermal waters are said to help rheumatism, skin diseases and respiratory tract disorders.

There's no public transport, but the spa is easily accessible by road, 10km north of Motovun and 11km south of Buzet on the main road that connects the two towns.

Grožnjan

POP 160

Until the mid-1960s, Grožnjan, 27km northeast of Poreč, was slipping towards oblivion. First mentioned in 1102, this hilltop town was a strategically important fortress for the 14th-century Venetians. They created a system of ramparts and gates, and built a loggia, a granary and several fine churches. With the collapse of the Venetian empire in the 18th century, Grožnjan suffered a decline in its importance and population.

In 1965 sculptor Aleksandar Rukavina and a small group of other artists 'discovered' the crumbling medieval appeal of Grožnjan and began setting up studios in the abandoned buildings. As the town crawled back to life, it attracted the attention of Jeunesses Musicales International, an international training program for young musicians. In 1969 a summer school for musicians was established in Grožnjan and it has been going strong ever since. Each year there are music, orchestra and ballet courses and recitals, with musical events almost daily throughout summer. You can hear the musicians practising while you browse the many craft shops and galleries of this tiny town, comprised of a jumble of crooked lanes and leafy squares.

◉ Sights & Activities

All the town's sights are marked with plaques that have English explanations. The Renaissance **loggia** is immediately to the right of the town gate by the tourist office. Keep going and on your right you'll see the baroque **Spinotti Morteani Palace**, its patio overtaken by the outdoor tables of the **Zigante Tartufi** (www.zigantetartufi.com; Umberta Gorjana 5; ⊙ 9am-10pm) shop. Next on the right comes the **Kaštel** (castle), where many concerts are held.

The town is dominated by the yellow sandstone bell tower of the **Church of St Vitus, St Modest & St Crescentia**, which was built in the 14th century and renovated in baroque style in 1770.

There are more than 30 galleries and studios scattered around town; most are open daily from May to September. **Fonticus Gallery** (Gradska Galerija Fonticus; Trg Lože 3; ⊙ 10am-1pm & 5-8pm Tue-Sun) promotes recent work of mainly Croatian artists. It doesn't have a permanent collection but does host a small display of heraldic paraphernalia that includes helmets, insignia and escutcheon.

★ Festivals & Events

Summer music concerts are organised by the **International Cultural Centre of Jeunesses Musicales Croatia** (www.hgm.hr). The concerts are free and no reservations are necessary. They are usually held in the church, the main square, the loggia or the Kaštel.

⌷ Sleeping & Eating

There are no hotels in Grožnjan, but the staff at the **tourist office** (☑ 052-776 131; Umberta Gorjana 3; ⊙ 10am-1pm & 5-8pm Tue-Sun) can put you in touch with private room owners. Count on spending at least 155KN per person.

Konoba Pintur　　　　　　ISTRIAN €
(Mate Gorjana 9; mains from 40KN; ⊙ 8am-11pm) On the main square, it has tables outside and acceptable and affordable food. It also rents rooms upstairs (single/double 160KN/360KN).

Bastia　　　　　　　　　　ISTRIAN €€
(1 Svibnja 1; mains from 60KN; ⊙ 8am-midnight) The town's oldest restaurant sits on the verdant main square. The decor is bright and cheerful, and the menu extensive and heavy on truffles. Try the local Favorit beer.

⚑ Drinking & Nightlife

Kaya Energy Bar & Design　　CAFE, BAR
(Vincenta iz Kastva 2; ⊙ 9am-11pm) This family-run hideaway at the entrance to town has many faces in one – it's a cafe, a bar, a shop, a showroom and a gallery, with a stylish stone interior, tables on the square and a lovely little terrace off to the side with fantastic valley views. It serves fresh-squeezed juices, smoothies, breakfasts, all-day snacks and good local *malvazija* wine.

Cafe Vero　　　　　　　　CAFE, BAR
(Trg Cornera 3; ⊙ 8am-10pm) The marvellous valley views below are the main draw of this cafe-bar at the end of the village, with wooden tables gracing its terrace.

❶ Getting There & Away

You will have to rely on private transport to get to Grožnjan, as there are no buses. If you're driving from Motovun, do not take the first marked turn-off for Grožnjan as it's unsealed and takes a lot longer. Continue along the road for another kilometre or so until you get to another sign for Grožnjan – this is a far-better approach.

Momjan

POP 283

The oft-skipped-over town of Momjan in northwestern Istria, just south of the Slovenian border, is situated on a hilltop commanding incredible vistas of Istria's interior and the sea. Its historic highlights include the 15th-century Church of St Martin and a clifftop castle from the 13th century.

Cyclists shouldn't miss the nearby **Parenzana bike trail** (www.parenzana.net), which runs along a defunct narrow gauge railway that operated from 1902 to 1935 between Trieste and Poreč. Today, it traverses three countries, Italy, Slovenia and Croatia (the Croatian stretch is 78km), and is becoming an increasingly popular way to take in the highlights of Istria, especially in spring and autumn.

A great place to bed down for cyclists in north Istria is **B&B Momjan** (☑ 098 689 127; bnbmomjan@gmail.com; Gorenja Vas 3; dm 137KN, s/d 190/265KN, cottage 380KN). It's run by a pair of cycling enthusiasts who are an excellent source of info about the best trails around the peninsula. Pick between two rooms in the main house, where bathrooms and kitchen are shared with the live-in owners, the garden house (that sleeps up to six) in the back with a lovely terrace, or the bunk beds in the downstairs apartment (for nine people, ideal for groups of friends or a family or two); all rates include a breakfast of French pastries and coffee roasted by the owner. Alternatively, stay at Agroturizam San Mauro (p130).

On top of the joys of cycling here, don't miss Momjan's gastro delights and its renowned *muscato di momiano*, a dry sweet white wine produced by local winemakers. The favourite, smack at the heart of town, is **Konoba Rino** (☑ 052-779 170; Dolinja Vas 23; mains from 55KN; ☺ noon-10pm Wed-Mon), a rustic tavern with wooden beams that whips up amazing local specialties, like pastas with *boškarin* (Istrian ox) and truffle gnocchi. For a fancier experience, take a five-minute drive out of town to **Stari Podrum** (☑ 052-779 152; Most 52, Momjan; mains from 70KN; ☺ noon-10pm Thu-Tue), where Istrian mainstays are served with a creative touch, and at higher prices; hence the flashy cars parked outside. Try its renowned tenderloin steak.

A little further afield, 9km southeast of Momjan on the Brtonigla–Buje road, **Konoba Morgan** (www.konoba morgan.eu; Bracanija 1; mains from 70KN; ☺ noon-10pm Wed-Mon) offers a fine gastronomic experience. It has a lovely terrace on a hill, with sweeping views of the countryside. The menu, which changes daily, focuses on game meat and seasonal ingredients such as truffles and asparagus.

To reach Momjan, you must get behind the wheel, as bus connections are practically nonexistent.

ISTRIA MOMJAN

Kvarner

Includes ➡

Rijeka 136
Opatija 142
Beli 147
Cres Town 148
Valun. 150
Lubenice 151
Osor 151
Mali Lošinj 152
Veli Lošinj. 156
Krk Island 157
Rab Island 163

Best Places to Eat

➡ Bistro Bukarica (p159)

➡ Kukuriku (p143)

➡ Konoba Valle Losca (p146)

➡ Bora Bar (p157)

➡ Mlinar (p140)

Best Places to Stay

➡ Mare Mare Suites (p154)

➡ Hotel Miramar (p144)

➡ Carnevale (p139)

➡ Hostel Dharma (p139)

➡ Hotel Manora (p154)

Why Go?

Sheltered by soaring mountains, the Kvarner Gulf has long been loved by visitors attracted by the mild climate and cobalt waters, and those in search of more than just beach appeal. In the days of the Austro-Hungarian Empire, the wealthy built holiday homes here, bestowing places like Rijeka and Opatija with a rich legacy of stately Habsburg-era architecture. From both of these neighbouring towns you can easily connect to hiking trails inside the protected forests of Učka Nature Park and Risnjak National Park.

The islands of Cres, Lošinj, Krk and Rab all have highly atmospheric old port towns and stretches of unspoiled coastline dotted with remote coves for superb swimming. Wildlife puts in an appearance too: Cres has an important griffon vulture population and Lošinj has a marine centre devoted to preserving the Adriatic's dolphins and turtles.

When to Go
Rijeka

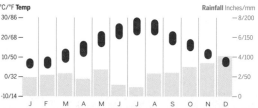

Jan–Mar Rijeka becomes 'Rio in Europe' during two weeks of carnival action.

May–Jun Dolphins are regularly spotted off the coast of Lošinj.

Jul–Aug Open-air performances and medieval fairs galore.

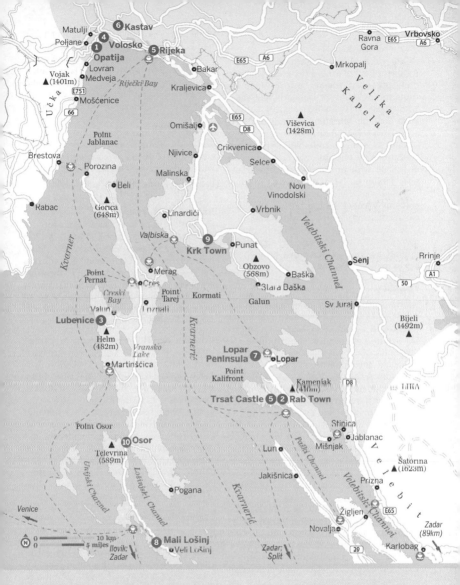

Kvarner Highlights

1 Adopting a Habsburg swagger as you stroll along the promenade in **Opatija** (p142).

2 Wandering the cobbled, church-lined streets of ancient **Rab Town** (p164).

3 Looking isolation in the eye at **Lubenice** and wondering at its harsh beauty (p151).

4 Sampling Croatian specialities in **Volosko** (p144), a diner's delight.

5 Taking in the panoramic views from **Trsat Castle** (p137) in Rijeka.

6 Heading to the hills for a memorable meal in **Kastav** (p143).

7 Lazing on sandy beaches in the remote reaches of the **Lopar Peninsula** (p168).

8 Enjoying summer on the **Mali Lošinj** (p152) waterfront.

9 Losing yourself in history in the streets of **Krk Town** (p159).

10 Exploring the tiny walled town of **Osor** (p151).

RIJEKA

♪ 051 / POP 129,000

Rijeka, Croatia's third-largest city, is an intriguing blend of gritty port and Habsburg grandeur. Most people rush through en route to the islands or Dalmatia, but those who pause will discover charm, culture, good nightlife, intriguing festivals and Croatia's most colourful carnival.

Despite some regrettable architectural ventures in the outskirts, much of the centre is replete with ornate Austro-Hungarian-style buildings. It's a surprisingly verdant city once you've left its concrete core, which contains Croatia's largest port, with ships, cargo and cranes lining the waterfront.

Rijeka is a vital transport hub, but as there's no real beach in the city (and hotel options are few) most people base themselves in nearby Opatija.

History

Following their successful conquest of the indigenous Illyrian Liburnians, the Romans established a port here called Tarsaticae. Slavic tribes migrated to the region in the 7th century and built a new settlement within the old Roman town.

The town changed feudal masters – from German nobility to the Frankopan dukes of Krk – before becoming part of the Austrian empire in the late 15th century. Rijeka was an important outlet to the sea for the Austrians and a new road was built in 1725 connecting Vienna with the Kvarner coast. This spurred economic development, especially shipbuilding, the industry that has remained the centrepiece of Rijeka's economy ever since.

In 1730 Rijeka was hit by a devastating earthquake which destroyed much of its medieval heart. Thirty years later the old town walls were removed to allow for the construction of a more modern commercial centre. Korzo, Rijeka's main pedestrian strip, was built as a grand avenue on the site of the demolished walls.

With the birth of the Austro-Hungarian Dual Monarchy in 1867, Rijeka was given over to the jurisdiction of the Hungarian government. Imposing municipal buildings were constructed and a new railway linked the city to Zagreb, Budapest and Vienna, bringing the first tourists to the Kvarner Gulf.

Between 1918, when Italian troops seized Rijeka and Istria, and 1945, when Rijeka became part of postwar Yugoslavia, it changed hands several times, with sporadic periods as a free city (known under its Italian name, Fiume). In 1991 Rijeka became part of independent Croatia but still retains a sizeable, well-organised Italian minority who have their own newspaper, *La Voce del Popolo*.

◉ Sights

The maze of streets and squares in the ancient core of Rijeka is excellently marked with multilingual plaques explaining the history of each sight. Pick up a map from the tourist office (p141).

Natural History Museum　　　MUSEUM
(Prirodoslovni Muzej; www.prirodoslovni.com; Lorenzov Prolaz 1; adult/concession 10/5KN; ⊙ 9am-7pm Mon-Sat, to 3pm Sun) Located in a very grand 19th-century villa, this museum is devoted to the geology, botany and sea life of the Adriatic area. There's a small aquarium, exhibits on sharks, taxidermied animals and lots of bugs. Don't miss the adjacent botanical garden, with over 2000 native plant species.

Maritime and History Museum　　　MUSEUM
(Pomorski i Povijesni Muzej; www.ppmhp.hr; Muzejski trg 1; adult/concession 15/10KN; ⊙ 9am-4pm Mon, 9am-8pm Tue-Fri, 9am-1pm & 4-8pm Sat, 4-8pm Sun) The star of this museum is the building itself, the former palace of the Austro-Hungarian governor. It's a splendid showcase of Hungarian architecture, with grand staircases, glittering chandeliers and many sumptuously restored rooms. The maritime collection includes Roman amphorae, model ships, sea charts, navigation instruments and portraits of captains; little of it is captioned in English.

Rijeka City Museum　　　MUSEUM
(Muzej Grada Rijeke; www.muzej-rijeka.hr; Muzejski trg 1/1; adult/concession 15/10KN; ⊙ 10am-8pm Mon-Fri, 9am-1pm Sat) Housed in a boxy 1970s structure, this small museum houses ever-changing themed exhibitions, ranging from art to aspects of local history.

**Our Lady of Lourdes
Capuchin Church**　　　CHURCH
(Kapucinska Crkva Gospe Lurdske; www.glurdska-kapucini.blogspot.com; Kapucinske Stube 5; ⊙ 8am-noon & 4-8pm) If you're arriving by bus, you won't help but notice this imposing church towering over the station. Dating from 1904, its ornate neo-Gothic facade stands above an elaborate Italianate double staircase.

Museum of Modern & Contemporary Art
GALLERY

(Muzej Moderne i Suvremene Umjetnosti; www. mmsu.hr; Dolac 1; adult/concession 20/10KN; ⊙10am-8pm Tue-Sun) On the 2nd floor of the university library, this small museum puts on high-quality rotating shows, from street photography to contemporary drawings and sculptures.

City Tower
TOWER

(Gradski Toranj; Korzo) One of the few buildings to have survived the 1750 earthquake, the distinctive yellow City Tower was originally a gate from the waterfront to the old town centre. The Habsburgs added the baroque decorations after the disaster, including the portal with coats of arms and busts of emperors. The still-functioning clock was mounted in 1873.

Roman Arch
GATE

(Rimski luk; Stara Vrata) This plain archway marks the former entrance to the Praetorium, an ancient military complex. Other Roman remains can be seen in a small excavation site nearby.

St Vitus' Cathedral
CATHEDRAL

(Katedrala Sv Vida; Trg Grivica 11; ⊙7am-noon & 4.30-7pm Mon-Sat, to noon Sun Jun Aug, 6.30am-noon daily Sep May) North of the Roman Gate is this unusual round cathedral, built by the Jesuit order in 1638 on the site of an older church and dedicated to Rijeka's patron saint. If it looks familiar, it's probably because it features on the reverse of the 100KN note. Massive marble pillars support the central dome under which are housed baroque altars and a 13th-century Gothic crucifix.

★ Trsat Castle
CASTLE

(Trsatska Gradina; Petra Zrinskoga bb; adult/concession 15/5KN; ⊙9am-8pm Jun-Oct, to 5pm Nov-May) High on a hill above the city, this semiruined 13th-century fortress offers magnificent vistas from its bastions and ramparts, looking down the Rječina river valley to the docks, Adriatic and distant island of Krk. The present structure was built by the Frankopan dukes of Krk, but the latest facelift was done in 1824 when Irish-born count Laval Nugent, a commander in the Austrian army, bought the castle and had it restored in a romantic neoclassical Biedermeier design.

Guarded by basilisks (which incidentally look nothing like the one in *Harry Potter*), the Ancient Greek–style Nugent family mausoleum houses a gallery, while underground a former dungeon hosts occasional exhibits. During summer, the fortress features concerts, theatre performances and fashion shows. The open-air cafe-bar (open until midnight in summer) is a wonderful spot to take in the views.

Our Lady of Trsat Church
CHURCH

(Crkva Gospe Trsatske; www.trsat-svetiste.com; Frankopanski trg; ⊙8am-5pm) According to legend, the angels carrying the house of Jesus' mother from Nazareth rested here in the late 13th century before moving it to Loreto in Italy. Pilgrims started trickling into the chapel erected on the site, and then pouring in when the Pope donated an icon of St Mary in 1367 (located on the main altar, behind a magnificent wrought-iron gate).

View offerings of votive gifts across in the baroque cloister and make an appointment to see the valuable sacral-art collection in the treasury, where you can watch a 15-minute film about the church.

To follow in the pilgrims' steps, climb the Petar Kružić Stairway from Titov trg, built in 1531 for the faithful on their way to the church, and lined with chapels once used as rest stops for the pilgrims. Alternatively, take a quick ride on city bus 2 to Trsat.

Astronomical Centre
OBSERVATORY

(Astronomski Centar; ☑051-455 700; www.rijeka sport.hr; Sv Križ 33; adult/child 20/10KN) High on a hill in the east of the city, Croatia's first astronomical centre is a striking modern complex encompassing an observatory, planetarium and study centre. Check the website for details of evening presentations, some of which are held in English, Italian, French, German, Russian and Spanish. To get here, catch bus 7A from the centre.

🏃 Activities

Paragliding Kvarner
PARAGLIDING

(☑095 85 49 995; www.paragliding-kvarner.com) Based in Crikvenica, 30km down the coast, this crew offers tandem flights taking off from 770m above the Kvarner Gulf. Choose between a 20-minute panoramic flight (€80) and 50 minutes riding the thermals (€120).

Yacht Rent
SAILING

(☑098 369 692; www.yacht-rent.com) With nearly 4000 boats on its books, this outfit can sort you out with a yacht, launch or catamaran, with or without a skipper and/or

KVARNER

Rijeka

200 m
0.1 miles

Opatija
(14km)

Trsat Castle (500m);
Our Lady of Trsat Church
(700m)

Bulevar Oslobođenja

Strossmayerova

Franje Brentinija

Milana Smokvine

Cindrića

Andrije Kačića Miošića

Rječina River

Youth Hostel Rijeka (700m);
Best Western Hotel Jadran (1.2km);
Hostel Dharma (3km);
Astronomical Centre (3km)

Križaniceva

⊙ 6

13 ✗

Titov trg

Školjić

21 🚇

Mrtvi Canal

Pavla Rittera Vitezovića

Agatićeva

Jelačićev
Trg

Bus Station
(Local)

Scarpina

Ante Starčevića

Veslarska

Matije Gupca

Ivana Zajca

Kazalíšni
Park

Wenzelova

22 ✪

15 ✗

Zagrebačka

Demetrova

Trpinjina

Ljubišina

Vatroslava

Verdjeva

Riva Boduli

Rijeka
Harbour

Jadrolinija

⊙ UTO
Kapetan
Luka

Žrtava Fašizma

Ivana Grohovca

Kalvarija

Park Vladimira
Nazora

Šetalište Vladimira Nazora

Lorenzov
Prolaz

Park Nikole
Hosta

4 🏛

Muzejski
trg

Laginjina

7 🏛

2 🏛

Pomerio

Erazma Barčića

Ivana Dežmana

Frana Supila

Slogina ulica

14 ✗

Frana Kurelca

R Strohala

Dolac

11

3

19

17 ✗

Knjižna

Jadranski
Trg

Splitska

Zanonova

Riva

Ciottina

Trpimirova

Zadarska

5 ✚

Trg
Žabica

Bus Station
(Intercity)

20

9 🏛

Trg Grivica

Gornja
Vrata

Đure
Šporera

Užarska

Stara
Vrata

8

Jadroagent

18

Trg Rječke
Revolucije

Marina

Petra Zrinjskog

Trg Ivana
Koblera

1

Korzo

Adamićeva

i

Herzka

16

🏛 23

Sokolkula

i

200 m
0.1 miles

crew (you'll need a valid skipper's license if you choose the 'bareboat' option). Expect to pay upwards of €1500 per week.

✨ Festivals & Events

Rijeka Carnival CARNIVAL
(Riječki Karneval; www.rijecki-karneval.hr; ⊙mid-Jan–early Mar) The largest carnival in Croatia involves pageants, street dances, concerts, masked balls, exhibitions and a parade. Check out the *zvončari*, masked men clad in animal skins who dance and ring loud bells to frighten off evil spirits. The festivities take place between mid-January and Ash Wednesday.

Rijeka Summer Nights THEATRE
(Riječke Ljetne Noći; www.rijeckeljetnenoci.com; ⊙Jun–Jul) Concerts are held at the Croatian National Theatre and on outdoor stages set up on the Korso and the beaches in June and July.

🛏 Sleeping

Prices are generally consistent year-round except at carnival time, when you can expect to pay a surcharge and you'll need to book well in advance. There are few private rooms in Rijeka itself; the tourist office lists these on its website. Nearby Opatija has a lot more accommodation, but it tends to be pricier.

★ Carnevale HOSTEL €
(☑051-410 555; www.hostelcarnevale.com; Jadranski trg 1; dm/r 175/385KN; ❄🖲) With silver paint on the walls, billowing fabric on the ceiling, animal-print bed linen and art everywhere, this centrally located hostel should put you in a festive mood. Towels are provided (and changed regularly) and there are nice big lockers.

★ Hostel Dharma HOSTEL €
(☑051-562 108; www.dharmahostels.com; Spinčićeva 2; dm/s/tw 135/270/370KN; 🅿❄🖲) A clever conversion of what was once an iron smelter on the eastern edge of town has produced this wonderful hostel, with a yoga studio and vegetarian restaurant attached. Start your day with a yoga class (free) and tuck into a substantial vege breakfast (20KN), before chilling out in the large garden.

Youth Hostel Rijeka HOSTEL €
(☑051-406 420; www.hfhs.hr; Šetalište XIII Divizije 23; dm/s/tw €21/37/52; @🖲) In the leafy residential area of Pečine, 1km east of the

Rijeka

◎ Sights
1 City Tower...D3
2 Maritime and History Museum...........D1
3 Museum of Modern &
   Contemporary Art.............................C2
4 Natural History Museum....................D1
5 Our Lady of Lourdes Capuchin
   Church..B2
6 Petar Kružić Stairway.........................F2
7 Rijeka City Museum.............................D1
8 Roman Arch...D2
9 St Vitus' Cathedral..............................D2

🛏 Sleeping
10 Carnevale..C2
11 Grand Hotel Bonavia.........................C2

🍴 Eating
12 City Market...D3
13 Konoba Nebuloza................................F2
14 Mlinar..C1
15 Na Kantunu..D4
16 Ristorante Spagho.............................D3
17 Zlatna Školjka......................................C2

🍷 Drinking & Nightlife
18 CukariKafe...D2
19 Filodrammatica Bookshop
   Cafe...C2
20 Nina 2...B2
21 Tunel...F1

🎭 Entertainment
22 Croatian National Theatre
   Ivan Zajc...E4

🛍 Shopping
23 Mala Galerija..D2
24 Što Da?...E2

centre, this renovated 19th-century villa has clean, spacious (if plain) rooms and a communal TV area. It can get block-booked by school groups so reserve ahead.

Best Western Hotel Jadran HOTEL €€
(☑051-216 600; www.bestwestern-ce.com/jadran; Šetalište XIII Divizije 46; s/d from €82/97; 🅿❄@🖲) Located 2km east of the centre, this attractive four-star hotel clings to a cliff above the Adriatic: book a sea view room and revel in the tremendous vistas from your balcony right above the water. There's a concrete-edged beach below too.

Grand Hotel Bonavia HOTEL €€
(☑051-357 100; www.bonavia.hr; Dolac 4; r from €99; 🅿❄🖲) Right in the heart of town, this striking glass-fronted boxy building has well-equipped, comfortable rooms that

WORTH A TRIP

RISNJAK NATIONAL PARK

Relatively isolated and rarely visited, despite being only 32km northeast of Rijeka, **Risnjak National Park** (Nacionalni park Risnjak; www.risnjak.hr; adult/concession 45/25KN) covers an area of 63 sq km and rises up to 1528m at its highest peak, Veliki Risnjak. The landscape is thickly forested with beech and pine trees, and carpeted with meadows and wildflowers. The bracing alpine breezes make it the perfect hideaway when the coastal heat and crowds become overpowering.

The park is named after the lynx (*ris* in Croatian), the fluffy eared, pad-footed wild cat which can still be found here. Other wildlife includes brown bears, wolves, wild cats, wild boar, deer, chamois and 500 species of butterfly. Most of the park is unspoiled virgin forest, with only a few settlements.

The **park information office** (☑ 051-836 133; Bijela Vodica 48; s/d 300/480KN; ⊙ 9am-5pm; 🛜) is just west of the village of Crni Lug. There's a restaurant attached and five simple, clean B&B rooms above (also available for half or full board). This is the starting point for the **Leska Path**, an easy and shady 4.2km trail punctuated by several dozen explanatory panels (with English translations) telling you all about the park's history, topography, geology, flora and fauna. You'll pass crystal-clear streams, forests of tall fir trees, bizarre rock formations, a feeding station for the deer and a mountain hut with a picnic table; allow two hours.

Another accommodation option is the **Hotel Risnjak** (☑ 051-508 160; www.hotel-risnjak.hr; Lujzinska 36; s/d €47/80; 🅿🛜) in **Delnice**, a scrappy little town 14km east of the park entrance. The three-storey, yellow building has its charm, and inside there are 21 rooms, a restaurant (known for its game meats), cafe-bar and a gym. The hotel also organises activities for groups of 10 or more (paragliding, rafting, canoeing, paintball, archery, skiing, canyon visits).

There's no public transport to the park but there are trains to Delnice from Rijeka (43KN, 1½ hours, six daily) and buses from Zagreb (106KN to 132KN, 1¾ hours, five to nine daily), Rijeka (34KN to 48KN, 45 minutes, roughly hourly), Opatija (48KN, 1½ hours, daily), Pula (111KN, 3½ hours, two daily) and Rovinj (126KN, four hours, daily). To get there by car, exit the main Zagreb–Rijeka motorway at Delnice and follow the signs.

are much more stylish than you'd expect. There's also a restaurant, a spa and a small gym.

✗ Eating

★ Mlinar
BAKERY €

(Frana Supila; items from 5KN; ⊙ 5.30am-8pm Mon-Fri, 6.30am-3pm Sat) The best bakery in town, with delicious filled baguettes, wholemeal bread, croissants and *burek* (pastry stuffed with meat, spinach or cheese). There are several branches around.

City Market
MARKET €

(Tržnica; Ivana Zajca 3; ⊙ 6.30am-2pm Mon-Sat, to noon Sun) Excellent for seasonal fruit and vegetables.

★ Konoba Nebuloza
CROATIAN €€

(☑ 051-374 501; www.konobanebuloza.com; Titov trg 2b; mains 48-120KN; ⊙ noon-midnight Mon-Sat) Straddling the line between modern and traditional Croatian fare, this upmarket little riverside restaurant serves

lots of seafood along with selected beef and turkey dishes. Specialities include *sous vide* swordfish and baby rump steak with prosciutto and cheese.

Na Kantunu
CROATIAN, SEAFOOD €€

(☑ 051-313 271; Demetrova 2; mains 55-95KN; ⊙ 8am-10pm) Fresh fish and seafood are the stars of the show at this bright and breezy restaurant in a somewhat grimy location by the port. It's a good place to try traditional fish or octopus stews, followed by crispy fruit pastries.

Ristorante Spagho
ITALIAN €€

(☑ 051-311 122; www.ristorantespagho.fullbusiness.com; Ivana Zajca 24; mains 35-160KN; ⊙ 10am-midnight Mon-Sat, to 10.30pm Sun) A stylish, modern Italian place with exposed brickwork, art and hip seating that offers delicious and filling portions of pasta, pizza, salads and meat dishes. There's even a whole section of the menu devoted to truffles!

Zlatna Školjka
CROATIAN, SEAFOOD €€

(☑ 051-213 782; www.zlatna-skoljka.hr; Kružna 12; mains 60-120KN; ⊙ 11am-11pm Mon-Sat) Savour the superbly prepared seafood and choice Croatian wines at this formal maritime-themed restaurant. Daily specials such as *pečena hobotnica* (roast octopus) are chalked up on a board.

Drinking & Nightlife

CukariKafe
CAFE, BAR

(Trg Jurja Klovica 2; ⊙ 7am-midnight Mon-Thu, 7am-2am Fri & Sat, 10am-10pm Sun) Tucked into a tiny lane in the old part of town, this is Rijeka's coolest cafe-bar. Grab a seat on the oversized white wooden furniture on the covered deck or head inside to admire the oddball knick-knacks.

Filodrammatica Bookshop Cafe
CAFE, BAR

(www.vbz.hr; Korzo 28; ⊙ 7am-11pm) A cafe-bar with luxurious decor, comfy sofas and a VBZ (Croatia's biggest publisher) bookshop at the back, Filodrammatica prides itself on specialist coffees and fresh, single-source beans. It also serves sandwiches and snacks.

Tunel
BAR, CLUB

(www.facebook.com/tunel.klub; Školjić 12, ⊙ 9am-midnight Mon-Wed, 9am-2am Thu & Fri, 6pm-2am Sat; ☎) Tucked beneath the railway tracks in an actual tunnel, this popular place morphs from a daytime cafe, to a comedy and live-music venue, to a late-night club. It gets jam-packed on the weekends.

Nina 2
BAR, CLUB

(www.nina2.com; Adamićev Gat; ⊙ 9am-4am Mon & Tue, to 10pm Wed, to 6am Thu & Fri, 4pm-6am Sat; ☎) This boat moored on the harbour front offers daytime drinking and lots of night-time action, including DJs and live bands.

☆ Entertainment

Croatian National Theatre Ivan Zajc
THEATRE

(Hrvatsko Narodnog Kažalište Ivana pl Zajca; ☑ 051-355 907; www.hnk-zajc.hr; Verdieva 5a) In 1885 the inaugural performance at this imposing theatre was lit by the city's first lightbulb. These days you can catch dramas in Croatian and Italian, as well as opera and ballet. Gustav Klimt painted some of the ceiling frescoes.

Shopping

Šta Da?
GIFTS

(Užarska 14; ⊙ 9am-8pm Mon-Fri, to 1pm Sat) Literally translating as 'what yes?', '*šta da*' is an idiom peculiar to Rijeka meaning something like 'you what!?' or 'really, you don't say!'. This cool little store stocks T-shirts, jewellery and clocks, including many emblazoned with images of its logo and of the distinctive orange local buses.

Mala Galerija
ARTS & CRAFTS

(www.mala-galerija.hr; Užarska 25; ⊙ 8am-8pm Mon-Fri, 9am-2pm Sat) This small art shop stocks the traditional Rijeka design known as *morčići*, a ceramic jewellery piece depicting a Moor wearing a turban.

ⓘ Information

You'll find free wi-fi access on the Korzo and at Trsat Castle.

Clinical Hospital Center Rijeka (Klinički bolnički centar Rijeka; ☑ 051 658 111; www.kbc-rijeka.hr; Krešimirova 42)

Post office (Korzo 13; ⊙ 7am-8pm Mon-Fri, to 2pm Sat) Has a telephone centre and an exchange office.

Tourist office (☑ 051-335 882; www.visitrijeka.hr; Korzo 14; ⊙ 8am-7.30pm Mon-Fri, to

KVARNER RIJEKA

CYCLING THE KVARNER

The Kvarner region offers a variety of options for biking enthusiasts, from gentle rides to heart-pumping climbs on steep island roads. There are several trails around Opatija; two easier paths depart from Mt Kastav (360m), while a challenging 4½-hour adventure goes from Lovran to Učka Nature Park. Lošinj offers a moderately difficult 2½-hour route that starts and ends in Mali Lošinj. On Krk, a leisurely two-hour ride from Krk Town shows you meadows, fields and hamlets of the island's little-visited interior. A biking route from Rab Town explores the virgin forests of the Kalifront Peninsula. On Cres, a 50km trail takes you from the marina at Cres Town past the medieval hilltop village of Lubenice and the seaside gem of Valun.

For details of these itineraries, ask at any tourist office for the *Kvarner by Bicycle* brochure, which outlines 19 routes across the region. The websites www.kvarner.hr and www.pedala.hr both have details of rides in this region.

BUSES FROM RIJEKA

DESTINATION	COST (KN)	DURATION (HR)	DAILY SERVICES
Dubrovnik	414	12½	2-3
Krk	51	1½	13
Pula	84-113	2½	19-25
Split	230-291	8	8-13
Zadar	145-185	4½	7-13
Zagreb	80-149	2½	27-35

1.30pm Sat) Has good colour city maps, lots of brochures and private accommodation lists.

ⓘ Getting There & Away

AIR

Rijeka Airport (Zračna luka Rijeka ; ☎ 051-842 040; www.rijeka-airport.hr; Hamec 1, Omišalj), located on the island of Krk, is only used for seasonal flights from April to October. There are international flights to Cologne, Stuttgart, Oslo, Stockholm and more. The only domestic routes are **Trade Air** (www.trade-air.com) services to Split and Zagreb.

BOAT

Jadroagent (☎ 051-211 276; www.jadroagent. hr; Trg Ivana Koblera 2; ☻) has information on all boats around Croatia.

Jadrolinija (☎ 051-211 444; www.jadrolinija. hr; Riječki Lukobran bb) a daily catamaran connects Rijeka to Rab Town (80KN, 1¾ hours) and Novalja on Pag (80KN, 2¾ hours).

From June to September a twice-weekly coastal car ferry heads south to Split (passenger/car €27/60, 12 hours), Stari Grad on Hvar (€33/66, 14¼ hours), Korčula (€40/74, 18 hours), Sobra on Mljet (€47/82, 20¼ hours) and Dubrovnik (€47/82, 22 hours).

UTO Kapetan Luka (☎ 021-645 476; www. krilo.hr) has daily passenger-only ferries to/ from Cres (45KN, 1¼ hours) and Mali Lošinj (60KN, three to 4½ hours) year-round, some of which also stop at Martinšćica (50KN, two hours), Unije (55KN, 2½ hours), Susak (60KN, three hours) and Ilovik (60KN, 3½ hours).

BUS

The **intercity bus station** (☎ 051-660 300; Trg Žabica 1) is in the town centre. Buses for Opatija leave from the local bus station on Jelačićeva trg.

TRAIN

The **train station** (Željeznički kolodvor; ☎ 060 333 444; www.hzpp.hr; Trg Kralja Tomislava 1) is a 10-minute walk east of the city centre. Direct services include Osijek (232KN, nine hours, daily), Zagreb (119KN, 3¾ hours, three daily), Delnice (43KN, 1½ hours, six daily) and Ljubljana (129KN, two hours, two daily).

ⓘ Getting Around

TO/FROM THE AIRPORT

Rijeka Airport is on Krk Island, 30km from town.

An airport bus meets all flights for the 30-minute ride to the intercity bus station; it leaves for the airport two hours and 20 minutes before flight times. You can buy a ticket (50KN) on the bus.

Taxis from the airport charge up to 350KN to the centre.

BUS

Rijeka has an extensive network of orange city buses run by **Autotrolej** (www.autotrolej.hr), operating from the local **bus station** (Jelačićev trg). Buy two-trip tickets for 18KN from any *tisak* (news-stand). A single ticket from the driver costs 12KN.

The same company also operates a 24-hour, colourful, open-topped, double-decker, hop-on hop-off sightseeing bus (adult/child 50/35KN) that runs between central Rijeka, Trsat and Opatija. The ticket is also valid for travel on all city buses.

OPATIJA

☎051 / POP 6660

Genteel Opatija, 13km west of Rijeka, was the most fashionable seaside resort for the Viennese elite during the days of the Austro-Hungarian Empire – as evidenced by many beautiful belle époque villas that remain. Although it lost some of its lustre during the Yugoslav period, the town has spruced itself up and once again attracts a mainly mature crowd, drawn to its grand spa hotels, spectacular location and agreeable year-round climate. Some excellent restaurants have sprung up to cater to them, with a particularly good cluster in the pretty Volosko neighbourhood.

The town sprawls along the coast between forested hills and the sparkling Adriatic, and the whole waterfront is connected by a promenade. Don't expect great beaches (there aren't any) but there's still excellent swimming in the sheltered bays.

History

Until the 1840s Opatija was a minuscule fishing village with 35 houses and a church, but the arrival of wealthy Iginio Scarpa from Rijeka turned things around. He built Villa Angiolina (named after his wife) and surrounded it with exotic subtropical plants. The villa hosted European aristocrats aplenty (including the Austrian queen Maria Anna, wife of Ferdinand) and Opatija's classy reputation was sealed.

Opatija's development was also assisted by the completion of a rail link on the Vienna–Trieste line in 1873. Construction of Opatija's first hotel, the Quarnero (today the Hotel Kvarner), began and wealthy visitors arrived en masse. It seemed everyone who was anyone was compelled to visit Opatija, including kings from Romania and Sweden, Russian tsars and celebrities of the day.

Today Opatija remains a refined (some would say conservative) resort, very popular with German and Austrian senior citizens. It's not the place for wild nights or round-the-clock clubbing, and that's just how the regulars like it.

◉ Sights

Lungomare PROMENADE
Lined with majestic villas and ample gardens, this wonderful path (more formally known as the Franz Joseph I Promenade) is a voyeur's dream and walker's delight. It winds along the coast, past villa after villa, for 12km from Volosko to Lovran via the villages of Ičići and Ika. Along the way you can peer into the homes of the wealthy and marvel at their seafront palaces.

The path weaves through exotic bushes, thickets of bamboo, a marina and rocky bays where you can throw down a towel and jump into the sea – a better option than Opatija's concrete beach.

Croatian Museum of Tourism MUSEUM
(Hrvatski muzej turizma; www.hrmt.hr; Park Angiolina 1; adult/concession 10/5KN; ⊘10am-9pm)
Spread between three historic buildings, this museum houses a permanent collection of old photographs, postcards, brochures and posters tracing the history of tourism, and there's always a well-presented travel-themed exhibition as well. But really, it's the buildings themselves that are the main attraction. The restored **Villa Angiolina** is one of Opatija's grandest structures – a marvel of trompe l'œil frescoes, Corinthian capitals, gilded mirrors and geometric floor mosaics – though the addition of modern windows is unforgivable.

Verdant gardens surround the villa, replete with gingko trees, sequoias, holm oaks, Japanese camellia (Opatija's symbol) and even a little open-air theatre where

KVARNER OPATIJA

WORTH A TRIP

GOING KUKURIKU IN KASTAV

A fortified hilltop town filled with stone churches and squares, Kastav isn't short on atmosphere. However, the main reason to drive the 10km from Rijeka (or /km from Opatija) is local slow-food pioneer Nenad Kukurin's wonderful hotel-restaurant, **Kukuriku** (☑051-691 519; www.kukuriku.hr; Trg Lokvina 3; 6-course meal 380-550KN; ⊘7am-midnight; P ❋ ☎).

There's no menu, so you need to be prepared to relinquish control to the staff. Tell them whether you prefer meat, fish or vegetarian dishes, and whether you have any particular dislikes or dietary requirements (or budget constraints). Then prepare for course after course of delicious, beautifully presented, innovative local cuisine.

To top it all off there are 15 extremely chic rooms here (s/d from €110/170) – which can be handy if you are planning to partake in the recommended matches from the excellent wine list. And if you're wondering about the rooster-themed paraphernalia that is scattered about, *kukuriku* is the Croatian take on 'cock-a-doodle-doo'.

costumed recitals are held. Neighbouring **Swiss House** (1875) was an outbuilding of the main villa, used partly as a buttery. Further west, past St James' Church, the **Juraj Šporer Artistic Pavillion** (1900) was originally built as a patisserie.

Volosko   VILLAGE

The former village of Volosko on the northern edge of Opatija is one of the prettiest places on this coastline and still maintains a local ambience. It's very scenic indeed – men repair fishing nets in the tiny harbour, while stone houses with flower-laden balconies rise up from the coast via a warren of narrow alleyways. From central Opatija it's best reached by a 2km, 30-minute stroll along Lungomare, past laurels, palms, fig trees, oaks and magnificent villas.

⚜ Festivals & Events

Festival Opatija   CULTURE, FILM

(☑ 051-271 377; Zert bb) From June to September, the open-air theatre by the waterfront plays host to live music (including classical, jazz and international pop acts), theatre, ballet and cinema.

🛏 Sleeping

There are few good budget or midrange hotels in Opatija and everything gets booked up over Christmas, so reserve ahead for this time. Private rooms are abundant but a little more expensive than in other areas.

Autocamp Medveja   CAMPGROUND €

(☑ 051-291 191; www.remisens.com; Medveja bb; camping per adult/child/site/car 54/34/38/38KN; r 562KN; ☺ Easter–mid-Oct; P ❄ @) Given the paucity of cheaper hotels in Opatija, the new mobile homes and simple en suite rooms at this peaceful camping ground are worth considering. It's set in a cleft in the mountains in a leafy valley leading to a pretty pebbly cove, 10km south of Opatija.

★ Hotel Miramar   HOTEL €€€

(☑ 051-280 000; www.hotel-miramar.info; Ive Kaline 11; r from €230; P ❄ @ 🛜 🏊) Glam almost to the point of kitsch but fabulous nonetheless, Miramar has spacious rooms spread between five pastel buildings, set amongst lovely gardens. There's a rocky little beach, indoor and outdoor pools, a spa centre and a surfeit of chandeliers.

Villa Kapetanović   HOTEL €€€

(☑ 051-741 355; www.villa-kapetanovic.hr; Nova Cesta 12a; r from 825KN; P ❄ 🛜 🏊 🐾) High on the hill above Volosko, this modern block offers 27 stylish rooms, extraordinary sea views, a fish restaurant and a particularly inviting outdoor pool area. A free shuttle takes the sting out of the walk from Opatija.

Villa Ariston   HOTEL €€€

(☑ 051-271 379; www.villa-ariston.hr; Ulica Maršala Tita 179; s/d/ste from 480/850/1300KN; P ❄ 🛜) With a gorgeous location beside a rocky cove, this historic hotel has celebrity cachet in spades (Coco Chanel and the Kennedys were former guests). The interior remains grand and impressive, with a sweeping staircase, chandeliers and plenty of period charm.

Design Hotel Astoria   HOTEL €€€

(☑ 051-706 350; www.hotel-astoria.hr; Ulica Maršala Tita 174; s/d from 775/1034KN; P ❄ @ 🛜) Bored with all that fussy Habsburg style? Then the sleek, understated, subtly hued rooms here should fit the bill nicely. The balconies offer magnificent views of the Kvarner coast.

Hotel Ambasador   HOTEL €€€

(☑ 051-710 444; www.remisens.com; Feliksa Perišića 1; s/d from €162/190; P ❄ @ 🛜 🏊) A thorough renovation has breathed new life into this Yugoslav-era monolith, bringing smart decor and considerable comfort to the 200 rooms in the 10-storey tower. The complex includes a spa centre, swimming pool, small beach terrace, bars and restaurants.

Hotel Mozart   HOTEL €€€

(☑ 051-718 260; www.hotel-mozart.hr; Obala Maršala Tita 138; s/d from €147/177; P ❄ 🛜 🏊) The beautifully decorated, comfortable, classic rooms harmonise perfectly with the Secession-style halls, dining room and rosy facade in this centrally located hotel. It has its own spa centre and fitness room.

🍴 Eating

Maršala Tita is lined with serviceable restaurants that offer pizza, grilled meat and fish, but don't expect anything outstanding. Head to Volosko for fine dining and regional specialities.

UČKA NATURE PARK

One of Croatia's best-kept natural secrets, this 160-sq-km park lies just 30 minutes from the Opatija Riviera. Comprised of the Učka mountain massif and the adjacent Ćićarija plateau, it's officially split between Kvarner and Istria. Vojak (1401m), its highest peak, affords sublime views of the Italian Alps and the Bay of Trieste on clear days.

Much of the area is covered by beech forest but there are also sweet chestnut trees, oaks and hornbeams. Sheep graze the alpine meadows, golden eagles fly overhead, brown bears roam and endemic bellflowers blossom.

Well-informed staff at the **park office** (☑051-293 753; www.pp-ucka.hr; Liganj 42, Lovran; ☺8am-4.30pm Mon-Fri) will help plan a trip. There are also two seasonal info points: one at **Poklon** (☑051-299 643; ☺9am-6pm mid-Jun–mid-Sep) and another at **Vojak** (☑091 89 59 669; ☺9am-6pm mid-Jun–mid-Sep).

The spectacular canyon of **Vela Draga** on the eastern side of the park is an astounding sight, its valley floor scattered with limestone pillars or 'fairy chimneys'. Raptors including kestrels and peregrine falcons can be seen cruising the thermals here, and eagle owls and wallcreepers are also present. From the highway, it's a lovely 15-minute descent along an interpretive trail to a viewpoint over the canyon.

Mala Učka, a half-abandoned village at over 995m above sea level, is intriguing. A few shepherds live here from May to October and you can buy delicious sheep's cheese from the house with green windows by the stream at the village's end. Just ask for *sir* (cheese).

Organised activities in the park include **mountain biking** and **trekking** on 150km of trails. Pick up a map from the park office or the tourist office in Opatija. There's also **free-climbing** in the Vela Draga canyon, **horse riding** and **birdwatching**. Paragliding and hang-gliding can be organised through **Homo Volans Free Flying Club** (www.homovolans.hr) in Opatija.

For country cooking, **Dopolavoro** (☑051-299 641; www.dopolavoro.hr; Učka 9; mains from 50KN; ☺noon-11pm) offers excellent game – deer steak with blueberries, wild boar with forest mushrooms, venison stew – as well as homemade pasta and delicious sweet platters.

✕ Central Opatija

Kaneta
ISTRIAN €

(☑051-291 643; www.kaneta.fullbusiness.com; Nova Cesta 80; mains 48-75KN; ☺10am-11pm Mon-Sat, noon-7pm Sun) This unassuming family restaurant specialises in big flavours and generous portions: feast on roast veal shanks, roast octopus, game stew, turkey, homemade pasta and risotto. The wine list is well chosen.

Istranka
ISTRIAN €€

(☑051-271 835; www.istranka.net; Bože Milanovića 2; mains 55-150KN) This atmospheric little family-run eatery specialises in Istrian cuisine such as *maneštra* (vegetable and bean soup) and, of course, you'll find plenty of truffles infusing the menu. There's a shady side terrace and live traditional folk music some evenings.

Bevanda
MODERN EUROPEAN €€€

(☑051-493 888; www.bevanda.hr; Zert 8; mains 130-320KN) A marble pathway leads to this amazing-looking restaurant, which enjoys a huge ocean-facing terrace complete with Grecian columns and hip monochrome seating. The contemporary menu features terrific fresh fish and meat dishes, including lots of indulgences (lobster etc).

✕ Volosko

Konoba Ribarnica Volosko
SEAFOOD €

(Andrije Štangera 5; mains 45-80KN; ☺9am-9pm Mon-Sat, 11am-5pm Sun) No cash to splash? This tiny shopfront has Volosko's cheapest fresh fish. Point to your desired sea creature – whatever is in season – and eat the well-prepared dish in a small downstairs dining room around the corner. It's located on the main village road, up from the harbour.

★ Konoba Valle Losca CROATIAN €€

(☑ 095 58 03 757; Andrije Štangera 2; mains 60-95KN; ⊘ 1-10pm Wed-Sat, 12.30-4.30pm Sun) The word *konoba* usually denotes a little family-run eatery – most of which have identikit menus. Here, French and Italian techniques combine with top-notch local ingredients to take things to another level entirely. Yet dishes remain deliciously rustic.

Tramerka CROATIAN €€

(Andrije Mohorovičića 15; mains 50-120KN; ⊘ 1pm-midnight Mon-Sat) It doesn't have sea views but this wonderful place scores on every other level. Actually, the setting is tremendous, a cavelike restaurant that occupies the cool interior of an ancient town house. Staff will expertly guide you through the short menu, chosen from the freshest available seafood and locally sourced meats.

Skalinada CROATIAN €€

(☑ 051-701 109; www.skalinada.org; Put Uz Dol 17; mains from 50-130KN; ⊘ 1pm-midnight Sun, Mon, Wed & Thu, 3pm-2am Fri & Sat) An intimate, highly atmospheric little eatery/bar with sensitive lighting, exposed-stone walls and a creative menu of Croatian food (small dishes or mains) using seasonal and local ingredients. Many local wines are available by the glass.

🍷 Drinking & Nightlife

Opatija is a sedate place. Hotel terraces and Viennese-style coffee houses are popular with the mature clientele, though there are a few stylish bars too.

Hemingway COCKTAIL BAR

(www.hemingway.hr/opatija; Zert 2) A very sleek bar ideal for a cocktail session with cool seating and distant views of the Rijeka skyline. It's the original venue of what's now a nationwide chain; there's an adjoining restaurant too.

Caffe Bar Surf BAR

(Supilova Obala bb; ⊘ 8am-midnight) Prefer somewhere very down to earth? This scruffy but friendly little waterfront bar in Volosko has a shady sea-facing terrace and a good mix of Rijeka trendies and fishing folk.

ℹ Information

Ulica Maršala Tita has numerous ATMs and travel agencies eager to change money. There's free wi-fi in central Opatija and Volosko.

Da Riva (☑ 051-272 990; www.da-riva.hr; Ulica Maršala Tita 170) A good source of private accommodation and excursions around Croatia.

GI Turizam (☑ 051-271 967; www.tourgit.com; Ulica Maršala Tita 65) Finds private accommodation, books excursions, rents cars and changes money.

Post office (Eugena Kumičića 4; ⊘ 7am-8pm Mon-Fri, to 2pm Sat) Behind the market.

Tourist office (☑ 051-271 310; www.opatija-tourism.hr; Ulica Maršala Tita 128; ⊘ 8am-8pm Mon-Sat, 11am-7pm Sun) This office has knowledgable staff and lots of maps, leaflets and brochures.

ℹ Getting There & Away

Bus 32 runs roughly every half hour from Rijeka to Opatija (16KN, 30 minutes) and as far as Lovran; some continue further south along the coast.

Other destinations include Zagreb (119KN to 134KN, three hours, five daily), Pula (72KN, two hours, eight to 10 daily), Zadar (150KN to 170KN, five hours, three daily) and Split (240KN to 278KN, eight hours, three daily).

CRES & LOŠINJ ISLANDS

Separated by only an 11m-wide canal and joined by a bridge, these two sparsely populated and highly scenic islands in the Kvarner archipelago are often treated as a single entity. Although their topography is different, the islands' identities are blurred by a shared history.

Nature lovers will be in heaven here. Both islands are criss-crossed by hiking and biking trails, and the surrounding waters are home to the only known resident population of dolphins in the Adriatic. Much of the sea off the eastern coast is protected by the Lošinj Dolphin Reserve, the first of its kind in the entire Mediterranean.

Wilder, greener Cres (Cherso in Italian) has remote camping grounds, pristine beaches and a handful of medieval villages. There's a real off-the-beaten-track feel to the place and even its most built-up settlement, pretty Cres Town, has a sleepy vibe in all but the height of summer. Note, the name 'Cres' is pronounced with a 'ts' sound – like 'tsar' – and not at all like the English 'cress'.

The more populated and touristy of the twin islands, 31km-long Lošinj (Lussino in Italian) has a more indented coastline than Cres, especially in the south where there are some beautiful bays. Vegetation is lush and varied, with 1100 plant species, 230 medicinal herbs and some atypical growths such as lemon, banana, cedar and eucalyptus brought from exotic lands by sea captains. Pine forests encircle the pretty port towns of Mali Lošinj and Veli Lošinj, both of which attract plenty of tourists in summer.

History

Excavations indicate that a prehistoric culture spread out over both islands from the Stone Age to the Bronze Age. The ancient Greeks called the islands the Apsyrtides. They were in turn conquered by the Romans, then put under Byzantine rule and settled by Slavic tribes in the 6th and 7th centuries.

The islands subsequently came under Venetian rule, followed by that of the Croatian-Hungarian kings, then back to the Venetians. By the time Venice fell in 1797, Veli Lošinj and Mali Lošinj had become important maritime centres, while Cres devoted itself to wine and olive production.

During the 19th century shipbuilding flourished in Lošinj, but with the advent of steamships it was replaced by health tourism as the major industry. Meanwhile, Cres had its own problems in the form of a phylloxera epidemic that wiped out its vineyards. Both islands were poor when they were annexed to Italy as part of the 1920 Treaty of Rapallo. They became part of Yugoslavia in 1945 and, most recently, Croatia in 1991.

Today, apart from a small shipyard in Nerezine in north Lošinj and some olive cultivation, sheep farming and fishing on Cres, the main source of income on both islands is tourism. Until very recently one of Cres' main income sources was rearing sheep (the island's lamb is famed for its flavour) but the introduction of wild boar for hunting has upset the unique environment and an age-old culture is now waning.

ⓘ Getting There & Away

BOAT

Jadrolinija (☑ 051-231 765; www.jadrolinija.hr; Riva Lošinjskih Kapetana 22, Mali Lošinj) runs the main car ferries between Brestova (on the mainland, 29km south of Opatija) and Porozina on Cres (per adult/child/car 18/9/115KN, 20 minutes, seven to 13 daily); and between Valbiska on Krk and Merag on Cres (18/9/115KN, 25 minutes, nine to 13 daily).

A weekly (daily in July and August) car ferry runs between Mali Lošinj and Zadar

(59/30/271KN, seven hours), stopping at some of the smaller islands en route.

There's also a passenger-only ferry which loops from Mali Lošinj to the islands of Unije (1½ hours) and Susak (one hour) twice daily.

UTO Kapetan Luka (☑ 021-645 476; www.krilo.hr) has daily passenger-only ferries from Rijeka to Cres Town (45KN, 1¼ hours) and Mali Lošinj (60KN, three to 4½ hours) year-round, some of which also stop at Martinšćica (50KN, two hours). Some of these boats also stop at the islands of Unije, Susak and Ilovik.

Venezia Lines (☑ 052-422 896; www.venezialines.com) runs a catamaran on Saturdays in July and August between Mali Lošinj and Venice (adult/child €78/48, 4¾ hours).

BUS

Most bus services in the islands begin (or end) in Veli Lošinj and stop in Mali Lošinj and Cres. Off-island destinations include Malinska on Krk (101KN to 126KN, 2½ hours, daily), Opatija (153KN, 3½ hours, daily), Rijeka (135KN, 3½ hours, weekdays) and Zagreb (233KN to 291KN, six hours, twice daily)

Beli

☑ 051 / POP 35

Clinging to a 130m hill above a lovely pebbly beach, Beli is one of Cres' oldest settlements. Its 4000-year history can be felt in its twisting lanes and austere stone town houses overgrown with plants. You can walk a loop around this evocative but diminutive settlement in five minutes or so, stopping at a viewpoint to take in incredible vistas over the Adriatic to the mainland mountains.

Even with its diminutive population, Beli is the main settlement in the Tramuntana region which covers the island's northern tip. It's a place that time forgot, with ancient virgin forests, abandoned villages, lone chapels and myths of good elves. Much of it is covered with dense oak, hornbeam

MOŠĆENIČKA DRAGA

Halfway between Opatija and the ferry port at Brestova, this little resort town (population 585) is particularly popular with families. There's a long pebbly beach, a little marina, several cafes and a few oversized Yugoslav-era hotels. The **tourist office** (☑ 051-739 166; www.tz-moscenicka.hr; Aleja Slatina bb) lists accommodation on its website.

KVARNER BELI

and chestnut forest and it's prime cruising terrain for the protected griffon vulture.

Note that the road leading to Beli is narrow and winding, and necessitates some tight squeezes if you pass vehicles coming in the other direction, but it's very scenic and ultimately worth it. The road to the beach is even more narrow, steep and terrifying but it still beats the walk back up.

🏃 Activities

Diving Beli   DIVING
(🖉051-840 519; www.diving-beli.com; beach/boat dives €15/25) Based at the beach below Beli, this local outfit offers boat- and beach-based dive trips; nondivers can come along too.

🛏 Sleeping & Eating

Autokamp Brajdi   CAMPGROUND €
(🖉051-840 532; www.perica666.wix.com/autokamp-brajdi; Sv Petar 1a; per adult/child 57/34KN; ☺May-Sep; 🅿) Situated in an olive grove right by the beach, this is a pretty spot to pitch a tent but the facilities are fairly basic. There's a summertime snack bar nearby.

Pansion Tramontana   B&B €€
(🖉051-840 519; www.beli-tramontana.com; s/d 413/600KN; ☺Mar-Dec; 🅿🌼@🛜) On the approach to Beli, this attractive place has 12 comfortable rooms upstairs and a fine rustic restaurant (mains 40KN to 150KN) below, where great chunks of meat are barbecued. Fish, pasta, risotto and superb organic salads are available too, as is draught Guinness.

ℹ Getting There & Away

On weekdays there's a bus from Cres Town to Beli (34KN, 30 minutes).

Cres Town

📲051 / POP 2880

Pastel-coloured terrace houses and Venetian mansions hug the medieval harbour of Cres Town, a beautiful sheltered bay encircled by vivid green hills of pine trees and Adriatic scrub. As you stroll along the seaside promenade and the atmospheric maze of old town streets, you'll notice reminders of Italian rule, including coats of arms of powerful Venetian families and Renaissance loggias.

The town's strong Italian influence dates back to the 15th century when Venetians relocated here after Osor fell victim to plague and pestilence. Public buildings and patricians' palaces were built along the harbour and a town wall was added in the 16th century.

⊙ Sights

Trg Frane Petrića   SQUARE
Right by the harbour, the main town square was the scene of public announcements, financial transactions and festivals under Venetian rule. It's now the site of a morning fruit-and-vegetable market. Look out for the graceful 16th-century **gate**, topped by a blue-faced clock and coats of arms.

THE HUNTERS & THE HUNTED

Cres' semiwild tramuntana sheep are unique to the island and perfectly adapted to the karst pastures that were first developed by the Illyrians over 1000 years ago. But now the island's culture of free-range sheep farming is on the slide. A couple of decades ago Cres had 100,000 tramuntana sheep; now it's around 15,000. One of the main factors in this decline has been the introduction of wild boar by Croatia's powerful hunting lobby. Boar numbers have grown exponentially (they have even spread as far as the campsites in Mali Lošinj). Wild boar prey on sheep and lambs – in the winter of 2006 Beli's Eco-Centre Caput Insulae documented 2500 lamb kills due to boar attacks, though the actual figure is thought to be much higher.

Declining sheep numbers have an impact on the environment in many ways. Griffon vultures now don't have enough sheep carrion to survive upon, and have to be fed at feeding sites by volunteers. As pastureland has dwindled, juniper and thornbush have replaced native grasses and wildflowers with a resulting drop in plant biodiversity. Low stone walls used by sheep farmers called *gromače* used to criss-cross Cres, acting as windbreaks and preventing soil erosion, but these are no longer maintained and many are crumbling away.

St Mary of the Snow Church
CHURCH

(Sv Marije Snježne; ⊘ Mass only) Just inside the main harbour gate, this church's facade is notable for the Renaissance portal with a relief of the Virgin and Child. A glassed-in foyer allows you to peer inside but the church is only open at Mass times. If you do find it open, look for the carved wooden pietà from the 15th century (now under protective glass) at the left altar.

Ruta
ARTS CENTRE

(☑ 051-571 835; www.ruta-cres.hr; Zazid 4; ⊘ sporadic or by appointment) This fascinating local collective promotes the island's cultural tradition of wool weaving and felting. Using the discarded wool of indigenous Cres sheep, the craftspeople make wonderful slippers, hats, handbags and clothes. If you're lucky enough to find someone here, you can see the workshop, learn about felting and maybe even try it yourself.

🏃 Activities

There's an attractive promenade on the west side of the bay with sunbathing zones and good swimming, and good beaches around Hotel Kimen. Drop by the tourist office for a map of walking and cycling trails around Cres.

Diving Cres
DIVING

(☑ 051-571 706; www.divingcres.de; Melin 1/20; boat dive incl equipment €50) Based in Kamp Kovačine, this German crew offers PADI (Professional Association of Diving Instructors) and SSI (Scuba Schools International) courses and fun dives.

🛏 Sleeping

For the cheapest accommodation, contact travel agencies for private room rentals. Single rooms in Cres Town start at around €29, doubles cost from €38.

Kamp Kovačine
CAMPGROUND €

(☑ 051-573 150; www.camp-kovacine.com; Melin 1/20; camping per adult/child/site €12/5/11, s/d €48/86, cabins from €81; ⊘ Easter–mid-Oct; P @ 🛜 🐾) With a fine location on the tip of a little wooded peninsula about 1km southwest of town, this large camping ground offers excellent bathrooms, beachside bathing platforms, a restaurant and activities galore. A quarter of the area is reserved for naturists, including some of the beach. Private rooms are available in Tamaris, a small guest house near the water.

A VILLAGE FEAST

Cres lamb gets the top billing at this down-to-earth village restaurant **Konoba Bukaleta** (☑ 051-571 606; Loznati 99; mains 40-100KN; ⊘ noon-11pm Apr-Sep), which has been run by the same family for over 30 years. Try it breaded, grilled or roasted on the spit, or tuck into homemade gnocchi and pasta instead. Bukaleta is in Loznati, 5km south of Cres Town, and signposted from the highway. It also rents out rooms (€40).

Hotel Kimen
HOTEL €€

(☑ 051-573 305; www.hotel-kimen.com; Melin 1/16; s/d from €81/94; P ❄ @ 🛜 🐾) With a beachside location and grounds shaded by pine trees, this large Yugoslav-era hotel has been thoroughly renovated and offers fresh-looking rooms with balconies. Rooms in the neighbouring 'Depandance' are cheaper, but the main hotel is much nicer.

🍴 Eating

Feral
CROATIAN €€

(☑ 051-573 101; Riva Creskih Kapetana 9; mains 50-120KN; ⊘ 7am-11pm) The name refers to a ship's lantern, not some kind of wild beast, so you can relax into a lazy harbourside reverie while tucking into local cheeses, pasta, grilled meat and seafood. Traditional favourites such as fish soup and grilled squid are deftly executed.

Riva
SEAFOOD €€

(Riva Creskih Kapetana 13; mains 60-70KN; ⊘ 10am-11pm) This well-established place spills onto the harbourside promenade and is many locals' choice for fish and seafood: scampi, squid and prawns.

ℹ Information

Cresanka (☑ 051-750 600; www.cresanka.hr; Varozina 25) Local travel agency which books private rooms, apartments, campsites and hotels.

Post office (Cons 3; ⊘ 7.30am-9pm Mon-Sat Jun-Aug, 7am-8pm Mon-Fri, to 2pm Sat Sep-May)

Tourist Agency Croatia (☑ 051-573 053; www.cres-travel.com; Cons 10; ⊘ 8am-1pm & 4-7pm Mon-Sat, 10am-1pm Sun) Travel agency which arranges private accommodation, has internet access and hires out boats, bikes, cars and scooters.

THE THREATENED GRIFFON VULTURE

With a wingspan of almost 3m, measuring about 1m from end to end, and weighing 7kg to 9kg, the Eurasian griffon vulture looks big enough to take passengers. It cruises comfortably at 40km/h to 75km/h, reaching speeds of up to 160km/h. The vulture's powerful beak and long neck are ideally suited to rummaging around the entrails of its prey, which is most likely to be a dead sheep.

Finding precious sheep carcasses is a team effort for griffon vultures. Usually a colony of birds will set out and fly in a comb formation of up to a kilometre apart. When one of the vultures spots a carcass, it circles as a signal for its neighbours to join in the feast. Shepherds don't mind griffons, reasoning that the birds prevent whatever disease or infection killed the sheep from spreading to other livestock.

The total known number of griffon vultures in Croatia is around 280, more than half of them living on the coastal cliffs of Cres, the others in small colonies on Krk and Prvić islands. The birds' dietary preferences mean that griffons tend to follow sheep although they will eat other dead mammals, to their peril: the last remaining birds in Paklenica National Park died after eating poisoned foxes, and in 2005 20 Cres vultures died after eating poisoned meat.

The griffon population now enjoys legal protection as an endangered species in Croatia. Killing a bird or disturbing it while nesting carries a €5000 fine. Intentional killing is rare but because the young birds cannot fly more than 500m on a windless day, tourists on speedboats who provoke them into flight often end up threatening their lives. The exhausted birds drop into the water and drown.

Breeding habits discourage a large population, as a pair of griffons only produces one fledgling a year and it takes five years for the young bird to reach maturity. During that time the growing griffons travel widely: one tagged in Paklenica National Park was found in Chad, 4000km away. When they're about five, the vultures head home to Cres (sometimes to the same rock where they were born) to find a mate, who will be a partner for life.

Captive vultures can live for over 55 years, but in the wild 20 to 30 years is more normal. The dangers facing young Cres vultures include the guns of Italian hunters, poison and power lines, but by far the biggest issue is the massive decline in sheep farming in Cres, which is reducing the birds' food source day by day.

If you want to find out more about Croatia's griffon vultures, contact the **Grifon Birds of Prey Conservation Centre** (Grifon centar za zaštitu ptica grabljivica; ☑ 091 357 123; www.supovi.hr) on the mainland, 14km south of Senj.

Tourist office (☑ 051-571 535; www.tzg-cres.hr; Cons 11; ⊘ 8am-noon & 3.30-8pm Mon-Sat, 9am-1pm Sun Jun-Aug, 8am-2pm Mon-Fri Sep-May) Well stocked with maps and brochures, including accommodation listings with photographs.

❶ Getting There & Away

Two to seven buses per day head to Osor (42KN, 45 minutes), Mali Lošinj (48KN to 60KN, 1¼ hours) and Veli Lošinj (52KN to 65KN, 1½ hours). There are also buses to Beli (34KN, 30 minutes) on weekdays and to Valun (30KN, 22 minutes) up to three times a week.

UTO Kapetan Luka has daily passenger-only ferries to/from Mali Lošinj (45KN, 1½ to 3¼ hours), some of which also stop at Martinšćica (20KN, 40 minutes).

❶ Getting Around

Gonzo Bikes (☑ 051-573 107; Turion 8; per hour/day 20/90KN; ⊘ Mar-Dec) rents out good-quality bikes and camping equipment from its Cres base, as well as bikes from Hotel Kimen and various campgrounds.

Valun

☑ 051 / POP 65

The pretty seaside hamlet of Valun, 14km southwest of Cres Town, is secluded at the foot of cliffs and surrounded by pebbly beaches. Its appeal lies in its tranquillity: its restaurants are rarely crowded, and there's a refreshing lack of souvenir stalls or touristy tack.

Park in the lot above the village and take the steep steps down. To the right of the harbour, a path leads to a beach and camping ground. About 700m in the other direction there's another lovely pebble beach bordered by pines.

◎ Sights

St Mary's Church   CHURCH
(⊘sporadic) The parish church houses the village's main sight, the 11th-century Valun Tablet. Inscribed in both Glagolitic and Latin, this tombstone reflects the ethnic composition of the island, which was inhabited by Roman descendants and newcomers who spoke Croatian.

✕ Eating & Drinking

Camping Zdovice   CAMPGROUND €
(☑051-571 161; www.cresanka.hr; per adult/child 103/42KN; ⊘May-Sep; 🕮) This idyllic camping ground is a small affair with pitches occupying old terraced fields right by a great swimming beach. There's also a volleyball court and a clean toilet block. The Cresanka agency handles the bookings and registrations.

Konoba Toš-Juna   SEAFOOD €€
(mains 45-95KN; ⊘10am-11pm) Of Valun's half a dozen restaurants, this one stands out for its seafood and attractive terrace emblazoned with Glagolitic writing. It's inside a converted olive mill with exposed-stone walls, right by the harbour and the church.

❶ Information

Cresanka (☑051-525 050; www.cresanka.hr; ⊘8am-8pm May-Sep) This branch of a Cres Town–based agency doubles as the village's tourist ofice, as well as booking private rooms and ferry tickets. Accommodation in Valun is scarce and usually reserved well in advance.

❶ Getting There & Away

Valun is not well served by public transport. Buses head to and from Cres Town (30KN, 22 minutes) on Monday, Wednesday and Friday in summer, with fewer services in winter.

Lubenice

☑051 / POP 24

Perched on an exposed rocky ridge, 378m above the western shore of the island, this medieval hilltop hamlet is one of the most evocative places in Cres. Semi-abandoned, Lubenice's maze of ancient austere stone houses and churches seems fused to the very bedrock of the island itself.

It sits above one of Kvarner's most remote and beautiful beaches, a secluded cove accessible by a steep path through the bush. The 45-minute descent is a breeze, but coming up is more of a challenge (you could consider taking a taxi boat from Valun or Cres).

✪ Festivals & Events

Lubenice Musical Evenings   MUSIC
(Lubeničke Glazbene Večeri; ⊘Jul-Aug) Alfresco classical concerts are held every Friday night in July and August.

✕ Eating & Drinking

Konoba Hibernicia   CROATIAN €
(Lubenice 17; mains 45-75KN; ⊘11am-8pm) Extremely rustic, with stone walls and an outdoor terrace popular with the village cats, this humble eatery is notable for its lamb dishes and local ham.

Lubenička Loza   CAFE, BAR
(⊘10am-8pm Jun-Sep) By the entrance to the village, this is a great spot to stop for a beer and a snack.

❶ Getting There & Away

If you've got the time and the inclination, the very best way to get here is on foot: it's a one-hour hike from Valun.

In summer two daily buses connect Lubenice with Cres Town (34KN, 30 minutes), except on Sunday. One also heads here from Valun (26KN, 31 minutes).

If you're driving up, note that the road is narrow and winding.

Osor

☑051 / POP 60

The tiny walled town of Osor is one of the most peaceful places you could imagine, despite its grand and troubled past. The village sits on the narrow channel dividing Cres and Lošinj, which is thought to have been dug by the Romans. Because of it, Osor was able to control a key navigational route.

In the 6th century a bishopric was established here, with authority over both islands throughout the Middle Ages. Until the 15th century Osor was a strong commercial, religious and political presence in the region, but a combination of plague, malaria and new sea routes devastated the town's economy and it slowly decayed.

Now it's becoming a kind of a museum-town of churches, open-air sculptures and lanes that meander from its 15th-century town centre. Look out for the Ivan Meštrović statue *Daleki akordi* (distant chords), one of the town's many modern sculptures on a musical theme.

When crossing from Lošinj to Osor, you may have to wait at the drawbridge spanning the Kavuada Canal, as the bridge is raised twice a day (at 9am and 5pm) to allow boats to pass.

◉ Sights

Entering through the gate on the canal, you pass old city walls and the remains of a castle before you hit the centre of town.

Osor Archaeological Collection   MUSEUM
(Arheološka Zbirka Osor; www.muzej.losinj.hr; adult/child 10/5KN; ⊘10am-1pm & 7-10pm Tue-Sun mid-Jun–mid Sep, 10am-2pm Tue-Sat Easter–mid-Jun & mid-Sep–Oct) On the main square in the 15th-century town hall, this outpost of the Lošinj Museum contains a collection of stone fragments, reliefs, ceramics and sculptures from the Roman, early Christian and medieval periods.

Church of the Assumption   CHURCH
(Crkva Uznešenja; ⊘10am-noon & 7-9pm Jun-Sep) Completed in 1498, this large church's rich Renaissance portal faces onto the main square. The baroque altar inside has relics of St Gaudentius, Osor's patron saint.

✯ Festivals & Events

Osor Musical Evenings   MUSIC
(Osorske glazbene večeri; www.osorskeveceri.org; ⊘mid-Jul–Aug) From mid-July to late August, high-calibre Croatian artists perform classical music in the cathedral and on the main square.

⊨ Sleeping & Eating

The tourist office (p155) in Mali Lošinj has listings of private rooms and apartments.

Camping Bijar   CAMPGROUND €
(☑051-237 147; www.camps-cres-losinj.com; camping per adult/child/site €9/6/6; ⊘May-Sep; ℗ 🛜 🏊) Set amongst the pines on a lovely pebbly cove 500m from Osor, this attractive camping ground offers fabulous swimming as well as table tennis, volleyball and basketball.

Osor Pansion   B&B €
(☑051-237 135; www.ossero.com; Osor 28; s/d 329/438KN; ℗ ❄ 🏊) Seven simple pine-trimmed rooms, each with its own bathroom, are available at this little guesthouse above a garden restaurant (mains 60KN to 200KN). Breakfasts are excellent, and it's worth calling back later for a meal of Cres lamb or Adriatic fish.

Konoba Bonifačić   CROATIAN €€
(Osor 64; mains 50-100KN; ⊘noon-11pm) Tuck into home cooking – such as dependable risottos, grilled meat and fish, and traditional pork with sage – in a particularly lovely garden setting. Have a shot of elderflower grappa while you're there.

ⓘ Getting There & Away

Depending on the time of the year and the day of the week, between two and seven buses a day pass through Osor en route to Cres Town (42KN, 45 minutes), Nerezine (19KN, five minutes), Mali Lošinj (32KN, 30 minutes) and Veli Lošinj (38KN, 45 minutes). Some also head to Martinšćica (35KN, 20 minutes).

Mali Lošinj
☑051 / POP 6100

Mali Lošinj is a stunner: a natural harbour ringed by graceful, gently weathered Mediterranean town houses and green surrounding hills. The town straddles both coasts on the narrowest section of the island, at the apex of a long protected harbour. A string of imposing 19th-century sea captains' houses lines the seafront, and even with the summer tourist commotion, this historic quarter still retains its charm and atmosphere.

All of the resort hotels are just out of town by the pebbly beaches **Sunčana Uvala** (meaning 'Sunny Bay') and **Čikat**. This leafy area started to flourish in the late 19th century, when the wealthy Vienna and Budapest elite, who gravitated to the 'healthy air' of Mali Lošinj, started building villas and luxurious hotels around Čikat. Some of these grand residences remain, but most of the current hotels are modern developments surrounded by pine forests that blanket the coves and its pretty beaches.

Although it's more relaxed visiting in spring and autumn, a visit to Mali Lošinj is worthwhile even in the hectic summer months. It's also a good base for excursions to the small islands of Susak, Ilovik and Unije nearby.

In 1996 an exquisite bronze statue was found on the seabed near Lošinj, thought to date from the 2nd or 1st century BC. It takes the form of a popular Ancient Greek subject known as *Apoxyomenos* ('The Scraper', *Apoksiomen* in Croatian), featuring a muscular naked male athlete scraping the dirt, oil and sweat from his body with a tool known as a *strigil*. At the time of writing it still resides in Zagreb's Mimara Museum but is expected to return to Lošinj once its specially designed museum opens inside the Kvarner Palace on the waterfront.

⊙ Sights

Fritzy Palace   MUSEUM
(Palača Fritzy; www.muzej.losinj.hr; Vladimira Gortana 35; adult/concession 10/5KN; ⊙ 10am-1pm & 7-10pm Tue-Sun Jul & Aug, 10am-1pm & 6-8pm Tue-Fri, 10am-1pm Sat Apr-Jun & Sep-Dec) The largest branch of the three-headed Lošinj Museum (the others are in Osor and Veli Lošinj), this grand mansion houses three distinct collections: a moderately interesting set of mainly 17th- and 18th-century paintings; a more interesting array of early 20th-century photographs; and a fascinating display of 20th-century art.

The most intriguing exhibit is one of the smallest: a 10cm-high, possibly Etruscan, clay statue dating from the 7th century BC, known as the 'Lady of Čikat'. In the modern section, look out for works by Croatia's three most important 20th-century sculptors: Ivan Meštrović, Frano Kršinić and Antun Augustinčić.

Garden of Fine Scents   GARDENS
(Miomirisni Otočki Vrt; www.miomirisni-vrt.hr; Bukovica 6; ⊙ 8.30am-12.30pm & 6-9pm Jul & Aug, 8am-3pm Mar-Jun & Sep-Dec) FREE This fragrant paradise on the southern edge of town has over 250 native plant varieties plus 100 exotic species, all framed with *gromače* (traditional stone fences). Natural fragrances, salts and liquors are sold too.

Church of the Nativity   CHURCH
(Župna Crkva Male Gospe; Sv Marije bb) The parish church (built 1696–1775) towers over the town from the ridge. Inside are some notable artworks, including a painting of the Nativity by an 18th-century Venetian artist, and relics of St Romulus. It's usually only open around Mass times.

Sea Turtle Rescue Centre   WILDLIFE CENTRE
(Oporavilište za Morske Kornjače; www.blue-world.org; Sunčana Uvala bb; ⊙ 10am-2pm Mon-Fri Jun-Sep) 🖉 FREE Small but extremely interesting, this centre is dedicated to rehabilitating injured sea turtles, most of which have been entangled in plastic or fishing nets. There aren't a lot of displays but the staff on hand will talk you through their work. You might even get to see some of the patients. It's located between the hotels Adriatic and Vespera, just up from the promenade.

🏃 Activities

Cycling and **hiking** have become increasingly popular on Lošinj. The tourist office (p155) has an excellent brochure, *Promenades & Footpaths,* with maps of 250km of trails and accurate walking times. All five islands of the archipelago (Lošinj, Cres, Ilovik, Susak and Unije) are covered. Climb the highest peak of Televrina (588m) for great views, hike to the remote coves south of Mali Lošinj or access secret bays on Susak.

Diver Sport Center   DIVING
(🖉 051-233 900; www.diver.hr) Lošinj has good diving with excellent visibility and good sea life. There's a wreck dating from 1917, a large, relatively shallow cave suitable for beginners, and the wonderful Margarita Reef off the island of Susak. Based by the water at Čikat, this centre offers a 'Discovery' course (€55) and the SSI Open Water certification (€340).

Croyak   KAYAKING, SAILING
(🖉 098 92 31 034; www.croyak.com; per 2hr/half-day/day €40/60/95) Rents out an odd tandem kayak-trimaran hybrid which can be propelled by both pedals and a sail. It is based by the dive shop and Konoba Cigale at Čikat.

BEACHSIDE CAMPING

Tucked away on the west coast of Cres by a nondescript fishing village called Martinšćica, **Campsite Slatina** (🖉 051-574 127; www.camps-cres-losinj.com; camping per adult/child/site from €9/5/7, unit from 820KN; ⊙ May-Sep) offers access to two lovely pebbly beaches. The complex includes restaurants, a pizzeria, cafes, a grocery shop, a dive school and boat and bike hire. Despite its large size (500 sites), it's well spaced out and doesn't feel too cramped.

KVARNER MALI LOŠINJ

NEREZINE

The first town on the Lošinj side of the bridge, little Nerezine has a pretty harbour lined with pastel houses and a few cafe-bars. It's Lošinj's third-biggest settlement, with a whopping great population of 353. All buses travelling the main highway stop here.

Hidden in its outskirts, cheerful wee **Hotel Manora** ([☎] 051-237 460; www.manora-losinj.hr; Magdalenska 26b; r €139; [P][✳][@][🤶][🏊]) is brightly painted inside and out, and extremely well set up for families. There's an enticing swimming pool, a sauna, an outdoor playground and even an indoor playroom for when the weather turns bad.

Sunbird   WINDSURFING, SAILING
([☎] 095 83 77 142; www.sunbird.de) Čikat is a good spot for windsurfing, with its narrow shingle beach and great wind exposure. This German outfit, based on the beach near the Hotel Bellevue, offers courses in windsurfing (from 970KN) and sailing catamarans (from 675KN). It also rents windsurfers (from 60KN per hour), kayaks (per hour/day 35/150KN) and bikes (20/95KN).

🛏 Sleeping

Camping Village Poljana   CAMPGROUND €
([☎] 051-231 726; www.poljana.hr; Rujnica 9a; camping per adult/child/site 69/61/54KN, units from 525KN; [P][✳][🤶]) Surrounded by mature trees, this complex on the northern approach to Mali Lošinj has power-fitted pitches, good air-conditioned units, a restaurant and a supermarket. There is also a small pebble beach and a rocky area for nude bathers.

Camping Čikat   CAMPGROUND €
([☎] 051-231 708; www.camps-cres-losinj.com; Dražica 1; camping per adult/child/site from 66/42/46KN, units from 122KN; [☉] Apr-Dec; [🤶][🏊]) More of a canvas and caravan city than a camping ground, this huge pine-shaded place has hundreds of pitches and dozens of units spread along a rocky coastline. There's also a restaurant and a grocery store.

Alaburić   B&B €€
([☎] 051-231 343; Stjepana Radića 17; r/apt €65/89; [P][🤶][🏊]) A welcoming family-run guesthouse with simple, well-equipped rooms and apartments, all with bathrooms – two have

distant sea views. It's in a suburban street just below the Garden of Fine Scents.

⭐**Mare Mare Suites**   HOTEL €€€
([☎] 051-232 010; www.mare-mare.com; Riva Lošinjskih Kapetana 36; s/d/apt 720/810/1200KN; [P][✳][@][🤶]) Enjoying a prime position towards the northern end of the harbour, this historic town house has been converted into immaculately presented, individually styled rooms and an apartment with a private terrace. There's a rooftop spa pool and free use of kayaks and bikes.

Hotel Aurora   RESORT €€€
([☎] 051-667 200; www.losinj-hotels.com; Sunčana Uvala bb; s/d/ste from 950/1262/2006KN; [☉] Feb-Dec; [P][✳][@][🤶][🏊]) ⚘ This former state-owned behemoth is now the very model of a modern resort hotel. Rooms are decorated in sunny shades and each has its own balcony. If you're not tempted by the brilliant blue waters of the beach below, there are indoor and outdoor pools, and a very good spa centre. The Aurora even has its own customised scent.

Hotel Vespera   RESORT €€€
([☎] 051-667 300; www.losinj-hotels.com; Sunčana Uvala bb; s/d/ste from 973/1292/2113KN; [☉] Easter-Oct; [P][✳][@][🤶][🏊]) Vespera is very much oriented to families. This huge hotel has excellent facilities including tennis courts, a large resort-style pool and two smaller kids' pools. Plus the beach is right at its doorstep.

Hotel Apoksiomen   HOTEL €€€
([☎] 051-520 820; www.apoksiomen.com; Riva Lošinjskih Kapetana 1; s/d from €108/144; [✳][🤶]) A well-run harbourside hotel where the 25 modern rooms have satellite TVs, safes and contemporary bathrooms. Staff are helpful and there's a cafe and restaurant on the ground floor. Book via the website for the best deals.

🍴 Eating & Drinking

Most of the harbourside restaurants have great views but they tend to serve bog-standard fare (pasta, seafood and grilled meats), with little variety in price or quality.

Baracuda   CROATIAN, SEAFOOD €€
([☎] 051-233 309; Priko 31; mains 60-140KN; [☉] noon-midnight) Baracuda is highly rated for the freshness of its fish, the skills of the chefs and the cheeky charm of the waiting staff. There's a large terrace and usually a daily special or two chalked up on the blackboard.

If you're ordering fish by the kilo, it pays to check the price first.

Konoba Cigale
CROATIAN €€

(☎051-238 583; Sabina Hausknecht bb; mains 70-140KN; ⊗9am-10pm) With a large terrace overlooking the water at Čikat, this laid-back eatery makes a good job of the usual selection of grilled meat, seafood, pasta and salads. Its homemade pasta with truffles is excellent, and if there's a group of you and you call ahead, they'll cook lamb under a *peka* (traditional domed baking lid).

Porto
CROATIAN, SEAFOOD €€

(Sveti Martin 33; mains 45-120KN; ⊗7am-midnight Mar-Sep) Up over the hill on the east side of town, this fine fish restaurant sits on a pretty bay next to a church. Fish fillet with sea urchins is the signature dish, but all seafood is expertly prepared and presented.

Konoba Bukaleta
CROATIAN €€

(☎098 17 08 155; Del Conte Giovanni; mains 45-130KN; ⊗10am-11pm) A great place for a casual lunch or dinner. Specialities include lamb cooked under a *peka*.

Priko
BAR

(Priko 2; 🖥) On summer evenings the terrace of this harbourside bar is the place to be, with live music most nights.

ℹ Information

Cappelli (☎051-231 582; www.cappelli-tourist. hr; Lošinjskih Brodograditelja 57) Travel agency which books private accommodation on Cres and Lošinj, and offers cruises and excursions.

Manora (☎051-520 100; www.manora-losinj. hr; Priko 29) Friendly agency associated with Nerezine's Hotel Manora, which hires scooters (per day 330KN) and mountain bikes (per day 120KN).

Post office (Vladimira Gortana 4; ⊗7.30am-9pm Mon-Sat Jun-Aug, 8am-7pm Mon-Fri Sep-May)

San Mar (☎051-238 293; Priko 24) Travel agency which rents out private accommodation, mountain bikes (per day 70KN), mopeds (250KN) and boats (from 1000KN, license required). It also exchanges foreign currencies.

Tourist office (☎051-231 884; www. tz-malilosinj.hr; Riva Lošinjskih Kapetana 29; ⊗8am-8pm Mon-Sat, 9am-1pm Sun Jun-Sep, 8am-3pm Mon-Fri Oct-May) A very useful office, with knowledgeable staff and tons of (practical and glossy) leaflets and maps, plus a comprehensive accommodation list with owners' emails and websites.

ℹ Getting There & Away

Island buses head to/from Veli Lošinj (12KN, 12 minutes, four to 16 daily), Nerezine (32KN, 30 minutes, two to nine daily), Osor (32KN,

---

ISLANDS AROUND LOŠINJ

The nearby car-free islands of Susak, Ilovik and Unije are the most popular day trips from Mali Lošinj. Tiny **Susak** (population 151, area 3.8 sq km) is unique for the thick layer of fine sand that blankets the underlying limestone and creates excellent beaches. It's the island's unusual culture that makes it particularly interesting. Islanders speak their own dialect, which is nearly incomprehensible to other Croats. On feast days and at weddings you can see the local women outfitted in traditional multicoloured skirts (a little like tutus) and red leggings. When you see the old stone houses on the island, consider that each stone had to be brought over from Mali Lošinj and carried by hand to its destination. The island has steadily lost its population in the last few decades (it was over 1600 in 1948), with many of its citizens settling in Hoboken, New Jersey.

In contrast to flat Susak, **Ilovik** (population 85, area 5.8 sq km) is a hilly island known for its profusion of flowers. Overgrown with oleanders, roses and eucalyptus trees, it's popular with boaters and has some secluded swimming coves.

The largest of the islands, **Unije** (population 88, area 18 sq km) has an undulating landscape that abounds with Mediterranean shrubs, pebble beaches and numerous coves and inlets. The island's only settlement is a picturesque fishing village of gabled stone houses.

Travel agencies in Mali Lošinj sell excursions to the islands or you can peruse the boats moored along the harbour and see which deal takes your fancy.

Otherwise, Jadrolinija has a passenger-only ferry which loops from Mali Lošinj to Unije (1½ hours) and Susak (one hour) twice daily. Most of UTO Kapetan Luka's daily Rijeka/ Cres Town/Martinšćica/Mali Lošinj ferries also service the islands, stopping at Unije and Susak five days a week and at Ilovik on two.

A COVE OF YOUR OWN

South of Mali Lošinj the island forms a glorious, barely inhabited, thumb-shaped peninsula that's blessed with exquisite natural bays and is perfect for hiking (pick up a map from the tourist office). One lonely road snakes down the spine of this hilly, wooded landmass, eventually fizzling out at Mrtvaška, Lošinj's land's end. You can circumnavigate the entire peninsula on foot in a full day, stopping to swim at deserted coves. If you only want to hit one beach, drive 5km to the turn-off for **Krivica**. It's a 30-minute descent from the parking area to this idyllic, sheltered bay which is ringed by pine trees. The water is emerald-tinged and superb for swimming.

30 minutes, two to seven daily) and Cres Town (48KN to 60KN, 1¼ hours, two to seven daily).

UTO Kapetan Luka has daily passenger-only ferries to/from Cres Town (45KN, 1½ to 3¼ hours), some of which also stop at Martinšćica (35KN, two hours).

❶ Getting Around

Between late April and mid-October there's an hourly shuttle bus (10KN) that runs from the town centre to the hotel district in Sunčana Uvala and Čikat.

Note that you have to pay to enter the centre of Mali Lošinj in a car (two hours 20KN).

Veli Lošinj

📞051 / POP 900

Despite the name (in Croatian, *veli* means big and *mali* means small), Veli Lošinj is much smaller, more languid and somewhat less crowded than Mali Lošinj, only 4km to the northwest. It's an exceptionally scenic place, really nothing more than a huddle of pastel-coloured houses, cafes, hotels and stores around a tiny harbour. Dolphins sometimes enter the narrow mouth of the bay in April and May. Don't miss a walk to Rovenska, another idyllic little bay, a 10-minute stroll along a coastal path to the southeast.

Like its neighbour, Veli Lošinj had its share of rich sea captains who built villas and surrounded them with gardens of exotic plants they brought back from afar. You can

glimpse these villas on a walk up the steep streets from the harbour. Sea captains also furnished the churches in town, most notably St Anthony's on the harbour.

You'll have to park up above the bay and hoof it down the narrow cobblestone streets in the summer months.

◉ Sights

Church of St Anthony the Hermit   CHURCH
(Obala Maršala Tita) Built in baroque style in 1774, this pretty-in-pink church is elaborately decked out with marble altars, a rich collection of Italian paintings (including on the ceiling), a pipe organ and relics of St Gregory. It's only open for Sunday Mass but you can catch a glimpse of the interior through its metal gate.

Tower Museum   MUSEUM
(Kula; adult/concession 10/5KN; ⊙10am-1pm & 4-10pm Tue-Sun Jul & Aug, 10am-1pm Tue-Sat Easter-Jun & Sep) This striking defence tower, in the maze of streets set back from the harbour, was built by the Venetians in 1455 to defend the town from pirates. It now contains a branch of the Lošinj Museum, dedicated to the island's maritime history. Browse the Roman ceramic fragments, sabres and old postcards before climbing up to the battlements for unrivalled Veli views.

Lošinj Marine Education Centre   WILDLIFE CENTRE
(📞051-604 666; www.blue-world.org; Kaštel 24; adult/concession 15/10KN; ⊙10am-9pm Jul & Aug, 10am-4pm Mon-Fri, to 2pm Sat May, Jun & Sep, 10am-2pm Mon-Fri Oct-Mar) 🐾 A companion piece to Blue World's practical conservation work (see p158), this enlightening attraction aims to educate locals and visitors about the marine environment and the threats it's facing. There's a highly informative video (in a variety of languages), the vertebra of an 11m fin whale (a baby) and some multimedia displays, including an acoustic room where you can hear dolphin click communications.

⨳ Sleeping

Youth Hostel Veli Lošinj   HOSTEL €
(📞051-236 234; www.hfhs.hr; Kaciol 4; dm/tw 150/360KN; ⊙May-Oct; 🛜) One of Croatia's best YHA-associated hostels, this converted town house has a friendly vibe and hospitable management. Dorms (all with lockers) are spacious, the pine-trimmed private rooms are quite classy and the front terrace is a great place to meet people and have an evening beer (12KN).

Villa Mozart B&B €€

(☑ 051-236 262; hotelvillamozart.mikrut357@ gmail.com; Kaciol 3; r from 470KN; ❄ 🌐) There are 18 characterful rooms available at this attractive guest house; all are smallish but they have TVs and tiny bathrooms, and some come with harbour views. The breakfast terrace overlooks the shimmering harbour waters and the church. English isn't the staff's strongpoint.

Pansion Saturn B&B €€

(☑ 051-236 102; www.val-losinj.hr; Obala Maršala Tita bb; r €60-70; ❄ 🌐) A recent renovation has left some rather odd bubbly gold walls (a space theme, perhaps?) but Saturn's eight rooms are spacious and the bathrooms are modern. It's above a popular terrace bar, so pack earplugs if you don't want to join the party.

🍴 Eating & Drinking

★ Bora Bar ITALIAN €€

(☑ 051-867 544; Rovenska Bay 3; mains 60-160KN; ☺ noon-10pm Mar-Oct) Truffle heaven, this casual-chic restaurant has a Tuscan chef and a passion for the magic fungi. Feast on delicious homemade pasta with a generous shaving of truffle, and finish with *panna cotta* with truffle honey. Istrian wines feature strongly.

Ribarska Koliba CROATIAN €€

(Obala Maršala Tita 1; mains 40-120KN; ☺ 9am-midnight Apr Oct) Just past the church, this old stone structure has a nice portside terrace and serves up flavoursome meat dishes (try the suckling lamb or pig on a spit) as well as seafood.

Saturn BAR

(Obala Maršala Tita bb; ☺ 8am 2am; 🌐) The best bar in town, this atmospheric little place has harbour-facing tables and an eclectic playlist of Western and Croatian music.

ℹ Information

Palma Tourist Agency (☑ 051-236 179; www. losinj.com; Vladimira Nazora 22) Offers information, currency exchange, internet access and private accommodation rentals.

Post office (Obala Maršala Tita 33; ☺ 7.30am-9pm Mon-Sat Jul & Aug, 8am-5pm Mon, to 3pm Tue-Fri Sep-Jun)

Turist (☑ 051-236 256; www.island-losinj.com; Obala Maršala Tita 17) Private travel agency which runs excursions to Susak and Ilovik (190KN), rents out private accommodation, bikes and scooters, and changes money.

Val Tourist Agency (☑ 051-236 604; www.val-losinj.hr; Vladimira Nazora 29) Books private accommodation, runs excursions, offers internet access and rents out bikes and scooters.

ℹ Getting There & Away

Buses head to/from Mali Lošinj (12KN, 12 minutes, four to 16 daily), Nerezine (35KN, 10 minutes, two to nine daily), Osor (38KN, 45 minutes, two to seven daily) and Cres Town (52KN to 65KN, 1½ hours, two to seven daily).

KRK ISLAND

Croatia's largest island, connected to the mainland by a toll bridge, Krk (Veglia in Italian) is also one of the busiest – in summer, Germans and Austrians stream over to its holiday houses, campsites and hotels. It's not the lushest or most beautiful island, though its landscape is quiet varied, ranging from forests in the west to sunburnt ridges in the east. The northwestern coast of the island is rocky and steep with few settlements because of the fierce *bura* (cold northeasterly) that whips the coast in winter. The climate is milder in the southwest and can be scorching in the southeast.

You'll find Krk an easy place to visit, with good transport connections and infrastructure. Rijeka Airport is at the northernmost tip of the island, though flights only land here from April to October.

History

The earliest known inhabitants of Krk were the Illyrian Liburnian tribe, followed by the Romans who settled on the northern coast. Krk was later incorporated into the Byzantine Empire, then passed between Venice and the Croatian-Hungarian kings.

In the 11th century Krk became a leading centre for the preservation of the Glagolitic alphabet, the original Slavic script introduced by Sts Cyril and Methodius in the 9th century. When the church in Rome demanded that the Croatian church fall into line and use the Latin script and language for divine services, the clergy in Krk staged a short-lived revolt. However, Rome eventually granted an exemption for some Croatian dioceses to continue using the vernacular (a rarity in the Catholic tradition until the reforms of the 1960s) and the Glagolitic alphabet was used here until the 19th century.

KVARNER KRK ISLAND

BLUE WORLD

The **Blue World Institute of Marine Research & Conservation** (www.blue-world. org) is a Veli Lošinj–based nongovernmental organisation founded in 1999 to protect the Adriatic's marine environment. As well as hands-on research and conservation work (including running the Sea Turtle Rescue Centre in Mali Lošinj), it promotes environmental awareness through lectures, media presentations and the organisation of the annual Dolphin Day, held in Veli Lošinj on 1 July. It's quite an event, involving photography exhibitions, an ecofair, street performances, water-polo contests, treasure hunts and displays of hundreds of children's drawings and paintings.

As part of the Adriatic Dolphin Project, Blue World studies bottlenose dolphins that frequent the Lošinj-Cres area. Each dolphin is named and catalogued by photos taken of the natural marks that can be seen on its dorsal fin.

Dolphins were hunted here in the 1960s and '70s, when each kill was rewarded by the local government – fishermen were paid by the tail. Protection began in 1995, but a steep decline in bottlenose dolphins was recorded between 1995 and 2003. Subsequently, Blue World worked to establish the Lošinj Dolphin Reserve. Numbers are now believed to be stable, though still critically endangered, at around 180 individuals. In August 2009 a pod of 60 dolphins was seen near the island of Trstenik, a record sighting. Occasionally other dolphin species are seen too, including striped dolphins. The giant basking shark has also been spotted.

The biggest threat to Lošinj's dolphins is boat traffic, which brings noise and disturbance. During July and August dolphins are never seen close to the shore and avoid their main feeding grounds south and east of Cres where hake is common. Overfishing is another big concern, reducing available prey.

You can get involved by adopting a dolphin (from 200KN), which supports the Adriatic Dolphin Project, or volunteering. From May to September it's possible to join a 10-day programme which starts at €800 per person (with discounts available for students), and includes food and accommodation.

KVARNER MALINSKA

In 1358 Venice granted rule over the island to the dukes of Krk, later known as the Frankopans, who became one of the richest and most powerful families in Croatia. Although vassals of Venice, they ruled with a measure of independence until 1480, when the last member of the line put the island back under the protection of Venice.

Although tourism is the dominant activity on the island, there are two small shipyards (in Punat and Krk) and some agriculture and fishing.

ℹ Getting There & Away

Buses head across the bridge from Rijeka to Malinska (50KN, one hour, six to 15 daily), Krk Town (51KN, 1½ hours, 13 daily), Punat (71KN, 1½ hours, four to nine daily) and Baška (84KN, two hours, four to seven daily). There's also at least one bus per day from Zagreb to Malinska (80KN to 150KN, three hours), Krk Town (95KN to 216KN, three hours), Punat (94KN to 222KN, 3½ hours) and Baška (95KN to 236KN, four hours), increasing to seven daily in summer.

The main ferry port is at Valbiska, with services to the islands of Cres and Rab; see those sections for details.

There are buses from Malinska to both Cres Town (77KN, 1¼ hours, two to three daily) and Mali Lošinj (101 to 126KN, 2½ hours, daily).

ℹ Getting Around

Malinska is something of a bus hub for the island; if you want to head to Cres or Lošinj you'll need to change here. Buses head from Malinska to Krk Town (30KN, 20 minutes, hourly in summer), Punat (35KN, 40 minutes, 15 daily in summer), Vrbnik (35KN, 45 minutes, one to two daily year-round) and Baška (42KN, one hour, 12 daily in summer).

Krk Town also has services to/from Punat (26KN, 12 minutes, hourly in summer), Vrbnik (30KN, 35 minutes, two daily in summer) and Baška (35KN, 40 minutes, 12 daily in summer).

Malinska

☑051 / POP 965

Once the main port for the export of wood on the island, Malinska is now basically a sprawl of colourful holiday apartments grouped around a little marina. Sheltered from the winds and averaging 260 sunny days per year, it became a popular holiday destination with the Viennese aristocracy in the dying days of the Austro-Hungarian Empire. Now the tidy gardens and well-kept abodes speak to a large population of retirees. The surrounding Dubašnica area is scattered with little lost-in-time villages.

Although it's a little removed from the island's main sights, the location is handy for the Cres–Rijeka buses and for its proximity to the airport.

🛏 Sleeping & Eating

Villa Haya APARTMENTS €
(☑ 051-604 021; www.villahaya.com; Linardići 28/4; apt from €50; P❄🐾🛜🏊) Located in a middle-of-nowhere village between Malinska and the ferry port, this block of nine apartments would make a good-value base, provided you've got your own car. It's got its own little blue-tiled pool and there are remote beaches within 40-minutes' walk.

Pinia HOTEL €€€
(☑ 051-866 333; www.hotel-pinia.hr; Porat bb; s/d from 1216/1430KN; P❄@🛜🏊) This curvy hotel gazes over a dining terrace and lush lawns to the beach, 4km west of the harbour. The rooms are very comfortable and there's an indoor pool and spa centre.

Malin HOTEL €€€
(☑ 051-850 234; www.hotelmalin.com; Kralja Tomislava 23; s/d from €72/108; P❄🛜) Popular with tour groups, this large old fashioned hotel offers comfortable rooms and a substantial breakfast buffet. It's right across from a little concrete-lined beach and only a 15-minute stroll along the coastal promenade from the town centre.

⭐ Bistro Bukarica MODERN EUROPEAN €€
(☑ 051-859 022; www.bistrobukarica.com; Nikole Tesle 61; mains 70-170KN; ⊙ 11am-11pm) Tucked away up the hill in an unlikely residential street, this inventive restaurant is well worth seeking out. Asian flavours make their way onto a solidly European menu, highlighting the best Croatian produce.

ℹ️ Information

Post office (Obala 48; ⊙ 7.30am-9pm Mon-Fri Jun-Aug, 7am-8pm Mon-Fri, to 2pm Sat Sep-May)
Tourist office (☑ 051-859 207; www.tz-malinska.hr; Obala 46; ⊙ 8am-9pm Mon-Sat, 9am-1pm & 5-8pm Sun, reduced hours in winter)

Krk Town
☑ 051 / POP 3730

On the island's southern coast, Krk Town clusters around an ancient walled centre. The newer part of town spreads out over the surrounding hills and bays, and includes a port, beaches, camping grounds and hotels. The seafront promenade can get seriously crowded in summer with tourists and weekending Croats, who spill into the narrow cobbled streets that make up the pretty old quarter.

Minus the crowds, this stone labyrinth is the highlight of Krk Town. The former Roman settlement still retains sections of the ancient city walls and gates, as well as a grand Romanesque cathedral and a 12th-century Frankopan castle.

You won't need more than a couple of hours to see these sights, but from a base in Krk Town it's easy to explore the rest of the island.

◉ Sights

Cathedral of the Assumption CATHEDRAL
(Katedrala Uznešenja; Trg Sv Kvirina; admission 10KN; ⊙ 9.30am-1pm) Built on the site of Roman baths and an early Christian basilica, this imposing Romanesque structure dates from the 12th century. Outside of Mass times, entry is possible by paying the admission to the cathedral treasury housed in adjoining **St Quirinus'**, another Romanesque church built of white stone and dedicated to the island's patron saint. Grafted onto the side is a pretty 18th-century **campanile** (bell tower), topped with an onion-shaped dome and a statue of an angel.

Inside the cathedral, note the rare early Christian carving of two birds eating a fish on the first column next to the apse. The left nave features a Gothic chapel from the 15th century, with the coats of arms of the Frankopan princes who used it as a place of worship. Amongst the art and vestments stored in St Quirinus' is a silver altarpiece depicting the Madonna dating to 1477.

Kaštel FORTRESS
(Trg Kamplin; ⊙ 9am-2pm) **FREE** This crumbling old seafront fortress guarded the Old Town from pirate attacks. It's free to wander around inside and check out the inscribed Liburnian and Roman stones displayed within. There's a 12th-century tower that was once used as a Frankopan

courtroom and another round defence tower built by Venetians (if you fancy checking out the views from the top, there's a 10KN admission charge). The castle is now an open-air venue used for summer concerts and plays.

🏄 Activities

Speed
CYCLING

(📞 051-221 587; www.bike-speed-krk.com.hr; Šetalište Sv Bernardina 3; ⏰ 8am-1pm & 5-8pm Mon-Fri, 8am-1pm Sat) Pick up an island map from the tourist office and get out and explore the lanes around Krk Town by bike. This crew rents and sells good-quality bikes from their shop by the bus station.

Fun Diving Krk
DIVING

(📞 051-222 563; www.fun-diving.com; Braće Juras 3; day tour incl 2 dives €55; ⏰ Easter-Oct) A German crew offering courses and dives around the island. Some of the best dive sites include *Peltastis*, the wreck of a 60m Greek cargo ship, and the Punta Silo and Kamenjak reefs, which are rich with sealife including sea snails and octopuses.

🎉 Festivals & Events

Krk Fair
CULTURAL

(⏰ 8-10 Aug) This Venetian-inspired event takes over the town for three days, with concerts, people dressed in medieval costumes and stalls selling traditional food.

🛏 Sleeping

Autocamp Ježevac
CAMPGROUND €

(📞 051-221 081; www.camping-adriatic.com; Plavnička bb; camping per adult/child/site €9/6/10, units from €120; ⏰ mid-Apr–Sep; 🅿️ �🐕) With shady pitches set on old farming terraces, this beachfront camping ground offers good swimming, barbecue sites and tip-top self-contained units. It's a 10-minute walk southwest of town.

Camping Bor
CAMPGROUND €

(📞 051-221 581; www.camp-bor.hr; Crikvenička 10; per adult/child/site 60/36/35KN; 🅿️ 📶 🏊) On a hill covered with olive trees, this tightly packed campground has well-kept shower blocks, a tiny swimming pool, a playground and a restaurant. It's a 10-minute walk west of the seafront.

Bor
HOTEL €€

(📞 051-220 200; www.hotelbor.hr; Šetalište Dražica 5; s/d/apt from €55/84/120; ⏰ Apr-Oct; 🅿️ ❄️ 📶) It's the location – by an attractive rocky shoreline and surrounded by mature pines – that's the main asset of this small hotel. The 22 rooms are modest and we noticed the odd bit of bathroom mould, but there's a lovely terrace cafe and it's only a 10-minute walk from the centre.

Hotel Marina
HOTEL €€€

(📞 051-221 128; www.hotelmarina.hr; Obala Hrvatske Mornarice 8; s/d from €107/180; 🅿️ ❄️ 📶) Marina is the only hotel in the Old Town, and it's a good one. It enjoys a prime waterfront location and you can gaze out over the yachts from the balconies of all of the 10 plush units (book a room with a terrace for the best views). All boast stylish contemporary decor and hip bathrooms.

🍴 Eating

Galija
CROATIAN, PIZZERIA €€

(📞 051-221 250; www.galijakrk.com; Frankopanska 38; mains 40-150KN) Set well back from the seafront at the top of the Old Town, this atmospheric stone building looks gloomy from the street but the convivial dining room opens on to a lovely internal garden. It's part traditional *konoba*, part pizzeria; we highly recommend the deli platter.

Konoba Nono
CROATIAN €€

(📞 051-222 221; www.nono-krk.com; Krčkih Iseljenika 8; mains 40-145KN; ⏰ noon-10pm) A rustic place that's renowned for its Krk cooking, Nona also produces its own olive oil, as evidenced by the large traditional press on the terrace. There's a smaller branch, Mali Nono, in the Old Town.

🍷 Drinking & Nightlife

⭐ Volsonis
BAR, CLUB

(Vela Placa 8; ⏰ 7am-2am May-Sep, to midnight Oct-Apr) This slick place has an outdoor terrace, a cavelike interior with a pool table, a delicious secret garden and there's even a collection of archaeological relics that were uncovered during the renovations. Live bands and DJs do their thing on weekend nights, or you can just chill on the terrace with a coffee or cocktail.

Caffettaria XVIII st.
CAFE, BAR

(Vela Placa 1; ⏰ 7am-2am May-Sep, to midnight Oct-Apr; 📶) Located right on the main square in the historic town hall, this is the perfect place for people-watching and a delicious coffee in the shade. There is good wi-fi and nice sofas to lounge on.

ℹ Information

Aurea (☑ 051-221 777; www.aurea-krk.hr; Vršanska 26l; ⊙8am-2pm & 3-8pm) A local agency offering island excursions and private accommodation bookings.

Autotrans (☑ 051-222 661; www.autotrans-turizam.com; Šetalište Sv Bernardina 3) Based in the bus station, this agency finds private accommodation and sells bus tickets.

Hospital (☑ 051-221 224; Vinogradska bb)

Post office (Bodulska bb; ⊙7.30am-9pm Mon-Sat Jun-Aug, 7am-8pm Mon-Fri, to 2pm Sat Sep-May)

Tourist office (☑ 051-220 226, www.tz-krk. hr; JJ Strossmayera 9; ⊙8am-9pm May-Sep, 8am-2pm Mon-Fri Oct-Apr)

Punat

☑ 051 / POP 1860

Six kilometres southeast of Krk, the small town of Punat has an attractive promenade lined with gelaterias, a marina much loved by yachties, and decent beaches on its outskirts. The main attraction here is the monastery islet of Košljun, only a 10-minute boat ride away.

◉ Sights & Activities

Košljun Franciscan Monastery   MONASTERY
(admission 20N; ⊙9 5pm Mon Sat, 10.30am-12.30pm Sun) The tiny island of Košljun contains a 16th-century Franciscan monastery built on the site of a 12th-century Benedictine abbey. Taxi boats wait on the Punat harbourside, ready to shuttle people across to the island (20KN return); in summer there'll be plenty of interested parties with whom you can share a ride.

Highlights include a large, appropriately chilling *Last Judgment*, painted in 1653 and housed in the monastery church. There's also a small museum with religious paintings, an ethnographic collection and a rare copy of Ptolemy's *Atlas* printed in Venice in the late 16th century. Allow extra time to stroll around the forested island and admire its 400 plant species.

Cable Krk Wakeboard Center   WAKEBOARDING
(☑ 091 32 71 221; www.wakeboarder.hr; per hour/day €14/31; ⊙10am-dark May-Sep) Adrenalin junkies can get their fix at this 650m-long cableway for wakeboarding and waterskiing, running at a speed of 32km/h. It's located just off the main road at the head of the bay (before the turn-off to Punat). The complex includes a restaurant, bar and board shop.

BEACH PEACE

Many of Krk's best beaches are heavily developed and crowded in summer. For more tranquillity, head south of Punat on the lonely road that heads to **Stara Baška** (not southeast to Baška). It's a superlative drive, through steep parched hills and lunar scenery. Stara Baška itself is a run-of-the-mill tourist sprawl of holiday homes and caravan parks but if you pull up 500m before the first campsite there is a series of gorgeous pebble and sand coves with wonderful swimming. You'll have to park on the road, and then walk down one of the rocky paths for five minutes to get to the coast.

⌂ Sleeping

Camping Pila   CAMPGROUND **€**
(☑ 051-854 020; www.hoteli-punat.hr; Šetalište Ivana Brusića 2; camping per adult/child/site 48/32/124KN; ⊙Apr-mid-Oct; ⌨ 🖥 🐾) ✿ Just south of the town centre, this midsized camping ground is positioned right by a concrete-edged, clear-water beach. Water is solar-heated.

Vrbnik

☑ 051 / POP 948

Perched on a 48m cliff overlooking the sea, Vrbnik is a beguiling medieval village of steep, arched streets. It's not a real secret (tour groups pass through from time to time) but most of the year it's a peaceful, unhurried place. Vrbnik was once the main centre where the Glagolitic script was used and was the repository for many Glagolitic manuscripts. It was kept alive by priests, who were always plentiful in the town since many young men entered the priesthood to avoid serving on Venetian galleys.

Now the town is a terrific place to soak up the vistas and sample the *žlahtina* white wine produced in the surrounding region. After wandering the tight-packed cobbled alleyways, head down to the town beach for a swim.

✕ Eating

Restaurant Nada   CROATIAN **€€**
(☑ 051-857 065; www.nada-vrbnik.hr; Glavača 22; mains 60-180KN; ⊙noon-10pm Apr-Oct) Nada is a great place to sample local favourites such as Krk lamb or *šurlice* (noodles) topped with

SENJ

The historic walled town of Senj (population 7190) is the largest town on the coast between Rijeka and Zadar. In the 16th century it became a base for the Uskoks, Croats driven from their homes by the Ottoman invasion. They became a feared fighting force, harassing both Turkish and Venetian vessels with their own pirate fleet, painted red and black – the colours of blood and death.

The story of the Uskoks is showcased in the dramatic setting of **Nehaj Castle** (Tvrđava Nehaj; adult/child 20/10KN; ⊙9am-9pm Jul & Aug, 10am-6pm May-Jun & Sep-Oct), a sturdy stone cube that looms above the town from a 62m-high hill to the south. It was completed in 1558 with funds supplied by the Austrian emperor; the current structure was largely reconstructed in 1970. Head up to the parapets for fine views along the coast and over the island of Krk.

meat goulash. There are two attractive dining terraces – one shaded and one overlooking the sea – plus a cellar where you can snack on deli treats surrounded by wine barrels. It also has some classy stone houses for rent.

ⓘ Information

Mare Tours (☑051-604 400; www.mare-vrbnik.com; Pojana 4; ⊙8am-8pm Mon-Sat) Travel agency that offers tourist information and rents out private rooms.

Baška

☑051 / POP 981

The drive to the southern end of Krk Island is extremely dramatic, passing through a fertile valley that's bordered by eroded mountains. Eventually the road peters out at Baška, where there's a fine crescent beach set below barren hills. With the peaks of the mainland directly opposite you're effectively enveloped by soaring highlands, giving the sea the impression of an alpine lake.

However, and this is a considerable caveat, in summer tourists are spread towel-to-towel and what's otherwise a pretty, if slimline, pebble beach turns into a fight for your place in the sun. Baška's promenade is also lined with a tatty excess of souvenir stalls.

The small 16th-century core of Venetian town houses is pleasant enough, but what surrounds it is a bland tourist development of modern apartment blocks and generic restaurants. Facilities are plentiful and there are nice hiking trails into the surrounding mountains, and more secluded beaches to the east of town, reachable on foot or by water taxi.

⊙ Sights

St Lucy's Church   CHURCH, MUSEUM
(Crkva Sv Lucija; admission 25KN; ⊙9am-7pm) More than just a village church, little St Lucy's was the site of one of the most important cultural discoveries in Croatia – the 11th-century Baška tablet – which was found in the floor of the church in 1851. Written in Glagolitic it contains the earliest reference in the Croatian language to a Croatian king. Visitors are invited to watch a video which tells the fascinating story of the tablet's discovery and eventual translation, before being shown around the church itself.

The squat, early Romanesque church was built on the foundations of a 4th-century villa and has a Roman column and gravestone built into its porch. The actual famous stone tablet is now in the Archaeological Museum in Zagreb, but a replica has been positioned in its original place where the rood screen would have once stood. On the feast of St Lucy (13 December), the sun strikes the inscription referring to the saint. Look out for the statue of St Lucy, depicted with an angel holding her gouged-out eyes on a plate – a reference to her gruesome martyrdom.

The church is in the village of Jurandvor and well signposted from the approach to Baška; it's only 2km from town, so easily reached on foot.

🏃 Activities

Several popular **trails** begin around Camping Zablaće, including an 8km walk over the stark, salt-washed limestone hills to Stara Baška. Along the way you'll see the flower-shaped stone pens traditionally used for mustering and shearing sheep. There are also two **rock-climbing** sites in the area.

Call into the tourist office for maps and information.

🛏 Sleeping

There's usually a four-night minimum stay requirement for private accommodation in summer (or a hefty surcharge) and rooms fill up quickly; for options, contact the tourist office or local travel agencies.

Naturist Camp Bunculuka CAMPGROUND €
(☑ 051-856 806; www.bunculuka.info; camping per adult/child/site from 52/24/124KN, units from 763KN; ⊙ Apr-Oct; 🅿 ✳ 🛜 🐾) This shady naturist camp is a 15-minute walk over the hill east of the harbour on a lovely beach. It's equipped with good facilities for kids including minigolf and a playground, as well as a restaurant, a fruit-and-veg market and a bakery.

Camping Zablaće CAMPGROUND €
(☑ 051-856 909; www.campzablace.com; camping per adult/child site from 52/24/85KN, units from 889KN; ⊙ Apr–mid-Oct; 🅿 ✳ 🛜) Spreads along the long pebble beach and has good showers, laundry facilities and units with barbecues.

Atrium Residence Baška HOTEL €€€
(☑ 051-656 111; www.hotelibaska.hr; Emila Geistlicha 39; r/apt from 1134/1246KN; 🅿 ✳ 🛜) Sleek and modern, this midsized beachside hotel has options ranging from rooms with mountain views to a two-bedroom apartment with a sauna and Jacuzzi on the deck overlooking the sea. Guests have use of the resort-style pool at sister hotel Corinthia-Baška.

Hotel Tamaris HOTEL €€€
(☑ 051-864 200; www.baska-tamaris.com; Emila Geistlicha 54b; r/apt from 820/1824KN; ⊙ Easter-Sep; 🅿 ✳ @ 🛜) Built as an Austro-Hungarian army barracks, this small hotel has decent, if smallish, carpeted rooms and apartments that are in good shape. It's right on the beach on the west side of town.

✖ Eating

Bistro Forza MEDITERRANEAN €€
(Zvonimirova 98; mains 40-130KN; ⊙ 7am-midnight; 🛜) A good cheap-bite option, this place dishes out pizza and the usual grilled meat, pasta and salad options.

Cicibela CROATIAN €€€
(☑ 051-856 013; www.cicibela.hr; Emila Geistlicha 22a; mains 46-198KN; ⊙ 9am-midnight Mar-Oct) At the heart of the beach promenade, this is Baška's top cat, with stylish seating and a massive and tempting menu of seafood and meat dishes. If you're ordering fish by the kilogram, ask for the price in advance to avoid nasty surprises.

❶ Information

PDM Guliver (☑ 051-864 007; www.pdm-guliver.hr; Zvonimirova 98) Travel agency letting private rooms and apartments.

Primaturist (☑ 051-856 132; www.primaturist.hr; Zvonimirova 98) Agency dealing in private rooms and apartments.

Tourist Office (☑ 051-856 817; www.tz-baska.hr; Zvonimirova 114; ⊙ 8am-9pm Mon-Sat Jun-Aug, to 2pm Mon-Fri Sep-May) Lists private accommodation on ITS website.

RAB ISLAND

Rab (Arbe in Italian) has some of the most diverse landscapes in the Kvarner region, leading to its declaration as a Geopark in 2008. The more densely populated southwest coast has pine forests and beaches, while the northeast coast is a windswept region with few settlements, high cliffs and a barren look. In the interior, fertile land is protected from cold winds by mountains, allowing the cultivation of olives, grapes and vegetables. The island's Lopar Peninsula offers the best sandy beaches.

The cultural and historical highlight of the island is enchanting Rab Town, characterised by four elegant bell towers rising from the ancient stone streets. Even at the peak of the summer season, when the island is overrun with visitors, you still get a sense of discovery wandering its old quarter and escaping to nearly deserted beaches just a quick boat ride away. In spring and autumn, Rab Island is a lovely place to visit, as the climate is famously mild and visitors are scarce.

History

Originally settled by the Illyrian Liburnian people in around 360 BC, Rab was declared a city in 10 BC by the Roman Emperor Augustus. It was Augustus who ordered the first walls to be built. The town first made its way into the history books in AD 70 when Pliny the Elder referred to it as Arba (meaning dark, obscure or green). It later became known as Felix Arba (Happy Arba).

After the Romans, Rab underwent periods of Byzantine and Croatian rule before being sold to Venice, along with Dalmatia, in 1409. Farming, fishing, vineyards and salt production were the economic mainstays, but most income ended up in Venice. Two plague epidemics in the 15th century nearly wiped out the population and brought the economy to a standstill.

When Venice fell in 1797, there was a short period of Austrian rule until the French arrived in 1805. After the fall of Napoleon in 1813, the power went back to the Austrians who favoured the Italianised elite and it was not until 1897 that Croatian was made an official language. The tourism industry began at the turn of the 20th century.

After the fall of the Austro-Hungarian Empire in 1918, Rab eventually became part of the Kingdom of Yugoslavia. Occupied by Italian and then German troops in the early 1940s, it was liberated in 1945. During Tito's rule Goli Otok ('Barren Island'), off the Lopar Peninsula, served as a notorious prison camp for fascists, Stalinists and other political opponents.

These days, tourism is Rab's bread and butter. Even during the 1990s war, Rab managed to hold on to its German and Austrian visitors.

ⓘ Getting There & Away

BOAT

Jadrolinija (🖉 051-666 111; www.jadrolinija.hr) A daily catamaran stops in Rab Town en route between Rijeka (80KN, 1¾ hours) and Novalja on Pag (80KN, 2¾ hours).

Linijska Nacionalna Plovidba (🖉 021-352 527; www.lnp.hr) A car ferry runs between Valbiska on Krk and Lopar (adult/child/car 37/18/225KN, 1½ hours) twice daily (October to May) and four times daily in high season; prices drop in winter.

Rapska Plovidba (🖉 051-724 122; www. rapska-plovidba.hr) A car ferry shuttles back and forth between Mišnjak on the island's southeastern tip and Stinica (adult/child/car 17/7/98KN, 15 minutes) on the mainland; even in winter there are a dozen boats a day, increasing to nearly double that in high season. There's also a passenger boat from Rab Town to Lun on the island of Pag, operating three days a week (daily from June to August).

BUS

Buses head to Rab Town from Rijeka (90KN, three hours, two daily) and Senj (74KN, 1½ hours, two to five daily); from Zadar you'll need to change at Senj. In the high season there are three direct buses a day from Zagreb to Rab (216KN, four hours); book ahead on this busy route.

ⓘ Getting Around

There are 11 buses a day (nine on Sunday) between Rab Town and Lopar (20KN, 15 minutes); some are timed to meet the Valbiska–Lopar ferry.

Taxi boats will take you to any island beach.

Rab Town

🖉 051 / POP 8070

Walled Rab Town is among the northern Adriatic's most spectacular sights. Crowded onto a narrow peninsula, its four instantly recognisable bell towers rise like exclamation points from a red-roofed huddle of stone buildings. A maze of streets leads to the upper town, where there are ancient churches and dramatic lookout points. It's quite a scene, the glinting azure waters of Rab's pocket-sized harbour set against the island's backbone of hills that shelter the bay from cool *bura* winds. Once you've soaked up the town vibe, there are excursion and taxi boats waiting to whisk you off to lovely beaches scattered around the island.

A five-minute walk north of the Old Town is the ageing, down-at-heel commercial centre, with stores and the bus station. Built-up suburbs sprawl along the coast, including Banjol and Barbat in the south and Palit and Kampor in the north.

⊙ Sights

It's a pure delight to meander through the narrow old alleys of Rab and explore the harbour front, upper town and parks. Rab's principal sights are its historic churches and towers, which are clustered together on the narrow lane of Ulica Gornja (Upper Street), which runs parallel to Srednja (Central) and Donja (Lower) streets. Most of the churches are usually only open for morning and evening Mass, but even when they're closed you can often peer through metal railings to view their interiors.

Komrčar Park   PARK
Leafy and deliciously cool on a summer's day, this 8.3-hectare park abuts the Old Town and stretches along the coast to the marina at Palit. It was originally used as a place to graze cattle, but was planted in forest in the 19th century, much to the consternation of the townsfolk.

Dominis Palace   HISTORIC BUILDING
(Srednja bb) Built at the end of the 15th century for a prominent patrician family who taught the public to read and write here, this building's facade is worth noting for its Renaissance windows and striking doorway decorated with the family coat of arms. It now houses a cafe.

Viewpoint VIEWPOINT

For a great view over the rooftops including all four bell towers, head to the northwesternmost corner of the Old Town and look for a small courtyard containing fragments of old monuments. Stone stairs lead up from here onto the walls and a lookout.

St John the Evangelist's Church RUINS

(Crkva Sv Ivana Evandelista; Gornja bb) It's thought that parts of this atmospherically ruined Romanesque basilica date as far back as the 5th century. Today, only a handful of columns are still standing, along with the restored 12th-century bell tower.

Holy Cross Church CHURCH

(Crkva Sv Križa; Gornja bb) This 13th-century church takes its current name from a crucifix upon which, in 1556, the image of Christ was said to have wept due to the immoral conduct of the people of Rab. The miraculous cross was lost in the early 20th century. Today the church is the venue for summer concerts during Rab Musical Evenings (p167).

St Justine's Church CHURCH

(Crkva Sv Justine; Gornja bb) This semiderelict church has a bell tower dating from 1672. It's located beside pretty Trg Slobode, which has a holm oak tree and sea vistas.

St Andrew's Monastery CHURCH

(Samostan Sv Andrije; Ivana Rabljanina bb) Founded in 1018, this Benedictine monastery has Rab's oldest bell tower (1181). Peer through the railings at the church's triple nave; some of the plasterwork has been uncovered to reveal the original stonework.

St Mary's Campanile TOWER

(Toranj Sv Marije; Ivana Rabljanina bb; admission 15KN; ☺9.30am-1pm & 7-9pm May-Sep) Dating from the 12th century, this is Rab's tallest bell tower and one of the most beautiful on the entire Croatian coast. The 26m edifice is topped with an octagonal pyramid surrounded by a Romanesque balustrade, and features a cross with five small globes and reliquaries of several saints. Climb up the very steep wooden staircase for glorious views over the Old Town rooftops and sea. You'll emerge right by the chiming mechanism itself.

Church of the Assumption CHURCH

(Crkva Uznesenjca; Ivana Rabljanina bb; ☺10.30am-1pm & 6-9pm) It hasn't been a cathedral since 1828 when the diocese was dissolved, but locals still refer to this, their grandest church, as the *katedrala*. Its striking facade

WORTH A TRIP

A HEAVENLY DESTINATION

Monastery of St Euphemia (Samostan Svete Eufemije; Kampor; adult/child 15/5KN; ☺10am-noon & 4-6pm Mon-Sat) A 2.5km walk heading north along the seaside promenade from Rab's Old Town will bring you to this peaceful Franciscan monastery, dating from the 13th century. The monks have a small museum here with old manuscripts and religious paintings. Check out the pleasant cloister and, inside the baroque church of St Bernardine, the ethereal painted ceiling – a stark contrast to the visceral agony depicted on the late-Gothic wooden crucifix in the side chapel. Note also the 15th-century polyptych by the Vivarini brothers.

has stripes of pink and cream stone, and a Gothic-style pietà over the door. Inside, key features include 15th-century choir stalls and weathered pillars. It's been remodelled a lot over the years but mosaics found here indicate this has been a Christian place of worship since the 4th or 5th century.

St Anthony the Abbot's Church CHURCH

(Crkva Svetog Antuna Opata; Ivana Rabljanina bb) At the eastern tip of the Old Town, this church attached to a still-operating Franciscan convent has lots of inlaid marble and a carving of a seated St Anthony decorating the altar. Steps lead down from here to a beautifully landscaped park, a great place for a break on a hot summer's day.

🏃 Activities

Rab is criss-crossed with 100km of marked **hiking trails** and 80km of **biking trails**, several of which can be accessed from Rab Town. Pick up the excellent *Biking & Trekking* map from the tourist office or call into the Geopark Visitor Centre (p168) for information on the new 'geotrails'. Bikes can be rented from several travel agencies.

From Rab Town there's a trail that leads northeast to the mountain peak of Sveti Ilija. It only takes about 30 minutes on foot and the view is great.

Diving sites are many and varied: the wreck of the *Rosa*, with its red gorgonian forest, conger eels and lobsters; various caves and tunnels; and a protected amphora field off the cape of Sorinj. **Mirko Diving Centre**

Rab Town

N

0 ———— 100 m
0 ———— 0.04 miles

14

Monastery of
St Euphemia
(2km)

Tamaris
(500m)

Tourist Office
Annexe

Bus
Station

Palit

11

Šetalište Mark Antuna Dominisa

Šetalište Kapetana Ivana Dominisa

5

Water Taxis

Blato

Gradska
Luka

Šetalište fra Odorika Badurine

Komrčar Park

Juraj Barakovića

Marina

Trg
Svetog
Kristofora

Camping
Padova III (1.5km);
Mišnjak (11km)

Obala Kralja Petra Krešimira IV

10

3

Bobotine

A Ugalje
Matije Pončuna

Geopark Visitor Centre

VAROŠ

1

4

Kneza Trpimira

Donja Srednja

15

13

Gornja

Kneza Domagoja

Trg
Municipium
Arba

8

Tourist
Office

Water Taxis

Trg Slobode

Put Kaldanca

12

6

9

Kaldanac

Ivana Rabljanina

Ferry Dock

2

Obala Svete
Eufemije

7

KVARNER

(☑ 051-721 154; www.mirkodivingcenter.com; Barbat 710), based in nearby Barbat, offers courses and fun dives.

A long pebbly beach stretches all around Rab Town, so take a towel and freshen up after sightseeing – just mind those sea urchins!

☞ Tours

Day tours of the island by boat, including swim stops and visits to nearby islands such as Sveti Grgur and the infamous Goli Otok, are offered by many travel agents; expect to pay about 200KN to 250KN, including lunch. You can also chat directly with skippers about trips: in the evening the main harbour front is lined with excursion boats. Trips to the islands of Lošinj and Krk are also possible.

✦ Festivals & Events

Rab Musical Evenings   MUSIC
(Rapske glazbene večeri; ⊙ Jun-Sep) Takes place from June to September and revolves around Thursday-night concerts at venues including Holy Cross Church.

Rab Fair   FIESTA
(Rapska Fjera; ⊙ 25-27 July) Witness Rab transporting itself back to the Middle Ages. Residents dress in period garb and there are drummers, processions, fireworks, medieval dancing and crossbow competitions.

Summer Festival   MUSIC
(⊙ early Aug) In early August, Croatian pop-stars and international DJs perform in the Old Town.

🛏 Sleeping

Campgrounds and hotels (though few of real quality) are relatively plentiful around Rab Town; many are managed by the **Imperial** (www.imperialrab.com) group. Contact travel agencies for private rooms and apartments or sniff one out yourself.

Camping Padova III   CAMPGROUND €
(☑ 051-724 355; www.rab-camping.com; Banjol 496; camping per adult/child/site 60/31/119KN; unit from 575KN; ⊙ Apr-Oct) About 2km east of town, this tightly packed camping ground sits right on a sandy beach – perfect for toddlers, painfully shallow for adults. The facilities aren't as new or well kept as some, but are perfectly adequate.

Tamaris   HOTEL €€
(☑ 724 925; www.tamaris-rab.com; Palit 285; s/d from 521/744KN; P ❄ 🛜) About a 10-minute

Rab Town

◉ Sights

1 St John the Evangelist's Church	B5
2 Church of the Assumption	C6
3 Dominis Palace	B4
4 Holy Cross Church	B5
5 Komrčar Park	A3
6 St Andrew's Monastery	C6
7 St Anthony the Abbotts Church	D7
8 St Justine's Church	C5
9 St Mary's Campanile	C6
10 Viewpoint	B4

🛏 Sleeping

11 Grand Hotel Imperial	B2
12 Hotel Arbiana	D6

✕ Eating

13 Konoba Rab	C5
14 Ristorante Ana	B1

✪ Entertainment

15 Dock 69	C5

walk north of town, this is a well-run little hotel, with attentive staff and a peaceful location near the sea. Rooms are simple but quite stylish with laminate floors and soft linen, and most have sea views from their balconies.

Hotel Arbiana   HOTEL €€€
(☑ 051-725 563; www.arbianahotel.com; Obala Kralja Petra Krešimira IV 12; s/d from 585/950KN; P ❄ 🛜) The classiest address in Rab, this historic hotel dates back to 1924 and retains plenty of period character and formal elegance. All 27 rooms have been updated and come with LCD TVs, desks and good-quality repro furniture.

Grand Hotel Imperial   HOTEL €€€
(☑ 051-724 522; www.imperial.hr; Šetalište Markantuna Dominisa 9; s/d from 575/960KN; ⊙ Apr-Nov; P ❄ @ 🛜 ☲) It's a little old-fashioned and not as grand as it makes out, but this large hotel enjoys a great location in shady Komrčar Park. It boasts tennis courts, a gym, a spa and a very appealing outdoor swimming pool.

✗ Eating

Rab cuisine revolves around fresh seafood and pasta. Quality and prices are fairly uniform, though there are some notable exceptions.

Konoba Rab   CROATIAN €€
(Kneza Branimira 3; mains 50-120KN; ⊙ 10am-2pm & 5-11pm Mon-Sat, 5-11pm Sun) For real country

cooking this place excels and the old stone building adds to the rustic appeal. Stick to grilled meat and fish staples or order the lamb baked under *peka* in advance.

Ristorante Ana   MEDITERRANEAN €€
(📞 051-724 376; Palit 80; mains 40-120KN; ⊗ 11am-3pm & 5.30pm-midnight) In the newer part of town, just around the corner from the bus station, this restaurant has a quiet internal terrace overlooking a garden. It serves pasta, pizza and grilled meat and fish; the spaghetti with scampi is particularly good.

🍷 Drinking & Nightlife

Hardcore clubbers often head to Zrće beach in Pag Island, catching the late-afternoon catamaran connection and returning on the 7.30am boat (note: when you get to Pag, it's still 20km from the ferry to the clubs).

Dock 69   BAR, CLUB
(Obala Kralja Petra Krešimira IV; ⊗ 7pm-3am Sat & Sun) This slick lounge bar has a harbour-facing terrace and clubby interior where DJs ramp up the volume on the weekends.

Santos Beach Club   CLUB
(www.sanantonio-club.com; Pudarica Beach; ⊗ 10am-dawn late Jun-early Sep) This summer-only beach club is about 10km from Rab Town, near the Mišnjak car ferry (shuttle boats run at night). DJs spin to a lively party crowd and there are live concerts and fashion shows. It also doubles as a daytime beach hang-out, with loungers and volleyball.

ℹ Information

There's free wi-fi around the tourist office and the Palit shops and bus station.

Geopark Visitor Centre (Bobotine bb; ⊗ 10am-5pm Mon, Tue & Thu-Sat, 3-8pm Sun) Call in for information on 'geotrail' paths, exploring the island's unique geology. There are also interactive information screens and samples of local rocks.

Katurbo (📞 051-724 495; www.katurbo.hr; Šetalište Markantuna Dominisa 5) Private accommodation, money exchange, bike rental (per hour/day 20/70KN), boat excursions and tours to places such as Plitvice Lakes National Park.

Numero Uno (📞 051-775 073; www.numero-uno.hr; Banjol 30) Books private accommodation, rents out bicycles and offers trekking trips, kayak (360KN) and bike tours (320KN).

Post office (Mali Palit 67; ⊗ 7.30am-9pm Mon-Sat Jun-Aug, 7am-8pm Mon-Fri, to 2pm Sat Sep-May)

Tourist office (📞 051-724 064; www.tzg-rab.hr; Trg Municipium Arba 8; ⊗ 8am-10pm Mon-

Sat, to 1pm Sun Easter-Oct, 8am-3pm Mon-Fri Nov-Easter) A well-organised office with helpful staff and loads of useful maps, brochures and leaflets. In summer, it operates a second branch (⊗ 8am-3pm Jun-Sep) around the corner from the bus station.

Lopar
📞 051 / POP 1270

At the northern tip of the island, the beach town of Lopar is still semirural around the edges, with garden plots and roses growing in front gardens. Even in early June it's a sleepy place, but in the school holidays Central European families flock here, as the sea is very shallow and perfect for small children. This is particularly so on 1500m-long **Paradise Beach** (Rajska Plaža) on Crnika Bay, right in the centre of town, where you can almost wade right across to a little offshore island.

There are 22 sandy beaches bordered by shady pine groves scattered around the peninsula, including nearby **Livačina Beach**. If you wish to shed your speedos, **Sahara Beach** is a popular nudist spot in a gorgeous but shallow bay. Look for the signpost pointing off the main road before you reach Paradise Beach; it's a 1.8km (half-hour) walk from here, or you can drive along the narrow lane and walk for 15 minutes from the parking area.

🛏 Sleeping & Eating

Hotel Epario   HOTEL €€
(📞 051-777 500; www.epario.net; Lopar 456a; s/d from €40/70; 🅿 🌐 @ 🛜) Laid-back and friendly Epario is a modern block sitting facing fields on the main road leading towards Paradise Beach. The rooms all have desks, balconies and good bathrooms.

Gostionica Laguna   MEDITERRANEAN €€
(📞 051-775 177; www.laguna-lopar.com; Lopar 547; mains 42-125KN; ⊗ noon-10pm) The terrace at this tavern is by far the nicest place to eat at this end of the island. House specialities include spit-roast or *peka*-cooked lamb, but there's also pasta, pizza and grilled meat and fish.

ℹ Information

Sahara Tours (📞 051-775 633; www.sahara-lopar.com; s/d/apt from €21/32/50) Has dozens of private rooms, houses and apartments on its books.

Tourist office (📞 051-775 508; www.lopar.com; ⊗ 8am-10pm Mon-Sat, to 2pm Sun Jul & Aug, to 11am Mon-Fri Sep-Jun)

Northern Dalmatia

Includes ➡

Lika 171
Plitvice Lakes &
Around 171
Paklenica National
Park 174
Pag Island 176
Zadar 179
Dugi Otok 186
Kornati Islands 188
Šibenik 190
Krka National Park ... 194
Knin 196

Why Go?

Serving that classic Dalmatian cocktail of historic towns, jewel like waters, rugged mountains, sun-kissed islands, gorgeous climate and Mediterranean cuisine, this region is a holidaymaker's paradise. Yet it's the cities and islands further south that hog all the limelight, leaving Northern Dalmatia, if not quite undiscovered, then certainly less over-run. Yachties can sail between unpopulated islands without a shred of development, lost in dreams of the Mediterranean of old, while hikers can wander lonely trails where bears and wolves still dwell, and explore three of Croatia's most impressive national parks, which shelter in the hinterland.

By contrast, Zadar is a cultured city rich with museums, Roman ruins, restaurants and hip bars. Meanwhile international clubbers gravitate to Zrće beach and Tisno, which together form the nucleus of Croatia's premier summer clubbing scene.

Best Places to Eat

➡ Pelegrini (p193)
➡ Mediteran (p194)
➡ Kaštel (p184)
➡ Pet Bunara (p184)
➡ Konoba Figurica (p177)

Best Places to Stay

➡ Art Hotel Kalelarga (p183)
➡ Boškinac (p178)
➡ House Župan (p173)
➡ Drunken Monkey (p183)
➡ Indigo (p193)

When to Go

Zadar

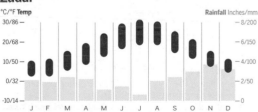

Apr–Jun Take advantage of the warming weather and cheaper prices.

Jul & Aug The peak party time in Zrće and Tisno.

Sep & Oct Watch the colours change in Plitvice and Krka National Parks.

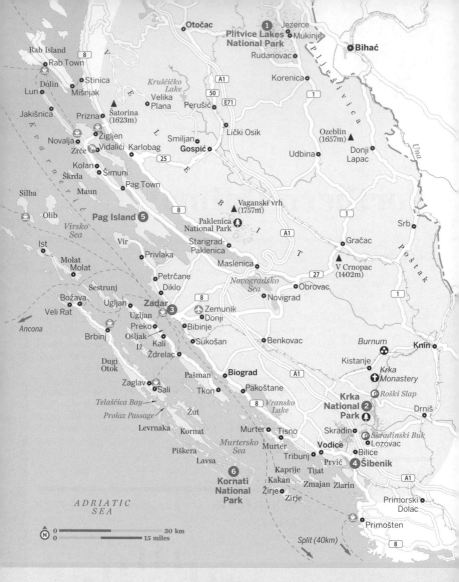

Northern Dalmatia Highlights

1 Marvelling at the otherworldly turquoise lakes and dramatic waterfalls of **Plitvice Lakes National Park** (p171).

2 Strolling alongside gurgling crystalline streams, swimming in a waterfall-fed lake and exploring historic monasteries in **Krka National Park** (p194).

3 Discovering Roman ruins, interesting museums, excellent eateries and hip bars within the marbled streets of **Zadar's** (p179) old town.

4 Stopping to admire the celebrated architecture of St James' Cathedral while wandering the medieval streets of **Šibenik** (p190).

5 Enjoying the sensory delights of **Pag Island** (p176) – sun-scorched scenery, fine wine, rustic cooking, pungent cheese and partying in the sun.

6 Seeing the Mediterranean as it looked to the ancients, boating between the unpopulated islands of **Kornati National Park** (p189).

LIKA

Covering a large swathe of the interior between the coastal mountains and the Bosnian border, this lightly populated region has blissful scenery ranging from lush farmland to dense forest and craggy uplands. In parts, the karstic nature of the underlying limestone has bequeathed a wonderland of caves, canyons, lakes and waterfalls.

Part of the Croatian heartland since the early 7th century, Lika was attacked by the Ottomans in the 16th century and was incorporated into the *vojna krajina* (military frontier). Vlach and Serb refugees, driven from Bosnia by the encroaching Ottomans, settled in the region with the blessing of the Habsburg monarchy, on the condition that they were prepared to fight. By the 1910 census the population was almost evenly split between the Orthodox and Catholic faiths, with many districts in the east having an outright Serbian majority.

During WWII, Lika's Serbian population suffered greatly at the hands of the Ustaše regime. In 1991, following Croatia's declaration of independence, the Serbs of the Krajina declared themselves an autonomous republic and it was in Lika that the first shots of the war rang out. Much of the local Croatian population was forced to abandon their homes and flee. When Croatian forces regained the area in 1995, most of the Serb population fled – leaving in their wake the many abandoned homes and villages that can still be seen today. Some, however, chose to return, and today the ethnic make-up of the region is 86% Croat and 12% Serb.

Plitvice Lakes & Around

The absolute highlight of Croatia's Adriatic hinterland, this glorious expanse of forested hills and turquoise lakes is excruciatingly scenic – so much so that in 1979 Unesco proclaimed it a World Heritage Site. The extraordinary natural beauty of the park merits a full day's exploration, but you can still experience a lot on a half-day trip from Zadar or Zagreb.

While the park is beautiful year-round, spring and autumn are the best times to visit. In spring and early summer the falls are flush with water, while in autumn the changing leaves put on a colourful display. Winter is also spectacular, although snow can limit access and the free park transport doesn't operate. Unquestionably the worst time to visit is in the peak months of July and August, when the falls reduce to a trickle, parking is problematic and the sheer volume of visitors can turn the walking tracks into a conga line and cause lengthy waits for the buses and boats which ferry people around the park.

History

A preservation society was founded in 1893 to ensure the protection of the lakes, and the first hotel was built here in 1896. The boundaries of the national park were set in 1951 and the lakes became a major tourist attraction until the civil war (which actually began in Plitvice on 31 March 1991, when rebel Serbs took control of the park headquarters). Croatian police officer Josip Jović became the war's first victim when he was killed here in the park. The Serbs held the area for the war's duration, turning the hotels into barracks. The Croatian army retook the park in August 1995, and subsequently the park's facilities have been fully restored.

◉ Sights

Plitvice Lakes National Park NATIONAL PARK
(☎053-751 015; www.np-plitvicka-jezera.hr; adult/child Jul & Aug 180/80KN, Apr-Jun, Sep & Oct 110/55KN, Nov-Mar 55/35KN; ☉7am-8pm) Within the boundaries of this heavily forested national park, 16 crystalline lakes tumble into each other via a series of waterfalls and cascades. The mineral-rich waters carve through the rock, depositing tufa in continually changing formations. Clouds of butterflies drift above the 18km of wooden footbridges and pathways which snake around the edges and under and across the rumbling water.

It takes upwards of six hours to explore the lakes on foot, or you can slice two hours off by taking advantage of the park's free boats and buses (departing every 30 minutes from April to October). From Entrance 2, catch the bus to the top of the upper lakes and wander back down to the shore of **Kozjak**, the park's largest lake (about 4km in length). A boat will whisk you from here to the lower lakes, where the circuit culminates in the aptly named **Veliki Slap**, the tallest waterfall in Croatia (78m). The path then climbs steeply (offering great views and photo opportunities)

THE NATURE OF PLITVICE LAKES

The Plitvice lake system is divided into upper and lower sections. The upper lakes, lying in a dolomite valley, are surrounded by dense forests and are linked by several gushing waterfalls. The lower lakes are smaller and shallower. Most of the water comes from the Bijela and Crna (White and Black) Rivers, which join south of Prošćansko Lake, but the lakes are also fed by underground springs. In turn, water disappears into the porous limestone at some points only to re-emerge in other places. All the water empties into the Korana River near Sastavci Falls.

The upper lakes are separated by dolomite barriers, which expand with the mosses and algae that absorb calcium carbonate as river water rushes through the karst. The encrusted plants grow on top of each other, forming travertine barriers and creating waterfalls. The lower lakes were formed by cavities created by the water of the upper lakes. They undergo a similar process, as travertine is constantly forming and reforming itself into new combinations so that the landscape is ever changing. This unique interaction of water, rock and plant life has continued more or less undisturbed since the last ice age.

The lakes' colours also change constantly. Most of the time they're a surreal shade of turquoise, but hues shift with the quantity of minerals and organisms in the water, rainfall and the angle of sunlight. On some days the lakes can appear more jade green or steely grey.

The luxuriant vegetation of the national park includes beech, fir, spruce and white pine forests, dotted with patches of whitebeam, hornbeam and flowering ash, which change colour in autumn.

The mammalian stars of the park are bears and wolves, but there are also deer, boar, rabbits, foxes and badgers. Look out for bird species including hawks, owls, cuckoos, kingfishers, wild ducks and herons, and occasionally black storks and ospreys.

to a bus stop, where you can grab a lift back to Entrance 2.

If you've got limited time, the upper lake section can be completed in two hours. The lower section takes about three, although we recommend that you start with the bus ride and end with the boat to save yourself a climb.

Rowboats can be hired from the shores of Lake Kozjak near Entrance 2 (50KN per hour). Note: swimming is not permitted in any of the lakes.

Barać's Caves CAVE
(Baraćeve špilje; ☑ 047-782 007; www.baraceve-spilje.hr; Nova Kršlja bb; adult/child Mar-May 50/25, Jun-Sep 60/30KN; ☺ 10am-6pm daily May-Sep, 10am-4pm Fri-Sun Mar, to 6pm Wed-Mon Apr) The same karstic limestone that created the Plitivice Lakes is responsible for these vast caverns hidden beneath verdant farmland 15km northeast of the national park (it's well signposted from the main road). Visits are by way of 45-minute guided tours (there is a minimum two people) through chambers with cheery names such as 'Dragon's Gorge' and 'Hall of Lost Souls'. Wear warm clothes and sensible shoes.

🛏 Sleeping

The four hotels operated by the national park are relatively charmless institutions but they're conveniently positioned right on the park's borders, making them a good option if you don't have your own wheels (see the park's website for details). Otherwise there are excellent guesthouses within walking distance in Mukinje and Jezerce (south of Entrance 2) and even better ones a little further away in the villages strung along the highway north of Entrance 1 (Selište Drežničko, Grabovac, Rakovica). For a particularly atmospheric alternative, hunt for private rooms in tiny Korana, an idyllic village set by a gurgling stream, reached by a narrow road north of the Korana bridge.

🛏 Mukinje & Jezerce

Plitvice Mirić Inn GUESTHOUSE €€
(☑ 099 21 42 250; www.plitvice-croatia.com; Jezerce 18/1; s/d €67/95; ☺ Apr-Oct; P ❄ 🏠) Run by a delightful family, this flower-strewn guesthouse has 13 rooms split between neighbouring buildings, only 1.5km from Entrance 2. Rooms are slightly bigger in the newer annex but they're all very com-

fortable. If you get a chance, try the home baking.

Villa Lika GUESTHOUSE €€
(📞 053-774 302; www.villa-lika.com; Mukinje 63; r €80-100; 🕙 Apr-Oct; 🅿️❄️🛜🏊) Right by the bus stop in Mukinje, these two large newly built houses have shiny white rooms offset with brightly coloured drapes and tiles. There are 15 rooms in total. When we visited they were busily landscaping a pool area.

Plitvice Etno-House GUESTHOUSE €€
(📞 053 774 760; www.plitviceetnohouse.com; Jezerce 21; r €100; 🅿️🛜🏊) Consisting of two large stone-and-wood houses hung with flowerboxes, this attractive complex has pine-trimmed rooms of real character and comfort. There's also a pool outside, with a little paddling area for children.

Selište Drežničko

Kamp Korana CAMPGROUND €
(📞 053-751 888; www.np-plitvicka-jezera.hr; site per adult/child/tent/car 67/47/15/22KN, bungalow s/d 148/252KN; 🕙 Apr-Oct; 🅿️) Spread over 35 hectares flanking the Korana River, this national park-run campground is about 6km north of Entrance 1, on the road to Zagreb. Facilities include a restaurant and a cafe-bar.

Hotel Degenija HOTEL €€€
(📞 047-782 143; www.hotel-degenija.com; Selište Drežničko 57a, s/d from €90/128; 🅿️❄️🛜) Still all very shiny and new, this small roadside hotel, 4km north of Entrance 1, has smart international-standard rooms and an attractive cafe grafted onto the side in its own wooden pavilion.

Grabovac & Rakovica

⭐ House Župan GUESTHOUSE €€
(📞 047-784 057; www.sobe-zupan.com; Rakovica 35; s/d 460/520KN; 🅿️❄️🛜) With an exceptionally welcoming hostess and clean, comfortable, contemporary rooms, this is an excellent choice. There's even a guest kitchen. It's set back from the highway in the small town of Rakovica, 11km north of the park.

House Tina GUESTHOUSE €€
(📞 047-784 197; www.housetina.com; Grabovac 175; r/bungalow €70/120; 🅿️❄️🛜) Smart and modern but with a rural ambience, this large family-run guesthouse offers first-rate family-friendly accommodation both in the main house and in two rustic wooden

bungalows in the yard. It's 9km from the park entrance, but shuttles are available (one way/return €5/7).

🍴 Eating

Eating options are limited in the national park itself, with a handful of options scattered about the entrances and the bus and boat stops.

Vila Velebita CROATIAN €€
(📞 053-755 040; www.vila-velebita.com; Rudanovac 12a; mains 56-85KN; 🕙 7am-11pm) Traditional meat grills are the speciality here, especially spit-roast lamb and suckling pig. If you've got your own transport, it's well worth the 14km trip south along the highway from Entrance 2.

Restaurant Degenija EUROPEAN €€
(📞 047-782 060; www.hotel-degenija.com; Selište Drežničko 57a; mains 45-115KN; 🕙 7am-11pm) The menu of the upmarket restaurant covers a lot of bases (pasta, pizza, fish) but meat is the star player. Traditional treats include turkey on gnocchi-like dumplings and, in summer, veal and potatoes slow-cooked under a *peka* (a dome-shaped cooking 'bell').

ℹ️ Information

Both of the park's two main entrances have parking (per hour/day 7/70KN) and an information office stocking brochures and maps.

ℹ️ Getting There & Away

Buses stop at both park entrances and there's a small ticket office at the stop near Entrance 2. Destinations include Zagreb (from 92KN, two hours, 14 daily), Zadar (from 85KN, 2½ hours, nine daily), Šibenik (107KN, 4½ hours, five daily), Trogir (120KN, five hours, four daily) and Split (from 132KN, 5½ hours, nine daily).

Around Gospić

The administrative capital of Lika-Senj county is a sleepy kind of place, but there are a couple of sights in the vicinity that are well worth seeking out. You'll need your own wheels though.

👁️ Sights

Nikola Tesla Memorial Centre MUSEUM
(📞 053-746 530; www.mcnikolatesla.hr; Smiljan; adult/child 50/20KN; 🕙 8am-8pm Tue-Sun Apr-Oct, 9am-3pm Tue-Sun Nov-Mar) It's extraordinary to think that one of the greatest minds

COWBOYS & CROATIANS

Linden Tree Retreat & Ranch
(☑053-685 616; www.lindenretreat.com; Velika Plana 3; s/d 297/456KN) Nestled within the wild reaches of the Velebit mountains, 27km northwest of Gospić, this remote dude ranch offers atmospheric accommodation in tepees or wooden chalets. The highlight here is horse riding (304KN for a two-hour jaunt, 912KN for a day trip), but you can also partake in wagon rides, guided hikes to nearby caves, mountain biking and mountain climbing.

of the modern world originated from such a peaceful and obscure place as the tiny village of Smiljan, 5km west of Gospić. Yet it was here that Nikola Tesla – the man responsible for bringing electricity into our homes and inventing wireless technology – was born. This fascinating museum includes displays about his life and working replicas of some of his most famous inventions.

Tesla's father was a Serbian Orthodox priest and sadly the family house, barn and church on this site were torched during the 1990s war. What stands here today is a reconstruction, financed by the Croatian government.

Grabovača Cave Park   CAVE
(Pećinski Park Grabovača; ☑053-679 233; www.pp-grabovaca.hr; Perušić; ⏰9am-8pm Jun-Aug, to 5pm Apr-May & Sep-Oct) The small town of Perušić, 12km north of Gospić, is notable for its pretty onion-domed church and its perfect chess-piece Turkish castle. However, the main attraction is this extraordinary cave complex on the edge of town.

The largest cave, **Samograd**, has four beautiful chambers – the biggest of which is large enough to host a concert every Easter Monday. Tours depart on the hour, descending 480 handmade stairs into the depths (not suitable for small children). Wear warm clothes and sensible footwear.

Paklenica National Park

Rising high above the Adriatic, the stark peaks of the Velebit Massif stretch for 145km and form a dramatic barrier between continental Croatia and the Adriatic coast.

Paklenica National Park (www.paklenica.hr; adult/child Jun-Sep 50/30KN, Oct-May 40/20KN; ⏰ entrance booths 6am-8.30pm Jun-Sep, 7am-3pm Oct-May) covers 95 sq km of this mountain chain. The park contains some of the country's finest mountain scenery, giving you the opportunity to trek up gorges, climb walls of stone and meander along shady paths next to a rushing stream.

The national park encompasses two deep gorges, Velika Paklenica (Great Paklenica) and Mala Paklenica (Small Paklenica), which scar the mountain range like giant hatchet marks, with cliffs over 400m high. The dry limestone karst that forms the Velebit Range is highly absorbent, but several springs at high altitudes provide a continuous source of water and nurture patches of lush vegetation. About half the park is covered with forests, mostly beech and pine followed by pubescent oak and varieties of hornbeam. The vegetation changes as you ascend, as does the climate, which progresses from Mediterranean to continental to subalpine. The lower regions, especially those with a southern exposure, can be fiercely hot in the summer, while the *bura* (cold northeasterly wind) that whips through the range in winter brings rain and sudden storms.

Animal life is scarce, but you may see golden eagles, striped eagles and peregrine falcons, which nest on the cliffs of the two gorges. Lynx, bears and wolves live in the park's upper regions, but your chances of seeing any are minuscule. There is, however, a high chance of seeing chamois near the main park entrances.

The best time to visit the park is in April, May, June or September. In late spring it's at its greenest and the streams become torrents. In July and August many of the streams dry up and it can be too hot to hike comfortably.

◉ Sights & Activities

Most hikes in the park are one-day affairs from either of the two main park entrances (accessed from Starigrad-Paklenica on the coast), or from one of the mountain huts. Given the nature of the terrain, most of them are reasonably challenging, although there are shorter routes suitable for novices. It's a good idea to ask at the national park office about walks that will suit your level of ability.

Landmines are a risk in some of the higher zones of the park. Follow only clearly marked paths and check with the park office before attempting any unusual routes.

Manita Peć CAVE
(adult/child 20/10KN; ☉10am-1pm Jul-Sep, reduced days Apr-Jun & Oct) The only cave in the park that's open to the public, Manita Peć has a wealth of stalagmites and stalactites enhanced by strategically placed lighting in the main chamber (40m long and 32m high). Entry is by way of a 30-minute tour.

This cave is about a 90-minute walk from the Entrance 1 car park. The path heads right up and into the Velika Paklenica gorge. When you pass a rocky waterfall with a stream on your right, you'll be at Anića Luka, a green, semicircular plateau. After another kilometre, a steep trail leads up to the cave.

Anića Kuk ROCK CLIMBING
Paklenica has rock-climbing routes ranging from beginner level to borderline suicidal. The firm, occasionally sharp limestone offers graded climbs, including 72 short sporto routes and 250 longer routes.

You'll see the beginner routes at the entrance to the park with cliffs reaching about 40m, but the best and most advanced climbing is on Anića Kuk, which offers over 100 routes up to a maximum of 350m. Most (though not all) of the routes are bolted. The most popular climbs here are Mosoraški (350m), Velebitaški (350m) and Klin (300m).

Spring is the best climbing season as summers can be very warm and winters too windy. A rescue service is also available. Consult Boris Čulić's *Paklenica* climber's guide for the complete rundown; it's available from the park office for 168KN.

🛏 Sleeping

Within the park's boundaries there's some rustic accommodation for hikers and climbers, but most people prefer to base themselves in the relative comfort of Starigrad-Paklenica, the small settlement that sprawls along the coastal road near the entrances to the park. It's neither particularly *stari* (old) or much of a *grad* (town) but it does have access to the sea for a cooling dip after a day's exertions.

🛏 National Park

Rugged types can avail themselves of three basic free-of-charge mountain shelters: Ivine Vodice, Struge and Vlaški Grad.

There's no electricity and you'll need your own sleeping bag but each has a spring which is reliable in all but the height of summer; check with the park office or at Planinarski Dom Paklenica before setting out.

Planinarski Dom Paklenica MOUNTAIN LODGE €
(☏023-301 636; www.pdpaklenica.hr; dm 65KN; ☉Sat & Sun year-round, daily mid-Jun–mid-Sep) Offering such luxuries as running water, a toilet and electricity, this lodge has 50 beds in four rooms; bring a sleeping bag. There's also a kitchen and dining room. The hut is a two-hour walk up from the Velika Paklenica canyon. Reservations are recommended on summer weekends.

🛏 Starigrad-Paklenica

Bluesun Camp Paklenica CAMPGROUND €
(☏023-209 050; www.bluesunhotels.com; Dr Franje Tudmana 14; camping per adult/child/site 73/45/122KN, mobile home from €99; ☉Apr Oct; ☷ ☷ ☷ ☷) Next to a pebbly beach and the national park office, this well-equipped campground has mobile homes and tent sites arranged under the pines. Guests have access to the resort pool at the Hotel Alan next door.

Hotel Rajna HOTEL €€
(☏023-359 121; www.hotel-rajna.com; Dr. Franje Tudjmana 105; s/d incl breakfast from €48/62; ☷ ☷ ☷) Simple and old fashioned but well-priced, this small family-run roadside hotel has rooms with balconies overlooking the sea and a downstairs restaurant that serves an excellent breakfast.

🍴 Eating

Taverna-Konoba Marasović CROATIAN €€
(Marasovići bb; mains 60-140KN; ☉110pm May-Oct) 🍴 A kilometre inland from Entrance 1, this eatery occupies a fantastic old village house with a terrace at the front and chunky tables in the dining room. All the food is locally sourced and, with advance notice, can be cooked in a traditional *peka*. The national park owns the property and usually has interesting displays upstairs.

Buffet Dinko CROATIAN €€
(Paklenička 1; mains 56-95KN) At the junction of the coastal highway and the access road to Entrance 1 in Starigrad, this popular restaurant has a shady terrace and a hefty menu of grilled meat and seafood. Serves are huge.

ℹ Information

Paklenica National Park Office (✆ 023-369 202; www.paklenica.hr; Dr Franje Tuđmana 14a; ⏱7am-3pm Mon-Fri) Sells booklets and maps and dispenses advice, both from the main office in Starigrad and at the park entrances. The *Paklenica National Park* guide (120KN) gives an excellent overview of the park and details walks. Three- and five-day passes are available.

Starigrad Tourist Office (✆ 023-369 245; www.rivijera-paklenica.hr; Trg Tome Marasovića 1; ⏱8am-9.30pm Jul & Aug, to 8pm Jun & Sep, to 2pm Mon-Fri Oct-May) In the town centre, across from the small marina.

ℹ Getting There & Around

Most buses travelling along the coastal highway stop at Starigrad-Paklenica. Destinations include Rijeka (from 138KN, 3½ hours, five daily), Zadar (45KN, one hour, five daily), Split (from 124KN, four hours, five daily), Dubrovnik (from 243KN, nine hours, three daily) and Zagreb (136KN, 3¾ hours, daily).

There are no taxis in Starigrad. Some hotels will drop off and pick up guests at the park's entrance gates.

PAG ISLAND

Pag is like something you'd find in a 1950s Italian film, perfect for a broody black-and-white Antonioni set – it's barren, rocky, and sepia coloured, with vast empty landscapes stretching across the horizon. The Adriatic is a steely blue around it and, when the sky is stormy, it's the most dramatic-looking place in the whole of Croatia. Its karstic rock forms a moonscape defined by two mountain ridges, patches of shrubs and a dozen or so villages and hamlets.

Nowadays it's connected to the mainland by a bridge – but in terms of culture and produce it's very independent and distinct. Islanders farm the miserly soil and produce some excellent wine. Tough local sheep graze on herbs and salty grasses, lending their meat and milk a distinctive flavour and producing *paški sir* (Pag cheese; soaked in olive oil and aged in stone). Intricate Pag lace is famed and framed on many a Croat's wall.

Pag has a new twist to its image as a place of centuries-old tradition and culture, in the form of the clubbing mecca of Zrće beach.

ℹ Getting There & Away

BOAT

A daily **Jadrolinija** (www.jadrolinija.hr) catamaran connects Novalja to Rab (45KN, 55 minutes) and Rijeka (80KN, 2¾ hours).

Regular Jadrolinija car ferries also link Žigljen on Pag's northeast coast to Prizna on the mainland (per adult/child/car 17/9/96KN, 15 minutes); these run roughly every 90 minutes, increasing to hourly in July and August. If you're coming from the north, this will save you at least 1½ hours driving time as opposed to taking the bridge.

BUS

Buses travel to Zadar year-round (79KN, two hours, three to five daily), and to Šibenik (117KN, 3½ hours, two daily), Split (174KN, five hours, two daily), Rijeka (72KN, three hours, daily) and Zagreb (from 168KN, four hours, seven daily) in summer.

ℹ Getting Around

Three to 11 buses a day make the 30-minute trip between Pag Town and Novalja (from 30KN).

Pag Town

POP 3850

Historic Pag Town enjoys a spectacular setting, fringing a narrow spit of land between sun-scorched hills, with an azure bay on its eastern flank and shimmering salt pans to its west. It's an intimate, somewhat shabby collection of narrow lanes and bleak-looking stone houses with pebble beaches close by.

In the early 15th century the prosperous salt business prompted the construction of Pag Town when adjacent Stari Grad could no longer meet the demands of its burgeoning population. Venetian rulers engaged the finest builder of the time, Juraj Dalmatinac, to design a new city – the first cornerstone was laid in 1443. In accordance with what were then the latest ideas in town planning, the main streets and the cross lanes intersect at right angles and lead to four city gates. In the centre, there's a square with a cathedral, a ducal palace and an unfinished bishop's palace. In 1499 Dalmatinac began working on the city walls, but only the northern corner, with parts of a castle, remains.

◉ Sights

Pag Lace Gallery   MUSEUM
(Galerija paške čipke; Trg Kralja Krešimira IV; admission 10KN; ⏱9.30am-6.30pm Jun-Sep) Housed in the spectacular restored Ducal Palace

(Kneževa Palača), designed by Juraj Dalmatinac, this museum showcases some remarkably intricate designs. The history of lacemaking in Pag and its importance to the community is skilfully illustrated with photographs and information panels.

Collegiate Church of the Assumption
CHURCH

(Zborna Crkva Marijinog Uznesenja; Trg Kralja Krešimira IV; ⊙9am-noon & 5-7pm May-Sep, Mass only Oct-Apr) Dalmatinac's Gothic church sits in perfect harmony with the modest structures surrounding it. The lunette over the portal shows the Virgin with women of Pag in medieval blouses and headdresses, and there are two rows of unfinished sculptures of saints. Completed in the 16th century, the interior was renovated with baroque ceiling decorations in the 18th century.

Salt Exhibition
MUSEUM

(Stalna Izlozba Solarstva; Stari Grad; admission 10KN; ⊙10am-1pm Jun-Sep) Over the bridge in what remains of ancient Stari Grad – which is very little – this exhibition (in a former salt warehouse) documents the production of salt in Pag with photography and artefacts.

⚝ Festivals & Events

Pag Carnival
CULTURAL

(⊙31 Jul) The last day of July is the Pag Carnival, a good chance to see the traditional *kolo* (a lively Slavic circle dance) and appreciate the elaborate traditional dress of Pag. The main square fills with dancers and musicians, and a theatre troupe presents the folk play *Paška Robinja* (The Slave Girl of Pag).

🛏 Sleeping & Eating

While Pag Town is an interesting place to visit, there are better places to stay. There are a few hotels scattered around the bay immediately north of the old town and plenty of private accommodation on offer; enquire at a travel agency or look for signs advertising '*sobe*'.

Bistro Na Tale
CROATIAN €€

(Radićeva 2; mains from 43-180KN; ⊙9am-11pm) This dependable, casual and highly popular place has a little front terrace facing the salt flats and another with plenty of shade. Pag lamb is a real speciality, or opt for the fresh fish of the day cooked in wine and herbs.

🔒 Shopping

It would be a shame to leave the island without buying lace, since the prices are relatively cheap and buying a piece helps keep the tradition alive. A small circle or star about 10cm in diameter takes a good 24 hours to make. If you walk down Kralja Tomislava or Kralja Dmitra Zvonimira you can buy directly from the lace makers, virtually all of whom have fixed prices.

Pag cheese is not as easy to find, although you should be able to get it at the morning market. Otherwise, look out for homemade '*Paški sir*' signs posted outside a house on a remote road somewhere.

ⓘ Information

Mediteran Pag (☑023-611 238; www.mediteran-pag.com; Zrinsko-frankopanska 8) Agency with a very wide selection of private accommodation and excursions.

Meridian 15 (☑023-612 162; www.meridijan15.hr; Ante Starčevića 1) Travel agency that runs island excursions and trips to national parks including Paklenica. Also books accommodation.

Post Office (Golija bb; ⊙8am-7pm Mon-Fri, to noon Sat)

Tourist Office (☑023-611 286; www.tzgpag.hr; Vela bb, ⊙8am-10pm Jun-Aug, 8am-8pm Mon-Fri, 9am-1pm & 4-8pm Sep-May)

Central Pag

After the crossing the bridge from Pag Town, the main road climbs sharply up the narrow spine of the island and then crosses to the slightly greener west coast and the small port of Šimuni. Before too long it ascends again to the sunburnt central ridge and the agricultural village of Kolan. Not only is this a great place to shop for Pag cheese, it's also home to some of the island's best traditional eateries.

🛏 Sleeping & Eating

Camping Šimuni
CAMPGROUND €

(☑023-697 441; www.camping-simuni.hr; Šimuni bb; camping per adult/child/site 68/44/113KN, unit from 743KN; 🅿✳) On a gorgeous cove with a shingle beach, about 12km from Pag Town in the direction of Novalja, this large complex has a good vibe and lots of activities on offer. All local buses stop here.

★Konoba Figurica
DALMATIAN €€

(Figurica 11, Kolan; mains 50-160KN; ⊙noon-10pm) This rustic restaurant occupies a covered terrace surrounded by olive trees, just below the lower road running through Kolan. Share a Pag cheese platter and then tuck into delicious grilled squid or *peka*-roasted Pag lamb.

Konoba Nono DALMATIAN €€
(☑ 023-698 059; http://konobanono.com; Rudina 1, Kolan; mains 45-120KN; ◉ 11am-11pm May-Sep) Grab a seat in the stone-walled front terrace and tuck into a tasty serve of old-fashioned home cooking, Dalmatian-style. Pag cheese and lamb feature prominently on the menu, as does pasta and grilled fish.

Novalja & Around

POP 3670

In a nation of sedate resorts, Novalja bucks the trend. Its bars and clubs offer nightlife as raucous as you'll find in Croatia and as a consequence it attracts a noticeably younger crowd. Depending on which side of 35 you sit on, this could be heaven or it could be hell. Cultural interest is confined to the incendiary club scene based on nearby Zrće beach; there are no historic sights. That said, the promenade has an appealing buzz, and there are fine beaches close by. In winter it reverts to being a pleasantly sleepy backwater.

✸ Festivals & Events

Hideout MUSIC
(www.hideoutfestival.com; ◉ late Jun-early Jul) The festival that put Zrće on the electronic dance music (EDM) map takes over the beach bars and clubs in late June/early July. Expect big-name DJs and multiple nights of mayhem.

Fresh Island MUSIC
(www.fresh-island.org; ◉ late Jul) Billing itself as 'Europe's #1 Beach Hip-Hop Festival', Fresh Island comes to Zrće's Papaya and Aquarius clubs for three nights in late July. Past headliners have included the likes of Rick Ross, Method Man and Redman.

Sonus MUSIC
(www.sonus-festival.com; ◉ mid-Aug) Five days and nights of EDM in mid-August on Zrće. In previous years it's featured the likes of John Digweed and Laurent Garnier.

🛏 Sleeping & Eating

Most of the best places to stay are a little out of the town centre. Accommodation

is incredibly hard to find during the summer party season, especially during the big events, so make sure you book ahead.

Within Novalja itself there are plenty of eateries catering to the foreign backpacker/clubber crowd, including an American burger bar, a Mexican joint and loads of places selling pizza slices. For a more memorable meal you're better off jumping in the car (if you've got one) and heading to Boškinac or Kolan.

Big Yellow Hostel HOSTEL €
(☑ 09 23 083 668; www.bigyellowhostel.com; Lokunje 1; dm/r from 230/460KN; P @ 🛜) The best of a new wave of hostels catering to the young party crowd, Big Yella offers a sweet vibe, free breakfast and basic four- to six-bed dorms, some of which have balconies and terrific sea views. It's not flash but it hits the spot.

Barbati HOTEL €€
(☑ 091 12 11 233; www.barbati.hr; Vidalići 39; r/apt from €60/130; P ✳ @ 🛜 ⛱) Located across the bay from Zrće (you'll hear it in the distance) within a scrappy development of beach apartments 6km from Novalja, this chic little hotel has well-designed rooms, a tiny covered pool and an attractive waterside bar-restaurant.

★ Boškinac HOTEL €€€
(☑ 053-663 500; www.boskinac.com; s/d 1125/1275KN; P ✳ @ 🛜 ⛱) Hands down the most sophisticated place to stay, eat and drink on Pag, this wonderful little winery hotel offers eight huge rooms and three suites in a blissful rural location surrounded by vines. Even if you're not staying here you should make the pilgrimage to sample the wine (cellar hours noon to 1am) and to dine at the acclaimed restaurant (mains 70KN to 160KN).

Its cabernet merlot blend is excellent and it's the only place in the world growing and making wine from Gegić, a grape endemic to Pag (producing an elegant white). It's about 3km north of Novalja; follow the signs towards Stara Novalja.

Luna HOTEL €€€
(☑ 053-654 700; www.lunaislandhotel.com; Jakišnica bb; r from 1381KN; P ✳ @ 🛜 ⛱) Right up the northern end of the island, 14km from Novalja, this big modern hotel is a good option for a poolside holiday. Rooms are spacious, and facilities include pools and a spa centre.

Drinking & Nightlife

About 3km southeast of Novalja, Zrće beach is staking its claim as the Ibiza of Croatia. Unlike Ibiza, the clubs and bars are right on the beach – but in terms of scale, it's got a long way to go. Basically there are three main clubs and a scattering of bars in between, all of which open in late June and close by mid-September. Entrance prices very much depend on the event: nights are usually free at the beginning of the season and as much as €35 for big-name DJs in mid-August

The beach itself is a picturesque 1km-long treeless crescent of pebbles overlooking a parched strip of eastern Pag, with the mountains of the mainland rearing up on the horizon – rent an umbrella for shade. Swimming is excellent, though you'll have to endure the buzz of jet skis (which are confined to certain sections).

Papaya CLUB

(www.papaya.com.hr; ⊙10am-6am) Rated by *DJ Mag* as the 23rd best club in the world in 2014, Papaya is the kingpin of the Zrće scene, complete with palm trees, waterfalls and a shell-like roof over the dancefloor. On big nights it can cram 5000 people onto its terraces.

Kalypso CLUB

(www.kalypso-zrce.com; ⊙10am-6am) Kalypso is the coolest-looking club on the strip, built into a cove at the north end of the beach with myriad cabana-like bars surrounded by palm trees. While the sun shines you can chill out on day beds by a small pool; after dark, DJs spin deep house mixes to a sophisticated crowd.

Aquarius CLUB

(www.aquarius.hr) The 82nd best club in the world (according to *DJ Mag*), Aquarius is a huge space with stylish alcoves, great views and a glassed-off area.

ℹ Information

Aurora (☑053-663 493; www.aurora-novalja. com; Slatinska 9; ⊙9am-8pm) Well-organised agency with rental apartments and rooms on its books. Excursions too.

Sunturist (☑053-661 211; www.sunturist. hr; Silvija Strahimira Kranjčevićeva bb) Books private accommodation and trips.

Tourist Office (☑056-661 404; www.tz-novalja. hr; Trg Brišćić 1; ⊙8am-8pm Jun-Sep, to 3pm Mon-Fri Oct-May) Stocks free town maps and timetables for boats and buses.

ZADAR

POP 75,100

Boasting a historic old town of medieval churches, Roman ruins, cosmopolitan cafes and quality museums set on a small peninsula, Zadar is an intriguing city. It's not too crowded, it's not overrun with tourists, and its two unique attractions – the sound-and-light spectacle of the *Sea Organ* and the *Sun Salutation* – need to be seen and heard to be believed.

While it's not a picture postcard kind of place, the mix of ancient relics, Habsburg elegance, coastal setting and unsightly tower blocks is what gives Zadar so much character. It's no Dubrovnik, but it's not a museum town either – this is a living, vibrant city, enjoyed by residents and visitors alike.

Zadar is also a key transport hub with superb ferry connections to the surrounding islands and to Italy.

History

Zadar was inhabited by the Illyrian Liburnian tribe as early as the 9th century BC. By the 1st century BC, it had become a minor Roman colony. Slavs settled here in the 6th and 7th centuries AD, and Zadar eventually fell under the authority of Croatian-Hungarian kings.

The rise of Venetian power in the mid-12th century was bitterly contested – there was a succession of citizens' uprisings over the next 200 years – but the city was finally acquired by Venice in 1409, along with the rest of Dalmatia.

Frequent Veneto-Turkish wars resulted in the building of Zadar's famous city walls in the 16th century, partly on the remains of the earlier Roman fortifications. With the fall of Venice in 1797, the city passed to Austrian rulers, who administered the city with the assistance of its Italianised ruling aristocracy. Italian influence endured well into the 20th century, with Zadar (or Zara as the Italians call it) captured by Italy at the end of WWI and officially ceded to Italy with the Treaty of Rapallo in 1920.

When Italy capitulated to the Allies in 1943, the city was occupied by the Germans and then bombed to smithereens by the Allies, with almost 60% of the old town destroyed. The city was rebuilt following the original street plan.

History repeated itself in November 1991 when Yugoslav rockets kept Zadar under siege for three months. Few war wounds

Zadar

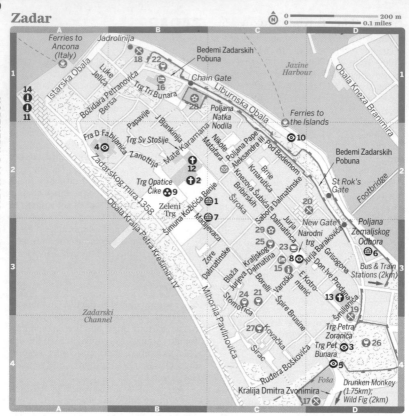

are now visible, however, and Zadar has re-emerged as one of Croatia's most dynamic towns.

◉ Sights

Land Gate   GATE
(Kopnena vrata; Ante Kuzmanića bb) The most elaborate of the city gates also has the prettiest setting, facing a sheltered little marina. Dating from 1543, its Renaissance-style decorations include St Chrysogonus (Zadar's patron saint) on horseback and the Venetian winged lion.

Five Wells Square   SQUARE
(Trg Pet Bunara) Built in 1574 on the site of a former moat, this square takes its name from the five wells that supplied Zadar with water until 1838. Set into the neighbouring bastion is Queen Jelena Madijevka Park, a lovely little garden with shady paths and views from the ramparts.

St Simeon's Church   CHURCH
(Crkva Sv Šime; Poljana Šime Budinića bb; ⊙8.30am-noon & 5-7pm Mon-Fri, 8.30am-noon Sat May-Oct) While this 17th-century baroque church is pretty enough, it's what lies inside that makes it truly noteworthy. Taking pride of place above the main altar, the sarcophagus of St Simeon is a masterpiece of medieval goldsmithery. Commissioned in 1377, the coffin is made of cedar and covered inside and out with finely executed gold-plated silver reliefs.

The middle relief showing the Presentation of Jesus to Simeon at the Temple is a copy of Giotto's fresco from Cappella dell'Arena in Padua, Italy. Other reliefs depict scenes from the lives of the saints and King Ludovic's visit to Zadar. The lid shows a reclining St Simeon.

Museum of Ancient Glass   MUSEUM
(Muzej antičkog stakla; www.mas-zadar.hr; Poljana Zemaljskog Odbora 1; adult/concession 30/10KN;

9am-9pm Mon-Sat May-Sep, to 4pm Oct-Apr) It's baffling that a medium as delicate as glass could survive the earthquakes and wars that have plagued this region over the millennia, but this impressive museum has thousands of objects on display: goblets, jars, vials, jewellery and amulets. Many of the larger glass urns were removed from the local Roman necropolis (cemetery) where they held cremated remains. The layout is superb, with large light boxes and ethereal music to heighten the experience.

People's Square
SQUARE

(Narodni trg) Traditionally the centre of public life, this pretty little square is constantly abuzz with the chatter from its many cafebars. The western side is dominated by the late-Renaissance **City Guard** building, dating from 1562; the clock tower was added under the Austrian administration in 1798. Public proclamations and judgments were announced from the 1565 **loggia** opposite, which is now an art exhibition space.

Archaeological Museum
MUSEUM

(Arheološki Muzej; www.amzd.hr; Trg Opatice Čike 1; adult/concession 30/15KN; 9am-9pm Jun-Sep, to 2pm Mon Sat Oct-May) A wealth of prehistoric, ancient and medieval relics, mainly from Zadar and its surrounds, awaits at this fascinating museum. Highlights include a 2.5m-high marble statue of Augustus from the 1st century AD, and a model of the Forum as it once looked.

Museum of Religious Art
MUSEUM

(Trg Opatice Čike bb; adult/concession 20/10KN; 10am-1pm & 6-8pm Mon-Sat, 10am-1pm Sun) This impressive museum in the Benedictine convent boasts a fine collection of reliquaries, sculpture, embroidery and paintings. Of particular note are works by Venetian masters Paolo Veneziano and Vittore Carpaccio.

Roman Forum
RUINS

(Zeleni trg) One of the most intriguing things about Zadar is the way Roman ruins seem to sprout randomly from the city's streets. Nowhere is this more evident than in the site of the ancient Forum, constructed between the 1st century BC and the 3rd century AD. As in Roman times it's still the centre of civic and religious life, with St Donatus' Church dominating one side of it.

Among the ruins of temples and colonnades stands one intact Roman column, which in the Middle Ages served as a shame post where wrongdoers were chained and

---

Zadar

⊙ Sights
1	Archaeological Museum	C2
2	St Donatus' Church	B2
3	Five Wells Square	D4
4	Franciscan Monastery	A2
5	Land Gate	D4
6	Museum of Ancient Glass	D3
7	Museum of Religious Art	C2
8	People's Square	C3
9	Roman Forum	B2
10	Sea Gate	C2
11	Sea Organ	A1
12	St Anastasia's Cathedral	B2
13	St Simeon's Church	D3
14	Sun Salutation	A1

⊙ Sleeping
| 15 | Art Hotel Kalelarga | C3 |
| 16 | Hotel Bastion | B1 |

⊗ Eating
17	Foša	D4
	Gourmet Kalelarga	(see 15)
	Kaštel	(see 16)
18	Kornat	B1
19	Pet Bunara	D4
20	Market	D2

⊙ Drinking & Nightlife
21	Galerija Dina	C3
22	Garden	B1
23	Kavana Lovre	C3
24	Kult Caffe	C3
25	La Bodega	C3
26	Ledana	D4
27	Zodiac	C4

⊕ Entertainment
| 28 | Arsenal | B1 |
| 29 | Croatian National Theatre | C3 |

---

publicly humiliated. Nearby are more Roman remains, including altars with reliefs of the mythical figures Jupiter Ammon and Medusa. On the top you can see the hollows used in blood sacrifices. It is believed that this area was a temple dedicated to Jupiter, Juno and Minerva dating from the 1st century BC.

St Donatus' Church
CHURCH

(Crkva Sv Donata; Šimuna Kožičića Benje bb; admission 15KN; 9am-9pm May-Sep, to 4pm Oct-Apr) Dating from the beginning of the 9th century, this unusual circular Byzantine-style church was named after the bishop who commissioned it. As one of only a handful of buildings from the early Croatian kingdom to have survived the Mongol invasion of the 13th century, it's a particularly important cultural relic. The simple and unadorned interior includes two complete Roman columns, recycled from the Forum. Also from the Forum are the paving slabs that were revealed after the original floor was removed.

The church hasn't been used for services for around 200 years and these days it often serves as a concert hall.

St Anastasia's Cathedral   CATHEDRAL
(Katedrala Sv Stošije; Trg Sv Stošije; ☉ 6.30-7pm Mon-Fri, 8-9am Sat, 8-9am & 6-7pm Sun) Built in the 12th and 13th centuries, Zadar's cathedral has a richly decorated facade and an impressive three-nave interior with the remains of frescoes in the side apses. The cathedral was badly bombed during WWII and has since been reconstructed. On the altar in the left apse is a marble sarcophagus containing the relics of St Anastasia, while the choir contains lavishly carved stalls. A glass vestibule allows you peer inside when the cathedral's closed.

Climb the **bell tower** (admission 15KN; ☉ 9am-10pm Mon-Sat) for old-town views.

Franciscan Monastery   MONASTERY
(Franjevački Samostan; www.svetifrane.org; Trg Sv Frane 1; adult/child 10/5KN; ☉ 9am-6pm) Entry to this historic monastery includes access to a lovely Renaissance cloister, the Gothic church (the oldest of its kind in Dalmatia, consecrated in 1280), the sacristy (where the 1358 treaty under which Venice relinquished its rights to Dalmatia in favour of the Croatian-Hungarian king Ludovic was signed) and a small treasury.

Highlights of the latter include a large 12th-century painted wooden crucifix, a 15th-century polyptych from the island of Ugljan and a 16th-century painting of the dead Christ by Jacopo Bassano.

Sea Organ   MONUMENT
(Morske orgulje; Istarska Obala) Zadar's incredible *Sea Organ*, designed by local architect Nikola Bašić, is unique. Set within the perforated stone stairs that descend into the sea is a system of pipes and whistles that exudes wistful sighs when the movement of the sea pushes air through it. The effect is hypnotic, the mellifluous tones increasing in volume when a boat or ferry passes by. You can swim from the steps off the promenade while listening to the sounds.

Sun Salutation   MONUMENT
(Pozdrav Suncu; Istarska Obala) Another wacky and wonderful creation by Nikola Bašić, this 22m-wide circle set into the pavement is filled with 300 multilayered glass plates that collect the sun's energy during the day. Together with the wave energy that makes the *Sea Organ*'s sound, it produces a trippy light show from sunset to sunrise that's meant to simulate the solar system. It also collects enough energy to power the entire harbour-front lighting system.

The place is packed with tourists, excited children and locals every night, especially at sunset, when the gorgeous sea views and the illuminated pavement make for a spectacular sight.

Sea Gate   GATE
(Morska vrata; Poljana Pape Aleksandra III bb) Also known as St Chrysogonus' Gate (Vrata Sv Krševana), this port-facing gate was built in 1573 and sports the Venetian lion and part of a Roman triumphal arch. The inscription is a memorial to the 1571 Battle of Lepanto, where the Ottoman fleet was defeated off western Greece.

 ## Activities

There's a **swimming area** with diving boards, a small park and a cafe on the coastal promenade south of the old town; from the Land Gate, follow the road as it curves to the right and continue on Kralja Dmitra Zvonimira. Bordered by pine trees and small parks, the promenade takes you to a beach in front of Hotel Kolovare and then winds on for about 1km along the coast.

Tours

Local travel agencies offer **boat cruises** to Telašćica Bay and the beautiful Kornati Islands; tours generally include lunch and a swim in the sea or a salt lake. Ask around on Liburnska Obala (where the excursion boats are moored) or contact Aquarius Travel Agency (p185). Organised trips to the national parks of Paklenica, Krka and Plitvice Lakes are also very popular, making it easy for visitors to access the parks without having to worry about organising transport.

Festivals & Events

St Donatus Musical Evenings   MUSIC
(Glazbene večeri u Sv Donatu; www.donat-festival.com; ☉ Jul & Aug) Classical-music performances featuring prominent artists from

across the globe, held in St Donatus' Church in July and August.

Zadar Dreams — THEATRE
(Zadar Snova; www.zadarsnova.hr; ☉ early Aug) International festival of contemporary theatre, held over a week in early August.

Full Moon Festival — CULTURAL
(Noć Punog Miseca; ☉ Aug) During this festival (held on the night of the full moon in August), Zadar's quays are lit with torches and candles, stalls sell local delicacies and boats lining the quays become floating fish markets.

🛏 Sleeping

There's little accommodation in the old town itself, but plenty in the surrounding city. A couple of terrific hostels have sprung up 1.5km south of the old town in the suburb of Arbanasi, home to the centuries-old Albanian community. It's a handy spot, close to the beach and only a 20-minute walk from the Land Gate.

Most visitors stay in the 'tourist settlement' of Borik, along the waterfront 4km north of the old town. Although it's a good 40-minute walk away, it has good swimming, a nice promenade and lots of greenery.

🛏 Old Town

★ Art Hotel Kalelarga — HOTEL €€€
(☎ 023-233 000; www.arthotel-kalelarga.com; Majke Margarite 3; s/d/ste 1360/1660/2580KN; ❄ 🛜) Built and designed under strict conservation rules due to its old-town location, this 10-room boutique hotel is an understated and luxurious beauty. Exposed stonework and mushroom hues imbue the spacious rooms with plenty of style and character.

Hotel Bastion — HOTEL €€€
(☎ 023-494 950; www.hotel-bastion.hr; Bedemi Zadarskih Pobuna 13; s/d/ste from 1560/1900/2490KN; P ❄ 🛜) Built over the remains of a Venetian fortress, Bastion radiates character and sophistication. The 23 rooms and five suites successfully combine a classic early-20th-century feel with a contemporary sensibility. It also boasts a top-drawer restaurant and a basement spa.

🛏 Arbanasi

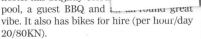

★ Drunken Monkey
(☎ 023-314 406; www.[...]com; Jure Kastriotica Skend[...] 193/500KN; ❄ @ 🛜 ☰) T[...] suburban neighbourhood [...] hostel has brightly colou[...] pool, a guest BBQ and a[...] around great vibe. It also has bikes for hire (per hour/day 20/80KN).

Wild Fig — HOSTEL €
(☎ 023-302 351; www.thewildfighostel.com; Uvala Bregdetti 14c; dm/r 150/480KN; ☉ Apr–mid-Nov; P ❄ @ 🛜) Run by a charming Aussie-Brit duo, this sociable hostel has attractive rooms, an excellent guest kitchen and a chilled-out terrace strung with hammocks. Help yourself to figs, mulberries and peaches in summer. The hostel van provides shuttles to Plitvice and Krka National Parks (250KN).

🛏 Borik

Apartmani Petra — APARTMENTS €€
(☎ 091 20 06 501; www.apartman-petra.com; Roberta Frangeša Mihanovića 63, apt 420 595KN; P ❄ 🛜) Hidden in a scrappy cluster of holiday homes up on the hill (not too far from the beach but a fair hike from the old town), this tidy apartment block is a real gem. The units are clean, quiet and secure and the hostess couldn't be more welcoming.

Hotel Adriana — HOTEL €€€
(☎ 023 555 600; www.adriana.falkensteiner.com; Majstora Radovana 7; r from 1690KN; ☉ mid-May–Oct; P ❄ @ 🛜 ☰) Aimed at grown-ups (as opposed to its neighbouring sister establishment), this upmarket hotel is centred on a handsome 19th-century villa with lovely shady grounds that extend down to the Adriatic. The rooms, in a 1960s extension, are suitably well appointed. Rates include half board.

Club Funimation Borik — RESORT €€€
(☎ 023-555 600; www.borik.falkensteiner.com; Majstora Radovana 7; s/d all-inclusive from €143/226; P ❄ @ 🛜 ☰) Families are well catered for in this beachfront hotel, with all-inclusive rates and an impressive indoor-outdoor pool complex. Kids can explore their own 'Falky Land', while mum and dad avail themselves of the outstanding spa and gym. Rooms are very spacious and suites are palatial.

...he island of Ugljan is easily accessible by boat from Zadar, making it a popular getaway for the locals and a kind of leafy island suburb for people who work in the city. It's densely populated, with over 6000 residents, and can get crowded on summer weekends. There are few forested areas but many *macchia* (shrubs), some pines and a good deal of farmland with vegetable gardens, olive groves and vineyards. The eastern coast is the most developed part of the island, while the west is relatively deserted.

The port of entry is **Preko**, directly across from Zadar, with two small harbours and a ferry port. Although there's a town beach, the best beach is on the little island of **Galovac**, only 80m from the town centre. Small, pretty and wooded, Galovac has a Franciscan monastery dating from the 15th century. If you have your own car, you could visit **Ugljan village**, positioned on a bay with a sandy beach; the fishing village of **Kali**; and the nearby islet of **Ošljak**, which is covered with pine and cypress trees.

Jadrolinija runs car ferries from Zadar to Preko (per adult/child/car 18/9/103KN, 25 minutes, 11 to 17 daily) year-round.

Hotel Niko
HOTEL €€€
(☑ 023-337 888; www.hotel-niko.hr; Obala Kneza Domagoja 9; s/d €100/140; ☐☀☎) The spacious rooms in this small, friendly, family-run hotel are kitted out with richly coloured carpets and good-quality furniture. All have balconies and some have lovely views over the Adriatic towards the old town.

Villa Hrešć
HOTEL €€€
(☑ 023-337 570; www.villa-hresc.hr; Obala Kneza Trpimira 28; s/d/apt from 650/850/1290KN; ☐☀☎☒) This attractive condo-style complex has a full-frontal view of the old town from its coastal garden. Some of the rooms have massive terraces. It's halfway between the old town and Borik, about a 20-minute walk along the coastal promenade from the footbridge.

🍴 Eating

Market
MARKET €
(Zlatarska; ☉7am-1pm) One of Croatia's best traditional markets, with seasonal, local produce at cheap prices: juicy watermelons and oranges, cured ham and Pag cheese.

★ Kaštel
MEDITERRANEAN €€
(☑ 023-494 950; www.hotel-bastion.hr; Bedemi Zadarskih Pobuna 13; mains 80-160KN; ☉7am-11pm) Hotel Bastion's fine-dining restaurant offers contemporary takes on classic Croatian cuisine (octopus stew, stuffed squid, Pag cheese). France and Italy also make their presence felt, particularly in the delectable dessert list. Opt for the white-linen experience inside or dine on the battlements overlooking the harbour.

★ Pet Bunara
DALMATIAN €€
(☑ 023-224 010; www.petbunara.hr; Stratico bb; mains 75-145KN; ☉11am-10.30pm) Boasting exposed-stone walls inside and a pretty terrace lined with olive trees, this is an atmospheric place to tuck into Dalmatian soups and stews, homemade pasta and local faves such as octopus and turkey. Save room for a traditional Zadar fig cake or cherry torte.

Kornat
MEDITERRANEAN €€
(☑ 023-254 501; www.restaurant-kornat.com; Liburnska Obala 6; mains 50-135KN; ☉noon-midnight) Sitting pretty in a prime harbour-front spot with lots of polished wood and a slim covered terrace, this elegant place is one of Zadar's best restaurants. The cooking marries fresh Croatian produce, rich French-style sauces and plenty of Italian touches.

Restaurant Niko
SEAFOOD €€
(☑ 023-337 888; www.hotel-niko.hr; Obala Kneza Domagoja 9; mains 58-170KN; ☉noon-midnight) This wildly popular hotel restaurant is great for grilled fish and other seafood, though the menu has red meat and vegetarian dishes too. It's your best bet down the Borik end of the city.

Gourmet Kalelarga
CAFE, DALMATIAN €€
(Široka 23; breakfast 18-50KN, mains 76-128KN; ☉7am-10pm) Beneath the Art Hotel Kalelarga, this chic little cafe is your best option for a cooked breakfast or a decadent cake. As the day progresses, the focus shifts towards more substantial Dalmatian fare.

Foša
SEAFOOD €€€
(☑ 023-314 421; www.fosa.hr; Kralja Dmitra Zvonimira 2; mains 85-230KN; ☉noon-1am) With

a gorgeous terrace that juts out into the harbour and a sleek interior that combines ancient stone walls with 21st-century style, Foša is a very classy place. The main focus is on fresh Adriatic fish, served grilled or salt-baked.

🍸 Drinking & Nightlife

Zadar has a lively and diverse bar scene, buoyed by a large student population. Head to the Varoš neighbourhood, on the southwest side of the old town, for interesting little cafe-bars popular with arty types.

Garden   BAR
(www.watchthegardengrow.eu; Bedemi Zadarskih Pobuna bb; ⊘10am-1am late May-Oct) Perched on top of the old city walls, this exceedingly cool bar-club-garden is very Ibiza-esque, with harbour views, day beds, secluded alcoves, billowing fabric and contemporary electronic music. The same crew runs the Garden Tisno.

La Bodega   WINE BAR
(www.labodega.hr; Široka 3; ⊘8am-midnight Sun-Tue, to 2am Wed-Sat) A slick, eccentric, semi-industrial fitout sets the scene for one of Zadar's hippest bars. There's a good selection of Croatian wines by the glass and an extraordinary selection by the bottle – to be enjoyed with a variety of cheese and prosciutto.

Zodiac   BAR
(Simana Ljubavca 2; ⊘8am-1.30am Mon-Sat, 6pm-1.30am Sun) Zadar HQ for artists and writers, daydreamers and doers, Zodiac's backstreet seats are full of interesting characters. The music's usually excellent too: indie, rock, ska, reggae etc.

Galerija Đina   BAR
(Varoška 2; ⊘7am-midnight) A lively hole-in-the-wall bar that spills out into a narrow lane in the heart of the Varoš action. It gets infectiously raucous at weekends.

Kult Caffe   BAR
(Stomorića 4; ⊘7.30am-midnight Sun-Thu, to 1.30am Fri & Sat) Kult's huge umbrella-shaded terrace is one of the old town's key meeting points. It's great for a quiet afternoon coffee or the start of a raucous night out.

Ledana   BAR, CLUB
(www.ledana.hr; Perivoj kraljice Jelene Madijevke; ⊘8am-4am Jun-Sep) Ledana's gorgeous garden setting and cheesy music choices make it a good place for a trashy night out. Party nights see guest DJs, dancers and (occasionally) live bands entertaining the troops. If it's chilly outside, grab a seat in the circular 19th-century *ledana* (ice house).

Kavana Lovre   CAFE
(Narodni trg 1; ⊘7.30am-11pm) Spilling onto People's Sq, Lovre is good for a light breakfast: munch on a croissant, sip a cappuccino and soak up the heart-of-the-city vibe. Added atmosphere comes courtesy of the remains of 12th-century St Lawrence's Church at the rear.

☆ Entertainment

Arsenal   CONCERT VENUE
(www.arsenalzadar.com; Trg Tri Bunara 1) This huge former shipping warehouse, complete with bars and a restaurant, is now mainly used for concerts, art exhibitions and private functions. Check its website to see if anything interesting is coming up.

Croatian National Theatre   THEATRE
(Hrvatsko narodno kazalište; ☑023-314 552; www.hnk-zadar.hr; Široka 8) Zadar's premier theatre venue.

ℹ️ Information

Aquarius Travel Agency (☑023 212 919; www.aquariuszadar.com; Nova Vrata bb) Books private accommodation and runs tours to the Kornati Islands (300KN including food and drink)

Post Office (Šimuna Kožičića Benje 1; ⊘7am-8pm Mon-Fri, to 1pm Sat)

Tourist Office (☑023-316 166; www.tzzadar.hr; Mihe Klaića 5; ⊘8am-11pm May-Sep, 8am-8pm Mon-Fri, 9am-2pm Sat & Sun Oct-Apr) Publishes a good colour map and rents out audioguides (35KN) for a self-guided tour around the town.

Zadar General Hospital (Opća Bolnica Zadar; ☑023-315 677; Bože Peričića 5)

ℹ️ Getting There & Away

AIR
Zadar Airport (☑023-205 800; www.zadar-airport.hr) is 12km east of the town centre. Croatia Airlines flies to Zadar from Zagreb and Pula. There are international flights to Brussels, Dublin, London, Munich, Paris, Warsaw and more.

BOAT
Ferries run by **Jadrolinija** (☑023-254 800; www.jadrolinija.hr; Liburnska Obala 7) pull right up to the old town, with the large international boats mooring on Istarska Obala and the smaller

boats on Liburnska Obala (where you'll also find the ticket office). Six car ferries per week head to/from the Italian port of Ancona from June to September, increasing to 14 in July and August (per passenger/car from €38/50).

Local car-ferry destinations include Mali Lošinj (per adult/child/car 59/30/271KN, 6¾ hours, daily July and August), Brbinj on Dugi Otok (per adult/child/car 30/15/176KN, 1¼ hours, two to three daily) and Preko on Ugljan (per adult/child/car 18/9/103KN, 25 minutes, 11 to 17 daily). Passenger-only catamarans also head to Božava on Dugi Otok (40KN, 1¼ hours, three daily).

G&V Line (www.gv-line.hr) has three daily passenger ferries to Dugi Otok, stopping at both Sali (50 minutes) and Zaglav (one hour).

BUS

The **bus station** (☎ 060 305 305; www.liburnija-zadar.hr; Ante Starčevića 1) is about 1km southeast of the old town.

Domestic destinations include Zagreb (from 107KN, 3½ hours, hourly), Pula (from 200KN, seven hours, two daily), Rijeka (from 145KN, 4½ hours, six daily), Split (from 80KN, 3½ hours, hourly) and Dubrovnik (from 264KN, eight hours, six daily).

TRAIN

The **train station** (☎ 023-212 555; www.hznet.hr; Ante Starčevića 3) is adjacent to the bus station but the only direct service is to/from Knin (56KN, 2¼ hours, two daily).

🛈 Getting Around

TO/FROM THE AIRPORT

Buses are timed around all Croatia Airlines flights, departing from outside the main terminal, and from the old town (Liburnska Obala) and the bus station (platform 8) one hour prior to flights (25KN).

A taxi will cost around 140KN to the old town and 170KN to Borik.

BUS

Local company **Liburnija** (www.liburnija-zadar.hr) runs buses on 10 routes, which all loop through the bus station. Tickets cost 10KN on board – or 15KN for two from a *tisak* (newsstand). Buses 5 and 8 (usually marked 'Puntamika') head to/from Borik regularly.

DUGI OTOK

POP 1700

The largest island in the Zadar area, Dugi Otok has a lost-in-time feel, with plenty of relatively untouched natural beauty to enjoy. The name means 'long island': stretching

from northwest to southeast it's 43km long and just 4km wide. The southeastern coast is marked by steep hills and cliffs, while the northern half is cultivated with vineyards, orchards and sheep pastures. In between is a series of karstic hills rising to 338m at Vela Straža, the island's highest point.

Good accommodation is in short supply, with a choice between private accommodation or some rather tired holiday resorts. There's a brief high season in the first three weeks of August, when Italian vacationers descend en masse.

History

Ruins on the island reveal early settlement by Illyrians, Romans and then early Christians, but the island wasn't documented until the mid-10th century. It later became the property of the monasteries of Zadar. Settlement expanded with the 16th-century Turkish invasions, which prompted immigration from elsewhere along the coast.

Dugi Otok's fortunes have largely been linked with Zadar as it changed hands between Venetians, Austrians and the French, but when Northern Dalmatia was handed over to Mussolini the island stayed within Croatia. Old-timers still recall the hardships they endured when the nearest medical and administrative centre was Šibenik, a long, hard boat ride along the coast.

Economic development has always been hampered by the lack of any freshwater supply – drinking water must be collected from rainwater or brought over by boat from Zadar. The population has drifted away over the last few decades, leaving only the hardiest souls to brave the dry summers and *bura*-chilled winters.

🛈 Getting There & Away

Jadrolinija (p185) has daily ferries from Zadar to Brbinj (per adult/child/car 30/15/176KN, 1¼ hours, two to three daily), as well as passenger-only catamarans to Božava (40KN, 1¼ hours, three daily).

G&V Line (p186) runs three daily passenger ferries from Zadar, stopping at both Sali (50 minutes) and Zaglav (one hour).

🛈 Getting Around

The only bus services in Dugi Otok are timed to coincide with boat connections, running between Božava and Brbinj in the north. You can rent scooters in both Sali and Božava.

Sali

POP 740

As the largest town, Sali is a positive metropolis when compared with the rest of the settlements scattered around the island. Named after a now-defunct salt works, the town has a rumpled, lived-in look. Its little harbour is a working fishing port and in summer it fills up with the small passenger boats and yachts that dock here on their way to and from Telašćica Bay and the Kornati Islands.

◎ Sights

Telašćica Nature Park OUTDOORS
(Park prirode Telašćica; www.telascica.hr; admission 25KN) South of Sali, the tip of Dugi Otok is split in two by deeply indented Telašćica Bay, dotted with five small islands and five even tinier islets. With superb sheltered azure waters, it's one of the largest, most beautiful and least spoilt natural harbours in the Adriatic. Consequently it's very popular with yachties.

The Kornati Islands extend nearly to the edge of Telašćica Bay and the topography of the two island groups is identical – stark white limestone with patches of brush. The western edge faces the sea where the wind and waves have carved out sheer cliffs dropping 166m. There are no towns or settlements on this part of Dugi Otok, only a couple of restaurants in Mir (Peace) Bay catering to boaties.

Next to Mir Bay is saltwater **Lake Mir**, fed by underground channels that run through limestone to the sea. The lake, which is clear but has a muddy bottom, is surrounded by pine forests and its water is much warmer than the sea. Like most mud in unusual places, it's supposed to be very good for your skin.

Despite being tantalisingly close to Sali, getting here is not straightforward. If you've got your own car, a sealed road leads to the edge of the bay (4km from Sali) and continues (partly unsealed) for another 5km to a small parking area where you can continue on foot to Lake Mir. Otherwise enquire with Adamo Travel about joining a small-group tour (per person 50KN), which drives right up to the lake and to the highest point of the park. Better still, book a boat trip (€40 including lunch), departing Sali at 9.30am and returning at 6.30pm, with swimming and snorkelling in between.

St Mary's Church CHURCH
(Crkva Sv Marije; Sv Marije bb; ⊘ Mass only) Built in the 15th century, the local parish church's wooden altar and Renaissance paintings are particularly impressive.

🏃 Activities

Kornati Diver DIVING
(☑ 098 16 93 107; www.kornati-diver.com; per 1/5/10 dives €25/110/200) Based in the neighbouring village of Zaglav, 3km to the north, this operator leads expeditions to caves, drop-offs and a wreck off the western coast of the island.

Tome BOATING
(☑ 023-377 489; www.tome.hr) Offers a full-day cruise to Telašćica Bay and the Kornati Islands (€300 for a maximum of six people), including food and entry fees, or you can hire a boat and skipper and set your own itinerary (€200). Fishing trips (from €300) can also be arranged.

🎆 Festivals & Events

Sali Fiesta CULTURAL
(Saljske Užance; ⊘ early Aug) The weekend before the Assumption, this celebration draws visitors from the entire region with donkey races and a candlelight procession of boats around the harbour. Men and women don traditional costumes, play instruments fashioned from cow horns and perform traditional village dances.

🍴 Eating & Drinking

Pizza Bruc PIZZA €
(Obala Petra Lorinija bb; pizzas 38-60KN; ⊘ Apr-Oct) The friendliest restaurant in town, it has a terrace right by the yachts. Try the spicy *pizza picante*.

Maritimo BAR
(Obala Petra Lorinija bb) The heart and soul of Sali, this bar has a vibrant buzz about it, rain or shine. It's got plenty of character, with a long wooden bar and photographs of yesteryear decorating the walls, plus a popular terrace that's good for a cocktail, coffee or draught beer.

❶ Information

Sali has the island's only ATM and pharmacy. The only petrol station is in Zaglav.
Adamo Travel (☑ 023-377 208; www.adamo.hr; Obala Kralja Tomislava bb) Sharing space with the tourist office, this very helpful agency rents out a good range of private rooms and

apartments, and sells tickets for car and boat excursions to Telašćica Bay.

Post Office (Obala Petra Lorinija bb; ⊙ 8am-5pm Mon, to 2pm Tue-Fri)

Tourist Office (📋 023-377 094; www.dugiotok. hr; Obala Kralja Tomislava bb; ⊙ 8am-8pm Mon-Sat, 11am-1pm Sun Jul & Aug, 8am-3pm Mon-Fri Sep-Jun) On the harbour front; call in for maps and brochures or to surf the internet (15KN per 30 minutes).

ⓘ Getting Around

Louvre (📋 098 650 026; Obala Kralja Tomislava bb) Hires scooters and mountain bikes.

Božava

POP 116

Božava is a peaceful little place huddled around a lovely natural harbour that's mutated from fishing village to holiday resort in a couple of generations. The village is overgrown with lush, flowering trees and there are lovely shady paths along the coast. Tourism now totally dominates the local economy in the shape of the four hotels of the Božava 'tourist village' and a couple of harbourside restaurants.

During the summer season a little land 'train' (10KN) tootles between the hotels and **Sakarun Bay**. Mainly pebbly with small strip of sand, this is one of the island's prettiest beaches – although there's not much shade and the water's painfully shallow. If you're driving, turn right onto the main island road and look for the turnoff on the left after 3km (parking per hour/day 10/40KN).

🛏 Sleeping

Hotel Mirta   HOTEL €€€
(📋 023-291 291; www.hoteli-bozava.hr; s/d from €74/128; P ✳ @) Of Božava's three three-star hotels, Mirta stands out as the most comfortable. It has a pretty setting amongst the pines and the rooms are spacious, although they would benefit from more attention to the cleaning. Prices include half board, but you're better off heading to one of the local restaurants.

Hotel Maxim   HOTEL €€€
(📋 023-291 291; www.hoteli-bozava.hr; s/d from €103/176; P ✳ @ ☲) Four-star Maxim is Božava's most upmarket option. The smart rooms and apartments all have satellite TV, fridges and balconies overlooking the sea. Plus there's an appealing little pool terrace

and access to floodlit tennis courts and a small spa centre.

ⓘ Information

Tourist Office (📋 023-377 607; www.dugiotok. hr; ⊙ 9am-1pm & 5-8pm Mon-Fri, to 2pm Sat Jun-Sep) Just above the tiny harbour; can help with bike, scooter and car rental, and finding private accommodation.

Veli Rat

POP 60

Veli Rat is a pretty village with a marina on a sheltered bay close to the northwestern point of the island. Aside from a solitary store-cum-bar, there's not a lot here. However, if you continue for 3km towards the tip of the island you'll reach the striking **Punta Bjanca** lighthouse (built 1849). At 42m, it's the largest such beacon on the Adriatic. A small **chapel** dedicated to St Nicholas, patron saint of sailors, is positioned nearby. Facing nearly due west, it's hard to imagine a more sublime spot to watch the sunset.

🛏 Sleeping

Camp Kargita   CAMPGROUND €
(📋 098 532 333; www.camp-kargita.hr; camping per adult/child/site from €8/6/5; ⊙ Apr-Oct) Virtually in the shadow of the lighthouse, this small campground has a terrifically remote feel and a rocky beach nearby. It's brand new, so the toilet block is in great shape, but the recently planted olive trees will need many more years before they provide much shade.

ŠIBENIK-KNIN COUNTY

Wedged between the bigger and more attention-grabbing cities of Zadar and Split, this slice of Croatia is often unfairly overlooked. Yet it's loaded with interesting attractions, including the incredible medieval heart of Šibenik and two national parks – the pristine Kornati Islands and the inland watery wonderland of Krka.

Kornati Islands

Composed of 147 mostly uninhabited islands, islets and reefs covering 69 sq km, the Kornatis are the largest and densest archipelago in the Adriatic. Due to its typically karstic terrain, the islands are riddled with cracks, caves, grottoes and rugged cliffs.

Since there are no sources of fresh water they are mostly barren, sometimes with a light covering of grass. The evergreens and holm oaks that used to be found here were long ago burned down. Far from stripping the islands of their beauty, the deforestation has highlighted startling rock formations – their stark whiteness against the deep blue Adriatic is an eerie and wonderful sight.

◎ Sights

The Kornati Islands form four groups running northwest to southeast. The first two groups of islands lie closer to the mainland and are known locally as Gornji Kornat. The largest of these islands is **Žut**.

The other two series of islands, facing the open sea, comprise **Kornati National Park** and have the most dramatically rugged coastline. **Kornat** is by far the largest island in the park, extending 25km in length but only 2.5km in width. Both the land and surrounding sea are protected. Fishing is strictly limited in order to allow the regeneration of fish shoals. Groper, bass, conger eel, sea bream, pickerel, sea scorpion, cuttlefish, squid, octopus and smelt are some of the sea life trying to make a comeback in the region.

The island of **Piškera**, also within Kornati National Park, was inhabited during the Middle Ages and served as a fishing collection and storage point.

Until the 19th century, the islands were owned by the aristocracy of Zadar, but about a hundred years ago peasant ancestors of the present residents of Murter and Dugi Otok bought them, built many kilometres of rock walls to divide their properties and used the land to raise sheep.

The islands remain privately owned: 90% belong to Murter residents and the remainder to residents of Dugi Otok. Although there are no longer any permanent inhabitants, many owners have cottages and fields that they visit from time to time to tend the land. Olive trees account for about 80% of the land under cultivation, followed by vineyards, orchards and vegetable gardens. There are about 300 buildings on the Kornati Islands, mostly clustered on the southwestern coast of Kornat.

🛏 Sleeping

If you'd like to stay on a Kornati island, Adamo Travel (p187) in Sali and KornatTurist (p190) in Murter both have private houses on their books. Small cottages start at around 4500KN per week including a boat transfer, gas for cooking and lighting, and the national-park admission fee.

ℹ Information

Entrance fees are priced by boat; a small vessel costs 150KN per day if the ticket is bought in advance. Scuba-diving permits cost 100KN per person per day.

Kornati National Park Office (⎘022-434 662; www.kornati.hr; Butina 2; ◷8.30am-5pm Mon-Fri) Located in Murter, the office is well stocked with information.

ℹ Getting There & Away

There is no ferry transport between the Kornatis and other islands or the mainland. Unless you have your own boat, you'll have to book an excursion from Zadar, Sali, Šibenik, Split or another coastal city, or arrange private accommodation from Sali or Murter.

The largest marina is on the island of Piškera, on the southern part of the strait between Piškera and Lavsa. There's another large marina on Žut and a number of small coves throughout the islands where boaters can dock.

Tisno & Murter Island

POP 5140

Tisno is a cute little town, straddling the bridge that connects the island of Murter to the mainland. Its newfound fame as host to a series of high-profile music festivals is totally out of keeping with its otherwise sleepy appeal.

On the island proper, the main settlement is **Murter village**, which although unremarkable in itself is an excellent base from which to explore the Kornati Islands. Murter's steep southwestern coast is indented by small coves, most notably **Slanica**, which is great for swimming.

🎊 Festivals & Events

Between July and August, Tisno is imbued with some of the globe's most celebrated electronic music. Styles are myriad and music is eclectic: cosmic disco, soul and funk, folk-tinged electronica, deep house and jazzy lounge. The ringmaster for all of these festivals is the Zadar-based Garden Bar.

The festival site is a grand affair, only 1km from town, with a private sandy beach, 80 apartments and a luxury campsite – with 30-sq-metre Indian Shikar cotton tents that have electric fans and lighting, real beds and mosquito nets, and even a separate dressing room and porch area. This is all for the revellers to stay in and make as much noise as they like without annoying the locals. There are shady chill-out zones and three different music areas, including the open-air Barbarella's club, a short bus or water-taxi ride away. Chuck in the infamous Argonaughty boat parties (and the sparkling Adriatic sea on tap) and it's quite a scene.

Electric Elephant MUSIC
(www.electricelephant.co.uk; ☉early Jul) Five days and nights of DJ-driven lunacy in early July. In 2014 it featured the likes of Derrick May, Ashley Beedle and Horse Meat Disco.

Soundwave MUSIC
(www.soundwavecroatia.com; ☉mid-Jul) Kicking off over five nights in the middle of July, Soundwave has more of a focus on live acts from the alternative, dub and world-music end of the dance music spectrum. Past headliners have included Fat Freddy's Drop and Huey Morgan.

SUNćeBeat MUSIC
(www.suncebeat.com; ☉late Jul) Spreading musical sunshine over eight days at the end of July, with a solid line-up of legendary DJs (the likes of David Morales, Dimitri from Paris, François K).

Stop Making Sense MUSIC
(www.stopmakingsense.eu; ☉early Aug) Four more days of dancing in the sun to underground DJs, in early August.

⌂ Sleeping

Hotel Tisno HOTEL €€€
(☑022-438 182; www.hoteltisno.com; Zapadna Gomilica 8, Tisno; r €120-190; ✸ 🛜) Creating a rather grand impression on the Tisno waterfront, this late-19th-century house has been converted into a great little hotel. The rooms are in keeping, with gathered crimson curtains and lots of polished wood – but the ambience isn't even remotely stuffy.

ⓘ Information

Coronata (☑022-435 933; www.coronata. hr; Žrtava Ratova 17, Murter) One of several agencies that rents out private apartments and runs full-day excursions to the Kornati Islands from Murter.

KornatTurist (☑022-435 854; www.kornatturist.hr; Hrvatskih Vladara 2, Murter) Rents private accommodation and a 17m yacht (per week 6000KN with skipper).

Tourist Office (☑022-434 995; www.tzomurter.hr; Rudina bb, Murter; ☉8am-10pm Jun-Aug, to 3pm Sep-May)

ⓘ Getting There & Away

Buses on the coastal highway stop at the Tisno turn-off, 6km from the centre. In summer two buses head to Tisno and Murter from Zagreb daily (170KN, 4¾ hours).

Šibenik

POP 46,400

Driving through the shabby outskirts of Šibenik you might find yourself questioning your choice of destination. However, that is guaranteed to change as soon as you reach the city's magnficent medieval heart, gleaming white against the placid waters of the bay. The stone labyrinth of steep backstreets and alleys is a joy to explore. Šibenik is also an important access point for Krka National Park and the Kornati Islands.

History

Unlike many other Dalmatian coastal communities, Šibenik was founded not by Illyrians, Greeks or Romans but by the Croatian king Petar Krešimir IV in the 11th century. The city was conquered by Venice in 1116, and tossed around between Venice, Hungary, Byzantium and Bosnia until Venice ultimately seized control in 1412. Ottomans periodically attacked the town, disrupting trade and agriculture in the 16th and 17th centuries.

Venetian control was usurped in 1797 by Austrian rule, which continued until 1918. Following on from the discoveries of compatriot Nikola Tesla, local engineer and inventor (and later mayor) Ante Šupak built one of the world's first hydroelectric plants on the Krka River in 1895, and Šibenik became only the third city in the world with an alternating current (AC) street-lighting system.

Šibenik fell under attack in 1991 from Yugoslav federal forces and was subject to shelling until its liberation as part of 'Operation Storm' by the Croatian army in 1995. Little physical damage is evident, but the city's aluminium industry was shattered and unemployment grew to over 50%. Šibenik has started to make a serious comeback in the past few years, and tourism is becoming a vital part of the local economy.

◉ Sights

Many of Šibenik's beautiful smaller churches are only open around Mass times.

St James' Cathedral
CATHEDRAL

(Katedrala Svetog Jakova; Trg Republike Hrvatske; adult/child 15KN/free; ⊙9.30am-7.30pm) The crowning architectural glory of the Dalmatian coast and the undisputed masterpiece of its principal designer Juraj Dalmatinac, this World Heritage Site is worth a detour to see. It was constructed entirely of stone quarried from the islands of Brač, Korčula, Rab and Krk, and is reputed to be the world's largest church built completely of stone without brick or wooden supports. The structure is also unique in that the interior shape corresponds exactly to the exterior.

Dalmatinac was not the first (nor the last) architect to work on the cathedral. Construction began in 1431 but, after 10 years of toying with various Venetian builders, the city appointed Dalmatinac, a Zadar native, who increased the size and transformed the conception of the church into a transitional Gothic-Renaissance style. The unusual domed-roof complex was completed after Dalmatinac's death by Nikola Firentinac, who continued the facade in a pure Renaissance style. It was all finally completed in 1536.

The cathedral's most unusual feature is the **frieze** of 71 heads on the exterior walls at the rear of the building. These portraits placid, annoyed, comical, proud and fearful – almost appear like caricatures, but are depictions of ordinary 15th-century citizens. The building cost a great deal of cash to construct, and it's said that the stingier the individual, the grosser the caricature.

Note also the **Lion's Portal** on the northern side, created by Dalmatinac and Bonino da Milano, in which two lions support columns containing the figures of Adam and Eve, who appear to be excruciatingly embarrassed by their nakedness.

Pick up the excellent brochure (available in various languages) as you enter the church, which provides a self-guided circuit of the many artworks and architectural features inside. A highlight is Dalmatinac's extraordinary **baptistery** in the rear corner, with its exquisitely carved ceiling and font supported by three angels.

Other interior artworks worth noting are the tomb of Bishop Šižigorić (by Dalmatinac), who supported the building of the cathedral; the altar painting of St Fabian and St Sebastian (by Filippo Zaniberti); and a particularly gruesome 15th-century Gothic crucifix (by Juraj Petrović).

Šibenik City Museum
MUSEUM

(Muzej grada Šibenika; www.muzej-sibenik.hr; Gradska Vrata 3; adult/child 30/10KN; ⊙10am-9pm Tue-Sat, to 3pm Sun) Focusing on the city and its surrounds, this well laid out museum has a permanent collection of artefacts dating from prehistory to the end of the Venetian period. There are English translations throughout and the odd bit of video to spice things up. When we last visited there were plans afoot to extend the coverage up until the present day.

Aquarium
AQUARIUM

(www.aquariumsibenik.com; Kralja Tomislava 15a; adult/child 37/27KN; ⊙10am-9pm) A useful rainy-day diversion for the kids, this little aquarium has a display of local and tropical fish, along with crabs, lobsters, rays, small sharks and the odd octopus.

Medieval Monastery
Mediterranean Garden
GARDENS

(Srednjevjekovni samostanski Mediteranski vrt; www.spg.hr; Strme stube 1; group tours adult/child 15/10KN; ⊙8am-11pm May-Oct, reduced hours Nov-Apr) Designed and completed by

WORTH A TRIP

ISLAND EXCURSIONS

Šibenik has good ferry connections to several small islands that can be explored on a day trip or overnight. **Zlarin** is only 30 minutes by boat from Šibenik and is known for the coral that used to be abundant before it was torn from the sea and sold for jewellery. Because there are no cars allowed on the island, it makes a tranquil retreat from Šibenik and boasts a sandy beach, pine woods and a spacious port.

Only 15 minutes further on from Zlarin, **Prvić** contains two villages, Prvić Luka and Šepurine, which retain the flavour of simple fishing settlements.

In July and August, **Jadrolinija** (☎ 022-213 468; www.jadrolinija.hr; Obala Franje Tuđmana 7; ⊙9am-6pm Mon-Fri) has five ferries per day to Zlarin, Prvić Luka and Šepurine, decreasing to at least two daily in winter.

Šibenik

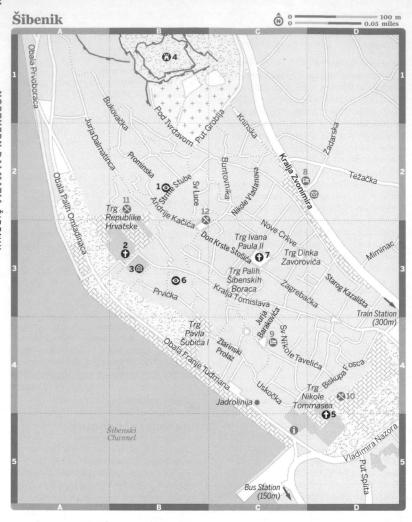

Dragutin Kiš (an award-winning landscape artist), this tiny recreated medieval garden has a formal layout, with herbs and medicinal plants in neat borders between pathways in the shape of a cross. The attached cafe is a pleasant spot to stop for an ice-cream sundae or coffee and cake before you continue your ascent to the fortress.

St Michael's Fortress   FORTRESS
(Tvrđava Sv Mihovila; adult/child 35/20KN; ⊙8am-10pm) Clamber up to this large medieval fort for magnificent views over Šibenik, the Krk River and the Adriatic islands from its battlements (they're particularly impressive at sunset). Parts of it date to the 13th century but the surviving shell has been shored up with a polished-concrete understructure and converted into a summer stage.

St John's Church   CHURCH
(Crkva Svetog Ivana; Trg Ivana Paula II) Dating from the end of the 15th century, this is a fine example of Gothic-Renaissance architecture but sadly the interior has mouldering paintwork and a rather unloved feel.

St Francis' Church
CHURCH

(Crkva Sv Frane; Trg Nikole Tommasea 1) The Franciscan monastery's mammoth church dates from the end of the 14th century. It has fine frescoes and an array of Venetian baroque paintings but the highlight is the painted wooden ceiling, dating from 1674. It's the principal shrine of St Nikola Tavilić, a Franciscan missionary who became the first Croatian saint when he was martyred in Jerusalem in 1391.

✦ Festivals & Events

Terraneo
MUSIC

(www.terraneofestival.com; ⊙ Jun Aug) In 2014, Terraneo morphed from a multiday music festival into a series of individual concerts by the likes of Thievery Corporation and Nouvelle Vague, held at St Michael's Fortress between June and August. Keep an eye on its website as it may morph back.

International Children's Festival
CHILDREN

(⊙ late Jun–mid-Jul) Šibenik hosts a renowned international children's festival, starting from the third Saturday in June and lasting for three weeks. There are craft workshops, along with music, dance, children's film and theatre, puppets and parades.

🛏 Sleeping

Apart from a couple of excellent hostels, there's very little accommodation actually in Šibenik, so you might like to consider basing yourself along the coast and heading to town on day trips. Tribunj, Vodice, Primošten and Rogonica are all good options. Contact the travel agencies for private digs.

★ Indigo
HOSTEL €

(☏ 022-200 159; www.hostel-indigo.com; Jurja Barakovića 3; dm 119KN; ❄ 🛜) Cute as a button, this friendly little hostel has a four-bed dorm with pine bunks and lockable drawers on each of its four floors. At the very top, the terrace has views over the rooftops to the sea. Blue jeans provide a kooky decoration throughout.

Hostel Mare
HOSTEL €

(☏ 022-215 269; www.hostel-mare.com; Kralja Zvonimira 40; dm 120-140KN, r 450KN; ❄ 🛜) A heavy door opens from the busy road onto a cobbled courtyard and behind that lies this breezy hostel. The decor is fresh, bright and modern, the dorms have lockers and there's one double room with its own bathroom.

Šibenik

⊚ Sights

1 Aquarium B3
2 Medieval Monastery
   Mediterranean Garden B2
3 Šibenik City Museum B3
4 St Michael's Fortress B1
5 St Francis' Church D5
6 St James' Cathedral B3
7 St John's Church C3

🛌 Sleeping
8 Hostel Mare C2
9 Indigo C4

🍴 Eating
10 Nostalgija D4
11 Pelegrini B2
12 Restoran Tinel B2

Solaris Camping Beach Resort
CAMPGROUND €

(☏ 022-361 017; www.campingsolaris.com; Solaris; camping per adult/child/site from €11/8/15, apt from €165; ⊙ mid-Mar–Nov; 🅿 ❄ @ 🛜 🐕 🏊) Part of a giant complex 6km south of Šibenik that includes five hotels, an excellent supermarket, a seawater pool, various sports courts, tons of facilities for kids, 10 bars and a spa. The sites and mobile homes are tightly arranged, but the toilet blocks are excellent. An attractive set of flower-trimmed apartments takes up one end of the beach.

✕ Eating

Nostalgija
EUROPEAN €

(www.nostalgija-sibenik.com; Biskupa Fosca 11; mains 54-69KN; ⊙ 8am-2pm & 6-10pm Mon-Sat, 6-10pm Sun; 🛜) With a pleasant covered terrace right by the Franciscan Monastery, this is an unpretentious option for breakfast (cereal, omelettes, pancakes), light lunches (soup, sandwiches) and simple rustic Croatian cuisine (local fish, grilled meat, pasta).

★ Pelegrini
MEDITERRANEAN €€

(☏ 022-213 701; www.pelegrini.hr; Jurja Dalmatinca 1; mains 87-153KN; ⊙ noon-midnight) Responsible for upping the culinary ante in Šibenik, this wonderful restaurant raids the globe for flavours, with influences from Japan and France, but its heart is in the Mediterranean. Dalmatian wines are very well represented on the list. Call ahead to bag one of the outside tables.

PRIMOŠTEN

Pretty little Primošten occupies what was once a little islet just off the coast, 28km south of Šibenik. During the Turkish threat of the 16th century it was fortified – and when the Turks disappeared, the drawbridge connecting it to the mainland was replaced by a causeway.

Sleepy to the point of inertia in winter, in the summer it comes alive, with bands playing in the main square, interesting gift shops selling their wares and excited kids racing around the cobbled streets. Romantics stroll up the hill to St George's Church to watch the sunset, and loop around the peninsula's perimeter after dark.

As if this wasn't enough reason to visit, Primošten is also home to one of the region's best restaurants. **Mediteran** (☑022-571 780; www.mediteran-primosten.hr; Put Briga 13; mains 70-240KN; ⊗1pm-midnight) centres on a lovely old stone building, although in summer the action moves into the courtyard and up to the little 1st-floor terrace. Chef Pero Savanović's dishes offer a modern take on Dalmatian traditions and highlight delicious local produce. Visit when Istrian truffles are in season and you're in for a treat.

Restoran Tinel   CROATIAN €€
(Trg Puckih Kapetana 1; mains 55-130KN) This well-regarded old-town restaurant has a lovely elevated terrace on a little square and dining rooms spread over two floors. You'll find lots of interesting dishes including octopus *à la tinel* (like a goulash).

Information

General Hospital Šibenik (Opća bolnica Šibenik; ☑ 022-641 641; www.bolnica-sibenik.hr; Stjepana Radića 83)

NIK Travel Agency (☑ 022-338 550; www.nik.hr; Ante Šupuka 5) Large agency offering excursions to Kornati and Krka, private accommodation and international bus and air tickets.

Post Office (Zadarska 2; ⊗7am-2pm Mon-Fri)

Tourist Office (☑ 022-214 441; www.sibenik-tourism.hr; Obala Franje Tuđmana 5; ⊗8am-9pm May-Oct, to 4pm Mon-Fri Nov-Apr)

Getting There & Away

BUS

Though it's pretty rundown, Šibenik's **bus station** (☑ 060 368 368; Draga 14) has plenty of regular services and is only a short walk from the old town.

Domestic destinations include Zagreb (from 130KN, 5¼ hours, at least 14 daily), Rijeka (185KN, six hours, at least seven daily), Zadar (51KN, 1½ hours, at least hourly), Split (from 52KN, 1½ hours, at least hourly) and Dubrovnik (from 149KN, 6½ hours, at least four daily).

TRAIN

If the bus station is rundown, Šibenik's **train station** (☑022-333 696; Fr Jerolima Milete bb) is nearly derelict. Up to five shabby trains a day run to Knin (51KN, two hours) where theoretically you could change for Zagreb or Split. But why would you?

Krka National Park

Stretching from the western foot of the Dinaric Range into the sea near Šibenik, the 73km Krka River and its wonderful waterfalls define the landscape of **Krka National Park** (☑022-201 777; www.npkrka.hr; adult/child 110/80KN Jun-Sep, 90/70KN May & Oct, 30/20KN Nov-Feb). The waterfalls are a karstic phenomenon: over millennia river water has created a canyon up to 200m deep through limestone hills, bringing dissolved calcium carbonate with it. Mosses and algae retain the calcium carbonate and encrust it in their roots. The material is called tufa and is formed by billions of plants growing on top of one another. These growths create barriers in the river that produce spectacular waterfalls.

There are five main entrances to the park. As most people visit from Šibenik, the two most popular starting points are Skradin and Lozovac at the southern end. The other three entrances are at Roški Slap, Krka Monastery and Burnum, which can all be reached by car.

Skradin is a pretty little riverside town with a combination of brightly painted and bare stone houses on its main street and a ruined fortress towering above. Apart from the opportunity to see the town itself, the advantage to starting in Skradin is that the park admission includes a boat ride through the canyon to Skradinski Buk. The disadvantage is that there can be queues for the boats in summer.

From the **Lozovac** entrance, buses (free with park admission) shuttle visitors from the large car park (also free) down a serpentine road to Skradinski Buk. Neither the free boats or buses operate from November to February, but in these months you're able to drive right down to the falls.

From Skradinski Buk boats head to Visovac Monastery (adult/child 100/70KN, two hours) and Roški Slap (130/90KN, 3½ hours); check the schedule and book tickets at the Skradin or Lozovac entrance. From Roški Slap, boats to Krka Monastery leave by arrangement (100/70KN, 2½ hours, April to October only).

⊙ Sights

Skradinski Buk   WATERFALL
The highlight of Krka, this hour-long loop follows boardwalks connecting little islands in the emerald green, fish-filled river and terminates at the park's largest waterfall. Skradinski Buk's 800m-long cascade descends by almost 46m before crashing into the lower lake, which is a popular swimming spot. Nearby, a cluster of historic mill cottages have been converted into craft workshops, souvenir stores and eateries. The whole area gets insanely busy in summer.

**Mother of Mercy
Franciscan Monastery**   MONASTERY
(Franjevački samostan Majke od Milosti; www.visovac.hr) Upstream of Skradinski Buk the river broadens out into Lake Viskovac, bordered by reeds and bulrushes sheltering marsh birds. At its centre is this lovely, tree-fringed, island monastery, founded in the 14th century by Augustinian hermits but expanded in 1445 by Franciscans escaping the Ottoman invasion of Bosnia. The church was extensively remodelled in the 17th century and the bell tower added in 1728. Boat trips from Skradinski Buk include 30 minutes on the island.

Roški Slap   WATERFALL
(adult/child 60/40KN, incl in park admission) Beginning with shallow steps and continuing in a series of branches and islets to become 23m-high cascades, this 650m-long stretch is another flamboyantly pretty part of the river. On the eastern side you can visit the water mills that used to grind wheat.

Krka Monastery   MONASTERY
(Manastir Krka; www.eparhija-dalmatinska.hr/Manastiri-Krka-E.htm; ☉10am-6pm) Not only is this the most important Serbian Orthodox monastery in Croatia, it ranks as one of that faith's most important sites full stop. Featuring a unique combination of Byzantine and Mediterranean architecture, it occupies a peaceful position above the river and a small lake. From mid-June to mid-October a national-park guide is at hand to show you around. At other times you're welcome to visit the church and wander the lakeside path.

Dedicated to the Archangel Michael, the monastery was founded in 1345 by Jelena Šubić, the wife of a local Croatian noble and half-sister to Emperor Dušan of Serbia. However its Christian origins are much older than that. Beneath the complex in a natural cave system are catacombs bearing early Christian graffiti, possibly from the 1st century. Local lore has it that this hidden church was visited by St Titus and possibly

---

WORTH A TRIP

RAPTOR RESCUE

Sokolarski Centre (☏091 50 67 610; www.sokolarskicentar.com; Škugori bb; adult/concession 45/35KN; ☉9am-7pm Apr-Nov) Dedicated to protecting birds of prey in Croatia, this centre performs a kind of rescue and rehab service for around 150 injured raptors each year. Visitors are treated to a highly entertaining and educational presentation from centre director Emilo Mendušić, who uses a tame eagle owl and harris hawks to demonstrate these birds' agility and skills. Rescued native birds aren't used for these shows; they're only kept at the centre until they're healthy enough to be released back into the wild.

Most of the patients at the centre have been involved in a collision on Croatian roads. Other threats include illegal poisoning, shooting and the use of pesticides.

The Sokolarski Centre is about 7km from Šibenik and is not served by public transport. It's a little tricky to find: to get there take the road to Krka National Park, turn east at Bilice and look for the signs.

even St Paul. The guided tours only visit a small section of cave, where the graffiti and human bones can be seen; the cave system continues for at least 100m and possibly for a couple of kilometres.

During the recent war, the monastery's substantial treasury – including priceless manuscripts and religious paraphernalia – was moved to Belgrade for safekeeping. A new museum has recently been constructed to display the items once they're returned – hopefully in the next couple of years. The monastery itself was protected during the fighting by the UN. The complex is also home to the Serbian Orthodox church's oldest seminary. It reopened in 2001 and now has 50 theological students.

Burnum RUINS
(adult/child 40/30KN with Krka Monastery, incl in park admission; ☉10am-6pm Apr-Oct) Just off the main road from Kistanje to Knin, 6km past the monastery turn-off, lies the remains of the only Roman military amphitheatre in Croatia. Earth mounds lined with brick form the distinctive oval shape of the structure, which once entertained the troops stationed here. A little further along the road, look out for the two elegant white arches of a ruined aqueduct. There are also a couple of viewpoints for waterfalls in the vicinity.

ⓘ Information

Krka National Park Office (☎022-771 688; www.npkrka.hr; Skradin; ☉8am-8pm) Near the harbour in Skradin; provides good maps and information, and can arrange excursions.
Skradin Tourist Office (☎022-771 306; www.skradin.hr; Trg Male Gospe 3; ☉9am-5pm Mon-Fri) The main tourist office is in the town hall but from Easter to October they also staff a kiosk by the national park office.

ⓘ Getting There & Away

Numerous agencies sell excursions to Krka from Šibenik, Zadar and other cities, but it's not hard to visit independently. In summer, seven daily buses (three on Sunday) from Šibenik head

to Lozovac and Skradin (25KN, 25 minutes). In winter the only buses are timed around the school run.

Knin
POP 15,400

Located on a historical hot seat on the borders of Dalmatia and Bosnia, Knin was an important trading centre in the Middle Ages, becoming the capital of the Croatian Kingdom in the 11th century. However, the huge Croatian flag flying from the top of the fortress is more to do with recent events than medieval history.

Ethnic Serbs made up 86% of the population when in 1991 Knin declared itself the capital of the breakaway Republic of Serbian Krajina. Most of the Serbs fled before Croatia recaptured the town in 1995 and it was subsequently repopulated with Croatian refugees from Bosnia. Knin's economy evaporated along with the Serbs and there's still a somewhat grim feel to the town today.

◉ Sights

Knin Fortress CASTLE
(Kninski Tvrđava) FREE Commenced from the 9th century and reaching its peak as a royal residence in the 11th century, this hulking fortress looms over the town from steep Spas hill. Its strategic importance is well demonstrated by the extraordinary views it offers over the valley to the mountains of Bosnia and Hercegovina.

When the Croatian kings fell, Knin was battered by a series of invaders until the Ottomans snatched it in 1522. Later, Venice swept in (note the republic's winged lion emblem over the main gate), followed by Austria, France and then Austria again. Much of the present structure dates from the 17th and 18th centuries.

ⓘ Information

Tourist Office (☎022-664 822; www.tz-knin.hr; Tuđmana 24; ☉7am-3pm Mon-Fri)

Split & Central Dalmatia

♪ 021

Includes ➡

Split	200
Trogir & Around	218
Trogir	218
Makarska	223
Brač Island	226
Supetar	227
Bol	233
Hvar Island	235
Hvar Town	236
Stari Grad	242
Jelsa	243
Vis Island	244
Vis Town	245

Best Places to Eat

➡ Pojoda (p247)
➡ Villa Spiza (p209)
➡ Antika (p243)
➡ Lola Konoba & Bar (p247)

Best Places to Stay

➡ Divota Apartment Hotel (p207)
➡ Goli + Bosi (p206)
➡ Hotel Adriana (p240)
➡ Hotel San Giorgio (p246)

Why Go?

Central Dalmatia is the most action-packed, sight-rich and diverse part of Croatia, with pretty islands, quiet ports, rugged mountains, dozens of castles and an emerging culinary scene, as well as Split's Diocletian's Palace and medieval Trogir (both Unesco World Heritage sites).

Roman ruins, a buzzing Mediterranean-flavoured city and chic dining, wining and partying on the most glamorous isle in the Adriatic, Hvar Island, all vie for visitors' attention. Let's not forget the slender and seductive sand beaches, secluded pebble coves on islands near and far, and gorgeous nudie hideaways. Whatever your bent, this part of Croatia, with the rugged 1500m-high Dinaric Range providing a dramatic background to the coastline, will grip even the pickiest of visitors.

Best of all: Dalmatia is always warmer than Istria or the Kvarner Gulf. You can plunge into the crystalline Adriatic from the middle of May right up until the end of September.

When to Go
Split

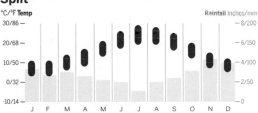

May The sea is already warm enough to swim in, so beat the crowds and enjoy sunshine aplenty.

Jul & Aug A full roster of festivals, lots of action wherever you go and the weather is tops.

Sep Come for warm seas and lower prices after the summer hordes have left.

Split & Central Dalmatia Highlights

1 Discovering Split's ancient heart in **Diocletian's Palace** (p200), a quarter that buzzes day and night.

2 Savouring the foodie scene and beautiful beaches of **Vis** (p244), among Croatia's most remote islands.

3 Stretching out on Croatia's sexiest beach, **Zlatni Rat** (p233), in Bol.

4 Soaking up the glamour and partying all out at the seafront bars in **Hvar Town** (p236).

5 Hiking up dramatic **Mt Biokovo** (p225) and enjoying views of Italy from the top.

6 Taking in the remarkably preserved ancient architecture of tiny **Trogir** (p218), the World Heritage star of Central Dalmatia.

7 Exploring the dreamy interior of **Hvar Island** (p235), with its endless fields of lavender, stretching sea vistas and abandoned hamlets.

SPLIT

POP 178,190

The second-largest city in Croatia, Split (Spalato in Italian) is a great place to see Dalmatian life as it's really lived. Always buzzing, this exuberant city has just the right balance of tradition and modernity. Step inside Diocletian's Palace (a Unesco World Heritage site and one of the world's most impressive Roman monuments) and you'll see dozens of bars, restaurants and shops thriving amid the atmospheric old walls where Split life has been going on for thousands of years. To top it off, Split has a unique setting. Its dramatic coastal mountains act as the perfect backdrop to the turquoise waters of the Adriatic. You'll get a chance to appreciate this gorgeous cityscape when making a ferry journey to or from the city.

Split is often seen mainly as a transport hub to the hip nearby islands (which, indeed, it is), but the city has been sprucing itself up and attracting attention by renovating the old Riva (seafront) and replacing the former cement strolling ground with a marble look. Even though the modern transformation hasn't pleased all the locals, the Riva is a beauty.

History

Split achieved fame when the Roman emperor Diocletian (AD 245–313), noted for his persecution of early Christians, had his retirement palace built here between 295 and 305. After his death the great stone palace continued to be used as a retreat by Roman rulers. When the nearby colony of Salona (now Solin) was abandoned in the 7th century, many of the Romanised inhabitants fled to Split and barricaded themselves behind the high palace walls, where their descendants live to this day.

First the Byzantine Empire and then Croatia controlled the area, but from the 12th to the 14th centuries medieval Split enjoyed a large measure of autonomy, which favoured its development. The western part of the old town around Narodni trg, which dates from this time, became the focus of municipal life, while the area within the palace walls remained the ecclesiastical centre.

In 1420 the Venetians' conquering of Split led to its slow decline. During the 17th century, strong walls were built around the city as a defence against the Ottomans. In 1797 the Austrians arrived; they remained until 1918, with only a brief interruption during the Napoleonic Wars.

◉ Sights

Obala Hrvatskog Narodnog Preporoda – commonly known as the Riva (waterfront promenade) – is your best central reference point in Split. Most of the large hotels and many restaurants, nightlife and beaches lie east of the harbour along Bačvice, Firule, Zenta and Trstenik bays. The wooded Marjan Hill dominates the western tip of the city and has many beaches at its foothills.

★ **Diocletian's Palace**   HISTORICAL CENTRE

(Map p208) Facing the harbour, Diocletian's Palace is one of the most imposing Roman ruins in existence and where you'll spend most of your time while in Split. Don't expect a palace though, nor a museum – this is the city's living heart, its labyrinthine streets packed with people, bars, shops and restaurants. A military fortress, imperial residence and fortified town, the palace measures 215m from east to west and is 181m wide at the southernmost point, altogether covering 31,000 sq metres.

Although the original structure was modified in the Middle Ages, the alterations have only served to increase the allure of this fascinating site. The palace was built from lustrous white stone from the island of Brač, and construction lasted 10 years. Diocletian spared no expense, importing marble from Italy and Greece, and columns and sphinxes from Egypt.

Each wall has a gate named after a metal: at the northern end is the Golden Gate, while the southern end has the Bronze Gate. The eastern gate is the Silver Gate and to the west is the Iron Gate. Between the eastern and western gates there's a straight road (Krešimirova; also known as Decumanus), which separates the imperial residence on the southern side, with its state rooms and temples, from the northern side, once used by soldiers and servants. The Bronze Gate, in the southern wall, led from the living quarters to the sea. Just beyond the palace walls are two city landmarks made by sculptor Ivan Meštrović; the medieval bishop Grgur Ninski guards the Golden Gate and the literary scholar Marko Marulić watches over Trg Braće Radić (Voćni Trg) just off Riva.

There are 220 buildings within the palace boundaries, home to about 3000 people. The narrow streets hide passageways and courtyards, some deserted and eerie, others thumping with music from bars and cafes, while the local residents hang out their washing overhead, kids play football amid the ancient walls, and grannies sit in their windows watching the action below. Each street has small signs at its beginning and end marking what you'll find upon it: bars, cafes, restaurants, shops, museums. It makes moving around much easier, though one of the best things you can do is get lost in the palace – it's small enough that you'll always find your way out easily.

➡ **Town Museum**

(Muzej Grada Splita; Map p208; www.mgst.net; Papalićeva 1; adult/concession 20/10KN; ⊘9am-9pm Tue-Fri, to 4pm Sat-Mon) Built by Juraj Dalmatinac for one of the many noblemen who lived within the palace in the Middle Ages, Papalić Palace is considered a fine example of late Gothic style, with an elaborately carved entrance gate that proclaimed the importance of its original inhabitants. The interior has been thoroughly restored to house this museum.

Captions are in Croatian, but wall panels in a variety of languages provide a historical framework for the exhibits. The museum has three floors, with drawings, heraldic coats of arms, 17th-century weaponry, fine furniture, coins and documents from as far back as the 14th century.

➡ **Cathedral of St Domnius**

(Katedrala Svetog Duje, Map p208; Duje 5; cathedral/treasury/belfry 15/15/10KN; ⊘8am-7pm Mon-Sat, 12.30-6.30pm Sun) **FREE** Split's octagonal-shaped cathedral was originally built as Diocletian's mausoleum, encircled by 24 columns, and is almost completely preserved to this day. Its round domed interior has two rows of Corinthian columns and a frieze showing Emperor Diocletian and his wife. Note that admission to the cathedral also gets you access to the Temple of Jupiter and its crypt. For 35KN you can get a ticket that includes access to all these highlights.

The oldest monuments in the cathedral are the remarkable scenes from the life of Christ on the wooden entrance doors. Carved by Andrija Buvina in the 13th century, the scenes are presented in 28 squares, 14 on each side, and recall the fashion of Romanesque miniatures of the time.

Notice the right altar carved by Bonino da Milano in 1427 and the vault above the altar decorated with murals by Dujam Vušković. To the left is the altar of St Anastasius (Sveti Staš; 1448) by Dalmatinac, with a relief of the Flagellation of Christ, which is one of the finest sculptural works of its time in Dalmatia.

The choir is furnished with 13th-century Romanesque seats that are the oldest in Dalmatia. Cross the altar and follow the signs to the treasury, rich in reliquaries, icons, church robes, illuminated manuscripts and documents in Glagolitic script. Part of the same structure, the Romanesque belfry was constructed between the 12th and 16th centuries and reconstructed in 1908 after it collapsed. Notice the two lion figures at the foot of the belfry and the Egyptian black-granite sphinx dating from the 15th century BC on the right wall. South of the mausoleum, there are remains of the Roman baths, a Roman building with a mosaic and the remains of the imperial dining hall, in various stages of preservation.

➡ **Temple of Jupiter**

(Map p208; admission temple/temple & cathedral 10/35KN; ⊘8am-7pm Mon-Sat, 12.30-6.30pm Sun) The headless sphinx in black granite guarding the entrance to the temple was imported from Egypt at the time of the temple's construction in the 5th century. Of the columns that supported a porch the temple once had, only one remains. Take a look at the barrel-vaulted ceiling and a decorative frieze on the walls. You can also pop into the crypt, which was used as a church back in the day.

➡ **Ethnographic Museum**

(Etnografski Muzej; Map p208; www.etnografski-muzej-split.hr; Severova 1; adult/concession 15/10KN; ⊘9.30am-7pm Mon-Sat, 10am-1pm Sun) This mildly interesting museum has a collection of photos of old Split, traditional costumes and memorabilia of important citizens, housed on two floors and an attic. The ground floor hosts temporary exhibits. Make sure you wander through this early medieval palace and climb the reconstructed Roman staircase that leads to the Renaissance terrace on the southern edge of the vestibule. The views from up there are reason enough to visit the museum.

➡ **Synagogue**

(Map p208; www.zost.hr; Židovski Prolaz 1) Built into the western wall of the palace, Split's synagogue is the third-oldest synagogue in Europe that's still in use. Created out of two medieval houses in the 16th century, in what was then the Jewish ghetto, it got its current appearance around 1728.

Split's Jewish community, which can be traced back to the Roman times, today has around 100 members. As there is no rabbi, the community is more traditional than religious. Split's first Jewish wedding in 70 years was held at the synagogue in September 2012, the first official ceremony since WWII. The previous wedding was in 1943, a year after the synagogue had been pillaged by Italian fascists.

➡ **Basement Halls**

(Map p208; adult/concession 40/20KN; ⊘9am-9pm) Although mostly empty, save an exhibit or two, the rooms and corridors underneath Diocletian's Palace exude a haunting timelessness that is well worth the price of a ticket. The cellars, filled with stands selling souvenirs and handicrafts, open onto the southern gate.

Gregorius of Nin   MONUMENT

(Grgur Ninski; Map p208) The 10th-century Croatian bishop Gregorius of Nin fought for the right to use old Croatian in liturgical services. Sculpted by Ivan Meštrović, this powerful work is one of the defining images of Split. Notice that his left big toe has been polished to a shine – it's said that rubbing the toe brings good luck and guarantees that you'll come back to Split.

Archaeological Museum   MUSEUM

(Arheološki Muzej; Map p204; www.mdc.hr; Zrinsko-Frankopanska 25; adult/concession 20/10KN; ⊘9am-2pm & 4-8pm Mon-Sat) Just over 1km north of the town centre, the Archaeological Museum is worth the leisurely 10-minute walk. The emphasis is on the Roman and early Christian period, with exhibits devoted to burial sculpture and excavations at Solin. The quality of the sculpture is high, and there are interesting reliefs based on Illyrian mythical figures. There are also jewellery, ceramics and coins on display.

Gallery of Fine Arts   GALLERY

(Galerija Umjetnina Split; Map p208; www.galum. hr; Kralja Tomislava 15; adult/concession 20/10KN; ⊘11am-4pm Mon, to 7pm Tue-Fri, to 3pm Sat) In the building that once housed the city's first hospital, this gallery exhibits nearly 400 works of art spanning almost 700 years. Upstairs is the permanent collection of mainly paintings and some sculpture, a chronological journey that starts with the old masters and continues with works of modern Croatian art by the likes of Vlaho Bukovac and Ignjat Job. Temporary exhibits downstairs change every few months. The pleasant cafe has a terrace overlooking the palace.

Meštrović Gallery   GALLERY

(Galerija Meštrović; Šetalište Ivana Meštrovića 46; adult/concession 30/15KN; ⊘9am-7pm Tue-Sun, closed Sun Oct-Apr) At this stellar art museum, you'll see a comprehensive, well-arranged collection of works by Ivan Meštrović, Croatia's premier modern sculptor, who built the gallery as a personal residence from 1931 to 1939. Although Meštrović intended to retire here, he emigrated to the US soon after WWII. Don't miss the nearby **Kaštelet** (Šetalište Ivana Meštrovića 39; admission by Meštrović Gallery ticket; ⊘9am-7pm Tue-Sat, 10am-7pm Sun), a fortress that Meštrović bought and restored to house his powerful *Life of Christ* wood reliefs.

Aquarium Split   AQUARIUM

(☑021-24 71 15; www.aquariumsplit.com; Mladih 1, Vranjic; adult/child 75/50KN; ⊘10am-10pm) Located on the ground floor of an old villa on the quaint little Vranjic peninsula 8km from Split, this is a lovely spot for a family outing or a rainy day alternative. Fishing enthusiast Kuzma from Vis and his seven kids have realised their dream. Croatia's biggest aquarium has 130 Adriatic species that swim among original amphorae and antique marine memorabilia in 20 tanks. You can stroke the rays, catch a fish to take home for dinner in their fishing pool or buy a shell in the gift shop.

🏃 Activities

Bačvice   SWIMMING

(Map p204) A flourishing beach life gives Split its aura of insouciance in summer. The pebbly **Bačvice** is the most popular beach, awarded with a Blue Flag eco label. You'll find good **swimming**, lively ambience and *picigin* (beach ball) games galore. There are showers and changing rooms at both ends of the beach. Bačvice is also a popular summer bar and club area for Split's younger crowd and for visitors.

Marjan   WALKING TRAIL

(Map p204) For an afternoon away from the city buzz, Marjan (178m) is the perfect destination. Considered the lungs of the city, this hilly nature reserve offers trails through fragrant pine forests, scenic lookouts and ancient chapels.

There are different ways of reaching Marjan. One is to head up Plinarska just behind the National Theatre, cross Nazorova and continue west down Mandalinski Put until you get to the Northern Gate (Spinutska Vrata). Otherwise, you can start the walk closer to the centre, from the stairway (Marjanske Skale) in Varoš, right behind the Church of Sveti Frane. It's a mild incline along old stone stairs and a scenic 10-minute trek to get to Vidilica cafe at the top. From here, right by the old Jewish cemetery, you can follow the marked trail, stopping en route to see the chapels, all the way to Kašjuni cove, a quieter beach option than buzzing Bačvice.

Seafront of Marjan
WALKING TRAIL

A particularly lovely walk is along the sea front of Marjan, starting at Riva, leading you to the shiny new Zapadna Obala (West Coast) promenade. You can rent a bike from Toto Travel for 75KN for four hours.

It then takes you to ACI Marina in the Meje neighbourhood, continuing on to Sustipan peninsula on the southwestern point of Split's harbour, passing by the Jadran swimming-pool complex, then Zvončac Bay and on to Kaštelet. From here, you climb up to Šetalište Ivana Meštrovića and continue west for another 20 minutes to Kašjuni, from where it's about 3.5km back along Šetalište Ivana Meštrovića to Riva, passing the Meštrović Gallery.

☞ Tours

Atlas
OUTDOORS

(Map p208; ☑info 021-34 30 55; Obala Lazareta 3; ☺8am-8pm Mon-Fri) Atlas runs excursions to the waterfalls at Krka National Park (390KN), Hvar (485KN) and Plitvice (590KN).

Toto Travel
OUTDOORS

(Map p208; ☑021-88 70 55; www.totosplit.com; Trumbićeva Obala 2; ☺9am-midnight) Offers a bunch of adventure activities as well as excursions to the waterfalls at Krka National Park (405KN), Hvar by boat (600KN) and Plitvice (570KN), plus a hardcore bike tour to Mosor (200KN) or an easier one to Marjan (100KN).

Summer Blues
BOAT TOUR

(☑021-332 500; www.summer-blues.com) If you are up for a little fun in the sun, hop aboard this mega-catamaran offering half-day sailings to Brač and Šolta, with dancers, cocktails and lunch included (from 350KN).

Secret Dalmatia
GUIDED TOUR

(www.secretdalmatia.com) Excellently run outfit that offers customised tours in Split and all around Dalmatia, including sailing trips,

cooking classes at a 13th-century palace in Trogir, wine tastings with local experts and unique outings to Dalmatia's uncharted interior.

Travel 49
WALKING TOUR

(Map p208; ☑021-572 772; www.splitwalking tour.com; Dioklecijanova 5) Offers a One-Penny walking tour (for 7.5KN) that departs from the Peristil five times daily; it also offers kayaking around Marjan (250KN).

croActive Holidays
KAYAKING

(Map p208; ☑021-277 344; www.croactive-holidays.com; Majstora Jurja 5) Runs a scenic half-day Marjan peninsula paddle (260KN) as well as multiday kayaking trips.

Šugaman Tours
BOAT TOUR

(Map p208; ☑095 1978 608; www.sugamantours. com; Dosud 6) Šugaman Tours operates a series of day trips by speedboat or other sea excursions such as a full-day trip to the Blue Cave on Vis (also takes you to the Green Cave and Palmižana), for 850KN per person.

★♣ Festivals & Events

The tourist office can give you information about all the festivals. From June through to September a variety of evening entertainment is presented in the old town, usually around the Peristil.

Carnival
CULTURE

(☺Feb) This traditional February event sees locals dressing up and dancing in the streets for two very fun days.

Feast of St Duje
RELIGIOUS

(☺May) Otherwise known as Split Day, this 7 May feast involves much singing and dancing all around the city.

World Championship in Picigin
SPORT

(☺Jun) For the last 10 years, locals have been showing off their *picigin* skills competitively at this fun early June event in Bačvice.

Mediterranean Film Festival
FILM

(www.fmfs.hr; ☺Jun) Week-long festival each June screening films from the Mediterranean region, spiced up with exhibitions and parties.

Festival of Pop Music
MUSIC

(☺Jun/Jul) Four days of music held around the end of June or early July.

Split

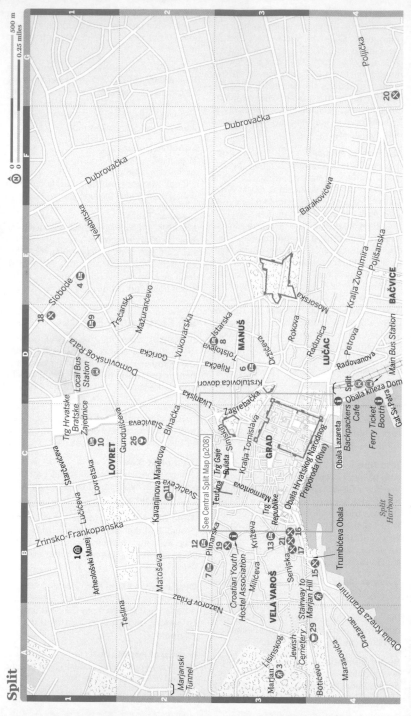

500 m
0.25 miles

G1 G2 G3 G4
F
E
D
C
B
A

1
2
3
4

Dubrovačka
Dubrovačka
Barakovićeva
Poljička
Poljišanska
Kralja Zvonimira
Petrova
Radovanova
Radunica
Rokova
Mosorska
BAČVICE
LUČAC
MANUŠ
Držićeva
Istarska
Rijeka
Tolstojeva
Vukovarska
Mažurančevo
Gorička
Trsćanska
Slobode
Velebtska
Domovinskog Rata
Krstulovica dovori
Livanjska
Zagrebačka
GRAD
Kralja Tomislava
Sinjska
Sinjska
Bulata
Trg Gaje
Teutina
Marmontova
Obala Hrvatskog Narodnog
Preporoda (Riva)
Obala Lazareta
Obala kneza Dom
Main Bus Station
Gat Sv Petra
Ferry Ticket Booth
Split
Backpackers Cafe
Split Harbour
Trg Republike
Križeva
Miličeva
Senjska
Stairway to Marjan Hill
Marjan
VELA VAROŠ
Plinarska
Croatian Youth Hostel Association
Nazorov Prilaz
Matoševa
Zrinsko-Frankopanska
Arheološki Muzej
Teslina
Lučićeva
Lovretska
Starčevićeva
Trg Hrvatske Bratske Zajednice
LOVRET
Gundulićeva
Slavićeva
Slaviceva
Kavanjinova Manœrova
Bihačka
Blhačka
Lisinskog
Jewish Cemetery
Marjanski Tunnel
Botićevo
Marasovića
Dažanac
Trumbićeva Obala
Obala Kneza Branimira

1 Arheološki Muzej
3 Marjan
4
6
7
8
9
10
11
12
13
15
16
17
18
19
20
21
26
29

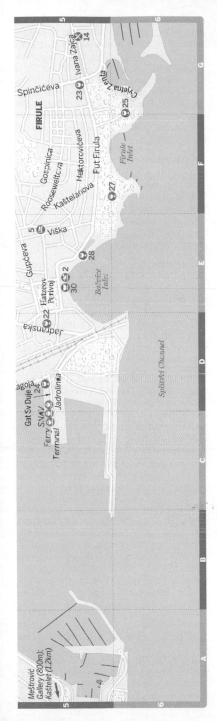

Split

⊙ Sights
1 Archaeological Museum B1

⊕ Activities, Courses & Tours
2 Bačvice E5
3 Marjan A3

⊜ Sleeping
4 Art Hotel E1
5 Beach Hostel Split E5
6 CroParadise Split Hostels D3
7 Divota Apartment Hotel B2
8 Hostel Emanuel D3
9 Hotel Consul D1
10 Hotel Globo C1
11 Tchaikovsky Hostel C2
12 Villa Baguc B2
13 Villa Varoš B3

⊗ Eating
14 Kadena G5
15 Kod Fife B4
16 Konoba Marjan B3
17 Konoba Matejuška B3
18 Konoba Stare Grede D1
19 Makrovega B3
20 Pimpinella C4
21 Šperun B3

⊜ Drinking & Nightlife
22 Cirkus II D5
23 Hedonist G5
24 Imperium D5
25 O'Hara G6
26 Quasimodo C2
27 Šumica F6
28 Tropic Club E5
29 Vidilica A4
30 Žbirac E5

⊕ Entertainment
Egoist ....(see 23)
Kino Bačvice ....(see 28)

Split Summer Festival   ARTS
(www.splitsko-ljeto.hr; ⊙ Jul-Aug) From mid-July
to mid-August, it features opera, drama, ballet and concerts on open-air stages.

Ultra Europe   MUSIC
(www.ultraeurope.com; ⊙ Jul) One of the world's
largest electronic-music festivals has set its
base in Split for the next five years, taking
over the city's Poljud stadium for three days
in July (and a fourth day on a beach somewhere outside the city). People from across
the world swarm to rave to the tunes of celebrity DJs. Atlas (p203) sell tickets (765KN
per day).

Split Film Festival FILM

(www.splitfilmfestival.hr; ☉ Sep) Focuses on new international films and screens lots of art-house movies; held in mid-September.

🛏 Sleeping

Quality budget accommodation has become more available in Split in the last couple of years but it's mostly comprised of hostels. Private accommodation is a good option and in summer you may be deluged at the bus station by women offering *sobe* (rooms available). Make sure you are clear about the exact location of the room or you may find yourself several bus rides from the town centre. The best thing to do is to book through one of the travel agencies, but there is little available within the heart of the old town.

Expect to pay between 300KN and 500KN for a double room; in the cheaper ones you will probably share the bathroom with the proprietor. If you have your own wheels and don't mind staying out of town, you will find a wealth of *pansions* (guesthouses) along the main Split–Dubrovnik road just south of town.

Also consider **Dalmatian Villas** (Map p208; ✆ 021-340 680; www.accommodationinsplit.com; Livanjska 6; d/apt 570/680KN), where you can rent rooms or apartments in renovated stone villas in the old town. It also has cottages (820KN to 1270KN) and villas (2660KN per day, for 11 people; minimum one week stay) on Brač.

Split has quite a few boutique hotels popping up in the old town. The swish Radisson Blu opened a couple of years ago, with an exclusive spa. So if you fancy relaxing in a Jacuzzi or an aromatic wellness centre after you've been lazing by the Adriatic all day long, Split is the place to be.

🛏 Central Split

CroParadise Split Hostels HOSTEL €

(Map p204; ✆ 091 444 4194; www.croparadise.com; Čulića Dvori 29; dm 200KN, s/d 250/500KN, apt from 500KN; ❇ @ 🗢) A great collection of three hostels – Blue, Green and Pink – inside converted apartments in the neighbourhood of Manuš. The shared bar Underground (open June to September) is a starting point for pub crawls (Monday to Saturday nights). Other facilities include laundry, bike and scooter rental. Five apartments are also available.

Silver Central Hostel HOSTEL €

(Map p208; ✆ 021-490 805; www.silvercentralhostel.com; Kralja Tomislava 1; dm 190KN; ❇ @ 🗢) In an upstairs apartment, this light-yellow-coloured boutique hostel has four dorm rooms and a pleasant lounge. It has a two-person apartment nearby (250KN to 520KN) and another hostel, **Silver Gate** (Map p208; ✆ 021-322 857; www.silvergatehostel.com; Hrvojeva 6; dm per person 180KN, double with kitchen 525KN), near the food market.

Tchaikovsky Hostel HOSTEL €

(Map p204; ✆ 021-317 124; www.tchaikovskyhostel.com; Petra Ilića Čajkovskog 4; dm 187KN; ❇ @ 🗢) Four-dorm hostel in the neighbourhood of Špinut, run by a German-born Croat. Rooms are neat and tidy, with bunks featuring built-in shelves. Freebies include cereal, espresso and tea.

Hostel Emanuel HOSTEL €

(Map p204; ✆ 021-786 533; Tolstojeva 20; dm 190-200KN; ❇ @ 🗢) Run by a friendly couple, this mini design-hostel has colourful contemporary interiors and retro accents. In the two dorms (one for five, the other for 10), each bunk has curtains, a reading light and a power outlet. In the morning, free croissants and coffee are served.

Split Hostel Booze & Snooze HOSTEL €

(Map p208; ✆ 021-342 787; www.splithostel.com; Narodni trg 8; dm 200-215KN; ❇ @ 🗢) Run by a pair of Aussie Croat women, this party place at the heart of town has four dorms, a terrace, book swap and boat trips. Its newer outpost, **Split Hostel Fiesta Siesta** (Map p208; Kružićeva 5; dm 200-215KN, d 560KN; ❇ @ 🗢), has five sparkling dorms and one double above the popular Charlie's Backpacker Bar.

★ Goli + Bosi HOSTEL €€

(Map p208; ✆ 021-510 999; www.gollybossy.com; Morpurgova Poljana 2; dm/s/d 240/700/800KN) Split's design hostel is the premier destination for flashpackers, with its sleek futuristic decor, hip vibe and a cool lobby cafe-bar-restaurant. For 1130KN you get the superior double (called Mala Floramy), with breakfast included and gorgeous views.

Hotel Bellevue HOTEL €€

(Map p208; ✆ 021-345 644; www.hotel-bellevue-split.hr; Bana Josipa Jelačića 2; s/d 500/700KN; 🅿 @ 🗢) This atmospheric old classic with a 2nd-floor reception has seen better days, but it remains one of the more character-filled hotels in town. It's all regal-patterned wallpaper, dark-brown wood, art-deco elements, billowing gauzy curtains and faded but well-kept rooms, some with sea views.

Villa Varoš
GUESTHOUSE €€

(Map p204; ☎021-483 469; www.villavaros.hr; Miljenka Smoje 1; d/ste 586/887KN; P❋🖤) Midrangers are getting a better deal in Split nowadays with places such as Villa Varoš around. Owned by a New Yorker Croat, Villa Varoš is central, the rooms are simple, bright and airy, and the apartment has a Jacuzzi and a small terrace.

B&B Villa Kaštel 1700
B&B €€

(Map p208; ☎021 343 912; www.kastelsplit.com; Mihovilova Širina 5; s/d 950/1030KN; ❋@🖤) Among Split's best value-for-money places, this B&B is in an alleyway within the palace walls. It's near the bars and has small tidy rooms and friendly service. Triple rooms are available, as are apartments with small kitchens.

★ Divota Apartment Hotel
HOTEL €€€

(Map p204; ☎091 404 1199; www.divota.hr; Plinarska 75; s/d 761/823KN; ❋🖤) Scattered across the Varoš neighborhood in eight restored fishers' houses, Divota, owned by an artsy Swiss Croat, provides a retreat from the nearby palace buzz. The six contemporary rooms, nine apartments (1508KN) and a stunning three-bedroom villa with a courtyard (5030KN) come with upscale amenities, original details and unique features, like a bedroom inside a vaulted well.

Hotel Vestibul Palace
HOTEL €€€

(Map p208; ☎021-329 329; www.vestibulpalace.com; Iza Vestibula 4; s/d 2660/2810KN; P❋@🖤) The poshest in the palace, this award-winning boutique hideaway has seven stylish rooms and suites, all with exposed ancient walls, leather and wood, and the full spectrum of upscale amenities. There's parking for 100KN per day. The hotel's annexe, Villa Dobrić, a stone's throw away, has four double rooms (single/double 1725/1875KN).

Hotel Peristil
HOTEL €€€

(Map p208; ☎021-329 070; www.hotelperistil.com; Poljana Kraljice Jelene 5; s/d 1000/1200KN; ❋@🖤) This lovely hotel overlooks the Peristil, in the midst of Diocletian's Palace. Service is warm and the 12 rooms are gorgeous – all have hardwood floors, antique details and good views but smallish bathrooms. Rooms 204 and 304 have small alcoves with a bit of the palace's ancient wall exposed *and* they overlook the Peristil.

Marmont Hotel
HOTEL €€€

(Map p208; ☎021-308 060; www.marmonthotel.com; Zadarska 13; s/d 1927/2126KN; ❋@🖤) A boutique hideaway with 21 rooms, this stylish spot features lots of marble, exposed stone, skylights and hardwood floors. The 2nd-floor terrace has great rooftop views. Rooms are spacious and contemporary, with dark walnut furniture, oak flooring and fancy bathrooms. The presidential suite is a steal at 8260KN.

Villa Baguc
GUESTHOUSE €€€

(Map p204; ☎021-770 456; www.baguc.com; Plinarska 29/2; s/d 860/970KN; ❋🖤) Four rooms on four floors of a restored 150-year-old family house in Varoš, with modern fittings combined with original details such as exposed stone walls. The villa is tucked away, yet only a five-minute walk to the town centre.

Hotel Adriana
HOTEL €€€

(Map p208; ☎021-340 000; www.hotel-adriana.com; Hrvatskog Narodnog Preporoda 8; s/d 750/1100KN; ❋🖤) Good value, excellent location smack in the middle of the Riva. The rooms are not massively exciting, with their navy curtains and beige furniture, but some come complete with lovely sea views.

🛏 Bačvice & the Coast

Beach Hostel Split
HOSTEL €

(Map p204; ☎098 945 0998; Viška 9; dm 200KN; 🕙Apr-Oct; @🖤) A hop and a skip from Bačvice beach, this no-frills hostel is managed by a friendly Norwegian called Ladybird, who gives the place soul. There's free coffee and tea, and a terrace with a guitar ready.

Camping Stobreč
CAMPGROUND €

(☎021-325 426; www.campingsplit.com; Lovre 6, Stobreč; sites per adult 59KN, mobile homes for 4 people 824KN; @🖤) Roughly halfway between Split and Solin, this well-equipped place has two beaches, three bars, a restaurant, a shop and a gazillion activities on offer nearby. Take bus 25 or 60. Bring your own tent.

Le Meridien Grand Hotel Lav
HOTEL €€€

(☎021-500 500; www.lemeridien.com; Grljevačka 2A; s/d 2265/2567KN; P❋@🖤🏊) The daddy of all Split hotels, this five-star giant sits 8km south of the city, at Podstrana, with 800m of beach, five interlinking buildings, 381 beautifully designed rooms, endless sea views and luscious gardens. Check out its excellent online rates.

SPLIT & CENTRAL DALMATIA SPLIT

Central Split

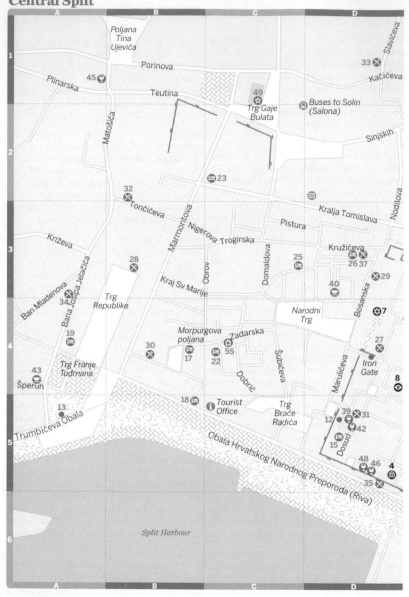

Poljana Tina Ujevića

Porinova

Plinarska

45

Teutina

Matošića

Trg Gaje Bulata

49

Buses to Solin (Salona)

33

Kačićeva

Slavićeva

Sinjskih

23

32

Tončićeva

Nigerova

Trogirska

Kralja Tomislava

Nodilova

Križeva

Ban Mladenova

Bana Josipa Jelačića

Marmontova

Obrov

Pistura

Domaldova

28

34

Trg Republike

Kraj Sv Marije

25

Kružićeva

26 37

29

40

Bosanska

19

30

Morpurgova poljana

Zadarska

Narodni Trg

7

17

55

22

Šubićeva

27

43

Trg Franje Tuđmana

Dobrić

Marulićeva

Iron Gate

8

Šperun

13

Trumbićeva Obala

18

Tourist Office

Trg Brače Radića

12

39

31

42

Dosud

15

35

48

46

4

Obala Hrvatskog Narodnog Preporoda (Riva)

Split Harbour

Outside the Centre

Hotel Consul
HOTEL €€€

(Map p204; ☎021-340 130; www.hotel-consul.net; Tršćanska 34; s/d 650/950KN; 🅿❄🛜) Situated a 1.3km walk from the city centre, Hotel Consul has spacious carpeted rooms that have flat-screen TVs and Jacuzzis (in some). It's quiet, with a leafy terrace, and is a good option for travellers who have their own set of wheels.

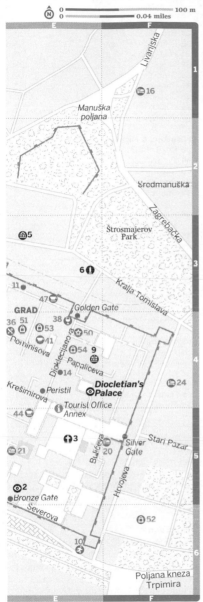

spa. Ask for a room on the quiet side. The annexe out the back has smaller, simpler rooms (single/double 675/900KN).

Hotel Globo   HOTEL €€€

(Map p204; ☎ 481 111; www.hotelglobo.com; Lovretska 18; s/d 1040/1330KN; P ✳ ?) Geared towards business travellers, this swish four-star hotel has a red-carpeted entrance, a marble reception and 33 elegantly decorated long rooms with high ceilings. It's just over 1km from the centre of town, in a slightly drab area.

🍴 Eating

🍴 Central Split

★ Villa Spiza   DALMATIAN €

(Map p208; Kružićeva 3; mains from 50KN; ⊙9am-midnight Mon-Sat) Locals' favourite within the palace walls, this low-key joint offers great-quality Dalmatian mainstays that change daily – think calamari, risotto, stuffed peppers – at low prices. It's fresh home cooking served at the bar inside or at a couple of benches outside. Service is slow but the food is prepared with care.

Šperun   SEAFOOD €

(Map p204; ☎ 021-346 999; Šperun 3; mains from 65KN; ⊙9am-11pm) A sweet little restaurant decked out with rustic details and exposed stone walls, Šperun is a favourite among foreigners – possibly because the waiters, clad in sailor T-shirts, seem to speak every language under the sun. The food is classic Dalmatian, with a decent *brujet* (seafood stew), fresh mussels in a tomato and parsley sauce, or grilled tuna with capers.

Figa   INTERNATIONAL €

(Map p208; ☎ 021-274 491; Buvinina 1; mains from 50KN; ⊙8.30am-1am) A cool little restaurant and bar, with a funky interior and tables on the stairs outside, Figa serves nice breakfasts, seafood dishes and a wide range of salads. There's live music some nights and the kitchen stays open late. Service can be slow but comes with smiles and jokes.

Konoba Matejuška   DALMATIAN €

(Map p204; ☎ 021-355 152; Tomića Stine 3; mains from 50KN; ⊙noon-midnight) Cosy, rustic tavern in an alleyway minutes from the seafront, it specialises in well-prepared seafood that also happens to be well-priced. The waitstaff are friendly. Wash down your meal

Art Hotel   HOTEL €€€

(Map p204; ☎ 021-302 302; www.arthotel.hr; Slobode 41; s/d 937/1237KN; P ✳ @ ?) This Best Western property sits between boutique and business, with four-star rooms sporting plush beds and minibars, plus a gym and a

Central Split

◎ **Top Sights**
1 Diocletian's Palace E4

◎ **Sights**
2 Basement Halls E5
3 Cathedral of St Domnius E5
4 Ethnographic Museum........................ D5
5 Gallery of Fine Arts E3
6 Gregorius of Nin E3
7 Synagogue...D4
8 Temple of Jupiter..................................D4
9 Town Museum..E4

⊕ **Activities, Courses & Tours**
10 Atlas...E6
11 croActive Holidays................................E3
12 Šugaman Tours D5
13 Toto Travel.. A5
14 Travel 49 ....E4

🛏 **Sleeping**
15 B&B Villa Kaštel 1700........................... D5
16 Dalmatian Villas F1
17 Goli + Bosi.. B4
18 Hotel Adriana..B5
19 Hotel Bellevue A4
20 Hotel Peristil..F5
21 Hotel Vestibul Palace E5
22 Marmont Hotel.......................................C4
23 Silver Central Hostel C2
24 Silver Gate F4
25 Split Hostel Booze & Snooze C3
26 Split Hostel Fiesta Siesta.................... D3

✴ **Eating**
27 Bajamont...D4
28 Bajamonti.. B3

29 Brokula...D3
30 Crème de la Crème B4
31 Figa D5
32 Galija... B2
33 Gušt.. D1
34 Paradigma...A3
35 Slastičarna Riva.................................... D5
36 UJE Oil Bar E4
37 Villa Spiza D3

● **Drinking & Nightlife**
38 Dva Tona Bar E4
39 Fluid...D5
40 Gaga D3
41 Galerija E4
42 Ghetto Club D5
43 Libar..A4
44 Luxor E5
    Mosquito.......................................(see 41)
45 Paradox... A1
    Porta ....(see 47)
46 Split Cirkus D5
47 Teak...E3
48 Tri Volta D5

✿ **Entertainment**
49 Croatian National Theatre.................... C1
50 Kinoteka Zlatna Vrata E4

🛍 **Shopping**
51 Arterija E4
    Diocletian's Cellars.......................... (see 2)
52 Food Market F6
53 GetGetGet E4
54 Nadalina...E4
55 Think Pink C4

with a glass of *kujundžuša,* a local white wine from Dalmatia's hinterland.

Kod Fife DALMATIAN €
(Map p204; ☎ 021-345 223; Trumbićeva 11; mains from 45KN; ☺ 6am-midnight) Dragan presides over a motley crew of sailors, artists and misfits who drop in for his simple Dalmatian home cooking (of hit-and-miss quality), especially the *pašticada* (stewed beef), the meat-stuffed courgettes, and his own brand of grumpy, slow hospitality.

Galija PIZZA €
(Map p208; ☎ 021-347 932; Tončićeva 12; pizzas from 38KN; ☺ noon-midnight) The go-to place for pizza, Galija is the sort of joint where locals take you for a good, simple meal, and where everyone relaxes on the wooden benches with the leftovers of a *quattro stagioni* in front of them.

Gušt PIZZA €
(Map p208; ☎ 021-486 333; Slavićeva 1; pizzas from 32KN; ☺ 9am-11pm Mon-Sat, 6-11pm Sun, closed Sun Jul-Sep) Split's die-hard pizza fans swear by this pizza joint – it's cheap and very local.

Makrovega VEGETARIAN €
(Map p204; ☎ 021-394 440; Leština 2; buffets from 60KN; ☺ 9am-8pm Mon-Fri, to 5pm Sat) This meat-free haven has a stylish, spacious interior and delicious buffets. À la carte food includes macrobiotic and vegetarian offerings. Think lots of seitan, tofu and tempeh and excellent cakes.

Brokula VEGETARIAN €
(Map p208; Bosanska 6; snacks from 10KN; ☺ 10am-8pm Mon-Sat) Tiny vegetarian takeaway counter serving daily changing soups, sandwiches, juices and the Split speciality, *soparnik,* a Swiss chard pie.

Crème de la Crème
PASTRIES €

(Map p208; Ilićev Prolaz 1; pastries 8-20KN; ☺ 7.30am-10pm) This chic French-inspired patisserie has delicious cakes and macarons crafted by a Cordon Bleu pastry chef, and also pours good coffee. Seats are on the Morpurgo square down at the end of the passageway.

Slastičarna Rlva
SWEETS €

(Map p208; Hrvatskog Narodnog Preporoda 20; pastries 8-12KN; ☺ 8am-midnight) Briocherie counter on the Riva serving great brioches, croissants, pastries, cakes, tarts and homemade ice cream to take away and savour on one of the benches that line the seafront.

Paradigma
MEDITERRANEAN €€

(Map p208; ☑ 021-645 103; Bana Josipa Jelačića 3; mains from 95KN; ☺ 8am-midnight) Bringing culinary innovation to Split, this new restaurant sports modern interiors with hand-painted murals and a rooftop terrace featuring Riva views, housed in an old building resembling a ship's bow. It's slightly hidden from the tourist scene. Highlights are its top-notch wine list and Mediterranean-inspired dishes, like olive oil *sorbetto*, sous vide steaks and *pršut* (prosciutto) powder.

Bajamonti
INTERNATIONAL €€

(Map p208; ☑ 021-341 033; Trg Republike 1, mains from 75KN; ☺ 7.30am-midnight) Sleek restaurant and cafe on Trg Republike, right off the Riva, with classic decor and excellent international fare featuring refined seafood dishes. Grab a table on the square or on the mezzanine level inside.

Bajamont
DALMATIAN €€

(Map p208; ☑ 021-355 356; Bajamontijeva 3; mains from 70KN; ☺ 11.30am-midnight) This tiny joint within the palace walls is like a granny's living room, with old-school sewing machines used as tables. There's no sign above the door, and the daily menu is written out in marker pen, often featuring *brujet* (seafood stew with wine, onions and herbs, served with polenta). There's an annexe across the alley.

UJE Oil Bar
DALMATIAN €€

(Map p208; Dominisova 3; mains from 70KN; ☺ 9am-midnight) A restaurant and olive oil/delicatessen shop with a small selection of mains, several tapas-style dishes and olive-oil tasting options. Rustic light-wood interiors are charming, as are alfresco seats in the alley. Service can be spotty though. Their recently opened wine bar next door is set against the original stone walls of Diocletian's Palace.

Konoba Marjan
DALMATIAN €€

(Map p204; Senjska 1; mains from 78KN; ☺ noon-11pm) Great-quality Dalmatian fare at this friendly little tavern in Varoš features daily specials like octopus *brujet*, goulash and other hearty dishes. The wine list is excellent, showcasing some local boutique wineries, and there are a few seats outside on the street leading up to the Marjan hill.

Bačvice & the Coast

Kadena
MEDITERRANEAN €€

(Map p204; ☑ 021-389 400; Ivana Zajca 4; mains from 80KN; ☺ noon-midnight) A restaurant, wine bar and lounge with a swank all-white contemporary design and an airy terrace overlooking the sea in Zenta. Food can be pretentious and overpriced but its fortes are the views and the superb wine list.

Outside the Centre

Pimpinella
DALMATIAN €

(Map p204; ☑ 021-389 606; Spinčićeva 2a; mains from 50KN; ☺ 9am-midnight Mon-Sat, to 5pm Sun) As local as you'll find in Split, this *konoba* (tavern) on the ground floor of a family house serves unfussy but tasty food on a terrace and in the no-frills dining room. Try the squid stuffed with shrimp, Dalmatian ham and squid tentacles.

Konoba Stare Grede
DALMATIAN €

(Map p204; ☑ 021-485 501; Domovinskog rata 46; mains from 45KN; ☺ 9am-11pm Mon-Fri, noon-11pm Sat & Sun) Located 1km up the busy main street out of town, this is a blue-collar hangout for *marenda*, a Dalmatian midday meal (starting at 29KN), with a rustic vibe – old beams, wooden benches and stone walls. The owner, who is a hunter, puts much effort into sourcing the very best meat and other ingredients

Konoba-Pizzeria Zora Bila
INTERNATIONAL €€

(☑ 021-782 711; Žnjanska 2; mains from 85KN; ☺ 11am-midnight Tue-Sun) Located near Žnjan beach about 4.5km east of the centre, this contemporary indoor-only tavern on the ground floor of a residential block has gained a following among local foodies. The daily menu of homemade pastas and grilled meats features fresh seasonal ingredients prepared with creative flair by a husband-wife team. Service can be slow.

SPLIT & CENTRAL DALMATIA SPLIT

Drinking & Nightlife

Split is great for nightlife, especially in spring and summer. The palace walls are generally throbbing with loud music on Friday and Saturday nights, and you can spend the night wandering the mazelike streets, discovering new places.

After all the bars in the palace go quiet at 1am (as people live within the palace walls), the entertainment complex of Bačvice kicks on with a multitude of open-air bars and clubs that stay open till the wee hours. Alternatively, look out for flyers in any of the late-night bars.

Daytime coffee sipping is best along the Riva or on one of the squares inside the palace walls.

Central Split

Ghetto Club
BAR

(Map p208; Dosud 10; ⏱6pm-midnight Mon-Thu, to 2am Fri-Sat) Head for Split's most bohemian and gay-friendly bar, in an intimate courtyard amid flower beds, a trickling fountain, great music and a friendly atmosphere.

Luxor
CAFE, BAR

(Map p208; Sveti Ivana 11; ⏱8am-midnight) Touristy, yes, but it's great to have coffee and delicious cake in the courtyard of the cathedral: cushions are laid out on the steps so you can watch the locals go about their business.

Tri Volta
BAR

(Map p208; Dosud 9; ⏱7am-midnight) A mixed crowd of misfits, fishers and bohos gathers at this legendary hang-out under three ancient vaults, with low-priced drinks and *sir i pršut* (cheese and prosciutto).

Vidilica
CAFE, BAR

(Map p204; Nazorov Prilaz 1; ⏱8am-midnight) It's worth the climb up the stone stairs through the ancient Varoš quarter for a sunset drink at this hilltop cafe with amazing city and harbour views.

Paradox
WINE BAR

(Map p208; Poljana Tina Ujevića 2; ⏱9am-1am Mon-Sat, 4pm-1am Sun) Stylish wine bar with cool wine-glass chandeliers inside, alfresco tables and a great selection of well-priced Croatian wines and local cheeses to go with them.

Gaga
CAFE, BAR

(Map p208; Iza Lože 9; ⏱7am-2am) Right behind the town hall on Narodni trg, this spot serves coffee during the day and transforms into a buzzy bar at night, with a cocktail station and DJs.

Galerija
CAFE, BAR

(Map p208; Vuškovićeva bb; ⏱8am-1am Sun-Thu, to 2am Fri-Sat) Catch up with friends without blasting music drowning out the conversation. The interior is granny chic, with pretty floral sofas and armchairs, paintings and little lamps everywhere.

Libar
CAFE, BAR

(Map p208; Trg Franje Tuđmana 3; ⏱7am-midnight) This fun little spot has a lovely upper terrace, great breakfasts and tapas all day plus a big-screen TV for sporting events. A relaxed place away from the palace buzz.

Mosquito
CAFE, BAR

(Map p208; Vuškovićeva 4) Sit on the big terrace, grab a cocktail, listen to music and hang out with the locals.

Teak
CAFE, BAR

(Map p208; Majstora Jurja 11; ⏱8am-midnight Mon-Thu, to 1am Fri-Sat, 10am-2pm & 7pm-midnight Sun) Located on a busy square, the Teak's terrace is superpopular for coffee and chats during the day, and gets busy in the evenings, too.

Porta
CAFE, BAR

(Map p208; Majstora Jurja 4; ⏱8am-midnight Mon-Thu, to 2am Fri-Sun) Come here for cocktails. On the same square are a couple of other bars, all of which end up merging into one when the night gets busy, so remember your waiter!

Fluid
BAR

(Map p208; Dosud 1; ⏱8am-midnight Mon-Thu, 1am Fri-Sat) This chic little spot is a jazzy party venue, pretty low-key and cool. Great for people watching.

Split Cirkus
BAR

(Map p208; Dosud 6; ⏱8pm-1am Mon-Thu & Sun, to 2am Fri-Sat) This watering hole in a narrow street gets animated and crowded in summer months.

Dva Tona Bar
BAR

(Map p208; Carrarina poljana 1; ⏱8am-1am Mon-Thu, to 2am Fri-Sat) Popular hangout among beer connoisseurs, with 35 international and local beers and sports on TV, inside three stone-walled rooms with dark wood chairs and tables.

Bačvice & the Coast

Žbirac
CAFE

(Map p204; Šetalište Petra Preradovića 1b; ⊘7am-1am Sun-Thu, to 2am Fri-Sat) This beachfront cafe is like the locals' open-air living room, a cult hang-out with great sea views, swimming day and night, *picigin* games and occasional concerts.

Cirkus II
BAR

(Map p204; Jadranska 1; ⊘9.30am-midnight Sun-Thu, to 1am Fri-Sat) A varied crowd of misfits and hipsters mingle under low ceilings in this basement hangout with an upstairs garden in Bačvice. It serves more than 25 flavours of *rakija* (local grappa).

O'Hara
CLUB

(Map p204, Uvala Zenta 3; ⊘8am 6am) For alfresco clubbing, head to this fun Zenta hang-out with a waterfront terrace. Come to boogie the night away to a mixed bag of music – from Dalmatian and club hits to house and reggae – depending on the night.

Šumica
CLUB

(Map p204; Put Firula 6; ⊘8am-11pm Sun-Thu, to 4am Fri Sat) Among pine trees just above Ovčice beach, with a large terrace overlooking the Adriatic, this spot draws a young moneyed crowd to its purple velvet interior, where DJs spin every night in summer.

Imperium
CLUB

(Map p204; Gat Sv Duje bb; ⊘8am-11pm Sun-Thu, to 4am Fri-Sat) Split's only megaclub overlooks the harbour from the 1st floor of the ferry terminal, with two large dance floors and an outdoor terrace with a bar. It's quiet on weekdays but fills up with a mixed crowd for concerts and DJ events on weekends.

Tropic Club
CLUB

(Map p204; Bačvice bb; ⊘11pm-5am) A beachfront terrace disco with a black, white and blue theme, house, pop or Croatian music (depending on the night) and the lapping of the Adriatic.

Hedonist
CLUB

(Map p204; Put Firula bb) The cashed-up crowd – iPhones and designer outfits required – comes out to play at this glitzy little club in Zenta, and its older brother, **Egoist** (Map p204), right next door.

Outside the Centre

Quasimodo
CLUB

(Map p204; Gundulićeva 26; ⊘7pm-2am Mon-Thu & Sun, 9pm-4am Fri-Sat Oct-May) Splićani have been partying at this 1st-floor miniclub for decades. There's live and DJ-spun alternative music: rock, indie rock, jazz, blues... It shuts down in summer months.

☆ Entertainment

Cinemas

Kino Bačvice
CINEMA

(Map p204; Put Firula 2) The after-dark entertainment zone of Bačvice is a perfect venue for the open-air cinema that runs nightly from July to September.

Kinoteka Zlatna Vrata
CINEMA

(Map p208; Dioklecijanova 7) Classic films, art flicks and retrospectives are screened at this university-affiliated cinema. It has few screenings during July and August.

Theatre

Croatian National Theatre
THEATRE

(Map p208; ☎021-306 908; www.hnk-split.hr; Trg Gaje Bulata 1) Opera, ballet and music performances are presented here year-round. Tickets start at 50KN and can be bought at the box office or online. Built in 1891, the theatre was fully restored in 1979 in the original style; it's worth attending a performance for the architecture alone.

🔒 Shopping

Shopaholics will find their habit hard to kick in Split – it has the most shoe and eyewear shops in Croatia. The Diocletian's Palace walls are packed with shops: small boutiques and international chains alike. Marmontova is equally popular among the locals for shopping.

Diocletian's Cellars (Map p208; ⊘9am-9pm), part of the palace's basement halls, is a market for crafted jewellery, reproductions of Roman busts, silver cigarette cases, candlestick holders, wooden sailing ships, leather goods and other odds and ends. Prices aren't too steep and you might find the perfect lightweight item to fulfill your back-from-a-trip gift-giving obligations.

You will find several boutiques selling Croatian design and arts within and just outside the palace walls. To name a few: **Arterija** (Map p208; Kružićeva 6; ⊘10am-9pm Mon-Sat) has Croatian fashion, design and

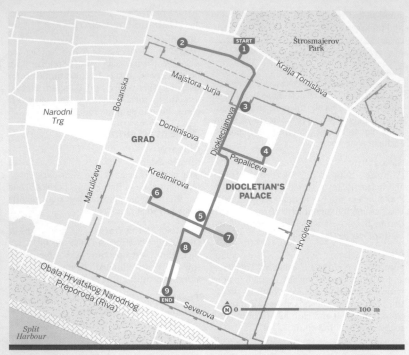

🏃 City Walk
Diocletian's Palace

START STATUE OF GREGORIUS OF NIN
END BASEMENT HALLS
LENGTH 500M; TWO HOURS

Begin just outside the palace at the imposing statue of **1 Gregorius of Nin** (p202), and rub his toe for good luck. Between the statue and the well-preserved corner tower of the palace are the remains of the pre-Romanesque church of St Benedict with the 15th-century **2 Chapel of Arnir**. Through the protective glass you'll see the altar slab and sarcophagus carved by the early Renaissance master Juraj Dalmatinac.

The statue is outside the **3 Golden Gate**, which features fragments of statues, columns and arches that once decorated it. Turn left at Papalićeva and at No 1 is Papalić Palace, housing the worthwhile **4 town museum** (p201).

Return to Dioklecijanova, turn left and look for the Peristil, the ceremonial entrance court, three steps below street level. The longer side is lined with six granite columns, linked by arches and decorated with a stone frieze. The southern side is enclosed by the **5 Protiron**, the entrance to the imperial quarters.

Turn right (west) onto the narrow Sveti Ivana, which leads to the palace's former ceremonial and devotional section. You can still see parts of columns and a few fragments of the two temples that once flanked these streets. At the end of the street is the **6 Temple of Jupiter** (p201), notable for its arched roof.

Returning to the Peristil, go up the eastern stairs to the **7 Cathedral of St Domnius** (p201). Immediately west of the cathedral are massive steps leading down through the Protiron into the well-preserved **8 vestibule**. The circular ground floor has such great acoustics that different *klapas* sing a cappella here in the mornings. To the left is the entrance to the palace's **9 basement halls** (p202). The story goes that Diocletian was so paranoid someone would kill him that he often slept in different rooms. To get to the sleeping quarters you had to pass a circular space with great acoustics so the echo would warn the emperor if anyone was coming. You can still hear the echo when you stand in the basement's circular room.

art; **GetGetGet** (Map p208; www.getgetget. hr; Dominisova 16; ☺9am-2pm & 5-8pm Mon-Fri, 9am-2pm Sat) is a concept store touting off-beat Croatian design items; **Nadalina** (Map p208; Dioklecijanova 6; ☺8.30am-8.30pm Mon-Fri, 9am-2pm Sun) sells 70% fine chocolates, made by a local punkstar-cum-chocaholic in nearby Solin, with Dalmatian flavours like olive oil, rosemary, fig and carob; and **Think Pink** (Map p208; Zadarska 8; ☺8.30am-10pm) has boho women's clothing made by home-grown designers.

There's a daily **market** (Map p208; ☺food market 6.30am-2pm) above Obala Lazareta where you can buy fruit, vegetables, shoes, confectionery, clothing, flowers, souvenirs and other products.

ℹ Information

INTERNET ACCESS
Several spots around town offer free wi-fi ac-cess, including Luxor and Twins on the Riva and Bajamonti on Trg Republike.

MEDICAL SERVICES
KBC Firule (☎021-556 111; Spinčićeva 1) Split's hospital.

MONEY
You can change money at travel agencies or at any post office. There are ATMs around the bus and train stations and throughout the city.

POST
Main Post Office (Map p208; Kralja Tomislava 9; ☺7.30am-7pm Mon-Fri, to 2.30pm Sat)

TELEPHONE
There's a telephone centre at the main post office.

TOURIST INFORMATION
Backpackers Cafe (Map p204; ☎021 338 548; Kneza Domagoja bb; internet 30N per hour; ☺7am-8pm) Sells used books, offers luggage storage and internet access, and provides information for backpackers.
Croatian Youth Hostel Association (Map p204; ☎021-396 031; www.hfhs.hr; Domilijina 8; ☺8am-4pm Mon-Fri) Sells HI cards and has information about youth hostels all over Croatia.
Tourist Office (Map p208; ☎021-360 066; www.visitsplit.com; Hrvatskog Narodnog Preporoda 9; ☺8am-9pm Mon-Sat, to 1pm Sun Jun-Sep) Has info on Split and sells the Split Card (35KN), which offers free and reduced prices to Split attractions and discounts on car rental, restaurants, shops and hotels. You get

the card for free if you're staying in Split more than three nights.
Tourist Office Annex (Map p208; ☎021-345 606; www.visitsplit.com; Peristil bb; ☺8am-9pm Mon-Sat, to 1pm Sun Jun-Sep) This tourist office annexe on Peristil has shorter hours.

TRAVEL AGENCIES
Daluma Travel (☎021-338 424; www.daluma-travel.hr; Kneza Domagoja 1) Arranges private accommodation, excursions and car rental.
Maestral (☎021-470 944; www.maestral.hr; Boškovića 13/15) Monastery stays, horse-riding excursions, lighthouse holidays, trekking, sea kayaking and more.
Split Tours (☎021-352 553; www.splittours. hr; Gat Sv Duje bb; ☺closed Sat & Sun after-noon) In the ferry terminal, it handles tickets to Ancona (Italy) on Blue Line, and finds private accommodation.
Touring (☎021-338 503; Kneza Domagoja 10) Near the bus station, it represents Deutsche Touring and sells bus tickets to German cities.
Turist Biro (☎021-347 100; www.turistbiro-split. hr; Hrvatskog Narodnog Preporoda 12) Its forte is private accommodation and excursions.

ℹ Getting There & Away

AIR
Split airport (www.split-airport.hr) Located 20km west of town, just 6km before Trogir.
Croatia Airlines (☎021-895 298; www. croatiaairlines.hr; Split airport; ☺5.15am-8pm) Operates one-hour flights to and from Zagreb several times a day and a weekly flight to Dubrovnik (during summer only).
Easyjet (www.easyjet.com)
European Coastal Airlines (www.ec-alr.eu) Brand-new airline with seaplanes that connect the mainland to Jelsa on Hvar. Destinations to come include Korčula, Dubrovnik, Rab, Lastovo and Vis.
Germanwings (www.germanwings.com)
Norwegian (www.norwegian.com)

BOAT
Car ferries and passenger lines depart from separate docks; the passenger lines leave from Obala Lazareta and car ferries from Gat Sv Duje. You can buy tickets from either the main Jadro-linija office in the large ferry terminal opposite the bus station, which handles all car-ferry services that depart from the docks around the ferry terminal, or at one of the two stalls near the docks. You can't reserve tickets ahead of time; they're only available for purchase on the day of departure. In summer it's usually necessary to arrive several hours before departure for a car ferry, and put your car in the line for boarding.

JADROLINIJA SERVICES FROM SPLIT

Note that the schedules listed for these ferries are for services between June and September. Service is reduced outside these months.

CAR FERRIES

Destination	Cost per person/car (KN)	Duration (hr)	Daily Services
Šolta	33/160	1	6
Stari Grad (Hvar)	47/318	2	6-7
Supetar (Brač)	33/160	1	12-14
Vela Luka (Korčula)	60/530	3	2

CATAMARANS

Destination	Cost (KN)	Duration (hr)	Daily Services
Bol (Brač)	55	1	1
Hvar Town	55	1	4-5
Jelsa (Hvar)	55	2	1
Vela Luka (Korčula)	65	2	1
Vis	50	1¼	1

There is rarely a problem or a long wait obtaining a space off-season.

Jadrolinija (Map p204; ☑ 021-338 333; www.jadrolinija.hr; Gat Sv Duje bb) Jadrolinija handles most of the coastal ferry lines and catamarans that operate between Split and the islands. There is also a twice-weekly ferry service between Rijeka and Split (147KN, 7.30pm Thursday and Sunday, arriving at 6am). Three times weekly a car ferry goes from Split to Ancona in Italy (397KN on weekdays, 433KN on weekends, nine to 11 hours).

BlueLine (www.blueline-ferries.com) Car ferries to Ancona (Italy), on some days via Hvar Town and Vis (per person/car from 480KN/540KN, 10 to 12 hours).

Krilo (www.krilo.hr) A fast passenger boat that goes to Hvar Town (70KN, one hour) twice daily and to Vis once a day (55KN, 2¾ hours); the Vis catamaran stops in Hvar on Tuesdays. There's also a new connection twice weekly to Dubrovnik from mid-May through mid-October (170KN, 4½ hours).

SNAV (Map p204; ☑ 021-322 252; www.snav.it) Daily ferries to Ancona (660KN, five hours) from June through mid-September. In the ferry terminal.

BUS

Bus tickets purchased in advance with seat reservations are recommended. There are buses from the **main bus station** (Map p204; ☑ 060 327 777; www.ak-split.hr) beside the harbour to a number of destinations. If you need to store bags, there's a **garderoba** (left luggage; 1st hour 5KN, then 1.50KN per hour; ⊘ 6am-10pm).

Bus 37 goes to Split airport and Trogir (21KN, every 20 minutes), also stopping at Solin; it leaves from a **local bus station** (Domovinskog Rata), 1km northeast of the city centre, but it's faster and more convenient to take an intercity bus heading north to Zadar or Rijeka.

Note that Split–Dubrovnik buses pass briefly through Bosnian territory, so keep your passport handy for border-crossing points.

CAR

Dollar Thrifty (☑ 021-399 000; www.thrifty.com.hr) Branches at Trumbićeva Obala 17 and Split airport.

TRAIN

There are five daily trains between Split **train station** (☑ 021-338 525; www.hznet.hr; Kneza Domagoja 9) and Zagreb (189KN, six to eight hours), two of which are overnight. There are three daily trains between Šibenik and Split (45KN, two hours), with a change in Perković. There are also two trains a day from Split to Zadar (107KN, five hours) via Knin.

If you need to store bags, there's a **garderoba** (left luggage; per day 15KN; ⊘ 6am-10pm).

🛈 Getting Around

The bus, train and ferry terminals are clustered on the eastern side of the harbour, a short walk from the old town.

You can rent scooters, bikes, speed boats and cars from **Split Rent Agency** (☑ 091 591 7111; www.split-rent.com).

TO/FROM THE AIRPORT

Taxis cost between 200KN and 250KN.

Bus 37 From the local bus station on Domovinskog Rata (21KN, 50 minutes).

Pleso Prijevoz (www.plesoprijevoz.hr) Buses depart to Split airport (30KN) from Obala Lazareta three to six times daily.

Promet Žele (www.split-airport.com.hr) Buses travel between Obala Lazareta and the airport 10 times daily from April to October, with slightly fewer services in the off season.

BUS

Local buses by Promet Split connect the town centre and the harbour with outlying districts; the city is broken up into four travel zones. A one-zone ticket costs 11KN for one trip in central Split; it's 21KN to the surrounding districts. A two-journey ticket in zone one costs 17KN if bought at a kiosk; it's 34KN for the zone-four two-journey ticket. Buses run about every 15 minutes from 5.30am to 11.30pm.

AROUND SPLIT

Šolta

This lovely, wooded island (just 59 sq km) is a popular getaway for Split inhabitants escaping the sultry summer heat. The island's main entry point is **Rogač**, where ferries from Split tie up in front of the **tourist office** (☑021-654 491; www.visitsolta.com; ⊙7am-9pm) on the edge of a large bay. A shady path leads around the bay to smaller coves with rocky beaches, and a small road leads uphill to the island's administrative centre of **Grohote**, with a market and shops. **Maslinica** is the island's prettiest settlement, with seven islets offshore, a luxury heritage hotel-spa, **Martinis Marchi** (www.martinis-marchi.com), with its own marina, a handful of restaurants (Šismiš is the best) and a good choice of private accommodation. Another gorgeous village is **Stomorska**, with its pretty sheltered harbour popular with yachters. The island's interior has several worthwhile family-run farm eateries; Kaštelanac in Gornje Selo does tastings of its olive oils, grappas and wines. The tourist offices have details on other inland options.

There are three ATMs on the island, in Stomorska, Rogač and Grohote.

In high season, six daily car ferries run between Split and Rogač (33KN, one hour) as well as two catamarans per day (28KN).

Solin (Salona)

The ruins of the ancient city of Solin (Roman Salona), among the vineyards at the foot of mountains just northeast of Split, are the most archaeologically important in Croatia.

Today Solin is surrounded by noisy highways and industry. It was first mentioned in 119 BC as the centre of the Illyrian tribe. The Romans seized the site in 78 BC and under the rule of Augustus it became the administrative headquarters of the Roman Dalmatian province.

When Emperor Diocletian built his palace in Split at the end of the 3rd century AD, it was the proximity to Solin that attracted him. Solin was incorporated into the Eastern Roman Empire in the 6th century, but was levelled by the Slavs and Avars in 614. The inhabitants fled to Split and neighbouring islands, leaving Solin to decay.

⊙ Sights

A good place to begin your visit to the city is at the main entrance near Caffe Bar Salona, where you'll see an info map of the complex. **Tusculum Museum** (admission 20KN; ⊙8am-7pm Mon-Sat, 9am-1pm Sun) is where you pay admission for the entire archaeological reserve, including the small museum with interesting sculpture embedded in the walls and in the garden. It also serves as an information centre and distributes a brochure about Salona. **Manastirine**, the fenced area behind the car park, was a burial place for early Christian martyrs prior to the legalisation of Christianity. The excavated remains of **Kapljuč Basilica** – built on one of the early Christian cemeteries – and the 5th-century **Kapjinc Basilica** that sits inside it are highlights, although this area was outside the ancient city itself.

A path bordered by cypresses runs south to the northern city wall of Solin. Notice the **covered aqueduct** located south of the wall. It was probably built around the 1st century AD and supplied Solin and Diocletian's Palace with water from the Jadro River. The ruins you see in front of you as you stand on the wall were an early Christian site; they include a three-aisled, 5th-century **cathedral** with an octagonal **baptistery**, and the remains of **Bishop Honorius'**

CHARTERING A YACHT OR BOAT

Yachting enthusiasts may wish to charter their own boat. Experienced sailors can charter a yacht on a bareboat basis, or you can pay for the services of a local captain for a skippered boat. The price depends upon the size of the boat, the number of berths and the season.

Cosmos Yachting (www.cosmosyachting.com) This UK company offers charters out of Dubrovnik, Pula, Rovinj, Split, Trogir, Zadar, Lošinj, Punat and other destinations.

Nautical Centre Nava (www.navaboats.com) Locally owned charter that has an impressive fleet of luxury Lagoon catamarans with bases in Split, Baška Voda and Kaštela.

Sunsail (www.sunsail.com) An international operator offering bareboat and skippered charters from Dubrovnik and Marina Agana, 40km west of Split.

Ultra Sailing (www.ultra-sailing.hr) Among the best and most reliable Croatian charters, plus it has a popular sailing school. The base marinas are in Dubrovnik, Kaštela, Split and Trogir.

Basilica with a ground plan in the form of a Greek cross. **Public baths** adjoin the cathedral on the east.

Southwest of Solin's cathedral is the 1st-century eastern city gate, **Porta Caesarea**, later engulfed by the growth of the city in all directions. Grooves in the stone road left by ancient wheels can still be seen at this gate. South of the city gate was the centre of town, the forum, with temples to Jupiter, Juno and Minerva, none of which are visible today.

At the western end of Solin is the huge 2nd-century **amphitheatre**, destroyed in the 17th century by the Venetians to prevent it from being used as a refuge by Turkish raiders. At one time it could accommodate 18,000 spectators, which gives an idea of the size and importance of this ancient city.

The southeastern corner of the complex contains the **Gradina**, a medieval fortress around the remains of a rectangular early Christian church.

ⓘ Getting There & Away

The ruins are easily accessible on Split city bus 1 (13KN), which goes all the way to the parking lot for Salona every half-hour from Trg Gaje Bulata.

From Solin you can continue on to Trogir by catching westbound bus 37 (17KN) from the Širine crossroad. Take city bus 1 back to Širine and then walk for five minutes on the same road to get to the stop for bus 37 on the adjacent highway.

TROGIR & AROUND

Trogir

POP 11,000

Gorgeous and tiny Trogir (formerly Trau) is beautifully set within medieval walls, its streets knotted and mazelike. It's fronted by a wide seaside promenade lined with bars and cafes, and yachts in the summer. Trogir is unique among Dalmatian towns for its profuse collection of Romanesque and Renaissance architecture (which flourished under Venetian rule); this, along with its magnificent cathedral, earned it World Heritage status in 1997.

Trogir is an easy day trip from Split and a relaxing place to spend a few days, taking an outing or two to nearby islands.

History

Backed by high hills in the north, the sea to the south and snug in its walls, Trogir (Tragurion to the Romans) proved an attractive place to settlers. The early Croats settled the old Illyrian town by the 7th century. Its defensive position allowed Trogir to maintain its autonomy throughout Croatian and Byzantine rule, while trade and nearby mines ensured its economic viability. In the 13th century sculpture and architecture flourished, reflecting a vibrant, dynamic culture. When Venice bought Dalmatia in 1409, Trogir refused to accept the new ruler and the Venetians were forced to bombard the town into submission. While the rest of Dalmatia stagnated under Venetian rule, Trogir continued to produce great artists who enhanced the beauty of the town.

◉ Sights

Even though it's a pocket-sized town, Trogir has plenty to see. The town has retained many intact and beautiful buildings from its age of glory, between the 13th and 15th centuries. The old town of Trogir occupies a tiny island in the narrow channel between Čiovo Island and the mainland, just off the coastal highway. Most sights can be seen on a 15-minute walk around this island.

Cathedral of St Lovro   CATHEDRAL
(Katedrala Svetog Lovre; Trg Ivana Pavla II; admission 25KN; ☺9am-noon & 4-/pm) The showcase of Trogir is the three-naved Venetian cathedral, one of the finest architectural works in Croatia, built from the 13th to 15th centuries. Note the **Romanesque portal** (1240) by Master Radovan. The sides of the portal depict lion figures (the symbol of Venice) with Adam and Eve above them, the earliest example of the nude in Dalmatian sculpture. At the end of the portico is another fine piece of sculpture – the 1464 **baptistery** sculpted by Andrija Aleši.

Enter the building through an obscure back door to see the richly decorated **Renaissance Chapel of St Ivan**, created by the masters Nikola Firentinac and Ivan Duknović from 1461 to 1497. Within the sacristy there are paintings of St Jerome and John the Baptist. Be sure to take a look at the treasury, which contains an ivory triptych and several medieval illuminated manuscripts. You can even climb the 47m-high cathedral tower for a delightful view.

A sign informs that you must be 'decently dressed' to enter the cathedral, which means that men must wear tops (women too, of course) and shorts are a no-no.

Kamerlengo Fortress   FORTRESS
(Tvrđava Kamerlengo; adult/concession 10/15KN; ☺9am-8pm) The fortress, once connected to the city walls, was built around the 15th century. At the furthest end, you'll see an elegant gazebo built by the French Marshal Marmont during the Napoleonic occupation of Dalmatia, where he used to sit and play cards amid the waves. At that time, the western end of the island was a lagoon; the malarial marshes were not drained until the 20th century. The fortress hosts concerts during the Trogir Summer festival.

Town Museum   MUSEUM
(Gradski Muzej; Gradska Vrata 4; adult/concession 15/10KN; ☺9am-1pm & 4.30-9.30pm) Housed in the former Garagnin-Fanfogna palace, the museum has five rooms that exhibit books, documents, drawings and period costumes from Trogir's long history.

Convent of St Nicholas   CONVENT
(Samostan Svetog Nikole; adult/concession 10/5KN; ☺8am-1pm & 3-7pm) The treasury of this Benedictine convent is home to a dazzling 3rd-century relief of Kairos, the Greek god of opportunity, carved out of orange marble. Access by appointment from October to May.

Town Hall   HISTORIC BUILDING
(Gradska Vijećnica; 7am-7pm Mon-Fri) This 15th-century building opposite the cathedral has a Gothic yard decorated with coats of arms and a monumental staircase. Its well features a preserved winged lion of St Mark (the coat of arms of the Venetian Republic).

Grand Cipiko Palace   PALACE
(Palaca Cipiko) This palace, originally a set of Romanesque structures and home to a prominent family during the 15th century, has a stunning carved gothic triforium, the work of Andrija Aleši.

☞ Tours

Portal Trogir   WALKING TOUR, KAYAKING
(☑021-885 016; www.portal-trogir.com; Bana Berislavića 3) Portal travel agency runs a 90-minute walking tour of Trogir's old town twice a day (morning and evening) from May to October, departing from outside the agency. It also rents out two-person kayaks for 250KN per day, which you can use to kayak around the island and to Pantan beach.

☆ Festivals & Events

Trogir Summer   MUSIC
(☺Jun-Sep) Every year from 21 June through early September, the town hosts Trogir Summer, a music festival with classical and folk concerts presented in churches, open squares and the fortress. Posters advertising the concerts are all around town.

⌸ Sleeping

Atlas (p221) can arrange private rooms from 300KN a double. Portal (p222) also has rooms and apartments, from 300KN for a double and 450KN for a two-person apartment. Also check out the offerings at www.trogir-online.com.

Trogir

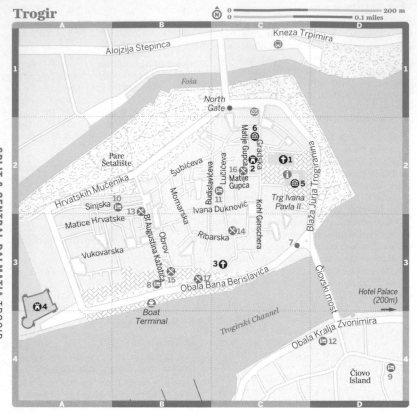

Hostel Trogir
HOSTEL €

(☑ 091 579 2190; www.hosteltrogir.com.hr; Trg Sv Jakova 7; dm 135KN; ✳ @ 🛜) Trogir's only hostel is located just across the bridge on Čiovo, so only 200m from the Riva. It has four clean dorms (of six and eight beds) with lockers, a small common room with a kitchenette and a shaded terrace out the front.

Seget
CAMPGROUND €

(☑ 021-880 394; www.kamp-seget.hr; Hrvatskih Žrtava 121, Seget Donji; per adult/site 54/120KN; ☺ Apr-Oct) Located just 2km west of Trogir, this intimate campground has a small shingle beach and a cemented diving point. It is just 2km from Hotel Medena, which offers tennis, cycling, windsurfing and other activities.

Concordia
HOTEL €€

(☑ 021-885 400; www.concordia-hotel.net; Bana Berislavića 22; s/d 450/755KN; P ✳ 🛜) The somewhat faded rooms here are clean but pretty basic, though the service and location,

right on the seafront, are lovely. Try to get a recently refurbished room with sea views. Boats to the beaches depart right outside.

Villa Tina
HOTEL €€

(☑ 021-888 305; www.vila-tina.hr; Cesta Domovinske Zahvalnosti 63, Arbanija; s/d 499/670KN; P ✳ @ 🛜) Tastefully decorated, with spacious and bright rooms, a Jacuzzi and infrared sauna, Villa Tina is excellent for those wanting to relax and swim. It's about 5km east of Trogir, steps from the beach.

Villa White
GUESTHOUSE €€

(☑ 091 221 4473; www.villawhite.net; Kralja Tomislava 22; r 570KN; P ✳ @ 🛜) This 14-room guesthouse is 1km from the town centre. With a minimalist black-and-white theme, it has small but inviting rooms with TVs and showers. Breakfast is included, as is a free supply of coffee and tea. To get here, take the bridge from Trogir to the mainland, crossing the main coastal road, and head north.

★**Hotel Tragos** HOTEL €€€
(📞021-884 729; www.tragos.hr; Budislavićeva 3; s/d 600/900KN; P❈@🛜) This medieval family house has been exquisitely restored, with lots of exposed stone and original details. Its 12 sleek, beautifully decorated rooms come with satellite TV and mini-bars. Even if you don't stay here, come for the wonderful home cooking served in the hotel restaurant (mains from 60KN); try the *trogirska pašticada* (Trogir-style beef stew).

Hotel Pašike HOTEL €€€
(📞021-885 185; www.hotelpasike.com; Sinjska bb; s/d 760/1140KN; ❈@🛜) This delightful hotel in a 15th-century house showcases 19th-century furniture, walnut timber and wrought-iron beds. Each of the 14 vividly painted rooms has a separate sitting area and a hydromassage shower. The friendly staff wear traditional outfits, there is a two-table roof terrace and upon arrival you get *rafioli,* a traditional Trogir almond cake.

Vila Sikaa HOTEL €€€
(📞021-881 223; www.vila-sikaa-r.com; Kralja Zvonimira 13; s/d 896/952KN; P❈@🛜) This hotel on Čiovo has 10 decent rooms with fantastic views of the old town. Some are equipped with saunas, massage showers and Jacuzzis. Room 14 has a balcony. Note that the rooms in the attic are claustrophobic and service can be sloppy. The reception also offers scooter, boat and car rental.

Hotel Palace HOTEL €€€
(📞021-685 555; www.trogir-palace.com; Put Gradine 8, s/d 940/1240KN; P❈@🛜) This upscale addition to Trogir's hotel scene sits in a pinkish-white building on Čiovo island, with lots of marble, hardwood floors and a restaurant. The 36 beige-coloured rooms sport tubs and balconies. Room 305 has great old town views across the way.

✖ Eating

Capo SEAFOOD €
(📞021-885 334; Ribarska 11; mains from 55KN; ⏱11am-11pm) Characterful family-run tavern tucked away in an old-town alleyway, with an alfresco area and a fishing-themed interior. Dishes focus on fish: specialities include sardines, *gavuni* (smelt fish) and anchovies, all served with veggies.

Pizzeria Mirkec PIZZA €
(📞021-883 042; Bana Berislavićeva 15; pizzas from 35KN; ⏱8am-midnight) Pizza at this seafront

Trogir

◉ **Sights**
1 Cathedral of St Lovro C2
2 Grand Cipiko Palace C2
3 Convent of St Nicholas C3
4 Kamerlengo Fortress A3
5 Town Hall C2
6 Town Museum....................................C2

◔ **Activities, Courses & Tours**
7 Portal Trogir C3

◍ **Sleeping**
8 Concordia B3
9 Hostel Trogir......................................D4
10 Hotel Pašike.....................................B2
11 Hotel Tragos......................................C2
12 Vila Sikaa..D4

✖ **Eating**
13 Alka...B2
14 Capo C3
15 Fontana B3
16 Konoba Trs C2
17 Pizzeria Mirkec..................................B3

joint comes out of a wood-burning oven and tastes pretty good. It also does breakfasts.

Konoba Trs DALMATIAN €€
(📞021-796 956; Matije Gupca 14; mains from 75KN; ⏱10am-midnight) Rustic little tavern with a welcoming courtyard shaded by grapevines. The interior has wooden benches and old stone walls. Its lamb *pašticada* stew, served with savoury pancakes stuffed with *pršut* and Swiss chard, is a signature dish.

Fontana SEAFOOD €€
(📞021-885 744; Obrov 1; mains from 70KN; ⏱8am-midnight) The large waterfront terrace is the main appeal of this long-standing restaurant. You can get almost anything, from inexpensive risotto and spaghetti to pricier grilled meat, but the speciality is fish (300KN per kilogram).

Alka INTERNATIONAL €€
(📞021-881 856; Augustina Kažotića 15; mains from 85KN) This restaurant has an outdoor terrace and a huge menu, with lots of meat specialities (such as chicken liver wrapped in bacon) and lobster.

❶ Information

Atlas Trogir (📞021-881 374; www.atlas-trogir.hr; Kralja Zvonimira 10) This travel agency arranges private accommodation and runs excursions.

Portal Trogir (☑ 021-885 016; www.portal-trogir.com; Bana Berislavića 3) Private accommodation; bike, scooter and kayak rental; excursions – from quad safaris and rafting to sea kayaking and canyoning – and an internet corner.

Post Office (Blaža Jurjeva Trogiranina 5; ⊘7.30am-7pm Mon-Fri, to 2.30pm Sat) There's a telephone centre here.

Tourist Office (☑ 021-885 628; www.tztrogir.hr; Trg Ivana Pavla II 1; ⊘8am-8pm Mon-Sat, 9am-2pm Sun) Hands out basic town maps.

❶ Getting There & Away

Southbound intercity buses from Zadar (130km) and northbound buses from Split (28km) will drop you off in Trogir. Getting buses from Trogir to Zadar can be more difficult, as they often arrive full from Split.

City bus 37 from Split leaves every 20 minutes throughout the day, with a stop at Split airport en route to Trogir. It leaves from the local bus station and takes longer than the intercity bus. You can buy the four-zone ticket (21KN) from the driver in either direction.

There are boats to and from Split six times daily (24KN) from mid-May to November from Čiovo (150m to the left of the bridge). A passenger boat also leaves from the boat terminal on Bana Berislavića, right in front of Hotel Concordia, to Okrug Gornji (20KN) hourly from 8.30am till 11.30pm as well as to Medena (15KN, 10 daily). A ferry goes to Drvenik Veli three times daily (15KN).

❶ Getting Around

The old town is just a few hundred metres from the bus station, which has a **garderoba** (left luggage; per day 15KN; ⊘7am-8pm) for those who need to store bags. After crossing the small bridge near the station, go through the North Gate. Turn left (east) at the end of the square and you'll come to Trogir's main street, Gradska. Trogir's finest sights are around Trg Ivana Pavla II, straight ahead. The seafront, Bana Berislavića, is lined with bars, restaurants and cafes, overlooking Čiovo Island. The old town is connected to Čiovo island to the south by a drawbridge.

Around Trogir

The area around Trogir is lined with beaches. The nearest is **Pantan**, 1.5km east of the old town, a gravel-and-sand beach on the estuary of Pantan River, surrounded by a protected nature reserve. To reach the beach, follow the path that leads from the old town to Pantan. The most popular beach, **Okrug**

Gornji, lies 5km south of Čiovo. Known as Copacabana, this 2km-long stretch of pebbles is lined with cafe-bars. It can be reached by road or boat. For the most extensive beach facilities, head 4km southwest to **Medena** beach on the Seget Riviera, home to the **Hotel Medena** (www.hotelmedena.com) megaresort.

For more isolation, it is better to head to the beaches on Drvenik Mali and Drvenik Veli islands, an easy boat trip from town. Both islands are sparsely inhabited and make idyllic getaways.

In addition there is the beautiful Kaštela area, with seven ports and several castles built by the Dalmatian nobility some 500 years ago.

Drvenik Mali & Drvenik Veli

Drvenik Mali, the smaller island, has olive trees, a population of 56 and a sandy beach that curves around the cove of Vela Rina. Drvenik Veli has secluded coves and olive trees plus a few cultural highlights to get you off the beach: the **Church of St George** dates from the 16th century and houses baroque furniture and a Venetian altarpiece. Outside Drvenik Veli village is the unfinished 18th-century **Church of St Nicholas**, whose builder never quite got past the monumental front.

To get to the islands from Trogir, take a **Jadrolinija ferry** (www.jadrolinija.hr). Three daily ferries operate from June through September (two on Friday). The return schedule makes it possible to visit Drvenik Veli on a day trip; Drvenik Mali is trickier. The journey to Drvenik Veli (15KN) takes one hour; it's a further 20 minutes to Drvenik Mali.

For those wanting to spend more time on the islands, Portal agency in Trogir can find private accommodation.

Kaštela

If you're looking to snuggle down in safety, you can't do much better than have the mountains behind you and the sea in front of you. At least that's what the Dalmatian nobility thought when they looked at the invading Ottomans in the 15th and 16th centuries. The 20km stretch of coast between Trogir and Split, backed by long, low Kozjak hill, looked like the perfect place to relax in a well-fortified castle. One after the other, rich families from Split filed down to Kaštela bay to build their mansions. The Turks never reached them and the castles remain today.

Kaštela is the name given to the seven little ports around these coastal fortified castles, and it is a delightful day trip from Split or Trogir. Starting in the west, from Trogir, you'll come first to **Kaštel Štafilić**, a castle on an islet connected to the mainland by a drawbridge. There's also a Renaissance church in town. Next up is **Kaštel Novi**, built in 1512, and then **Kaštel Stari**, built in 1476 and the oldest in the bay. An arcaded cloister stands in the middle. Further on is **Kaštel Lukšić**, the most impressive of all and the only one you can enter. Built in a transitional Renaissance-baroque style in 1487, it now houses municipal offices, a small museum and the regional tourist office. It's also the site of a rather involved tale of thwarted lovers who were married and buried here. Continue east to **Kaštel Kambelovac**, a cylindrically shaped defense castle built in 1517 by local noblemen and landowners, and then on to **Kaštel Gomilica**, built by Benedictine nuns and surrounded by shallow, sandy beaches. Finish at **Kaštel Sućurac**, then take the path that runs past the cemetery, climbing to the refuge at Putalj (480m), where you can climb to the ridge of Kozjak.

For details on accommodation in Kaštela, contact the **tourist office** (☑ 021-227 933; www.kastela-info.hr; Kaštel Lukšić; ☺ 8am-8pm Mon-Fri, 8am-noon & 6-8pm Sat, 8am-noon Sun).

To get to Kaštela, take bus 37 from Split to Trogir (21KN, every 20 minutes) – this bus stops in all the towns along the bay. It's best to get off at Kaštel Štafilić and walk eastward along the coastal promenade through the towns, until you've had enough. Then catch a bus back from the main road.

MAKARSKA RIVIERA

The Makarska Riviera is a 58km stretch of coast at the foot of the Biokovo Range, where a series of cliffs and ridges forms a dramatic backdrop to a string of beautiful pebble beaches. The foothills are protected from harsh winds and covered with lush Mediterranean greenery, including pine forests, olive groves and fruit trees. The seaside towns here are orientated towards package tourism; this is one of the most developed stretches of Dalmatian coast. It is a great place for families as facilities are vast, and it offers some active holiday possibilities. Note that in July and especially August the entire Riviera is jam-packed with holidaymakers, and many hotels impose a seven-night minimum stay. To avoid the hubbub, head to Makarska before or after the summer rush.

Makarska

POP 17,000

Makarska is a pretty port town with a limestone centre that turns peachy orange at sunset. It's an active place – there's an abundance of hiking, climbing, paragliding, mountain hiking, windsurfing and swimming opportunities – with a spectacular natural setting, backed by the gorgeous Mt Biokovo. It's the locus of Croatia's package tourism, focused on the town's long pebbly beach, which is filled with a feast of activities, from beach volleyball to screaming-children's games.

Makarska is favoured by tourists from neighbouring Bosnia and Hercegovina, who descend in huge numbers during summer. It's also popular with seniors as a 'medical tourism' destination, for the great climate and facilities. The high season is pretty raucous, with many rocking nightlife spots, but also a lot of fun for those with children. If you're interested in hanging around beach bars and clubs, playing beach volleyball and generally lounging about with beach bodies, you'll like Makarska. Outside the high season, things are pretty quiet.

Being the largest town in the region, Makarska has very good transport connections, making it a good base for exploring the coast and neighbouring Bosnia and Hercegovina. Don't miss venturing up Mt Biokovo.

◉ Sights

Franciscan Monastery
MONASTERY

(Franjevački Samostan; Franjevački put 1; museum admission 15KN; ☺ 9am-noon & 5-8pm) Just east of the centre, the single-nave church of this monastery has a huge contemporary mosaic in its apse and a well-presented **shell museum** in the cloister, with reportedly the largest collection of snails and shells in the world.

Biokovo Botanical Garden
BOTANICAL GARDEN

Just up from the village of Kotišina on Biokovo, this once-major regional highlight doesn't offer much to look at except some

SPLIT & CENTRAL DALMATIA MAKARSKA

indigenous flora and stunning views of the islands of Brač and Hvar. The scenic walk is worth it – follow the marked trail northeast of town that passes under a series of towering peaks.

Town Museum MUSEUM
(Gradski Muzej; Kralja Tomislava 17/1; admission 10KN; ⊘9am-1pm & 6-10pm Mon-Fri, 6-10pm Sat) On a rainy day when indoors beckons, trace the town's history by checking out this less-than-gripping collection of photos, old stones and nautical relics.

Beaches

Makarska is located on a large cove bordered by Cape Osejava in the southeast and the Sveti Petar peninsula in the northwest. The long pebble **town beach**, lined with hotels, stretches from the Sveti Petar park at the beginning of Kralja Tomislava northwest along the bay. To the southeast are rockier and lovelier beaches, such as **Nugal**, popular with nudists (take the marked trail from the eastern end of the Riva). For a party atmosphere all day long, head to **Buba beach** to the west of Sveti Petar peninsula, near Hotel Rivijera, where music pumps all day during the summer.

🛏 Sleeping

There's an overwhelming blandness to Makarska's hotels, which are geared for package tourism. Be prepared for nothing special, though comfortable beds and good views are reliable in the more upmarket spots. Private accommodation is, as always, the best bet for budget lodging.

Hostel Makarska HOSTEL €
(☑091 256 7212; www.hostelmakarska.com; Prvosvibanjska 15; dm/d 140/260KN; P ❋ @ 🛜) A five-minute walk to the waterfront, this basic spot has doubles and a 10-person dorm plus a shared kitchen and an outdoor area. It's open May through September.

Makarska HOTEL €€
(☑021-616 622; www.makarska-hotel.com; Potok 17; s/d 410/660KN; P ❋ @ 🛜) About 300m from the beach, it has well-equipped if chintzy rooms and friendly hosts.

Hotel Osejava HOTEL €€€
(☑021-604 300; www.osejava.com; Šetalište fra Jure Radića bb; s/d 1250/1680KN; P ❋ 🛜 🏊) Sweetest four-star in town, this contemporary property on the harbour to the south of the Riva has white-washed interiors featuring lots of light wood and B&W photos of Dalmatian themes. On the premises is a restaurant, a mini-spa and an outdoor pool, plus a cliff beach right in front.

Biokovo HOTEL €€€
(☑021-615 244; www.hotelbiokovo.hr; Kralja Tomislava 14; s/d 560/1000KN; P ❋ @ 🛜) One of the better hotels in Makarska, right on the promenade. Get a sea-view room with balcony for excellent vistas of the town.

Park HOTEL €€€
(☑021-608 200; www.parkhotel.hr; Petra Krešimira IV bb; s/d 1425/1900KN; P ❋ @ 🛜 🏊) This sleek spot is a top choice in Makarska, if luxury is what you seek. Mingle with Croatian celebs at the pool deck. There's a spa and a full spectrum of facilities.

🍴 Eating

Konoba Kalalarga DALMATIAN €
(Kalalarga 40; mains from 45KN; ⊘9am-2am) Traditional Dalmatian tavern with dim lighting, dark woods and alfresco bench seating in an alleyway tucked away at the end of Kalalarga street, which leads from Makarska's main square. It serves food the way grandma would make it, and dishes out the best *pašticada* (beef stewed in wine and spices, served with gnocchi) in town.

Decima DALMATIAN €
(☑021-611 374; Trg Tina Ujevića bb; mains from 40KN; ⊘noon-1am) Well-prepared Dalmatian staples and occasional live *klapa* (singing group) performances are served up at this family-run *konoba* just behind the Riva.

Konoba Ranč DALMATIAN €€
(☑021-623 563; Kamena 62, Tučepi; mains from 70KN; ⊘6pm-midnight) This cosy spot away from the tourist buzz is worth the 10-minute drive south at the end of Tučepi; follow the sign left and ascend along winding lanes. Dine on log chairs under olive trees, feasting on meat and fish on grill, *peka* on order, house wine and sporadic *klapa* performances.

Riva SEAFOOD €€
(☑021-616 829; Kralja Tomislava 6; mains from 75KN; ⊘10am-1am) Linger in the quiet leafy courtyard of this classy restaurant just off the main drag, feasting on fresh fish and seafood. Good wine list, too.

Jeny Restaurant
INTERNATIONAL €€€

(☑ 021-623 704; www.restaurant-jeny.hr; Čovići 1, Gornji Tučepi; mains from 130KN; ☺ 6pm-midnight) A fine dining restaurant on the slopes of Biokovo mountain in the village of Gornji Tučepi, where the culinary focus is Mediterranean, with a French touch. Splurge on the five-course tasting menu for 575KN. The stunning Riviera views make up for the passable decor.

🍷 Drinking & Nightlife

Grabovac
WINE BAR

(Kačićev trg 11; ☺ 9am-2am) Right in front of the city's church, it serves regional wines by the glass, plus tidbits such as local cheeses and *pršut*, and also does tastings of local wine varieties like *kujundžuša*.

Yeti
CAFE

(Dalmatinska 1) A cosy, much-loved spot for local bohos, misfits and alternative types, right on the main square. It closes for siesta between 3pm and 5pm in summer.

Grota
CLUB

(Šetalište Svetog Petra bb; ☺ 8pm-5am) On Sveti Petar peninsula, just after the port, this popular disco tucked into a cave welcomes local DJs plus an array of jazz, blues and rock bands.

Deep
CLUB

(Fra Jure Radića 21; ☺ 9am-5am; 🕾) A club inside a cave, on Osejava. It attracts a super-trendy set who sip cocktails as a DJ spins the latest beats in the background.

Rockatansky
BAR

(Fra Filipa Grabovca bb; ☺ 6pm-2am) Makarska's most alternative spot, where a diverse crowd gathers to hear live rock, grunge, metal and jazz on a small stage.

ℹ Information

There are many banks and ATMs along Kralja Tomislava and you can change money at the travel agencies on the same street.

Atlas Travel Agency (☑ 021-617 038; www. atlas-croatia.com; Kralja Tomislava 17) At the far end of town; finds private accommodation.

Biokovo Active Holidays (☑ 021-679 655; www.biokovo.net; Kralja Petra Krešimira IV 7b) A fount of information on Mt Biokovo, it organises hiking, cycling, rafting and kayaking trips.

Marivaturist (☑ 021-616 010; www.marivaturist. hr; Kralja Tomislava 15a) Has money-exchange facilities, and books excursions and private accommodation along the whole Makarska coast.

Tourist Office (☑ 021-612 002; www.makarska-info.hr; Kralja Tomislava 16; ☺ 8am-9pm Mon-Sat) Publishes a useful guide to the city with a map; pick it up here or at any of the travel agencies.

ℹ Getting There & Away

In July and August there are five ferries daily between Makarska and Sumartin on Brač (33KN, one hour), reduced to four in June and September. The **Jadrolinija stall** (Kralja Tomislava bb) is near the Hotel Biokovo.

From the **bus station** (☑ 021-612 333; Ante Starčevića 30), 300m uphill from the centre of the old town, there are 12 buses daily to Dubrovnik (110KN, three hours), 50 to Split (50KN, 1¼ hours), four to Rijeka (313KN to

---

ADVENTURE ON MT BIOKOVO

The limestone massif of Mt Biokovo, which is administered and protected by **Biokovo National Park** (www.biokovo.com; admission 40KN; ☺ 7am-8pm), offers wonderful hiking opportunities. If you're hiking independently, you have to enter the park at the beginning of 'Biokovo Rd' – basically the only road that runs up the mountain and impossible to miss – and buy an admission ticket there.

Vošac peak (1422m), only 2.5km from Makarska, is the nearest target for hikers. From St Mark's Church on Kačićev trg, you can walk or drive up Put Makra, following signs to the village of Makar, where a trail leads to Vošac. From Vošac a good marked trail leads to **Sveti Jure** (four hours), the highest peak at 1762m, from where you can get spectacular views of the Croatian coast and, on a clear day, the coast of Italy on the other side of the Adriatic. Take plenty of water, sunscreen, a hat and waterproof clothes – the weather on top is always a lot colder than it is by the sea.

Biokovo Active Holidays (p225) offers guided walks and drives on Mt Biokovo at all levels of physical exertion. You can go partway up the mountain by minibus and then take a short hike to Sveti Jure peak, take a 5½-hour trek through black pine forests and lush fields, or enjoy an early drive to watch the sun rise over Makarska.

393KN, seven hours) and six to Zagreb (190KN, six hours). There are also five daily buses to Mostar (100KN, 2¼ hours) and two to Sarajevo (200KN, four hours) in Bosnia and Hercegovina.

Brela

The longest and arguably loveliest coastline in Dalmatia stretches through the tiny town of Brela, which has a more chic flavour than neighbouring Makarska, 14km southeast. Six kilometres of pebble beaches curve around coves thickly forested with pine trees, where you can enjoy beautifully clear seas and fantastic sunsets. A shady promenade lined with bars and cafes winds around the coves, which are on both sides of the town. The best beach is Dugi Rat, a gorgeous stretch of pebbles about 300m southwest of the town centre.

🛏 Sleeping & Eating

Most of the private accommodation options from the tourist office or travel agencies are really small *pansions,* where double rooms start at 350KN in high season.

The four large hotels are managed by Blue Sun Hotels & Resorts (www.bluesun hotels.com). The most secluded of those is Hotel Berulia (☑021-603 599; Frankopanska bb; s/d 674/1056KN; P❄@🛜❄), a four-star giant 300m east of the town centre. Hotel Marina (☑021-608 608; s/d 608/927KN; P❄🛜) is the most affordable of the four properties and the best for families, with a wall of pine trees to separate it from the Brela beach.

Hostel Casa Vecchia   HOSTEL €
(☑099 196 7518; www.hostel-casa.com; Breljanska Cesta 40; dm/d 110/300KN; P🛜) The most affordable place in Brela is also its most adorable, the funky Hostel Casa Vecchia on the coastal highway (Magistrala), typically open from May through September. The friendly Aussie owner will even let you set up a tent for 37KN if space allows, and there's a restored wooden boat that docs daily booze cruises for hostel guests.

Konoba Feral   DALMATIAN €
(☑021-618 909; Obala Domagoja 30; mains from 60KN; ☉noon-11pm) For well-prepared seafood and fish, head to Konoba Feral, a friendly tavern with wooden tables; try the line-caught squid grilled with garlic and parsley.

Konoba Galinac   DALMATIAN €€
(☑021-618 251; Sv Jurja 52; mains from 70KN; ☉6pm-1am) For a scenic meal, head up above the coastal highway and follow the signs to Konoba Galinac, located in an abandoned hamlet of small stone houses. The restaurant has a large terrace with unobstructed views of the Adriatic islands and Brela below. It provides free transport from Brela and nearby towns.

ℹ Information

Berulia Travel (☑021-618 519; www.berulia travel-brela.hr; Frankopanska 111) Finds private accommodation, changes money, books excursions and arranges airport transfers.
Tourist Office (☑021-618 455; www.brela.hr; Trg Alojzija Stepinca bb; ☉8am-9pm) Provides a town map and a regional cycling map. Has an ATM outside.

ℹ Getting There & Away

All buses running between Makarska and Split stop at Brela, making it an easy day trip from either town. The bus stop (no left-luggage office) is behind Hotel Soline, a short walk downhill to Kneza Domagoja, the harbour street and the town centre.

BRAČ ISLAND

POP 14,435

Brač is famous for two things: its radiant white stone, from which Diocletian's Palace in Split and the White House in Washington, DC (oh, yes!) are made, and Zlatni Rat, the long pebbly beach at Bol that sticks out lasciviously into the Adriatic and adorns 90% of Croatia's tourism posters. It's the largest island in central Dalmatia, with two towns, several sleepy villages and a dramatic Mediterranean landscape of steep cliffs, inky waters and pine forests. The interior of the island is full of piles of rocks – the result of the back-breaking labour of women who, over hundreds of years, gathered the rocks in order to prepare the land for the cultivation of vineyards and olive, fig, almond and sour-cherry orchards.

The tough living conditions on the island meant that a lot of people moved to the mainland in search of work, leaving the interior almost deserted. Driving around and exploring Brač's stone villages is one of the loveliest experiences. The two main centres, Supetar and Bol, differ greatly from one another: Supetar has the appearance of a transit town, while Bol revels in its more exclusive appeal.

History

Remnants of a Neolithic settlement have been found in Kopačina cave near Supetar, but the first recorded inhabitants were the Illyrians, who built a fort in Škrip to protect against Greek invasion. The Romans arrived in 167 BC and promptly set to work exploiting the stone quarries near Škrip and building summer mansions around the island. During the four centuries of Venetian rule (1420–1797), the interior villages were devastated by plague and the inhabitants moved to the 'healthier' settlements along the coast, revitalising the towns of Supetar, Bol, Sumartin and Milna. After a brief period under Napoleonic rule, the island passed into Austrian hands. Wine cultivation expanded until the phylloxera epidemic at the turn of the 20th century ravaged the island's vines and people began leaving for North and South America, especially Chile. The island endured a reign of terror during WWII when German and Italian troops looted and burned villages, imprisoning and murdering their inhabitants. Although the tourism business took a hit in the mid-1990s, it has rebounded well and the island is now crowded in summer.

ⓘ Getting There & Away

AIR

Brač's **airport** (☑ 021-559 711; www.airport-brac.hr) is 14km northeast of Bol and 30km southeast of Supetar. There is one weekly flight from Zagreb during the high season, but there's no transport from the airport to Supetar so you'll need to take a **taxi** (☑ 098 781 377), which costs about 300KN (150KN to Bol).

BOAT

There are 14 daily car ferries between Split and Supetar in July and August (33/160KN per person/car, 50 minutes) and 12 daily in June and September (fewer in winter). The ferry drops you off in the centre of town, only steps from the bus station. Make bookings at **Jadrolinija** (☑ 021-631 357; www.jadrolinija.hr; Hrvatskih Velikana bb, Supetar), about 50m east of the harbour.

There's a Jadrolinija catamaran in summer between Split and Bol (55KN, one hour) that goes on to Jelsa on Hvar; buy your ticket in advance in Bol, as these can sell out fast in high season. There are also five daily summer car ferries between Makarska and Sumartin (33KN, one hour), reduced to four daily in June and September and two a day in winter. Note that you may have to wait an hour or two in Sumartin for a bus connection to Supetar.

ⓘ Getting Around

Public transport to the island's highlights is sparse, so you may wish to have your own wheels if you want to see a few sites in a short time. You can hire cars from travel agencies on the island or bring them from the mainland (which is pricey due to ferry costs).

Supetar is the hub for bus transport around the island. There are several daily buses that connect Supetar with Dol (50 minutes) and with Sumartin (1½ hours). Note that the bus schedule is reduced on Sundays.

Supetar

POP 4082

Supetar is not a great beauty – it feels more like a transit town than a living place in itself. However, it's a great hub for transport and a short stroll around the town will reveal some nice stone streets and a pretty church and square. The pebbly beaches are an easy stroll from the town centre, making it a popular destination for families.

Supetar is easy to navigate since most offices, shops and travel agencies are on the main road that runs roughly east–west from the harbour. Called Porat at the harbour, the road becomes Hrvatskih Velikana in the east and Vlačica on to Put Vele Luke as it travels west. The bus station (no left-luggage office) is next to the Jadrolinija office.

◉ Sights & Activities

There are five pebbly beaches on the coast. **Vrilo beach** is about 100m east of the town centre. Walking west, you'll come first to **Vlačica** then **Banj** beach, lined with pine trees. Next is **Bili Rat**, site of the water-sports centre, then if you cut across St Nikolaus Cape you come to **Vela Luka** beach, with soft pebbles on a peaceful bay.

Fun Dive Club   DIVING
(☑ 098 13 07 384; www.fundiveclub.com) The best diving on the island is found off the southwestern coast between Bol and Milna, making Bol a better base for divers. Still, you can book dives, take a diving course and rent equipment at this dive club located at plush Waterman Supetrus Resort Hotel, better known to locals as Hotel Kaktus.

(Continued on page 232)

SPLIT & CENTRAL DALMATIA SUPETAR

Croatia's Coast

From the tip of Istria to dazzling Dubrovnik, Croatia is blessed with one of the most unrelentingly gorgeous stretches of coast in the entire Mediterranean region. The crystalline waters provide a constant presence as the backdrop changes from mountains to walled towns to low-slung islands and back again.

Walled Towns

Since ancient times the people of this coast have encased their towns in sturdy walls of stone as a protection against the attacks that came all too frequently. Although the purpose may have been purely defensive, the end result is spectacular; the sight of these stone bastions rising from the sea is one of the most memorable images of the Adriatic coast. Even when the walls themselves have been largely removed, exposing the nest of medieval streets within, they still make for an impressive sight.

Most people know all about Dubrovnik, but there are many mini-Dubrovniks scattered all along the coast. One of the most magical is Trogir, west of Split, occupying a little islet anchored by bridges to the mainland. Split itself has at its heart an ancient fortress growing out of the remains of a Roman imperial palace – although from the water it's hard to distinguish from the sprawl surrounding it. Šibenik's fortified old town arcs up a hill to an imposing castle, while at Ston the fortifications rise up and over the mountainous terminus of the Pelješac peninsula.

Historic Rovinj was once an island, separated from the mainland by a narrow channel which was subsequently filled in – much like Dubrovnik itself. In Zadar's case the walls enclosed the tip of a peninsula – although these days only about half of them remain. The islands, too, have many such impressive sites;

the old towns of Cres, Krk, Rab, Pag and Korčula being principal amongst them.

Apart from all the well-known places, you might find yourself stumbling on to your own little walled treasure. Like sleepy wee Osor, watching over the channel separating the islands of Cres and Lošinj. Or pretty little Primošten, jutting out over a rocky shore south of Šibenik.

Island Life

Croatia's 1244 islands range from little more than rocks poking out of the sea, to large, populated places supporting agriculture and small towns. Two of the biggest, Krk and Pag, are joined to the mainland by bridges, yet they still maintain their own distinct island culture and way of life.

The more popular and populated islands are well-served by ferries all year round, although there can be lengthy queues for the car ferries in July and August, and during weekends in June and September. If you're planning on island-hopping at those times, you're better off doing so as a foot passenger and hiring a car or scooter when you arrive. Note, locals only tend to use the term 'ferries' when talking about car ferries; the faster passenger-only boats are generally listed on schedules as 'catamarans'.

....

1. Rovinj (p108) 2. Valun (p150)

For the clusters of smaller islands, such as the Kornatis, organised tours are popular; enquire at travel agencies, tourist offices and marinas anywhere along the coast. Yachties will find themselves in sailing heaven, with plenty of deserted bays on unpopulated islets to seek out. If, perchance, you haven't managed to bring your own yacht with you, it's possible to hire one, either with a skipper or without (provided you have a licence). There are numerous island-hopping package sailing tours available, including some specifically targeted to backpackers.

Beaches

Although it's only about 600km long as the crow flies, if someone were to iron out all the indentations and unwind the numerous islands, Croatia's Adriatic coastline would stretch for 1778km. The lure of the clear water and the balmy weather sees literally millions of tourists descend on the beaches each summer, with the peak being during the European school holidays in July and August.

If you're expecting long sandy beaches to compete with Bondi, Malibu or Copacabana, you'll be disappointed. Mostly you'll find pretty little rocky or pebbly coves, edged by pines, olives or low scrub. There are some beautiful sandy beaches – mainly on the islands – but the water is often painfully shallow, requiring a lengthy walk to get even your knees wet. It's partly for this reason that the locals tend to prefer the rocky bays.

What is particularly striking all the way along the coast is the clarity and colour of the water, at times seeming almost unnaturally blue or green. Currently there are 97 Blue Flag–rated beaches in the country (a measure of water quality and environmental standards), with the majority in Istria (43) and the Kvarner region (27).

Swimmers should watch out for sea urchins, which are common along the coast. The sharp spines are painful to tread on and can break off in your skin and become infected. If you're planning on swimming, you're well advised to wear water shoes, which are easily purchased on urchin-infested beaches.

Croatia is not short of places to let it all hang out, with naturist beaches all along the coast, often accompanied by campsites. Look for the signs reading 'FKK', which stands for *freikörperkultur,* meaning 'free body culture' in German. Just don't forget those water shoes!

Snorkelling & Diving

Do yourself a favour and pack your mask and snorkel – the clear, warm waters and the abundance of small fish make for lots to see. Serious divers will also find plenty to keep them busy, with numerous wrecks (dating from ancient times to WWII), drop-offs and caves. Popular sites include the wreck of the *Taranto* near Dubrovnik, the Margarita Reef off the island of Susak, the wreck of the *Rosa* off Rab and around the islands of Brač, Vis, Dugi Otok and Lošinj.

1. Brela (p226) **2.** Vis Island (p244) **3.** Pag Island (p176)

(Continued from page 227)

Rent a Robert's
WATER SPORTS, BOAT RENTAL

(☑091 534 7575; www.rentaroberts.com; Petra Jakšića 31) On the main beach, this friendly and reliable agency rents small boats, jet skis and scooters. They also have a taxi boat.

🏄 Tours

Adriatic Experience
GUIDED TOUR

(www.adriaticexperience.com) This travel agency offers the most authentic look at Brač with day sailings, stonemason workshops, wine jaunts and a Brač tour through the back roads of the island.

🎊 Festivals & Events

Supetar Summer
MUSIC

(⊙ Jun-Sep) The Supetar Summer festival lasts from mid-June through mid-September, when folk music, dances and classical concerts are presented several times a week in public spaces and churches. Tickets to festival events are usually free or cost very little. There are also frequent art exhibitions around town.

🛏 Sleeping

Most of the big hotels are in a tourist complex a few kilometres west of the port on Vela Luka bay. For a sprawling development of this kind, the landscaping is surprisingly pleasant, with pine trees, shrubbery and a nearby beach.

Travel agencies can find you good-quality rooms. Check www.supetar.hr for details of rooms and villas available.

Pansion Palute
GUESTHOUSE €

(☑021-631 541; palute@st.t-com.hr; Put Pašike 16; s/d 190/360KN; P❄) This small, family-run *pansion* has clean and tidy rooms (most with balconies), wooden floors, TVs and a voluble proprietor. Outstanding homemade jam is served with breakfast.

Funky Donkey
HOSTEL €

(☑021-630 937; www.brachostels.net; Polanda 20; dm 140-160KN; d 360KN; ⊙ May-Aug; ❄@🛜) This party hostel in the old town offers up dorms and doubles, laundry service, a kitchen, a terrace with sea views and tours around the island, including cliff jumping.

Camping Supetar
CAMPGROUND €

(☑091 194 02 46; per adult/site 22/30KN; ⊙ Jun-Sep) A midsized autocamp about 300m east of town, with access to a small rocky beach.

Bračka Perla
HOTEL €€€

(☑021-755 530; www.brackaperla.com; Put Vele Luke 53; d/ste 2526/3192KN; P❄🅿@🛜🏊) This exclusive little 'art hotel' showcases eight suites and three rooms, each painted by renowned artist Srećko Žitnik. The garden terrace is lovely, as are the sea vistas and the facilities, which include an open-air pool and a small wellness centre.

Hotel Amor
HOTEL €€€

(☑021-606 606; www.velaris.hr; Put Vele Luke 10; s/d 967/1290KN; P❄🅿@🛜🏊) This upscale hotel features 50 rooms, all with balconies, decked out in yellows, olives and bright greens. The complex, surrounded by peaceful olive and pine woods and close to the beach, has a spa and a dive centre.

🍴 Eating

Punta
SEAFOOD €

(☑021-631 507; Punta 1; mains from 60KN; ⊙8am-midnight) This fabulously located restaurant has a beach terrace overlooking the sea. Choose from seafood, dive into some meat or just have a pizza as you watch the waves and windsurfers play around.

★ Konoba Kopačina
DALMATIAN €€

(☑021-647 707; Donji Humac 7, Donji Humac; mains from 70KN; ⊙10am-midnight) In the village of Donji Humac, a 10-minute drive inland from Supetar, this tavern serves the best island food. Other than traditional *konoba* fare, they do bizarre Brač specialities such as *vitalac* (skewered lamb offal wrapped in lamb meat) and *puh* (dormouse). The terrace has panoramic valley views.

Vinotoka
SEAFOOD €€

(☑021-630 969; Jobova 6; mains from 80KN; ⊙noon-midnight) One of the best places in Supetar, Vinotoka is decorated with marine-inspired pieces and has a glassed-in terrace and a wooden boat in the middle. The seafood is excellent, best accompanied by some local white. Try the tuna prosciutto.

🍸 Drinking & Nightlife

Benny's Bar (Put Vela Luke bb; ⊙10am-2am) and **Day n' Night** (Put Vela Luke bb; ⊙10am-5am) are popular hangout spots. For a bohemian vibe, head to **Bravura Art Café** (Petra Jakšića 1; ⊙7am-10pm Mon-Thu, to midnight Fri, to 2am Sat), an artsy retreat with a stone courtyard tucked away from the buzz of the coastal promenade, with jazz nights, poetry readings, workshops, exhibits and live music.

ℹ️ Information

Atlas (☑ 021-631 105; Porat 10) Books excursions and private accommodation. Near the harbour.

Maestral (☑ 021-631 258; www.travel.maestral.hr; IG Kovačića 3) Source of private accommodation.

Radeško (☑ 021-756 694; Put Barba Maškova 11) Finds private accommodation, books hotels and changes money.

Tourist Office (☑ 021-630 900; www.supetar.hr; Porat 1; ☺8am-10pm) Has a full array of brochures on the activities and sights in Supetar, as well as up-to-date bus and ferry timetables. A few steps east of the harbour.

Bol

POP 1900

The old town of Bol is an attractive place, with small stone houses and winding streets dotted with pink and purple geraniums. Bol's real highlight is Zlatni Rat, the seductive pebbly beach that 'leaks' into the Adriatic and draws crowds of swimmers and windsurfers in the summer months. A long coastal promenade lined with pine trees connects the beach with the old town, and along it are most of the town's hotels. It's a great, buzzing place in summer – one of Croatia's favourites, and perennially popular.

The town centre is a pedestrian area that stretches east from the bus station. Sights in the old town are marked with interpretative panels, each explaining the cultural and historical heritage. Zlatni Rat beach is 2km west of town and in between are Borak and Potočine beaches. Behind them are several hotel complexes, including Hotel Borak, Elaphusa and Bretanide.

⊙ Sights

Zlatni Rat
BEACH

Most people come to Bol to soak up the sun or windsurf at Zlatni Rat, which extends like a tongue into the sea for about 500m from the western end of town. It's a gorgeous beach made up of smooth white pebbles, its tip shuffled by the wind and waves. Pine trees provide shade and rocky cliffs rise sharply behind the beach, making the setting one of the loveliest in Dalmatia.

To get there, follow the marble-paved seafront promenade, fringed with subtropical gardens. Note, though, that the beach gets jam-packed in the high season.

Galerija Branislav Dešković
GALLERY

(admission 10KN; ☺10am-noon & 6-10pm Tue-Sun) This gallery, inside a Renaissance-baroque townhouse right on the seafront, displays work by 20th-century Croatian artists, amounting to around 300 paintings and sculptures. A great place to pop in on a cloudy day.

Dragon's Cave
CAVE

You can go by foot to Dragon's Cave, an extremely unusual set of reliefs believed to have been carved by an imaginative 15th-century friar. Carved angels, animals and a gaping dragon decorate the walls of this strange cave in a blend of Christian and Croat pagan symbols.

First walk 6km to Murvica; from there it's a 3km walk. Note that the cave can only be visited by prior arrangement with a guide who has a key. He's best reached via the tourist office. It costs about 50KN per person to reach the cave from Murvica but there's a four-person minimum.

🏃 Activities

Bol is undoubtedly the **windsurfing** capital of Croatia and most of the action takes place at Potočine beach, west of town. Although the *maestral* (strong, steady westerly wind) blows from April to October, the best time to windsurf is at the end of May and the beginning of June, and at the end of July and the beginning of August. The wind generally reaches its peak in the early afternoon and then dies down at the end of the day.

If you fancy hiking, try the two-hour walk up to **Vidova Gora** (778m), the area's highest peak. There are also mountain-biking trails leading up. The local tourist office can give you info and basic maps.

Big Blue
WINDSURFING

(☑021-635 614; www.big-blue-sport.hr) Big Blue is a large operation that rents windsurfing boards (per half day 290KN) and offers beginners' courses (990KN). It also rents mountain bikes (per hour/day 40/120KN) and kayaks (50/180KN). It has three locations: inside a shop next to the tourist office on the seafront, on Borak beach and by Bretanide Hotel.

Big Blue
DIVING

(☑021-306 222; www.big-blue-diving.hr; Hotel Borak, Zlatni Rat; dives from 200KN, with equipment rental 300KN) Another operation named Big Blue, this company organises diving of coral reefs at 40m depth and a large cave, but no wrecks; boats go out regularly during the high season.

Nautic Center

Bol Stall BOAT RENTAL, WATER SPORTS
(☑ 021-635 367; www.nautic-center-bol.com; Potočine beach; per day from 400KN) Rent boats from the Nautic Center Bol stall, which sits opposite the Bretanide Hotel during the day. In the evening you can find the stall at the harbour, where it moves to attract more customers. It also has lots of water-sports activities such as wakeboarding, jet-skiing, waterskiing, tube riding and parasailing.

Tennis Centre Potočine TENNIS
(☑ 021-635 222; Zlatni Rat; per hr 100KN) There are professional-quality clay tennis courts at the Tennis Centre Potočine, along the road to Murvica. Rackets and balls can be rented.

⭐ Festivals & Events

Bol Summer Festival MUSIC, DANCE
(⊘ Jun-Sep) The Bol Summer Festival is held from the middle of June through late September each year, with dancers and musicians from around the country performing in churches and open spaces.

Cultural Festival Imena CULTURE
(⊘ Jun) An annual event that takes place in late June, Cultural Festival Imena gathers writers, artists and musicians for a few days of exhibits, readings, concerts and happenings.

Our Lady of Carmel Feast Day TRADITIONAL
(⊘ Aug) The patron saint of Bol is Our Lady of Carmel; on her feast day (5 August), there's a procession with residents dressed up in traditional costumes, as well as music and feasting on the streets.

🛏 Sleeping

There are few small hotels but several large tourist complexes, which, surprisingly, blend in well with the landscape. Several hotels are 'all-inclusive'. Reservations for most hotels are handled by **Blue Sun Hotels** (www.bluesunhotels.com).

Travel agencies can arrange private accommodation with en-suite bathrooms for around 150KN to 200KN per person. Two-person studio apartments cost around 350KN to 400KN in the high season; other sizes are available.

Campgrounds in Bol are small and familial. West of town and near the big hotels you'll find **Camp Kito** (☑ 021-635 551; www.camping-brac.com; Bračke Ceste bb; per adult/tent 60/22KN; ⊘ mid-Apr–mid-Sep; P 🛜), which is well kept and placed in a scenic spot.

Funky Donkey HOSTEL €
(☑ 021-635 026; www.brachostels.net; Domovinskog Rata 62; dm 150-170KN, d 380KN; ⊘ May-Sep; P @ 🛜) Bol's best budget option, the offshoot of Supetar's Funky Donkey, sits a 1.5km walk from Zlatni Rat and a 750m walk to the town centre. It has four dorms and three doubles, plus three kitchens and a barbecue area.

Hotel Kaštil HOTEL €€
(☑ 021-635 995; www.kastil.hr; Frane Radića 1; s/d 540/800KN; P ❄ 🛜) All 32 carpeted rooms have sea views in this central hotel in an old baroque townhouse. The decor is sparse but pleasant. Balconies adorn some of the units. There's a lovely restaurant terrace where hotel guests get 10% off the price of their meals.

Villa Giardino GUESTHOUSE €€€
(☑ 021-635 900; www.bol.hr/online/VillaGiardino.htm; Novi Put 2; s/d 635/850KN; P ❄ 🛜) An iron gate opens onto a luxuriant garden at the end of which is this elegant white villa. Ten tastefully restored and spacious rooms are furnished with antiques; some overlook the garden while others have sea views. It's an oasis of peace, with a secluded garden out the back. It is cash only,

Hotel Bol HOTEL €€€
(☑ 021-635 660; www.hotel-bol.com; Hrvatskih domobrana 19; s/d 963/1482KN; P ❄ 🛜 🏊) Contemporary boutique hotel, a few minutes from the town centre and 400m from the sea, where most rooms showcase sea-facing balconies. The decor is swish, featuring Dalmatian highlights like an olive sculpture and artsy photography of fishing boats, plus there's a free shuttle to Zlatni Rat beach.

Hotel Borak HOTEL €€€
(☑ 021-306 202; www.brachotelborak.com; Zlatni Rat; s/d 820/1100KN; P ❄ @ 🛜 🏊) Close to Zlatni Rat and sporting activities, this place lacks character thanks to its size and the socialist-style architecture. It is, however, a comfortable spot to relax after your windsurfing, mountain biking, kayaking, swimming...

Elaphusa HOTEL €€€
(☑ 021-306 200; www.hotelelaphusabrac.com; Put Zlatnog Rata bb; s/d 1024/1815KN; P ❄ @ 🛜 🏊)

Enormous and glistening, four-star Elaphusa feels like the inside of a cruise ship. It's all smooth interiors, glass partitions, saltwater pools, slick rooms and every possible amenity, including a wellness centre. If you like glam and glitz, this (although quite soulless) is it.

Eating

Bol's restaurant scene is decent although unexciting. Expect plenty of fresh fish and seafood, and some attempts at creative cooking.

★Konoba Mali Raj   DALMATIAN €

(Iza Loze 5; mains from 50KN; ⊙noon-midnight) Lovely little spot away from the tourist buzz, above the parking lot for Zlatni Rat, this alfresco tavern has a leafy garden with plenty of nooks and crannies to enjoy the delicious dishes such as sea anemone risotto, seafood skewers or monkfish in champagne sauce. It's cash only.

Taverna Riva   DALMATIAN €€

(☑021-635 236; Frane Radića 5; mains from 70KN; ⊙11am-midnight) This terrace right above the Riva is where locals go for a good meal. If you're feeling adventurous, try the *vitalac* (skewered lamb offal wrapped in lamb meat) or order ahead for the delicious lamb or octopus under *peka* (domed baking lid).

Ribarska Kućica   SEAFOOD €€

(☑021-635 033; Ante Starčevića bb; mains from 70KN; ⊙9am-1am) A lobster extravaganza is in order at this seaside restaurant, where you sit on the waterfront terrace or under straw sun umbrellas on a small pebble beach, gorging on well-prepared seafood. Service can be slow.

Terasa Ciccio   DALMATIAN €€

(Divulje bay; mains from 80KN; ⊙11am-8pm) Casual terrace tavern nestled on the edge of a rocky beach outside Bol, away from the hubbub, serving mostly fresh fish. Use their boat transfer, or follow the coastal road from Bol toward Murvica; after it turns into a dirt road, you'll see a sign on the left.

Konoba Dalmatino   DALMATIAN €€

(Frane Radića 14; mains from 65KN; ⊙noon-midnight) This tavern offers good, informal dining in a setting of burnished wood, old photos and knick-knacks. The seafood and meat dishes are prepared simply but well.

Drinking & Nightlife

Varadero   COCKTAIL BAR

(Frane Radića bb; ⊙May-Nov) At this open-air cocktail bar on the seafront you can sip coffee and fresh OJ under straw umbrellas during the day and return in the evening for fab cocktails, DJ music and lounging on wicker sofas and armchairs.

Marinero   CAFE, BAR

(Rudina 46) A cult gathering spot for Bol locals, up the stairs from the seafront (follow the sign), with a leafy terrace on a square, live music on some nights and a diverse merry-making crowd.

❶ Information

There are several ATMs in town, and many money changers in the port area. Most cafes have wi-fi and there are several hotspots around town (for a fee).

Adria Bol (☑021-635 966; www.adria-bol.hr; Bračka cesta 10) At the entrance to Bol, this is a great source for tours, day trips, transfers, apartments, rental boats and cars – very reliable, with good service.

Bol Tours (☑021-635 693; www.boltours.com; Vladimira Nazora 18) Books excursions, rents cars, changes money and finds private accommodation.

Interactiv (☑091 572 5855; Rudina 6; per hr 30KN; ⊙May-Oct) A dozen fast computers and a call centre.

More (☑021-642 050; www.more-bol.com; Vladimira Nazora 28) Private accommodation, scooter rental, island tours and excursions.

Tourist Office (☑021-635 638; www.bol.hr; Porat Bolskih Pomoraca bb; ⊙8.30am-10pm Jul & Aug, 8.30am-2pm & 4-9pm Mon-Sat May-Jun & Sep-Oct) Inside a Gothic 15th-century townhouse; a good source of information on town events and distributes plenty of brochures.

HVAR ISLAND

POP 11,080

Hvar is the number-one holder of Croatia's superlatives: it's the most luxurious island, the sunniest place in the country (2724 sunny hours each year) and, along with Dubrovnik, the most popular tourist destination. Hvar Town, the island's capital, is all about swanky hotels, elegant restaurants, trendy bars and clubs, posh yachties and a general sense that, if you care about seeing and being seen, this is the place to be. The

TOP FIVE BEACHES OF CENTRAL DALMATIA

→ **Zlatni Rat** (p233) The famous beach finger that appears in nearly all of Croatia's tourist publicity.

→ **Brela** A string of palm-fringed coves with ultrasoft pebbles.

→ **Pakleni Islands** Rocky islands near Hvar with clothing-optional coves.

→ **Šolta** Quiet, rocky coves not far from noisy Split.

→ **Stiniva** Stunning and secluded pebble cove on Vis Island, flanked by high rocks.

coastal towns of Stari Grad and Jelsa, the cultural and historical centres of the island, are the more serene and discerning spots.

Hvar is also famed for the lilac lavender fields that dot its interior, as well as for other aromatic plants such as rosemary and heather. You'll find that some of the really deluxe hotels use skin-care products made out of these gorgeous-smelling herbs.

The interior of the island hides abandoned ancient hamlets, towering peaks and verdant, largely uncharted landscapes. It's worth exploring on a day trip, as is the southern end of the island, which has some of Hvar's most beautiful and isolated coves.

❶ Getting There & Away

The local Jadrolinija car ferry from Split calls at Stari Grad (47KN, two hours) six times a day in summer. Jadrolinija also has three to five catamarans daily to Hvar Town (55KN to 70KN, one hour) and two to Jelsa (40KN, 1½ hours). **Krilo** (www.krilo.hr), the fast passenger boat, travels twice a day between Split and Hvar Town (70KN, one hour) in summer. You can buy tickets at Pelegrini Tours (p242) in Hvar.

There are at least 10 car ferries (fewer in the low season) running from Drvenik, on the mainland, to Sućuraj (16KN, 35 minutes) on the tip of Hvar Island. The **Jadrolinija agency** (☑021-741 132; www.jadrolinija.hr) is beside the landing in Stari Grad.

Connections to Italy are available in the summer season. Two Jadrolinija ferries a week (on Saturday and Sunday night) go from Stari Grad to Ancona in Italy. Blue Line also runs boats to Ancona from Hvar Town in August and September. Pelegrini Tours sells these tickets.

In Hvar Town, **garderoba** (left luggage; per hr 20KN; ⊗24hr) facilities are available in the public bathroom next to the bus station.

❶ Getting Around

Buses meet most ferries that dock at Stari Grad and go to Hvar Town (27KN, 20 minutes) and Jelsa (33KN, 40 minutes). There are 10 buses a day between Stari Grad and Hvar Town in summer, but services are reduced on Sunday and in the low season. A taxi to Hvar Town costs around 275KN; try **Radio Taxi Tihi** (☑098 338 824), which can also work out cheaper if there are a number of passengers to fill up the minivan. It's easy to recognise, with a picture of Hvar painted on the side.

If you're driving from Stari Grad to Hvar Town, be aware that there are two routes: the scenic route, which is a narrow road winding through the interior mountains; and the direct route, which is a modern roadway (2960) that gets you to town rapidly.

Hvar Town

POP 3770

The island's hub and busiest destination, Hvar Town is estimated to draw around 20,000 people a day in the high season. It's odd that they can all fit in the small bay town, where 13th-century walls surround beautifully ornamented Gothic palaces and traffic-free marble streets, but fit they do. Visitors wander along the main square, explore the sights on the winding stone streets, swim on the numerous beaches or pop off to the Pakleni Islands to get into their birthday suits, but most of all they party at night.

There are several good restaurants here and a number of great hotels, but thanks to the island's appeal to well-heeled guests, the prices can be seriously inflated. Don't be put off if you're on a lower budget though, as private accommodation and a couple of hostels cater to a younger, more diverse crowd.

◉ Sights

The main street is the long seaside promenade, dotted with small, rocky beaches, sights, hotels, bars and some restaurants. The town square is called Trg Svetog Stjepana and the bus stop is minutes away from here. On the northern slope above the square, and within the old ramparts, are the remains of several palaces that belonged to the Hvar aristocracy. From the bus station to the harbour the town is closed to traffic, which preserves the medieval tranquillity.

Hvar is such a small, manageable town that it only recently got street names, although nobody really uses them.

St Stephen's Square
SQUARE

(Trg Svetog Stjepana) The centre of town is this rectangular square, which was formed by filling in an inlet that once stretched out from the bay. At 4500 sq metres, it's one of the largest old squares in Dalmatia. The town first developed in the 13th century to the north of the square and later spread south in the 15th century. Notice the well at the square's northern end, which was built in 1520 and has a wrought-iron grill dating from 1780.

Franciscan Monastery & Museum
MONASTERY

(admission 25KN; ⊙ 9am-1pm & 5-7pm Mon-Sat) This 15th-century monastery overlooks a shady cove. The elegant bell tower was built in the 16th century by a well-known family of stonemasons from Korčula. The Renaissance cloister leads to a refectory containing lace, coins, nautical charts and valuable documents, such as an edition of *Ptolemy's Atlas*, printed in 1524.

Your eye will immediately be struck by *The Last Supper*, an 8m by 2.5m work by the Venetian Matteo Ingoli dating from the end of the 16th century. The cypress in the cloister garden is said to be more than 300 years old. The adjoining church, named Our Lady of Charity, contains more fine paintings such as the three polyptychs created by Francesco da Santacroce in 1583, which represent the summit of this painter's work.

Fortica
FORTRESS

(admission 25KN; ⊙ 9am-9pm) Through the network of tiny streets northwest of St Stephen's Square, climb up through a park to the citadel built on the site of a medieval castle to defend the town from the Turks. The Venetians strengthened it in 1557 and then the Austrians renovated it in the 19th century by adding barracks. Inside is a tiny collection of ancient amphorae recovered from the seabed. The view over the harbour is magnificent, and there's a lovely cafe at the top.

Arsenal
HISTORIC BUILDING

(Trg Svetog Stjepana) On the southern side of St Stephen's Square, the Arsenal was built in 1611 to replace a building destroyed by the Ottomans. Mentioned in Venetian documents as 'the most beautiful and the most useful building in the whole of Dalmatia', the Arsenal once served as a repair and refitting station for war galleons.

Renaissance Theatre
HISTORIC BUILDING

(Trg Svetog Stjepana; admission 15KN; ⊙ 8am-2pm & 3-9pm) Built in 1612, this theatre is reportedly the first theatre in Europe open to plebeians and aristocrats alike. It remained a regional cultural centre throughout the centuries. Plays were still staged here right up until 2008. Although much of the theatre is still under renovation, you can wander around the atmospheric interior and take in the faded frescoes and baroque loggias.

Cathedral of St Stephen
CATHEDRAL

(Katedrala Svetog Stjepana; Trg Svetog Stjepana, admission 10KN; ⊙ 9am-1pm & 5-9pm) The cathedral forms a stunning backdrop to the square. The bell tower rises four levels, each more elaborate than the last. The cathedral was built in the 16th and 17th centuries at the height of the Dalmatian Renaissance on the site of a cathedral destroyed by the Turks. Parts of the older cathedral are visible in the nave and in the carved 15th-century choir stalls.

Bishop's Treasury
MUSEUM

(Riznica; admission 10KN; ⊙ 9am-noon & 5-7pm Mon-Fri, 9am-noon Sat) Adjoining the Cathedral of St Stephen, the treasury houses silver vessels, embroidered Mass robes, numerous Madonnas, a couple of 13th-century icons and an elaborately carved sarcophagus.

Benedictine Monastery
MONASTERY

(admission 10KN; ⊙ 9am-noon & 5-7pm Mon-Sat) Northwest of St Stephen's Square, this monastery has a re-creation of a Renaissance house and a collection of lace painstakingly woven by the nuns from dried agave leaves.

🏃 Activities

There are several diving outfits in town, including Marinesa Dive Centre (☑ 091 515 7229) and Diving Centre Viking (☑ 091 568 9443; www.viking-diving.com). Both offer PADI certification courses and dives (from 250KN and up to 500KN for a full-day trip with two dives).

You can rent scooters at Navigare (☑ 021-718 721; www.renthvar.com; Trg Svetog Stjepana) for between 200KN and 250KN per day. They also rent cars (from 450KN per day) and boats (from 400KN per day).

There are coves around the hotels Amfora and Dalmacija for swimming, as well as the fancy Bonj Les Bains beach run by Sunčani

Hvar Town

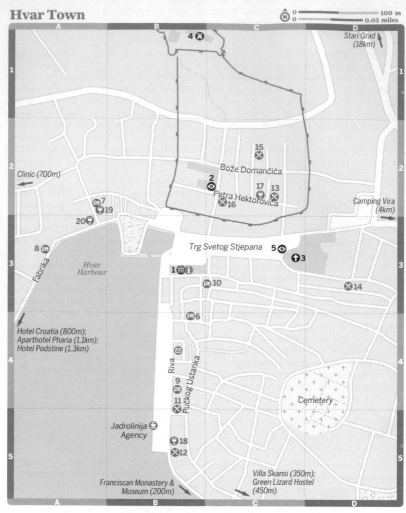

Hvar Hotels, with stone beach cabanas for open-air massages and expensive lounge chairs (650KN per day for two chairs).

A popular boat excursion (40KN, 20 minutes) is to **Mekićevica** bay on the south side of the island, where there's a great beachfront restaurant called **Robinson** (www.robinson-hvar.hr). Taxi boats also run to **Milna** (50KN, 30 minutes). Also on the south side are other great beaches such as Zaraće, Dubovica, Lušišće and Sveta Nedelja/Ivan Dolac.

Contact **Hvar Adventure** (📞 021-717 813; www.hvar-adventure.com; Obala bb) for ad-

venture activities such as sailing (half day 420KN), sea kayaking (half day 350KN), cycling (half day 500KN), hiking and rock climbing.

There are 120km of hiking trails and 96km of marked biking trails within easy access of Hvar Town. Maps are on sale from travel agencies and Tisak stores.

👉 Tours

Secret Hvar   GUIDED TOURS
(📞 021-717 615; www.secrethvar.com) Don't miss the great off-road tour with Secret Hvar (600KN, including lunch in a traditional

Hvar Town

◎ Sights
1 Arsenal B3
2 Benedictine Monastery C2
  Bishop's Treasury .... (see 3)
3 Cathedral of St Stephen C3
4 Fortica B1
  Renaissance Theatre..................... (see 1)
5 St Stephen's Square C3

⊜ Sleeping
6 Helvetia Hostel B4
7 Hostel Marinero A2
8 Hotel Adriana.. A3
9 Hotel Riva... B4
10 Hvar Out Hostel..................................... C3

✗ Eating
11 Divino B5
12 Gariful B5
13 Giaxa C2
14 Konoba Luviji.. D3
15 Konoba Menego C2
  Nonica .... (see 10)
16 Zlatna Školjka C2

⊙ Drinking & Nightlife
17 3 Pršuta C2
18 Carpe Diem B5
19 Kiva Bar... A2
20 Nautica.. A3

tavern), which takes in hidden beauties of the island's interior, including abandoned villages, scenic canyons, ancient stone huts, endless fields of lavender and the island's tallest peak, Sveti Nikola (626m). They also do wine tours (550KN with snacks and samplings) and island tours (450KN).

✯ Festivals & Events

Hvar's **Summer Festival**, which runs from late June to early September, includes classical concerts in the Franciscan monastery. **Lavender Festival** takes place in Velo Grablje village on the last weekend in June every year, with exhibits, concerts, wine tastings and a lavender fair – a fun local event.

⊨ Sleeping

As Hvar is one of the Adriatic's most popular destinations, don't expect many bargains. Most Hvar hotels are managed by **Sunčani Hvar Hotels** (www.suncanihvar.com) and many have undergone a total transformation.

Accommodation in Hvar is extremely tight in July and August, even though many houses have been renovated or constructed to accommodate the crush of tourism. Try the travel agencies for help. If you arrive without a reservation, you will be offered rooms at the ferry dock; there are also many *sobe* (rooms available) signs in town. If you rent a room or apartment from someone at a dock, make sure the house sports a blue *sobe* sign. Otherwise, they are renting illegally and you'll be unprotected in case of a problem. Get a business card if possible. It is amazingly easy to get lost in the warren of unnamed streets hanging over and around the old town and you may need to call the owner for help. Expect to pay anywhere

from 150KN to 300KN per person for a room with a private bathroom in the town centre. Outside the high season you can negotiate a much better price.

Family-run private-apartment options are so many in Hvar that the choice can be overwhelming. Here are a few reliable, good-value apartments: **Apartments Ukić** (www.hvar-apartments-center.com), **Apartments Komazin** (www.croatia-hvar-apartments.com), **Apartments Ivanović** (www.ivanovic-hvar.com) and **Apartments Bracanović** (www.hvar-jagoda.com).

Helvetia Hostel HOSTEL €
(☑ 091 34 55 556; hajduk.hvar@gmail.com; Grge Novaka 6; dm/d 230KN/500KN; ❀ 🛜) Run by a friendly islander, this hostel inside his family's old stone house just behind Riva has three dorms and two doubles. The highlight is the giant rooftop terrace where guests hang out and enjoy undisturbed views of Hvar bay and the Pakleni Islands.

Hostel Marinero HOSTEL €
(☑ 091 174 1601; Put Sv Marka 7; dm 240-320KN; ❀ 🛜) Location is the highlight at this six-dorm hostel right off the seafront. Dorms are basic but clean. There is no shared kitchen but the restaurant downstairs is a good place to mingle. The hostel wristband gets you discounts and perks at spots around town. Be ready for some noise as the Kiva Bar is right next door.

Hvar Out Hostel HOSTEL €
(☑ 021-717 375; hvarouthostel@gmail.com; Burak 23; dm 250-320KN; ❀ @ 🛜) By the same owners as Split Hostel Booze & Snooze, this party place, steps from the harbour in the maze of the old town, has seven well-equipped

DON'T MISS

PAKLENI ISLANDS

Most visitors to Hvar Town head to the Pakleni Islands (Pakleni Otoci), which got their name – 'Hell's Islands' in Croatian – from paklina, the resin that once coated boats and ships. This gorgeous chain of 21 wooded isles has crystal-clear seas, hidden beaches and deserted lagoons. Taxi boats leave regularly during the high season from in front of the Arsenal to the islands of **Jerolim** and **Stipanska** (40KN, 10 to 15 minutes), which are popular naturist islands (although nudity is not mandatory). They continue on to **Ždrilca** and **Mlini** (40KN) and, further out, **Palmižana** (60KN), which has a pebble beach and the **Meneghello Place** (www.palmizana.hr), a beautiful boutique complex of villas and bungalows scattered among lush tropical gardens. Run by the artsy Meneghello family, the estate holds music recitals, and features two excellent restaurants and an art gallery. Also on Palmižana are two top restaurant-cum-hang-out spots, Toto and Laganini.

dorms, a small shared kitchen and a terrace on the top floor. Book ahead through Hostelworld or Hostelbookers, or do a walk-in.

Villa Skansi HOSTEL €
(021-741 426; hostelvillaskansi1@gmail.com; Lučica bb; dm 150-200KN, d 400-500KN; ❄ @ ﹫) Popular hostel a short walk uphill from the seafront, with superclean dorms and doubles, fancy bathrooms, a great terrace with sea views, a bar and barbecue. There's a book exchange, laundry service, scooter, boat and bike rental and booze cruises. Run by a friendly couple.

Luka's Lodge HOSTEL €
(021-742 118; www.lukalodgehvar.hostel.com; Šime Buzolića Tome 75; dm 150-190KN, d 350-400KN; ❄ @ ﹫) Friendly owner Luka really takes care of his guests at this homey hostel, a five-minute walk from town. All rooms come with fridges, some with balconies. There's a living room, two terraces and a kitchen and laundry service. Upon request, Luka does pick-up from the ferry dock.

Green Lizard HOSTEL €
(021-742 560; www.greenlizard.hr; Domovinskog Rata 13; dm/d 200/460KN; ☺ Apr-Oct; @ ﹫) A friendly and cheerful budget option, a short walk from the ferry. Dorms are simple and clean, there's a communal kitchen and laundry service, and a few doubles are available (with private or shared facilities).

Camping Vira CAMPGROUND €
(021-717 776; www.campingcroatiahvar.com; campsite per adult/site 60/172KN; ☺ May–mid-Oct; P @ ﹫) This four-star campground on a beautiful wooded bay 4km from town is one of the best in Dalmatia. There's a gorgeous beach, a lovely cafe and restaurant, and a

volleyball court. The facilities are well kept and good quality. You can rent tents, too.

Hotel Croatia HOTEL €€€
(021-742 400; www.hotelcroatia.net; Majerovica bb; s/d 962/1283KN; P ❄ @ ﹫) Only a few steps from the sea, this medium-sized, rambling 1930s building sits among gorgeous, peaceful gardens. The rooms – with a yellow, orange and lavender colour scheme – are simple and old-fashioned. Many (pricier ones) have balconies overlooking the gardens and the sea. There's a sauna, too.

Hotel Adriana HOTEL €€€
(021-750 200; www.suncanihvar.com; Fabrika 28; s/d 3032/3131KN; ❄ @ ﹫ ☒) All of the bright, swanky rooms of this deluxe spa hotel overlook the sea and the medieval town. Facilities include Sensori Spa, a gorgeous rooftop pool next to the rooftop bar, a plush restaurant, 24-hour room service and more.

Hotel Riva HOTEL €€€
(021-750 100; www.suncanihvar.com; Riva 27; s/d 1884/1968KN; ❄ @) The luxury veteran on Hvar's hotel scene, this 100-year-old hotel has 54 smallish rooms that play with blacks, reds and whites, with black-and-white posters of movie stars, and glass walls between bedrooms and bathrooms. Rooms 115 and 215 are most spacious. The harbourfront location is perfect for watching the yachts glide up and away.

Aparthotel Pharia HOTEL €€€
(021-778 080; www.orvas-hotels.com; Put Podstina 1; s/d/apt 532/1254/1292KN; P ❄ ﹫) This sparkling complex is only 50m from the sea in a quiet neighbourhood slightly west of the town centre, behind Hotel Croatia. All the rooms and apartments have balconies, some

sea-facing. There are also four eight-person villas, each with a pool, and bikes for rent.

Hotel Podstine
HOTEL €€€

(021-740 400; www.podstine.com; Put Podstina 11; s/d 1460/1700KN; [P][※][@][⊛][≋]) Just 2km southwest of the town centre on the secluded Podstine cove lies this family-run cheerful hotel with its own beach and a spa and wellness centre. The hotel has regular transfers to and from town, or you can rent a bike, scooter or motorboat. The cheapest rooms have no sea views.

✖ Eating

Hvar's eating scene is good and relatively varied, though, as with the hotels, restaurants often target affluent diners. Make sure you try *hvarsku gregada,* the island's traditional fish stew served in many restaurants. At most places, it must be ordered in advance. Note that many restaurants close between lunch and dinner.

Self-caterers can head to the supermarket next to the bus station, or pick up fresh supplies at the vegetable market next door.

Nonica
PASTRIES, CAKES €

(021-718 041; Burak 23; ⊗8am-2pm & 5-11pm Mon-Sat, 8am-2pm Sun) Savour the best cakes in town at this tiny storefront cafe right behind the Arsenal. Try the old-fashioned local biscuits such as *rafioli* and *forski koloc* and the Nonica tart with choco mousse and orange peel.

Konoba Menego
DALMATIAN €

(021-742 036; www.menego.hr; Kroz Grodu 26; mains from 60KN; ⊗11.30am-2pm & 5.30pm-midnight) This rustic old house on the stairway towards Fortica is kept as simple and authentic as possible. As they say: no grill, no pizza, no Coca-Cola. The place is decked out in Hvar antiques, the staff wear traditional outfits, the service is informative and the marinated meats, cheeses and vegetables are prepared the old-fashioned Dalmatian way.

Konoba Luviji
DALMATIAN €

(091 519 8444; Jurja Novaka 6; mains from 50KN; ⊗7pm-1am) Food brought out of the wood oven at this tavern is simple, unfussy and tasty, although portions are modestly sized. Downstairs is the *konoba* where Dalmatian-style tapas are served, while the restaurant is upstairs on a small terrace, with old-town and harbour views.

Zlatna Školjka
MEDITERRANEAN €€

(098 16 88 797; Petra Hektorovića 8; mains from 90KN; ⊗noon-3pm & 7-11pm) In a narrow alley packed with restaurants, this slow-food hideaway stands out for its creative fare conjured up by a local celebrity chef. A family-run affair, it has a stone interior and a terrace out back. Innovative dishes include squid in wild-orange sauce and an unbeatable *gregada* (seafood stew) with lobster, sea snails and whatever first-class fish was freshly caught.

Gariful
SEAFOOD €€

(021-742 999; www.hvar-gariful.hr; Riva; mains from 95KN; ⊗noon-11pm) This is the place to mingle with celebrities coming off their glitzy yachts parked right across the way, over some of Hvar's best-prepared fish and seafood. Prices match the clientele.

Giaxa
SEAFOOD €€

(021-741 073; www.giaxa.com; Petra Hektorovića 3; mains from 90KN; ⊗noon-midnight) This top-end restaurant inside a 15th-century palazzo has a reputation as the place to be seen in Hvar. There is a lovely garden at the back. The food is excellent, with lobster being a popular choice.

Divino
MEDITERRANEAN €€€

(021 717 541; www.divino.com.hr; Put Križa 1; mains from 130KN; ⊗10am-1am) The fabulous location and the island's best wine list are reason enough to splurge at this swank restaurant. Add innovative food (think rack of lamb with crusted pistachio) and dazzling views of the Pakleni Islands and you've got a winning formula for a special night out. Or have some sunset snacks and wine on the gorgeous terrace. Book ahead.

🍷 Drinking & Nightlife

Hvar has some of the best nightlife on the Adriatic coast, mostly centred on the harbour. People come here to party hard, so expect plenty of action come nightfall.

★ Falko
BEACH BAR

(⊗8am-9pm mid-May–mid-Sep) A 3km walk from the town centre brings you to this adorable hideaway in a pine forest just above the beach. A great unpretentious alternative to the flashy spots closer to town, it serves yummy sandwiches and salads from a hut, as well as its own limoncello and *rakija*. Think low-key artsy vibe, hammocks and a local crowd.

Carpe Diem
LOUNGE BAR

(www.carpe-diem-hvar.com; Riva; ⊙9am-2am)
Look no further – you have arrived at the
mother of Croatia's coastal clubs. From
a groggy breakfast to pricey late-night
cocktails, there is no time of day when this
swanky place is dull. The house music spun
by resident DJs is smooth, there are drinks
aplenty, and the crowd is of the jet-setting
kind.

Carpe Diem Beach
BEACH CLUB

(www.carpe-diem-beach.com; ⊙10am-7pm &
midnight-6am) On the island of Stipanska, this
is the hottest place to party (from June to
September), with daytime beach fun, a restaurant, a spa and all-night parties (100KN
for boat transfers; admission is extra and
varies depending on the DJ).

3 Pršuta
WINE BAR

(Petra Hektorovića bb; ⊙6pm-2am) An unpretentious little wine bar in an alley behind
the main square. Sink into the couch by the
bar and feel as if you're in a local's living
room while sampling some of the best island
wines, paired with Dalmatian snacks.

Hula-Hula
BEACH BAR

(www.hulahulahvar.com; ⊙9am-11pm) *The* spot
to catch the sunset to the sound of techno
and house music, Hula-Hula is known for its
après-beach party (4pm to 9pm), where all
of young trendy Hvar seems to descend for
sundowner cocktails.

Kiva Bar
BAR

(www.kivabarhvar.com; Fabrika bb; ⊙9pm-2am) A
happening place in an alleyway just off the
Riva. It's packed to the rafters most nights,
with a DJ spinning old dance, pop and rock
classics that really get the crowd going.

Nautica
BAR

(Fabrika bb; ⊙5pm-2am) With the latest cocktails and nonstop dance music – ranging
from techno to hip hop – this disco-style bar
is an obligatory stop on Hvar's night-crawl
circuit.

🛍 Shopping

Lavender, lavender and more lavender is
sold in small bottles, large bottles or flasks,
or made into sachets. Depending on the
time of year, there will be anywhere from
one to 50 stalls along the harbour selling
the substance, its aroma saturating the air.
Various herbal oils, potions, skin creams and
salves are also hawked.

ℹ Information

Atlas Hvar (☑021-741 911; www.atlas-croatia.
com) On the western side of the harbour, this
travel agency finds private accommodation,
rents bikes and boats, and books excursions to
Vis, Bol and Dubrovnik.

Clinic (☑021-741 280; Trg Svetog Stjepana
16) Medical clinic about 700m from the town
centre, best for emergencies.

Del Primi (☑091 583 7864; www.delprimi-
hvar.com; Burak 23) Travel agency specialising in private accommodation. Also rents jet
skis.

Fontana Tours (☑021-742 133; www.happy
hvar.com; Riva 18) Finds private accommodation, runs excursions, books boat taxis around
the island and handles rentals. It has a romantic and isolated two-person apartment on
Palmižana (600KN per night).

Luka Rent (Riva 24; per hr 10KN; ⊙9am-9pm)
Internet cafe and call centre right on the Riva.

Pelegrini Tours (☑021-742 743; www.
pelegrini-hvar.hr; Riva bb) Private accommodation, boat tickets to Italy with Blue Line,
excursions (its daily trips to the Pakleni
Islands are popular) and bike, scooter and
boat rental.

Post Office (Riva 19; ⊙7am-8pm Mon-Sat)
Make phone calls here.

Tourist Office (☑021-741 059; www.tzhvar.
hr; Trg Svetog Stjepana 42; ⊙8am-2pm &
3-9pm Jul & Aug, 8am-2pm & 3-7pm Mon-Sat,
8am-noon Sun Jun & Sep) Right on Trg Svetog
Stjepana.

Stari Grad

POP 2685

Stari Grad (Old Town), on the island's north
coast, is a more quiet, cultured and altogether sober affair than its stylish and stunning
sister. If you're not after pulsating nightlife
and thousands of people crushing each other along the streets in the high season, head
for Stari Grad and enjoy Hvar at a more leisurely pace.

Although most ferries connecting the island to the mainland list Stari Grad as their
port of call, the town is actually a couple of
kilometres northeast of the new ferry terminal. Stari Grad lies along a horseshoe-shaped
bay, with the old quarter on the southern
side of the horseshoe. The bus station (no
left-luggage office) is at the foot of the bay.
The northern side is taken up by residences,
a small pine wood and the sprawling Helios
hotel complex.

Sights

Tvrdalj
FORTRESS

(Trg Tvrdalj; admission 20KN; ⊙10am-1pm & 6-8pm) Tvrdalj is Petar Hektorović's 16th-century fortified castle. The leafy fish pond reflects the poet's love for fish and fishers. His poem *Fishing and Fishermen's Chat* (1555) paints an enticing portrait of his favourite pastime. The castle also contains quotes from the poet's work inscribed on the walls in Latin and Croatian.

Dominican Monastery
MONASTERY

(Dominikanski Samostan; admission 20KN; ⊙10am-1pm & 6-8pm) This old Dominican monastery was founded in 1482, damaged by the Turks in 1571 and later fortified with a tower. In addition to the library and archaeological findings in the monastery museum, there is a 19th-century church with *The Interment of Christ*, attributed to Tintoretto, and two paintings by Gianbattista Crespi.

Sleeping & Eating

One of the agencies arranging private accommodation is **Hvar Touristik** (☑717 580; www.hvar-touristik.com; Šiberija 31), which will find doubles with private facilities for between 300KN and 500KN in July and August.

Hostel Sunce
HOSTEL €

(☑091 27 07 986; www.hostelsunce.freshcreator. com; Don Mihovila Pavlinovića 2; dm 130KN; 🛜) Stari Grad's only hostel has a great location in the old town and a variety of basic but pleasant rooms, from singles to dorms. There's a shared kitchen and dining room, and bike rental. The beach is just 1km away.

Kamp Jurjevac
CAMPGROUND €

(☑021-765 843; www.heliosfaros.hr; Njiva bb; per adult/tent 33/33KN; ⊙Jun-Sep) Near swimming coves off the harbour just east of the old town.

Helios
HOTEL €€

(☑021-765 866; www.heliosfaros.hr; 🅿) This large, rather soulless complex commandeers the northern wing of the town. Hotels include the three-star **Lavanda** (☑021-306 330; r 520KN) and the two-star **Arkada** (☑021-306 306; s/d 495/740KN) as well as **Studio Helios** (☑021-765 019; apt from 400KN) and **Trim Apartments** (☑021-765 019; 4-person apts 600KN).

Antika
DALMATIAN €

(Donja Kola 24; mains from 45KN; ⊙noon-1am) One of Hvar's loveliest restaurants and bars. It has three separate spaces in an ancient, rickety townhouse, tables lining the alleyway and an upstairs terrace that houses a bar. It's the place to hang out at night.

Eremitaž
DALMATIAN €

(Put Rudine 2; mains from 50KN; ⊙noon-3pm & 6pm-midnight) A 1km walk from town along the seafront, this 15th-century hermitage houses a stellar restaurant serving well-prepared Dalmatian staples and more creative dishes in an exposed stone interior and on the seafront terrace.

Shopping

Stari Grad has a small but growing art-gallery scene in the old town.

Little Horse & Baby Beuys
GIFTS

(www.littlehorseandbabybeuys.com; Moria Gallery, Vagonj 1; ⊙7-11pm) Super-cool clothing for children (and adults) as well as shoes and paintings by a pair of super-creative sisters behind this seasonal pop-up store.

Fantazam
JEWELLERY

(www.fantazam.com; Ivana Gundulića 6; ⊙11am-3pm & 5pm-1am) Stocks bizarre and stunning jewellery

Maya Con Dios
ART

(Škvor 5; ⊙8-10pm) Marine-themed paintings.

Information

Tourist Office (☑021-765 763; www.stari grad-faros.hr; Dr Franje Tuđmana 1; ⊙8am-2pm & 3-9pm Mon-Sat, 9am-1pm & 5-9pm Sun) Distributes a good local map.

Jelsa
POP 1600

Jelsa is a small town, port and resort 27km east of Hvar Town, surrounded by thick pine forests and high poplars. Although it lacks the Renaissance buildings of Hvar, the intimate streets and squares are pleasant and the town is within easy reach of swimming coves and sand beaches.

Jelsa is wrapped around a bay with several large hotels on each side; the old town sits at the foot of the harbour.

Activities include diving and boat outings. Find out more about the best nearby beaches, private accommodation (around 150KN per person) and hotels at the local **tourist** office (☑021-761 017; www.tzjelsa.hr; Riva bb; ⊘8am-2pm & 3-10pm Mon-Sat, 10am-noon & 7-9pm Sun Jul & Aug, 8am-2pm & 3-9pm Mon-Sat May-Jun & Sep-Oct). A favourite for food is Konoba Nono (mains from 80KN; ⊘6pm-midnight), a charming family-run tavern which serves traditional island fare. Don't miss the creative take on Dalmatian cuisine at Me & Mrs Jones (Mala Banda bb; mains from 64KN; ⊘noon-midnight Jun-Jul & Sep-Oct, 5pm-midnight Aug) at the edge of the harbour, where traditional stone and wood interiors merge with retro accents.

VIS ISLAND

POP 3430

Of all the Croatian islands, Vis is the most mysterious – even to locals. The furthest of the main central Dalmatian islands from the coast, Vis spent much of its recent history serving as a military base for the Yugoslav National Army, cut off from foreign visitors from the 1950s right up until 1989. The isolation preserved the island from development and drove much of the population to move elsewhere in search of work, leaving it underpopulated for many years.

As has happened with impoverished islands across the Mediterranean, Vis' lack of development has become its drawcard as a tourist destination. International and local travellers alike now flock to Vis, seeking authenticity, nature, gourmet delights and peace and quiet. Vis produces some of Croatia's best-known wines – *vugava* (white) in particular – and you'll see miles of vineyards across the island. You'll also taste some of the freshest seafood here, thanks to a still-thriving fishing tradition.

Vis is divided between two beautiful small towns at the foot of two large bays: Vis Town, in the northeast; and Komiža, in the southwest. There is friendly rivalry between the two – Vis Town is historically associated with the upper-class nobility while Komiža is proud of its working-class fishing heritage and pirate tales. The rugged coast around the island is dotted with gorgeous coves, caves and a couple of sand beaches. The island's remnants of antiquity, displayed in the Archaeological Museum and elsewhere around Vis Town, offer a fascinating insight into the complex character of this tiny island, which has become a destination for in-the-know travellers.

History

Inhabited first in Neolithic times, Vis Island was settled by the ancient Illyrians, who brought the Iron Age to Vis in the 1st millennium BC. In 390 BC a Greek colony was formed on the island, known then as Issa, from which the Greek ruler Dionysius the Elder controlled other Adriatic possessions. The island eventually became a powerful city-state and established its own colonies on Korčula and at Trogir and Stobreč. Allying itself with Rome during the Illyrian wars, the island nonetheless lost its autonomy and became part of the Roman Empire in 47 BC. By the 10th century Vis had been settled by Slavic tribes and was sold to Venice along with other Dalmatian towns in 1420. Fleeing Dalmatian pirates, the population moved inland from the coast.

With the fall of the Venetian Empire in 1797, the island fell under the control of Austria, France, Great Britain, Austria again and then Italy during WWII, as the great powers fought for control of this strategic Adriatic outpost. Over the course of its history, it belonged to nine nations! Perhaps that explains why such a small island has no less than four distinct dialects.

Vis was an important military base for Tito's Partisans. Tito established his supreme headquarters in a cave on Hum Mountain, from where he coordinated military and diplomatic actions with Allied forces and allegedly made his legendary statement: 'We don't want what belongs to others, but we will not give up what belongs to us.'

❶ Getting There & Around

Vis Town is best reached by car ferry from Split (50KN, 2½ hours, two to three daily) or by a fast passenger boat (55KN, 1¼ hours, one daily). Note that it's possible to visit on a day trip during the summer season, but irregular boat hours in low season make it impossible to visit Vis on a daily excursion.

The local **Jadrolinija office** (☑021-711 032; www.jadrolinija.hr; Šetalište Stare Isse; ⊘8.30am-7pm Mon-Fri, 9am-noon Sat) is in Vis Town. It opens one hour before boat departures.

The only bus transport on the island connects Vis Town with Komiža. The bus meets the Jadrolinija ferries at Vis Town. The connections are prompt in July and August, but you may have to wait in the low season.

Vis Town

POP 1660

On the northeast coast of the island, at the foot of a wide, horseshoe-shaped bay, lies the ancient town of Vis, the first settlement on the island. In only a short walk you can see the remains of a Greek cemetery, Roman baths and an English fortress. Ferry arrivals give spurts of activity to an otherwise peaceful town of coastal promenades, crumbling 17th-century townhouses and narrow alleyways twisting gently uphill from the seafront.

The town, on the southern slope of Gradina hill, is a merger of two settlements: 19th-century Luka on the northwestern part of the bay and medieval Kut in the southeast. The ferry ties up at Luka, from where a harbourside promenade runs scenically all the way to Kut. Small beaches line this promenade, although the busiest town beach lies on the west side of the harbour in front of Hotel Issa. Beyond it are nudist coves and a series of wild swimming spots. On the other side, past Kut and the British Naval Cemetery, is the popular pebble beach of Grandovac, which has a beach bar (look out for occasional late-night parties), a small stretch of pebbles and a string of rocky beaches on either side.

◎ Sights

Archaeological Museum　　　MUSEUM
(Arheološki Muzej; Šetalište Viški Boj 12; admission 20KN; ☺9am-1pm & 5-9pm Mon-Fri, to 1pm Sat) In addition to extensive archaeological exhibitions, this museum also features a healthy ethnographic collection, including the lowdown on the island's fishing, winemaking, shipbuilding and recent history. The 2nd floor has the largest collection of Hellenistic artefacts in Croatia, with Greek pottery, jewellery and sculpture, including an exquisite 4th-century bronze head of a Greek goddess.

A leaflet gives an overview of the exhibits, the history of Vis and a useful map showing the locations of the ruins around town.

🏃 Activities

Scenic coastal roads, with their dramatic cliffs and hairpin turns, make it worth renting your own wheels for a day. You can hire mountain bikes (per hour/day 20/100KN) from Ionios (p248), while **Navigator** (☑021-717 786; www.navigator.hr; Šetalište Stare Isse 1) has scooters (per three hours/

day 150/250KN) and cars (per six hours/day 290/490KN). Note that most cars for rent on the island are beat-up old things, including the cool-looking cabrios.

Diving is excellent in the waters around Vis. Fish are plentiful and there's a wreck of an Italian ship dating from the 1866 naval battle between Austria and Italy. **ANMA** (☑091 521 3944; www.anma.hr) has extensive dive programs; one tank dives start from 220KN.

👉 Tours

The handful of agencies in town offer tours, which are more or less identical. The most interesting is the tour of the island's **top-secret military sights** abandoned by the Yugoslav National Army in 1992. The trip takes in rocket shelters, bunkers, weapon storage spaces, submarine 'parking lots', Tito's Cave (which housed ex-Yugoslav president Tito during WWII) and nuclear shelters that served as communication headquarters for Yugoslavia's secret service. These sites occupy some of the island's most beautiful spots, only recently made accessible to the public. This tour is offered by **Vis Special** (☑021 711 524; www.vis-special.com; Šetalište Stare Isse 10), starting at 280KN for a two-hour jaunt.

Agencies in town also offer caving in the grottoes around the island, trekking, island tours with food and wine tasting and boat trips to outer islands that take in the Blue Grotto, the Green Grotto and other great outlying spots.

🛏 Sleeping

There are no camping grounds in Vis Town and only a few hotels, but you should have no trouble finding private lodging, either rooms or apartments, which is the best way to go. Browse www.info-vis.net for the most extensive listings. In summer, accommodation needs to be booked in advance, as the capacity is limited. Navigator can find private accommodation. You'll pay around 250KN for a double with shared bathroom and 380KN for a double with a private bathroom and terrace. Apartments cost between 380KN and 500KN. The agency also has 14 **luxury seafront villas** (www.visvillas.com; villa 1950-8000KN) for two to 17 people.

Villa Vis　　　GUESTHOUSE €€
(☑098 948 7490; www.villaviscroatia.com; Jakšina 11; s/d 600/750KN; ❋🅰) Stylish option in

WORTH A TRIP

SWIM & EAT ON VIS

While there are beaches around Vis Town and Komiža, some of the island's best are a boat or scooter ride away. Several require downhill walking, so bring comfortable shoes. The tourist offices and travel agencies can provide you with maps; many also organise transport.

The most unspoilt beaches are found on the south side of the island. **Stiniva** is Vis' most spectacular cove. Its very narrow rock entrance opens to a pebble beach flanked by rocks 35m high. Also worth a trip are **Srebrna** and **Milna**, as well as the sandy **Stončica** bay east of Vis, where you'll find a beachside tavern serving excellent barbecued lamb. Another great bay is **Rukavac**, with a gorgeous little beachside tavern and taxi boats ready to shuttle you to the island of Ravnik across the way, known for its Green Grotto (50KN) and the islet of Budikovac (100KN, with a visit to the cave).

For a special slow-food meal bordering on a performance, see if you can catch Senko Karuza, the local star poet, philosopher, bon vivant and chef, on a good day. He cooks up mean seafood meals at his house perched over **Mala Travna** bay. Call ahead on ☑ 099 352 5803 to see if he's in the mood to have you over. If he is, you're in for a treat.

The interior of the island and its isolated coves are becoming a foodie's dream. In recent years a number of rural households have started offering local homemade food worth travelling for. These include **Golub** (☑ 098 96 50 327; mains from 50KN; ☺ 1pm-1am), in the hamlet of Podselje, 5km from Vis Town. Specialities include lamb and octopus under *peka* (domed baking lids) and all sorts of marinated and smoked fish, such as the tuna carpaccio. Don't miss the homemade grappas, which come in all flavours, from cactus to nettle and sage. **Konoba Pol Murvu** (☑ 091 56 71 990; mains from 50KN; ☺ 2pm-midnight), in the village of Žena Glava, is known for its amazing tuna *pašticada*, a slow-cooked stew with wine and spices. **Roki's** (☑ 098 303 483; www.rokis.hr; peka meal per person from 135KN; ☺ 2pm-midnight) in Plisko Polje is owned by a local winemaker, so the delicious smoked eel and under-*peka* fare can be washed down with some of the island's best *plavac* (red wine) or *vugava* (white wine). Many of these places will pick you up, often for free, and drop you back in town after the meal. A more recent addition to the island's culinary scene is **Kod Magića** (☑ 091 898 4859; entire meal for 230KN; ☺ 5-11pm), a 4km drive east of Vis Town. This family-run affair, smack in the middle of fields and vineyards, does homemade dishes using fresh local ingredients and serves great house wine. Don't skip its broad-bean stew with cuttlefish and *savur*, a Vis speciality with marinated sardines.

Kut, with four colour-themed rooms (green, cream, chocolate and red), occasional yoga classes and a great location close to beaches and restaurants, all inside an old traditional townhouse with all-modern interiors. This is the place for hipsters who want style without a hefty price tag.

Dionis B&B €€
(☑ 021-711 963; www.dionis.hr; Matije Gubca 1; s/d 450/525KN; ❄) Above the pizzeria with the same name, just off the seafront, is this renovated old stone house with eight rooms and one apartment. All units at the family-run B&B come with TVs and fridges; some have balconies. The triple room in the attic has a lovely terrace with mountain and town vistas.

Hotel San Giorgio HOTEL €€€
(☑ 021-711 362; www.hotelsangiorgiovis.com; Petra Hektorovića 2; s/d 758/1145KN; P❄❅) A gorgeous Italian-owned hotel in Kut, with 10 swish, colourful rooms and suites in two buildings. The rooms have wooden floors, great beds and all sorts of upscale perks. Some come with Jacuzzis and sea-facing terraces. The restaurant (dinner only) serves creative Mediterranean cuisine, breakfast for nonguests and wine tastings each evening (150KN). Massages are available, too.

Hotel Tamaris HOTEL €€€
(☑ 021-711 350; www.hotelsvis.com; Svetog Jurja 30; s/d 540/820KN; ❄❅) The best thing about this hotel is the location, in an attractive old building right on the seafront,

about 100m southeast of the ferry dock. Its 25 smallish rooms are comfortable, with phone and TV. It's worth paying 30KN per person extra for a sea-view room and even getting half-board (lunch ends up costing you 15KN). The same hotel company manages Hotel Issa across the bay, which has 128 rooms with balconies.

Eating

Vis has some of Dalmatia's best restaurants in the two small towns as well as the island's interior. There are a few local specialities to try: *viška pogača,* a flatbread filled with salted fish and onions, and *viški hib,* dried grated figs mixed with aromatic herbs. Several restaurants on the island also serve excellent tuna prosciutto.

Karijola   PIZZA €

(Šetalište Viškog Boja 4; pizzas from 48KN; ☺noon-midnight Jul & Aug, 5pm-midnight Jun & Sep) The island's best pizza by the team that runs the namesake pizzeria in Zagreb. This thin-crust concoction comes with high-quality ingredients. The speciality pizza is Karijola, with tomato, garlic, mozzarella and prosciutto. Or try the surprisingly good sauceless white pizza.

Buffet Vis   SEAFOOD €

(Svetog Jurja 35; mains from 40KN; ☺9am-3pm & 6pm-1am Mon-Fri & Sun, 6pm-1am Sat) This is the cheapest place in town, right by the ferry dock. It's tiny and unadorned, with a few tables outside. It's no frills but great value, with a local vibe and delicious seafood.

★ Pojoda   SEAFOOD €€

(☏021-711 575; Don Cvjetka Marasovića 8; mains from 70KN; ☺noon-1am) Croats in the know rave about this seafood restaurant with a leafy yard dotted with bamboo, orange and lemon trees. It surely does some mean tricks in its kitchen with fish, shellfish and crustaceans. Try *orbiko,* its special dish with orzo, peas and shrimp. For dinner, reserve a table.

Kantun   DALMATIAN €€

(Biskupa Mihe Pušića 17; mains from 70KN; ☺5pm-midnight) The small menu at this seafront tavern offers flavourful local fare made with top-quality ingredients. The garden area is vine-covered and intimate, while the interior is a tasteful rustic space of exposed stone, and the outside tables overlook the seafront. Try the tuna prosciutto, and the artichokes with peas.

Val   DALMATIAN €€

(Don Cvjetka Marasovića 1; mains from 70KN; ☺noon-midnight) Set in an old stone house, with a shady terrace overlooking the sea. The seasonal menu has an Italian twist; try the offerings of wild asparagus in spring time, wild boar and mushrooms in winter, and lots of fish in summer. Don't miss the *pašta fazol* (Dalmatian bean stew) with fish, and local carob cake for dessert.

Lola Konoba & Bar   MEDITERRANEAN €€

(Matije Gupca 12; mains from 90KN; ☺6pm-midnight) Marked by an old-timer bicycle on its wall, Lola (in Luka, steps from the ferry) is tucked away into a garden courtyard, with eclectic furniture set against old stone walls and a Meštrović fountain. The owner from Vis and his Spanish wife stir up creative bites inspired by the Mediterranean coastline, with a lot of influence from Spain.

Villa Kaliopa   MEDITERRANEAN €€€

(☏091 27 11 755; Vladimira Nazora 32; mains from 120KN; ☺1-4pm & 5pm-1am) In the exotic gardens of the 16th-century Gariboldi mansion, Villa Kaliopa is an upmarket restaurant full of yachting enthusiasts. Tall palm trees, bamboo and classical statuary provide the setting for a menu of Dalmatian specialities, which changes daily. It hosts occasional concerts and exhibits.

Drinking & Entertainment

Paradajz Lost   BAR

(Pod Kulom 5; ☺8am-2am) Vis Town's boho spot draws in a colourful crowd of artists, hippies and misfits to its cool stone courtyard that lies in the shadow of the tower, steps from the ferry landing in Luka. Pop into the adjacent gallery of a local art collective and listen to old records the quirky owner plays on an old gramophone.

Lambik   BAR

(Pod Ložu 2; ☺8am-2am) Kut's best bar has alfresco seating in a lovely vine-covered stone passageway under an ancient colonnade, and tables outside on a small square only steps from the seafront. Acoustic bands and singers perform on some nights.

Bejbi   CAFE, BAR

(Pod Ložu 4; ☺7am-3pm & 5pm-2am) This cafe-bar in Kut is the place to sip coffee between outings to the beach during the day, and have cocktails at night.

Summer Cinema
CINEMA

(tickets 20-25KN; ⊗ Jun-Sep) Look out for posters advertising the program of the summer cinema, which sprouts on a terrace roughly halfway between Kut and Luka and attracts a mixed crowd of locals.

❶ Information

You can change money at the bank, post office or any travel agency.

Vis has several wi-fi hotspots, including the Tamaris Bar at the hotel, which has free wi-fi and charges 40KN per hour for using the internet terminals.

Ionios Travel Agency (☑ 021-711 532; Svetog Jurja 37 & Pod Ložu 5) Finds private accommodation, changes money, rents cars, bikes and scooters, runs excursions and sells wi-fi vouchers (40KN for one day).

Post Office (Svetog Jurja 25; ⊗ 7am-9pm Mon-Fri, to 2pm Sat)

Tourist Office (☑ 021-717 017; www.tz-vis.hr; Šetalište Stare Isse 5; ⊗ 8am-8pm Jun-Sep, 8am-2pm Mon-Fri) Right next to the Jadrolinija ferry dock.

Komiža
POP 1519

On the west coast, at the foot of Hum mountain, Komiža is a captivating small town on a bay, with sand and pebble beaches at the eastern end. Komiža has die-hard fans among Croats, who swear by its somewhat bohemian, rough-around-the-edges ambience.

Narrow back streets that are lined with tawny 17th- and 18th-century townhouses twist uphill from the port, which has been used by fishers since at least the 12th century.

◉ Sights & Activities

East of town is a 17th-century church on the site of a Benedictine monastery, and at the end of the main wharf is a Renaissance citadel dating from 1585 known as the Kaštel.

The town's most popular beach, fringed with pine trees, is right below Hotel Biševo, stretching to Gospa Gusarica church at the far end.

Darlić & Darlić rents out scooters (300KN per day), mountain bikes (100KN per day), cabrio cars (350KN per day) and quads (400KN per day).

☞ Tours

Darlić & Darlić
TOURS

(☑ 021-713 760; www.darlic-travel.hr; Riva Svetog Mikule 13) Just off the Riva as you're entering town from the bus stop, Darlić & Darlić runs a fun sunset tour to Hum, the island's highest point (200KN for two hours).

Alter Natura
TOURS

(☑ 021-717 239; www.alternatura.hr; Hrvatskih Mučenika 2) Alter Natura specialises in adventure tourism, including paragliding, trekking, kayaking and abseiling. It also offers excursions to the Blue Grotto, the islands of Brusnik, Sveti Andrija, Jabuka, Sušac and even the far-out Palagruža. It offers boat transfers to the island's best beaches, including Stiniva and Porat.

🛏 Sleeping & Eating

Darlić & Darlić finds private accommodation from 200KN per double.

Villa Nonna
GUESTHOUSE €€

(☑ 098 380 046; www.villa-nonna.com; Ribarska 50; apt 630-825KN; ❋ 🛜) This lovely old townhouse has seven renovated apartments, each with wooden floors and a kitchen; some have balconies or patios. Next door is another gorgeous old house, Casa Nono, which can sleep six to nine people (from 1760KN to 2400KN per day), with a lovely garden, three bathrooms, a living room with exposed stone walls and self-catering facilities.

Hotel Biševo
HOTEL €€€

(☑ 021-713 279; www.hotel-bisevo.com.hr; Ribarska 72; s/d from 394/487KN; ❋ @ 🛜) Facilities here are modest and the decor reminiscent of the socialist era, but it's located right near the beach. Try for a renovated room (with fridge and TV), with a sea-facing balcony (60KN extra).

Komiža
DALMATIAN €

(Riva 17; mains from 50KN; ⊗ 7am-midnight) This nondescript seafront restaurant has been around forever, with its old-school naval theme, old-school waiters and simple downhome food, such as grilled sardines. Plus the views are lovely.

Bako
SEAFOOD €€

(Gundulićeva 1; mains from 90KN; ⊗ 4pm-2am) The town's best restaurant, with a seaside terrace and excellent food – try the lobster *brodet* (seafood stew with polenta) or *komiška pogača* (fish-filled homemade bread). The cool stone interior contains a fish pond and a collection of Greek and Roman amphorae.

Konoba Jastožera SEAFOOD €€
(☑ 021-713 859; Gundulićeva 6; mains from 100KN; ⊙ noon-1am Jul & Aug, 5pm-1am May-Jun & Sep-Oct) Scaly delicacies are served at this town classic where you sit on wooden planks over the water, amid old furniture and fishing paraphernalia. Lobster from a live tank is the speciality (from 900KN per kilogram) – grilled, gratin, boiled...you name it. Reserve ahead.

☻ Drinking & Nightlife

Most of the town action is along the Riva and around Škor, the small square right as you get to the seafront.

For daytime chill-out and late-night parties, head to Kamenica beach, which is home to the seasonal **Aquarius Club**, hosting well-known DJs who spin anything from house to funk tunes.

❶ Information

Walking all the way around the harbour, past the Kaštel, you'll come to the municipal **tourist office** (☑ 021-713 455; www.tz-komiza.hr; Riva Svetog Mikule 2; ⊙ 9am-9pm), which gives out very basic info.

Darlić & Darlić has internet terminals (30KN per hour) and wireless access.

❶ Getting There & Away

The bus from Vis Town stops at the edge of town next to the post office and a few blocks away from the citadel.

Darlić & Darlić runs a taxi service, costing 12KN per kilometre (about 150KN to Vis Town).

Biševo

The tiny islet of Biševo has little other than vineyards, pine trees and the spectacular **Blue Grotto** (Modra Špilja). Between 11am and noon the sun's rays pass through an underwater opening in this coastal cave to bathe the interior in an unearthly blue light. Beneath the crystal-blue water, rocks glimmer in silver and pink to a depth of 16m. The only catch is that the water can be too choppy for you to enter the cave outside the summer months or when the *jugo* (southern wind) is blowing. When the tourist season is at its peak in July and August, the cave can be woefully crowded and the line of boats waiting to get in discouragingly long. Outside of the high season, you may be able to swim here.

There's a regular boat from Komiža to Biševo (30KN per person) that leaves daily throughout July and August at 8am, returning at 4.30pm, or you can book an excursion through one of the travel agencies. Another alternative is to rent a boat from one of the agencies and go on your own (admission 40KN). Many tours also offer excursions to the less-crowded **Green Grotto** (Zelena Špilja), located on the small island of Ravnik.

Dubrovnik & Southern Dalmatia

Includes ➡

Dubrovnik 251
Cavtat. 270
Lokrum Island. 271
Elafiti Islands 272
Pelješac Peninsula . . .274
Central Pelješac 275
Orebić. 276
Korčula Island. 277
Korčula Town. 279
Vela Luka 284

Best Places to Eat

➡ Konoba Koraćeva Kuća (p272)

➡ Bugenvila (p271)

➡ Konoba Mate (p278)

➡ Restaurant 360° (p267)

➡ Atlantic Kitchen (p267)

Best Places to Sleep

➡ MirÓ Studio Apartments (p263)

➡ Karmen Apartments (p262)

➡ Villa Klaić (p263)

➡ Lešić Dimitri Palace (p282)

➡ Apartments Silva (p266)

Why Go?

Dubrovnik is simply unique; its beauty is bewitching, its setting sublime. Not that it's a secret, quite the contrary: thousands of visitors walk along its marble streets every day of the year, gazing, gasping and happily snapping away.

The remarkable old town, ringed by mighty defensive walls, is a highlight of any trip to Croatia, capturing the very essence of a medieval Mediterranean fantasy. It's little wonder that in recent years it's featured so prominently in the *Game of Thrones* TV series. View it from Mt Srđ above and you'll understand why poets have so liberally showered it with epithets over the centuries, Byron's 'pearl of the Adriatic' being the most enduring.

Dubrovnik is also an ideal launching pad for expeditions throughout southern Dalmatia. From the island of Korčula in the northwest to the dreamy plains of Konavle in the southeast, this is a region to be savoured by beach seekers, wine lovers and history buffs alike.

When to Go
Dubrovnik

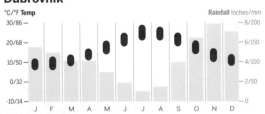

May & Jun Warm sunny days, without the scorching heat or crowds of mid-summer.

Jul & Aug Sate your cultural appetite during Dubrovnik's prestigious Summer Festival.

Sep & Oct Still warm enough for swimming and the beaches aren't as crowded.

DUBROVNIK

POP 28,500

Regardless of whether you are visiting Dubrovnik for the first time or the hundredth, the sense of awe never fails to descend when you set eyes on the beauty of the old town. Indeed it's hard to imagine anyone becoming jaded by the city's marble streets, baroque buildings and the endless shimmer of the Adriatic, or failing to be inspired by a walk along the ancient city walls that have protected a civilised, sophisticated republic for centuries.

Although the shelling of Dubrovnik in 1991 horrified the world, the city has bounced back with characteristic vigour to enchant visitors again. Take the revamped cable car up to Mt Srđ; marvel at the Mediterranean lifestyle and the interplay of light and stone; trace the rise and fall of Dubrovnik in museums replete with art and artefacts; exhaust yourself retracing history – then plunge into the azure sea.

History

The story of Dubrovnik begins with the 7th-century onslaught of the Slavs that wiped out the Roman city of Epidaurum (site of present-day Cavtat). Residents fled to the safest place they could find, which was a rocky islet (Ragusa) separated from the mainland by a narrow channel. Building walls was a matter of pressing urgency due to the threat of invasion; the city was well fortified by the 9th century when it resisted a Saracen siege for 15 months.

Meanwhile, another settlement emerged on the mainland, stretching from Zaton in the north to Cavtat in the south, and became known as Dubrovnik, named after the *dubrava* (holm oak) that carpeted the region. The two settlements merged in the 12th century, and the channel that separated them was filled in.

By the end of the 12th century Dubrovnik had become an important trading centre on the coast, providing an important link between the Mediterranean and Balkan states. Dubrovnik came under Venetian authority in 1205, finally breaking away from its control in 1358.

By the 15th century the Respublica Ragusina (Republic of Ragusa; Republic of Dubrovnik) had extended its borders to include the entire coastal belt from Ston to Cavtat, having previously acquired Lastovo Island, the Pelješac Peninsula and Mljet Island. It was now a force to be reckoned with. The city turned towards sea trade and established a fleet of its own ships, which were dispatched to Egypt, the Levant, Sicily, Spain, France and Istanbul. Through canny diplomacy the city maintained good relations with everyone – even the Ottoman Empire, to which Dubrovnik began paying tribute in the 16th century.

Centuries of peace and prosperity allowed art, science and literature to flourish, but most of the Renaissance art and architecture in Dubrovnik was destroyed in the earthquake of 1667, which killed 5000 people and left the city in ruins, with only the Sponza Palace and the Rector's Palace surviving. The earthquake also marked the beginning of the economic decline of the town.

The final coup de grâce was dealt by Napoleon whose troops entered Dubrovnik in 1808 and announced the end of the Republic. The Vienna Congress of 1815 ceded Dubrovnik to Austria; though the city maintained its shipping, it succumbed to social disintegration. It remained a part of the Austro-Hungarian Empire until 1918 and then slowly began to develop its tourism industry.

Caught in the cross-hairs of the war that ravaged former Yugoslavia, Dubrovnik was pummelled with some 2000 shells in 1991 and 1992, suffering considerable damage. All of the damaged buildings have now been restored.

◉ Sights

Today Dubrovnik is the most prosperous, elegant and expensive city in Croatia. In many ways it still feels like a city state, isolated from the rest of the nation by geography and history. It's become such a tourism magnet that there's even talk of having to limit visitor numbers in the old town – when several cruise ships disgorge people at the same time the main thoroughfares can get impossibly crowded.

Dubrovnik extends about 6km from north to south. The bulbous leafy promontory of Lapad in the northwest of the city contains many of the town's resorts. All of the sights are in or near the old town, which is entirely closed to cars. Looming above the city is Mt Srđ, which is connected by cable car to Dubrovnik.

Pile Gate is the main entrance to the old town and the terminus for many local buses from Lapad and the bus station.

Dubrovnik & Southern Dalmatia Highlights

1 Revelling in the most fascinating and touristy of activities: seeing Dubrovnik from its **city walls** (p253).

2 Catching the **cable car** (p258) up Mt Srđ for breathtaking views of Dubrovnik from above.

3 Visiting the affecting **War Photo Limited** (p253) gallery in Dubrovnik.

4 Soaking up the medieval atmosphere of the walled town of **Korčula** (p279).

5 Escaping the crowds while exploring the intriguing island of **Lokrum** (p271).

6 Sampling fine wine in the heart of the **Pelješac Peninsula** (p274).

7 Watching the sunset shadows dance across the mountains from the terrace of the restaurant **Konoba Koračeva Kuća** (p272), in the heart of the Konavle wine region.

8 Dining on oysters in the fascinating old port of **Ston** (p275).

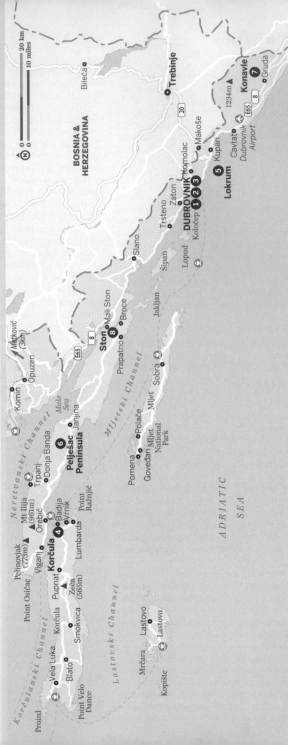

Pile Gate

GATE

(Map p260) The natural starting point to any visit to Dubrovnik, this fabulous city gate was built in 1537. Crossing the drawbridge at the gate's entrance, imagine that this was once actually lifted every evening, the gate closed and the key handed to the rector. Notice the statue of St Blaise, the city's patron saint, set in a niche over the Renaissance arch.

As you pass through the outer gate you come to an inner gate dating from 1460, and soon after you're struck by the gorgeous view of the main street, Placa, or as it's commonly known, Stradun, Dubrovnik's pedestrian promenade.

Onofrio Fountain

FOUNTAIN

(Map p260) One of Dubrovnik's most famous landmarks, Onofrio Fountain was built in 1438 as part of a water-supply system that involved bringing water from a well 12km away. Originally the fountain was adorned with sculpture, but it was heavily damaged in the 1667 earthquake and only 16 carved masks remain. Water gushes from their mouths into a drainage pool.

St Saviour Church

CHURCH

(Crkva Svetog Spasa; Map p260; Placa) Built between 1520 and 1528, this church was one of the few buildings to survive the earthquake of 1667. It's open for occasional exhibitions and regular candlelight concerts.

★ City Walls & Forts

FORT

(Gradske Zidine; Map p260; adult/child 100/30KN; ◷9am-6.30pm Apr-Oct, 10am-3pm Nov-Mar) No visit to Dubrovnik would be complete without a walk around the spectacular city walls, the finest in the world and the city's main claim to fame. From the top, the view over the old town and the shimmering Adriatic is sublime. You can get a good handle on the extent of the shelling damage done in the 1990s by gazing over the rooftops: those sporting bright new terracotta suffered damage and had to be replaced.

The first set of walls to enclose the city was built in the 9th century. In the middle of the 14th century the 1.5m-thick defences were fortified with 15 square forts. The threat of attacks from the Turks in the 15th century prompted the city to strengthen the existing forts and add new ones, so that the entire old town was contained within a stone barrier 2km long and up to 25m high. The walls are thicker on the land side – up to 6m – and range from 1.5m to 3m on the sea side.

The round **Minčeta Tower** (Map p260) protects the northern edge of the city from land invasion, while the western end is protected from land and sea invasion by the detached **Lovrjenac Fort** (Map p260). Pile Gate is protected by the **Bokar Tower** (Map p260), and the **Revelin Fort** (Map p260) guards the eastern entrance.

There are entrances to the walls from near the Pile Gate, the Ploče Gate and the Maritime Museum. The Pile Gate entrance tends to be the busiest, and entering from the Ploče side has the added advantage of getting the steepest climbs out of the way first (you're required to walk in an anticlockwise direction). Don't underestimate how strenuous the wall walk can be, especially on a hot day. There's very little shelter and the few vendors selling water on the route tend to be overpriced.

Franciscan Monastery & Museum

MONASTERY

(Muzej Franjevačkog Samostana; Map p260; Placa 2; adult/child 30/15KN; ◷9am-6pm) Within this monastery's solid stone walls is a gorgeous mid-14th-century cloister, a historic pharmacy and a small museum with a collection of relics and liturgical objects, including chalices, paintings, gold jewellery and pharmacy items such as laboratory gear and medical books. Artillery remains that pierced the monastery walls during the 1990s war have been saved, too.

Before you head inside, stop to admire the remarkable pietà over the door, sculpted by the local masters Petar and Leonard Andrijić in 1498. Unfortunately, the portal is all that remains of a richly decorated church, which was destroyed in the 1667 earthquake.

The cloister is one of the most beautiful late-Romanesque structures in Dalmatia. Notice how each capital over the incredibly slim dual columns is topped by a different figure, portraying human heads, animals and floral arrangements. At the centre is a small square garden that's shaded by orange and palm trees.

Further inside is the third-oldest functioning pharmacy in Europe, which has been in business since 1391. It may have been the first pharmacy in Europe open to the general public.

★ War Photo Limited

GALLERY

(Map p260; ☎020-322 166; www.warphotoltd.com; Antuninska 6; adult/child 40/30KN; ◷10am-10pm daily Jun-Sep, 10am-4pm Tue-Sun May & Oct) An

DUBROVNIK IN...

Two Days

Two days is plenty of time to explore the compact old town. Start early and take a walk along the **city walls** before it gets too hot. Spend the rest of the day wandering the marbled streets and calling into whichever church, palace or museum takes your fancy. Head to **Buža II** for a sunset tipple before dinner.

The next day, start by taking the **cable car** up Mt Srđ, stopping at the top to visit the **Homeland War exhibition**. Afterwards, pick up where you left off in the old town. When it starts to bake, wander along to **Banje Beach** for a dip. Spend your last evening splurging on a romantic meal at **Restaurant 360°**, before sampling fine Croatian wines at **D'vino**.

Four Days

With another couple of days up your sleeve, you'll have the luxury of confining your old town explorations to the evenings, when the cruise-ship hordes have returned to their boats. On day three, plan to spend the middle of the day on the island of **Lokrum**. On your final day, jump on a boat to **Cavtat**, allowing a couple of hours to stroll around the historic town before tucking into lunch at **Bugenvila**.

---

immensely powerful experience, this gallery features intensely compelling exhibitions curated by New Zealand photojournalist Wade Goddard, who worked in the Balkans in the 1990s. Its declared intention is to 'expose the myth of war...to let people see war as it is, raw, venal, frightening, by focusing on how war inflicts injustices on innocents and combatants alike'. There's a permanent exhibition on the upper floor devoted to the wars in Yugoslavia, but the changing exhibitions cover a multitude of conflicts.

Synagogue   SYNAGOGUE
(Sinagoga; Map p260; Žudioska 5; admission 35KN; ⊘10am-8pm May-Oct, to 3pm Nov-Apr) Dating to the 15th century, this is the second-oldest synagogue (the oldest Sephardic one) in the Balkans. Inside is a museum that exhibits religious relics and documentation on the local Jewish population, including records relating to their persecution during WWII.

Sponza Palace   PALACE
(Map p260; Placa bb) This superb 16th-century palace is a mixture of Gothic and Renaissance styles beginning with an exquisite Renaissance portico resting on six columns. The 1st floor has late-Gothic windows and the 2nd-floor windows are in a Renaissance style, with an alcove containing a statue of St Blaise. Sponza Palace was originally a customs house, then a mint, a state treasury and a bank.

It now houses the **State Archives** (Državni Arhiv u Dubrovniku; Map p260; www.dad.

hr; admission 25KN; ⊘8am-3pm Mon-Fri, to 1pm Sat), which contain a priceless collection of manuscripts dating back nearly a thousand years. Although there are some English translations, the displays aren't particularly interesting.

Just inside the entrance is the **Memorial Room of the Defenders of Dubrovnik** (Map p260; ⊘10am-10pm Mon-Fri, 8am-1pm Sat) **FREE**, a heartbreaking collection of black-and-white photographs of the mainly young men who perished between 1991 and 1995.

Orlando Column   MONUMENT
(Map p260; Luža Sq) Luža Sq once served as a marketplace, and this stone column – carved in 1417 and featuring the image of a medieval knight – used to be the spot where edicts, festivities and public verdicts were announced. The knight's forearm was the official linear measure of the Republic – the ell of Dubrovnik (51.1cm). Folk groups occasionally perform in the square.

St Blaise's Church   CHURCH
(Crkva Svetog Vlahe; Map p260; Luža Sq) Dedicated to the city's patron saint, this imposing church was built in 1715 in the ornate baroque style. The interior is notable for its marble altars and a 15th-century silver gilt statue of St Blaise, who is holding a scale model of pre-earthquake Dubrovnik.

Rector's Palace   PALACE
(Map p260; Pred Dvorom 3; admission via multi-museum pass, adult/child 80/25KN; ⊘9am-6pm May-Oct, to 4pm Nov-Apr) Built in the late 15th

century for the elected rector who governed Dubrovnik, this Gothic-Renaissance palace contains the rector's office, his private chambers, public halls, administrative offices and a dungeon. During his one-month term the rector was unable to leave the building without the permission of the senate. Today the palace has been turned into the **Cultural History Museum**, with artfully restored rooms, portraits, coats of arms and coins, evoking the glorious history of Dubrovnik.

The building retains a striking compositional unity despite being rebuilt many times. Notice the finely carved capitals and the ornate staircase in the atrium, which is often used for concerts during the Summer Festival. Also in the atrium is a statue of Miho Pracat, who bequeathed his wealth to the Republic and was the only commoner in the 1000 years of the Republic's existence to be honoured with a statue (1638). We may assume that the bequest was considerable.

Gundulićeva Poljana   SQUARE
(Map p260) The narrow street opposite the Rector's Palace opens onto this square, where a bustling morning produce market is held. The monument at its centre commemorates Dubrovnik's famous poet, Ivan Gundulić. Reliefs on the pedestal depict scenes from his epic poem, *Osman*.

Dulčić Masle Pulitika Gallery   GALLERY
(Map p260; www.ugdubrovnik.hr; Držićeva Poljana 1; admission via multimuseum pass, adult/child 80/25KN; ⊙9am-8pm Tue-Sun) This small offshoot of the city's main gallery unites three friends beyond the grave: local artists Ivo Dulčić, Antun Masle and Đuro Pulitika, who all came to the fore in the 1950s and 1960s. There's a permanent collection featuring the trio's work on the lower floor, while the upper gallery is given over to temporary exhibitions by current artists.

Maritime Museum   MUSEUM
(Pomorski Muzej; Map p260; www.dumus.hr; Tvrđava Sv Ivana; admission via multimuseum pass, adult/child 80/25KN; ⊙9am-6pm Tue-Sun May-Sep, to 4pm Oct-Apr) Inside the vaulted chambers of St John Fort, this well-presented museum traces the history of navigation in Dubrovnik with ship models, maritime objects and paintings.

Studio Pulitika   GALLERY
(Map p260; www.ugdubrovnik.hr; Tvrđava Sv Ivana; admission via multimuseum pass, adult/child 80/25KN; ⊙9am-8pm) The former studio of

Đuro Pulitika (1922–2006) has been preserved much as it might have looked in the artist's lifetime, although one room is devoted to changing exhibitions by local artists. It's not very well signed; look for it near the entry to the Maritime Museum.

Cathedral of the Assumption   CATHEDRAL
(Stolna Crkva Velike Gospe; Map p260; Poljana M Držića; ⊙7.30am-6pm) Built on the site of a 7th-century basilica, Dubrovnik's original cathedral was enlarged in the 12th century, supposedly funded by a gift from England's King Richard I, the Lionheart, who was saved from a shipwreck on the nearby island of Lokrum. Soon after the first cathedral was destroyed in the 1667 earthquake, work began on this, its baroque replacement, which was finished in 1713.

The cathedral is notable for its fine altars, especially the altar of St John Nepomuk, made of violet marble. The most striking of its religious paintings is the polyptych of the *Assumption of the Virgin*, hanging behind the main altar, made in the workshop of 16th-century Italian painter Titian.

It's difficult to see the Titian painting without purchasing a ticket to the **treasury** (Riznica; admission 20KN), located to the side of the main altar. Dripping in gold and silver, it contains relics of St Blaise as well as 138 other reliquaries largely made in the workshops

---

① MUSEUMS OF DUBROVNIK PASS

Perhaps a cunning plan to get you through the doors of some of the town's smaller museums, nine of Dubrovnik's institutions can only be visited by buying a multimuseum pass (adult/child 80/25KN); individual tickets aren't available. Cleverly the Rector's Palace is one of them – one of the city's higher profile sights.

If you've bought the ticket mainly to visit the Rector's Palace and want to get your money's worth in a limited amount of time, we suggest you prioritise the rest in the following order: Museum of Modern & Contemporary Art, Maritime Museum, Revelin Archaeological Exhibition, Dulčić Masle Pulitika Gallery, Natural History Museum, Ethnographic Museum, Marin Držić's House, Studio Pulitika.

Dubrovnik

N

0 — 1 km
0 — 0.5 miles

Airport (25km)

Jadranska Cesta

PLOČE

Petra Krešimira IV

Old Harbour

2
18
9
Frana Supila
7

PILE

Gornji

Petra Bakića

Zagrebačka

DANČE

Vladimira Nazora

1

Gronji Kono

12
3

Od Gaja

Braniteja Dubrovnika

Gradac Park

See Dubrovnik Old Town Map (p260)

Jadranska Cesta

Andrije Hebranga

Ante Starčevića

Bana Josipa Jelača

14

8

Iva Vojnovića

Obala Pape Ivana Pavla II

Obala Stjepana Radica

Ferry Terminal

Lapadska Obala

16

Dalmatinska

Nikole Tesle

Od Batale

Sv Mihajla

Josipa Kosora

Liechtensteinov Put

Dubrovnik Bus Station

Gruž Harbour

Riječka

Šetalište Kralja Zvonimira

Šetalište K Tomislava

Ispod Petke

Lapad Peninsula

Vatroslava Lisinskog

11

LAPAD

15
4
13
17

Masarykov Put

Iva Dulči

Kardinala Stepinca

Mika i Meda Pucića

10

Lapad Bay

6

Adriatic Sea

of Dubrovnik's goldsmiths between the 11th and 17th centuries.

Natural History Museum MUSEUM
(Prirodoslovni Muzej; Map p260; www.pmd.hr; Androvićeva 1; admission via multimuseum pass, adult/child 80/25KN; ⊙10am-6pm Mon-Sat) Spread over four sparsely populated floors, this low-key museum has displays on invasive fish species and a very cool arrangement of seashells suspended in plastic orbs.

St Ignatius' Church CHURCH
(Crkva Svetog Ignacija; Map p260; Uz Jezuite) Dramatically poised at the top of a broad flight of stairs, this Jesuit church was built in the same style as the cathedral and completed in 1725. Inside, frescoes display scenes from the life of St Ignatius, founder of the Society of Jesus. Abutting the church is the Jesuit College.

Ethnographic Museum MUSEUM
(Etnografski Muzej; Map p260; www.dumus.hr; Od Rupa; admission via multimuseum pass, adult/child 80/25KN; ⊙9am-4pm Wed-Mon) Inhabiting the 16th-century Rupe Granary, the Ethnographic Museum contains mildly interesting exhibits relating to agriculture and local customs.

Marin Držić's House MUSEUM
(Dom Marina Držića; Map p260; www.muzej-marindrzic.eu; Široka 7; admission via multimuseum pass, adult/child 80/25KN; ⊙9am-8.30pm Tue-Sun) Educational but not terribly interesting (unless you're a fan of 16th-century Croatian theatre), this small museum occupies the house of Marin Držić (c 1508–1567), Dubrovnik's famous priest-playwright. The museum houses manuscripts and editions of his plays, and one room has been set up to replicate his original cell.

Church of the Annunciation CHURCH
(Crkva Sv Blagovještenja; Map p260; Od Puča 8; ⊙8am-7.30pm) The old town's sole Serbian Orthodox church provides an interesting contrast to the numerous Catholic churches scattered about. Dating from 1877, it suffered substantial damage during the most recent war and was only fully restored in 2009.

Dominican Monastery & Museum MONASTERY
(Muzej Dominikanskog Samostana; Map p260; off Sv Dominika 4; admission 30KN; ⊙9am-5pm) This imposing structure is an architectural highlight, built in a transitional Gothic-Renaissance style, and containing an im-

Dubrovnik

⊙ Sights
1 Dubrovnik During the Homeland War G3
2 Museum of Modern & Contemporary Art G4

⊙ Activities, Courses & Tours
Blue Planet Diving .... (see 6)

⊙ Sleeping
3 Apartments & Rooms Biličić F3
4 Apartments Silva C2
5 Begović Boarding House C2
6 Dubrovnik Palace B2
7 Grand Villa Argentina G4
8 Hotel Bellevue E3
9 Hotel Excelsior G4
10 Royal Princess Hotel A1
11 Solitudo C1
12 Villa Klaić F3
13 Villa Wolff C2
14 Youth Hostel Dubrovnik E3

⊙ Eating
15 Atlantic Kitchen C2
16 Blidinje D2

⊙ Drinking & Nightlife
17 Cave Bar More B2
18 EastWest G4

pressive art collection. Constructed around the same time as the city wall fortifications in the 14th century, the stark exterior resembles a fortress more than a religious complex. The interior contains a graceful 15th-century cloister constructed by local artisans after the designs of the Florentine architect Maso di Bartolomeo.

The large, single-naved church features some bright, modern, stained glass and a painting by Vlaho Bukovac above one of the side altars. Other priceless pieces of art are hung in rooms off the cloister, including 15th- and 16th-century works by Lovro Do bričević, Nikola Božidarević and Titian.

Revelin Archaeological Exhibition MUSEUM
(Arheološke Izložbe; Map p260; www.dumus.hr; Sv Dominika 3; admission via multimuseum pass, adult/child 80/25KN; ⊙9am-4pm Thu-Tue) Fragments of masonry and sculpture are presented in this small museum under the Revelin Fort. There are some good examples of medieval plait-work *(pleter)* – psychedelic squiggles somewhat similar to those associated with Celtic art.

LOCAL KNOWLEDGE

ENTER THE GAME OF THRONES

Dubrovnik is like a fantasy world for most people, but fans of *Game of Thrones* have more reason to indulge in flights of fancy than most, as a large chunk of the immensely popular TV series was filmed here. The Lovrjenac Fort, the sea walls and the Trsteno Arboretum were all used for key King's Landing scenes, while the Rector's Palace atrium (with the staircase and statue clearly visible) appeared in Qarth. Lokrum Island also features, as do further afield destinations such as Diocletian's Palace in Split.

At the time of writing, Šibenik's old town was gearing up for its cameo in a future season.

Museum of Modern & Contemporary Art   MUSEUM
(Umjetnička Galerija; Map p256; www.ugdubrovnik. hr; Frana Supila 23; admission via multimuseum pass, adult/child 80/25KN; ☺9am-8pm Tue-Sun) Spread over three floors of a significant modernist building east of the old town, this excellent gallery showcases Croatian artists, particularly painter Vlaho Bukovac from nearby Cavtat. Head up to the sculpture terrace for excellent views.

★ Cable Car   CABLE CAR
(Map p260; www.dubrovnikcablecar.com; Petra Krešimira IV bb; adult/concession return 100/50KN; ☺9am-5pm Nov-Mar, to 8pm Apr, May & Oct, to midnight Jun-Aug, to 10pm Sep) Dubrovnik's cable car whisks you from just north of the city walls to Mt Srđ in under four minutes. Operations cease if there are high winds or a thunderstorm brewing. At the end of the line there's a stupendous perspective of the city from a lofty 405m, taking in the terracotta-tiled rooftops of the old town and the island of Lokrum, with the Adriatic and distant Elafiti Islands filling the horizon.

Telescopes help you pick out details far, far below. There's also a snack bar and a restaurant.

Dubrovnik During the Homeland War   MUSEUM
(Dubrovnik u Domovinskom Ratu; Map p256; adult/child 30/15KN; ☺8am-10pm) Set inside a Napoleonic fort near the cable-car terminus, this permanent exhibition is dedicated to the siege of Dubrovnik during the 'Homeland War', as the 1990s war is dubbed in Croatia. The local defenders stationed inside this fort ensured the city wasn't captured. If the displays are understandably one-sided, they still provide in-depth coverage of the events, including plenty of video footage.

If the cable car's not operating, it's possible to drive up here on a narrow road off the main highway (follow the signs to Bosanka).

🏃 Activities

Swimming
There are several city beaches, but many people take a boat to Lokrum Island or one of the Elafitis for more seclusion.

Banje Beach, around 300m east of the Ploče Gate, is the most popular (read 'crowded') city beach. A kilometre further on is **Sveti Jakov**, a good little beach that doesn't get too rowdy and has showers, a bar and a restaurant.

On the west side of the city, beaches past the Pile Gate include the pebbly **Šulići** and the rocky **Danče**. The nicest beach that's walkable from the old town is below Hotel Bellevue, where you'll find a lovely sheltered cove backed by high cliffs (which cast a shadow over its pebbled shore by late afternoon). It's fun watching kids high-dive into the sea here.

Lapad Bay is brimming with hotel beaches that you can use without a problem; try the bay by Hotel Kompas. A little further on is **Copacabana Beach** on Babin Kuk peninsula, a good shallow beach with a slide for kids. If you're a naturist, head down to **Cava**, signposted near Copacabana Beach.

In the old town, you can also swim below the two Buža bars, on the outside of the city walls. Steps help swimmers get in and out, and sunbathers can make use of cemented space between the rocks.

Diving & Kayaking
Blue Planet Diving   DIVING
(Map p256; ☎091 89 90 973; www.blueplanet-diving.com; Dubrovnik Palace, Masarykov Put 20; beginners/certified divers per dive €65/55, PADI Open Water course €345) There's some great diving around Dubrovnik, including the wreck of the *Taranto*, an 1899 Italian merchant ship that hit a mine during WWII. Blue Planet offers recreational dives and courses.

Adriatic Kayak Tours
KAYAKING, CYCLING

(Map p260; ☑ 091 72 20 413; www.adriatickayak tours.com; Zrinsko Frankopanska 6; half-day kayaking €35) Offers sea kayak excursions (ranging from a half-day paddle to a weeklong trip), stand-up paddleboarding, cycling tours and Montenegro getaways (including rafting).

☞ Tours

Dubrovnik Walks
WALKING TOUR

(Map p260; ☑ 095 80 64 526; www.dubrovnik walks.com; ☺ Apr-Oct) Excellent guided walks in English. Ninety-minute old-town tours (90KN) run daily at 10am and either 6pm (May, June, September and October) or 7pm (July and August). The 90-minute 'Walls & Wars' tour (190KN) departs daily at 9.30am and 3.30pm (5.30pm in July and August). The meeting place is just west of the Pile Gate. No reservations necessary.

Adriatic Explore
BUS TOUR

(Map p260; ☑ 020-323 400; www.adriatic-explore. com; Poljana Paska Miličevića 4) Day trips to Mostar and Montenegro (both 360KN) are very popular. Excursions to Split, Korčula and Pelješac, Mljet and the Elefiti Islands are offered, too.

✹ Festivals & Events

Feast of St Blaise
CULTURE

(☺ 3 Feb) A city-wide bash marked by pageants and processions.

Carnival
CARNIVAL

(☺ Feb) Venetian-style masked high jinks, which is held in the lead-up to Lent (usually February).

Libertas Film Festival
FILM

(☺ Jun-Jul) Feature films, documentaries and shorts screened in the open air at old-town venues between 29 June and 4 July.

Dubrovnik Summer Festival
CULTURE

(Dubrovačke ljetne Igre; ☑ 020-326 100; www. dubrovnik-festival.hr; tickets 30-350KN; ☺ Jul-Aug) From 10 July to 25 August, the most prestigious summer festival in Croatia presents a program of theatre, opera, concerts and dance on open-air stages throughout the city. Tickets are available online, from the festival office on Placa, and on site one hour before the beginning of each performance.

Park Orsula Music Festival
MUSIC

(www.parkorsula.du-hr.net; ☺ Jul-Aug) A series of concerts held between mid-July and late August in a park overlooking the old town, featuring local and regional musicians.

🛏 Sleeping

Dubrovnik is not a large city but accommodation is scattered all over the place; there's limited accommodation in the compact old town itself. Ploče, immediately east of the old town, has a strip of upmarket waterfront hotels, while Pile, on the town's other flank, has good private apartments. If you want to combine a beach holiday with your city stay, consider the leafy Lapad peninsula, 4km

---

DUBROVNIK: DESTRUCTION & RECONSTRUCTION

From late 1991 to May 1992, images of the shelling of Dubrovnik dominated the news worldwide. While memories may have faded for those who watched it from afar, those who suffered through it will never forget – and the city of Dubrovnik is determined that visitors don't either. You'll see reminders of it on several plaques throughout the old town, especially at the main gates.

Shells struck 68% of the 824 buildings in the old town, leaving holes in two out of three tiled roofs. Building facades and the paving stones of streets and squares suffered 314 direct hits and there were 111 strikes on the great wall. Nine historic palaces were completely gutted by fire, while the Sponza Palace, Rector's Palace, St Blaise's Church, Franciscan Monastery and the carved fountains Amerling and Onofrio all sustained serious damage. The reconstruction bill was estimated at US$10 million. It was quickly decided that the repairs and rebuilding would be done with traditional techniques, using original materials whenever feasible.

Dubrovnik has since regained most of its original grandeur. The town walls are once again intact, the gleaming marble streets are smoothly paved and famous monuments have been lovingly restored, with the help of an international brigade of specially trained stonemasons.

Dubrovnik Old Town

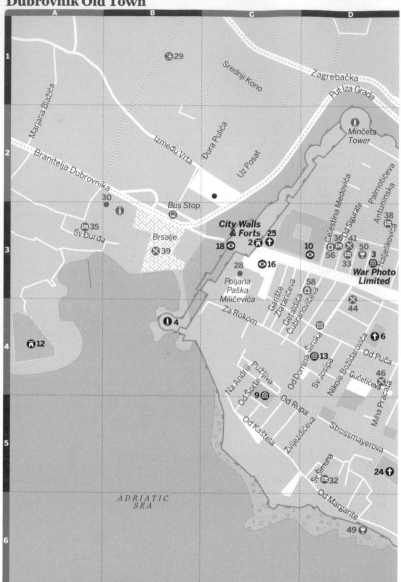

west of the centre. The bus connections are good, so you needn't feel cut off from the old town and there are lots of spots for sunbathing and swimming.

Book all accommodation well in advance, especially in summer. It's the most expensive city in the country, so expect to pay more for a room here (even most of the hostels fall into our midrange category).

If you're on a budget, private accommodation is a good alternative; contact local travel agencies or the tourist office for options.

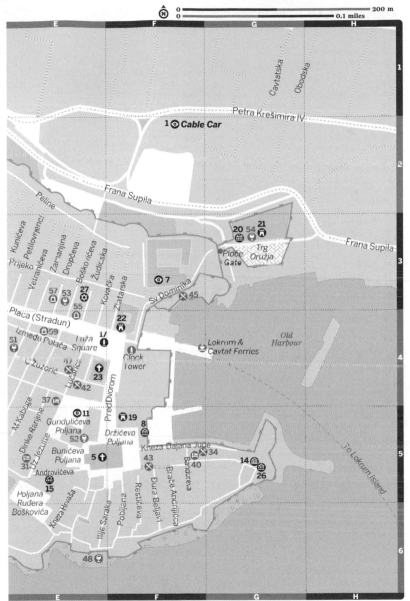

Beware the scramble of private owners at the bus station and ferry terminal. Some provide what they say they offer, others are scamming – try to pin down the location in advance if you want to be able to walk to the old town. Note that if you stay in unlicensed accommodation you are unprotected in case of a problem; all registered places should have a blue *sobe* (rooms available) sign. In high season, expect to pay from 300KN for a double room, or from 500KN for an apartment.

Dubrovnik Old Town

◉ Top Sights
1 Cable Car F2
2 City Walls & Forts C3
3 War Photo Limited D3

◉ Sights
4 Bokar Tower B4
5 Cathedral of the Assumption E5
6 Church of the Annunciation D4
7 Dominican Monastery & Museum F3
8 Dulčić Masle Pulitika Gallery F5
9 Ethnographic Museum C4
10 Franciscan Monastery & Museum D3
11 Gundulićeva Poljana E5
12 Lovrjenac Fort A4
13 Marin Držić's House D4
14 Maritime Museum G5
   Memorial Room of the
      Defenders of Dubrovnik .... (see 22)
15 Natural History Museum E5
16 Onofrio Fountain C3
17 Orlando Column E4
18 Pile Gate C3
19 Rector's Palace F5
20 Revelin Archaeological Exhibition G3
21 Revelin Fort G3
22 Sponza Palace F4
23 St Blaise's Church E4
24 St Ignatius' Church D5
25 St Saviour Church C3
   State Archives .... (see 22)
26 Studio Pulitika G5
27 Synagogue E3

◉ Activities, Courses & Tours
28 Adriatic Explore.................................. C3
29 Adriatic Kayak Tours B1
30 Dubrovnik Walks B3

◉ Sleeping
31 Apartments Amoret E5
32 Fresh Sheets D5
33 Hotel Stari Grad D3
34 Karmen Apartments F5
35 MirÓ Studio Apartments A3
36 Old Town Hostel D3
37 Pucić Palace E4
38 Rooms Vicelić...................................... D3

◉ Eating
39 Dubravka 1836 .... B3
40 Konoba Ribar....................................... F5
41 Lucin Kantun D3
42 Oliva Pizzeria E4
43 Oyster & Sushi Bar Bota Šare.............. F5
44 Proto... D3
45 Restaurant 360° F3
46 Taj Mahal.. D4
47 Zuzori E4

◉ Drinking & Nightlife
48 Buža... E6
49 Buža II D6
50 D'vino... D3
51 Gaffe E4
52 Jazz Caffe Troubadour E5
53 Malvasija E3
54 Revelin.. G3

◉ Shopping
55 Algoritam E4
56 Dubrovnik Treasures........................... D3
57 Lega-Lega E3
58 Magnolika D3
59 Uje E4

Old Town (Stari Grad)

★**Karmen Apartments**   APARTMENT €€
(Map p260; ☑ 098 619 282; www.karmendu.com; Bandureva 1; apt €95-175; ❄ 🛜) These four inviting apartments enjoy a great location a stone's throw from Ploče harbour. All have plenty of character with art, splashes of colour, tasteful furnishings and books to browse. Apartment 2 has a little balcony while apartment 1 enjoys sublime port views. Book well ahead.

Apartments Amoret   APARTMENT €€
(Map p260; ☑ 091 53 04 910; www.dubrovnik-amoret.com; Dinke Ranjine 5; apt €100-160; ❄ 🛜) Spread over four historic buildings in the heart of the old town, Amoret offers 13 high-quality studio apartments with kitchenettes, and two 'royal' apartments, sleeping four, with full kitchens. Elegant decor, tasteful furniture, a dash of art and parquetry flooring feature throughout. Amoret 2 has a pleasant guests' terrace.

Rooms Vicelić   GUESTHOUSE €€
(Map p260; ☑ 095 52 78 933; www.rooms-vicelic.com; Antuninska 10; r €90-110; ❄ 🛜) Situated on one of the steeply stepped old town streets, this friendly, family-run place has four atmospheric stone-walled rooms with private bathrooms. Guests have use of a shared kitchenette with a microwave and a kettle.

Old Town Hostel   HOSTEL €€
(Map p260; ☑ 020-322 007; www.dubrovnikold-townhostel.com; Od Sigurate 7; dm/s/d 325/350/650KN; ☉ Mar-Nov; 🛜) Converted from a historic residence – some rooms even have ceiling paintings – this centrally

located hostel isn't short on charm. Dorms range from four to six beds (including a female-only one), and there's a small kitchen. There's no air-conditioning, only fans.

Fresh Sheets
HOSTEL €€

(Map p260; ☑091 79 92 086; www.freshsheets hostel.com; Sv Šimuna 15; dm/r from €36/76; ❄@🛜) Tucked away by the city walls, this classic backpackers is warm and welcoming with a lively atmosphere. Downstairs there's space for socialising. Upstairs you'll find clean and simple dorms and a cosy double with a sea view. The same welcoming crew also runs a B&B near the cathedral.

Hotel Stari Grad
HOTEL €€€

(Map p260; ☑020-322 244; www.hotelstarigrad. com; Od Sigurate 4; s/d 1650/2100KN; ❄🛜) The eight rooms at this well-located boutique hotel are smallish, but they're well presented and don't fall short on comfort. Staff are sweet and you'll enjoy the dramatic city views from the rooftop terrace. Note: there are many flights of stairs to negotiate (and no lift).

Pucić Palace
HOTEL €€€

(Map p260; ☑020-326 222; www.thepucicpalace. com; Od Puča 1; s/d/ste from €300/465/690; ❄🛜) Located in a converted aristocrat's mansion, Pucić has well furnished rooms with an antique sensibility and high comfort levels (Egyptian cotton sheets etc). Guests have free use of the facilities at Banje Beach.

▣ Ploče

Hotel Excelsior
HOTEL €€€

(Map p256; ☑020-353 353; www.adriaticluxury hotels.com; Frana Supila 12; r from €459; P❄🛜🏊) A Yugoslav-era mash-up of a classic 1913 hotel with a modern annexe, this luxury place has top-notch leisure facilities (indoor and outdoor pools) and fully renovated rooms, many of which have remarkable views of the walled city. The decor is understated and the bathrooms are great.

Grand Villa Argentina
HOTEL €€€

(Map p256; ☑020-440 555; www.adriaticluxury hotels.com; Frana Supila 14; r from €302; P❄🛜🏊) Perhaps not as grand as it sounds, this hotel has good, comfortable, upmarket rooms with enviable views nonetheless. There are indoor and outdoor pools, and a spa centre – and it's only a 10-minute walk east of the old town.

▣ Pile

★ Villa Klaić
B&B €€

(Map p256; ☑020-411 144; www.villaklaic dubrovnik.com; Šumetska 11; r/apt from €100/140; P❄🛜🏊) Just off the main coast road, high above the old town, this outstanding guesthouse offers comfortable modern rooms and wonderful hospitality courtesy of the owner, Milo Klaić. Extras include a small swimming pool, continental breakfast, free pick-ups and free beer!

Apartments & Rooms Biličić
GUESTHOUSE €€

(Map p256; ☑098 802 111; www.dubrovnik-online. com/apartments_bilicic; Privežna 2, r/apt €60/120; ❄🛜) A highly atmospheric place to stay, partly due to the green fingers of the friendly host, whose subtropical garden is a delight. Rooms are bright, clean and pleasant, though bathrooms are not en suite. There's a guest kitchen on the terrace.

★ Miró Studio Apartments
APARTMENT €€€

(Map p260; ☑099 42 42 442; www.mirostudio apartmentsdubrovnik.com; Sv Đurđa 16; apt €140; ❄🛜) Located in a quiet residential nook only metres from the sea, hidden between the old town walls and Lovrjenac Fort, this schmick complex is an absolute gem. The decor marries ancient stone walls and whitewashed ceiling beams with design features such as uplighting, contemporary bathrooms and sliding-glass partitions.

▣ Montovjerna

Youth Hostel Dubrovnik
HOSTEL €

(Map p256; ☑020-423 241; www.hfhs.hr; Vinka Sagrestana 3; dm 157KN; @🛜) Thankfully there are now better, cosier hostels in the old town, but this Hostelling International establishment is considerably cheaper. The location is pretty good, in a quiet area 1.4km west of the Pile Gate. Dorms are spacious if plain, and can get hot. Rates include breakfast.

Hotel Bellevue
HOTEL €€€

(Map p256; ☑020-330 000; www.hotel-bellevue. hr; Petra Čingrije 7; d from 1900KN; P❄@🛜🏊) Positioned on a cliff near the very beginning of the Lapad peninsula (only a 20-minute walk west of Pile Gate), this classy hotel has modern decor (despite its dated smoky-glass facade), excellent facilities and a top-notch restaurant. Best of all, the hotel's lift offers direct access to the gem of a cove below.

(Continued on page 266)

Dubrovnik's Old Town

Nothing quite prepares you for your first sight of Dubrovnik's Old Town. From a distance, the compact nest of terracotta roofs enclosed by honey-coloured walls jutting out into the cerulean sea is overwhelmingly picturesque. The effect doesn't diminish as you pass through the ancient gates and stride forth on the marbled lanes.

JASON MAEHL / GETTY IMAGES ©

1. Walled City
Enjoy a stroll around the city's historic stone walls and walkways (p253).

2. Views over the Old Town
Take in stellar views of the Old Town and Adriatic Sea from the city's fort lookouts (p253).

3. Old Town Rooftops
Many of the Old Town rooftops were replaced with new terracotta after shelling damage in the 1990s (p253).

4. Street Dining
Relax at an outdoor table and enjoy local cuisine at an Old Town restaurant (p266).

RASPU / GETTY IMAGES ©

JOSEP BERNAT SANCHEZ MONER / GETTY IMAGES ©

(*Continued from page 263*)

Lapad

★Apartments Silva GUESTHOUSE €
(Map p256; ☎098 244 639; silva.dubrovnik@yahoo.com; Kardinala Stepinca 62; s/d 220/440KN, apt from 440KN; ❄) Lush Mediterranean foliage lines the terraces of this lovely hillside complex, a short hop up from the beach at Lapad. The rooms are comfortable and well-priced but best of all is the spacious top-floor apartment (sleeping five). The charming host is happy to arrange free pick-ups from the bus station.

Begović Boarding House GUESTHOUSE €
(Map p256; ☎020-435 191; www.begovic-boarding-house.com; Primorska 17; dm/r/apt 200/440/460KN; P❄@📶) A longstanding budget favourite, this welcoming family-run place has simple, tidy rooms and a communal terrace with amazing views. The apartments have kitchenettes and the other rooms have use of a guest kitchen. Free bus station pick-ups are included.

Solitudo CAMPGROUND €
(Map p256; ☎020-448 686; www.camping-adriatic.com; Vatroslava Lisinskog 17; per adult/child/site from €12/6/16, units from €69; ⏲Apr-Nov; P📶🏊🐾) Solitudo is a strange name for a giant campground that's filled to the gills in summer, but to its credit it has bright, modern shower blocks, it's close to Copacabana Beach and guests have access to a pool at a nearby hotel. Tenters will find the ground hard and rocky – or muddy and rocky when it rains.

Royal Princess Hotel HOTEL €€€
(Map p256; ☎020-440 100; www.importanneresort.com; Kardinala Stepinca 31; ste from €475; P❄@📶🏊) The classiest sister in a family of resort-style hotels grouped on a pretty stretch of Lapad Bay, the Royal Princess is deliciously low-slung and plush. There's an old-fashioned luxurious feel to the suites, all of which have balconies.

Dubrovnik Palace HOTEL €€€
(Map p256; ☎020-430 000; www.dubrovnikpalace.hr; Masarykov Put 20; r from €232; P❄@📶🏊) Spilling down the side of a hill by the bay, this large modern hotel has the best Adriatic views you could ever hope for. Service is good and facilities are excellent: there's a spa, indoor/outdoor pools and a dive shop. It's right by the No 4 bus terminal, which has buses running until late to/from the old town.

Villa Wolff HOTEL €€€
(Map p256; ☎020-438 710; www.villa-wolff.hr; Nika i Meda Pucića 1; r/ste from €144/174; ❄@📶) On a lovely seaside promenade, Wolff has six tasteful rooms, a verdant garden and high service standards. The front two rooms have balconies overlooking the sea.

Eating

Old Town (Stari Grad)

You have to choose carefully when dining out in the old town. Many places ride on the assumption that you're here just for a day (as many cruise ship passengers are) and that you won't be coming back. The two streets where average fodder is the norm are Stradun and Prijeko; head to the back streets for more interesting restaurants.

Oliva Pizzeria PIZZERIA €
(Map p260; ☎020-324 594; www.pizza-oliva.com; Lučarica 5; mains 40-89KN; ⏲noon-10pm) There are a few token pasta dishes on the menu, but this attractive little place is really all about pizza. And the pizza is worthy of the attention. Grab a seat on the street and tuck in.

Konoba Ribar DALMATIAN €€
(Map p260; ☎020-323 194; Kneza Damjana Jude bb; mains 60-120KN; ⏲10am-midnight) Serving local food the way locals like it, at more or less local prices, this little family-run eatery is a blissfully untouristy choice. They don't attempt anything fancy or clever, just big serves of traditional favourites such as risotto and stuffed squid. It's set in a little lane pressed hard up against the city walls.

Oyster & Sushi Bar Bota Šare SUSHI €€
(Map p260; ☎020-324 034; www.bota-sare.hr; Od Pustijerne bb; oysters/sushi per piece from 14/15KN; ⏲noon-10pm Tue-Sun) It's fair to say that most Croatians don't have much of an interest in or aptitude for Asian cooking, yet fresh seafood is something that they understand very well, as this little place demonstrates. Grab a terrace table with a view of the cathedral and tuck into Ston oysters (fresh or in tempura) and surprisingly good sushi and sashimi.

Taj Mahal BOSNIAN €€
(Map p260; ☎020-323 221; Nikole Gučetićeva 2; mains 70-150KN; ⏲10am-2am) This tiny restaurant is like an Aladdin's cave, with an interior loaded with Ottoman decorations.

Order the *džingis kan* (dried beef, sausage, peppers and spring onions with curdled milk) and get a taste of everything Bosnian or feast on spicy *sudžukice* (beef sausage).

Lucin Kantun
CROATIAN €€

(Map p260; ☑ 020-321 003; Od Sigurate bb; mains 80-110KN; ☺11.30am-11pm) With an open kitchen dominating the interior and a few pavement tables outside, this modest-looking place exceeds first impressions, delivering a creative menu of locally influenced tapas and larger mains. The stuffed squid is particularly good.

Dubravka 1836
EUROPEAN €€

(Map p260; ☑ 020-426 319; www.dubravka1836.hr; Brsalje 1; mains 59-178KN; ☺8am-11pm) Spilling on to a square right by the Pile Gate, this place is indisputably touristy. Still, it's a good spot for a light breakfast, and the locals rate the fresh fish, risotto, salads, pizza and pasta. The views are great too.

★ Restaurant 360°
MODERN EUROPEAN €€€

(Map p260; ☑ 020-322 222; www.360dubrovnik. com; Sv Dominika bb; mains 240-320KN, 5-/7-course set menu 780/970KN; ☺6.30-11pm Tue-Sun) Dubrovnik's glitziest restaurant offers fine dining at its best, with flavoursome, beautifully presented, creative cuisine and slick, professional service. The setting is unmatched, on top of the city walls with the tables positioned so you can peer through the battlements over the harbour. If you can't justify a splurge, it's still worth calling in for a drink.

Zuzori
DALMATIAN €€€

(Map p260; ☑ 020-450 000; www.zuzori.com; Cvijete Zuzorić 2; mains 99-179KN; ☺noon-10pm; 🖋) Serving 'traditional food with a modern twist', this excellent little bistro introduces international flavours and techniques into Dalmatian classics with considerable success. Local produce is celebrated, with the menu divided into 'from our sea' and 'from our land' sections.

Proto
SEAFOOD €€€

(Map p260; ☑ 020-323 234; www.esculap-teo.hr; Široka 1; mains 152-192KN; ☺11am-11pm) This elegant place is known for its fresh fish and seafood, with light sauces and bags of old-town atmosphere. To say it's 'long-standing' is an understatement – it opened its doors in 1886 and has served the likes of Edward VII and Wallis Simpson.

✖ Lapad

★ Atlantic Kitchen
MEDITERRANEAN €€

(Map p256; ☑ 020-435 726; www.facebook.com/atlantickitchen; Kardinala Stepinca 42; mains 89-139KN; ☺9am-11pm Apr-Nov) With its checked tablecloths and handwritten blackboard menus, there's a distinctly French feel to this breezy bistro – although the food meanders from France to Spain, Italy and Croatia. It's all excellent, and the service is great too.

Blidinje
CROATIAN €€

(Map p256; ☑ 020-358 794, Lapadska Obala 21; mains 60-140KN; ☺10am-1am) This locals' local is perfect for a meat feast. Call first and order lamb or veal slow-cooked under hot coals, then turn up a couple of hours later and it'll be cooked to perfection.

🍸 Drinking & Nightlife

Cave Bar More
BAR

(Map p256; www.hotel-more.hr; below Hotel More, Kardinala Stepinca 33; ☺10am-midnight) This little beach bar serves coffee, cocktails and snacks to bathers reclining by the dazzlingly clear waters in Lapad. But that's not the half of it: the main bar is set in an actual cave. Cool off beneath the stalactites in the side chamber, where a glass floor exposes a water-filled cavern.

Buža
BAR

(Map p260; off Ilije Sarake; ☺8am-late) Finding this ramshackle bar-on-a-cliff feels like a real discovery as you duck and dive around the city walls and finally see the entrance tunnel. Emerging by the sea, it's quite a scene with tasteful music (soul, funk) and a mellow crowd soaking up the vibes and views. Grab a cool drink in a plastic cup, perch on a concrete platform and enjoy.

Buža II
BAR

(Map p260; off Od Margarite; ☺10am-late) Just a notch more upmarket than the original Buža, this one is lower on the rocks and has a shaded terrace where you can snack on crisps, peanuts or a sandwich and lose a day quite happily, mesmerised by the Adriatic vistas.

Jazz Caffe Troubadour
BAR

(Map p260; Bunićeva Poljana 2; ☺9am-1am) Tucked into a corner behind the cathedral, Troubadour looks pretty nondescript during the day. That all changes on summer nights, when jazz musicians set up outside and quickly draw the crowds.

D'vino
WINE BAR

(Map p260; www.dvino.net; Palmotićeva 4a; ☉10am-midnight) If you're interested in sampling top-notch Croatian wine, this upmarket little bar is the place to go. As well as a large and varied wine list, it offers themed tasting flights (multiple wine tastings; three wines for 60KN) accompanied by a thorough description by the knowledgeable staff.

Malvasija
WINE BAR

(Map p260; Dropčeva 4; ☉9am-1am) Named after the white wine produced in the neighbouring Konavle area, this tiny bar is a good spot to sample the local drop. Cheese and olives may appear unbidden as you imbibe.

Gaffe
IRISH PUB

(Map p260; Miha Pracata bb; ☉9am-2am) The busiest place in town (especially when there's football on), this Croatian-run Irish pub has a homely interior and a covered side terrace. The food's good too (try the black risotto).

EastWest
BAR, CLUB

(Map p256; www.ew-dubrovnik.com; Frana Supila 8; ☉10am-4am May-Sep) By day this upmarket outfit on Banje Beach rents out sun loungers and umbrellas and serves drinks to the bathers who come here to relax and rehydrate. Later on, the cocktail bar comes into its own, morphing into a club as the night progresses.

Revelin
CLUB

(Map p260; www.clubrevelin.com; Dominika 3; ☉11pm-6am daily Jun-Sep, Fri & Sat Oct-May) Housed within the vast vaulted chambers of the Revelin Fort, this is Dubrovnik's most impressive club space, with famous international DJs dropping in during summer. Shame about the plastic glasses and the women dancing in cages.

🛍 Shopping

Stradun is mostly lined with tacky souvenir shops; the most interesting stores are hidden down the side lanes. Check out the morning market at Gundulićeva Poljana (p255) for local craft and produce.

★ Lega-Lega
CLOTHING, GIFTS

(Map p260; www.lega-lega.com; Dropčeva 3; ☉9am-8pm) An outlet for a Croatian design collective originating from Osijek, this is a hip place to shop for gifts with a difference, such as very cool tees, hoodies, notebooks, posters and coasters. The fantastic T-shirt packaging – in a Tetra Pak–like box, stored in a 'fridge' – has won an international design award.

Dubrovnik Treasures
JEWELLERY

(Map p260; www.dubrovniktreasures.com; Celestina Medovića 2; ☉9am-9pm Mar-Nov) An Aussie-born, Croatian-bred, locally based brother-and-sister team are behind this treasure trove of cool, well-crafted, handmade, contemporary jewellery.

Algoritam
BOOKS

(Map p260; www.algoritam.hr; Placa 8; ☉9am-9pm Mon-Sat, 10am-2pm Sun) A great bookshop with a wide range of English-language books and a good variety of guides on Dubrovnik and Croatia.

Uje
FOOD

(Map p260; www.uje.hr; Placa 5; ☉9am-9pm Mon-Sat, to 3pm Sun) Uje specialises in olive oils – among the best is Brachia, from the island of Brač. It also sells some excellent jams (the lemon spread is divine), pickled capers, and local herbs and spices.

Magnolika
JEWELLERY, GIFTS

(Map p260; www.magnolika.com; Getaldićeva 7; ☉10am-1pm & 6-8pm Tue-Fri, 10am-2pm Sat) A tiny space that sells jewellery and knick-knacks by young Croatian designers. It's great for finding affordable, beautiful pieces to hang on your wall, or yourself.

ℹ Information

General Hospital Dubrovnik (Opća Bolnica Dubrovnik; ☎020-431 777; www.bolnica-du.hr; Dr Roka Mišetića bb; ☉emergency department 24hr) On the southern edge of the Lapad peninsula.

Post Office (Map p260; www.posta.hr; Široka 8; ☉8am-8pm Mon-Fri, 10am-5pm Sat mid-Jun–Aug, 8am-7pm Mon-Fri, to noon Sat Sep–mid-Jun)

Tourist Office (www.tzdubrovnik.hr) Pile (Map p260; ☎020-312 011; Brsalje 5; ☉8am-9pm Jun-Sep, 8am-7pm Mon-Sat, 9am-3pm Sun Oct-May); Gruž (Map p256; ☎020-417 983; Obala Pape Ivana Pavla II 1; ☉8am-9pm Jun-Sep, to 3pm Mon-Sat Oct-May); Lapad (Map p256; ☎020-437 460; Kralja Tomislava 7; ☉8am-8pm Jun-Sep, to 3pm Mon-Sat Oct-May) Maps, information and advice.

ℹ Getting There & Away

AIR

Both Croatia Airlines and British Airways fly to Dubrovnik all year round. In summer they're joined by dozens of other airlines flying seasonal routes and charter flights. Croatia Airlines has domestic flights to/from Zagreb (up to five daily) and Osijek (weekly).

BUSES FROM DUBROVNIK

DESTINATION	COST (KN)	DURATION (HR)	DAILY SERVICES
Korčula	75-94	3	3
Kotor (Montenegro)	91-135	2½	4-5
Mostar (Bosnia & Hercegovina)	115	3	5
Pula	601	15	1
Rijeka	411-518	11¾-13¼	4
Sarajevo (Bosnia & Hercegovina)	175	6½	4
Split	113-135	4	24
Trieste (Italy)	459	15	1
Zadar	213-271	7½-8½	8
Zagreb	219	9¼-11½	14

BOAT

The **ferry terminal** (Map p256; Obala Pape Ivana Pavla II 1) is in Gruž, 3km northwest of the old town. Boats for Cavtat and Lokrum depart from the Old Harbour.

Jadrolinija (☑ 020-418 000; www.jadrolinija. hr) From April to October, two to six car ferries per day travel between Dubrovnik and Bari, Italy (passenger/car from €44/59, nine hours). From June to September a twice-weekly coastal car ferry heads north to Sobra on Mljet (passenger/car from €14/49, two hours), Korčula (€18/49, 3½ hours), Stari Grad on Hvar (€20/53, 7¾ hours), Split (€20/53, 9¾ hours) and Rijeka (€47/82, 22 hours).

G&V Line (☑ 060 100 000, www.gv-line.hr) Has a daily catamaran to Šipanska Luka on Šipan (35KN, 40 minutes) and Sobra on Mljet (60KN, 1¼ hours). There's another daily service to Sobra (one hour) along with Polače (70KN, 1¾ hours) on Mljet, with four per week continuing on to Korčula (90KN, 2½ hours) in summer.

UTO Kapetan Luka (www.krilo.hr) Has a fast boat to/from Korčula (90KN, two hours), Hvar (170KN, 3½ hours), Milna on Brač (170KN, 4¼ hours) and Split (170KN, 4¾ hours) on Tuesdays and Thursdays from mid-May to mid-October.

BUS

Buses out of **Dubrovnik Bus Station** (Map p256; ☑ 060 305 070; Obala Pape Ivana Pavla II 44a) can be crowded, so book tickets in advance in summer.

Split–Dubrovnik buses pass briefly through Bosnian territory, so keep your passport handy for border-crossing points.

All bus schedules are detailed at www.libertas-dubrovnik.hr.

ⓘ Getting Around

TO/FROM THE AIRPORT

Dubrovnik Airport (Zračna Luka Dubrovnik; www.airport-dubrovnik.hr) is in Čilipi, 19km southeast of Dubrovnik.

Atlas runs the airport bus service (35KN, 30 minutes), timed around flights. Buses to Dubrovnik stop at the Pile Gate and the bus station; buses to the airport pick up from the bus station and from the bus stop near the cable car.

A taxi to the old town costs about 250KN.

BUS

Dubrovnik has a superb bus service; buses run frequently and generally on time. The key tourist routes run until after 2am in summer, so if you're staying in Lapad there's no need to rush home. The fare is 15KN if you buy from the driver, and 12KN if you buy a ticket at a tisak (news stand). Timetables are available at www.libertas-dubrovnik.hr.

To get to the old town from the bus station, take buses 1a, 1b, 3 or 8. To get to Lapad, take bus 7.

From the Pile Gate, take bus 4, 5, 6 or 9 to get to Lapad.

CAR

The entire old town is a pedestrian area and all of the street parking surrounding it is metered.

There's a large parking garage on Zagrebačka – it's a short walk down to the old town, but a hard slog back up. It charges 20KN per hour and has a prepay rate of 220KN per day or 660KN per week. Note the daily and weekly rates are for prepay only; the machines don't make this clear and we've witnessed several people stung with hefty bills as a result.

All of the usual hire-car companies are represented at the airport and most also have city branches.

AROUND DUBROVNIK

Dubrovnik is an excellent base for day trips in the surrounding region – and even in the surrounding countries of Montenegro and Bosnia. You can hop over to Lokrum or the Elafiti Islands for a day of peaceful sunbathing, wander through the gardens at Trsteno or pop down to Cavtat for a day of sights and swimming. Alternatively, Cavtat makes a cheaper and quieter base from which to explore Dubrovnik.

Cavtat

POP 2150

Without Cavtat, there'd be no Dubrovnik, as it was refugees from the original Cavtat who established the city of Dubrovnik in 614. But Cavtat is interesting in itself. A lot more 'local' than Dubrovnik – read, not flooded by tourists on a daily basis – it has its own charm. Wrapped around a very pretty harbour that's bordered by beaches and backed by a curtain of imposing hills, the setting is lovely.

Cavtat's most famous personality is the painter Vlaho Bukovac (1855–1922), one of the foremost exponents of Croatian modernism. His paintings are liberally distributed around the town's main sights.

History

Originally a Greek settlement called Epidaurus, Cavtat became a Roman colony around 228 BC and was later destroyed during the 7th-century Slavic invasions. Throughout most of the Middle Ages it was part of the Republic of Dubrovnik and shared the cultural and economic life of the capital city.

◉ Sights

St Nicholas Church CHURCH
(Crkva Svetog Nikole; Obala Ante Starčevića bb) Peek inside this 15th-century church to view its impressive wooden altars and Bukovac painting.

Baltazar Bogišić Collection MUSEUM
(Obala Ante Starčevića 18; adult/concession 20/10KN; ⊙9am-1pm Mon-Sat) The former Rector's Palace houses the rich library belonging to 19th-century lawyer and historian Baltazar Bogišić, as well as lithographs and a small archaeological collection. One of the main draws is a painting by Bukovac, depicting the Cavtat Carnival in the 19th century.

Our Lady of the Snow Monastery MONASTERY
(Samostan Snježne Gospe; Bukovćeva bb) The church attached to this Franciscan Monastery (founded 1484) is worth a look for some notable early Renaissance paintings and a wonderful Bukovac work above the entrance to the sanctuary, depicting the Madonna and child gazing at the Cavtat skyline at sunset.

Bukovac House MUSEUM
(Kuća Bukovac; www.kuca-bukovac.hr; Bukovćeva 5; admission 20KN; ⊙10am-1pm & 4-8pm Tue-Sat, 4-8pm Sun May-Oct, 9am-5pm Tue-Sat, 2-5pm Sun Nov-Apr) The house where Vlaho Bukovac was born and raised has been converted into an interesting little museum devoted to his work. The early-19th-century architecture provides a fitting backdrop to his mementos and paintings. The house itself was actually the artist's first canvas – his earliest painting, a frieze of animals running around the walls, was only uncovered in 1998.

Račić Family Mausoleum MONUMENT
(Mauzolej Obitelji Račić; admission 10KN; ⊙10am-5pm Mon-Sat Apr-Nov) Built in 1921, this beautiful white stone tomb is the handiwork of pre-eminent Croatian sculptor Ivan Meštrović. It's located in the town cemetery, in the wooded area near the tip of the peninsula; take the path leading up from the monastery.

⌁ Sleeping & Eating

Castelletto B&B €€
(✆020-479 547; www.dubrovnikexperience.com; Frana Laureana 22; r €95-125; P✻@ ᐧ ᐧ) This very-well-run family-owned place has 13 spacious, immaculately presented rooms with tasteful modern furnishings in a converted villa. All have air-con and satellite TV and many have sweeping bay views. Airport transfers are free.

Galija SEAFOOD, DALMATIAN €€
(✆020-478 566; www.galija.hr; Vuličelićeva 1; mains 70-150KN; ⊙noon-10pm) Long-established and very well-regarded, this restaurant has a sea-facing terrace shaded by pines, and an atmospheric interior of exposed stone walls. The menu majors in fish and seafood – try the excellent sea platter (with fish, scallops, lobster, shrimps and scampi).

WORTH A TRIP

CROSS-BORDER JAUNTS

Dubrovnik is an easy bus ride away from **Montenegro** and the towns of Herceg Novi, Kotor and Budva. All three have wonderful historic centres, with curving marble streets and impressive architecture. If you really want to take your time and explore the region, you should hire a car, but you can also get there by public transport with daily buses crossing the border. The checkpoint can be very slow in summer; allow two hours to get to Herceg Novi by bus and a further hour for Kotor. Citizens of most European nations, Australia, New Zealand, Canada and the US don't need a visa to enter Montenegro; other nationalities should check with their embassy.

Buses also go to **Mostar**, giving you a chance to glance at its emblematic bridge and dip your toe into the world of Bosnia and Hercegovina. It's possible to go by public transport, but easier on an organised day excursion in private minibuses (around 380KN); enquire at local travel agencies. These leave around 8am and travel via the incredibly pretty fortified village of Počitelj, arriving in Mostar around 11.30am. After a (typically very brief) guided tour you'll be left to your own devices until 3pm – which doesn't leave a lot of time to have lunch and explore the town. Mostar is still divided along Croat/Bosnian lines (with the river acting as border), but most of the historic sights are on the Bosnian side.

★ **Bugenvila** MODERN EUROPEAN €€€
(☑ 020-479 949; www.bugenvila.eu; Obala Ante Starčevića 9; mains lunch 80-110KN, dinner 130-190KN; ☺ noon-4.15pm & 6.20-11pm) The coolest place on Cavtat's seafront strip – with brightly painted signs outside and colourful art on bare stone walls upstairs – Bugenvila is also the town's culinary trendsetter. Local ingredients are showcased in an adventurous and highly delicious menu. Visit at lunchtime to take advantage of the three-course specials (125KN to 145KN).

ℹ Information

Post Office (www.posta.hr; Trumbićev Put 10; ☺ 7am-9pm Mon-Fri, 8am-noon & 6-9pm Sat Jun-Aug, 7am-7pm Mon-Fri, 8am-noon Sat Sep-May)

Tourist Office (☑ 020-479 025; www.visit.cavtat-konavle.com; Zidine 6; ☺ 8am-8pm May-Sep, to 7pm Mon-Sat Apr & Oct, to 3pm Mon-Fri Nov-Mar) Very well stocked with leaflets and a good colour map.

ℹ Getting There & Away

BOAT

From June to September, there are 11 sailings a day between Dubrovnik's Old Harbour and Cavtat (one-way/return 50/80KN, 45 minutes). For the rest of the year this reduces to three to five a day, weather dependent.

BUS

Bus 10 runs roughly hourly to Cavtat (25KN, 45 minutes) from Dubrovnik's bus station; the last buses return at about 1am.

Lokrum Island

A ferry shuttles roughly hourly in summer (half-hourly in July and August) on the 10-minute trip from Dubrovnik's Old Harbour to lush Lokrum Island (adult/child return 56/16KN). It's a beautiful, forested place of holm oaks, black ash, pines and olive trees, and an ideal escape from urban Dubrovnik. Swimming is excellent, though the beaches are rocky. The nudist beach (marked FKK) is also Dubrovnik's de facto gay beach.

Check out the ruined medieval **Benedictine monastery** and the fine **botanical garden**, which has a cacti section with some giant agaves, and palms native to Brazil and South Africa.

Before you leave the boat, make sure you check what time the last boat to the mainland departs. Note that no one can stay overnight and smoking is not permitted anywhere on the island. The island is only open to the public from April to November.

Trsteno Arboretum

Just 14km northwest of Dubrovnik, these leafy gardens are the oldest of their kind in Croatia and well worth a visit. It was during the 16th century that Dubrovnik's noblesse started to pay extra attention to the appearance of their gardens. Ivan Gučetić planted the first seeds here and started the trend, and his descendants maintained the garden throughout the centuries. The land was

WORTH A TRIP

KONAVLE CALLING

After the dry and rugged coast around Dubrovnik, the lush fields and orderly vineyards of Konavle are quite a surprise. Here, in this hidden nook between the Bosnian and Montenegrin borders, east of Cavtat, the mountains have taken half a step back, providing a dramatic backdrop to the fertile agricultural region. It's best known for *malvasija*, an endemic grape producing a very pleasant white wine.

There's no better place to soak up the scenery than on the terrace of **Konoba Koraćeva Kuća** (☑020-791 557; Gruda bb; mains 55-130KN; ⊘noon-10pm Apr-Sep) in the village of Gruda, an exceptional family-run restaurant specialising in modern takes on Dalmatian traditions. At sunset, you can gaze over the fields and watch the colours dance across the mountains of Bosnia. Call ahead to arrange for lamb or veal to be slow-roasted under a *peka* (a metal dome covered in hot charcoal), or just call in to see what's on the menu. We highly recommend the bruschetta, the stuffed *pršut* (local prosciutto) and the wild boar stew with gnocchi.

eventually taken over by the (former Yugoslav and now Croatian) Academy of Sciences, which turned it into a public **arboretum** (☑020-751 019; adult/concession 40/25KN; ⊘8am-7pm Jun-Sep, to 4pm Oct-May).

The garden has a Renaissance layout, with a set of geometric shapes made with Mediterranean plants and bushes (lilac lavender, green rosemary, fuchsia, bougainvillea), while citrus orchards perfume the air. It's only partially landscaped, though – quite a bit of it is wonderfully wild. There's a **maze** that children enjoy, a fine palm collection (including Chinese windmill palms) and a gorgeous **pond** overlooked by a statue of Neptune and rich with white water lilies and dozens of bullfrogs.

Don't miss the two **giant plane trees** at the entrance to Trsteno village – each is more than 500 years old and around 50m high. They're amongst the largest of their kind in Europe.

To get to Trsteno, catch local bus 12, 15, 22 or 35 from Dubrovnik's bus station. Otherwise any intercity bus bound for Split will stop here.

Elafiti Islands

A day trip to an island in this archipelago northwest of Dubrovnik makes a perfect escape from the summer crowds. The most popular islands are Koločep, Lopud and Šipan. One way to see all three in one day is to take one of the 'Three Islands & Fish Picnic' tours (250KN including drinks and lunch), offered by several operators at Dubrovnik's Old Harbour. However, as these leave around 10am and return before 6pm, you don't get more than a quick glimpse of each island.

Koločep is the nearest of the islands and is inhabited by a mere 150 people. There are several sand-and-pebble beaches, steep cliffs and sea caves, as well as centuries-old pine forests, olive groves, and orchards filled with orange and lemon trees.

Car-free **Lopud** has interesting churches and monasteries dating from the 16th century, when the inhabitants' seafaring exploits were legendary. Lopud village is composed of stone houses surrounded by exotic gardens. You can walk across the spine of the island to beautiful and sandy **Šunj beach**; here a little bar serves griddled sardines and other types of fish.

Šipan is the largest of the islands and was a favourite with the Dubrovnik aristocracy, who built houses here in the 15th century. The village of **Šipanska Luka** has the remains of a Roman villa and a 15th-century Gothic duke's palace. Head to **Kod Marka** (☑020-758 007; Šipanska Luka; mains from 50KN) for gloriously prepared seafood – try the Korčula-style fish stew.

❶ Getting There & Around

Four **Jadrolinija** (www.jadrolinija.hr) car ferries (per adult/child/car 23/12/160KN) head from Dubrovnik to the Elafiti Islands every day, year-round (two on Sundays in winter), stopping at Koločep (35 minutes), Lopud (55 minutes) and Suđurađ on Šipan (1¼ hours). An additional one to two ferries per day head directly to Lopud and then Suđurađ.

G&V Line (www.gv-line.hr) also has a daily catamaran connecting Šipanska Luka to Dubrovnik (35KN, 40 minutes) and Mljet (30KN, 35 minutes).

All of these services depart from Dubrovnik's Gruž Harbour.

Mljet Island

POP 1090

Mljet is one of the most seductive of all the Adriatic islands. Much of the island is covered by forests and the rest is dotted with fields, vineyards and small villages. The northwestern half contains Mljet National Park, where the lush vegetation, pine forests and spectacular saltwater lakes are exceptionally scenic. It's an unspoiled oasis of tranquillity that, according to legend, captivated Odysseus for seven years. We're sure he didn't regret a moment.

History

Ancient Greeks called the island 'Melita' or 'honey' for the many bees humming in the forests. It appears that Greek sailors came to the island for refuge against storms and to gather fresh water from the springs. At that time the island was populated by Illyrians, who erected hill forts and traded with the mainland. They were conquered by the Romans in 35 BC, who expanded the settlement around Polače by building a palace, baths and servants' quarters.

The island fell under the control of the Byzantine Empire in the 6th century and was later subjected to the 7th-century invasions of Slavs and Avars. After several centuries of regional rule from the mainland, Mljet was given to the Benedictine order in the 13th century. Dubrovnik formally annexed the island in 1410.

Although Mljet's fortunes were thereafter tied to those of Dubrovnik, the inhabitants maintained their traditional activities of farming, viticulture and seafaring. Farming and viticulture remain key occupations today. The establishment of the national park in 1960 put Mljet on the tourist map, but the island is anything but overrun and visitors are almost entirely drawn to the tourist enclave around Pomena. If you're searching for tranquillity, you won't have to look hard.

◎ Sights & Activities

Mljet National Park   PARK

(www.mljet.hr; adult/concession 100/50KN) Kiosks in Pomena and Polače both sell admission tickets to the national park. From both villages you can walk or cycle (cars are forbidden) to **Malo Jezero** (Little Lake) and **Veliko Jezero** (Big Lake). In the middle of Veliko Jezero is an islet with a **Benedictine** monastery, that incorporates **St Mary's Church** (Crkva Svete Marije). A boat leaves for the island regularly from Mali Most, about 1.5km from Pomena (the trip is included in the park fee).

The monastery was originally built in the 12th century but has been rebuilt several times, adding Renaissance and baroque features to the Romanesque structure. In addition to building the monastery, the Benedictine monks deepened and widened the channel connecting the two lakes, taking advantage of the tidal surge to build a mill at the entrance to Veliko Jezero. The monastery was abandoned in 1869 and the mill housed the island's forest-management offices until 1941. It was then converted into a hotel, which was trashed during the 1990s war. Now it contains an atmospheric restaurant.

Veliko Jezero is connected to the sea by the Soline Canal, which makes the lakes subject to tidal flows. There's no bridge over the canal, so it's not possible to walk right around the larger lake. If you decide to swim it, keep in mind that the current can be strong.

Polače   VILLAGE

Polače features a number of remains dating from the 1st to the 6th centuries. Most impressive is the **Roman palace**, probably from the 5th century. The floor plan is rectangular and on the front corners are two polygonal towers separated by a pier. On a hill over the town you can see the remains of a late-antique **fortification** and northwest of the village are the remains of an early **Christian basilica** and a 5th-century **church**.

Aquatica   DIVING

(☏ 099 81 14 090; www.aquatica-mljet.hr; next to Hotel Odisej, Pomena) Mljet offers some interesting diving opportunities, including a German WWII torpedo boat and several walls. There's also a 3rd-century Roman wreck in relatively shallow water. The remains of the ship, including amphorae, have calcified over the centuries and this has protected them from pillaging.

⌲ Tours

Agencies in Dubrovnik and Korčula offer excursions to Mljet. Tours (around 390KN and 245KN respectively) last from about 8.30am to 6pm and include the park entry fee.

📖 Sleeping & Eating

The Polače tourist office arranges private accommodation (from around 250KN per double), but it's essential to make arrangements before peak season. You'll find more *sobe* signs around Pomena than Polače, and practically none at all in Sobra.

Pomena has the largest choice of eateries, with a lovely strip of places right by the sea. Fish and seafood are very fresh and readily available, though not cheap. Kid and lamb are also popular, cooked in a *peka* (a metal dome covered in hot charcoal). A tip for boaters: you can moor at any of the restaurants for free if you eat there.

Stermasi   APARTMENT, DALMATIAN €€
(📞098 93 90 362; www.stermasi.hr; Saplunara; apt €65-140, mains 70-180KN; 🅿️ ❄️) On the eastern side of Mljet, Stermasi's 10 apartments are bright and modern, and either have a terrace or private balcony. But the big draw here is the restaurant, serving flavoursome, authentic Dalmatian food prepared with love and skill. House specialities include vegetables, octopus or kid cooked under a *peka*, wild boar with gnocchi and Mljet-style fish stew.

Soline 6   APARTMENT €€
(📞020-744 024; www.soline6.com; Soline; d €80)
🖊 Within the confines of the national park, this very green place is quite a concept and an undertaking. Everything has been built from recycled products, rainwater is reused and organic waste composted. If you're expecting a hippie commune, think again: the four studios are modern and clean and each has a private bathroom, a balcony and a kitchen.

ℹ️ Information

Polače Tourist Office (📞020-744 186; www.mljet.hr; ⏰8am-1pm & 5-7pm Mon-Sat, 9am-noon Sun Jun-Sep, 8am-1pm Mon-Fri Oct-May) Stocks brochures and a good walking map. There's an ATM nearby.

Babino Polje Tourist Office (📞020-746 025; www.mljet.hr; Zabrježe 2; ⏰9am-5pm Mon-Fri) Babino Polje, 18km east of Polače, is the island's main settlement. You'll also find a post office here.

ℹ️ Getting There & Away

The quickest connection from the mainland to Mljet is the **Jadrolinija car ferry** (www.jadrolinija.hr) from Prapratno on the Pelješac Peninsula to Sobra (per adult/child/car 30/15/140KN, 45 minutes, four to five daily).

G&V Line (www.gv-line.hr) has a daily catamaran from Dubrovnik (60KN, 1¼ hours) and Šipan (30KN, 35 minutes) to Sobra, and another from Dubrovnik to Sobra (70KN, one hour) and Polače (70KN, 1¾ hours), with four per week continuing on to Korčula (50KN, 45 minutes) in summer. You cannot reserve tickets in advance for these services; get to the harbour ticket office well in advance in high season to secure a seat (bicycles are not permitted either).

From June to September the twice-weekly Jadrolinija coastal car ferry stops in Sobra en route between Dubrovnik (passenger/car from €14/49, two hours) and Rijeka (€47/82, 20¼ hours); other stops include Korčula (€14/49, two hours), Stari Grad on Hvar (€20/53, six hours) and Split (€20/53, eight hours).

ℹ️ Getting Around

Infrequent buses connect Sobra and Polače.

Renting a bicycle is an excellent way to explore the national park. Be aware that Pomena and Polače are separated by a steep hill. The bike path along the lake is an easier and very scenic pedal.

Mini Brum (📞020-745 084; www.rent-a-car-scooter-mljet.hr) rents scooters (per two hours/day 120/240KN) and cars (per five hours/day from 270/380KN) from Sobra, Polače and Pomena.

PELJEŠAC PENINSULA

The slender fingerlike peninsula of Pelješac is coastal Croatia at its most relaxed. Blessed with a spine of craggy mountains, sweeping valleys, idyllic coves and fine wines, it's a glorious place to visit.

Ston & Mali Ston

POP 549 & 139

Ston and its little buddy Mali Ston sit 50km northwest of Dubrovnik on an isthmus that connects the Pelješac Peninsula with the mainland. Formerly part of the Republic of Dubrovnik, Ston was and is an important salt-producing town. Its economic importance to Dubrovnik led, in 1333, to the construction of a 5.5km wall, one of the longest fortifications in Europe. Architects including Juraj Dalmatinac were involved in the design and construction, which included 40 towers and five forts. The walls are still standing, sheltering a cluster of medieval buildings in the town centre.

Mali Ston, a little village and harbour situated 1km northeast of Ston, was built along with the wall as part of the defensive system. Both towns are major gastronomic destinations, famed for the oysters and mussels that have been farmed here since Roman times.

Sights & Activities

The major sight in Ston is the 14th-century **wall** (adult/child 40/20KN; ☉8am-7pm) that stretches from both towns far up the hill. It has been fully restored and you can walk the ramparts for long stretches.

You could also drop by and see the Ston **salt pans** (www.solanaston.hr; Peljeski Put 1; admission 15KN; ☉7am-7pm May-Oct), which brought so much wealth and are still operational today. Salt is gathered between late July and September and volunteers are needed to help out. It's a kind of working holiday; check the website for info.

There are no beaches in town but **Prapratno**, 4km southwest of Ston, has a wonderful pebbly beach. Watch out for sea urchins in the shallow water though.

Sleeping

Camping Prapratno   CAMPGROUND €
(☏020-754 000; www.duprimorje.hr; Prapratno; per adult/car/site 50/42/40KN; ☐ ☎) Sites are arranged under the shade of olive trees at this attractive campground, right by the sparkling beach at Prapratno. It has good facilities including tennis and basketball courts, a shop and a restaurant.

Ostrea   HOTEL €€€
(☏020-754 555; www.ostrea.hr; Mali Ston; s/d from 690/990KN; ☐ ☀ ☎) Behind the stone walls and green shutters of this historic building are elegant rooms with polished timber floors and modern bathrooms. Staff are welcoming and professional and it's just steps from Mali Ston's pretty harbour.

Eating

Stagnum   DALMATIAN €
(Imena Isusova 23, Ston; mains 30-110KN; ☉11am-midnight May-Oct) Grab a seat in the lovely garden courtyard where you can watch and smell the fish and meat sizzling on the barbecue. Tasty portions of fresh mussels and risotto are also served up.

Kapetanova Kuća   SEAFOOD €€
(☏020-754 269; www.ostrea.hr; Mali Ston; mains 85-130KN; ☉noon-10pm) The 'Captain's House' is one of the most venerable seafood restaurants in the region. Dine on Ston oysters and mussels on the shady terrace.

ℹ Information

Tourist Office (☏020-754 452; www.ston.hr; Peljestki Put bb, Ston; ☉8am-7pm Mon-Sat, 9am-noon & 4-7pm Sun Jul-Sep, 8am-2pm Mon-Sat Oct-Jun) Has brochures and bus timetables and can help you find private accommodation. The bus stop and post office are nearby.

ℹ Getting There & Away

Bus destinations include Orebić (from 38KN, 1½ hours, four daily), Dubrovnik (60KN, 1½ hours, four daily), Split (90KN, 2½ hours, three daily), Zadar (135KN, six hours, daily) and Zagreb (219KN, nine hours, two daily).

Central Pelješac

The drive from Ston to Orebić takes a good hour and it's a very pleasant one indeed. What many travellers might not be aware of as they zip along the winding road is that they're passing through the realm of the king of Croatian red wines: *plavac mali*.

A descendant of *crljenak kaštelanski* (more commonly known as *zinfandel*) and little-known *dobričić*, this little *(mali)* blue *(plavac)* grape produces big, flavoursome wine (called *primitivo* in Italy). The more inhospitable the terrain, the more flavour-laden the grapes, which is why the very best *plavac mali* is grown on the barren, sunbaked slopes of **Dingač** and **Postup** on the peninsula's southern coast. The vines are so difficult to access that all of the grapes must be harvested by hand. Both of these regions are now recognised appellations, protected by a 'stamp of geographic origin'.

The peninsula's third largest settlement after Ston and Orebić is pretty little palm-lined **Trpanj** on the northern coast. Car ferries run between here and Ploče.

🍷 Drinking

★ Peninsula   WINE BAR
(www.peninsula.hr; Donja Banda; tastings from 4KN; ☉9am-11pm; ☎) Located in Donja Banda, near where the road from Trpanj branches off from the main peninsula road, this wonderful roadside wine bar is the best place to sample a wide range of high-quality local wine. There are over 60 wines to choose from, as well as a selection of locally produced olive oils, *rakija* (brandies) and liqueurs.

WINDSURFING IN VIGANJ

If you're into windsurfing, Viganj has some of the best conditions in Croatia. The village is strung out along the coast 7km west of Orebić, near the tip of the Pelješac Peninsula.

The weirdly named **Antony-Boy** (☑ 021-719 077; www.antony-boy.com; per adult/child/tent/car 36/22/30/36KN; @ 🛜 🐾), set beside a pebble beach, is a good camping choice and has a windsurf school. It also rents bikes.

Viganj is a low-key place, but there are a couple of restaurants and **Karmela** (☑020-719 097; Viganj 36; ⊘7am-midnight; 🛜), a lively beach bar with a great vibe, which also serves food in the high season. There's a little summertime **tourist office** (☑020-719 059; ⊘9am-2pm Mon-Sat mid-Jun–mid-Sep) right next door.

Taverna Domanoeta   TAVERNA
(Janjina; ⊘7pm-1am Jul & Aug) You couldn't hope for a more authentically rustic spot to sample a local drop than this stone-walled cellar bar in Janjina, a small village at the very centre of the peninsula. If it's sunny, grab a table in the garden and order some *plavac mali,* accompanied by local cheese and *pršut* (prosciutto).

❶ Getting There & Away

Jadrolinija (www.jadrolinija.hr) runs the Ploče-Trpanj car ferry (per adult/child/car 32/16/138KN, five to seven daily). If you're coming from (or heading to) the north, this ferry cuts around 90 minutes off the drive, but takes an hour for the crossing.

Orebić

POP 1980

Orebić, on the southern coast of the Pelješac Peninsula, has some of the best beaches in southern Dalmatia – sandy coves bordered by groves of tamarisk and pine. Only 2.5km across the water from Korčula Town, it makes a perfect day trip or an alternative base. After lazing on the beach, you can take advantage of some excellent hiking up and around Mt Ilija (961m) or poke around a couple of churches and museums. Mt Ilija protects the town from harsh northern winds, allowing vegetation to flourish. The temperature is usually a few degrees warmer than Korčula; spring arrives early and summer leaves late.

History

Orebić and the Pelješac Peninsula became part of Dubrovnik in 1333 when it was purchased from Serbia. Until the 16th century the town was known as Trstenica (the name of its eastern bay) and was an important maritime centre. The name Orebić comes from a wealthy seafaring family, who, in 1658, built a citadel as a defence against the Turks. Many of the houses and exotic gardens developed by prosperous sea captains still grace the area. The height of Orebić seafaring occurred in the 18th and 19th centuries when it was the seat of one of the largest companies of the day: the Associazione Marittima di Sabioncello. With the decline of shipping, Orebić began to turn to tourism.

◉ Sights & Activities

Trstenica   BEACH
There's a slim beach west of the dock, but the best beach is the long stretch at Trstenica about 700m east of the dock. A beautiful broad crescent of sand and fine shingle, it's fringed by mature trees and its sheltered waters are a near-Caribbean shade of turquoise.

Maritime Museum   MUSEUM
(Pomorski Muzej; Obala Pomoraca; adult/child 15/10KN; ⊘10am-noon & 5-8pm Mon-Sat Jul-Oct, 7am-3pm Mon-Fri Nov-Jun) This moderately interesting museum contains paintings of ships, boating memorabilia, navigational aids and prehistoric finds from archaeological excavations in nearby Majsan. Few captions are in English.

Walks   HIKING
Orebić is great for hiking, so pick up a trail map from the tourist office. A track through the pine trees leads from Hotel Bellevue to a 15th-century **Franciscan monastery** on a ridge 152m above the sea. From this vantage point, Dubrovnik patrols could keep an eye on the Venetian ships moored on Korčula and notify the authorities of any suspicious movements.

The village of Karmen near the monastery is the starting point for walks to picturesque upper villages and the more daring climb up **Mt Ilija**, the bare, grey massif that hangs over Orebić. The reward for climbers is a sweeping view of the entire coast. On a hill east of the monastery is **Our Lady of Carmel Church** (Gospa od Karmena), next to several huge cypresses, as well as a baroque loggia and the ruins of a duke's castle.

🛏 Sleeping

Enquire about private accommodation at the tourist office or Orebić Tours. Private rooms start at around 170KN per person.

Glavna Plaža   CAMPGROUND, APARTMENT €
(☑020-713 399; www.glavnaplaza.com; Kneza Domogoja 49; camping per adult/child/site/car €7/4/6/6, apt from €50; ☺May-Sep; P ⌖) This small family-run campground is tucked away down the Orebić end of sandy Trstenica beach. As well as sites, there are four simple apartments available (three studios and one that can sleep six).

Hotel Adriatic   HOTEL €€€
(☑020-714 488; www.hoteladriaticorebic.com; Šetalište Kneza Domagoja 8; s/d from 912/1140KN; ⌗⌖) Right by the water, this converted ship-captain's mansion has comfortable rooms with exposed stone walls, wooden floors and fantastic, ample bathrooms. All rooms have great sea views. An excellent breakfast is served on the seaside terrace.

Hotel Indijan   HOTEL €€€
(☑020-714 555; www.hotelindijan.hr; Šetalište, Škvar 2; s/d from 817/1417KN; P ⌗⌖) A contemporary feel pervades this well-designed hotel. Rooms are modern and well equipped, and some have balconies with views over the Adriatic to Korčula. The small circular heated pool has a retractable glass roof, so it's usable all year round.

🍴 Eating

Dalmatino   DALMATIAN €
(Jelačića 47; mains 40-90KN; ☺noon-10pm; ⌖) Right on the seafront just west of the harbour, this popular place has a pleasant atmosphere and tables shaded by pines. The menu includes squid, fish, shrimp, steak, pizza and pasta. It's a good place to while away a few minutes if you're waiting for a boat. There's a kids' play area.

Panorama Jerković   DALMATIAN €€
(Celestinov Put; mains 70-115KN; ☺6-9pm) This very basic family-run place sits high on the slopes past the monastery, providing staggeringly good views of Korčula Town. If you're thinking of dining here, it's best to call in the day before to order the house speciality: octopus, veal or lamb cooked *ispod peka* ('under the bell'). The rest of the limited menu is very average.

ℹ Information

Orebić Tours (☑020-713 367; www.orebic-tours.hr; Bana Josipa Jelačića 84a) Rents private accommodation, changes money and books excursions, including wine tours and boat cruises.

Post Office (Obala Pomoraca 13; ☺8am-9pm Mon-Fri, 8am-noon & 6-9pm Sat Jul & Aug, 7.30am-5pm Mon-Fri, 9am-1pm Sat Sep-Jun)

Tourist Office (☑020-713 718; www.visit orebic-croatia.hr; Zrinsko Frankopanska 2; ☺8am-10pm Jul & Aug, 8am-8pm May, Jun, Sep & Oct, 8am-4pm Mon-Fri Nov-Apr) Has a good hiking and biking map of the peninsula and plenty of brochures.

ℹ Getting There & Away

Ferries from Korčula tie up just steps from the tourist office and bus stop.

Buses head to/from Ston (from 38KN, 1½ hours, four daily), Dubrovnik (from 69KN, 2½ hours, three daily), Split (94KN, 4½ hours, daily), Zadar (188KN, 7¼ hours, daily) and Zagreb (250KN, 10¾ hours, daily).

KORČULA ISLAND

Rich in vineyards, olive groves and small villages, and harbouring a glorious old town, the island of Korčula is the sixth-largest Adriatic island, stretching nearly 47km in length. The dense woods led the original Greek settlers to call the island Korkyra Melaina (Black Korčula). Quiet coves and small sandy beaches dot the steep southern coast while the northern shore is flatter and more pebbly.

Tradition is alive and kicking on Korčula, with age-old religious ceremonies, folk music and dances still being performed to an ever-growing influx of tourists. Oenophiles will adore sampling its wine. Arguably the best of all Croatian whites is produced from *pošip* grapes, which are only grown here and to a lesser extent on the Pelješac Peninsula. The *grk* grape, cultivated around Lumbarda, also produces quality dry white wine.

History

A Neolithic cave (Vela Spila) located near Vela Luka, on the island's western end, points to the existence of a prehistoric settlement, but it was the Greeks who first began spreading over the island somewhere around the 6th century BC. Their most important settlement was in the area of today's Lumbarda around the 3rd century BC.

> **DON'T MISS**
>
> ## RURAL EATS
>
> Some of Korčula's best eating experiences can be found in the surrounding villages. If you've got your own transport, it's well worth seeking out the following.
>
> **Konoba Mate** (☎020-717 109; Pupnat 28; mains 50-80KN; ⊙11am-2pm & 7-11pm Mon-Sat, 7-11pm Sun) Our favourite place to eat on the entire island has the unlikely setting of the sleepy farming village of Pupnat, just off the main island road, 11km west of Korčula Town. The menu is short but universally tempting, offering unusual twists on true-blue traditions, including kid goat cooked under a *peka* (domed baking lid). The antipasto platter is sublime.
>
> **Konoba Belin** (☎091 50 39 258; Prvo Selo Žrnovo; mains 50-120KN; ⊙10am-2pm & 5pm-midnight) It's all about the barbecue (which dad is firmly in control of) at this friendly family-run place in the old part of Žrnovo, 2.5km west of Korčula Town. Expect lots of grilled fish and meat; if you call ahead they'll chuck an octopus in the *peka*.
>
> **Konoba Maslina** (Lumbarajska bb; mains 60-130KN; ⊙11am-10pm) With everything you'd want from a rural *konoba* (tavern), this traditional place offers rustic character and honest country cooking: fresh fish, lamb and veal, and local ham and cheese feature strongly. It's about 3km out of town on the road to Lumbarda.

Rome conquered Korčula in the 1st century, giving way to the Slavs in the 7th century. The island was conquered by Venice in AD 1000 and then passed under Hungarian rule. It was briefly part of the Republic of Dubrovnik before again falling to the Venetians in 1420, who remained until 1797. Under Venetian control the island became known for its stone, which was quarried and cut for export. Shipbuilding also flourished.

After the Napoleonic conquest of Dalmatia in 1797, Korčula's fortunes followed those of the region, changing hands among the French, British, Austro-Hungarians and Italians before becoming a part of the first Yugoslavia in 1921. Today Korčula is one of Croatia's most prosperous islands, its historic capital drawing visitors in increasing numbers.

ℹ Getting There & Around

BOAT

The island has three major entry ports: Korčula Town's West Harbour, Dominče (3km east of Korčula Town) and Vela Luka.

Jadrolinija (☎020-715 410; www.jadrolinija.hr) The main route to the island is the car ferry from Orebić to Dominče (per adult/child/car 16/8/76KN, 20 minutes), which departs roughly hourly year-round. A daily catamaran heads between Korčula Town's West Harbour and Split (120KN, three hours), stopping at Hvar (80KN, two hours) on the way.

A twice-daily car ferry also heads from Split to Vela Luka (per adult/child/car 60/30/530KN, 2¾ hours) and on to the island of Lastovo.

There's also a daily catamaran on this route that stops in Hvar (55KN, 45 minutes) en route from Split (65KN, 2¼ hours).

From June to September the twice-weekly coastal car ferry between Dubrovnik (passenger/car from €18/49, 3½ hours) and Rijeka (€40/74, 18 hours) stops at Dominče. Other stops include Mljet (€14/49, two hours), Stari Grad on Hvar (€18/49, 3¾ hours) and Split (€18/49, 5¾ hours).

G&V Line (☎060 100 000; www.gv-line.hr) Has four catamarans per week in summer between Korčula Town's West Harbour and Dubrovnik (90KN, 2½ hours), also stopping at Polače (50KN, 55 minutes) and Sobra (60KN, 1½ hours) on Mljet.

Linijska Nacionalna Plovidba (www.lnp.hr) Runs a car ferry between Drvenik (on the mainland halfway between Makarska and Ploče) and Dominče three times a day from mid-July to the end of August (per adult/child/car 57/29/298KN, 2¼ hours).

UTO Kapetan Luka (☎021-645 476; www.krilo.hr) Has a fast boat to Korčula Town's West Harbour from Dubrovnik (90KN, two hours), Hvar (80KN, 1¼ hours), Milna on Brač (90KN, two hours) and Split (90KN, 2½ hours) on Tuesdays and Thursdays from mid-May to mid-October.

BUS

Buses between the mainland and Korčula Town use the Orebić car ferry. Destinations include Ston (48KN, two hours, four daily), Dubrovnik (75KN, three hours, one to three daily), Split (100KN, five hours, daily), Zadar (157KN, 7¾ hours, daily) and Zagreb (261KN, 11¼ hours, daily). Book ahead in summer.

Korčula Town

POP 2860

Korčula Town is a stunner. Ringed by imposing defences, this coastal citadel is dripping in history, with marble streets rich in Renaissance and Gothic architecture. Its fascinating fishbone layout was cleverly designed for the comfort and safety of its inhabitants: western streets were built straight in order to open the city to the refreshing summer *maestral* (strong, steady westerly wind), while the eastern streets were curved to minimise the force of the winter *bura* (cold, northeasterly wind). The town cradles a harbour, overlooked by round defensive towers and a compact cluster of red-roofed houses.

There are rustling palms all around and several beaches are an easy walk away. This being a favourite family island, you'll need to get out of town to more remote beaches if you want some peace.

History

Although documents indicate that a walled town existed on this site in the 13th century, it wasn't until the 15th century that the current city was built. Construction coincided with the apogee of stone-carving skills on the island, lending the buildings and streets a distinctive style. In the 16th century masons added decorative flourishes such as ornate columns and coats of arms to building facades, which gave a Renaissance look to the original Gothic core.

People began building houses south of the old town in the 17th and 18th centuries as the threat of invasion diminished and they no longer needed to protect themselves behind walls. The narrow streets and stone houses in the 'new' suburb attracted merchants and artisans, and this is still where you'll find most commercial activity.

◉ Sights

City Defences   FORT

Korčula's towers and remaining city walls look particularly striking when approached from the sea – their presence warned pirates the town would be no pushover. Originally these defences would have been even more foreboding, forming a complete stone barrier against invaders that consisted of 12 towers and 20m-high walls.

From the western harbour the conical **Large Governor's Tower** (1483) and **Small Governor's Tower** (1449) protected the port, shipping and the Governor's Palace, which used to stand next to the town hall. Continuing clockwise around the edge of the old town peninsula, the **Sea Gate Tower** has an inscription in Latin from 1592 stating that Korčula was founded after the fall of Troy. Next you'll come to the renovated **Kanavelić Tower**, its semicircular profile topped with battlements, and then a smaller tower that has now been converted into a cocktail bar.

The entrance to the old city is through the southern land gate in the **Veliki Revelin Tower**. Built in the 14th century and later extended, this fortification is adorned with coats of arms of the Venetian doges and Korčulan governors. There was originally a

---

MOREŠKA SWORD DANCES

One of the island's most colourful traditions, the sword dance has been performed in Korčula since the 15th century. Although it's probably of Spanish origin, Korčula is now the only place in the world that it is performed. It tells the story of two kings – the White King (dressed in red) and the Black King – who fight for a princess abducted by the Black King. In the spoken introduction the princess declares her love for the White King, and the Black King refuses to relinquish her. The two armies draw swords and 'fight' in an intricate dance accompanied by a band.

Enthusiastic townspeople perform the dance, which takes place outside the southern gate. Although traditionally performed only on Korčula's town day (29 July), the dance now takes place at 9pm every Thursday evening between June and September, and every Monday in July and August. Tickets cost 100KN and can be purchased on the spot or from any travel agency.

Kumpanija dances in the villages of Pupnat, Smokvica, Blato and Čara also make a fun night out, but you'll need your own transport to see them. These dances also involve a 'fight' between rival armies and culminate in the unfurling of a huge flag. They're accompanied by the *mišnice* (like a bagpipe) and drums.

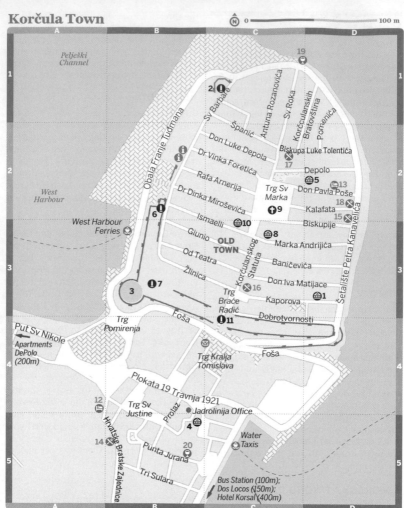

wooden drawbridge here, but it was replaced in the 18th century by the wide stone steps that give a sense of grandeur to the entrance. The best remaining part of the defence walls stretches west from here. The upper section of this tower is home to the small **Moreška Museum** (admission 20KN; ⊙9am-3pm May-Oct) dedicated to the Moreška dance tradition; it has some costumes and old photos.

Icon Museum   MUSEUM
(Muzej Ikona; Trg Svih Svetih; admission 15KN; ⊙9am-2pm & 6-7pm Mon-Sat) The modest Icon Museum has a small collection of interesting Byzantine icons painted on gilded wood, and 17th- and 18th-century ritual objects. As a bonus, visitors also have access to the beautiful **All Saints' Church** (Crkva Svih Svetih) next door. This 18th-century baroque church features a carved and painted 15th-century wood screen and a late-18th-century pietà, along with a wealth of local religious paintings.

Town Museum   MUSEUM
(Gradski Muzej; www.gm-korcula.com; Trg Sv Marka 20; adult/child 20/6KN; ⊙10am-9pm Jul-Sep, to 1pm Oct-Mar, to 2pm Apr-Jun) Occupying the 16th-

century Gabriellis Palace, this museum traces the history and culture of Korčula throughout the ages. It's not that well organised but there are some interesting curios scattered over its four floors – including a tablet recording the Greek presence on the island in the 3rd century BC. Explanations are in English.

Displays cover stonemasonry, shipbuilding, archaeology, art, furniture, textiles and examples of Korčulan traditional dress.

St Mark's Abbey Treasury MUSEUM
(Opatska Riznica Svetog Marka; Trg Sv Marka; admission 25KN; ⏰9am-7.30pm Mon-Sat May-Nov) The 14th-century Abbey Palace houses a collection of icons and Dalmatian art, with an excellent selection of 15th- and 16th-century paintings. The most outstanding work is the polyptych of *The Virgin* by Blaž Trogiranin. There are also liturgical items, jewellery, furniture and ancient documents relating to the history of Korčula.

St Mark's Cathedral CATHEDRAL
(Katedrala Svetog Marka; Trg Sv Marka; bell tower adult/child 20/15KN; ⏰9am-9pm Jul & Aug, Mass only Sep-Jun) Dominating the little square at Korčula's heart is this magnificent 15th-century cathedral, built from Korčula limestone in a Gothic-Renaissance style by Italian and local artisans. The sculptural detail of the facade is intriguing, particularly the naked squatting figures of Adam and Eve on the door pillars, and the two-tailed mermaid and elephant on the triangular gable cornice at the very top. The bell tower is topped by a balustrade and ornate cupola, beautifully carved by Korčulan Marko Andrijić.

Inside, the nave soars 30m in height and is lined with a twin colonnade of exposed limestone pillars. Look out for the ciborium, also carved by Andrijić, and behind it the altarpiece painting *Three Saints* by Tintoretto. Another painting attributed to Tintoretto or his workshop, *The Annunciation,* is by the baroque altar of St Anthony.

Other noteworthy artworks include a bronze statue of St Blaise by Ivan Meštrović near the altar on the northern aisle, and a painting by the Venetian artist Jacopo Bassano in the apse of the southern aisle. Check out the modern sculptures in the baptistery too.

Before leaving the square, notice the elegantly ornamented **Arneri Palace** opposite the cathedral, at the corner of the narrow street of the same name.

Korčula Town

⦿ **Sights**
1 Icon Museum...D3
2 Kanavelić Tower....................................C1
3 Large Governor's Tower B3
4 Marco Polo Museum B5
5 Marco Polo Tower................................D2
Moreška Museum ....(see 11)
6 Sea Gate Tower...................................B2
7 Small Governor's Tower B3
8 St Mark's Abbey Treasury C3
9 St Mark's Cathedral............................C2
10 Town Museum C3
11 Veliki Revelin Tower C4

⊟ **Sleeping**
12 Korčula Royal Apartments A4
13 Lešić Dimitri Palace D2

⊗ **Eating**
14 Cukarin..B5
15 Filippi...D2
16 Gradski Podrum...................................C3
17 Konoba Adio Mare D2
18 LD Terrace..D2

⦿ **Drinking & Nightlife**
19 Cocktail Bar Massimo C1
20 Vinum Bonum B5

🏃 Activities

There are some excellent biking and hiking trails around Korčula; pick up an island map from the tourist office. In the summer, water taxis offer trips to **Badija Island**, which has a 15th-century Franciscan monastery and a naturist beach.

👉 Tours

Local travel agencies can set you up on an island tour or a trip to Mljet and offer mountain biking, sea-kayaking and snorkelling trips.

🎆 Festivals & Events

A schedule of events is available at the tourist office. Holy Week celebrations are particularly elaborate in Korčula. Beginning on Palm Sunday, the entire week before Easter is devoted to ceremonies and processions organised by the local religious brotherhoods dressed in traditional costumes. The townspeople sing medieval songs and hymns, biblical events are re-enacted and the city gates are blessed. The most solemn processions are on Good Friday evening when members of all brotherhoods parade through the streets.

DUBROVNIK & SOUTHERN DALMATIA KORČULA TOWN

🛏 Sleeping

Hajduk 1963   GUESTHOUSE €
(☑ 020-711 267; www.hajduk1963.com; ul 67 br 6; r from 390KN; P ✳ 🕸 🛰 🖛) It's a couple of kilometres from town, off the road to the car ferry, but you get a warm welcome, air-con rooms with TVs and even a swimming pool. The in-house restaurant is also decent and there are a few swings for kids.

Apartments DePolo   GUESTHOUSE €
(☑ 020-711 621; tereza.depolo@du.t-com.hr; Sv Nikole 28; r from 300KN; ✳ 🕸) A great budget option, these small but attractive rooms have comfortable beds; one has a terrace with amazing views. There's a 30% surcharge in the summer for short stays.

Camping Kalac   CAMPGROUND €
(☑ 020-726 336; www.korculahotels.com; Dubrovačka 19; adult/child/site/car 60/30/60/40KN; ☺ May-Oct) The closest campground to the old town (a 20-minute walk away), Kalac has an attractive setting in a dense pine grove by a slim beach. The toilet block is serviceable and there are tennis courts, but it does get crowded in summer.

Korčula Royal Apartments   APARTMENT €€
(☑ 098 18 40 444; www.korcularoyalapartments. com; Trg Petra Šegedina 4; apt from €80; ✳ 🕸) The setting for these smart, well-equipped apartments couldn't be better, occupying an old stone villa facing a little square by the water, just outside the old town. And the Canadian-Croatian owners couldn't be more welcoming – you might even find wine and cheese awaiting your arrival.

★ Lešić Dimitri Palace   APARTMENT €€€
(☑ 020-715 560; www.lesic-dimitri.com; Don Pavla Poše 1-6; apt €480-1410; ✳ 🕸) In a class of its own, this extraordinary place has five impeccable 'residences' spread over several old mansions. All are themed after Marco Polo's travels – China, India etc – while original features (including exposed beams, stone walls and flagstones) reflect the old town setting.

Hotel Korsal   HOTEL €€€
(☑ 020-715 722; www.hotel-korsal.com; Šetalište Frana Kršinića 80; s/d from €108/180; ✳ 🕸) Near the marina, this newbie has 18 comfortable but unremarkable rooms spread between three buildings. The two older blocks have been fully renovated and have sea views, while the new one is set back behind the others and has only partial views.

✖ Eating

Cukarin   DELI €
(www.cukarin.hr; Hrvatske Bratske Zajednice bb; cakes from 10KN; ☺ 8.30am-noon & 5-7.30pm Mon-Sat) This deli-style place bakes amazing Korčulan creations such as *klašun* (walnut pastry) and *amareta* (a round cake with almonds). It also sells wine, jam and olive oil from the island.

Konoba Adio Mare   DALMATIAN €€
(☑ 020-711 253; www.konobaadiomare.hr; Sv Roka bb; mains 60-130KN; ☺ noon-11pm Mon-Sat, 5-11pm Sun) Right in the heart of the old town, this popular restaurant's covered rooftop terrace might just be the busiest place in Korčula. The menu focuses on Korčulan specialities such as *brodetto* (fish stew), *pašticada* (spicy meat stew) and beef with dumplings.

Gradski Podrum   DALMATIAN €€
(Kaporova bb; mains from 70KN; ☺ 5-11pm) Atmospheric old-town eatery worth trying for its Korčula-style fish stew.

★ LD Terrace   MEDITERRANEAN €€€
(☑ 020-601 726; www.lesic-dimitri.com; Don Pavla Poše 1-6; mains 190KN; ☺ 8am-11pm) The LD stands for Lešić Dimitri and it's no surprise that Korčula's most elegant accommodation should also have its finest restaurant. The setting is magnificent, with a chic upstairs dining room as well as romantic tables set right above the water. The modern Mediterranean menu is well matched by a fine wine list, featuring many wonderful Croatian choices.

Filippi   DALMATIAN €€€
(☑ 020-711 690; www.restaurantfilippi.com; Šetalište Petra Kanavelića bb; mains 100-190KN; ☺ noon-10pm) Upmarket Filippi has arguably the best building on the east promenade, with beautiful Renaissance windows, but on a summer's night you're going to want to nab a table under the pines overlooking the water. The menu, which focuses on traditional Korčulan fare, hits much more often than it misses.

🍷 Drinking & Nightlife

Vinum Bonum   WINE BAR
(Punta Jurana 66; ☺ 11am-2.30pm & 6pm-midnight Mon-Sat, 6pm-midnight Sun) Tucked away on a little pedestrianised lane just off the harbour, this casual place allows you to sample some of the island's best wines.

Cocktail Bar Massimo   COCKTAIL BAR
(Šetalište Petra Kanavelića; ☺ 6pm-2am May-Oct) This bar is lodged in the turret of the Zakerjan Tower and is accessible only by ladder;

MARCO POLO: ITALY VERSUS CROATIA

In 2011, nearly 700 years after his death, Marco Polo was the subject of a minor diplomatic row between Italy, Croatia and China, when former Croatian president Stjepan Mesić spoke at the opening of a museum dedicated to the explorer in Yangzhou. Mesić described Polo as a 'world explorer, born in Croatia, who opened up China to Europe'. This immediately sent the Italian media into a frenzy, accusing Croatia of the cultural theft of one of their national treasures.

While it's uncertain exactly where Marco Polo was born (both Venice and Korčula claim him), it's generally agreed that it was within the Venetian Republic. It certainly wasn't in Croatia (which was ruled by Hungary at the time and didn't include Korčula) or in Italy (which didn't even exist).

One of Korčula's historic families went by the surname Pilić (meaning 'chicken' in Croatian). It was common at the time for merchants and the aristocracy to use both Croatian and Italian versions of their names; hence Marko Pilić would become Marco Polo (*pollo* meaning chicken in Italian).

Despite the lack of proof one way or another, Korčula trumpets its Marco Polo claim stridently, so much so that there are now two Marco Polo museums in town, neither of which is particularly good.

Marco Polo Tower (Depolo bb; admission 20KN; ⊙ 9am-3pm May-Oct) Located in the skinny tower of the house that is supposed to have been his, this tiny museum has a few displays, but perhaps the real appeal of the building is its views. Climb the very steep steps for a vista over the rooftops to the sea. Note that the access staircase can be a challenge, so those with dodgy knees or young children may decide to skip it.

Marco Polo Museum (www.marcopolo.com.hr; Plokata 19 Travnja 1921 br 33; adult/child 60/30KN; ⊙ 9am-10pm) One for the kiddies, this somewhat tacky museum tells the story of Polo's extraordinary life by way of seven life-sized waxwork tableaux illustrating key scenes. Some of the commentary is a little dubious.

the drinks are brought up by pulley. Visit for the novelty and the views, not for the tacky cocktail list and certainly not for the surly service.

Dos Locos   BAR
(Šetalište Frana Kršinića 14; ⊙ 7am-1am; 🛜) A popular hang-out for young Korčulans that spills out into the street behind the bus station.

ℹ Information

Atlas Travel Agency (✆ 020-711 060; www.atlas-korcula.com; Plokata 19 Travnja 1921 bb) Represents American Express, runs excursions and books private accommodation.

Health Centre (Dom Zdravlja; ✆ 020-711 137; www.dom-zdravlja-korcula.hr; ul 57 br 5)

Post Office (www.posta.hr; Trg Kralja Tomislava 24; ⊙ 7am-9pm Mon-Sat Jul & Aug, 7am-8pm Mon-Fri, 8am-1pm Sat Sep-Jun)

Tourist Office (✆ 020-715 701; www.visitkorcula.eu; Obala Franje Tuđmana 4; ⊙ 8am-8pm Mon-Sat, 9am-1pm Sun Jul & Aug, 8am-3pm & 5-8pm Mon-Sat, 9am-1pm Sun May, Jun & Sep, 8am-3pm Mon-Fri, 8am-noon Sat Oct-Apr) An excellent source of information.

ℹ Getting There & Away

While smaller ferries stop in the West Harbour, the main car ferry terminal is 3km east of town. Taxis from the terminal are expensive (around 80KN). There's a **Jadrolinija Office** (✆ 020-715 410; Plokata 19 Travnja 1921 br 19) just outside the old town.

The bus station is on Obala Korčulanskih Brodograditelja, right by the marina and only 200m from the old town. Regular buses head to/from Lumbarda (15KN, 15 minutes, four to 10 daily) and Vela Luka (from 30KN, one hour, seven daily).

Lumbarda
POP 1220

Surrounded by vineyards and coves, Lumbarda is a laid-back town set around a harbour on the southeastern end of Korčula Island. The sandy soil is perfect for vineyards, and wine from the *grk* grape is Lumbarda's most famous product. In the 16th century, aristocrats from Korčula built summer houses here, and it remains a quieter retreat from the more urbanised Korčula Town. The town beaches are small but sandy. A good beach,

Plaza Pržina, is on the other side of the vineyards beyond the supermarket.

🛏 Sleeping & Eating

There are several small, inexpensive campgrounds up the hill from the bus stop.

Pansion Marinka   GUESTHOUSE €€
(📞098 344 712; www.bire.hr; Lumbarda 261; r/apt from 500/600KN; ⊗May-Nov) On the outskirts of Lumbarda, this working farm and vineyard rents simple rooms and apartments. The owners produce excellent wines, olive oil and cheese, and catch and smoke their own fish.

Agroturizam Zure   APARTMENT, DALMATIAN €€
(📞020-712 008; www.zure.hr; Lumbarda 239; apt from 610KN; ⊗May-Nov; 🅿⊛) *Grk* and *plavac mali* wines, liqueurs, olive oil, vegetables, cheese and dried ham are produced at this family-run farm, and the owners also catch fish on an almost daily basis. If you want to experience a slice of this self-sufficient lifestyle, book one of the two well-equipped apartments, or stop by for a meal (mains from 70KN).

ℹ Information

Post Office (www.posta.hr; Lumbarda 546; ⊗8am-noon & 5-8pm Mon-Fri Jul & Aug, 8-11am Mon-Fri Sep-Jun)
Tourist Office (📞020-712 005; www.tz-lumbarda.hr; ⊗8am-7pm Mon-Sat, 8am-noon & 3-7pm Sun mid-Jun–Aug, reduced hours rest of year)

ℹ Getting There & Away

In Korčula Town, water taxis wait around the eastern port for passengers to Lumbarda.

In summer, around 10 buses run to/from Korčula Town (15KN, 15 minutes) from Monday to Saturday, dropping to four on Sundays.

Vela Luka

POP 4140

Vela Luka, close to the western tip of Korčula, is a pretty little port set in a lovely natural harbour. There are coves for swimming but no beaches around town. Small boats can take you to the idyllic islands of Proizd and Osjak.

Vela Luka is surrounded by hills covered with olive trees, and the production and marketing of Korčula's famous olive oil is vital to the local economy. Tourism and fishing are the other main employers.

◉ Sights & Activities

Vela Luka's harbourfront is a pleasant place for a stroll, with a few sculptures and mosa-ics scattered about. **Gradina**, 5km northwest of Vela Luka, is a peaceful bay very popular with yachties. There are no beaches at Gradina but there's decent swimming in very shallow water and a popular restaurant. You'll need your own wheels (or sails) to reach it.

Vela Spila   CAVE
(www.velaspila.hr; admission 10KN; ⊗4-8pm Mon-Sat) Spacious enough to make cave-dwelling seem like a viable accommodation option, this large domed cavern, high on a cliff above the harbour, has been continuously occupied since the last ice age – about 18,000 years. It's open to the sky, so even the most claustrophobic shouldn't baulk at visiting. There's not actually an awful lot to see here, but information panels (in English and Croatian) explain the ongoing archaeological work taking place.

🛏 Sleeping

Mindel   CAMPGROUND €
(📞020-813 600; www.mindel.hr; Stani 192; adult/child/tent/car 30/15/25/25KN; ⊗May-Oct; 🅿) Set in an olive grove 5km north of town, this compact, inexpensive, friendly site is an ideal base for country walks; the beach is a 10-minute stroll. There's no bus service here.

Hotel Korkyra   HOTEL €€€
(📞020-601 000; www.hotel-korkyra.com; Obala 3 br 21; s/d €76/120; ⊛🔊⊛) The thorough refurb of this hotel has seriously upped accommodation standards in Vela Luka. The 58 rooms are finished to a very high standard, and have hip, contemporary decor and modish bathrooms. There's a fitness room with bay views, an outdoor pool at the rear and a good restaurant.

ℹ Information

Atlas Travel Agency (📞020-812 078; www.atlas.com.hr; Obala 3 br 21) On the quay near Hotel Korkyra; rents private accommodation and offers internet access.
Post Office (www.posta.hr; Obala 2 br 1; ⊗8am-9pm Mon-Fri, 8-noon & 6-9pm Sat Jul & Aug, 7.30am-5pm Mon-Fri, 8am-noon Sat Sep-Jun)
Tourist Office (📞020-813 619; www.tzvelaluka.hr; Obala 3 br 19; ⊗8am-2.30pm & 5.30-8pm Mon-Fri, 8am-12.30pm Sat Jun-Sep, 8am-3pm Mon-Fri Oct-May) Right on the waterfront, with helpful staff.

ℹ Getting There & Away

Seven buses head to/from Korčula Town daily (from 30KN, one hour).

Understand Croatia

CROATIA TODAY...........................286
Despite recently joining the European Union, Croatia is still struggling to heal its ailing economy.

HISTORY 288
The country's long and complex backstory plays a surprisingly large role in the Croatia of today.

THE CROATIAN MINDSET....................303
Meet the Croats: a religious, style-conscious, sports-mad people.

THE CUISINE...............................308
With its truffle hunting, wild asparagus, slow food and fine local wine, Croatia is a foodie's delight.

ARCHITECTURE IN CROATIA.................314
Almost the entire history of European architecture is on display in this compact country.

THE NATURAL ENVIRONMENT 316
Learn about Croatia's critters, karst and national parks, and get the low-down on current challenges.

THE ARTS 319
The arts are a cherished aspect of Croatian life; learn all about the traditional and the contemporary.

Croatia Today

Tourism may be booming, but a short time on from entering the European Union (EU), Croatia's economy remains in a sickly state. For nigh on a thousand years Croatia's fortunes were at the mercy of decisions made in Budapest or Venice or Vienna or Belgrade. Now, with control over its own destiny and no one left to blame, the road to recovery looks like it's going to be a bumpy one.

Best in Print

Black Lamb and Grey Falcon (Rebecca West; 1941) Recounts the writer's journeys through the Balkans in 1941.
The Fall of Yugoslavia (Misha Glenny; 1992)
A Paper House (Mark Thompson; 1992)
Cafe Europa – Life After Communism (Slavenka Drakulić; 1996) Wittily details the infiltration of Western culture into Eastern Europe.
The Death of Yugoslavia (Laura Silber and Allan Little; 1996)
Another Fool in the Balkans (Tony White; 2006) White retraces Rebecca West's journey, juxtaposing the region's modern life with its political history.
Croatia: A Nation Forged in War (Marcus Tanner; 3rd edition 2010)

Best on Film

You Only Love Once (*Samo jednom se ljubi*; 1981) Rajko Grlić
Cyclops (*Kiklop*; 1982) Antun Vrdoljak
How the War Started on My Island (*Kako je počeo rat na mom otoku*; 1996) Vinko Brešan
Number 55 (*Broj 55*; 2014) Kristijan Milić
Happily Ever After (2014) Tatjana Bozić

Brand New to the European Union

With the war behind them and their independence won, Croats ticked off another milestone in July 2013 when they formally joined the EU. In January 2012 about 44% of Croats turned up to vote in the referendum on the EU accession, which passed by a margin of two to one. Yet a great deal of scepticism towards the benefits of the move remained, particularly amongst the younger generation.

A short time on, there's certainly been little cause for that scepticism to dissipate, as Croatia heads into its sixth year in recession with the highest unemployment rate in the EU. It's estimated that economic output has decreased by 13% since 2008 and that one in five people is out of a job (for young people, that figure is closer to 50%).

Following on from the global financial crisis and the European debt crisis, it's not surprising that the hoped-for increase in foreign investment (such as that experienced by Bulgaria and Romania when they joined the EU in 2007) never eventuated. In fact, it's estimated that foreign investment has decreased by 60% since Croatia joined the EU. Factors such as an unfriendly business culture filled with bureaucracy and red tape have been cited as possible reasons for the decline.

At the same time, Croatia's farmers and manufacturers no longer enjoy the customs exemptions that were in place with their former Yugoslav neighbours, while also facing stiffer competition from imports from other EU states.

Croatia's budget deficit is high and public debt now stands at 68% of gross domestic product (GDP). Some pundits have been calling on the government to cut what they see as a bloated public sector, which employs more than 400,000 people. Yet others argue that such cut-backs in the midst of a recession would only increase unemployment and would ultimately be counterproductive. Certainly they would be deeply unpopular.

Even for those people with work, there's no guarantee of actually getting paid. It's estimated that in 2014 more than 5400 companies were withholding more than one month's pay from their employees, most of whom have little option but to keep working.

Many also decry the effect that foreign companies are having on the traditional southern Mediterranean way of life. Early starts and early finishes in time for big family lunches and afternoon siestas are slowly but surely fading away.

The Tourism Juggle

In the face of all this gloom, tourism is continuing to boom. In 2013 nearly 13 million travellers visited Croatia, and the industry now generates around 15% of the country's GDP, bringing in €7.2 billion annually. Despite this, Croatia hasn't completely given in to mass tourism. The 'Mediterranean as it Once Was' motto of Croatia's tourist board may seem a little overblown in popular destinations where development has taken a firm hold, but pockets of authentic culture remain and there's still plenty to discover off the grid.

The Croatian government hopes to double tourism revenue by 2020 and create 32,000 new jobs in the process. The challenge will be to develop the industry while preserving the natural and cultural assets that make Croatia such an appealing destination. Locals are keen to avoid the overdevelopment so evident in other parts of the Mediterranean, such as Spain's Costa Brava. Development is currently subject to strict regulations, and there are 444 specially protected areas in the country, including eight national parks.

Dubrovnik's Old Town is already full to bursting in the peak season, so much so that lanes have to be erected at the Pile Gate to funnel people in and out. A congestion charge has been mooted, although it would surely need to be quite substantial for it to dissuade people from visiting such an extraordinary place.

Part of the problem is the proliferation of cruise ships, whose passenger numbers are now four times higher than they were a decade ago. Dubrovnik enforces a limit of 8000 passengers per day outside of the peak season, and while this brings plenty of money into the local economy, it's estimated that land-based visitors spend three times as much per day and stay for much longer. It will be important to ensure that the huge numbers of the former don't start to put off the latter.

Many of these problems would be solved if tourists could be encouraged to visit outside of the peak season and to move on from the coast to the beauty spots of the interior, particularly in Zagorje and Slavonia.

POPULATION: **4.3 MILLION**

GDP PER CAPITA: **US$14,800**

GDP GROWTH: **-0.8%**

INFLATION: **2.2%**

UNEMPLOYMENT: **21.6%**

LITERACY RATE: **98.9%**

population per sq km

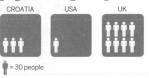

CROATIA   USA   UK

= 30 people

religious groups
(% of population)

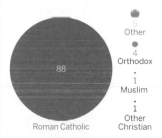

Other

4
Orthodox

1
Muslim

1
Other
Christian

88

Roman Catholic

if Croatia were 100 people

90 would be Croat
6 would be Other
4 would be Serb

History

Trampled over by invading armies, passed back and forth between empires, split up then put back together again in various different shapes: Croatia's history is more convoluted than most. In this part of the world, echoes of the past are ever-present, both in the built environment and as the subtext to any serious discussion about the present – not to mention the future.

Early Inhabitants

Around 30,000 years ago, Croatia was the haunt of Neanderthals (an early human species), who roamed through the hills of Slavonia. The Croatian Natural History Museum in Zagreb displays relics of this distant era, and the Museum of the Krapina Neanderthal in Krapina offers a faithful picture of Neanderthal life. By the end of the last ice age (around 18,000 years ago) modern humans were living in places such as the Vela Spila cave on the island of Korčula.

By around 1000 BC, the Illyrians took centre stage in the area now comprised of Slovenia, Croatia, Serbia, Kosovo, Montenegro and Albania. It's thought that the modern Albanian language, a linguistic oddity unrelated to any other language, is derived from ancient Illyrian. The often-warring tribes erected hill forts and created distinctive jewellery made from amber and bronze. In time they established a loose federation of tribes.

The Illyrians had to contend with the Greeks, who established trading colonies on the Adriatic coast at Epidaurus and Korčula in the 6th century BC, and on the islands of Vis and Hvar in the 4th century BC. In the meantime Celts were pushing down from the north.

In the rd 3century BC, Queen Teuta of the Illyrian Ardiaei tribe committed a fatal tactical error in seeking to conquer various Greek colonies. The put-upon Greeks asked the Romans for military support. The Romans pushed their way into the region and by 168 BC they defeated Gentius, the last Illyrian king. And so, gradually, the Illyrians were Latinised.

The word Adriatic is thought to be linked to the ancient Etruscan town of Adria, near Venice, but may also be related to the Illyrian word for water.

TIMELINE	6th century BC	4th century BC	229 BC
	Greek colonies are founded on the island of Korčula and at Epidaurus (modern-day Cavtat, south of Dubrovnik), within an area already populated by people the Greeks refer to as Ilyrians.	Illyrian tribes such as the Histri (the old name of Istria) and the Liburnians achieve supremacy in the Balkans, founding several kingdoms and establishing themselves as maritime powers.	Rome goes to war against Illyrian queen Teuta, at the behest of the Greeks who were being harried by state-sponsored Illyrian pirates. Following her defeat, the Illyrians pay annual tributes to Rome.

When in Rome

Following the fall of Gentius, the southern part of Illyria officially became an independent Roman protectorate known as Illyricum. It later became a Roman province and was enlarged as Rome pushed north in what was known as the Pannonian Wars. In AD 9, Illyricum was split into two separate Roman provinces: Pannonia (present-day Slovenia, northern Croatia and Bosnia, and bits of Austria, Slovakia, Hungary and Serbia) and Dalmatia (the rest of modern-day Croatia and Bosnia, Montenegro, and bits of Albania and Serbia).

Roman rule centred on the administrative headquarters of Salona (now Solin, near Split). It eventually brought peace and prosperity to the region, and cities such as Iader (Zadar), Felix Arba (Rab Town), Curicum (Krk Town), Tarsaticae (Rijeka), Parentium (Poreč), Polensium (Pula) and Siscia (Sisak) gained all the cultural accoutrements of Roman life, such as temples, baths and amphitheatres. The Romans built a series of roads reaching to the Aegean and Black Seas and the Danube, facilitating trade and the expansion of Roman culture. The roads also accelerated the later spread of Christianity.

These provinces even produced important figures in Roman history. Diocletian was born near Salona around AD 244 and distinguished himself as a military commander before becoming emperor in 285. As ruler, Diocletian attempted to simplify the unwieldy empire by dividing it into two administrative halves, thus sowing the seeds for the later division into the Eastern and Western Roman Empires. He is also remembered as a great persecutor of the Christians. In 305 he retired to the grand seaside palace he had built for himself near where he was born. Today, Diocletian's Palace is Croatia's greatest Roman remnant, forming the heart of the old town of Split. The Christians eventually had the last laugh, turfing the deceased emperor out of his mausoleum and converting it into a cathedral.

Christianity reached this region in its very earliest days. In the Bible, St Paul talks of preaching in Illyricum in his letter to the Romans (written in about AD 56), while his second letter to Timothy states that St Titus is in Dalmatia. Early Christian catacombs can be found under the Serbian Orthodox Monastery in Krka National Park, and local lore states that Titus and possibly even Paul himself visited the community here. In 313, only two years after Diocletian's death, the Emperor Constantine decriminalised Christianity, and in 380 it became the only tolerated religion under Theodosius the Great.

Theodosius was the last Roman leader to rule a united empire. On his death in AD 395, the empire was formally divided into eastern and western realms. The dividing line fell down the middle of present-day

Best Roman Ruins

....

Diocletian's Palace in Split, Central Dalmatia

....

Salona/Solin on the outskirts of Split

....

Arena in Pula, Istria

HISTORY WHEN IN ROME

168 BC	27 BC	11 BC	AD 9
The last Illyrian king, Gentius, is defeated by the Romans near his capital Shkodra (present-day Albania), and Rome takes control over all of Dalmatia.	After nearly 500 years, the Roman Republic officially becomes the Roman Empire when Octavian is granted extraordinary powers and takes on the name Augustus.	The Roman province of Illyricum, covering present-day Dalmatia, is extended to the Danube after the defeat of Pannonian tribes. The new province takes in all of modern-day Croatia except Istria.	Illyricum is split into two provinces: Dalmatia to the south and Pannonia to the north. What we now call Croatia is split between the two.

Montenegro, leaving present-day Croatia in the western half and Serbia in the east. The eastern half became the Byzantine Empire, which persisted until 1453. The Western Roman Empire fell in 476, following invasions by various 'barbarian' tribes, such as the Visigoths, Huns and Lombards. The Goths took control of Dalmatia until 535 when the Byzantine Emperor Justinian booted them out.

Hello Slavs, Adios Avars

While the Croats are clearly related to other Slavic nations, the name by which they know themselves – Hrvat – is not a Slavic word. One theory posits that Hrvat is a Persian word, and the Croats are a Slavic tribe who were briefly ruled – and named – by a ruling cast of Persian-speaking Alans from Central Asia.

In the wake of the collapse of the Western Roman Empire, various Slavic tribes headed south from their original territory north of the Carpathians. Around the same time, the Avars (a nomadic Central Asian people known for their brutality) were sallying around the Balkan fringes of the Byzantine Empire. The Avars ravaged the former Roman towns of Salona and Epidaurus, whose inhabitants took refuge in Diocletian's Palace and Ragusa (Dubrovnik), respectively. They then progressed all the way to the mighty Byzantine capital of Constantinople itself (present-day Istanbul), where the Byzantines duly crushed them and they faded into history (to 'die away like Avars' is a common Balkan saying).

Controversy surrounds the role that the Slavs had in the defeat of the Avars. Some claim that Byzantium called on the Slavs to help in the fight against the Avar assault, while others think that they merely filled the void left when the Avars disappeared. Whatever the case, the Slavs spread rapidly through the Balkans, reaching the Adriatic by the early 7th century.

Two closely related Slavic tribes settled along the Adriatic Coast and its hinterland: the Croats and the Serbs. The Croats settled in an area roughly equivalent to present-day Croatia and Bosnia. By the 8th century, they had formed two powerful tribal entities, each led by a *knez* (duke). The Duchy of Croatia included most of present-day Dalmatia, parts of Montenegro and western Bosnia, while the Duchy of Pannonia included present-day Slavonia, Zagorje and the area around Zagreb. The Byzantines maintained control of several coastal cities, including Zadar, Split and Dubrovnik, as well as the islands of Hvar and Krk.

Christianity & the Croat Kings

Charlemagne's Franks gradually encroached on central Europe from the west and in AD 800 they seized Dalmatia, baptising the previously pagan Croats en masse. After Charlemagne's death in AD 814, the Pannonian Croats revolted unsuccessfully against Frankish rule, without the support of the Dalmatian Croats, whose major coastal cities remained under the influence of the Byzantine Empire. The big breakthrough for the Croats happened when Duke Branimir revolted against Byzantine control and won recognition from Pope John VIII. This brought them

257	395	614	800
The city of Salona becomes the first diocese in Roman Dalmatia, thus creating a toehold for Catholicism in the region; within 30 years the Bishop of Salona had become pope.	After Theodosius the Great dies, the Roman Empire is split in two. Slovenia, Croatia and Bosnia fall into the Western Roman Empire, with Serbia, Kosovo and Macedonia in the Byzantine Empire.	Central Asian marauders, the Avars, sack Salona and Epidaurus. Some contend that the Croats followed in their wake; others that they were invited by Emperor Heraclius to fend off the Avars.	The Franks, led by King Charlemagne, seize control of Dalmatia and forcibly baptise the pagan Croats. The Byzantines recognise Frankish rule but retain control of several key coastal cities.

closer to the Vatican, and Catholicism became a defining feature of Croatian national identity.

Trpimir, who was *knez* from 845 to 864, is widely considered to have founded the first Croatian dynasty, but it was his grandson Tomislav who first crowned himself *kralj* (king) in 925, and united Pannonia and Dalmatia. His kingdom included virtually all of modern Croatia as well as parts of Bosnia and the coast of Montenegro.

But the glory days were not to last. During the 11th century, the Serbs, Byzantines and Venetians imposed themselves on the Dalmatian coast, and new adversaries, the Hungarians, emerged in the north and advanced into Pannonia. Krešimir IV (r 1058–74) turned the tables and regained control of Dalmatia but Croatia's rebound was only temporary and Krešimir was succeeded by Zvonimir and Stjepan, neither of whom produced an heir. Seeing an opportunity, the Hungarian King Laszlo claimed the throne by virtue of being the brother of Zvonimir's widow, Queen Jelena. He managed to take control of a large area of northern Croatia but died before he could cement his claims in the south.

Covetous Neighbours: Hungary versus Venice

Laszlo's brother Koloman succeeded him to the Hungarian throne and continued in his drive to take the Croatian throne as well. In 1097 he defeated his rival claimant Petar Svačić, thus ending the era of native-born Croat kings. In 1102 he imposed the *Pacta conventa,* ostensibly stating that Hungary and Croatia were separate entities under a single – Hungarian – monarchy. In practice, while Croatia maintained a *ban* (viceroy or governor) and a *sabor* (parliament), the Hungarians steadily

Dalmatian dogs are thought to be one of the oldest breeds, but there's no conclusive evidence that they originated in Dalmatia. Some experts believe the dogs may have been brought to Dalmatia by the Roma.

THE VENETIAN YOKE

For nearly 800 years the doges of Venice sought to control, colonise and exploit the Croatian coast. Coastal and island towns from Rovinj in the north to Korčula in the south still show a marked Venetian influence in architecture, cuisine and culture. However, as in Venice's other dominions, the period was not a happy time.

Venetian rule in Dalmatia and Istria was a record of virtually unbroken economic exploitation. The Venetians systematically denuded the landscape in order to provide timber for their ships. State monopolies set artificially low prices for olive oil, figs, wine, fish and salt, thus ensuring cheap commodities for Venetian buyers, while local merchants and producers were impoverished. Shipbuilding was effectively banned, since Venice tolerated no competition with its own ships. No roads or schools were built, and no investment was made in local industry.

845–64	869	910–28	1000
Trpimir establishes Croatia's first royal line. He fights and defeats the powerful Bulgarian state, and inflicts major defeats on the Byzantines. Croatian territory expands well into what is now Bosnia.	At the behest of Byzantium, Macedonian monks Methodius and Cyril create the Glagolitic alphabet, specifically with a view to speeding the spread of Christianity among the Slavic peoples.	Tomislav proclaims himself king while expanding territory at the expense of the Hungarians and defeating Bulgarian Tsar Simeon in modern Bosnia. Tomislav unites Pannonian and Dalmatian Croats.	Venice capitalises on a lack of stability in Croatia to begin encroaching on the Dalmatian coast. So begins the tussle between Venice and other powers for control of Dalmatia.

marginalised the Croatian nobility. Under Hungarian rule, Pannonia became known as Slavonia, and the interior towns of Zagreb, Vukovar and Varaždin became thriving centres of trade and culture. In 1107, Koloman persuaded the Dalmatian nobility to bring the coast, long coveted by land-locked Hungarian kings, into his realm.

Upon Koloman's death in 1116, Venice launched new assaults on Biograd and the islands of Lošinj, Pag, Rab and Krk. Meanwhile, Zadar had grown to become the largest and most prosperous Dalmatian city and had successfully fended off two Venetian naval expeditions in the 1190s. But in 1202 a vengeful Venetian doge paid the soldiers of the Fourth Crusade to sack Zadar, despite Pope Innocent III specifically banning the crusaders from attacking Christian states. After this they rumbled on to brutally sack Constantinople, the great bastion of Eastern Christianity.

The Mongolian juggernaut ravaged the Croatian interior in 1242, but not before King Bela IV of Hungary fled the onslaught and took refuge in Trogir. The Venetians used the chaos to consolidate their hold on Zadar, and upon the death of King Bela in 1270, added Šibenik and Trogir to their possessions.

King Ludovic (Louis) I of Hungary (r 1342–82) re-established control over the country and even persuaded Venice to relinquish Dalmatia. But new conflicts emerged upon his death. The Croatian nobility rallied around Ladislas of Naples, who was crowned king in Zadar in 1403. Short of funds, Ladislas sold Zadar to Venice in 1409 for a paltry 100,000 ducats and renounced his rights to Dalmatia. In the early 15th century, Venice strengthened its grip on the Dalmatian coastline south from Zadar and remained in control until the Napoleonic invasion of 1797. Only the wily citizens of Ragusa managed to retain their independence.

The Ottoman Onslaught

Croatia had plenty to contend with as Venetians, Hungarians and others picked at the remnants of the original Croatian state, yet another threat loomed from the east. The Ottoman Turks had emerged out of Anatolia in the early 14th century and rapidly swallowed up the Balkans.

The Serbs were rolled at Kosovo Polje in 1389, a hastily choreographed anti-Turkish crusade was garrotted in Hungary in 1396, and Bosnia was despatched in 1463. When the Croatian nobility finally faced up to the Ottomans in 1493 in Krbavsko Polje, they too were pummelled.

Despite a sudden show of unity among the remaining noble families, one city after another fell to the Ottoman sultans. The important bishopric at Zagreb heavily fortified the cathedral in Kaptol, which remained untouched, but the gateway town of Knin fell in 1521. Five years later, the Ottomans engaged the Hungarians in Mohács. Again the Turks won and the Hungarian army was destroyed. The Turks threatened the Adriatic

Best Gothic Buildings

St James' Cathedral, Šibenik

St Mark's Cathedral, Korčula

St Anastasia's Cathedral, Zadar

Cathedral of the Assumption of the Blessed Virgin Mary, Zagreb

1058–74	1091–1102	1242	1300s
Soon after the 1054 split of the church into Orthodox and Catholic strands, the pope recognises Krešimir IV as king of Dalmatia and Croatia. This places Croatia within the Catholic sphere.	Hungarian King Laszlo, related to the late King Zvonimir, claims the Croatian throne; his successor, Koloman, defeats the last Croatian king and cements Hungarian control of Croatia with the *Pacta conventa*.	The Mongols devastate the royal houses of Hungary and Croatia. The noble Šubić and Frankopan families step in to assume a degree of political and economic power that persists for centuries.	The Hungarian Anjou dynasty under Carl (Charles) and Ludovic (Louis) reasserts royal authority in Croatia and seeks to expel the Venetians who had taken Dalmatian territory.

coast but never actually captured it, while Ragusa maintained its independence throughout the turmoil.

Turkish assaults on the Balkans caused massive havoc. Cities and towns were destroyed, people were enslaved and commandeered to the Ottoman war machine, and refugees scattered around the region.

Enter the Habsburgs

With the Hungarians out of the picture, the Croats turned to the Austrians for protection. The Habsburg Empire, ruled from Vienna, duly absorbed a narrow strip of territory around Zagreb, Karlovac and Varaždin. The Habsburgs sought to build a buffer against the Ottomans, creating the Vojna Krajina (Military Frontier). In this region composed of a string of forts south of Zagreb, a standing army comprised largely of Vlachs and Serbs faced down the Ottomans.

Exactly a century after their defeat by the Ottomans, the Croats managed to turn the tables on the Turks. At Sisak in 1593 the Habsburg army, including Croat soldiers, finally inflicted a defeat on the Ottomans. In 1699 in Sremski Karlovci the Ottomans sued for peace for the first time, and the Turkish stranglehold on central Europe was loosened. Bosnia remained within the Ottoman Empire but Venice regained the coast, apart from a thin strip of land around Neum that gave the Ottoman's access to the Adriatic and provided a buffer between the territories of Venice and Ragusa.

The Habsburgs reclaimed Slavonia soon after, thus expanding the Krajina. This period saw a return to stability and advances in agricultural production, but Croatian culture and language languished.

> The neck tie is a descendant of the cravat, which originated in Croatia as part of military attire and was adopted by the French in the 17th century. The name 'cravat' is a corruption of both Croat and Hrvat.

THE REPUBLIC OF RAGUSA

While most of the Dalmatian coast struggled under Venetian rule, Ragusa (now Dubrovnik) led a charmed life, existing as a republic in its own right. A ruling class, abounding in business acumen and diplomatic skill, ensured that this minuscule city-state punched well above its weight and played a significant role in the immediate region and beyond.

The Ragusans asked the pope for permission to trade with the Turks in 1371 and subsequently established trade centres throughout the Ottoman Empire. Burgeoning trade led to a flowering in the arts and sciences. The Ragusans, once described as 'mild and noble', were extremely liberal for the time, abolishing the slave trade in the 15th century. They were also scientifically advanced, establishing a system of quarantine in 1377.

However, the Ragusans had to maintain a perilous position sandwiched between Ottoman and Venetian interests. An earthquake in 1667 caused a great deal of damage, from which they never fully recovered, and Napoleon finally swallowed up the republic in 1808.

1358	1409	1493	1526–27
Ragusa (modern Dubrovnik) frees itself of Venice and becomes an independent city republic. It grows to become an advanced and liberal society, while cannily fending off Venetians and Ottomans.	Ladislas of Naples assumes the Croatian throne but is scared off by dynastic squabbling and sells Dalmatia to Venice for 100,000 ducats. Venetian control soon extends from Zadar to Ragusa.	At Krbavsko Polje a joint Croatian-Hungarian army engages the Turks but is obliterated, leaving Croatia open to Turkish raids. The Turkish advance brings turmoil, as populations flee and famine ensues.	The Battle of Mohács sees the Ottoman Turks annihilate the Hungarian nobility, ending Hungarian control of Croatia. Hungarian King Louis dies heirless, allowing the Austrian Habsburgs control.

Napoleon & the Illyrian Provinces

Šibenik-born Faust Vrančić (1551–1617) made the first working parachute.

Habsburg support for the restoration of the French monarchy provoked Napoleon to invade the Italian states in 1796. After conquering Venice in 1797 he agreed to transfer Dalmatia to Austria in the Treaty of Campo Formio in exchange for other concessions. The Croats' secret hopes that Dalmatia would be united with Slavonia were soon dashed, as the Habsburgs made it clear that the two territories would retain separate administrations.

Austrian control of Dalmatia only lasted until Napoleon's 1805 victory over Austrian and Prussian forces at Austerlitz, which forced Austria to cede the Dalmatian coast to France. Ragusa quickly surrendered to French forces, which also swallowed up the Bay of Kotor in present-day Montenegro. Napoleon renamed his conquest the 'Illyrian provinces' and moved swiftly to reform the neglected territory. A tree-planting program was implemented to reforest the barren hills. Roads and hospitals were built and new crops introduced. Since almost the entire population was illiterate, the new government set up primary schools, high schools and a college at Zadar. Yet the French regime remained unpopular.

After Napoleon's Russian campaign and the fall of his empire, the 1815 Congress of Vienna recognised Austria's claims to Dalmatia and placed the rest of Croatia under the jurisdiction of Austria's Hungarian province. For the Dalmatians the new regime meant a return to the status quo, since the Austrians restored the former Italian elite to power, whereas the Hungarians imposed the Hungarian language and culture on the northern Croatian population.

A South Slavic Consciousness

Croatia Through History (2007) by Branka Magaš is a highly detailed doorstop of a history, focusing on pivotal events and clearly delineating the gradual development of Croatian national identity.

Traditionally, upper-class Dalmatians spoke Italian, and the northern Croatian nobility spoke German or Hungarian, but flush with the Enlightenment fervour, Napoleon had sown the seeds of creating a south Slavic consciousness. This sense of a shared identity eventually manifested itself in an 'Illyrian' movement in the 1830s, which centred on the revival of the Croatian language. Napoleon's grand plan was to foster Serbian culture, too, but Serbia remained under Ottoman occupation.

The establishment of the first Illyrian newspaper in 1834, written in the Zagreb dialect, prompted the Croatian *sabor* to call for the teaching of Slavic languages in schools.

Following the 1848 revolution in Paris, the Hungarians began to press for change within the Habsburg Empire. The Croats saw this as an opportunity to regain some control and unify Dalmatia, the Krajina and Slavonia. The Habsburgs paid lip service to Croatian sentiments and appointed Josip Jelačić *ban* (viceroy or governor) of Croatia. Jelačić

1537–40	1593	1671	1699
The Turks take Klis, the last Croatian bastion in Dalmatia. The Turkish advance continues to Sisak, just south of Zagreb. For reasons unknown, the Turks never push on to Zagreb.	At Sisak, previously the Ottoman high-tide mark, the Habsburgs inflict the first major defeat on the Ottomans, thus prefiguring the long, slow Turkish retreat from central Europe.	A deputation led by Franjo Frankopan and Petar Zrinski, with the aim of ridding Croatia of Hungarian domination, is cut short. Both are hanged, their lands confiscated by the Habsburgs.	At the Treaty of Karlovci, the Ottomans renounce all claims to Croatia. Venice and Hungary reclaim all freed lands over the next 20 years.

promptly called elections, claimed a mandate and declared war on Hungarian agitators in order to curry favour with the Habsburgs, but his demands for autonomy fell on deaf ears. Jelačić is immortalised in a martial pose in the heart of Zagreb.

Disillusionment spread after 1848, and amplified after the birth of the Austro-Hungarian Dual Monarchy in 1867. The monarchy placed northern Croatia and Slavonia within the Hungarian administration, while Dalmatia remained within Austria. Whatever limited form of self-government the Croats enjoyed under the Habsburgs disappeared.

Dreams of Yugoslavia

The river of discontent forked into two streams that dominated the political landscape for the next century. The old 'Illyrian' movement became the National Party, dominated by Bishop Josip Juraj Strossmayer. Strossmayer believed that the Habsburgs and the Hungarians set out to emphasise the differences between Serbs and Croats, and that only through Jugoslavenstvo (literally, 'Southslavism' – or south Slavic unity) could the aspirations of both peoples be realised. Strossmayer supported the independence struggle in Serbia but favoured a Yugoslav (ie south Slavic) entity within the Austro-Hungarian Empire rather than complete independence.

By contrast, the Party of Rights, led by the militantly anti-Serb Ante Starčević, envisaged an independent Croatia made up of Slavonia, Dalmatia, the Krajina, Slovenia, Istria, and part of Bosnia and Hercegovina. At the same time, the Orthodox Church was encouraging the Serbs to form a national identity based upon their religion. Until the 19th century, Orthodox inhabitants of Croatia identified themselves as Vlachs, Morlachs, Serbs, Orthodox or even Greeks. With the help of Starčević's attacks, the sense of a separate Serbian Orthodox identity within Croatia developed.

Under the 'divide and rule' theory, the Hungarian-appointed ban of Croatia blatantly favoured the Serbs and the Orthodox Church, but his strategy backfired. The first organised resistance formed in Dalmatia. Croats in Rijeka and Serbs in Zadar joined together in 1905 to demand the unification of Dalmatia and Slavonia, with a formal guarantee of Serbian equality as a nation. The spirit of unity mushroomed, and by 1906 Croat–Serb coalitions had taken over local government in Dalmatia and Slavonia, forming a serious threat to the Hungarian power structure.

WWI & the First Yugoslavia

With the outbreak of WWI, Croatia's future was again up for grabs. Sensing that they would once again be pawns to the Great Powers, a Croatian delegation called the 'Yugoslav Committee' talked the Serbian

Dubrovnik: A History (2003) by Robin Harris is a thoughtful and thorough look at the great city, investigating events, individuals and movements that have contributed to the architectural and cultural fabric of the 'pearl of the Adriatic'.

1780s	1797–1815	1830–50	1867
The Habsburgs begin a process of Germanisation, ordering all administration be conducted in German. This leads to rising nationalist feelings among the Habsburg's non-German subjects.	Napoleon brings the Venetian Republic to an end; Venetian dominions are initially given to the Habsburgs, but in 1806 Napoleon gains the Adriatic coast, which he dubs the 'Illyrian provinces'.	The south Slavic consciousness is awakened, aiming to reverse the processes of Hungarianisation and Germanisation under the Habsburgs. An offshoot is the Croatian National Revival.	The Habsburg throne devolves to become the Austro-Hungarian Dual Monarchy. Croatian territory is divided between them: Dalmatia is awarded to Austria, and Slavonia is under Hungarian control.

FINGERPRINTS

government into establishing a parliamentary monarchy that would rule over the two countries. Although many Croats were unclear about Serbian intentions, they were sure about Italian intentions, since Italy lost no time in seizing Pula, Rijeka and Zadar after the war. Effectively given a choice between throwing in their lot with Italy or Serbia, the Croats chose Serbia.

The Yugoslav Committee became the National Council of Slovenes, Croats and Serbs after the collapse of the Austro-Hungarian Empire in 1918. The council quickly negotiated the establishment of the Kingdom of Serbs, Croats and Slovenes to be based in Belgrade (the unwieldy name was changed to the Kingdom of Yugoslavia in 1929). The previously independent kingdom of Montenegro was also subsumed into the new entity. Montenegro's King Nikola had escaped to France during the war, and France refused to allow him to leave, thus ending the 300-year-old Petrović dynasty.

Problems with the kingdom began almost immediately. As under the Habsburgs, the Croats enjoyed scant autonomy. Currency reforms benefited Serbs at the expense of the Croats. A treaty between Yugoslavia and Italy gave Istria, Zadar and several islands to Italy. The new constitution abolished Croatia's *sabor* and centralised power in Belgrade, while new electoral districts severely under-represented the Croats.

Opposition to the new regime was led by the Croat Stjepan Radić, who favoured the idea of Yugoslavia but wished to transform it into a federal democracy. His alliance with the Serb Svetozar Pribićević proved profoundly threatening to the regime and Radić was assassinated in 1928. Exploiting fears of civil war, Yugoslavia's King Aleksandar ended any hope of democratic change by proclaiming a royal dictatorship, abolishing political parties and suspending parliamentary government. Meanwhile, during the 1920s the Yugoslav Communist Party arose; Josip Broz Tito was to become leader in 1937.

Ivan Vučetić (1858–1925), who developed dactyloscopy (fingerprint identification), was born on the island of Hvar in the Adriatic.

The Rise of Ustaše & WWII

One day after the proclamation of the royal dictatorship, a Bosnian Croat, Ante Pavelić, set up the Ustaše Croatian Liberation Movement in Zagreb, inspired by Mussolini. The stated aim was to establish an independent state, by force if necessary. Fearing arrest, he first fled to Sofia in Bulgaria and made contact with anti-Serbian Macedonian revolutionaries. He then moved on to Italy, where he established training camps for his organisation under Mussolini's benevolent eye. In 1934, he and the Macedonians assassinated King Aleksandar in Marseilles. Italy responded by closing down the training camps and imprisoning Pavelić and many of his followers.

1905	1908	1918	1920
Burgeoning Croatian national consciousness becomes visible in the Rijeka Resolution, which calls for increased democracy as well as the reunification of Dalmatia and Slavonia.	The Austro-Hungarian Empire takes control of Bosnia and Hercegovina, bringing the Slavic Muslims of the Balkans within its sphere of responsibility, thus creating the nucleus of the future Yugoslav federation.	The Kingdom of Serbs, Croats and Slovenes is created after the dismantling of the Austro-Hungarian Empire following WWI. Serbian Prince Aleksandar Karađorđević assumes the throne.	Stjepan Radić establishes the Croatian Republican Peasant Party, which becomes the primary voice for Croatian interests in the face of Serb domination.

When Germany invaded Yugoslavia on 6 April 1941, the exiled Ustaše were quickly installed by the Germans and the Italians, the latter of which hoped to see their own territorial aims in Dalmatia realised. Within days the Independent State of Croatia (Nezavisna Država Hrvatska; NDH), headed by Pavelić, issued a range of decrees designed to persecute and eliminate the regime's 'enemies', a thinly veiled reference to the Jews, Roma and Serbs. The majority of the Jewish population was rounded up and packed off to extermination camps between 1941 and 1945.

Serbs fared little better. The Ustaše program explicitly called for 'one-third of Serbs killed, one-third expelled and one-third converted to Catholicism', an agenda that was carried out with appalling brutality. Villages conducted their own pogroms against Serbs and extermination camps were set up, most notoriously at Jasenovac (south of Zagreb), where Jews, Roma and antifascist Croats were killed. The exact number of Serb victims is uncertain and controversial, although it is likely to have been in the hundreds of thousands.

Tito & the Partisans

Not all Croats supported these policies, and some spoke out against them. The Ustaše regime drew most of its support from the Lika region, southwest of Zagreb, and western Hercegovina. Pavelić's agreement to cede a good part of Dalmatia to Italy was highly unpopular and the Ustaše had almost no support in that region. Likewise, the Ustaše had little support amongst Zagreb's intellectuals.

Serbian 'Četnik' formations led by General Draža Mihailović provided armed resistance to the regime. The Četniks began as an antifascist rebellion but soon retaliated against the Ustaše with in-kind massacres of Croats in eastern Croatia and Bosnia.

The most effective antifascist struggle was conducted by the National Liberation Partisan units lead by Josip Broz, known as Tito. The Partisans, which had their roots in the outlawed Yugoslav Communist Party, attracted long-suffering Yugoslav intellectuals, Croats disgusted with Četnik massacres, Serbs disgusted with Ustaše massacres, and antifascists of all kinds. The Partisans gained wide popular support with their early manifesto, which envisioned a postwar Yugoslavia based on a loose federation.

Although the Allies initially backed the Serbian Četniks, it became apparent that the Partisans were waging a far more focused and determined fight against the Nazis. With the diplomatic and military support of Churchill and other Allied powers, the Partisans controlled much of Croatia by 1943. They established functioning local governments in the territory they seized, which later eased their transition to power. On 20 October 1944, the Partisans entered Belgrade alongside the Red Army.

The Balkans (2000), by noted historian Mark Mazower, is a highly readable short introduction to the region. It offers clearly discussed overviews of geography, culture and the broad historical sweep of the Balkans.

1934	1939	1941	1943
Ustaše and Macedonian revolutionaries conspire to assassinate Yugoslavia's King Aleksandar. He's shot in Marseilles while on a state visit to France. The crown passes to his 11-year-old son Petar.	Nazi Germany invades Poland and WWII begins. Yugoslavia, headed by the regent Prince Paul, attempts to stay neutral. Two years later, when Hitler pressures him to sign a pact, he is deposed in a coup.	Germany invades Yugoslavia. Ante Pavelić proclaims the Independent State of Croatia (Nezavisna Država Hrvatska; NDH), a Nazi puppet state. His Ustaše followers begin exterminating Serbs, Roma and Jews.	Tito's communist Partisans achieve military victories and build a popular antifascist front. They reclaim territory from retreating Italian brigades. The British and the USA lend military support.

When Germany surrendered in 1945, Pavelić and the Ustaše fled and the Partisans entered Zagreb.

The remnants of the NDH army, desperate to avoid falling into the hands of the Partisans, attempted to cross into Austria. A small British contingent met the 50,000 troops and promised to intern them outside Yugoslavia. It was a trick. The troops were forced into trains that headed back into Yugoslavia, where the Partisans awaited them. The ensuing massacre claimed the lives of at least 30,000 men (although the exact number is in doubt) and left a stain on the Yugoslav government.

The Second Yugoslavia

Clearly explaining centuries of complicated events, Marcus Tanner's *Croatia: A Nation Forged in War* (3rd edition 2010) sallies forth from the arrival of the Slavs to the present day, presenting in a lively, readable style the trials and tribulations of Croatian history.

Tito's attempt to retain control of the Italian city of Trieste and parts of southern Austria faltered in the face of Allied opposition. Dalmatia and most of Istria did, however, become a permanent part of postwar Yugoslavia. In creating the Federal People's Republic of Yugoslavia, Tito was determined to forge a state in which no ethnic group dominated the political landscape. Croatia became one of six republics – along with Macedonia, Serbia, Montenegro, Bosnia and Hercegovina, and Slovenia – in a tightly configured federation. However, Tito effected this delicate balance by creating a one-party state and rigorously stamping out all opposition.

During the 1960s, the concentration of power in Belgrade was an increasingly complicated issue as it became apparent that money from the more prosperous republics of Slovenia and Croatia was being distributed to the poorer autonomous province of Kosovo and the republic of Bosnia and Hercegovina. The problem seemed particularly blatant in Croatia, which saw money from its prosperous tourist business on the Adriatic coast flow into Belgrade. At the same time, Serbs in Croatia were over-represented in the government, armed forces and police.

In Croatia the unrest reached a crescendo in the 'Croatian Spring' of 1971. Led by reformers within the Communist Party of Croatia, intellectuals and students called for a loosening of Croatia's ties to Yugoslavia. In addition to calls for greater economic autonomy and constitutional reform for Croatia, nationalistic elements manifested themselves too. Tito fought back, clamping down on the liberalisation that had gradually been gaining momentum in Yugoslavia. Serbs viewed the movement as the Ustaše reborn; in turn, jailed reformers blamed the Serbs for their troubles. The stage was set for the rise of nationalism and the war of the 1990s.

The Death of Yugoslavia

Tito left a shaky Yugoslavia upon his death in May 1980. With the economy in a parlous state, a presidency that rotated among the six republics could not compensate for the loss of Tito's steadying hand at the

1945	1948	1960s	1971
Germany surrenders, the Partisans enter Zagreb and the Federal People's Republic of Yugoslavia is founded. Croatia becomes a constituent member of a federation of six republics.	Tito breaks with Stalin and Yugoslavia is expelled from the Cominform, the Soviet-dominated forum of Communist states. Tito begins to steer a careful course between the Eastern and Western blocs.	Croatian unrest about the centralisation of power in Belgrade builds. The use of Croatian money to support poorer provinces is resented, along with the over-representation of Serbs in the public service and military.	In the 'Croatian Spring', Communist Party reformers, intellectuals, students and nationalists call for greater economic and constitutional autonomy for Croatia.

helm. The authority of the central government sank along with the economy, and long-suppressed mistrust among Yugoslavia's ethnic groups resurfaced, coinciding with the rise to power of nationalist Slobodan Milošević in Serbia.

In 1989 repression of the Albanian majority in Serbia's Kosovo province sparked renewed fears of Serbian hegemony and precipitated the end of the Yugoslav Federation. With political changes sweeping Eastern Europe and in the face of increasing provocations from Milošević, Slovenia embarked on a course for independence. For Croatia, remaining in a Serb-dominated Yugoslavia without the counterweight of Slovenia would have been untenable.

TITO

Josip Broz was born in Kumrovec in 1892 to a Croat father and a Slovene mother. When WWI broke out, he was drafted into the Austro-Hungarian army and was taken prisoner by the Russians. He escaped just before the 1917 revolution, became a communist and joined the Red Army. He returned to Croatia in 1920 and became a union organiser while working as a metalworker.

As secretary of the Zagreb committee of the outlawed Communist Party, he worked to unify the party and increase its membership. When the Nazis invaded in 1941, he adopted the name Tito and organised small bands of guerrillas, which formed the core of the Partisan movement. His successful campaigns attracted military support from the British and the Americans, but the Soviet Union, despite sharing his communist ideology, repeatedly rebuffed his requests for aid.

In 1945 he became prime minister of a reconstituted Yugoslavia. Although retaining a communist ideology, and remaining nominally loyal to Russia, Tito had an independent streak. In 1948 he fell out with Stalin and adopted a conciliatory policy towards the West.

Yugoslavia's rival nationalities were Tito's biggest headache, which he dealt with by suppressing all dissent and trying to ensure a rough equality of representation at the upper echelons of government. As a committed communist, he viewed ethnic disputes as unwelcome deviations from the pursuit of the common good.

Yet Tito was well aware of the ethnic tensions that simmered just below the surface in Yugoslavia. Preparations for his succession began in the early 1970s as he aimed to create a balance of power among the ethnic groups of Yugoslavia. He set up a collective presidency that was to rotate annually but the system proved unworkable. Later events revealed how dependent Yugoslavia was on its wily, charismatic leader.

When Tito died in May 1980, his body was carried from Ljubljana (Slovenia) to Belgrade (Serbia). Thousands of mourners flocked to the streets to pay respects to the man who had united a difficult country for 35 years. It was the last communal outpouring of emotion that Yugoslavia's fractious nationalities were able to share.

1980	1981	1984	1986
President Tito dies. There is a genuine outpouring of grief, and tributes are paid from around the world. Yugoslavia is left beset by inflation, unemployment and foreign debt.	Future president Franjo Tuđman is sentenced to three years in jail following interviews with foreign newspapers about the position of Croats within Yugoslavia.	Yugoslavia hosts a successful Winter Olympic Games in Sarajevo, avoiding the Cold War–inspired boycotts that marred the Summer Olympics of both 1980 and 1984.	Slobodan Milošević becomes the head of the Serbian Communist Party. The following year he comes to public attention following a fiery address to minority Serbs in Kosovo.

In the Croatian elections of April 1990, Franjo Tuđman's Croatian Democratic Union (Hrvatska Demokratska Zajednica; HDZ) secured 40% of the vote, to the 30% won by the Communist Party, which retained the loyalty of the Serbian community as well as voters in Istria and Rijeka. On 22 December 1990, a new Croatian constitution changed the status of Serbs in Croatia from that of a 'constituent nation' to a national minority.

The constitution failed to guarantee minority rights and caused mass dismissals of Serbs from the public service. This stimulated Croatia's 600,000-strong ethnic Serb community to demand autonomy. In early 1991, Serb extremists within Croatia staged provocations in order to force federal military intervention. A May 1991 referendum (boycotted by the Serbs) produced a 93% vote in favour of Croatian independence. When Croatia declared independence on 25 June 1991, the Serbian enclave of Krajina proclaimed its independence from Croatia.

The War for Croatia

Misha Glenny's *The Balkans: Nationalism, War & the Great Powers, 1804–1999* (2000) explores the history of outside interference in the Balkans. His *The Fall of Yugoslavia* (1992) deciphers the complex politics, history and cultural flare-ups that led to the wars of the 1990s.

Under pressure from the EU, Croatia declared a three-month moratorium on its independence, but heavy fighting broke out in Krajina, Baranja and Slavonia. This initiated what Croats refer to as the Homeland War. The Yugoslav People's Army, dominated by Serbs, began to intervene in support of Serbian irregulars under the pretext of halting ethnic violence. When the Croatian government ordered a shutdown of federal military installations in the republic of Croatia, the Yugoslav navy blockaded the Adriatic coast and laid siege to the strategic town of Vukovar on the Danube. During the summer of 1991, a quarter of Croatia fell to Serb militias and the Serb-led Yugoslav People's Army.

In late 1991, the federal army and the Montenegrin militia moved against Dubrovnik, and the presidential palace in Zagreb was hit by rockets from Yugoslav jets in an apparent assassination attempt on President Tuđman. When the three-month moratorium ended, Croatia declared full independence. Soon after, Vukovar finally fell when the Yugoslav army moved in, in one of the more bloodthirsty acts in all of the Yugoslav wars. During six months of fighting in Croatia, 10,000 people died, hundreds of thousands fled and tens of thousands of homes were destroyed.

The United Nations Gets Involved

Beginning on 3 January 1992, a UN-brokered ceasefire generally held. The federal army was allowed to withdraw from its bases inside Croatia and tensions diminished. At the same time, the EU, succumbing to pressure from Germany, recognised Croatia. This was followed by US recognition, and in May 1992 Croatia was admitted to the UN.

1989	1990	1991	1992
The communist system begins to collapse in Eastern Europe; Franjo Tuđman establishes Yugoslavia's first non-communist party, the Croatian Democratic Union (HDZ).	Disagreements between Slovenia and Serbia lead to the disintegration of the Yugoslav Communist Party. The Croatian Communist Party allows multiparty elections, which are won by HDZ.	The Croatian *sabor* (parliament) proclaims the independence of Croatia; Krajina Serbs declare independence from Croatia, with the support of Milošević. War breaks out between Croats and Serbs.	A first UN-brokered ceasefire takes effect temporarily. The EU recognises Croatian independence and Croatia is admitted into the UN. War breaks out in neighbouring Bosnia.

CORRUPTION, CRIME & PUNISHMENT

The struggle against rife corruption came into the spotlight in late 2010, when Ivo Sanader – who had stepped down from serving a second term as prime minister in July 2009 without an explanation – was charged with corruption and fled the country overnight. He denied fleeing but was arrested in Austria a few days later. He was found guilty and is currently serving an 8½-year prison term.

The UN peace plan in Krajina was intended to bring about the disarming of local Serb paramilitary formations, the repatriation of refugees and the return of the region to Croatia. Instead, it only froze the existing situation and offered no permanent solution. In January 1993, the Croatian army suddenly launched an offensive in southern Krajina, pushing the Serbs back in some areas and recapturing strategic points. The Krajina Serbs vowed never to accept rule from Zagreb and in June 1993 they voted overwhelmingly to join the Bosnian Serbs (and eventually Greater Serbia). A mass expulsion left only about 900 Croats in Krajina out of an original population of 44,000. In early 2004, a comprehensive ceasefire substantially reduced the violence in the region. Demilitarised 'zones of separation' between the parties were established.

Troubles in Bosnia & Hercegovina

Meanwhile, neighbouring Bosnia and Hercegovina had been subjected to similar treatment at the hands of the Yugoslav army and Serbian paramilitaries, potentially preparing the ground for the creation of a Greater Serbia including the Serb-controlled parts of Bosnia and Croatia. Initially, in the face of Serbian advances, Bosnia's Croats and Muslims had banded together but in 1993 the two sides fell out and began fighting each other. The Bosnian Croats, with tacit support from Zagreb, were responsible for several horrific events in Bosnia, including the destruction of the old bridge in Mostar. This conflagration was extinguished when the USA fostered the development of the Muslim–Croatian federation in 1994, as the world looked on in horror at the Serb siege of Sarajevo.

While these grim events unfolded in Bosnia and Hercegovina, the Croatian government quietly began procuring arms from abroad. On 1 May 1995, the Croatian army and police entered occupied western Slavonia, east of Zagreb, and seized control of the region within days. The Krajina Serbs responded by shelling Zagreb in an attack that left seven people dead and 130 wounded. As the Croatian military consolidated its hold in western Slavonia, some 15,000 Serbs fled the region despite assurances from the Croatian government that they were safe from retribution.

In July 1995, upwards of 8000 Muslim men and boys were slaughtered by the Bosnian Serb Army in the Bosnian town of Srebrenica. UN Secretary General Kofi Annan described the genocide as the 'worst on European soil since WWII'.

1993	1994	1995	2005
Bosnian Croats and Muslims, previously aligned in fighting the Bosnian Serbs, start fighting each other. Croatia's reputation is sullied by the massacre of Muslim and Serb civilians.	US-brokered talks lead to the creation of a Muslim-Croat Federation in Bosnia. Pope John Paul II visits Croatia and calls for a rejection of nationalism and a culture of peace.	The 'Oluja' military campaign sees Croatian forces reclaim lost Croatian territory in the Krajina; most of the region's Serbs flee. The Dayton Accords bring peace and confirm Croatia's borders.	War-crimes suspect Croatian General Ante Gotovina is captured and handed to the International War Crimes Tribunal. He is later cleared of all charges.

Belgrade's silence throughout the campaign showed that the Krajina Serbs had lost the support of their Serbian sponsors, encouraging Croats to forge ahead. On 4 August, the military launched an assault on the rebel Serb capital of Knin. The Serb army fled towards northern Bosnia, along with 150,000 civilians whose roots in the Krajina stretched back centuries. The military operation ended in days but was followed by months of terror, including widespread looting and burning of Serb villages.

The Dayton Peace Accords signed in Paris in December 1995 recognised Croatia's Yugoslav-era borders and provided for the return of eastern Slavonia. The transition proceeded relatively smoothly, but the two populations still regard each other with suspicion and hostility.

Postwar Croatia

A degree of stability returned to Croatia after the hostilities. A key provision of the peace agreement was the guarantee by the Croatian government to facilitate the return of Serbian refugees, and although the central government in Zagreb made the return of refugees a priority in accordance with the demands of the international community, its efforts have often been subverted by local authorities intent on maintaining the ethnic singularity of their regions. The most recent census (2011) has Serbs at 4.4% of the population, slightly down on the previous census 10 years earlier, and less than a third of their 1991 numbers.

The handover of General Ante Gotovina in 2005 to the International Court of Justice in the Hague to answer war crimes charges was a major condition for the beginning of Croatia's negotiations to join the EU. In 2011 Gotovina and fellow ex-general Mladen Markač were sentenced to 24 and 18 years in jail respectively, but the decision was overruled in November 2012, after an appeal court ruled there had been no conspiracy to commit war crimes.

In the spring of 2008, Croatia was officially invited to join NATO at the summit in Bucharest; exactly a year later, it joined the alliance. In 2012, Croats voted in a referendum to join the EU and in 2013 the country officially became a member.

Richard Holbrooke's *To End a War* (1998) recounts the events surrounding the Dayton Accords. As the American diplomat who prodded the warring parties to the negotiating table to hammer out a peace accord, Holbrooke was in a unique position to evaluate the personalities and politics of the region.

2009	2010	2012	2013
Croatia officially joins NATO. Ivo Sanader suddenly resigns as prime minister. His deputy, former journalist Jadranka Kosor, takes over as the country's first female prime minister.	Slovenia votes in a referendum regarding a border dispute with Croatia. A narrow majority of Slovenes supports the compromise resolution, clearing way for Croatia's entry into the EU.	A referendum on whether Croatia should join the EU results in a 'yes' vote by a margin of two to one, though voter turnout is low at about 44%.	Croatia officially joins the EU, becoming the 28th member state and only the second of the former Yugoslav republics (behind Slovenia) to be admitted.

The Croatian Mindset

With Germanic influences in the north and larger-than-life Mediterranean tendencies in the south, Croats aren't completely cut from the same mould. Yet from one tip of the Croatian horseshoe to the other, there are constants. Wherever you go, family and religion loom large, social conservatism is the norm and sport is the national obsession.

Croatia: West or East?

The vast majority of Croats have a strong cultural identification with Western Europe and draw a distinction between themselves and their 'eastern' neighbours in Bosnia, Montenegro and Serbia. The idea that Croatia is the last stop before the Ottoman/Orthodox east is prevalent in all segments of the population. Describing Croatia as part of Eastern Europe will not win you any friends. Some locals even baulk at the term 'Balkan', given the negative connotations that it carries. They'll be quick to point out that Zagreb is actually further west than Vienna; that the nation is overwhelmingly Catholic, rather than Orthodox; and that they use the Latin alphabet, not Cyrillic.

Despite the different alphabet used, Croatian and Serbian are more akin to related dialects than separate languages. This doesn't stop both sides stressing the differences between them though. In Croatia in particular, a French style of linguistic nationalism has seen old Yugoslav-era words like '*aerodrom*' (airport) dropped from signs in favour of the Croatian-derived '*zračna luka*' (*zrak* means air and *luka* means port – but most people still say *aerodrom* regardless). And should you ask for *hljeb* or *hleb* (the Montenegrin and Serbian words for bread, respectively) instead of *kruh* if you're dining in Dubrovnik, it won't go down well.

In 2014, a petition garnered 500,000 signatures calling for a referendum to restrict the use of Cyrillic on public signs in Croatia. At present Cyrillic is used alongside the Latin script in areas where Serbs make up more than 30% of the population, but the petition sought to increase this to 50%. A court rejected the petition, stating that such a referendum would be unconstitutional. Supporters of the referendum saw this as a slap in the face for war veterans and the victims of Serbian aggression in places like Vukovar.

All of this stands in stark relief to the overwhelming popularity of Serbian turbo folk in Croatia, a type of music frowned upon and avoided during the 1990s war. It seems that ethnic tensions have eased to the point where connecting Balkan elements are again being embraced in some unexpected aspects of Croatian society.

Croatia's Split Personality

With its capital inland and the majority of its big cities on the coast, Croatia is torn between a more serious *Mitteleuropean* mindset in Zagreb, Zagorje and Slavonia (with meaty food, Austrian architecture and a strong interest in personal advancement over pleasure) and the coastal Mediterranean character which is more laid-back and open. Istrians are strongly Italian influenced and tend to be bilingual in Italian and Croatian.

Nikola Tesla (1856–1943), the father of the radio and alternating electric current technology, was born in the village of Smiljan in Croatia to Serbian parents (his father was an Orthodox priest). Both Croatia and Serbia celebrate him as a national hero.

The Dalmatians are only slightly less Italianised and are generally a relaxed and easygoing bunch: many offices empty out at 3pm, allowing people to enjoy the long hours of sunlight on a beach or at an outdoor cafe.

Most people involved in the tourist industry speak German, English and Italian, though English is the most widely spoken language among the young.

Family Matters

Family is very important to Croats and extended-family links are strong and cherished. First cousins tend to be very close and connections are maintained with more distant cousins as well.

It's traditional and perfectly normal for children to live with their parents until well into their adult life. This extends particularly to sons, who in rural and small-town areas will often move their wives into their parents' home when they marry. The expectation that you'll stay at home until you're married makes life particularly difficult for gays and lesbians or anyone wanting a taste of independence. Many young people achieve a degree of this by leaving to study in a different town.

Most families own their own homes, bought in the postcommunist years when previously state-owned homes were sold to the tenants for little money. These properties are often passed down from grandparents, great-aunts and other relatives.

Daily Life

Lounging in cafes and bars is an important part of life here, and you often wonder how the country's wheels are turning with so many people at leisure rather than work. But perhaps it's all that coffee that makes them work twice as fast once they're back in the office.

Croats like the good life and take a lot of pride in showing off the latest fashions and mobile phones. High-end fashion labels are prized by both women and men – the more prominent the label, the better. Even with a tight economy, people will cut out restaurant meals and films in order to afford a shopping trip to Italy or Austria for some new clothes. For young men, looking good and dressing well is all part of the macho swagger. Croat men don't like to lose face by acting stupidly in public, so while they'll drink, they generally don't drink to get drunk. Most local women don't drink much at all.

The cult of celebrity is extremely powerful in Croatia – the trashy tabloids are full of wannabe celebs and their latest shenanigans.

Manners & Mannerisms

Croats can come across as uninterested and rude (even those working in the tourist sector) and some people find their directness confronting. False pleasantries are regarded as just that – false. Smiles and exhortations to 'have a nice day' are reserved for people they actually care about. The idea of calling a complete stranger 'dear' at the start of a letter just seems weird to them, as does the antipodean habit of referring to people they've only just met as 'mate'.

This is just the way Croats operate, so don't take it personally. At least you'll always know where you stand. Once you graduate from the stranger category to friend, you'll find them warm, gregarious, generous and deeply hospitable. You might even make friends for life.

Never ask a Croat how they are if you don't want to know the answer. 'Fine' just doesn't cut it. Dalmatians, in particular, are prone to the dramatic: they'll either be full of the joys of life or in deep despair. Either way, if you ask, you'll hear about it.

Etiquette Tips

Dress modestly when visiting churches.

Wait to be invited to use a person's first name.

Whoever does the inviting (for dinner or a drink) pays the bill.

Religion

According to the most recent census, 86.3% of the population identifies itself as Catholic, 4.4% Orthodox (this corresponds exactly with the percentage of Serbs), 4% 'other and undeclared', 3.8% atheist and 1.5% Muslim.

The main factor separating the otherwise ethnically indistinguishable Croats and Serbs is religion: Croats overwhelming adhere to the Roman Catholic faith, while Serbs are just as strongly linked to the Eastern Orthodox Church. The division has its roots in the split of the Roman Empire at the end of the 4th century. Present-day Croatia found itself on the western side, ruled from Rome, while Serbia ended up on the Greek-influenced eastern side, ruled from Constantinople (now Istanbul). As time went on, differences developed between western and eastern Christianity, culminating in the Great Schism of 1054, when the churches finally parted ways. In addition to various doctrinal differences, Orthodox Christians venerate icons, allow priests to marry and do not accept the authority of the pope.

It would be difficult to overstate the extent to which Catholicism shapes the Croatian national identity. The Croats pledged allegiance to Roman Catholicism as early as the 9th century and were rewarded with the right to conduct Mass and issue religious writings in the local language, using the Glagolitic script. The popes supported the early Croatian kings, who in turn built monasteries and churches to further promote Catholicism. Throughout the long centuries of Croatia's domination by foreign powers, Catholicism was the unifying element in forging a sense of nationhood.

The Church enjoys a respected position in Croatia's cultural and political life, and Croatia is the subject of particular attention from the Vatican. The Church is also the most trusted institution in Croatia, rivalled only by the military.

Croats, both within Croatia and abroad, provide a stream of priests and nuns to replenish the ranks of Catholic clergy. Religious holidays are celebrated with fervour and Sunday Mass is strongly attended.

Equality in Croatia

Women continue to face some hurdles in Croatia, although the situation is improving. Under Tito's brand of socialism, women were encouraged to become politically active and their representation in the Croatian *sabor* (parliament) increased to 18%. Currently 24% of the parliament is comprised of women.

The Croatian church once fought against Rome to retain the use of the Glagolitic alphabet, upon which Cyrillic was partially based. It continued to be used on the island of Krk until the 19th century.

Croatian women weren't granted the vote until 1945. Following this election, Yugoslavia became a one-party state. Elections continued to be held but the League of Communists selected the candidates; sometimes there was only one name on the ballot.

THE CROATIAN MINDSET RELIGION

A SLICE OF CROATIA TO BRING BACK HOME

The finest artisan product from Croatia is the intricate lace from Pag Island, part of a centuries-old tradition that is still going strong. On the island, you can buy pieces of lace directly from the women who make them.

Embroidered fabrics are featured in many souvenir shops. Croatian embroidery is distinguished by cheerful red geometric patterns set against a white background, which you'll see on tablecloths, pillowcases and blouses.

Lavender and other fragrant herbs made into scented sachets or oils make popular and inexpensive gifts. You can find them on most central Dalmatian islands, but especially on Hvar, which is known for its lavender fields.

Brač Island is known for its lustrous stone. Ashtrays, vases, candlestick holders and other small but heavy items carved from Brač stone are on sale throughout the island.

> ### CROATS: NORMAL PEOPLE
>
> The word 'normal' pops up frequently in Croats' conversations about themselves. 'We want to be a normal country', they might say. Croats will frequently make a distinction between rabid, flag-waving nationalists and 'normal people' who only wish to live in peace. This is among the reasons Croatia bowed to international pressure to turn over its suspected war criminals.

More and more wives and mothers must work outside the home to make ends meet, but they still perform most household duties. Women are under-represented at the executive level.

Women fare worse in traditional villages than in urban areas, and were hit harder economically than men after the Homeland War. Many of the factories that closed, especially in eastern Slavonia, had a high proportion of female workers.

Both domestic abuse and sexual harassment at work are quite common in Croatia, but the legal system is not yet adequate for women to seek redress.

Although attitudes are slowly changing towards homosexuality, Croatia is an overwhelmingly Catholic country with highly conservative views of sexuality. Most homosexuals are very closeted, fearing harassment if their sexual orientation were revealed. In 2013, a group called *U ime obitelji* (In the Name of the Family) campaigned for a referendum in which 65% of voters approved a constitutional ban on same-sex marriage. The following year, parliament passed a law creating civil partnerships for same-sex couples, granting limited relationship rights.

The current crop of football stars includes Luka Modrić (who plays for Real Madrid), Dejan Lovren (Liverpool FC), Mario Pašalić (Chelsea, currently on loan to Elche CF) and Dejan Srna (FC Shakhtar Donetsk).

Good Sports

In 2013, Croatia was ranked the world's 10th-greatest sporting nation per head of population (neighbouring Slovenia topped the list). Football, basketball and tennis are enormously popular, and sporty Croatia has contributed a disproportionate number of world-class players in each sport.

Football

By far the most popular spectator sport in Croatia is football (soccer), which frequently serves as an outlet for Croatian patriotism and, occasionally, as a means to express political opposition. When Franjo Tuđman came to power he decided that the name of Zagreb's football club, Dinamo, was 'too communist', so he changed it to 'Croatia'. Waves of outrage followed the decision, led by angry young football fans who used the controversy to express their opposition to the regime. Even though the following government restored the original name, you will occasionally see *Dinamo volim te* (Dinamo, I love you) graffiti in Zagreb. Dinamo's bitterest rival is Hajduk Split; there are often brawls when the two teams meet.

By far the biggest name in Croatian football, Davor Šuker scored 46 international goals by the end of his career, 45 of them for Croatia. He is the Croatian national team's all-time leading goal-scorer and the current president of the Croatian Football Federation. Back in 2004, football great Pelé named him one of the top 125 greatest living footballers.

Be like the sporty locals and keep up with Croatian football by following the fortunes of Hajduk Split (www.hajduk.hr) and Dinamo Zagreb (www.gnkdinamo.hr).

Tennis

'I don't know what's in the water in Croatia, but it seems like every player is over 7ft tall' – Andy Roddick.

Not quite. Yet Croatia is producing some mighty big players, in every sense of the word.

The 2001 victory of 6ft 4in Goran Ivanišević at Wimbledon provoked wild celebrations throughout the country, especially in his home town of Split. The charismatic serve-and-volley player was much loved for his engaging personality and on-court antics, and dominated the top 10 rankings during much of the 1990s. Injuries forced his retirement in 2004, but Croatia stayed on the court with a 2005 Davis Cup victory led by 6ft 4in Ivan Ljubičić and 6ft 5in Mario Ančić. At the time of writing, Croatia's highest ranked tennis player was 6ft 6in Marin Čilić, who won his first Grand Slam title, the US Open, in 2014.

On the women's side, Zagreb-born Iva Majoli won the French Open in 1997 with an aggressive baseline game, but failed to follow up with other Grand Slam victories. She retired from tennis in 2004.

Tennis is more than a spectator sport in Croatia. The coast is amply endowed with clay courts. The biggest tournament in Croatia is the Umag Open in Istria, held in July.

Basketball

The most popular sport after football, basketball is followed with some reverence. The teams of Split, Zadar and Zagreb's Cibona are known across Europe, though no one has yet equalled the star team of the 1980s, when Cibona became European champion. For the thorough low-down on Croatian basketball, go to www.kosarka.hr.

Skiing

If Croatia had a national goddess it would be Janica Kostelić, the most accomplished skier to have emerged from Croatia. After winning the Alpine Skiing World Cup in 2001, Kostelić won three gold medals and a silver in the 2002 Winter Olympics – the first Winter Olympic medals ever for an athlete from Croatia. At the age of 20 she became the first female skier ever to win three gold medals at one Olympics. In 2002, Kostelić was plagued by a knee injury and the removal of her thyroid, but this didn't stop her from winning a gold medal in the women's combined and a silver in the Super-G at the 2006 Winter Olympics in Torino. In 2007, Kostelić announced her retirement from competitive racing.

Maybe it's in the genes. Her brother Ivica Kostelić took the men's slalom World Cup title in 2003 and brought home a silver medal in the men's combined in each of the 2006, 2010 and 2014 Winter Olympics, and a silver in the slalom in 2010.

The celebrated Croatian athlete Blanka Vlašić is the second-highest-flying female high jumper of all time. Despite receiving gold medals at various world championships, her only ever Olympics medal was a silver in Beijing.

THE CROATIAN MINDSET GOOD SPORTS

The Cuisine

While holding firm to its Eastern European roots, Croatian food echoes the varied cultures that have influenced the country over its history. There's a sharp divide between the Italian-style cuisine along the coast and the flavours of Hungary, Austria and Turkey in the continental parts. From grilled sea bass smothered in olive oil in Dalmatia to robust, paprika-heavy meat stews in Slavonia, each region proudly touts its own specialty, but regardless of the region you'll find tasty food made from fresh, seasonal ingredients.

Foodie Culture

Although Croats are not overly experimental when it comes to food, they're particularly passionate about it. They'll spend hours discussing the quality of the lamb or the first-grade fish, and why it overshadows all food elsewhere. Foodie culture is on the rise here, inspired largely by the slow-food movement, which places emphasis on fresh, local and seasonal ingredients and the joy of slow-paced dining. The Istria and Kvarner regions have quickly shot to the top of the gourmet ladder but other places aren't lagging far behind. Wine and olive-oil production have been revived, and there's now a network of signposted roads around the country celebrating these precious nectars.

A number of restaurants around Croatia now offer slow-food menus and if you're willing to pay a little more, you can spend hours feasting on slow-food delicacies or savouring the innovative concoctions of up-and-coming chefs. There is a limit to what the local crowd can afford to pay, so restaurants still cluster in the middle of the price spectrum – few are unbelievably cheap and few are exorbitantly expensive. Whatever your budget, it's hard to get a truly bad meal anywhere in Croatia. Another plus is that food is often paired with alfresco dining in warm weather.

For excellent reviews of restaurants all around Croatia and info about small producers, browse the excellent www.tasteofcroatia.org and download the app.

Regional Specialities

Zagreb & Northwestern Croatia

Zagreb and northwestern Croatia favour the kind of hearty meat dishes you might find in Vienna. Juicy *pečenje* (spit-roasted and baked meat) features *janjetina* (lamb), *svinjetina* (pork) and *patka* (duck), often accompanied by *mlinci* (baked noodles) or *pečeni krumpir* (roast potatoes). Meat slow cooked under a *peka* (domed baking lid) is especially delicious, but needs to be ordered in advance at many restaurants. *Purica* (turkey) with *mlinci* is an institution on Zagreb and Zagorje menus, along with *zagrebački odrezak* (veal steak stuffed with ham and cheese,

COOKING COURSES

Cooking courses in Croatia are becoming increasingly popular. **Culinary Croatia** (www.culinary-croatia.com) is a great source of information, and offers a variety of cooking classes and culinary and wine tours, mainly in Dalmatia. **iCroatiaTravel** (www.icroatiatravel.com/zagreb-gourmet-experience) organises a five-hour Zagreb gourmet experience. Istria-based **Eat Istria** (www.eatistria.com) offers cooking classes and wine tours around the peninsula.

DISHES & DRINKS TO TRY

Bazga Homemade elderflower juice is a classic of continental Croatia, fresh and lovely – a singular imbibing joy.

Bermet Intense herbal liqueur made only in the town of Samobor, with dried carob and figs, wormwood, orange zest, sage and mustard seeds, all soaked in red wine.

Boškarin Don't skip a taste of Istria's indigenous ox, nearly extinct by the late 20th century but brought back to life recently as a meat delicacy.

Gregada Fish stew made with different types of white fish, potatoes, white wine, garlic and spices. Hvar whips up Croatia's most famous *gregada*.

Komiška pogača Savoury focaccia-like pie from Korniža on Vis island, stuffed with onion, tomatoes and anchovies. If tomatoes are missing, then it's *viška pogača* (from the town of Vis).

Rogačica Among the many *rakija* (grappa) delights Croatia is known for, this Dalmatian liqueur made of carob is perfect if you like your drinks sweet.

Vitalac This offal delight from the island of Brač is not for the faint-hearted – think lamb intestines on a spit, grilled on hot coal.

then crumbed and fried) – another calorie-laden specialty. Another mainstay is *sir i vrhnje* (fresh cottage cheese and cream), bought at local markets and paired well with bread. For those with a sweet tooth, *palačinke* (thin pancakes) with various fillings and toppings are a common dessert.

Slavonia

Spicier than the food of other regions, Slavonian cuisine uses liberal amounts of paprika and garlic. The Hungarian influence is most prevalent here: many typical dishes, such as *čobanac* (a meat stew), are in fact versions of *gulaš* (goulash). The nearby Drava River provides fresh fish, such as carp, pike and perch, which is stewed in a paprika sauce and served with noodles in a dish known as *fiš paprikaš*. Another specialty is *šaran u rašljama* (carp on a forked branch), roasted in its own oils over an open fire. The region's sausages are particularly renowned, especially *kulen*, a paprika-flavoured sausage cured over a period of nine months and usually served with cottage cheese, peppers, tomatoes and often *turšija* (pickled vegetables).

> The salt extracted at the Pag and Ston salt pans is considered the cleanest in the entire Mediterranean region.

Istria

Istrian cuisine has been attracting international foodies in recent years for its long gastronomic tradition, fresh ingredients and unique specialities. Typical dishes include *maneštra*, a thick vegetable-and-bean soup similar to minestrone, *fuži*, hand-rolled pasta often served with *tartufi* (truffles) or *divljač* (game meat), and *fritaja* (omelette often served with seasonal veggies, such as wild asparagus). Thin slices of dry-cured Istrian *pršut* (prosciutto) – also excellent in Dalmatia – are often on the appetiser list; it's expensive because of the long hours and personal attention involved in smoking the meat. Istrian olive oil is highly rated and has won awards. The tourist board has marked an olive-oil route along which you can visit local growers, tasting oils at the source. The best seasonal ingredients include white truffles, picked in autumn, and wild asparagus, harvested in spring.

> Research shows that the prized oysters in the Ston area on Pelješac Peninsula have been farmed since Roman times.

Kvarner & Dalmatia

Coastal cuisine in Kvarner and Dalmatia is typically Mediterranean, using a lot of olive oil, garlic, fresh fish and shellfish, and herbs. Along the coast, look for lightly breaded and fried *lignje* (squid) as a main course; Adriatic squid is generally more expensive than squid from further afield, and tastier for its freshness. Meals often begin with a first course of pasta such as spaghetti or *rižoto* (risotto) topped with seafood. For a special

THE OLIVE OIL BOOM OF ISTRIA

There's an olive tree on Veli Brijun in the Brijuni Islands proven to be 1600 years old. Early Greek and Roman manuscripts praised the quality of Istrian olive oil. Now there's a revival of this ancient agricultural activity, with 94 listed growers on the Istrian Peninsula and a network of sign-posted olive-oil roads. In Istria, the plant is cultivated with special attention, and each tree given love and care. Several growers have received prestigious international awards and top marks for their fruity nectars, which is no small feat in the competitive world olive-oil market.

Duilio Belić is a relative newbie on the scene. The son of a miner, he grew up in Raša and went on to become a successful Zagreb businessperson before starting olive-oil production. With his wife, Bosiljka, an agriculture specialist, he bought an old grove near Fažana a decade ago and started what has become a real hit among gourmets. He now has five olive groves in three locations in Istria, with a total of 5500 trees. Under the brand name Oleum Viride, they produce 11 single-variety extra-virgin olive oils, four of which are made of indigenous varietals – Buža, Istarska Bjelica, Rosulja and Vodnjanska Crnica. Their showcase oil is Selekcija Belić, a blend of six varieties with a flavour of vanilla and chicory.

Over a coffee at a Fažana cafe, Duilio reminds me of a simple fact most people forget: the olive is a fruit and olive oil is a fruit juice. Just as with wine, certain oils can be combined with certain dishes to enhance the flavours. Selekcija Belić, for example, is a great accompaniment to lamb and veal cooked under a *peka* (domed baking lid), or a wild-asparagus omelette. The highly prized Buža oil pairs wonderfully with raw fish and meat, as well as mushrooms and grilled vegetables. The golden-green Istarska Bjelica, with its scent of mown grass and a hint of radicchio, goes well with chocolate ice cream or a dark-chocolate hazelnut cake.

It's all sounding quite abstract to me so we move on to Vodnjanka, a restaurant in Vodnjan, where Duilio pulls out a box with a selection of his oils and orders a range of hors d'oeuvres. There, I learn to taste olive oil. A small sample is poured into a wine glass, which you warm up with your hand in order for the oil to reach body temperature. You then cover the glass with your hand to release the oil's natural aroma. Next, you place a small sip of the oil at the front of your mouth, mix it gently and then swallow in one go.

Such tastings have become a trend among Croatian foodies. Duilio organises the gatherings for his wider circle of friends and for groups of enthusiasts at his olive grove or his tasting room in Zagreb. His oils can also be sampled at Croatia's top restaurants: Bevanda (p145) in Opatija, Milan (p105) in Pula, Kukuriku (p143) in Rijeka, Foša (p184) in Zadar and Damir & Ornella (p122) in Novigrad.

I ask Duilio my last questions as we sample Vodnjanska Crnica in *maneštra* (a vegetable-and-bean soup). I wonder what makes Istria such prime territory for growing olives. 'It's the microlocation,' Duilio says. 'Plus we harvest the olives early, unlike in Dalmatia, to preserve the natural antioxidants and nutrients. The oils may taste more bitter but they're also healthier.'

As we're parting ways, fascinated by the man's passion for olive oil, I wonder what made him enter this whole new world. 'It's simple – I love food, I love wine, I love all good things in life,' he replies. 'Olive oil is one of them.'

by Anja Mutić

appetiser, try *paški sir* (Pag cheese), a pungent hard sheep-milk cheese from the island of Pag. Dalmatian *brodet* (stewed mixed fish served with polenta; also known as *brodetto*) is another regional treat, but it's often only available in two-person portions. Dalmatian *pašticada* (beef stewed in wine and spices and served with gnocchi) appears on menus on the coast as well as in the interior. Lamb from Cres and Pag is deemed Croatia's best, as it's fed on fresh herbs, which makes the meat delicious.

Vegetarians & Vegans

A useful phrase is *Ja ne jedem meso* (I don't eat meat), but even then you may be served soup with bits of bacon swimming in it. That is slowly changing and vegetarians are making inroads in Croatia, but changes are mostly happening in the larger cities. Zagreb, Rijeka, Split and Dubrovnik now have vegetarian restaurants, and even standard restaurants in the big cities are beginning to offer vegetarian menus. Vegetarians may have a harder time in the north (Zagorje) and the east (Slavonia), where traditional fare has meat as its main focus. Specialities that don't use meat include *maneštra od bobića* (bean and fresh maize soup) and *juha od krumpira na zagorski način* (Zagorje potato soup). Other options include *štrukli* (baked cheese dumplings) and *blitva* (Swiss chard boiled and often served with potatoes, olive oil and garlic). Along the coast you'll find plenty of pasta dishes and risotto with various vegetable toppings and delicious cheese. If fish and seafood are part of your diet, you'll eat royally nearly everywhere.

The secret behind the pungent taste of *paški sir* (Pag cheese) is the diet of wild herbs on which the sheep feast.

Drinks

Croatia is famous for its *rakija* (grappa), which comes in different flavours. The most commonly drunk are *loza* (grape brandy), *šljivovica* (plum brandy) and *travarica* (herbal brandy). Istrian grappa is particularly excellent, and ranges in flavour from *medica* (honey) to *biska* (mistletoe) and various berries. The island of Vis is famous for its delicious *rogačica* (carob brandy). It's customary to have a small glass of brandy before a meal. Other popular drinks include *vinjak* (cognac), maraschino (cherry liqueur made in Zadar), *prosecco* (sweet dessert wine) and *pelinkovac* (herbal liqueur).

The two most popular types of Croatian *pivo* (beer) are Zagreb's Ožujsko and Karlovačko from Karlovac. The small-distribution Velebitsko has a loyal following among in-the-know beer drinkers but only some bars and shops carry it, and they're mostly in continental Croatia. You'll want to practise saying *živjeli!* (cheers!).

Strongly brewed *kava* (espresso-style coffee), served in tiny cups, is popular throughout Croatia. You can have it diluted with milk (macchiato) or order a cappuccino. Although some places have decaf options this is considered somewhat sacrilegious, as Croats love their coffee. Herbal teas are widely available but regular tea *(čaj)* is apt to be too weak for aficionados. Tap water is drinkable.

The Zadar sour-cherry liqueur maraschino was conjured up in the early 16th century by pharmacists working in Zadar's Dominican monastery.

Wine

Wine from Croatia may be new to international consumers but *vino* has been an embedded part of the region's lifestyle for more than 25 centuries. Today the tradition is undergoing a renaissance in the hands of a new generation of winemakers with a focus on preserving indigenous varieties and revitalising ancestral estates. Quality is rising, exports are increasing and the wines are garnering global awards and winning the affections of worldly wine lovers thirsty for authentic stories and unique terroirs.

Croatia is roughly divided into four winemaking regions: Slavonia and Croatian Uplands in the continental zone with a cooler climate; and Istria/Kvarner and Dalmatia along the Adriatic with a Mediterranean climate. Within each lie multiple *vinogorje* (sub-regions), comprised of more than 300 geographically defined appellations.

Continental Zone

White varieties such as *graševina*, *traminac*, pinot blanc, chardonnay and sauvignon blanc dominate the continental zone. Styles range from fruity, mildly aromatic, refreshing wines from cool northern areas to rich, savoury, age-worthy whites from warmer Slavonia, as well as luscious *predikatno* (dessert) wines. Kutjevo is a particular sweet spot for vine-growing with many wineries located within the hamlet. Look for bottles by Enjingi, Krauthaker, Kutjevo d.d. and Mihalj.

Ensconced in the pastoral hills of Međimurje, Plešivica and Zagorje, Croatian Uplands is a land of crisp, food-friendly whites (although pinot noir does well in spots). Beside *graševina* and native *škrlet*, international varieties like chardonnay, pinot blanc, pinot gris and sauvignon blanc thrive.

The Wine coverage was written by Cliff Rames, a Croatian-American sommelier and founder of Wines of Croatia (www.winesofcroatia.com).

For a regional sampler, check out wines from Bolfan, Korak and Tomac. For *ledeno vino* (ice wine), a coveted bottle of Bodren makes a delicious souvenir.

Coastal Zone

Crowning the northern Adriatic coast is Istria, home of *malvazija istarska*, a variety capable of award-winning wines with diverse profiles: lean and light to unctuous and sweet; crisp and unoaked to acacia wood-aged and orange wines. Benvenuti, Clai, Degrassi, Kozlović, Matošević, Piquentum and Trapan offer delightful examples. Istria also boasts a fiery signature red: *teran*. Look for Arman, Coronica, Geržinić, Roxanich and Terzolo.

Just below Istria is Kvarner, home of *žlahtina*, a seafood-friendly white found in abundance on Krk. Katunar, PZ Vrbnik, Šipun and Toljanić are leading producers.

Going south, the rugged beauty of Dalmatia, with its island vineyards (Hvar, Vis, Brač, Korčula), fosters a fascinating array of indigenous grape varieties that prosper in the Mediterranean climate, yielding full-bodied wines of rich character. Here *plavac mali*, scion of *crljenik kašteljanski* (zinfandel) and the obscure *dobričić*, is king of reds. Recommended labels include Korta Katarina, Miloš, Stina, Tomić and Zlatan Otok. Wines labelled 'Dingač' are *plavac mali* from a specific vineyard on Pelješac that clings to a mountainside high above the sea. Production is tiny and good examples command premium prices. Benchmark bottlings include Bura, Kiridžija and Saints Hills. Other indigenous varieties worth seeking are *babić* (red) and *pošip* (white). For easy-chair quaffing, the lovely rosés of Dalmatia evoke visions of the Mediterranean life. Look for examples from Sladić, Vuina and Senjković.

Visiting Wineries

When planning a visit, keep in mind that most Croatian wineries are family-owned estates; not all have visitor-ready facilities. Below is a selection of recommended wineries with public tasting rooms. Appointments are highly recommended.

There are 17,000 registered vine growers in Croatia, 2500 wines of controlled origin and 880 wineries.

➡ **Slavonia** (p93)

➡ **Croatian Uplands: Bolfan-Vinski Vrh** (www.bolfanvinskivrh.hr; Hraščina); **Cmrečnjak** (☑040-830 103; Štrigova); **Korak** (www.vino-korak. hr; Plešivica); **Tomac** (www.tomac.hr; Jastrebarsko); Vuglec Breg (p80).

➡ **Istria/Kvarner: Cossetto** (www.cossetto.net; Kaštelir); **Degrassi** (www. degrassi.hr; Savudrija); **Geržinić** (www.gerzinic.com; Vižinada); **Kozlović** (www. kozlovic.hr; Momjan); **Matošević** (www.matosevic.com; Krunčići); **Toljanić-Gospoja** (www.gospoja.hr; Vrbnik, Krk); **Trapan** (www.trapan.hr; Šišan).

➡ **Dalmatia: BIBICh** (☑022-775 597; Skradin); **Bire** (☑020-712 007; Lumbarda, Korčula); **Boškinac** (p178); **Carić** (www.vinohvar.hr; Hvar); **Grgić** (☑020-748 090; Trstenik, Pelješac); **Jako Vino** (www.stina-vino.hr; Bol, Brač); **Korta Katarina** (www.kortakatarinawinery.com; Orebić, Pelješac); **Matuško** (www.matusko-vina.hr; Potomje, Pelješac); **Tomić** (www.bastijana.hr; Jelsa, Hvar).

Croatian-Style Celebrations

As in other Catholic countries, most Croats don't eat meat on Badnjak (Christmas Eve); instead they eat fish. In Dalmatia, the traditional Christmas Eve dish is *bakalar* (dried, salted cod). Christmas dinner may be roast suckling pig, turkey with *mlinci* or another meat. Also popular at Christmas is *sarma* (sauerkraut rolls stuffed with minced meat). Fresh Christmas Eve bread, also known as *badnji kruh,* is the centrepiece: it's made with honey, nuts and dried fruit. Another tradition is the Christmas braid, glazed dough made with nutmeg, raisins and almonds and shaped into a braid. It's often decorated with wheat and candles and left on the table until Epiphany (6 January), when it is cut and eaten. *Orahnjača* (walnut cake), *fritule* (fritters) and *makovnjača* (poppy-seed cake) are popular desserts at celebrations.

THE YEAR IN FOOD

While local food and wine festivals go into full swing come autumn, there's never a bad time to chow down in Croatia.

Spring (March–May) Wild asparagus and fresh berries, plus a handful of festivals like Zagorje's Festival of Traditional Cakes in April and Istria's open wine cellars on the International Wine Day in late May.

Summer (June–August) Time for freshly caught seafood by the sea. Beat the heat with gelato and cocktails, and check out what Croatian elders ate at the festival of traditional foods in the town of Vrbovec just northeast of Zagreb.

Autumn (September–November) Food festivals aplenty feature wine, truffles and chestnuts. Truffle and grappa lovers head to Istria while wine connoisseurs hit wine harvests in their chosen region. Don't miss Kvarner's sweet chestnut festival in October.

Winter (December–February) Time for Christmas and Carnival treats, and a seafood delight – the Days of Seashells, which takes place each February in northwestern Istria.

The most typical Easter dish is ham with boiled eggs, served with fresh veggies. *Pinca,* a type of hard bread, is another Easter tradition, especially in Dalmatia.

Where to Eat

A *restauracija* or *restoran* (restaurant) is at the top of the food chain, generally presenting a more formal dining experience and an elaborate wine list. A *gostionica* or *konoba* is usually a traditional family-run tavern – the produce may come from the family garden. A *pivnica* is more like a pub, with a wide choice of beer; sometimes hot dishes or sandwiches are available. A *kavana* is a cafe, where you can nurse your coffee for hours and, if you're lucky, have cakes and ice cream. A *slastičarna* (pastry shop) serves ice cream, cakes, strudels and sometimes coffee, but you usually have to gobble your food standing up or take it away. Self-service *samoposluživanje* (cafeterias) are good for a quick meal. Though the quality may vary, all you need to do is point to what you want.

Throughout former Yugoslavia, the *doručak* (breakfast) of the people was *burek* (heavy pastry stuffed with meat or cheese). Modern Croats have opted for a lighter start to their day, usually just coffee and a pastry with some yoghurt and fresh fruit. If you're staying in hostels or at private accommodation, the easiest thing to do is to get coffee at a cafe and pastries from a bakery. Otherwise, buy some bread, cheese and milk at a supermarket and have a picnic. If you're staying in a hotel you'll be served a buffet breakfast that includes cornflakes, bread, yoghurt, a selection of cold meat, powdered 'juice' and cheese. More upmarket hotels have better buffets that include eggs, sausages and homemade pastries.

Restaurants open for *ručak* (lunch) around noon and usually serve until midnight, which can be convenient if you're arriving in town at an odd hour or just feel like spending more time at the beach. Croats tend to eat either a *marenda* (early lunch) or *gablec* (cheap, filling lunch) or a large, late lunch. Fruit and vegetables from the market and a selection of cheese, bread and ham from a grocery store can make a healthy picnic lunch. If you ask nicely, the person behind the deli counter at supermarkets or grocery stores will usually make a *sir* (cheese) or *pršut* (prosciutto) sandwich (*sendvič*, in Croatian) and you only pay the regular price of the ingredients.

Večera (dinner) is typically a light affair, but most restaurants have adapted their schedules to the needs of tourists, who tend to load up at night. Few Croats can afford to eat out regularly; when they do, it's likely to be a large family outing on Saturday night or Sunday afternoon.

On 1 April each year, the town of Ludbreg in the north of Croatia has wine instead of water flowing in its city fountain.

Architecture in Croatia

After they came, saw and conquered, most of Croatia's conga-line of invaders stuck around long enough to erect buildings. From the walled towns of the coast to the baroque splendour of Varaždin in the north – via Roman ruins, Gothic cathedrals, Renaissance palaces and Viennese villas – Croatia's architectural legacy is varied and extremely impressive.

Roman Riches

No substantial buildings survive from before the Romans' arrival, but reminders of the 650 years of Roman rule are scattered all over the country: an intact archway in the centre of Rijeka; a turf-covered amphitheatre in Krka National Park; columns from the ancient forum in Zadar.

All of these pale in comparison with what is one of the best-preserved remnants of Roman architecture still standing in the world today: Diocletian's Palace in Split. This oversized complex was built by the retiring emperor at the end of the 3rd century AD, and although it was converted into a walled town and has been continuously inhabited for nearly two millennia, some parts are still wonderfully evocative of the era in which it was built. Quite unlike the crumbling ruins we associate with Roman remains, the former Mausoleum and Temple of Jupiter even have their roofs intact.

Croatia's other Roman highlights can both be found in Istria. The remarkable amphitheatre in Pula is Croatia's answer to Rome's Colosseum. This imposing 1st-century-AD arena still has a complete circuit of nearly 30m-high walls and is once again used for public entertainment – albeit of a less bloodthirsty kind than that for which it was built. The other Istrian treasure is the Euphrasian Basilica in Poreč. Built in the 6th century, this early Christian church incorporates layers of older buildings within its walls, and a precious mosaic decorates its apse.

The Cathedral of St Domnius (3rd and 4th centuries AD) in Split is the oldest cathedral building in the world, thanks to it inhabiting the original mausoleum of the Emperor Diocletian.

Pre-Romanesque Churches

The Slavs arrived in Croatia in the early 7th century, heralding what is known in architectural terms as the Old Croatian, pre-Romanesque period. Not much survives from this time as most of it was destroyed during the Mongol invasion of the 13th century. The best remaining examples are found along the Dalmatian coast, beginning with the impressive 9th-century St Donatus' Church in Zadar, built on the ruins of the Roman forum. It has a round central structure, unique for late antiquity, and three semicircular apses.

Two other considerably smaller but similarly curvaceous churches survive nearby. The 11th-century Holy Cross Church in Nin has a cross-shaped plan, two apses and a dome above the centre point. Just outside of Nin, teensy St Nicholas' is a postcard-perfect, fortress-like stone church perched atop a small hill.

St James' Cathedral in Šibenik (1431–1535) is the only building of its time constructed using the technique of mounting prefabricated stone elements.

Croatia Goes Gothic

The Romanesque tradition of the Middle Ages, with its semicircular arches and symmetrical forms, persisted along the coast long after the pointy-arched Gothic style had swept the rest of Europe. In the 13th century the earliest examples of Gothic were still combined with Romanesque forms. The most beautiful work from this period is the portal of the Cathedral of St Lovro in Trogir, carved by the master artisan Radovan in 1240. The Cathedral of the Assumption in Zagreb was the first venture into the Gothic style in northern Croatia. Although reconstructed several times, the remnants of 13th-century murals are still visible in the sacristy.

The late-Gothic period was dominated by the builder and sculptor Juraj Dalmatinac, who was born in Zadar in the 15th century. His most outstanding work was Šibenik's St James' Cathedral, which marked a transition from the Gothic to the Renaissance period. Dalmatinac constructed the church entirely of stone, and adorned its outer walls with a wreath of realistically carved portraits of local people. Another beauty from this period is the 15th-century St Mark's Cathedral in Korčula.

The Renaissance flourished in Croatia, especially in independent Ragusa (Dubrovnik). By the second half of the 15th century, Renaissance influences (harking back to ancient Roman architecture) were appearing on late-Gothic structures. The Sponza Palace is a fine example of this mixed style. By the mid-16th century, Renaissance features began to replace the Gothic style in the palaces and summer residences built in and around Ragusa by the wealthy nobility. Unfortunately, much was destroyed in the 1667 earthquake.

Baroque to Brutalism

Northern Croatia is well known for the baroque style, which was introduced by Jesuit priests in the 17th century. The city of Varaždin was a regional capital in the 17th and 18th centuries, which, because of its location, enjoyed a steady interchange of artists, artisans and architects with northern Europe. The combination of wealth and creativity eventually led to Varaždin becoming Croatia's foremost city of baroque art. You'll notice the theatrical, sometimes frilly style in the elaborately restored houses, churches and especially the impressive castle.

In Zagreb, fine examples of the baroque style are found in the Upper Town, including the Jesuit Church of St Catherine and the restored mansion that is now the Croatian Museum of Naïve Art. Wealthy families built their baroque mansions in the countryside around Zagreb, including at Brezovica, Miljana, Lobor and Bistra.

The influence of the Austro-Hungarian Empire is also on display in the capital, particularly in the grand neoclassical public buildings, but also in smaller art-nouveau apartments and townhouses. Other examples are the former governor's palace in Rijeka and the holiday mansions of the Viennese elite scattered around neighbouring Opatija and some of the nearby islands.

During the modernist period, Croatian architecture fell in sync with the International Style. The socialist period saw many highly sophisticated and aesthetically mature examples of residential and civic architecture produced, particularly in planned suburbs such as Novi Zagreb. However, the more brutalist concrete structures, once seen as futuristic and modern, aren't to everyone's taste and many have been left to decay. Sadly, the sepia-tinged nostalgia surrounding 1970s Yugoslavia hasn't extended to preserving the wonderfully evocative hotels of the period.

The first distinctively Croatian design is *pleter* (plaited ornamentation), which appeared around AD 800. Resembling the interlaced squiggles found on Celtic crosses and in medieval manuscripts, *pleter* appears frequently on church entrances and furniture from the early medieval (Old Croatian) period.

Today's Croatia has a vibrant architecture scene. In the rebuilding that followed the 1990s war, numerous open competitions were organised and young architects were suddenly given an opportunity to show their talents. Some of the more important examples of their work are the Gymnasium in Koprivnica and Hotel Lone in Rovinj.

The Natural Environment

Croatia is shaped like a boomerang, curving from the fertile farmland of Slavonia in the north, down through hilly central Croatia to the Istrian peninsula, and then south through Dalmatia along the rugged Adriatic coast. Most visitors focus their attention on the narrow coastal belt at the foot of the Dinaric Alps and the numerous gorgeous islands just offshore, but there's a whole lot more natural beauty to explore back up the boomerang.

Karst, Caves, Chasms & Waterfalls

Croatia's most outstanding geological feature is the prevalent highly porous limestone and dolomitic rock called karst, which stretches along the coast and covers large parts of the hinterland. Karst is formed by acidic water dissolving the surface limestone, which then allows the water to seep into the harder layer underneath. Eventually the water forms underground streams, carving out fissures and caves before resurfacing, disappearing into another cave and eventually emptying into the sea.

Caves and springs are common interior features of karstic landscapes, which explains Croatia's Pazin Chasm, Plitvice Lakes and the Krka waterfalls, as well as the Manita Peć cave in Paklenica. When the limestone collapses, a kind of basin (known as *polje*) is formed. These are then cultivated, despite the fact that this kind of field drains poorly and can easily turn into a temporary lake.

There are 1244 islands and islets along the tectonically submerged Adriatic coastline, only 50 of them inhabited. The largest are Cres, Krk, Pag and Rab in the north; Brač, Hvar, Dugi Otok and Vis in the middle; and Korčula and Mljet in the south.

National Parks

When the Yugoslav federation collapsed, eight of its finest national parks ended up in Croatia. The national parks cover 1.3% of the country and have a total area of 961 sq km, of which 742 sq km is land and 219 sq km is water. Around 8% of Croatia is given over to its protected areas, including nature parks and the like.

On the Mainland

By far the most popular of the eight national parks is Unesco World Heritage–listed Plitvice Lakes National Park, near the Bosnian border, midway between Zagreb and Zadar. Its chain of exquisitely picturesque lakes and waterfalls were formed by mosses that retain calcium carbonate as river water rushes through the karst. The falls are at their watery best in spring. The park's popularity comes at a price though: the main paths get terribly congested in the peak months.

Krka National Park is an even more extensive series of lakes and waterfalls set along the Krka River, north of Šibenik. The main access point is Skradinski Buk, where the largest cascade covers 800m. Like Plitvice, this part of the park can get uncomfortably crowded in July and August, but there are many stretches that are more peaceful. The park also includes important cultural relics in the form of a Serbian Orthodox and a Roman Catholic monastery.

The dramatically formed karstic gorges and cliffs make Paklenica National Park, along the Adriatic coast near Zadar, a rock-climbing favourite. Large grottoes and caves filled with stalactites and stalagmites make it an interesting park for cave explorers, and there are many kilometres of hiking trails. Tourist facilities are well developed but there are large tracts of wilderness.

At the other end of the same mountain range, rugged Northern Velebit National Park is a patchwork of forests, peaks, ravines and ridges that backs the coast on the mainland opposite the island of Rab.

Risnjak National Park, northeast of Rijeka, is the most untouched forested park, partly because the climate at its higher altitudes is somewhat inhospitable, with an average temperature of 12.6°C in July. The winters are long and snowy but, when spring finally comes in late May or early June, everything blooms at once. The park has been kept deliberately free of tourist facilities, with the idea that only mountain lovers need venture this far. The main entrance point is the motel and information facility at Crni Lug.

On the Islands

The Kornati Islands consist of 140 sparsely vegetated, uninhabited islands, islets and reefs scattered over 300 sq km, 89 of which are included in the Kornati Islands National Park. The unusual form and extraordinary rock formations of the islands make them an Adriatic highlight. Unless you have your own boat, you'll need to join an organised tour from Zadar, Dugi Otok or Murter Island.

Mljet National Park, on the northwestern half of the island of the same name, incorporates two highly indented saltwater lakes surrounded by lush vegetation. Maquis shrubland is thicker and taller on Mljet than nearly anywhere else in the Mediterranean, which makes it a natural refuge for many animals.

The Brijuni Islands are the most cultivated national park, as they were developed as a tourist resort in the late 19th century. They were the getaway paradise for Tito and now attract the glitterati and their yachts. Most of the animals and plants were introduced, but the islands are lovely. Access to the islands is restricted – you can only visit on an organised tour.

Wildlife
Animals

Of the 59 mammal species present in Croatia, seven are listed as vulnerable: the garden dormouse and six species of bat. Red and roe deer are plentiful in the dense forests of Risnjak National Park, and there are also chamois, brown bears, wild cats and *ris* (Eurasian lynx), from which the park gets its name. Rarely, a grey wolf or wild boar may appear. Plitvice Lakes National Park, however, is an important refuge for wolves. The rare Eurasian otter is also protected in Plitvice Lakes National Park, as well as in Krka National Park.

The temperature of the Adriatic Sea varies greatly: it rises from an average of 7°C (45°F) in December up to a balmy 23°C (73°F) in September.

The website of the Ministry of Environmental & Nature Protection (www.mzoip.hr) is the place to go for the latest news on Croatia's environment.

REFUGE FOR YOUNG BEARS

In the village of Kuterevo in the northern Velebit Range lies the **Kuterevo Refuge** (www.kuterevo-medvjedi.org) for young bears. Founded in 2002 by an association called Velebit Association Kuterevo (Velebitska Udruga Kuterevo; VUK), it works together with the villagers to protect orphaned bears that are endangered due to traffic, hunting and poaching. From spring to late autumn, it's possible to visit the baby bears at the refuge, which attracts some 10,000 visitors per year. The website is in Croatian, but emails will be answered in English.

BIRDWATCHING

The griffon vulture, with a wingspan of up to 2.6m, has permanent colonies on the islands of Cres, Krk and Prvić. Paklenica National Park is rich in peregrine falcons, goshawks, sparrow hawks, buzzards and owls. Krka National Park is an important winter habitat for migratory marsh birds such as herons, wild ducks, geese and cranes, as well as rare golden eagles and short-toed eagles. Kopački Rit Nature Park, near Osijek in eastern Croatia, is an extremely important bird refuge.

Two venomous snakes are endemic in Paklenica: the nose-horned viper and the European adder. The non-venomous leopard snake, the four-lined snake, the grass snake and the snake lizard can be found in both Paklenica and Krka National Parks.

The waters around the islands of Lošinj and Cres are home to the Adriatic's only known resident pod of bottlenose dolphins. Striped dolphins and basking sharks are sometimes also sighted here. A centre has been set up in Mali Lošinj devoted to rehabilitating injured loggerhead, leatherback and green turtles.

Plants

The country's richest plant life is found in the Velebit Range, part of the Dinaric Alps, which provides the backdrop to the central Dalmatian coast. Botanists have counted around 2700 species and 78 endemic plants there, including the increasingly threatened edelweiss. Risnjak National Park is another good place to find edelweiss, along with black vanilla orchids, lilies and hairy alpenroses, which look a lot better than they sound. The dry Mediterranean climate along the coast is perfect for maquis, a low brush that flourishes all along the coast but especially on the island of Mljet. You'll also find oleander, jasmine and juniper trees along the coast, and lavender is cultivated on the island of Hvar. Mediterranean olive and fig trees are also abundant.

Environmental Issues

The lack of heavy industry in Croatia has had the happy effect of leaving its forests, coasts, rivers and air generally fresh and unpolluted. An increase in investment and development, however, brings forth problems and threats to the environment.

Reaching up to 95cm in length, the nose-horned viper is the largest and most venomous snake in Europe. It likes rocky habitats and has a zigzag stripe on its body and a distinctive scaly 'horn' on its nose. If you're close enough to spot the horn you're probably a little too close.

With the tourist boom, the demand for fresh fish and shellfish has risen exponentially. The production of farmed sea bass, sea bream and tuna (for export) is rising substantially, resulting in environmental pressure along the coast. Croatian tuna farms capture the young fish for fattening before they have a chance to reproduce and replenish the wild-fish population.

Coastal and island forests face particular problems. First logged by Venetians to build ships, then by local people desperate for fuel, the forests experienced centuries of neglect, which have left many island and coastal mountains barren. The dry summers and brisk *maestrals* (strong, steady westerly winds) also pose substantial fire hazards along the coast. In the last 20 years, fires have destroyed 7% of Croatia's forests.

In 2014, the Croatian government opened up for tender licences for gas and oil exploration in the Adriatic. Local environmental group Zelena Akcija (Green Action) is protesting the move due to concerns about the potentially devastating effect an oil spill would have in the relatively enclosed body of water.

The Arts

Croatia views itself very much as a cultured central European nation, steeped in the continent's finest artistic traditions and imbued with its own unique folk styles, but equally unafraid of the avant-garde. Even if they're virtually unknown elsewhere, local artists are highly regarded at home.

Literature

Poets & Playwrights

The first literary flowering in Croatia took place in Dalmatia, which was strongly influenced by the Italian Renaissance. The works of the scholar and poet Marko Marulić (1450–1524), from Split, are still venerated in Croatia. His play *Judita* was the first work produced by a Croatian writer in his native tongue. The plays of Marin Držić (1508–67), especially *Dundo Maroje*, express humanistic Renaissance ideals and are still performed, especially in Dubrovnik. Ivan Gundulić's (1589–1638) epic poem *Osman* celebrated the Polish victory over the Turks in 1621, a victory that the Dubrovnik-based author saw as heralding the destruction of Ottoman rule.

The most significant figure in the period after the 1990s war was the lyrical and sometimes satirical Vesna Parun (1922–2010). Although Parun was often harassed by the government for her 'decadent and bourgeois' poetry, her published work *Collected Poems* has reached a new generation, which finds solace in her vision of wartime folly.

Ivan Gundulić (1589–1638) from Ragusa (Dubrovnik) is widely considered to be the greatest Croatian poet. A more recent contender for the title is Tin Ujević (1891–1955), whose work remains extremely popular today.

Novelists

Croatia's towering literary figure is 20th-century novelist and playwright Miroslav Krleža (1893–1981). Always politically active, Krleža broke with Tito in 1967 over the writer's campaign for equality between the Serbian and Croatian literary languages. Depicting the concerns of a changing Yugoslavia, his most popular novels include *The Return of Philip Latinowicz* (1932) and *Banners* (1963–65), a multivolume saga about middle-class Croatian life at the turn of the 20th century.

Mention should also be made of Ivo Andrić (1892–1975), who won the 1961 Nobel Prize for Literature for his Bosnian historical trilogy *The Bridge on the Drina*, *Bosnian Story* and *Young Miss*. Born as a Catholic Croat in Bosnia, the writer used the Serbian dialect and lived in Belgrade, but identified himself as a Yugoslav.

Gold, Frankincense and Myrrh by Slobodan Novak (b 1924), originally published in Yugoslavia in 1968, has been translated into English. The book is set on the island of Rab, where an elderly lady is dying, and her carer – the narrator – reminisces about life, love, the state, religion and memory.

Some contemporary writers have been strongly marked by the implications of Croatian independence. Goran Tribuson (b 1948) uses the thriller genre to examine the changes in Croatian society after the war. In *Oblivion*, Pavao Pavličić (b 1946)uses a detective story to explore the problems of collective historical memory. Canadian-based Josip

Award-winning writer Dubravka Ugrešić and four other female writers were accused of being 'witches' by a Croatian magazine for not wholeheartedly supporting the Croatian war for independence.

Novakovich's (b 1956) work stems from nostalgia for his native Croatia. His most popular novel, *April Fool's Day* (2005), is an absurd and gritty account of the recent wars that gripped the region. Slavenka Drakulić (b 1949) writes novels and essays that are often politically and sociologically provocative, and always witty and intelligent. Look out for *How We Survived Communism and Even Laughed* (1992) and *Cafe Europa* (1999).

Expat writer Dubravka Ugrešić (b 1949) has been a figure of controversy in Croatia and is acclaimed elsewhere. Now living in the Netherlands in self-imposed exile, she is best known for her novels *The Culture of Lies* (1998) and *The Ministry of Pain* (2006).

Miljenko Jergović (b 1966), born in Sarajevo but living in Croatia, is a witty, poignant writer whose *Sarajevo Marlboro* (1994) and *Mama Leone* (1999) powerfully describe the atmosphere in prewar Yugoslavia.

> Vedrana Rudan's novel *Night* (2004) perfectly illustrates the strong language and controversial antipatriarchal themes that are often ruffling feathers in the Croatian literary establishment.

Cinema

By far the most prominent person in the Croatian film industry is Branko Lustig, winner of Academy Awards for producing both *Schindler's List* and *Gladiator*. Born in Osijek to Croatian Jewish parents in 1932, he survived Auschwitz as a child and went on to work for state-owned Jadran Film alongside the likes of director Branko Bauer (1921–2001).

Another luminary is writer and director Veljko Bulajić (b 1928), whose debut movie *Vlak bez voznog reda* (Train without a Timetable) was nominated for the Golden Palm at Cannes in 1959, while *Bitka na Neretvi* (Battle of Neretva) was nominated for an Academy Award 10 years later.

More recently Vinko Brešan's (b 1964) *Kako je počeo rat na mom otoku* (How the War Started on My Island; 1996) and *Maršal* (Marshal Tito's Spirit; 1999) were massively popular in Croatia. Goran Rušinović's (b 1969) stylish *Mondo Bobo* (1997) was the first independent feature film made in Croatia, while his *Buick Riviera* (2008) went on to win awards at the Pula and Sarajevo film festivals.

> On the world stage, Croatia's most famous actors are Mira Furlan (*Babylon 5, Lost*) and Goran Višnjić (*ER, The Girl with the Dragon Tattoo*). Actors of Croatian heritage include John Malkovich and Eric Bana (born Banadinović).

Music

Folk

Although Croatia has produced many fine classical musicians and composers, its most original musical contribution lies in its rich tradition of folk music. This music reflects a number of influences, many dating back to the Middle Ages when the Hungarians and the Venetians vied for control of the country. Franz Joseph Haydn (1732–1809) was born near a Croat enclave in Austria and his compositions were strongly influenced by Croatian folk songs.

The instrument most often used in Croatian folk music is the *tamburica,* a three- or five-string mandolin that is plucked or strummed. Introduced by the Turks in the 17th century, the instrument rapidly gained a following in eastern Slavonia and came to be closely identified with

---

RECOMMENDED FOLK RECORDINGS

➡ *Croatie: Music of Long Ago* is a good starting point as it covers the whole gamut of Croatian music.

➡ *Lijepa naša tamburaša* is a selection of Slavonian chants accompanied by *tamburica* (a three- or five-string mandolin).

➡ *Omiš 1967–75* is an overview of *klapa* (an outgrowth of church-choir singing) music.

➡ *Pripovid O Dalmaciji* is an excellent selection of *klapa* in which the influence of church-choral singing is especially clear.

FOLK DANCES

In dance, look for the *drmeš*, a kind of accelerated polka danced by couples in small groups. The *kolo*, a lively Slavic round dance in which men and women alternate in the circle, is accompanied by Roma-style violinists. In Dalmatia, the *poskočica* is also danced by couples creating various patterns.

Like folk music, Croatian traditional dances are kept alive at local and national festivals. The best is the International Folklore Festival in Zagreb in July. If you can't make it to that, not to worry: music and folklore groups make a circuit in the summer, hitting most coastal and island towns at one point or another. Ask at a local tourist office for a current schedule.

Croatian national aspirations. *Tamburica* music continued to be played at weddings and local festivals during the Yugoslav period, too.

Vocal music followed the *klapa* tradition. Translated as 'group of people', *klapa* is an outgrowth of church-choir singing. The form is most popular in Dalmatia, particularly in Split, and can involve up to 10 voices singing in harmony about love, tragedy and loss. Traditionally the choirs were all-male, but now women are getting involved, although there are very few mixed choirs.

Another popular strain of folk music, which is strongly influenced by music from neighbouring Hungary, emanates from the region of Medimurje in northeastern Croatia. The predominant instrument is a *citura* (zither). The tunes are slow and melancholic, frequently revolving around themes of lost love. New artists have breathed life into this traditional genre, including Lidija Bajuk and Dunja Knebl, female singers who have done much to resuscitate the music and who have gained large followings in the process.

Pop, Rock & the Rest

There's a wealth of home-grown talent in Croatia's pop and rock music scene. One of the most prominent bands is Hladno Pivo (Cold Beer), which plays energetic punky music with witty, politically charged lyrics. Then there's the indie rock band Pips, Chips & Videoclips, whose breakthrough single '*Dinamo ja te volim*' (Dinamo, I Love You) referred to Tuđman's attempts to rename Zagreb's football team, but whose music has generally been apolitical since.

The band Gustafi sings in the Istrian dialect and mixes Americana with local folk sounds, while the deliciously insane Let 3 from Rijeka is (in)famous for its nutty tunes and live performances at which the band members often show up naked, with only a piece of cork up their backsides (yes, really). TBF (The Beat Fleet) is Split's answer to hip hop, using Split slang to talk about current issues, family troubles, heartbreak and happy times. Bosnian-born but Croatia-based hip-hop singer Edo Maajka is another witty voice.

The fusion of jazz and pop with folk tunes is very popular in Croatia. One of the more prominent names in this scene is talented Tamara Obrovac from Istria, who sings in an ancient Istrian dialect that is no longer spoken.

The Croatian queen of pop is Severina, famous for her good looks and eventful personal life, which is widely covered by local celebrity and gossip magazines. Gibonni is another massively popular singer, and his major influence is Oliver Dragojević, a legendary singer of loveable schmaltz. All three (Severina, Gibonni and Dragojević) are from Split.

For more about Croatian roots music, including the hot names on the contemporary scene, check out www.croatian rootsmusic.com.

Painting & Sculpture

The painter Vincent of Kastav was producing accomplished church frescoes in Istria during the 15th century. The small St Mary's Church near Beram contains his work, most notably the *Dance of Death*. Another notable Istrian painter of the 15th century is John of Kastav, who has left frescoes throughout Istria, mostly in the Slovenian part.

Many artists born in Dalmatia were influenced by, and in turn influenced, Italian Renaissance style. The sculptors Lucijan Vranjanin (1420–79) and Frano Laurana (1420–1502), the miniaturist Julije Klović (c 1510–63) and the painter Andrija Medulić left Dalmatia while the region was under threat from the Ottomans in the 15th century and worked in Italy. Museums in London, Paris and Florence contain examples of their work, but few of their creations remain on display in Croatia.

Vlaho Bukovac (1855–1922) was the most notable Croatian painter in the late 19th century. After working in London and Paris, he came to Zagreb in 1892 and produced portraits and paintings on historical themes in a lively style. Early-20th-century painters of note include Miroslav Kraljević (1885–1913) and Josip Račić (1885–1908), but the most internationally recognised artist was the sculptor Ivan Meštrović (1883–1962), who created many masterpieces on Croatian themes. Antun Augustinčić (1900–79) was another internationally recognised sculptor, whose *Monument to Peace* is outside New York's UN building. A small museum of his work can be visited in the town of Klanjec, north of Zagreb.

> Nirvana bass player Krist Novoselic was born in California to Croatian parents and spent part of his teenage years living in Zadar.

Naive Art

Post-WWI artists experimented with abstract expressionism, but this period is best remembered for the naive art that began with the 1931 Zemlja (Soil) exhibition in Zagreb, which introduced the public to works by Ivan Generalić (1914–92) and other peasant painters. Committed to producing art that could be easily understood and appreciated by ordinary people, Generalić was joined by painters Franjo Mraz (1910–81) and Mirko Virius (1889–1943), and sculptor Petar Smajić (1910–85) in a campaign to gain acceptance and recognition for naive art.

Abstract Art

Abstract art infiltrated the postwar scene. The most celebrated modern Croatian painter is Edo Murtić (1921–2005), who drew inspiration from the countryside of Dalmatia and Istria. In 1959 a group of artists – Marijan Jevšovar (1922–88), Ivan Kožarić (b 1921) and Julije Knifer (1921–2004) – created the Gorgona group, which pushed the boundaries of abstract art. Đuro Pulitika (1922–2006), known for his colourful landscapes, was a well-regarded Dubrovnik painter, as were Antun Masle (1919–67) and Ivo Dulčić (1916–75).

> For a thorough rundown of cultural events in Croatia, check out the informative www.culturenet.hr.

Contemporary Art

The post-WWII trend towards avant-garde art has evolved into installation art, minimalism, conceptualism and video art. Contemporary Croatian artists worth seeing include Lovro Artuković (b 1959), whose highly realistic painting style is contrasted with surreal settings, and video artists Sanja Iveković (b 1949) and Dalibor Martinis (b 1947). The multimedia works of Andreja Kulunčić (b 1968), the installations of Sandra Sterle (b 1965) and the video art of Paris-based Renata Poljak (b 1974) are attracting international attention. The performances of Dubrovnik-born multimedia artist Slaven Tolj (b 1964), including his installations and video art, have received international acclaim. Lana Šlezić (b 1973) is a Toronto-based photographer whose excellent work is often shot in Croatia.

Survival Guide

DIRECTORY A–Z....324

Accommodation........ 324

Activities 326

Customs Regulations ... 326

Discount Cards......... 326

Electricity 327

Embassies &
Consulates 327

Gay & Lesbian
Travellers 327

Health.................327

Insurance.............. 328

Internet Access......... 328

Legal Matters 328

Maps.................. 328

Money................. 328

Opening Hours 329

Photography 330

Public Holidays......... 330

Safe Travel............. 330

Telephone 330

Time 331

Tourist
Information 331

Travellers with
Disabilities.............331

Visas..................331

Volunteering 331

Women Travellers........331

TRANSPORT 332

GETTING THERE &
AWAY 332

Entering the Country.... 332

Air 332

Land 332

Sea 334

GETTING AROUND......334

Air 334

Bicycle 334

Boat 334

Bus 335

Car & Motorcycle....... 335

Local Transport......... 336

Tours.................. 336

Train 336

LANGUAGE 337

Directory A–Z

Accommodation

Budget accommodation includes campgrounds, hostels and some guesthouses. Private accommodation is a lot more affordable in Croatia, and is often great value. If you don't mind forgoing hotel facilities, it's a great way to travel.

Accommodation providers will handle travellers' registration with the police, as required by Croatian authorities. To do this, they will need to take your passport away overnight.

Along the coast, accommodation is priced according to four seasons, which vary from place to place:

Nov–Mar The cheapest months – there may only be one or two hotels open in a coastal resort but you'll get great rates.

Apr, May & Oct These are generally the next cheapest months.

Jun & Sep These months are the shoulder season, so prices range in the middle.

Jul & Aug The peak period runs from late July to mid- or late August – and you'll be paying top price. In these months you should make arrangements in advance.

Note that many establishments add a 30% charge for stays shorter than three nights, and also include a 'sojourn tax', which is around 7KN per person per day.

Accommodation is generally cheaper in Dalmatia (except in Dubrovnik and Hvar) than in Kvarner or Istria.

Booking Accommodation

Once you know your itinerary it pays to start calling around to check prices and availability. Most receptionists speak English.

It can be difficult to get a confirmed reservation without a deposit, particularly in the high season. Hotels are equipped to reserve rooms using a credit-card number.

Some guesthouses might require a SWIFT wire transfer (where your bank wires directly to their bank). Banks charge fees for the transaction, usually in the range of US$15 to US$30. The only way around it is to book online through an agency.

Camping

Over 500 campgrounds are along the Croatian coast, including four-star camps and small, family-run sites.

Most operate from mid-April to mid-September only, although a few are open from March to October.

In spring and autumn, it's best to call ahead to make sure that the campground is open. Don't go only by the opening and closing dates given by local tourist offices, travel brochures or even this guide, as these can change.

CAMPGROUNDS

➡ Many campgrounds in Istria are gigantic 'autocamps' with restaurants, shops and rows of caravans, but in Dalmatia they're smaller and often family owned.

➡ If you want a more intimate environment, the town tourist office should be able to refer you to smaller campgrounds (but you may have to insist upon it).

➡ Naturist campgrounds (marked FKK) are among the best because their secluded locations ensure quietness.

➡ Freelance camping is officially prohibited.

➡ See www.camping.hr for camping info and links.

PRICES

➡ Prices listed in this book are per adult and site. Expect to pay up to 100KN for the site at some of the larger camps. Most campgrounds charge from 40KN to 60KN per person per night.

→ The tent charge is sometimes included in the price, but occasionally it's an extra 10KN to 15KN. The vehicle charge is sometimes included; it may be an extra 10KN to 50KN.

→ Caravan sites cost about 30% more; electricity is not always included and may cost an extra 15KN per night.

→ The sojourn tax (also called the residence tax) costs about 7KN extra per person per night, depending on the season and the region.

Hostels

The **Croatian YHA** (Map p46; ☑01-48 29 294; www. hfhs.hr; Savska 5, Zagreb) operates youth hostels in Rijeka, Dubrovnik, Pula, Veli Lošinj, Zadar and Zagreb. Non-members pay an additional 10KN per person per day for a stamp on a welcome card; six stamps entitle you to membership. The Croatian YHA can also provide information about private youth hostels in Poreč, Hvar, Zadar and Zagreb.

Most hostels are now open in winter but may not be staffed all day. It's wise to call in advance.

Prices given in this book are for the high season in July and August; prices drop the rest of the year.

Hotels

The majority of hotels in Croatia are midrange: around 800KN for a double in high season along the coast; around 450KN in late spring or early autumn. At that price you can get a private bathroom, a telephone and sometimes a TV with a satellite hook-up. Double hotel rooms are a good size, and nearly all rooms in Croatian hotels have private bathrooms. Formerly state-owned hotel complexes dating from the 1970s and 1980s are very similar to each other.

Most hotels offer half-board. In a 'tourist settlement' far from town, half-board may be the only dining possibility. Meals centre on cheaper cuts of meat, although some hotels are starting to offer a vegetarian menu.

There is usually a sur-charge for short stays (fewer than three or four nights) during summer along the coast and on the islands.

The star-rating system for Croatian hotels is inconsistent and not very helpful.

Family-run *pansions* (guesthouses) offer excellent value and a more personal experience. Ask at the local tourist office as more *pansions* pop up each season.

Apartments are self-contained units that include equipped kitchens, a bed or beds, and a bathroom.

Private Accommodation

Croatia's hotels are typically overpriced, especially along the coastline in the peak summer season. Staying in private accommodation is the best way to save considerable cash and also to have a glimpse at Croatia's own brand of hospitality – many of the owners treat their guests like long-lost friends. Some even offer the option of eating with them, which is a great way to get to know the culture.

Finding the right private room or apartment takes a little effort though. It's best to research your options online or by word of mouth before going. Prefer on-the-fly travel? Once you've arrived in your destination, visit a handful of properties through a travel agency before booking. You can also deal directly with proprietors who meet you at the local bus or ferry station, or knock on the doors of houses with *sobe, zimmer* or *apartmani* (rooms available) signs.

Note that in high season many private accommodation owners impose a surcharge for stays of less than three or four nights.

PRICES

→ Rates are usually fixed by the local tourist association and don't vary from agency to agency, though some agencies may not handle rooms in the cheapest category, and some only handle apartments.

→ In legally rented accommodation there's often a 'registration tax' to register you with the police.

→ Any prices quoted in this book assume a four-night stay in high season. Prices fall mainly outside July and August.

WHAT TO EXPECT

→ Travel agencies classify private accommodation according to a star system:

Three stars The most expensive; includes a private bathroom.

Two stars The bathroom is shared with one other room.

One star The bathroom is shared with two other rooms or with the owner.

→ Studios with cooking facilities cost more than a double room, but self-catered meals are not cheap in Croatia. If you're travelling in a small group, it may be worth getting an apartment.

TIPS FOR PRIVATE ACCOMMODATION

➡ If you decide to go with proprietors (usually women) at the bus or ferry station, get an exact location first or you could find yourself stuck way out of town.

➡ Clarify whether the price is per person or per room. Don't hesitate to bargain, especially if you're staying for a week.

➡ Avoid a surcharge by specifying the exact number of days you plan to stay and what time of day you plan to check out. In high season along the coast, it may be impossible to find a proprietor willing to rent you a room for one night only.

➡ If you land in a room or apartment without a blue *sobe, zimmer* or *apartmani* sign outside, the proprietor is renting to you illegally (ie not paying sojourn tax). They will probably be reluctant to give their full name or phone number and you'll have no recourse in case of a problem.

➡ Under no circumstances will private accommodation include a telephone, but satellite TV is becoming increasingly common.

➡ Single rooms are scarce.

BOOKING THROUGH AGENCIES

➡ Any accommodation you book through an agency will have been professionally vetted.

➡ Agencies can handle complaints (often in English) if things go wrong.

➡ Stays of fewer than four nights will attract an agency surcharge of at least 30%; some will insist on a seven-night minimum stay in the high season.

BOOKING WITH OWNERS

➡ Look for houses with signs that say *sobe, zimmer* or *apartmani* to know which ones offer private accommodation.

➡ Start early in the day, as proprietors may be out on errands in the afternoon.

➡ Leave your luggage in a *garderoba* (left-luggage office) before heading out – you'll be more comfortable and in a better position to negotiate a price.

BOOKING HALF-BOARD

If possible, it may be worthwhile to take a half-board option and stay with a family. Most families on the coast have a garden, a vineyard and access to the sea – you could find yourself savouring a homemade aperitif before dining on garden-fresh vegetables and grilled fresh fish, all washed down with your host's very own wine.

Activities

Adventure Sports

Cro Challenge (www.cro challenge.com) Extreme sports association.

Croatian Aeronautical Federation (www.caf.hr) Parachuting club.

Huck Finn (www.huckfinn croatia.com) Specialises in adventure travel and runs the gamut of adrenaline-lifting tours around Croatia: river and sea kayaking, rafting, canoeing, caving, cycling, fishing, hiking and sailing.

Outdoor (www.outdoor.hr) Adventure and team-building travel.

Cycling

NGO Bicikl (www.mojbicikl. hr) Cycling information.

Diving

Croatian Diving Association (www.diving-hrs.hr)

Rock Climbing

Croatian Mountaineering Association (www.hps.hr) Rock climbing, caving and hiking information.

Sailing

Adriatic Croatia International Club (www.aci.hr) Manages 21 coastal marinas.

Association of Nautical Tourism (Udruženje Nautičkog Turizma; www.croatia charter.com) Represents all Croatian marinas.

Customs Regulations

➡ Travellers from EU countries can bring their personal effects into the country along with 10L of liquor, 90L of wine, 800 cigarettes and 110L of beer.

➡ Travellers from non-EU countries can bring their personal items into the country along with 4L of wine, 200 cigarettes and 16L of beer.

➡ Camping gear, boats and electronics should be declared upon entering the country.

➡ There is no quarantine period for animals brought into the country, but you should have a recent vaccination certificate. Otherwise, the animal must be inspected by a local vet, who may not be immediately available.

Discount Cards

➡ Most museums, galleries, theatres and festivals in Croatia offer student discounts of up to 50%. For youth travel and the cards listed below, contact the travel section of **Croatian YHA** (☑ 01-48 29 294; www.hfhs.hr; Savska 5, Zagreb).

➡ An International Student Identity Card (ISIC) is the best international proof of student status. People under the age of 26 who are not students qualify for the International Youth Travel Card (IYTC).

➡ Croatia is a member of the **European Youth Card Association** (www.eyca. org), which offers reductions in shops, restaurants and libraries in participating countries. The card can be used at around 1400 places of interest in Croatia.

Electricity

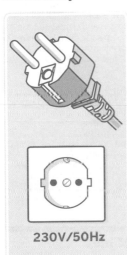

230V/50Hz

Embassies & Consulates

Albanian Embassy (☑01-48 10 679; www.ambasadat. gov.al/croatia; Boškovićeva 7a, Zagreb)

Australian Embassy (☑01-48 91 200; www.croatia. embassy.gov.au; Nova Ves 11/3, Centar Kaptol, Zagreb)

Bosnian & Hercegovinan Embassy (☑01-45 01 070; ambasada-bh-zg@zg.htnet.hr; Torbarova 9, Zagreb)

Bulgarian Embassy (☑01-46 46 609; www.mfa.bg/ embassies/croatia; Nike Grškovića 31, Zagreb)

Canadian Embassy (☑01-48 81 200; zagrb@ international.gc.ca; Prilaz Gjure Deželića 4, Zagreb)

Czech Embassy (☑01-61 77 246; www.mzv.cz/zagreb; Radnička 47/6, Zagreb)

Dutch Embassy (☑01-46 42 200; http://croatia.nlembassy. org; Medvešćak 56, Zagreb)

French Embassy (☑01-48 93 600; www.ambafrance-hr. org; Andrije Hebranga 2, Zagreb)

German Embassy (☑01-63 00 100; www.zagreb.diplo.de; Grada Vukovara 64, Zagreb)

Hungarian Embassy (☑01-48 90 900; www.mfa. gov.hu/kulkepviselet/CR/en/; Pantovčak 255-257, Zagreb)

Irish Consulate (☑01-63 10 025; irish.consulate.zg@inet.hr, Miramarska 23 (Eurocenter), Zagreb)

New Zealand Consulate (☑01-46 12 060; nzealand consulate@email.t-com.hr; Vlaška 50a, Zagreb)

Polish Embassy (☑01-48 99 444; www.zagrzeb.msz.gov. pl, Krležin Gvozd 3, Zagreb)

Romanian Embassy (☑01-46 77 550; zagreb.mae.ro; Mlinarska 43, Zagreb)

Serbian Embassy (☑01 45 79 067; www.zagreb.mfa.gov.rs; Pantovčak 245, Zagreb)

Slovakian Embassy (☑01-48 77 070; www.mzv.sk/ zagreb; Prilaz Gjure Deželića 10, Zagreb)

Slovenian Embassy (☑01-63 11 000; www.zagreb. veleposlanistvo.si; Alagovićeva 30, Zagreb)

UK Embassy (☑01-60 09 100; www.ukincroatia.fco.gov. uk; I Lučića 4, Zagreb)

US Embassy (☑01-66 12 200; http://zagreb.usembassy.gov; Thomasa Jeffersona 2, Zagreb)

Gay & Lesbian Travellers

Homosexuality has been legal in Croatia since 1977 and is tolerated, but not welcomed with open arms. Public displays of affection between same-sex couples may be met with hostility, especially outside the major cities.

Exclusively gay clubs are a rarity outside Zagreb, but many of the large discos attract a mixed crowd. On the coast, Rovinj, Hvar, Split and Dubrovnik are popular with gay male travellers, who often frequent naturist beaches.

➡ In Zagreb, the last Saturday in June is Gay Pride Zagreb day.

➡ Most Croatian websites devoted to the gay scene are in Croatian only, but www. croatia-gay.com and www. friendlycroatia.com are good starting points.

➡ **LORI** (www.lori.hr) is a lesbian organisation based in Rijeka.

Health

Good-quality health care is readily available in Croatia. Pharmacists can give valuable advice and sell over-the-counter medication for minor illnesses.

The standard of dental care is usually good, but it's sensible to have a dental check up at home before taking a long trip.

Infectious Diseases

Tick-borne encephalitis, a serious brain infection, is spread by tick bites. Vaccination is advised for those in areas of risk who are unable to avoid tick bites (such as campers and hikers). Two doses of vaccine will give a year's protection; three doses, up to three years.

Environmental Hazards

➡ Dehydration is already happening by the time you feel thirsty – aim to drink sufficient water to produce pale, diluted urine. To treat heat exhaustion, replace lost fluids by drinking water

PRACTICALITIES

Newspapers & Magazines Widely read newspapers include *Večernji List, Jutarnji List* and *Slobodna Dalmacija*.

Radio The most popular radio station is Narodni Radio, which airs only Croatian music, followed by Antena Zagreb and Otvoreni Radio. Public broadcaster Croatian Radio broadcasts news in English daily at 8am and noon on HR2 (98.5 FM) and at 8pm on HR1 (92.1 FM).

Electricity Electrical supply is 220V, 50Hz AC. Croatia uses the standard European (round-pronged) plugs.

Weights & Measures Croatia uses the metric system.

TV & Video The video system is PAL.

and/or fruit juice, and cool the body with cold water and fans. Treat salt loss with salty fluids such as soup or Bovril, or add a little more table salt to foods than usual.

➡ Heat exhaustion is caused by excessive fluid loss and inadequate replacement of fluids and salt. Symptoms include headache, dizziness and tiredness.

➡ Heatstroke is much more serious, resulting in irrational and hyperactive behaviour and eventually loss of consciousness, and death. Rapid cooling by spraying the body with water and fanning is ideal. Emergency fluid and electrolyte replacement by intravenous drip is recommended.

➡ Watch for sea urchins around rocky beaches. If you get some of their needles embedded in your skin, olive oil will help to loosen them. If they are not removed, they could become infected. As a precaution, wear rubber shoes while walking on the rocks or bathing.

➡ To avoid getting bitten by snakes, do not walk barefoot or stick your hands into holes or cracks. Half of those bitten by venomous snakes are not actually injected with poison (envenomed). If bitten by a snake, do not panic. Immobilise the bitten limb with a splint (eg a stick)

and apply a bandage over the site firmly, similar to a bandage over a sprain. Do not apply a tourniquet, or cut or suck the bite. Get medical help as soon as possible so that an antivenin can be administered if necessary.

Insurance

Worldwide travel insurance is available at www.lonelyplanet.com/travel_services. You can buy, extend and claim online any time – even if you're already on the road.

Internet Access

➡ Most cafes, restaurants and bars across Croatia have free wi-fi; just ask for the password.

➡ Internet access at cybercafes costs around 30KN per hour.

➡ Local tourist offices should have the latest information on local internet access.

➡ Hotels and most private guesthouses are almost always equipped with wi-fi.

Legal Matters

Although it is highly unlikely that you'll be hassled by the police, you should keep identification with you at all times

as the police have the right to stop you and demand ID.

By international treaty, you have the right to notify your consular official if arrested. Embassies and consulates can normally refer you to English-speaking lawyers, although they will not pay for one.

Maps

Freytag & Berndt publishes a series of country, regional and city maps. Its 1:600,000 map of Croatia, Slovenia and Bosnia and Hercegovina is particularly useful if you're travelling in the region. Others include *Croatia, Slovenia* (1:800,000) by GeoCenter and *Hrvatska, Slovenija, Bosna i Hercegovina* (1:600,000) by Naklada Naprijed in Zagreb.

For cities other than Zagreb, Split, Zadar, Rijeka and Dubrovnik, there are few top-quality maps.

Local tourist offices usually publish helpful maps. Regional tourist offices often publish good regional driving maps.

Money

Croatia uses the kuna (KN). Commonly circulated banknotes come in denominations of 500, 200, 100, 50, 20, 10 and five kuna, bearing images of Croat heroes such as Stjepan Radić and Ban Josip Jelačić. Each kuna is divided into 100 lipa. You'll find silver-coloured 50- and 20-lipa coins, and bronze-coloured 10-lipa coins.

The kuna has a fixed exchange rate tied to the euro and the rate varies little from year to year. However, to amass hard currency, the government makes the kuna more expensive in summer when tourists visit. You'll get the best exchange rate from mid-September to mid-June.

➡ You can pay for a meal or small services in euros, but the rate is not as good. You can pay for most private accommodation in euros.

➡ International boat fares are priced in euros, although you pay in kuna.

ATMs

➡ Automatic teller machines (ATMs) are prevalent nearly everywhere in Croatia and can be a convenient way of changing money. Most are tied in with Cirrus, Plus, Diners Club and Maestro.

➡ Most ATMs also allow you to withdraw money using a credit card; note that you pay interest on the amount immediately and are charged a withdrawal fee. Privredna Banka usually has ATMs for cash withdrawals using American Express cards.

➡ All post offices will allow you to make a cash withdrawal on MasterCard or Cirrus, and a growing number work with Diners Club as well.

Credit Cards

Credit cards (Visa, Diners Club, MasterCard, American Express) are widely accepted in hotels but rarely accepted in any kind of private accommodation. Many smaller restaurants and shops do not accept credit cards.

American Express cardholders can contact

Atlas travel agencies in Dubrovnik, Opatija, Poreč, Pula, Split, Zadar and Zagreb for the full range of Amex services, including cashing personal cheques and holding mail. Privredna Banka is a chain of banks that handles many services for Amex clients.

Local credit-card websites:

American Express www.americanexpress.hr

Diners Club www.diners.com.hr

MasterCard/Eurocard www.zaba.hr

Visa www.splitskabanka.hr

Moneychangers

➡ There are numerous places to change money in Croatia, all of them offering similar rates; ask at any travel agency for the location of the nearest exchange. Post offices also change money and are open longer hours.

➡ Most places deduct a commission of 1% to 1.5% to change cash, though some banks do not.

➡ Travellers cheques may be exchanged only in banks.

➡ Kuna can be converted into hard foreign currency only at a bank and only if you submit a receipt of a previous transaction.

Taxes & Refunds

Travellers from non-EU countries who spend more than 740KN in one shop are entitled to a refund of the value-added tax (VAT), which is equivalent to 22% of the purchase price. In order to claim the refund, the merchant must fill out the Tax Cheque (a required form), which you must present to the customs office upon leaving the country. Mail a stamped copy to the shop within six months, which will then credit your credit card with the appropriate sum.

There is also a service called the Global Refund System, which will give you your refund in cash at the airport or at participating post offices. Post offices in Zagreb, Osijek, Dubrovnik, Split, Rijeka, Pula and a few other towns participate in the system. For a complete list, see www.posta.hr.

Tipping

Bills in restaurants include a service charge, but it's common to round up as a tip.

Opening Hours

Croats are early risers: by 7am there will be lots of people on the street and many places already open.

STREET NAMES

Particularly in Zagreb and Split, you may notice a discrepancy between the names used on maps and the names you'll actually see on the street.

In Croatian, a street name can be rendered either in the nominative or the possessive case. The difference is apparent in the name's ending. Thus, Ulica Ljudevita Gaja (street of Ljudevita Gaja) becomes Gajeva ulica (Gaja's Street). The latter version is the one most commonly seen on the street sign and used in everyday conversation. The same principle applies to a trg (square), which can be rendered as Trg Petra Preradovića or Preradovićev trg.

Some of the more common names are Trg Svetog Marka (Markov trg), Trg Josipa Jurja Strossmayera (Strossmayerov trg), Ulica Andrije Hebranga (Hebrangova), Ulica Pavla Radića (Radićeva), Ulica Augusta Šenoe (Šenoina), Ulica Nikole Tesle (Teslina) and Ulica Ivana Tkalčića (Tkalčićeva). Be aware also that Trg Nikole Šubića Zrinskog is almost always called Zrinjevac.

In an address, the letters 'bb' following a street name (such as Placa bb) stand for *bez broja* (without number), which indicates that the building has no street number.

Along the coast, life is more relaxed – shops and offices frequently close around noon for an afternoon break and reopen at about 4pm.

Coastal travel agencies open from 8am or 9am until 9pm or 10pm daily in high season, shortening their hours as the tourist season wanes. In continental Croatia, most agencies keep office hours.

Banks From 8am or 9am to 8pm weekdays, and 7am to 1pm or 8am to 2pm on Saturdays.

Bars & Cafes Usually 8am or 9am to midnight.

Nightlife In Zagreb and Split discos and nightclubs are open year-round, but many places along the coast are only open in summer.

Offices 8am to 4pm or 8.30am to 4.30pm Monday to Friday.

Post Offices 7am to 8pm on weekdays and 7am to 1pm on Saturday. (They keep longer hours in coastal towns during the summer season.)

Restaurants Open long hours, often from noon to 11pm or midnight. They often close on Sunday outside peak season.

Shops 8am to 8pm on weekdays and until 2pm or 3pm on Saturday. Shopping malls have longer hours.

Supermarkets 8am to 8pm Monday to Friday. On Saturday, some close at 2pm while others stay open until 8pm. Only some supermarkets are open on Sunday during the summer season.

Photography

➡ Photo printing from memory cards is available in Zagreb and other large cities, but few places develop rolls of film.

➡ Military installations may not be photographed, and you may have a lot of angry naked people after you if you try to take pictures in a naturist resort.

Public Holidays

Croats take their holidays very seriously. Shops and museums are shut and boat services are reduced. On religious holidays, the churches are full; it can be a good time to check out the artwork in a church that is usually closed.

New Year's Day 1 January

Epiphany 6 January

Easter Monday March/April

Labour Day 1 May

Corpus Christi 10 June

Day of Antifascist Resistance 22 June

Statehood Day 25 June

Homeland Thanksgiving Day 5 August

Feast of the Assumption 15 August

Independence Day 8 October

All Saints' Day 1 November

Christmas 25 & 26 December

Safe Travel
Landmines

The former confrontation line between Croat and federal forces was heavily mined in the early 1990s, and over a million mines were laid in eastern Slavonia around Osijek, and in the hinterlands north of Zadar. Although the government has invested heavily in demining operations, it's a slow job. In general, the mined areas are well signposted with skull-and-crossbones symbols and yellow tape, but don't go wandering off on your own in sensitive regions before checking with a local. Never go poking around an obviously abandoned and ruined house.

Telephone
Area Codes

➡ To call Croatia from abroad, dial your international access code, then ✆385 (the country code for Croatia), then the area code (without the initial 0) and the local number.

➡ To call from region to region within Croatia, start with the area code (with the initial zero); drop it when dialling within the same code.

➡ Phone numbers with the prefix ✆060 can be either free or charged at a premium rate, so watch out for the fine print.

➡ Phone numbers that begin with ✆09 are mobile phone numbers, calls to which are billed at a much higher rate than regular numbers.

Mobile Phones

➡ If you have an unlocked 3G phone, you can buy a SIM card for about 20KN to 50KN, which includes 15 to 30 minutes of connection time. You can choose from three network providers: **VIP** (www.vip.hr), **Hrvatski Telekom** (www.hrvatskitelekom.hr) and **Tele2** (www.tele2.hr).

➡ You can also buy a special prepaid SIM starter pack for tourists; these are available during the high season (June to September) for about 50KN, with data or minutes included.

➡ You can buy a mobile and phonecard package at any telecom shop from about 150KN, which includes connection time.

➡ Mobile phone rental is not available in Croatia.

Phonecards

➡ You'll need a phonecard to use public telephones. Many phone boxes are equipped with a button on the upper left with a flag symbol. Press the button for instructions in English.

➡ Phonecards are sold according to *impulsi* (units); cards are available in 25 (15KN), 50 (30KN), 100 (50KN) and 200 (100KN) units. These can be purchased at any post office and most tobacco shops and newspaper kiosks.

➡ A call from Croatia using a phonecard will cost from around 3KN to 10KN per minute. Local calls cost 0.80KN per minute and calls to mobile networks cost 2KN per minute.

➡ For local and national calls, the mark-up is negligible from cheaper hotels but significantly more from four-star establishments. Private accommodation never includes a private telephone, but you may be able to use the owner's for local calls.

➡ You can call from a post office without a phonecard.

Time

➡ Croatia is on Central European Time (GMT/UTC plus one hour). Daylight saving comes into effect at the end of March, when clocks are turned forward an hour. At the end of September they're turned back an hour.

➡ Croatia uses the 24-hour clock.

Tourist Information

Regional tourist offices supervise tourist development. Local tourist offices have free brochures and good information on local events. Tourist information is also dispensed by commercial travel agencies.

Croatian National Tourist Board (www.croatia.hr) The best starting point to plan your holiday.

Dubrovnik-Neretva County (www.visitdubrovnik.hr)

Istria County (www.istra.hr)

Krapina-Zagorje County (www.tzkzz.hr)

Osijek-Baranja County (www.tzosbarzup.hr)

Primorje-Gorski Kotar (Kvarner) County (www.kvarner.hr)

Šibenik-Knin County (www.sibenikregion.com)

Split-Dalmatia County (www.dalmatia.hr)

Zadar County (www.zadar.hr)

Zagreb County (www.tzzz.hr)

Travellers with Disabilities

More attention is being paid to the needs of people with disabilities in Croatia due to the number of wounded war veterans. For further information, get in touch with **Croatian Association for the Physically Disabled** (Hrvatski Savez Udruga Tjelesnih Invalida; ☑01-48 12 004; www.hsuti.hr; Šoštarićeva 8, Zagreb).

➡ Public toilets at bus stations, train stations, airports and large public venues are usually wheelchair-accessible. Large hotels are wheelchair-accessible, but very little private accommodation is.

➡ Bus and train stations in Zagreb, Zadar, Rijeka, Split and Dubrovnik are wheelchair-accessible, but the local Jadrolinija ferries are not.

Visas

Citizens of the EU, the USA, Canada, Australia, New Zealand, Israel, Ireland, Singapore and the UK do not need a visa for stays of up to 90 days. South Africans must apply for a 90-day visa in Pretoria. Contact any Croatian embassy, consulate or travel agency abroad for information. Your passport must be valid for at least another three months after the planned departure from

Croatia, as well as issued within the previous 10 years. (Note that you're only allowed to stay in Croatia for a total of 90 days in a 180-day period, so leaving the country just to get a stamp and return isn't a legal option.)

Citizens of EU countries and the UK can enter Croatia with only their ID card.

Croatian authorities require all foreigners to register with the local police when they arrive in a new area of the country, but this is a routine matter normally handled by the hotel, hostel, campground or agency securing your private accommodation. If you're staying elsewhere (eg with relatives or friends), your host should take care of it for you.

Volunteering

For short-term volunteering programmes, consider the **Kuterevo Refuge** (www.kuterevo-medvjedi.org) for young bears in the Velebit Range, the **Sokolarski Centre** (☑091 50 67 610; www.sokolarskicentar.com) near Šibenik, and the **Lošinj Marine Education Centre** (☑051-604 666; www.blue-world.org) on Lošinj Island.

Women Travellers

➡ Women face no special danger in Croatia. There have been cases in large coastal cities of some lone women being harassed and followed, but this is not common.

➡ Police will not always take reports of sexual assault by an acquaintance (aka 'date rape') very seriously. Be careful about being alone with an unfamiliar man.

➡ Topless sunbathing is tolerated, but you're better off on one of the numerous nudist beaches.

Transport

GETTING THERE & AWAY

Getting to Croatia is becoming ever easier, especially if you're arriving in summer. Low-cost carriers have established routes to Croatia – you can now fly to Dubrovnik, Split, Zadar, Rijeka, Pula and Zagreb on budget airlines. A plethora of bus and ferry routes also shepherd holidaymakers to the coast. Flights, tours and rail tickets can be booked online at www.lonelyplanet.com/bookings.

Entering the Country

With an economy that depends heavily on tourism, Croatia has wisely kept red tape to a minimum for foreign visitors. The most serious hassle is likely to be long lines at immigration checkpoints.

Air

There are direct flights to Croatia from a variety of European cities. There are no nonstop flights from North America to Croatia, however.

Dubrovnik Airport (DBV; www.airport-dubrovnik.hr) Nonstop flights from Brussels, Cologne, Frankfurt, Hanover, London (Gatwick and Stansted), Manchester, Munich, Paris, Stuttgart and many more.

Pula Airport (PUY; www.airport-pula.com) Nonstop flights from London (Gatwick and Stansted), Manchester, Oslo, Stockholm, Munich, Edinburgh, Copenhagen and more.

Rijeka Airport (RJK; www.rijeka-airport.hr) Nonstop flights from Cologne, Stuttgart, Oslo, Stockholm and more.

Split Airport (SPU; www.split-airport.hr) Nonstop flights from Berlin, Cologne, Copenhagen, Frankfurt, London, Munich, Prague, Stockholm, Rome, Venice and many more.

Zadar Airport (ZAD; www.zadar-airport.hr) Nonstop flights from Brussels, Dublin, London, Munich, Paris, Warsaw and more.

Zagreb Airport (ZAG; www.zagreb-airport.hr) Direct flights from all European capitals, as well as Cologne, Doha, Istanbul, Hamburg, Madrid, Munich, Moscow and Tel Aviv.

Land

Croatia has border crossings with Hungary, Slovenia, Bosnia and Hercegovina, Serbia and Montenegro.

Austria
BUS

Eurolines (www.eurolines.com) operates buses from Vienna to several destinations in Croatia.

Rijeka €42, eight hours, two weekly June to September

CLIMATE CHANGE & TRAVEL

Every form of transport that relies on carbon-based fuel generates CO_2, the main cause of human-induced climate change. Modern travel is dependent on aeroplanes, which might use less fuel per kilometre per person than most cars but travel much greater distances. The altitude at which aircraft emit gases (including CO_2) and particles also contributes to their climate change impact. Many websites offer 'carbon calculators' that allow people to estimate the carbon emissions generated by their journey and, for those who wish to do so, to offset the impact of the greenhouse gases emitted with contributions to portfolios of climate-friendly initiatives throughout the world. Lonely Planet offsets the carbon footprint of all staff and author travel.

BUSES FROM BOSNIA & HERCEGOVINA

FROM	TO	APPROXIMATE COST (€)	DURATION (HR)	SERVICES
Međugorje	Dubrovnik	20	3	1 daily
Mostar	Dubrovnik	19	3	4 daily
Sarajevo	Dubrovnik	24	5–7	4 daily
Sarajevo	Rijeka	41	10	1 daily
Sarajevo	Split (via Mostar)	28	7	3 daily
Sarajevo	Zagreb	26	7–8	4 daily

Split €44, 12 hours, two weekly in summer, one weekly in winter

Zadar €37, nine hours, two weekly

Zagreb €28, five to seven hours, three daily (one direct, the others via Varaždin)

TRAIN

There are two daily and two overnight trains between Vienna and Zagreb, via Slovenia and via Hungary. The price is between €70 and €80 and the journey takes between 5¾ and 6½ hours. Once in Zagreb, you can connect to other cities in Croatia.

Bosnia & Hercegovina

There are dozens of border crossings between Bosnia and Hercegovina and Croatia. Major destinations, such as Sarajevo, Mostar and Međugorje, are all accessible from Zagreb, Split and Dubrovnik.

BUS

Buses run to Croatia from a number of destinations in Bosnia and Hercegovina.

TRAIN

Trains from Sarajevo service the following destinations:

Ploče (via Capljina) €15, four hours, two daily

Zagreb €30, 10 hours, one daily

Germany
BUS

Bus services between the two countries are good, and fares are cheaper than the train. All buses are handled by **Deutsche Touring**

GmbH (www.deutsche-touring. de). There are no Deutsche Touring offices in Croatia, but numerous travel agencies and bus stations sell its tickets.

Scheduled departures to/ from Germany:

Istria To/from Frankfurt weekly; from Munich twice weekly.

Rijeka To/from Berlin twice weekly.

Split To/from Cologne, Dortmund, Frankfurt, Main, Mannheim, Munich, Nuremberg and Stuttgart daily; from Berlin (via Rijeka) twice a week.

Zagreb To/from Cologne, Dortmund, Frankfurt, Main, Mannheim, Munich, Nuremberg and Stuttgart daily; from Berlin two times a week.

TRAIN

There are two trains daily from Munich to Zagreb (€45 to €100, 8½ to nine hours) via Salzburg and Ljubljana. Reservations are required southbound, but not northbound.

Hungary

These are the main highway entry and exit points between Hungary and Croatia (the most important are Donji Miholjac and Goričan):

Donji Miholjac Located 7km south of Harkány.

Gola Located 23km east of Koprivnica.

Goričan Between Nagykanizsa and Varaždin.

Terezino Polje Opposite Barcs.

TRAIN

There are three daily trains from Zagreb to Budapest (€35 return, six to seven hours).

Italy
BUS

Trieste is well connected with the Istrian coast. Note that there are fewer buses on Sundays.

Dubrovnik 470KN, 15 hours, one daily

Poreč 87KN, two hours, four to six daily

Pula 120KN, 2½ to 3¾ hours, four to eight daily

Rijeka 70KN, two hours, five daily

Rovinj 110KN, three hours, two daily

Split 325KN, 10½ hours, two daily

Zadar 221KN, 7½ hours, one daily

There's also a bus from Padua that makes stops in Venice, Trieste and Rovinj and ends up in Pula (245KN, six hours). It runs Monday to Saturday.

TRAIN

There are several trains that run between Venice and Zagreb (€45 to €66, 7½ hours), passing through Ljubljana and Villach.

Montenegro

There are two daily buses from Kotor to Dubrovnik (105KN to 150KN, 2½ hours), which start at Bar and stop at Herceg Novi.

Serbia

Border crossings abound, many off the main Zagreb–Belgrade highway.

BUS

There are seven daily buses from Zagreb to Belgrade (220KN, six hours).

TRAIN

One daily train connects Zagreb with Belgrade (188KN, 6½ hours).

Slovenia

There are 26 border-crossing points between Slovenia and Croatia.

BUS

Slovenia is well connected with the Istrian coast. The following destinations are serviced by buses from Ljubljana:

Rijeka 200KN, 2½ hours, three daily

Rovinj 200KN, four hours, three daily

Split 400KN, 10 hours, one daily

There's also one bus each weekday that connects Rovinj with Koper (105KN, 2¾ hours), stopping at Poreč, Portorož and Piran.

TRAIN

Trains run to Croatia from Ljubljana:

Rijeka 120KN, 2½ hours, two daily

Zagreb 120KN, 2½ hours, four daily

Sea

Regular ferries connect Croatia with Italy.

Blue Line (www.blueline-ferries.com)

Commodore Cruises (www.commodore-cruises.hr)

Jadrolinija (www.jadrolinija.hr)

SNAV (www.snav.com)

Ustica Lines (www.ustica lines.it)

Venezia Lines (www.venezia lines.com)

GETTING AROUND

Air

Croatia Airlines (☑01-66 76 555; www.croatiaairlines.hr) is the national carrier. There are daily flights between Zagreb and Dubrovnik, Osijek, Pula, Rijeka, Split and Zadar.

The new **Trade Air** (www.trade-air.com) has domestic flights, with flights to Split, Rijeka, Osijek, Dubrovnik and Zagreb. Also new, **European Coastal Airlines** (www.ec-air.eu) has seaplanes that fly between mainland and island destinations.

Note that all batteries must be removed from checked luggage when leaving from any airport in Croatia.

Bicycle

Bicycles are easy to rent along the coast and on the islands, and cycling can be a great way to explore the islands. Relatively flat islands such as Pag and Mali Lošinj offer the most relaxed biking, but the winding, hilly roads on other islands offer spectacular views. Cycling on the coast or the mainland requires caution: most roads are busy, two-lane highways with no bicycle lanes.

Some tourist offices, especially in the Kvarner and Istria regions, have maps of routes and can refer you to local bike-rental agencies.

If you have some Croatian language skills, www.pedala.hr is a great reference for cycling routes around Croatia.

Boat

Jadrolinija Ferries

Jadrolinija (www.jadrolinija.hr) operates an extensive network of car ferries and catamarans along the Adriatic coast. Ferries are a lot more comfortable than buses, though somewhat more expensive.

Frequency Year-round. Services are less frequent in winter.

Reservations Cabins should be booked a week ahead. Deck space is usually available on all sailings.

Tickets You must buy tickets in advance at an agency or a Jadrolinija office. Tickets are not sold on board. Tickets for selected catamaran lines can now be bought online.

Cars Check in two hours in advance in summer months.

Food Somewhat mediocre fixed-price menus in on-board restaurants cost about 100KN; the cafeteria offers only ham-and-cheese sandwiches (30KN). Do as the Croats do: bring some food and drink on board with you.

Local Ferries

Local ferries connect the bigger offshore islands with each other and with the mainland, but you'll find many more ferries going from the mainland to the islands than from island to island.

Frequency On most lines, service is less frequent between October and April. Extra passenger boats are added in the summer; these are usually faster, more comfortable and more expensive.

Reservations On some shorter routes (eg Jablanac to Mišnjak), ferries run nonstop in summer and advance reservation is unnecessary.

Tickets Buy at a Jadrolinija office or at a stall near the ferry (usually opens 30 minutes prior to departure). There are no tickets sales on board. In summer, arrive one to two hours prior to departure, even if you've already bought your ticket.

Cars Incur a charge, which is calculated according to the size of car and often very pricey. Reserve as far in advance as possible. Check in several hours in advance.

Bicycles Incur a small charge.

Food There is no meal service; you can buy drinks and snacks on board. Most locals bring their own food.

Bus

Bus services are excellent and inexpensive. There are often a number of different companies handling each route, so prices can vary.

Luggage stowed in the baggage compartment under the bus costs extra (7KN to 10KN a piece, including insurance).

Bus Companies

Autotrans (☏051-660 660; www.autotrans.hr) Based in Rijeka. Connections to Istria, Zagreb, Varaždin and Kvarner.

Brioni Pula (☏052 535 155; www.brioni.hr) Based in Pula. Connections to Istria, Padua, Split, Trieste and Zagreb.

Clissa (☏021-262 090; www.clissa-bus.hr) Only has Zagreb–Split routes but they have electrical sockets, wi-fi, newspapers and water for passengers.

Contus (☏023-317 062) Based in Zadar. Connections to Split and Zagreb.

Croatiabus (☏01-61 13 073; www.croatiabus.hr) Connects Zagreb with towns in Zagorje and Istria.

Samoborček (☏01-63 21 190; www.samoborcek.hr) Connects Zagreb with towns in Dalmatia.

Tickets & Schedules

➡ At large stations, bus tickets must be purchased at the office, not from drivers.

➡ Try to book ahead to be sure of a seat, especially in summer.

➡ Departure lists above the various windows at bus stations tell you which window sells tickets for your bus.

➡ On Croatian bus schedules, *vozi svaki dan* means 'every day', and *ne vozi nedjeljom i blagdanom* means 'no service on Sunday and holidays'.

➡ Some buses travel overnight, saving you a night's accommodation. Don't expect to get much sleep, though, as the inside lights might be on and music might be blasting the whole night.

➡ Take care not to be left behind at meal or rest stops, which usually occur about every two hours.

Car & Motorcycle

Croatia's motorway connecting Zagreb with Split is only a few years old and makes some routes much faster. Zagreb and Rijeka are connected by motorway, and an Istrian motorway has shortened the travel time to Italy considerably.

Although the new roads are in excellent condition, there are stretches where service stations and facilities are scarce.

Car Hire

In order to rent a car:

➡ You must be 21.

➡ You must have a valid driving licence.

➡ You must have a major credit card.

Independent local companies are often much cheaper than the international chains, but the big companies offer one-way rentals. Sometimes you can get a lower rate by booking the car from abroad, or by booking a fly/drive package.

Car Insurance

Third-party public liability insurance is included by law with car rentals, but make sure your quoted price includes full collision insurance, known as a collision damage waiver (CDW). Otherwise, your responsibility for damage done to the vehicle is usually determined as a percentage of the car's value, beginning at around 2000KN.

Driving Licences

Any valid driving licence (no matter what its language) is sufficient to drive legally and rent a car; an international driving licence is not necessary.

The **Hrvatski Autoklub** (HAK, Croatian Auto Club; ☏01-46 40 800; www.hak.hr; Avenija Dubrovnik 44) offers help and advice. For help on the road, you can contact the nationwide **HAK road assistance** (Vučna Služba; ☏1987).

On the Road

➡ Petrol stations are generally open from 7am to 7pm, and often until 10pm in summer. Options are Eurosuper 95, Super 98, normal or diesel. See www.ina.hr for up-to-date fuel prices.

➡ You have to pay tolls on all motorways, to use the Učka tunnel between Rijeka and Istria, to use the bridge to Krk Island, and on the road from Rijeka to Delnice.

➡ For general news on Croatia's motorways and tolls, see www.hak.hr.

ROAD DISTANCES (KM)

	Dubrovnik	Osijek	Rijeka	Split	Zadar	Zagreb
Dubrovnik	---					
Osijek	495	---				
Rijeka	601	459	---			
Split	216	494	345	---		
Zadar	340	566	224	139	---	
Zagreb	572	280	182	365	288	---

USEFUL TRAIN TERMS

Some terms you might encounter posted on timetables at train stations include the following:

brzi – fast train

dolazak – arrivals

polazak – departures

ne vozi nedjeljom i blagdanom – no service on Sunday and holidays

poslovni – business-class train

presjedanje – change of trains

putnički – economy-class/local train

rezerviranje mjesta obvezatno – compulsory seat reservation

vozi svaki dan – daily services

➡ The radio station HR2 broadcasts traffic reports in English every hour on the hour from July to early September.

Road Rules

➡ In Croatia you drive on the right, and use of seatbelts is mandatory.

➡ Unless otherwise posted, the speed limits for cars and motorcycles are as follows: 50km/h in built-up areas; 100km/h on main highways; 130km/h on motorways.

➡ On two-lane highways, it's illegal to pass long military convoys or a line of cars caught behind a slow truck.

➡ It's illegal to drive with blood-alcohol content higher than 0.05%.

➡ You are required to drive with your headlights on even during the day; in Dalmatia, this applies only from October to June.

➡ All foreign cars must have their nationality sticker on the back, even if your EU license plate states it.

Local Transport

The main form of local transport is bus (although Zagreb and Osijek also have well-developed tram systems).

Buses in major cities such as Dubrovnik, Rijeka, Split and Zadar run about once every 20 minutes, less often on Sunday. A ride is usually 10KN to 15KN, with a small discount if you buy tickets at a *tisak* (newsstand).

Small medieval towns along the coast are often closed to traffic and have infrequent links to outlying suburbs.

Bus transport within the islands is infrequent since most people have their own cars.

Tours

Atlas Travel Agency (www. atlas-croatia.com) Offers a wide variety of bus tours, fly/drive packages and excursions all around Croatia.

Huck Finn (www.huckfinn croatia.com) Specialises in adventure travel and runs the gamut of adrenaline-lifting tours around Croatia: river and sea kayaking, rafting, canoeing, caving, cycling, fishing, hiking and sailing.

Inselhüpfen (www.islandhop ping.com) This German company combines boating and cycling and takes an international crowd through southern Dalmatia, Istria or the Kvarner islands, stopping every day for a bike ride.

Katarina Line (www.katarina-line.hr) Offers week-long cruises from Opatija to Split, Mljet, Dubrovnik, Hvar, Brač, Korčula, Zadar and the Kornati Islands on an attractive wooden ship.

Southern Sea Ventures (www.southernseaventures. com) This Australia-based outfitter offers 10- to 14-day sea-kayaking trips in Croatia, including a gourmet kayaking tour.

Train

Trains are less frequent than buses but more comfortable. Note that delays are a regular occurrence on Croatian trains, sometimes for a matter of hours. For information about schedules, prices and services, contact **Croatian Railways** (Hrvatske Željeznice; ☎ 060 333 444; www.hznet.hr).

Zagreb is the hub for Croatia's less-than-extensive train system. No trains run along the coast and only a few coastal cities are connected with Zagreb. For travellers, the main lines of interest are the following:

➡ Zagreb–Osijek

➡ Zagreb–Rijeka–Pula (via Lupoglava, where passengers switch to a bus)

➡ Zagreb–Varaždin–Koprivnica

➡ Zagreb–Zadar–Šibenik–Split

Classes Domestic trains are either 'express' or 'passenger' (local). Any prices quoted in this book are for unreserved, 2nd-class seating. Express trains have 1st- and 2nd-class cars; they are more expensive than passenger trains and a reservation is advisable.

Sleeping Cars There are no couchettes on domestic trains. There are sleeping cars on overnight trains between Zagreb and Split.

Baggage Bringing baggage is free on trains; most stations have left-luggage services charging around 15KN a piece per day.

Passes Travellers with a European InterRail pass can use it in Croatia for free travel. Those travelling only in Croatia are unlikely to do enough train travel to justify the cost.

Language

WANT MORE?

For in-depth language information and handy phrases, check out Lonely Planet's *Croatian Phrasebook*. You'll find it at **shop. lonelyplanet.com**, or you can buy Lonely Planet's iPhone phrasebooks at the Apple App Store.

Croatian belongs to the western group of the South Slavic language family. It's similar to other languages in this group, namely Serbian, Bosnian and Montenegrin.

Croatian pronunciation is not difficult – in the Croatian writing system every letter is pronounced and its sound does not vary from word to word. The sounds are pretty close to their English counterparts. Note that in our pronunciation guides n' is pronounced as the 'ny' in 'canyon', and zh as the 's' in 'pleasure'. Keeping these points in mind and reading our coloured pronunciation guides as though they were English, you'll be understood.

Word stress is also relatively easy in Croatian. In most cases the accent falls on the first vowel in the word – the last syllable of a word is never stressed in Croatian. The stressed syllable is indicated with italics in our pronunciation guides.

Some Croatian words have masculine and feminine forms, indicated after the relevant phrases in this chapter by 'm' and 'f'. Polite ('pol') and informal ('inf') alternatives are also shown for some phrases.

BASICS

Hello.	*Bog.*	bog
Goodbye.	*Zbogom.*	zbo·gom
Yes./No.	*Da./Ne.*	da/ne
Please.	*Molim.*	mo·leem
Thank you.	*Hvala.*	hva·la
You're welcome.	*Nema na čemu.*	ne·ma na che·moo
Excuse me.	*Oprostite.*	o·pro·stee·te
Sorry.	*Žao mi je.*	zha·o mee ye

How are you?
Kako ste/si? — ka·ko ste/see (pol/inf)

Fine. And you?
Dobro. — do·bro
A vi/ti? — a vee/tee (pol/inf)

My name is ...
Zovem se ... — zo·vem se ...

What's your name?
Kako se zovete/ — ka·ko se zo·ve·te/
zoveš? — zo·vesh (pol/inf)

Do you speak (English)?
Govorite/ — go·vo·ree·te/
Govoriš — go·vo·reesh
li (engleski)? — lee (en·gle·skee) (pol/inf)

I (don't) understand.
Ja (ne) razumijem. — ya (ne) ra·zoo·mee·yem

ACCOMMODATION

Do you have any rooms available?
Imate li slobodnih — ee·ma·te lee slo·bod·neeh
soba? — so·ba

Is breakfast included?
Da li je doručak — da lee ye do·roo·chak
uključen? — ook·lyoo·chen

How much is it (per night/per person)?
Koliko stoji — ko·lee·ko sto·yee
(za noć/po osobi)? — (za noch/po o·so·bee)

Do you have a ... room?	*Imate li ... sobu?*	ee·ma·te lee ... so·boo
single	*jednokrevetnu*	yed·no· kre·vet·noo
double	*dvokrevetnu*	dvo· kre·vet·noo

campsite	*kamp*	kamp
guest house	*privatni smještaj*	pree·vat·nee smyesh·tai
hotel	*hotel*	ho·tel
room	*soba*	so·ba
youth hostel	*prenoćište za mladež*	pre·no·cheesh·te za mla·dezh
air-con	*klima- uređaj*	klee·ma· oo·re·jai
bathroom	*kupaonica*	koo·pa·o·nee·tsa
bed	*krevet*	kre·vet
cot	*dječji krevet*	dyech·yee kre·vet
wi-fi	*bežični internet*	be·zheech·nee een·ter·net
window	*prozor*	pro·zor

DIRECTIONS

Where is ...?
Gdje je ...?　　gdye ye ...

What's the address?
Koja je adresa?　　ko·ya ye a·dre·sa

Can you show me (on the map)?
Možete li mi to　　mo·zhe·te lee mee to
pokazati (na karti)?　　po·ka·za·tee (na kar·tee)

at the corner	*na uglu*	na oo·gloo
at the traffic lights	*na semaforu*	na se·ma·fo·roo
behind	*iza*	ee·za
in front of	*ispred*	ees·pred
far (from)	*daleko (od)*	da·le·ko (od)
left	*lijevo*	lee·ye·vo
near	*blizu*	blee·zoo
next to	*pored*	po·red
opposite	*nasuprot*	na·soo·prot
right	*desno*	de·sno
straight ahead	*ravno naprijed*	rav·no na·pree·yed

EATING & DRINKING

What would you recommend?
Što biste nam　　shto bee·ste nam
preporučili?　　pre·po·roo·chee·lee

What's in that dish?
Od čega se　　od che·ga se
sastoji ovo jelo?　　sa·sto·yee o·vo ye·lo

That was delicious!
To je bilo izvrsno!　　to ye bee·lo eez·vr·sno

Please bring the bill/check.
Molim vas,　　mo·leem vas
donesite račun.　　do·ne·see·te ra·choon

KEY PATTERNS

To get by in Croatian, mix and match these simple patterns with words of your choice:

When's (the next day trip)?
Kada je (idući　　ka·da ye (ee·doo·chee
dnevni izlet)?　　dnev·nee eez·let)

Where's (a market)?
Gdje je (tržnica)?　　gdye ye (trzh·nee·tsa)

Where do I (buy a ticket)?
Gdje mogu　　gdye mo·goo
(kupiti kartu)?　　(koo·pee·tee kar·too)

Do you have (any others)?
Imate li　　ee·ma·te lee
(kakve druge)?　　(kak·ve droo·ge)

Is there (a blanket)?
Imate li (deku)?　　ee·ma·te lee (de·koo)

I'd like (that dish).
Želim (ono jelo).　　zhe·leem (o·no ye·lo)

I'd like to (hire a car).
Želio/Željela　　zhe·lee·o/zhe·lye·la
bih (iznajmiti　　beeh (eez·nai·mee·tee
automobil).　　a·oo·to·mo·beel) (m/f)

Can I (take a photograph of you)?
Mogu li (vas/te　　mo·goo lee (vas/te
slikati)?　　slee·ka·tee) (pol/inf)

Could you please (help)?
Molim vas,　　mo·leem vas
možete li　　mo·zhe·te lee
(mi pomoći)?　　(mee po·mo·chee)

Do I have to (pay)?
Trebam li (platiti)?　　tre·bam lee (pla·tee·tee)

I'd like to reserve a table for ...	*Želim rezervirati stol za ...*	zhe·leem re·zer·vee·ra·tee stol za ...
(eight) o'clock	*(osam) sati*	(o·sam) sa·tee
(two) people	*(dvoje) ljudi*	(dvo·ye) lyoo·dee
I don't eat ...	*Ja ne jedem ...*	ya ne ye·dem ...
fish	*ribu*	ree·boo
nuts	*razne orahe*	raz·ne o·ra·he
poultry	*meso od peradi*	me·so od pe·ra·dee
red meat	*crveno meso*	tsr·ve·no me·so

Key Words

appetiser	*predjelo*	pre·dye·lo
baby food	*hrana za bebe*	hra·na za be·be
bar	*bar*	bar

Signs

Izlaz	Exit
Muškarci	Men
Otvoreno	Open
Ulaz	Entrance
Zabranjeno	Prohibited
Zahodi	Toilets
Zatvoreno	Closed
Žene	Women

bottle	boca	bo·tsa
bowl	zdjela	zdye·la
breakfast	doručak	do·roo·chak
cafe	kafić/ kavana	ka·feech/ ka·va·na
(too) cold	(pre)hladno	(pre·)hlad·no
dinner	večera	ve·che·ra
dish (food)	jelo	ye·lo
food	hrana	hra·na
fork	viljuška	vee·lyoosh·ka
glass	čaša	cha·sha
knife	nož	nozh
lunch	ručak	roo·chak
main course	glavno jelo	glav no ye lo
market	tržnica	trzh·nee·tsa
menu	jelovnik	ye·lov·neek
plate	tanjur	ta·nyoor
restaurant	restoran	re·sto·ran
spicy	pikantno	pee·kant·no
spoon	žlica	zhlee·tsa
with/without	sa/bez	sa/bez
vegetarian meal	vegetarijanski obrok	ve·ge·ta·ree· yan·skee o·brok

Meat & Fish

beef	govedina	go·ve·dee·na
chicken	piletina	pee·le·tee·na
fish	riba	ree·ba
lamb	janjetina	ya·nye·tee·na
pork	svinjetina	svee·nye·tee·na
veal	teletina	te·le·tee·na

Fruit & Vegetables

apple	jabuka	ya·boo·ka
apricot	marelica	ma·re·lee·tsa
(green) beans	mahuna	ma·hoo·na
cabbage	kupus	koo·poos
carrot	mrkva	mrk·va

corn	kukuruz	koo·koo·rooz
cherry	trešnja	tresh·nya
cucumber	krastavac	kra·sta·vats
fruit	voće	vo·che
grape	grožđe	grozh·je
lentils	leća	le·cha
lettuce/salad	zelena salata	ze·le·na sa·la·ta
mushroom	gljiva	glyee·va
nut	orah	o·rah
onion	luk	look
orange	naranča	na·ran·cha
peach	breskva	bres·kva
pear	kruška	kroosh·ka
peas	grašak	gra·shak
plum	šljiva	shlyee·va
potato	krumpir	kroom·peer
pumpkin	bundeva	boon·de·va
strawberry	jagoda	ya·go·da
tomato	rajčica	rai·chee·tsa
vegetable	povrće	po·vr·che
watermelon	lubenica	loo·be·nee·tsa

Other

bread	kruh	krooh
butter	maslac	ma·slats
cheese	sir	seer
egg	jaje	ya·ye
honey	med	med
jam	džem	jem
oil	ulje	oo·lye
pasta	tjestenina	tye·ste·nee·na
pepper	papar	pa·par
rice	riža	ree·zha
salt	sol	sol
sugar	šećer	she·cher
vinegar	ocat	o·tsat

Drinks

beer	pivo	pee·vo
coffee	kava	ka·va
juice	sok	sok
milk	mlijeko	mlee·ye·ko
(mineral) water	(mineralna) voda	(mee·ne·ral·na) vo·da
tea	čaj	chai
(red/white) wine	(crno/bijelo) vino	(tsr·no/bye·lo) vee·no

EMERGENCIES

Help!
Upomoć! — oo·po·moch

I'm lost.
Izgubio/
Izgubila sam se. — eez·goo·bee·o/
eez·goo·bee·la sam se (m/f)

Leave me alone!
Ostavite me na miru! — o·sta·vee·te me na *mee*·roo

There's been an accident!
Desila se nezgoda! — de·see·la se *nez*·go·da

Call a doctor!
Zovite liječnika! — zo·vee·te lee·*yech*·nee·ka

Call the police!
Zovite policiju! — zo·vee·te po·*lee*·tsee·yoo

I'm ill.
Ja sam bolestan/
bolesna. — ya sam *bo*·le·stan/
bo·le·sna (m/f)

It hurts here.
Boli me ovdje. — *bo*·lee me *ov*·dye

I'm allergic to ...
Ja sam alergičan/
alergična na ... — ya sam a·*ler*·gee·chan/
a·*ler*·geech·na na ... (m/f)

SHOPPING & SERVICES

I'd like to buy ...
Želim kupiti ... — *zhe*·leem koo·pee·tee ...

I'm just looking.
Ja samo razgledam. — ya sa·mo *raz*·gle·dam

May I look at it?
Mogu li to pogledati? — mo·goo lee to po·gle·da·tee

How much is it?
Koliko stoji? — ko·*lee*·ko *sto*·yee

That's too expensive.
To je preskupo. — to ye pre·*skoo*·po

Do you have something cheaper?
Imate li nešto
jeftinije? — ee·ma·te lee *nesh*·to
yef·*tee*·nee·ye

There's a mistake in the bill.
Ima jedna greška
na računu. — ee·ma *yed*·na *gresh*·ka
na ra·*choo*·noo

ATM	*bankovni automat*	*ban*·kov·nee a·oo·*to*·mat
credit card	*kreditna kartica*	kre·*deet*·na *kar*·tee·tsa
internet cafe	*internet kafić*	een·ter·net ka·feech

Question Words

How?	*Kako?*	*ka*·ko
What?	*Što?*	shto
When?	*Kada?*	*ka*·da
Where?	*Gdje?*	gdye
Who?	*Tko?*	tko
Why?	*Zašto?*	*za*·shto

post office	*poštanski ured*	*posh*·tan·skee *oo*·red
tourist office	*turistička agencija*	too·*ree*·steech·ka a·*gen*·tsee·ya

TIME & DATES

What time is it?
Koliko je sati? — ko·*lee*·ko ye sa·tee

It's (10) o'clock.
(Deset) je sati. — (*de*·set) ye sa·tee

Half past (10).
(Deset) i po. — (*de*·set) ee po

morning	*jutro*	*yoo*·tro
afternoon	*poslijepodne*	po·slee·ye·*pod*·ne
evening	*večer*	*ve*·cher
yesterday	*jučer*	*yoo*·cher
today	*danas*	*da*·nas
tomorrow	*sutra*	*soo*·tra

Monday	*ponedjeljak*	po·*ne*·dye·lyak
Tuesday	*utorak*	oo·*to*·rak
Wednesday	*srijeda*	*sree*·ye·da
Thursday	*četvrtak*	chet·*vr*·tak
Friday	*petak*	*pe*·tak
Saturday	*subota*	*soo*·bo·ta
Sunday	*nedjelja*	*ne*·dye·lya

January	*siječanj*	*see*·ye·chan'
February	*veljača*	*ve*·lya·cha
March	*ožujak*	*o*·zhoo·yak
April	*travanj*	*tra*·van'
May	*svibanj*	*svee*·ban'
June	*lipanj*	*lee*·pan'
July	*srpanj*	*sr*·pan'
August	*kolovoz*	*ko*·lo·voz
September	*rujanj*	*roo*·yan'
October	*listopad*	*lee*·sto·pad
November	*studeni*	*stoo*·de·nee
December	*prosinac*	*pro*·see·nats

TRANSPORT

Public Transport

boat	*brod*	brod
bus	*autobus*	a·oo·*to*·boos
plane	*avion*	a·*vee*·on
train	*vlak*	vlak
tram	*tramvaj*	*tram*·vai

Numbers

1	*jedan*	ye·dan
2	*dva*	dva
3	*tri*	tree
4	*četiri*	che·tee·ree
5	*pet*	pet
6	*šest*	shest
7	*sedam*	se·dam
8	*osam*	o·sam
9	*devet*	de·vet
10	*deset*	de·set
20	*dvadeset*	dva·de·set
30	*trideset*	tree·de·set
40	*četrdeset*	che·tr·de·set
50	*pedeset*	pe·de·set
60	*šezdeset*	shez·de·set
70	*sedamdeset*	se·dam·de·set
80	*osamdeset*	o·sam·de·set
90	*devedeset*	de·ve·de·set
100	*sto*	sto
1000	*tisuću*	tee·soo·choo

I want to go to ...
Želim da idem u ...   zhe·leem da ee·dem oo ...

Does it stop at (Split)?
Da li staje u (Splitu)?   da lee sta·ye oo (splee·too)

What time does it leave?
U koliko sati kreće?   oo ko·lee·ko sa·tee kre·che

What time does it get to (Zagreb)?
U koliko sati stiže   oo ko·lee·ko sa·tee stee·zhe
u (Zagreb)?   oo (zag·reb)

Could you tell me when we get to (the Arena)?
Možete li mi reći   mo·zhe·te lee mee re·chee
kada stignemo kod   ka·da steeg·ne·mo kod
(Arene)?   (a·re·ne)

I'd like to get off at (Dubrovnik).
Želim izaći   zhe·leem ee·za·chee
u (Dubrovniku).   oo (doob·rov·nee·koo)

A ... ticket.	Jednu ... kartu.	yed·noo ... kar·too
1st-class	*prvorazrednu*	pr·vo· raz·red·noo
2nd-class	*drugorazrednu*	droo·go· raz·red·noo
one-way	*jednosmjernu*	yed·no· smyer·noo
return	*povratnu*	po·vrat·noo
the first	*prvi*	pr·vee
the last	*posljednji*	pos·lyed·nyee
the next	*sljedeći*	slye·de·chee

aisle seat	*sjedište do* *prolaza*	sye·deesh·te do pro·la·za
delayed	*u zakašnjenju*	oo za·kash· nye·nyoo
cancelled	*poništeno*	po·neesh·te·no
platform	*peron*	pe·ron
ticket office	*blagajna*	bla·gai·na
timetable	*red vožnje*	red *vozh*·nye
train station	*željeznička* *postaja*	zhe·lyez·neech·ka pos·ta·ya
window seat	*sjedište* *do prozora*	sye·deesh·te do pro·zo·ra

Driving & Cycling

I'd like to hire a ...	Želim iznajmiti ...	zhe·leem eez·nai·mee·tee ...
4WD	*džip*	jeep
bicycle	*bicikl*	bee·tsee·kl
car	*automobil*	a·oo·to·mo·beel
motorcycle	*motocikl*	mo·to·tsee·kl
bicycle pump	*pumpa za* *bicikl*	poom·pa za bee·tsee·kl
child seat	*sjedalo za* *dijete*	sye·da·lo za dee·ye·te
diesel	*dizel gorivo*	dee·zel go·ree·vo
helmet	*kaciga*	ka·tsee·ga
mechanic	*auto-* *mehaničar*	a·oo·to· me·ha·nee·char
petrol/gas	*benzin*	ben·zeen
service station	*benziska* *stanica*	ben·zeen·ska sta·nee·tsa

Is this the road to ...?
Je li ovo cesta za ...?   ye lee o·vo tse·sta za ...

(How long) Can I park here?
(Koliko dugo)   (ko·lee·ko doo·go)
Mogu ovdje   mo·goo ov·dye
parkirati?   par·kee·ra·tee

The car/motorbike has broken down (at Knin).
Automobil/   a·oo·to·mo·beel/
Motocikl   mo·to·tsee·kl
se pokvario   se pok·va·ree·o
(u Kninu).   (oo knee·noo)

I have a flat tyre.
Imam probušenu   ee·mam pro·boo·she·noo
gumu.   goo·moo

I've run out of petrol.
Nestalo mi je   ne·sta·lo mee ye
benzina.   ben·zee·na

I've lost the keys.
Izgubio/   eez·goo·bee·o/
Izgubila   eez·goo·bee·la
sam ključeve.   sam *klyoo*·che·ve **(m/f)**

GLOSSARY

(m) indicates masculine gender, (f) feminine gender and (pl) plural

amphora (s), **amphorae** (pl) – large, two-handled vase in which wine or water was kept

apse – altar area of a church

autocamps – gigantic campgrounds with restaurants, shops and row upon row of caravans

Avars – Eastern European people who waged war against Byzantium from the 6th to 9th centuries

ban – viceroy or governor

bb – in an address the letters 'bb' following a street name (such as Placa bb) stand for *bez broja* (without number), which indicates that the building has no street number

bura – cold northeasterly wind

cesta – road

crkva – church

fortica – fortress

galerija – gallery

garderoba – left-luggage office

Glagolitic – ancient Slavonic language put into writing by Greek missionaries Cyril and Methodius

gora – mountain

HDZ – Hrvatska Demokratska Zajednica; Croatian Democratic Union

Illyrians – ancient inhabitants of the Adriatic coast, defeated by the Romans in the 2nd century BC

karst – highly porous limestone and dolomitic rock

klapa – an outgrowth of church-choir singing

konoba – the traditional term for a small, intimate dining spot, often located in a cellar; now applies to a wide variety of restaurants; usually a simple, family-run establishment

knez – duke

maestral – strong, steady westerly wind

mali – small

maquis – dense growth of mostly evergreen shrubs and small trees

muzej – museum

nave – central part of a church flanked by two aisles

NDH – Nezavisna Država Hrvatska; Independent State of Croatia

obala – waterfront

otok (s), **otoci** (pl) – island

pansion – guesthouse

plaža – beach

polje – collapsed limestone area often under cultivation

put – path, trail

restoran – restaurant

rijeka – river

sabor – parliament

šetalište – walkway

sobe – rooms available

sveti – saint

svetog – saint (genitive case – ie of saint, as in the Church of St Joseph)

tamburica – a three- or five-string mandolin

tisak – news-stand

toplice – spa

trg – square

turbo folk – a techno version of Serbian folk music

ulica – street

uvala – bay

velik – large

vrh – summit, peak

zimmer – rooms available (a German word)

Behind the Scenes

SEND US YOUR FEEDBACK

We love to hear from travellers – your comments keep us on our toes and help make our books better. Our well-travelled team reads every word on what you loved or loathed about this book. Although we cannot reply individually to your submissions, we always guarantee that your feedback goes straight to the appropriate authors, in time for the next edition. Each person who sends us information is thanked in the next edition – the most useful submissions are rewarded with a selection of digital PDF chapters.

Visit **lonelyplanet.com/contact** to submit your updates and suggestions or to ask for help. Our award-winning website also features inspirational travel stories, news and discussions.

Note: We may edit, reproduce and incorporate your comments in Lonely Planet products such as guidebooks, websites and digital products, so let us know if you don't want your comments reproduced or your name acknowledged. For a copy of our privacy policy visit lonelyplanet.com/privacy.

OUR READERS

Many thanks to the travellers who used the last edition and wrote to us with helpful hints, useful advice and interesting anecdotes:

Aidan Kennedy, Alan Addison, Anto Vukovic, Andreas Vilic, Beata Åhall, Calum Munro, Carlo Iossa, Cristiana Constantinescu, Dale Hattey, David Carrizo, David Grimwood, Dudley McFadden, Elaine Crowe, Emily Durham, Gayle Galletta, George Moss, Gill Ludkiewicz, Gregoire Labbe, Jack Downton, Jane Ramsell, Kate Sandey, Lynn Hopchet, Marcel Albornoz, Maria Carmona, Mike Gerber, Nuria Zantman, Patrick Reid, Paul Dekleva, Samantha Kent, Teresa Oldham

AUTHOR THANKS

Anja Mutić

Hvala mama, for your inspiring laughter. Obrigada, Hoji, for being there before, during and after. A huge *hvala* to my friends in Croatia who gave me endless recommendations – this book wouldn't be the same without you. Special thanks go to Mila in Split. Finally, to the inspiring memory of my father who travels with me still.

Peter Dragicevich

Company on the road is always a treat, so many thanks to Len and Anne Erceg, Manda Wilson and Tim Moyes. Special thanks to the extended Dragičević family in Split and Vrgorac for their warm welcome and exceptional hospitality, especially Vojko and Marija Dragičević.

ACKNOWLEDGMENTS

Climate map data adapted from Peel MC, Finlayson BL & McMahon TA (2007) 'Updated World Map of the Köppen-Geiger Climate Classification', *Hydrology and Earth System Sciences*, 11, 163344

Cover photograph: Rovinj, Istria, Alan Copson/ Getty Images

THIS BOOK

This 8th edition of Lonely Planet's *Croatia* guidebook was researched and written by Anja Mutić and Peter Dragicevich. The previous edition was written by Anja Mutić and Vesna Maric.

Destination Editor
Anna Tyler

Product Editor
Alison Ridgway

Regional Senior Cartographer
Anthony Phelan

Book Designer
Katherine Marsh

Assisting Editors
Michelle Bennett, Melanie Dankel, Ali Lemer, Kate Mathews, Rosie Nicholson, Charlotte Orr, Erin Richards, Gabrielle Stefanos

Assisting Cartographer
Alison Lyall

Assisting Book Designers
Virginia Moreno, Jennifer Mullins

Cover Researcher
Naomi Parker

Thanks to Justin Flynn, Luna Soo, Saralinda Turner, Amanda Williamson

Index

A

accommodation 324-6, 337, see also individual locations
activities 326, see also individual activities
Ada 95
air travel
  airports 17
  to/from Croatia 332
  within Croatia 334
Ančić, Mario 307
Anića Kuk 175
animals 317-18, see also individual species
Aquarium Split 18, 202
archaeological & historic sites
  Burnum 196
  Diocletian's Palace 14, 200-2, 214, **214**, **14**
  Polače 273
  Poreč 116
  Pula 99-102
Archaeological Museum of Osijek 87
architecture 20-1, 314-15
area codes 17, 330
art galleries, see museums & galleries
arts 319-22
ATMs 329

B

Badija Island 281
Bale 115
Banj 227
Banje Beach 258
Barać's Caves 172
Baranja 91-4
Baška 162-3
basketball 307

Map Pages **000**
Photo Pages **000**

Batina 94
beaches 21, 230
  Ada 95
  Bale 115
  Brela 226, **230**
  Dubrovnik 258
  Galovac 184
  Kolombarica Beach 103
  Komiža 248
  Krivica **156**
  Lopar 168
  Lubenice 151, **20**
  Makarska 224
  Medena 222
  Okrug Gornji 222
  Orebić 276
  Pakleni Islands 240
  Pantan 222
  Prapratno 275
  Pula 103
  Sakarun Bay 188
  Stara Baška 161
  Supetar 227
  Sveti Andrija 114
  Vis Island 246
  Zlatni Rat 233
bears 317
beer 311
Beli 147-8
Beram 122
bicycle travel, see cycling
Bili Rat 227
Bilje 92
Biokovo National Park 225
birdwatching 318
  Kopački Rit Nature Park 92
  Učka Nature Park 145
Biševo 12, 249
Blue Grotto 12, 249, **12**
Blue World Institute of Marine Research & Conservation 158
boat travel 334, see also canoeing & kayaking, sailing

boat trips 12, **12**
  Badija Island 281
  Crveni Otok 114
  Hvar Town 238
  Rovinj 111
  Sali 187
  Šibenik 191
  Sveti Nikola 116
  Zadar 182
  Bol 11, 233 5, **11**
border crossings
  Austria 332-3
  Bosnia & Hercegovina 333
  Hungary 333
  Montenegro 333
  Serbia 334-5
  Slovenia 334
  Božava **188**
Brač Island 19, 226-35
Brela 226, **230**
Brijuni Islands 107-8
Broz, Josip (Tito) 297, 298, 299
Buba 224
budget 17
Burnum 196
bus travel
  to/from Croatia 332-4
  within Croatia 335
business hours 17, 329-30
Buzet 126-8

C

camping 324
canoeing & kayaking
  Dubrovnik 259
  Mali Lošinj 153
  Rovinj 111
car travel 335-6, 341
Carnival 22
castles
  Kaštel Gomilica 223
  Kaštel Kambelovac 223
  Kaštel Lukšić 223
  Kaštel Novi 223

  Kaštel Štafilić 223
  Kaštel Stari 223
  Kaštel Sućurac 223
  Knin Fortress 196
  Morosini-Grimani Castle 124
  Trakošćan Castle 14, 79-81
  Trsat Castle 137
  Veliki Tabor Castle 14, 82-3, **14**
cathedrals, see churches & cathedrals
Cava 258
caves
  Barać's Cave 172
  Dragon's Cave 233
  Grabovača Cave Park 174
  Manita Peć 175
  Pazin Chasm 125
Cavtat 270-1
cell phones 16, 330
Central Dalmatia 38, 197-249, **198-9**
  climate 197
  highlights 198
Cest is D'Best 23, 54
children, travel with 34-5
  International Children's Festival 193
  Zagreb 59
churches & cathedrals
  Cathedral of St Lovro 219
  Cathedral of the Assumption (Dubrovnik) 255-7
  Cathedral of the Assumption (Krk Town) 159
  Cathedral of the Assumption of the Blessed Virgin Mary 41
  Church of St Euphemia 110
  Euphrasian Basilica 116
  Marija Bistrica Church 83
  Our Lady of Trsat Church 137
  St Blaise's Church 123

churches & cathedrals
continued
St James' Cathedral 191
St John the Evangelist's
Church 165
St Lucy's Church 162
St Mark's Cathedral 281
St Mark's Church 44
Čikat 152
Čilić, Marin 307
cinema 320
climate 16, see also
individual locations
climate change 332
coffee 311, **10**
consulates 327
cooking courses 308
credit cards 329
Cres Island 15, 19, 146-
57, **15**
Cres Town 148-50
Crikvenica 137
Croatian Association of
Artists 52
Croatian Museum of
Tourism 143-4
Crveni Otok 114
culture 303-7
currency 16, 328
customs regulations 326
cycling 19, 326, 334, 341
Bilje 92
Krk Town 160
Kvarner 141
Mali Lošinj 153
Momjan 133
Poreč 118
Pula 102
Rab Town 165
Rovinj 111
Učka Nature Park 145

D
Đakovački Vezovi 90
Đakovo 90
dance 321
Dančé 258
Dance & Nonverbal
Theatre Festival 23-4,
124
dangers, see safety
Days of Jules Verne 125
deer 317
Delnice 140
Dingač 275

Map Pages **000**
Photo Pages **000**

Diocletian's Palace 14, 200-
2, 214, **214**, **14**
disabilities, travellers
with 331
discount cards 326-7
diving & snorkelling 19,
231, 326
Beli 148
Bol 233-4
Cres 149
Dubrovnik 258
Hvar Town 237
Krk Town 160
Mali Lošinj 153
Maškin 114
Mljet Island 274
Poreč 118
Pula 102
Rab Town 165-7
Rovinj 111
Sali 187
Supetar 227
Vis Town 245
Dolac Market 41
dolphins 158
Dragon's Cave 233
drinks 21, 311-12, 339
driving, see car travel
driving licences 335
Drvenik Mali 222
Drvenik Veli 222
Dubrovnik 9, 38, 251-70,
256, **260-1**, 5, 9, **264**,
265
accommodation 259-66
activities 258-9
climate 250
drinking & nightlife
267-8
festivals & events 259
food 266-7
information 268
medical services 268
shopping 268
sights 251-8
tourist information 269
tours 259
transport 269-70
Dubrovnik Summer
Festival 23
Dugi Otok 186-8
Dugi Rat 226

E
economy 286
Elafiti Islands 272
electricity 328
embassies 327
emergencies 17

environment 316-18
environmental issues 318
Euphrasian Basilica 116
events 22-3
exchange rates 17

F
Feast of St Blaise 22
Feast of St Martin 25
ferries 334
Festival of Subotina 127
Festival Opatija 144
festivals 22-3, see also
individual locations
films 320
flora 318
food 12, 21, 308-13, 338, **11**,
12, see also individual
locations
football 306
For Festival 23
Fritzy Palace 153
Fuliranje 55
Full Moon Festival 24-5

G
galleries, see museums &
galleries
Galovac 184
Game of Thrones 258
gardens, see parks &
gardens
gay travellers 62, 306,
327
Gospić 173-4
Grabovača Cave Park 174
Gračišće 126
Gradina 284
Green Grotto 249
griffon vultures 148, 150
Grohote 217
Grožnjan 132-3
Gustafi 321

H
health 327-8
Hideout 23, **24**
hiking 19
Biokovo National Park
225
Gračišće 126
Mali Lošinj 153
Medvednica Nature
Park 70
Orebić 276-7
Paklenica National
Park 174
Poreč 118

Rab Town 165
Risnjak National Park
140
Samobor 69
Split 202-3
Učka Nature Park 145
historic sites, see
archaeological &
historic sites
history 288-302
Bosnia & Hercegovina
301-2
Christianity 290-1
early inhabitants 288
EU recognition 300-1
Habsburgs 293
Homeland War 300
Napoleonic invasion
294
Ottoman Turks 292-3
Romans 289-90
WWI 295-6
WWII 296-7
Yugoslavia 295-6, 297,
298-300
holidays 330
Holy Week 23
horseback riding 19, 145
hot springs 78, 82
Hrelić 65
Hum 128-9
Hvar Island 235-44
Hvar Town 10, 19, 236-42,
238, **10**, **28**

I
Ilok 96
Ilovik 155
INmusic Festival 23, 54
insurance 328, 335
International Children's
Festival 193
International Folklore
Festival 54
International Puppet
Theatre Festival 54-5
internet access 328
internet resources 17
Istria 11, 37, 97-133, **98**
climate 97
highlights 98
itineraries 26-33
Ivanišević, Goran 307

J
Jadrolinija 155
Jelsa 243-4
Jerolim 240

K

Karanac 93-4
Kaštel Gomilica 223
Kaštel Kambelovac 223
Kaštel Lukšić 223
Kaštel Novi 223
Kaštel Štafilić 223
Kaštel Stari 223
Kaštel Sućurac 223
Kaštela 222-3
kayaking, see canoeing & kayaking
Klanjec 83
Knin 196
Knin Fortress 196
Koločep 272
Kolombarica Beach 103
Komiža 248
Komrčar Park 164
Konavle 272
Kopačevo 92
Kopački Rit Nature Park 15, 91-2, **15**
Korčula Island 277-84
Korčula Town 19, 279-84, **280**
Kornat 189
Kornati Islands 19, 188-9
Kornati National Park 189
Košljun 161
Kostelić, Ivica 307
Kostelić, Janica 307
Kotli 128
Krapina 81-2
Krivica 156
Krk Island 157-63
Krk Town 159-61
Krka Monastery 195-6
Krka National Park 13, 194-6, **13**
Krleža, Miroslav 319
Kumrovec 83
Kvarner 37, 134-68, **135**
   climate 134
   highlights 135

L

Labin 121-3
Lake Mir 187
landmines 330
language 16, 303, 337-41
Lapad Bay 258
legal matters 328
lesbian travellers 62, 306, 327
Lighting Giants 18
Lika 171-6
Limska Draga Fjord 115

literature 319-20
Ljeto na Strossu 23, 54
Ljubičić, Ivan 307
Lokrum Island 271
Lonjsko Polje Nature Park 68-70
Lopar 168
Lopud 272
Lošinj Island 19, 146-57
Lozovac 195
Lubenice 151, **20**
Lumbarda 284

M

Makarska 223-6
Makarska Riviera 223-6
Maksimir Park 50
Mala Učka 145
Mali Lošinj 152-6
Mali Plac na Tavanu 65
Mali Ston 275
Malinska 158-9
Manita Peć 175
maps 328
Marija Bistrica 83
markets 65
   Dolac Market 41
   Fulir anje 55 Hrelić 65
   Mali Plac na Tavanu 65
Marulić, Marko 319
Maskın 114
measures 328
Medena 222
medical services 327
Međimurje 79
Medvedgrad 50
Medvednica Nature Park 70
Mekićevica 238
Milna 246
Mlini 240
Mljet Island 10, 19, 273-4, **10**
Mljet National Park 273
mobile phones 16, 330
Momjan 133
money 16, 17, 328-9
Montenegro 271
Morosini-Grimani Castle 124
Mošćenička Draga 147
Mostar 271
motorcycle travel 335-6
Motovun 129-31
Motovun Film Festival 24, 129
mountain biking, see cycling
Mt Biokovo 225

Mt Kastav 141
Murter Island 189-90
museums & galleries
   Archaeological Museum of Osijek 87
   Croatian Association of Artists 52
   Croatian Museum of Tourism 143-4
   Fritzy Palace 153
   Museum of Broken Relationships 41
   Museum of Contemporary Art 50
   Museum of Slavonia 85-7
   Museum of the Krapina Neanderthal 81
   Staro Selo Museum 83
   Street Art Museum 54
   War Photo Limited 253-4
music 320-1
Music Biennale Zagreb 22, 53
Mužilovčica 70

N

national parks 21, 316-17
   Biokovo National Park 225
   Kornati National Park 189
   Krka National Park 13, 194-6, **13**
   Mljet National Park 273
   Paklenica National Park 174-6
   Plitvice Lakes National Park 9, 171-2, **8, 33**
   Risnjak National Park 140
nature parks
   Kopački Rit Nature Park 15, 91-2, **15**
   Lonjsko Polje Nature Park 68-70
   Medvednica Nature Park 70
   Telašćica Nature Park 187
   Učka Nature Park 145
naturism 104
Nerezine 154
newspapers 328
Northern Dalmatia 38, 169-96, **170**
   climate 169
   highlights 170
Novalja 178-9
Novigrad 122
Nugal 224

O

Okrug Gornji 222
olive oil 310, **20**
Opatija 142-6
opening hours 17, 329-30
Oprtalj 122
Orebić 276-7
Osijek 85-91, **88**
Ošljak 184
Osor 151-2
otters 317
Our Lady of Trsat Church 137

P

Pag Island 19, 176-9, **231**
Pag Town 176-7
painting 322
Pakleni Islands 240
Paklenica National Park 174-6
Palmižana 240
Pantan 222
paragliding
   Crikvenica 137
   Motovun 129
   Samobor 69
   Učka Nature Park 145
parks & gardens, see also national parks, nature parks
   Komrčar Park 164
   Maksimir Park 50
   Punta Corrente Forest Park 110
Parun, Vesna 319
passports 331
Pazin 124-6
Pazin Chasm 125
Pelješac Peninsula 274-84
phonecards 330-1
photography 330
Piškera 189
planning
   budgeting 17
   calendar of events 22
   children 34-5
   Croatia basics 16-17
   Croatia's regions 36-8
   internet resources 17
   itineraries 26-33
   repeat visitors 18
   travel seasons 16
plants 318
Plitvice Lakes National Park 9, 171-3, **8, 33**
Polače 273
politics 301-2

Polo, Marco 283
population 287
Poreč 115-20, **117**
Postup 275
Prapratno 275
Preko 184
Premantura Peninsula 103
Primošten 194
Prvić 191
public holidays 330
Pula 99-107, **100**, **30**
Pula Film Festival 102
Punat 161
Punta Bjanca 188
Punta Corrente Forest Park 110

R
Rab Island 19, 163-8
Rab Town 164-8, **166**, **29**
radio 328
rafting 19
Ragusa 293
rakija 311
Raša 122
religion 287, 305
Rijeka 136-42, **138**
Risnjak National Park 140
road rules 336
Roč 128
rock climbing 19, 326
  Baška 162
  Paklenica National Park 175
  Rovinj 111
  Samobor 69
Rogač 217
Roški Slap 195
Rovinj 108-14, **109**, **31**, **229**
Rt Kamenjak 13, 103, **13**
ruins, *see* archaeological & historic sites
Rukavac 246

S
safety 330
sailing 326
Sakarun Bay 188
Sali 187-8
same-sex marriage 306
Samobor 69
scuba diving, *see* diving & snorkelling

Map Pages **000**
Photo Pages **000**

sculpture 322
Sea Turtle Rescue Centre 18, 153
Severina 321
sheep 148
shopping, *see* individual locations
Šibenik 190-4, **192**
Šibenik-Knin County 188-96
Siege of Vukovar 95
Šipan 272
Šipanska Luka 272
skiing 22, 307
Skradin 194
Skradinski Buk 195
Slanica 189
Slavonia 37, 84-96, **86**
  climate 84
  highlights 86
Sljeme 53, 70
snakes 318
snorkelling, *see* diving & snorkelling
soccer 306
Sokolarski Centre 195
Solin 217-18
Šolta 217
Sonus 25
Soundwave 24
Southern Dalmatia 38, 250-84, **252**
  climate 251
  highlights 252
Sovinjsko Polje 129
Špancirfest 25, 76
Split 14, 38, 200-17, **204-5**, **208-9**
  accommodation 206-9
  activities 202-3
  climate 197
  drinking & nightlife 212-13
  entertainment 213
  festivals & events 203-6
  food 209-11
  internet access 215
  medical services 215
  shopping 213-15
  sights 200-2
  tourist information 215
  tours 203
  transport 215-17
  travel agencies 215
  walking tour 214, **214**
sports 306-7
Srebrna 246
St Blaise's Church 123
St James' Cathedral 191

St John the Evangelist's Church 165
St Lucy's Church 162
St Mark's Cathedral 281
St Mark's Church 44
Stara Baška 161
Stari Grad 242-3
Staro Selo Museum 83
Stiniva 246
Stipanska 240
Stomorska 217
Ston 275
Stončica 246
Street Art Museum 54
street names 329
Subversive Festival 23
Šuker, Davor 306
Šulići 258
Sunčana Uvala 152
Šunj 272
Supetar 227-33
Supetar Summer 232
Susak 155
Sveta Katarina 114
Sveti Andrija 114
Sveti Jakov 258
Sveti Jure 225
Sveti Nikola 116
Svetvinčenat 124
sword dance 279

T
Tabor Film Festival 82
taxes 329
tea 311
Telašćica Nature Park 187
telephone services 330-1
tennis 306-7
time 16, 331, 340
tipping 329
Tisno 189-90
Tito 297, 298, 299
tourist information 331
tours 336, *see also* boat trips, walking tours, *individual locations*
train travel
  to/from Croatia 333-4
  within Croatia 336
Trakošćan Castle 14, 79-81
travel to/from Croatia 332-4
travel within Croatia 334-6
trekking, *see* hiking
Trogir 218-22, **220**
Trpanj 276
Trpimir 291
Trsat Castle 137

Trsteno Arboretum 272-3
truffles 127
turtles 18, 153
TV 328
Tvrđa 85-7

U
Učka Nature Park 145
Ugljan 184
Ultra Europe 24
Unije 155
Unknown Festival 25
Urban Festival 53-4

V
vacations 330
Valun 150-1, **229**
Varaždin 74-8, **75**
Varaždin Baroque Evenings 25, 76
Varaždinske Toplice 78-9
vegan travellers 60, 310-11
vegetarian travellers 60, 310-11
Vela Draga 145
Vela Luka 227, 284
Vela Spila 284
Veli Lošinj 156-7
Veli Rat 188
Veliki Tabor Castle 14, 82-3, **14**
Verne, Jules 125
Verudela Peninsula 103
video 328
Vidova Gora 233
Viganj 276
Vis Island 19, 244-9, **231**
Vis Town 245-8
visas 16, 331
Vlačica 227
Voloska 144
volunteering 331
Vošac peak 225
Vrbnik 161-2
Vrilo 227
Vrsar 122
Vukovar 94-6
Vukovar Film Festival 25

W
walking, *see* hiking
walking tours
  Diocletian's Palace 214, **214**
  Zagreb 51, **51**
War Photo Limited 253-4
water 311

weather 16, *see also individual locations*
websites 17
weights 328
white-water rafting 19
wi-fi 328
Wild Asparagus Harvest 23
wildlife 317-18
windsurfing 19
  Bol 233
  Viganj 276
wine 21, 311-12
wine regions 311-12
  Ilok 96

Međimurje 79
Slavonia 93
women in Croatia 305-6
women travellers 331
World Festival of Animated Film 54
World Theatre Festival 25, 55

Z
Zadar 15, 179-86, **180**, **15**, **27**, **33**
Zagorje 36, 71-83, **72-3**
  climate 71
  highlights 72

Zagreb 36, 40-68, **42-3**, **46-7**
  accommodation 55-7
  activities 53
  climate 40
  drinking & nightlife 10, 60-4
  entertainment 64-5
  festivals & events 53-5
  food 57-60
  highlights 42
  internet access 66
  medical services 66
  shopping 65-6
  sights 41-52

tourist information 66
tours 53
transport 66-8
travel agencies 66
walking tour 51, **51**
Zagreb Film Festival 25, 55
Zagrebdox 22
Ždrilca 240
Zlarin 191
Zlatni Rat 233
Zoo Osijek 87
Zrće Beach Festivals 18
Zrenj 122
Žut 189

Map Legend

Sights

- Beach
- Bird Sanctuary
- Buddhist
- Castle/Palace
- Christian
- Confucian
- Hindu
- Islamic
- Jain
- Jewish
- Monument
- Museum/Gallery/Historic Building
- Ruin
- Shinto
- Sikh
- Taoist
- Winery/Vineyard
- Zoo/Wildlife Sanctuary
- Other Sight

Activities, Courses & Tours

- Bodysurfing
- Diving
- Canoeing/Kayaking
- Course/Tour
- Sento Hot Baths/Onsen
- Skiing
- Snorkelling
- Surfing
- Swimming/Pool
- Walking
- Windsurfing
- Other Activity

Sleeping

- Sleeping
- Camping

Eating

- Eating

Drinking & Nightlife

- Drinking & Nightlife
- Cafe

Entertainment

- Entertainment

Shopping

- Shopping

Information

- Bank
- Embassy/Consulate
- Hospital/Medical
- Internet
- Police
- Post Office
- Telephone
- Toilet
- Tourist Information
- Other Information

Geographic

- Beach
- Hut/Shelter
- Lighthouse
- Lookout
- Mountain/Volcano
- Oasis
- Park
- Pass
- Picnic Area
- Waterfall

Population

- Capital (National)
- Capital (State/Province)
- City/Large Town
- Town/Village

Transport

- Airport
- Border crossing
- Bus
- Cable car/Funicular
- Cycling
- Ferry
- Metro station
- Monorail
- Parking
- Petrol station
- S-Bahn/S-train/Subway station
- Taxi
- T-bane/Tunnelbana station
- Train station/Railway
- Tram
- Tube station
- U-Bahn/Underground station
- Other Transport

Note: Not all symbols displayed above appear on the maps in this book

Routes

- Tollway
- Freeway
- Primary
- Secondary
- Tertiary
- Lane
- Unsealed road
- Road under construction
- Plaza/Mall
- Steps
- Tunnel
- Pedestrian overpass
- Walking Tour
- Walking Tour detour
- Path/Walking Trail

Boundaries

- International
- State/Province
- Disputed
- Regional/Suburb
- Marine Park
- Cliff
- Wall

Hydrography

- River, Creek
- Intermittent River
- Canal
- Water
- Dry/Salt/Intermittent Lake
- Reef

Areas

- Airport/Runway
- Beach/Desert
- Cemetery (Christian)
- Cemetery (Other)
- Glacier
- Mudflat
- Park/Forest
- Sight (Building)
- Sportsground
- Swamp/Mangrove

OUR STORY

A beat-up old car, a few dollars in the pocket and a sense of adventure. In 1972 that's all Tony and Maureen Wheeler needed for the trip of a lifetime – across Europe and Asia overland to Australia. It took several months, and at the end – broke but inspired – they sat at their kitchen table writing and stapling together their first travel guide, *Across Asia on the Cheap*. Within a week they'd sold 1500 copies. Lonely Planet was born.

Today, Lonely Planet has offices in Franklin, London, Melbourne, Oakland, Beijing and Delhi, with more than 600 staff and writers. We share Tony's belief that 'a great guidebook should do three things: inform, educate and amuse'.

OUR WRITERS

Anja Mutić

Coordinating Author, Zagreb, Zargoje, Slavonia, Istria, Split & Central Dalmatia
It's been more than two decades since Anja left her native Croatia. The journey took her to several countries before she made New York City her base 15 years ago. But the roots are a'calling. She's been returning to Croatia frequently for work and play, intent on discovering a new place on every visit, be it a nature park, an offbeat town or a remote island. She's happy that Croatia's beauties are appreciated worldwide but secretly longs for the time when you could head to Hvar and hear the sound of crickets instead of blasting music. Anja is online at www.everthenomad.com.

Read more about Anja at:
lonelyplanet.com/members/anjamutic

Peter Dragicevich

Kvarner, Northern Dalmatia, Dubrovnik & Southern Dalmatia After a dozen years working for newspapers and magazines in both his native New Zealand and Australia, Peter ditched the desk and hit the road. Since then he's contributed to literally dozens of Lonely Planet titles, including writing our first guide to Montenegro. Returning to Croatia this year was especially poignant for him, as it's exactly 100 years since his grandfather left his village in Dalmatia to seek a better life on the other side of the world. Peter also wrote the Welcome to Croatia, Travel with Children, Croatia's Coast, Croatia Today, History, The Croatian Mindset, Architecture in Croatia, The Natural Environment and The Arts chapters.

Read more about Peter at:
lonelyplanet.com/members/peterdragicevich

Published by Lonely Planet Publications Pty Ltd
ABN 36 005 607 983
8th edition – April 2015
ISBN 978 1 74321 402 2
© Lonely Planet 2015   Photographs © as indicated 2015
10 9 8 7 6 5 4 3 2 1
Printed in China